I0823140

Funny Stuff

HOW *Comedy* SHAPED AMERICAN HISTORY

EDITED BY

LAURA LAPLACA AND RYAN LINTELMAN

FOREWORD BY MEL BROOKS

R

RUTGERS UNIVERSITY PRESS
NEW BRUNSWICK, CAMDEN, AND NEWARK, NEW JERSEY
LONDON

Rutgers University Press is a department of Rutgers, The State University of New Jersey, one of the leading public research universities in the nation. By publishing worldwide, it furthers the University's mission of dedication to excellence in teaching, scholarship, research, and clinical care.

978-1-9788-3796-6 (cloth)
978-1-9788-3797-3 (epub)

Cataloging-in-publication data is available from the Library of Congress.
LCCN 2025017752

A British Cataloging-in-Publication record for this book is available from the British Library.

∞ The paper used in this publication meets the requirements of the American National Standard for Information Sciences—Permanence of Paper for Printed Library Materials, ANSI Z39.48-1992.

rutgersuniversitypress.org

CONTENTS

CHAPTER 2

Comedy Creates American Identity

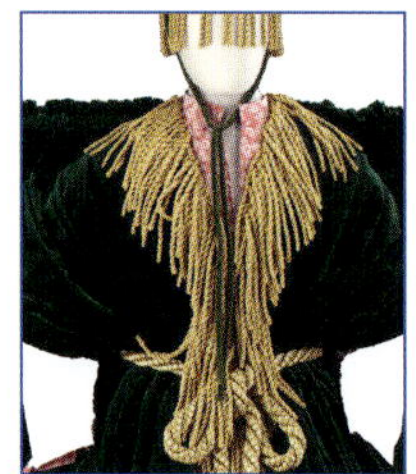

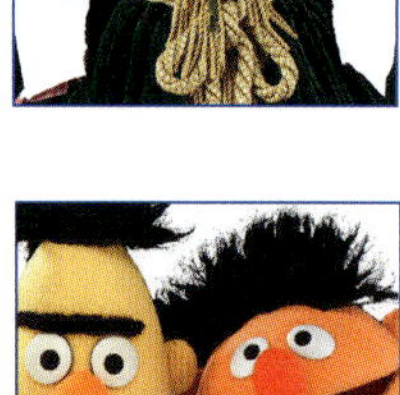

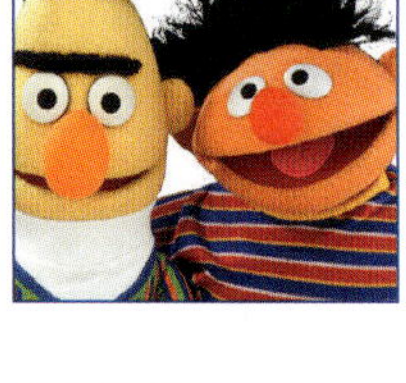

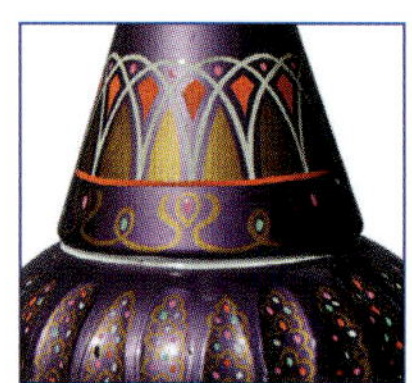

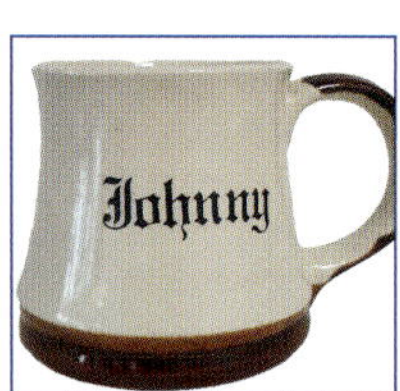

CHAPTER 3

Comedy Provokes Conversations

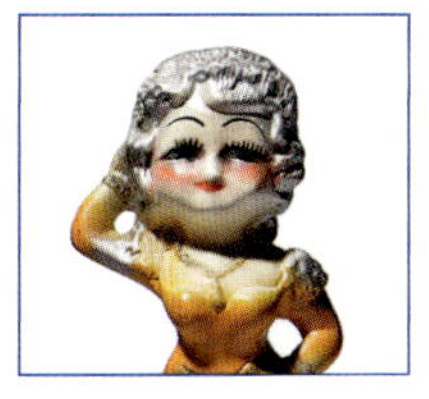

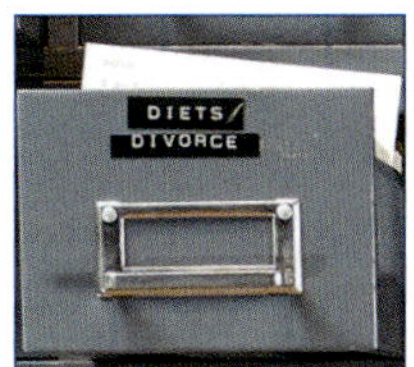

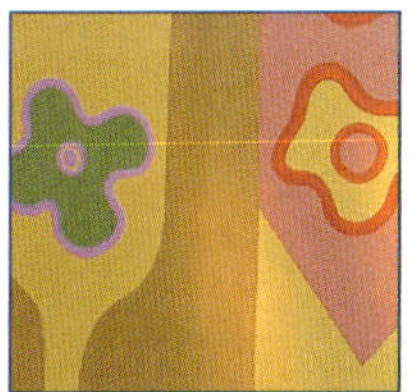

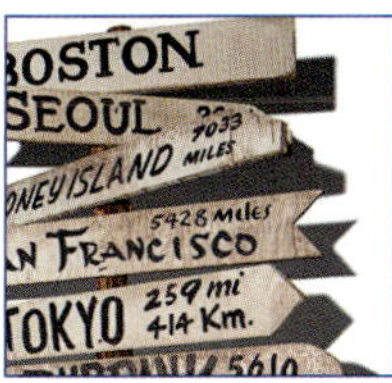

CHAPTER 4

Comedy Breaks the Mold

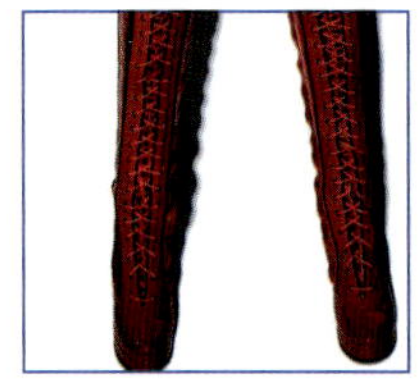

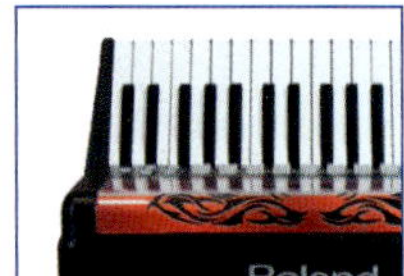
Roland

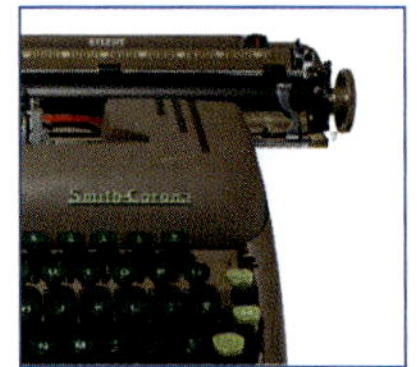

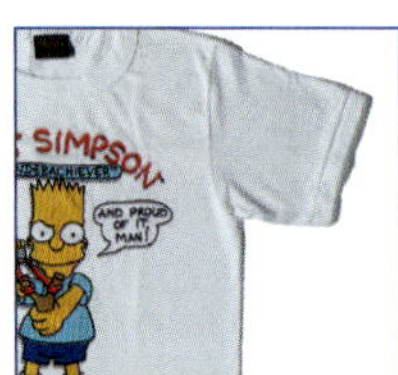
SIMPSON

FOREWORD

MEL BROOKS

In my 1982 film *My Favorite Year*, which is loosely based on my own adventures as a comedy writer, Peter O'Toole's character Alan Swann quotes the great English actor Edmund Kean, who on his deathbed said, "Dying is easy. Comedy is hard."

Indeed, comedy *is* hard. That's why it's so valuable. Not every attempt at it succeeds, but when it does something wonderful happens—laughter! There is nothing in the world quite like laughter. It can transport you from worry and despair to joy and jubilation. It blows the dust off your soul.

I was born in Brooklyn, New York, during the Great Depression. And depression was the right word for it, both for our bank accounts and our national state of mind. One of the things that got us through was comedy, and at that time it came through our radios. Comics like Eddie Cantor, Fred Allen, Jack Benny, George Burns, and Gracie Allen lifted our spirits and let us laugh in the face of hardship.

But what is comedy? When Carl Reiner and I were doing our 2000-Year-Old Man routine, one of his questions as the interviewer to me as the 2000-Year-Old Man was, "You've lived a long time and you've seen a lot. Can you tell us the difference between comedy and tragedy?"

"That's easy!" I replied. "If I cut my finger, that's tragedy. If you walk into an open sewer and die . . . that's comedy!"

I met Carl in the early 1950s in a writer's room that consisted of some of the most talented and funny people who ever lived. Like Emmy- and Peabody Award–winning head writer Mel Tolkin, Lucille Kallen, one of the first female comedy writers in television history, Larry Gelbart, who created *M*A*S*H* and had the fastest comedy mouth in the West, Neil Simon, the guy who wrote dozens of the funniest plays that ever ran on Broadway, Mike Stewart, who wrote the books for Tony-winning musicals like *Bye Bye Birdie* and *Hello, Dolly!*, Joe Stein, the cocreator of *Enter Laughing* and *Fiddler on the Roof*, and another funny guy you might have heard of named Woody Allen—just to name a few. We were all there writing for *Your Show of Shows*, starring Sid Caesar, Imogene Coca, Carl Reiner, and Howard Morris and produced by the tough but wonderful Max Liebman (and also later its successor, *Caesar's Hour*). We were writing thirty-nine hour-and-a-half comedy shows in every TV season, recorded live and broadcast to over sixty million people across America every Saturday night. The show was so successful that businesses like restaurants and theaters and taxicab drivers pleaded with NBC to move the show to a Monday so it wouldn't hurt their normal weekend take. For a time, watching *Your Show of Shows* was the most beloved shared comic experience in America.

Some might say a job writing comedy wasn't a serious career, but none of us in that writer's room took it lightly. To comedy writers it is life and death. Either you get a big laugh or die in ignominy. But those in the know understand that laughter has enormous real value.

As I wrote in my memoir, *All About Me!*, "Comedy is a weird but very beautiful thing. Even though it seems foolish and silly and crazy, comedy has the most to say about the human condition. Because if you can laugh, you can get by. You can survive when things are bad if you have a sense of humor."

I think I am most happy when I am sitting in a Broadway theater watching a musical comedy like maybe (excuse the indulgence) *The Producers*, which by the way to this day holds the record for winning the most Tony Awards ever for a Broadway musical. I love looking around and seeing that everyone in the theater is laughing their heads off. It fills me with comfort and joy and makes me glad I was born.

DIRECTOR'S NOTE

JOURNEY GUNDERSON
EXECUTIVE DIRECTOR
NATIONAL COMEDY CENTER

I know enough about comedy to know you generally don't want to follow Mel Brooks. Yet here I am.

The National Comedy Center opened in 2018 and is the nation's first official museum dedicated to the art form of comedy. Its archive is our country's congressionally designated hub for the preservation of comedy's history, home to thousands of artifacts representing its artistic, social, and cultural impacts. (Was building a formal institution about comedians—the people most apt to lampoon anything formal or institutional—a potentially perilous mission? You bet! And yet here we are.)

Our role, whether inside the National Comedy Center's galleries or within this volume, is to address why comedy *matters*, and to take seriously the project of preserving its heritage *because* it matters.

How do we know comedy matters? Because Mel said so. No, truly: Mel said it made him feel happy to be alive, and the key to survival in the bleakest of times is the *will* to go on.

Comedy has always been a fundamental factor in American survival. It's also been a key part of the system of unofficial checks and balances on power, a source of the all-too-rare alchemy that creates connection and common ground, and a vehicle singularly well-suited to deliver new perspectives. Laughter's physiological effect is the opposite of fight-or-flight: It brings down one's walls, the result of which is a receptive mind. I'd say that matters. Power, connection, progress—through "mere" jokes.

Mel referenced comedy healing us through the Great Depression, and entertaining his fellow troops during the horrors of World War II. The day that a person can laugh again after experiencing grief is the day they start to realize there is hope. The smallest smirk can be the first glimmer on the horizon that better days lie ahead, no matter how far off that otherwise may seem.

Comedy is not just an elixir that makes us feel better, it's a cerebral art that makes us think. Anyone with the dedication to hone the craft of comedy can harness its force and, in making others laugh, reset the balance of power in a room, or in a society.

Among my favorite things about this art form is that one need not come from a position of privilege to step into the authority of the comedian, an attractive proposition for anyone who's an underdog. American comedy was born, in many ways, of the demand to populate thousands of stages during the vaudeville era, creating a robust training ground for a generation of comedians who used their platform to punch up. These artists, many with working-class or immigrant roots, offered a fractured nation a means of reckoning with the assimilationist experience and finding community in a shared popular culture.

As you consume the chapters in this book, and when you visit the (excuse the indulgence) award-winning National Comedy Center in Jamestown, New York, I hope you will consider a new category of American hero: the comedian.

The National Comedy Center is a total immersion in the art that has soothed, challenged, and given voice to the American people—a tribute to the innovators who have revealed and defined our national mood across centuries of shared history—a tribute to the truth-tellers, the tension-breakers, and the connection-makers.

Whether you are exploring the artistic process as you delve into hand-scrawled joke notes from comedy's prolific artists, stepping into the shoes of a comedian in our participatory galleries, or reflecting on the temporal nature and trajectory of the art form's most boundary-pushing material on our "Blue Room" level, the National Comedy Center is the place to experience all facets of the vital story of comedy in America.

In our galleries you'll find immersive exhibits that celebrate comedy's great minds, unique voices, and the time-honed creative processes that have elevated comedy to an art.

Also, there's a fart bench.

DIRECTOR'S NOTE

ANTHEA M. HARTIG
ELIZABETH MACMILLAN DIRECTOR
NATIONAL MUSEUM OF AMERICAN HISTORY
SMITHSONIAN INSTITUTION

When Jerry Seinfeld's long-running and lucrative tenure of his self-named television show ended, he could have written his proverbial ticket to the next big comedic success. He sat atop humor's heap. Instead, he chose to do the two things he loved most—writing and stand-up. Thus does this remarkable new volume bring forth far-ranging explorations of comedy's history in the United States, uniting words and laughs.

Coeditors and primary authors Laura LaPlaca of the National Comedy Center and Ryan Lintelman of the Smithsonian's National Museum of American History join nine expert colleagues in delving into the stories, the objects, the cringe, and the joyous release afforded by comedic genres and performers across the past nearly two hundred years.

From maestro Mel Brooks's foreword onward, the authors explore the wit, the wisdom, and the hard work of comedy. Importantly, they do not shy away from its misogyny, racism, elitism—understanding that these contours have helped create, sustain, and shatter the pervasive stereotypes and biases we inherit and hold. On inheritances, I spoke to my ninety-year-old Irish American mother (b. 1933) about this new volume. She shared that above all, radio and minstrel shows transmitted comedy to her very funny family (no one could beat Aunt Marie's timing!). That her Catholic high school in Providence, Rhode Island, continued the ugly tradition of blackface minstrelsy should not have surprised me, but it did nonetheless. How then did that contribute to her formation of racialized biases? To my own? Our conversation also brought back memories of listening to Flip Wilson and Bill Cosby records and watching *Laugh-In*, *All in the Family*, and *M*A*S*H* as a girl.

Of course, *Saturday Night Live* and I grew up together and continue to do so.

This volume's sibling, fraternal twin even, is the museum's *Entertainment Nation | Nación del espectaculo* exhibition, opened in late 2022, and in particular the brilliantly produced "What's So Funny?" micro-gallery curated by Ryan Lintelman and a team of colleagues. As well, the material culture of comedy forms a critical through line of the entire exhibition's layered archaeology of popular culture since the 1840s. Unsurprisingly, as I am the museum's first woman director, stories and objects of Mae West, Phyllis Diller, and Ellen DeGeneres resonate with me.

There is such richness to this book, but by its very nature it is incomplete. It's always important to ask what and who are missing. Certainly, more on gender's complexity and construction can be written, and on class and demographics in comedy. Moreover, the chapters on Latino/a comedy by Ashley Mayor set the stage for further scholarship on performers and their impact and resonance. This does not detract from the fabulous and often challenging histories behind the laughs that this book brings. Rather, it sets the stage for ongoing contextualization and scholarship, for which this historian remains ever grateful. And in the context of the cyclone of crises and pain of the pandemic years in particular, and in a time of increasing strife, let us hold on to humor, live in laughter, and meddle in malaprops together to add meaningful levity to our lives.

FUNNY STUFF

INTRODUCTION

PRESERVING THE FUNNY "STUFF"

The arrival of this book marks a milestone: Comedy is finally being recognized as an art form with a history worthy of preservation on a national scale.

The National Comedy Center and the Smithsonian have come together to share an unprecedented range of artifacts in this volume. What follows is your invitation to explore America's living, growing comedy archives for the very first time—and as we continue in our long, never-complete effort to safeguard this art form's history for generations to come.

We're just getting started. Indeed, the National Comedy Center was still in its early years when this project began and major acquisitions continue to arrive as this book is going to press. At the same time, the Smithsonian's landmark *Entertainment Nation* exhibition and collecting initiatives continue to evolve, reshaping how comedy is presented alongside other cultural forms within the walls of its National Museum of American History. It's an exciting time to be a comedy nerd.

Of course, as curators and archivists responsible for preserving comedy's heritage, we spend a lot of time thinking about the impact this art form has had on American life. Comedy can be a conduit for truth, a release valve for society, an avenue for liberation, or a crucible for new ways of thinking. It's a unique force that prompts us to examine our most closely held beliefs and contemplate others' perspectives. When we take a seat at a comedy club, turn on a funny movie, or crack open a work of literary humor, we are signing an unwritten social contract. Most of us agree to let our guard down, turn off our moral indignation, and reconsider the world around us.

We won't be theorizing about the nature of comedy in this book—psychoanalyzing or probing the anthropological origins of humor. Instead, we'll examine performance and impact: discussing how comedians and their bodies of work have shaped historical developments and debates from the nation's founding to today. At our respective institutions, we're building incredible collections of objects representing these stories, and we study comedy to better understand how it functions to create and undergird social change. Sadly, this doesn't mean *we're* funny people, we're just historians who study funny people. As Bob Newhart once said, "The closer you get to understanding humor, the more you begin to lose your sense of humor."[1] That's not totally fair though!

We decided to organize this book in a unique way: we don't present a chronological story of the history of comedy through time, nor have we separated out different genres or styles of comedy. Instead, we've grouped stories about some of the most illuminating, novel, and provocative moments in comedy history into chapters that reflect some of the key ways in which comedy has intervened in our national discourse:

Comedy Shapes How We See Each Other

Comedy Creates American Identity

Comedy Provokes Conversations

Comedy Breaks the Mold

In these chapters, you'll read about stand-up, cinema, and sitcoms; theater, improv, and internet memes; puppets, roasts, and novelty songs; cartoons, sketch shows, and late-night television. All of these forms—and more—are well documented in our institutions' collections. Even though we're reaching far and wide across all genres and eras of comedy history, you might not see your favorite comedian or a show you think is the funniest of all time in this book. We're here to share some of the treasures that fill our shelves today—with more work to be done, more volumes to be written, and our collections growing richer with holdings that document the vitality and range of this powerful art form.

1

Comedy

SHAPES HOW WE SEE EACH OTHER

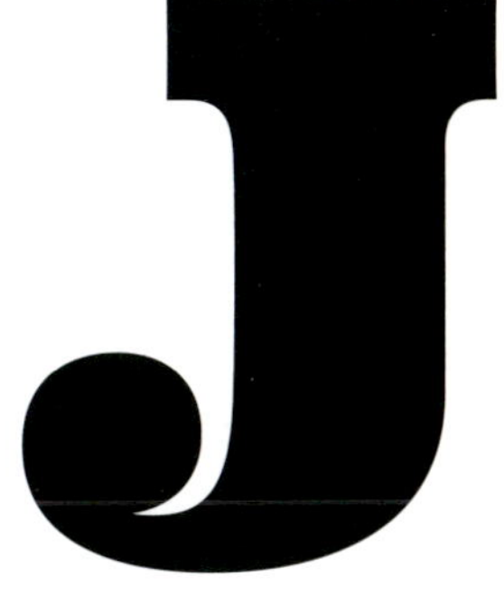

ack Soo believed that he could be funny, be Japanese American, and fight stereotypes all at the same time. That was a tall order in the mid-twentieth century, when Americans were more likely to see a white actor in "yellowface" performing grotesque racial caricature (like actor Mickey Rooney's depiction of Japanese landlord Mr. Yunioshi in *Breakfast at Tiffany's*) than an actual Asian American actor performing on-screen. But Soo was an extremely talented comedian who worked his way through the business. From entertaining fellow internees at the Topaz War Relocation Center during World War II to becoming a beloved emcee at Chinatown nightclubs across the United States, earning stage and screen roles in productions, all while refusing to play stereotypical roles or engage with racist tropes for cheap laughs, he excelled in turning those stultifying stereotypes on their heads, finding humor in others' misconceptions and limited understanding of Asian American life.

Soo (born Goro Suzuki) displayed his versatility in roles ranging from the handsome, charming, swinging bachelor nightclub owner Sammy Fong in 1961's *Flower Drum Song* to the role he's best remembered for today, the unflappable, wisecracking New York police detective Nick Yemana on the 1970s television sitcom *Barney Miller*. In each of these roles, he fully embraced his identity and background, but rather than fulfilling preconceived notions of what a Japanese American character should be like, he demonstrated the full range of characteristics, personalities, abilities—the full humanity—of his community. And his work is all the more hilarious for it.

Publicity photograph of Jack Soo as Nick Yemana on *Barney Miller*.

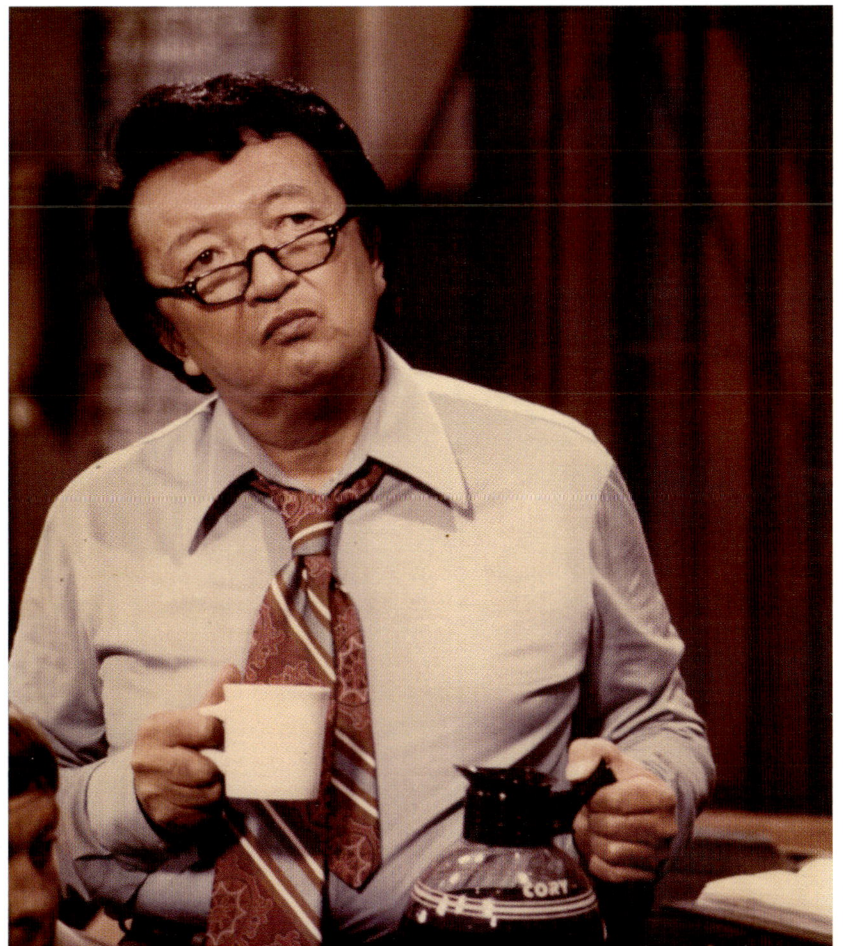

In a memorable scene from *Barney Miller*, the 12th Precinct detective squad is discussing the fate of a defector from the Soviet Union seeking asylum in the United States. Some of Yemana's colleagues wonder if the defector will end up returning home. Detective Sergeant Arthur Dietrich (Steve Landesberg) turns to Yemana.

Dietrich: What about you, Nick?

Yemana: Huh?

Dietrich: You ever feel any longing to return to your home? Back to the ancient cultures and traditions? Back to the shrines and temples of your ancestors? Back to the terraced hillsides and cherry trees?

Yemana: (after a long pause, tiredly) I was born in Omaha.

Dietrich: (disbelieving) We got a city in Nebraska sounds just like that![1]

Like all forms of popular entertainment, comedy has a remarkable ability to shape viewers' understanding of others. Despite its liberating, transgressive potential, through its play with stereotypes, representation, and expectations, comedy has often helped create and enforce oppressive and essentialist definitions of identity: what it means to be an American, a man or woman, a member of a racial or ethnic group, young or old, urban or rural, rich or poor.

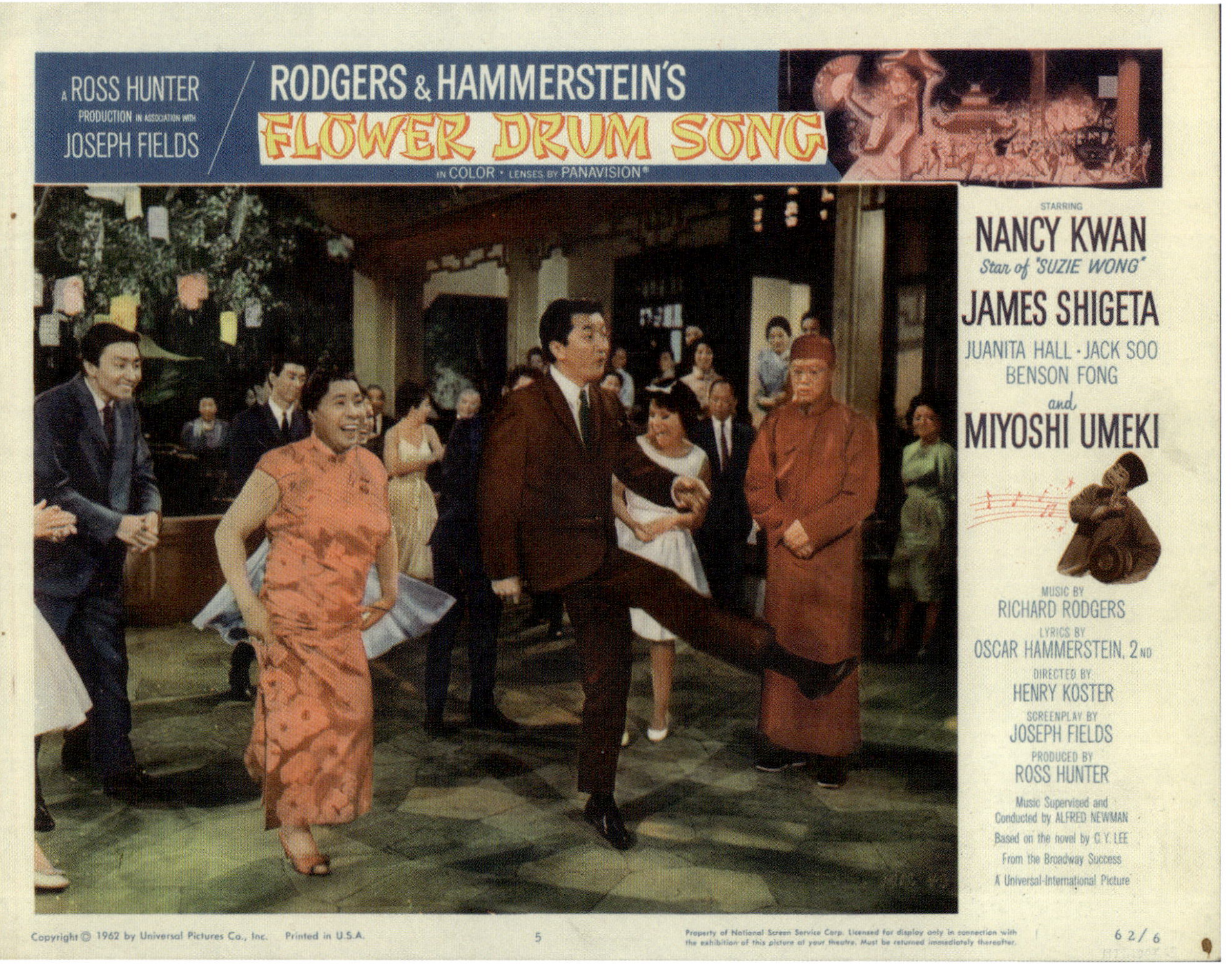

Lobby card for the 1961 musical comedy film *Flower Drum Song*, featuring Jack Soo as nightclub owner and emcee Sammy Fong.

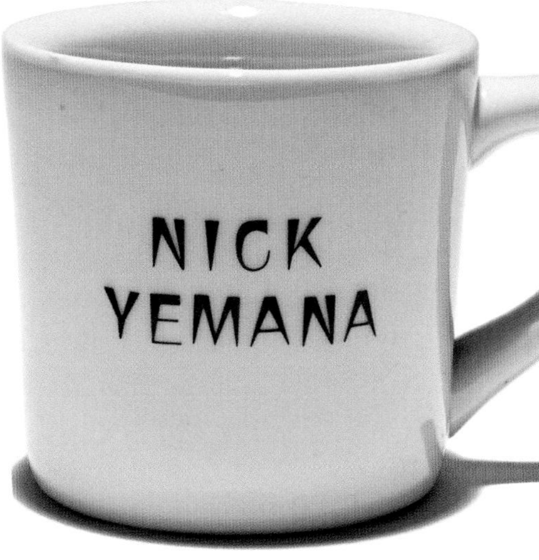

On *Barney Miller*, Jack Soo portrayed Nick Yemana, a competent, somnolent detective with deadpan sardonic wit who invariably made horrible coffee for the rest of the squad. When Soo died suddenly of esophageal cancer at the age of sixty-one in 1979, his fellow cast members raised their mugs in a special episode to honor their friend and colleague.

For instance, a nineteenth-century white New Englander who had little personal exposure to Black life or slavery might have seen a traveling minstrel show and drawn conclusions about an entire population based on the stereotyped jokes and songs of the performance. A city dweller later that century might have had their prejudices about immigrant newcomers reinforced while laughing at the ethnic acts so popular on the vaudeville stage. In the twentieth century, radio, film, and television comedy programs broadcast narrow and offensive representations of Black, Hispanic, Asian, and Native Americans to every corner of the country, perpetuating negative stereotypes and supporting white supremacist ideology. And Americans' normative understandings of gender and sexuality have frequently been shaped and affirmed by mocking dismissals of people who risked their lives and livelihoods by living outside traditional ideals of masculinity and femininity. Plays, movies, and television shows have often been marred by distorted and offensive portrayals of effeminate men, butch women, or "depraved" homosexuals.

While some comedians have reinforced strict categories and performances of identity, others have pushed back against reductive norms and stereotypes, using their craft to challenge prejudice and reclaim their communities' full humanity. The writers and cast of *The Beverly Hillbillies* played with the traditional rube and hillbilly tropes to indict the wealthy elite class for its greed and selfishness. Ellen DeGeneres and the cast of *Will & Grace* subverted stereotypes about gay and lesbian people, helping to change minds about LGBTQ+ rights by situating their characters in the mainstream. Disruptors like the Marx Brothers, Phyllis Diller, and Hari Kondabolu challenged prevailing norms, using laughter to open Americans' minds and get them to reconsider the structures and strictures that limit our lives and constrain our creativity. Bob Hope and Martha Raye, among the many other comedians who have dedicated themselves to service through the USO, used comedy not only to entertain soldiers, sailors, and airmen but also to imagine a broader community of Americans bound by healing laughter.

Of course, harmful stereotypes and prejudice still inform comedy today, and debates have raged especially strongly in recent years as comics and commentators contest the limits of free speech, the dynamics of power and privilege, and the importance of positive representation in building a more just and inclusive society. Some comedians have bemoaned "the death of comedy" in a politically correct, overly sensitive society of too-powerful and plentiful morality police who can destroy a career over a misspoken word or off-color joke. Others, however, have seized the moment to engage comedy fans in a conversation about the legacy of racist entertainment and comedy's power to confront and destroy systems of oppression. They ask, is an insensitive joke acceptable when a member of the targeted group makes it? Are some groups "off-limits" as targets of humor due to their history and status in society? Is it always acceptable to "punch up" by mocking the elite and powerful? Is it ever acceptable to "punch down" by poking fun at the disadvantaged? And above all, what is the impact of making someone the butt of a joke?

Today, comics like Keegan-Michael Key and Jordan Peele, Ali Wong, Leslie Jones, Wanda Sykes, Sarah Silverman, Bobby Lee, Nikki Glaser, Nicole Byer, Sheng Wang, Cristela Alonzo, and Joel Kim Booster, to name just a few, continue to challenge the notion that comedy must either ignore or embrace stereotypes. Instead, these comedians play with and subvert these preconceived notions to craft hilarious bombs to lob at the remaining bastions of privilege and prejudice. Their work proves the enduring power of comedy to shape how we see each other.

Introduction by Ryan Lintelman

PETROLEUM VESUVIUS NASBY AKA DAVID ROSS LOCKE

"There is a chap out in Ohio," explained Abraham Lincoln at the height of the Civil War, who had been writing hilarious satires of Lincoln's critics under the name "Petroleum Vesuvius Nasby." Lincoln planned to write to "Petroleum" and ask how he did it. If Nasby could teach him, Lincoln joked, "I will swap places with him!"[2]

It's little wonder that the embattled president would like to swap places with Petroleum V. Nasby, because in the middle of a grinding civil war, no humorist was bolder, or funnier, in their attack on slavery, racism, secession, and their apologists in the Union. Nasby was free to write so boldly because he didn't exist. Instead, he was the comedic

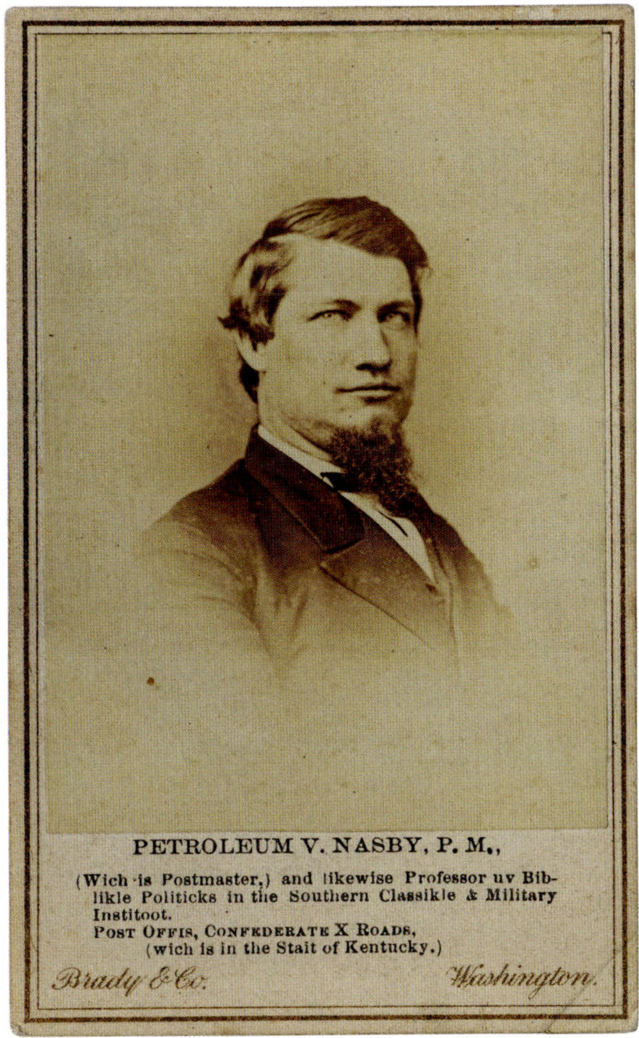

This carte de visite photograph of David Ross Locke by Mathew Brady's studio identifies the humorist by his pen name, "Petroleum V. Nasby."

persona created by the Ohio newspaperman David Ross Locke, used—in his friend Mark Twain's words—to "promote liberal causes by seeming to oppose them." Penning insane exaggerations of the worst traits of his political opponents, Locke made Nasby the Stephen Colbert of the Civil War.[3]

Locke was just one of the many journeyman newspaper printers bouncing around nineteenth-century America. He got his start as an apprentice "printer's devil" at age twelve. One of his first tasks was to mix drinks for the boozy guys who cranked out the news.[4] Alcohol played a big role in his life after that: when a friend later told Locke that he had never met a drunker man, Locke famously retorted, "Get somebody to introduce you to me in an hour."[5] Locke also stood out, even in the shabby world of editors, as the "most slovenly of all employees." Friends described him as a hulking man, with smirking eyes but "abominably nasty" clothing.[6]

But this drunken mess had a sparkling mind. Locke had long been on the antislavery side of American politics, and as the Civil War began he found himself incensed by the pro-Confederate backlash he heard in his small Ohio town. Attending a funeral for a Union soldier, Locke heard the preacher mourn "another victim of this goddamned abolitionist war." He knew he had to strike back, not at the distant Confederacy but at the "traitorous secessionist slime" in his midwestern backyard.[7]

Locke invented Petroleum Vesuvius Nasby to caricature the type of northerner who sympathized with the Confederacy—petty and selfish, drunken and illiterate, willfully ignorant and eye-wateringly racist. He kicked off his letters with a routine in which Nasby's town secedes from Ohio. His wannabe secessionists complained that no one from town was ever appointed to "any offis where theft wuz possible." Skewering the grand oratory—and banal realities—of the age, Nasby swore to secede, "armed with justice and shot-guns."[8]

Newspapers from Ohio to San Francisco to London started printing Nasby's letters. British fans came to believe that all Americans talked in Nasby's ragged vernacular. And he "wrote strong," getting away with jokes that would never fly in a later age. Nasby admired the failing Union general George B. McClellan for inadvertently killing off so many abolitionist soldiers with his defeats, though he later complained that McClellan's escapes left some soldiers "to live and vote agin us" in the future.[9] Nasby could not serve in the military himself, of course, on account of his dandruff. But he was willing to fight—at the polling place—spending election day engaged in "the patryotik biznis uv knockin down the opposition voters."[10] At a time when the Democratic party was stereotyped as the less educated, less sober movement, Nasby bragged "no man hez drunk more whisky for the party."[11]

It was his writing on race that hit the hardest. At a time when most Americans—including Lincoln—openly espoused white supremacy, Nasby was willing to attack such bigotry. It was "soothing to a ginooine, constooshnel, Suthern-rites Dimekrat to be constantly told that ther is a race uv men meaner than he is."[12] He mocked abolitionist stretches of the North as places "wher evry boddy redes and rites."[13] He worried that if freed slaves immigrated to Ohio, "our kentry will be no fit place for men uv educhashen and refinement" like himself.[14] African Americans might begin to "tyrannize over us, even as we tyrannize over them."[15] Instead of earnest argument for essential equality of all mankind, Locke used Nasby to make a funnier, angrier case for the essential stupidity of those who would claim superiority.

His starkest jokes are essentially unquotable today, noxiously loaded with satirical use of the N-word. Few comedians ever hit harder at white supremacy in their day, but few ever did so in a way that is less palatable now.

Locke even joked about Lincoln's assassination. The two had become friendly, and Lincoln read Nasby's stories at dinner on the night of April 14, 1865, before heading to Ford's Theatre. It was the last book he read. After his murder, Locke had Nasby wail and moan, but it soon turned out that he was mourning the fact that the assassination took place *after* the Confederacy was already defeated. "The tragedy," Nasby whined, "cum at the wrong time!"[16]

Locke kept writing as Nasby after the war. Soon he got caught up in the growing network of traveling humorists, crisscrossing the country by cattle car to lecture in small towns. These proto-stand-ups lived grueling lives. Mark Twain recalled that Locke spoke on the road twenty-five nights a month (Twain also noted Locke's filthy attire). It paid the bills, but his era was ending, as the furious tensions of the war years slowly receded. Nasby's wit was probably too pointed for peacetime. At the same time, the world of nineteenth-century persona comedians—primarily relying on the written word—was slowly replaced by the brighter performers of early vaudeville.

But during the Civil War, when the republic was at its lowest and its people were at their angriest, Locke's "letters were copied everywhere, from the Atlantic to the Pacific, and read and laughed over by everybody," Twain recalled, from soldiers in trenches to the president in the White House.[17]

Jon Grinspan

PIPPS AMONG THE WIDE AWAKES

Political violence is not supposed to be funny. Partisan gangs are not supposed to be funny. Civil war is not supposed to be funny. Yet in the midst of America's ugliest election, on the brink of secession, one of America's strangest comedians took a shot at making an anxious public laugh.

Pipps Among the Wide Awakes is one of those shards of American history that takes an awful lot of background to piece back into a coherent narrative, a weird forgotten satire of a weird forgotten movement by a weird forgotten man. But once you make sense of it, it cuts directly to what is funny and maddening and compelling about both democracy and comedy.

Pipps Among the Wide Awakes was written to mock the Wide Awakes, a mass movement that came to define the pivotal 1860 presidential election. The Wide Awakes were clubs of young men (and a few women) who wore militaristic black capes, lit torches, and marched at night to protest against slavery. They campaigned aggressively for a little-known Republican presidential candidate named Abraham Lincoln. Their supporters considered the Wide Awakes the "largest and most soul-inspiring organization the country has ever seen," while their enemies warned that the movement was plotting "an invasion of the South for murder, rape, lust, and similar unamiable intentions."[18]

However inspiring or menacing, the young men who joined the movement mostly spent their time trying on capes, growing out mustaches,

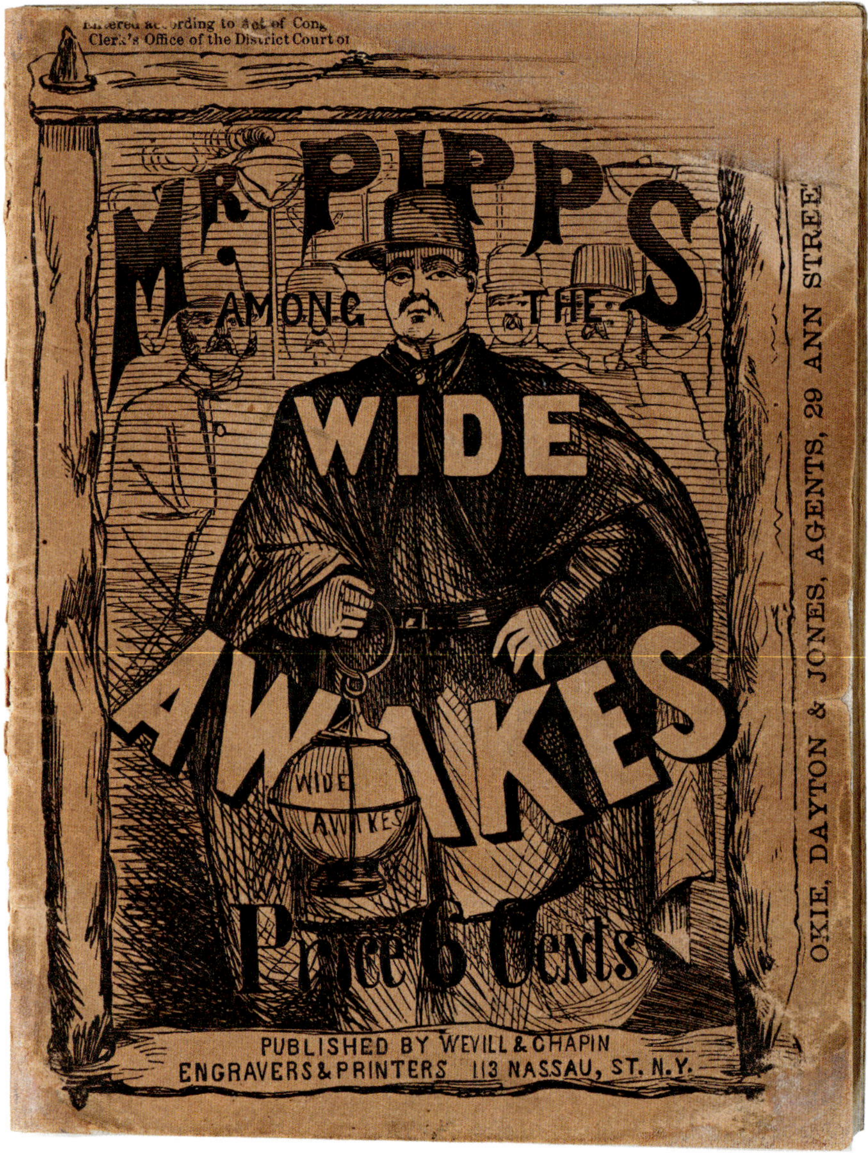

Charles Godfrey Leland's *Mr. Pipps Among the Wide Awakes* features a cover illustration of a Wide Awake parade, with participants wearing the recognizable uniform of oilcloth hats and capes, holding the lanterns and torches that were characteristic of their nighttime marches through American cities.

giving long speeches, and marching *very seriously* through northern cities. In this self-important context, a cheeky humorist saw a perfect opportunity.

Charles Godfrey Leland is one of those nineteenth-century figures who hardly seems real. Raised by an elite Philadelphia family, he made his name alternately writing for America's chief humor publications, like *Vanity Fair*, and revolutionizing the study of folklore. He traveled the world, fought in the 1848 revolutions in Europe and in the American Civil War, and produced piles of not-entirely-trustworthy books on magic, sorcery, fairy tales, and other Gothic themes. One of his works inspired modern Wiccanism. Another seems to have coined the term "emancipation," as a more saleable replacement for "abolitionism." And he liked to tell people that after a mysterious initiation ceremony as a boy, he was destined for a long career as a "scholar and a wizard."[19]

This wizard spent the furious campaign season of 1860 writing one of the first comic books. Political cartoons of his day were usually stiff one-panel affairs, with a single broad joke and little sense of movement or narrative. Leland chose to tell a story over more than a dozen pages, relying on humorous repetition and laughable pomposity to skewer the very serious Wide Awakes.

Pipps tells the story of "Mr. Pipps," a young man excited to cast his "virgin vote" in the upcoming election. The cover offers a hint of what readers are in for, promising the tale of "How he Fit, Bled, and Died / And how he got over it." Nineteenth-century audiences loved this kind of explosion of puffery, juxtaposing grandiose language with banal

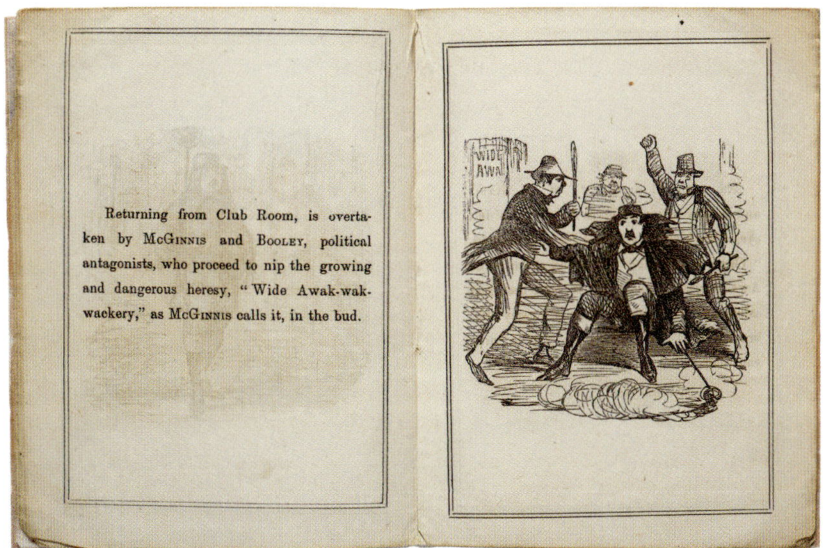
Returning from Club Room, is overtaken by McGinnis and Booley, political antagonists, who proceed to nip the growing and dangerous heresy, "Wide Awak-wak-wackery," as McGinnis calls it, in the bud.

Capturing the frequent violence of nineteenth-century street politics (and bursting the bubble of a self-impressed movement), Charles Godfrey Leland's *Mr. Pipps Among the Wide Awakes* depicts young "Mr. Pipps" being beaten by rival partisans—drawn as Irish Democratic stereotypes. Nasty nativism, cartoonish behavior, and very real threats to democracy combine in this one articulate little cartoon.

results. In a repeated satire of the dramatic language being thrown around, the book promised to show "Correct and Entire Method of Being: WIDE AWAKE, AWOKE, AND AWAKEN. WONDERFUL! TERRIBLE!! FIRST-RATE! Ahead of Anything Out! Or any other man!" Leland repeats that last phrase—"Or any other man"—over and over across the pages, laughing at the movement's sweaty self-assertion, wearing increasingly thin with each repetition.

Leland takes us through Pipps's development, from growing out his first mustache to marching in a Wide Awake company and listening to meaningless orations packed with over-the-top 1860s slang ("Go it, Lemons!" "Show the World You're Pumpkins!"). Once Pipps puts on his Wide Awake uniform he is immediately set upon by atrocious stereotypes of the Irish Catholic Democrats, who were seen as the Republicans' main antagonists in the guerrilla warfare of nineteenth-century urban politics. Even this thuggery Leland handles with tongue-in-cheek formality, referring to "the powerful arguments of McGinnis and Booley being observable on Pipps' left eye." The nasty stereotyping continues when Pipps finally tries to vote, facing down a "*ferocious Irishman*."

But Pipps perseveres. There is, tellingly, no mention of slavery, or the South, or race in the little book. Pipps's fight to cast his ballot becomes the driving issue, at a time of mass voter intimidation and election-day violence. At the polls he is, in Leland's magic phrase, "sworn in a little, and sworn at considerably." Yet he succeeds, casting his virgin vote for Lincoln. Suddenly his chest swells, and the little pipsqueak from the beginning of the comic is drawn standing tall, finally "a Man of the World and a Politician." The simple illustrations carry as much punch as the text, showing Pipps reading partisan newspapers until his hair frizzles and his feet fly into the air, or alternating between a proud, haughty Wide Awake marcher in one panel and a stunned victim of McGinnis and Booley's pummeling in the next. Leland seems to be mocking and affirming the transformative power of democratic participation at the same time.

Perhaps most impressive, Charles Godfrey Leland uses *Pipps Among the Wide Awakes* to skewer a movement that he supported. The "scholar and wizard" was an abolitionist Republican, in line with the Wide Awakes' goals for the country. But as a humorist, he just couldn't let these kids go marching around in uniforms without poking some fun. Even in a nation on the brink of civil war, Leland the Wizard felt a needling compulsion to chuckle at the way democracy turns humans into monuments. *Pipps Among the Wide Awakes* stands as a testament to the irreverent streak in American political humor, sketched out by a scholar almost mysteriously attuned to language and ritual.

Jon Grinspan

BRET HARTE AND "THE HEATHEN CHINEE"

Bret Harte's satirical poem "Plain Language from Truthful James" was one of the most popular works of written humor of the nineteenth century, but also one of the most tragically misunderstood. Written to expose and skewer contemporary anti-immigrant sentiment, the poem instead inspired reactionary anti-Chinese ethnic prejudice, giving birth to an enduring nativist caricature and adding a harmful, racist phrase to the nation's cultural vernacular.

Harte was a New York–born journalist and humorist best known for his "local color" stories and articles written in Northern California in the 1860s and 1870s. He was alarmed by the nativist movement and racist violence against Chinese immigrants in the American West and wrote a narrative poem to satirize anti-Chinese white Californians, "Plain Language from Truthful James," first published in the *Overland Monthly* magazine in September 1870. In the poem, three men are playing the card game euchre: Irish miners James and Bill Nye (no relation to the Science Guy) and Chinese laundryman Ah Sin, who seems not to understand the game and is therefore taken as an easy mark by his companions. Nye is cheating, with a sleeve "stuffed full of aces and bowers," and thinks he has the upper hand.

When Ah Sin wins the game, however, and is revealed to have been cheating as well, Nye exclaims, "Can this be? We are ruined by Chinese cheap labor," a mocking reference to a contemporary political slogan.

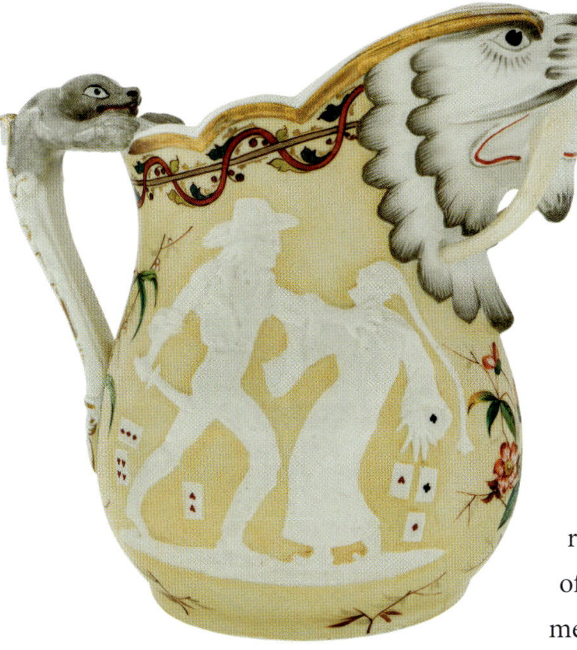

In November 1875, Union Porcelain Works in Long Island began manufacturing a pitcher decorated with figures from the poem they incorrectly titled "The Heathen Chinee." Bill Nye is shown in heroic frontiersman's clothing brandishing a knife to threaten Ah Sin, depicted with cards falling from his sleeve.

Though the poem doesn't explicitly state that Nye attacks Ah Sin, it's clear that there is an altercation, as James narrates:

In the scene that ensued
I did not take a hand,
But the floor it was strewed
Like the leaves on the strand
With the cards that Ah Sin had been hiding,
In the game "he did not understand."

The poem enjoyed immediate and overwhelming success, reprinted in newspapers across the country, and made Bret Harte one of the nation's most famous writers nearly overnight. "By any objective measure—the frequency with which it was reprinted, the number of parodies it inspired, the times it was quoted or set to music," one scholar wrote, "'Plain Language from Truthful James,' more commonly known as 'The Heathen Chinee,' was one of the most popular poems ever published."[20] Its popularity even inspired a merchandising boom, with illustrated reprints, sheet music adaptations, and even water pitchers decorated with scenes of the card game, especially playing up the implied violent ending, becoming bestsellers across the United States.

The meaning of the poem, that the hypocritical white card players saw Ah Sin's cheating as worse than their own, mirroring Irish immigrant laborers' prejudice against their Chinese counterparts, was lost on an American public that interpreted the story as a simple exposé of Chinese treachery. That misunderstanding was heightened by its frequent reprinting under the title "The Heathen Chinee" and its celebration by public officials like California Senator Eugene Casserly, an opponent of Chinese immigration who also took its satire literally. The poem was mentioned in congressional debates about banning Asian immigration and likely increased support for anti-immigrant legislation like the Chinese Exclusion Act of 1882, which banned all immigration by Chinese laborers for ten years, and the 1892 Geary Act, requiring Chinese residents to register and obtain a certificate of residence—or face deportation.[21]

Although Harte originally wrote "Truthful James" to criticize anti-Chinese violence, he would ultimately join in on the commercialization of the poem despite its widespread misinterpretation. He tried to cash in on its popularity by writing uninspired sequels and even collaborated with Mark Twain on a racial-caricature-laden theatrical

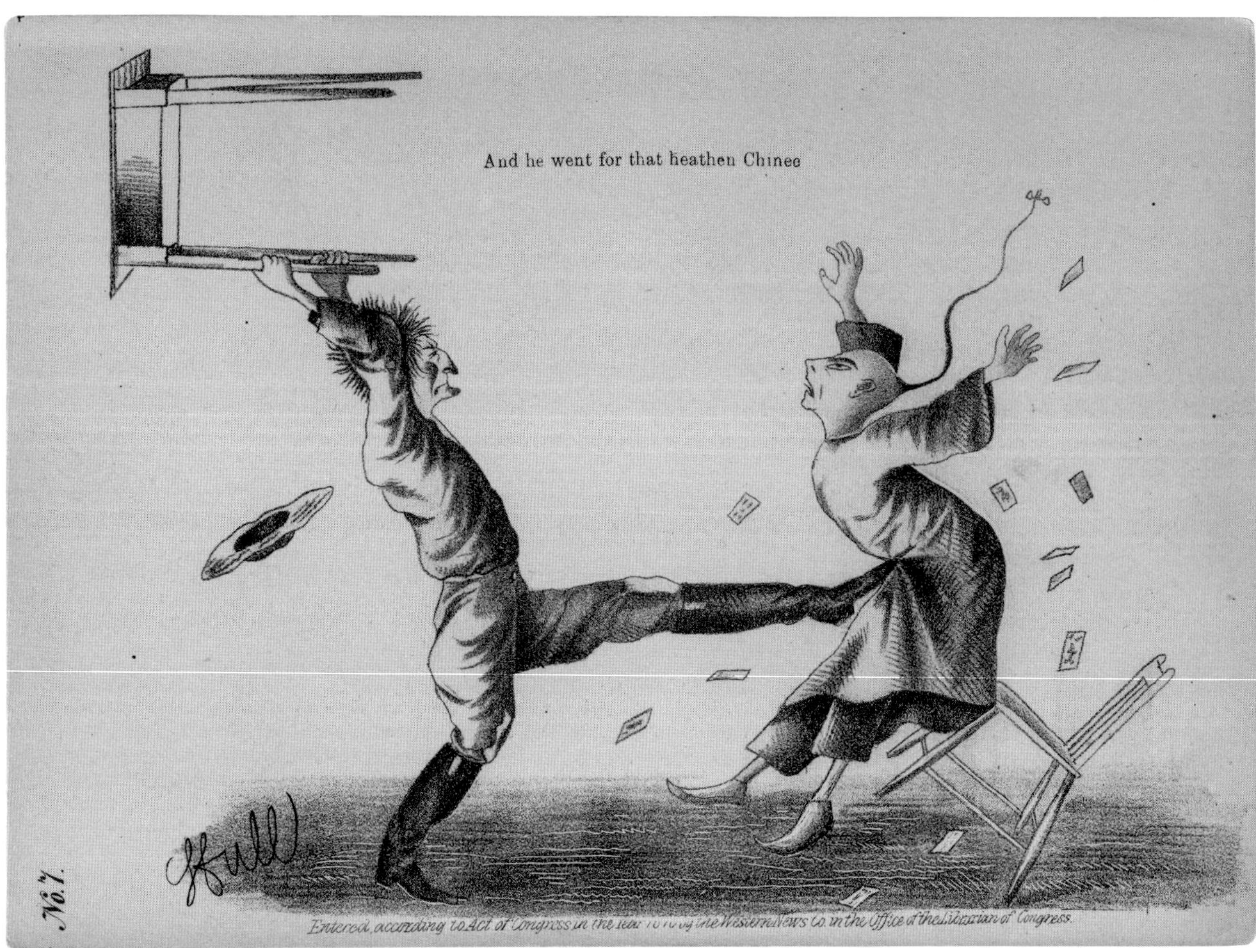

Part of a set of nine illustrations by Joseph Hull printed by the Western News Company and sold in a set suggested for framing. The exaggerated, political-cartoon-style drawings helped popularize the misunderstanding of the poem's original meaning.

adaptation titled *Ah Sin*, which closed quickly after opening at the National Theatre in Washington, D.C., in 1877.[22] While Harte profited from his poem financially and reputationally for decades, when asked about "Truthful James" in later years, Harte called the poem "trash" and "the worst poem I ever wrote, possibly the worst poem anyone ever wrote."[23]

But the damage was done. Harte's satire was misconstrued by anti-Chinese reactionaries to give license to their zealous xenophobia. A testament to the power of comedy to shape an audience's idea of an entire community, the legacy of "Truthful James" resonates in modern debates about free speech and comics' responsibility to the individuals and groups they target for humor and casts a long shadow over modern violence against Asian American and Pacific Islander communities still unfairly regarded with suspicion in American society.

Ryan Lintelman

VAUDEVILLE: THE VOICE OF THE CITY

What do Bob Hope, the Marx Brothers, Sammy Davis Jr., Buster Keaton, Milton Berle, Moms Mabley, Mae West, Jack Benny, and *The Wizard of Oz*'s Cowardly Lion (Bert Lahr), Scarecrow (Ray Bolger), Tin Man (Jack Haley), and Wizard (Frank Morgan) have in common? They all got their start in the entertainment business performing comedy on the vaudeville stage.

The most popular form of theatrical entertainment for five decades, from the 1880s to the 1920s, vaudeville was the crucible of American popular culture. Combining aspects of traveling entertainments like circuses and sideshows, concert hall and burlesque variety shows, blackface minstrelsy, and dime museums, vaudeville was as diverse as America itself. Vaudeville theaters across the country featured varied bills of entertainments including singers, dancers, acrobats, musicians, animal trainers, plate spinners, ventriloquists, body builders, contortionists, jugglers, magicians, hypnotists, male and female impersonators, and comedians, all available for low prices to a heterogenous, multiethnic, interclass audience.

In its endless variety and novelty, it was likewise a testament to the nation's restless creativity and entrepreneurial spirit. Taking advantage of new transportation networks, inexpensive printing technology and expansive visual culture, and the efficiency of industrial incorporation, vaudeville was a product of its time that created the twentieth-century entertainment industry.

Vaudeville also gave birth to modern American comedy. On its stages, comedy performance evolved from its incidental dramatic and musical roots to something resembling today's stand-up, sketch, and musical comedy forms. In this democratic artistic arena, comics had to capture and hold an audience's attention or get the hook—sometimes literally (as in the case of poor performers who were physically removed from the stage with a shepherd's hook during the amateur nights at Miner's Bowery Theatre).[24] That meant that they became masters of quick wordplay, slapstick gags, and constantly evolving routines that resonated with the medium's diverse and demanding audience. The broad, physical, "slapstick" comedy that many vaudeville

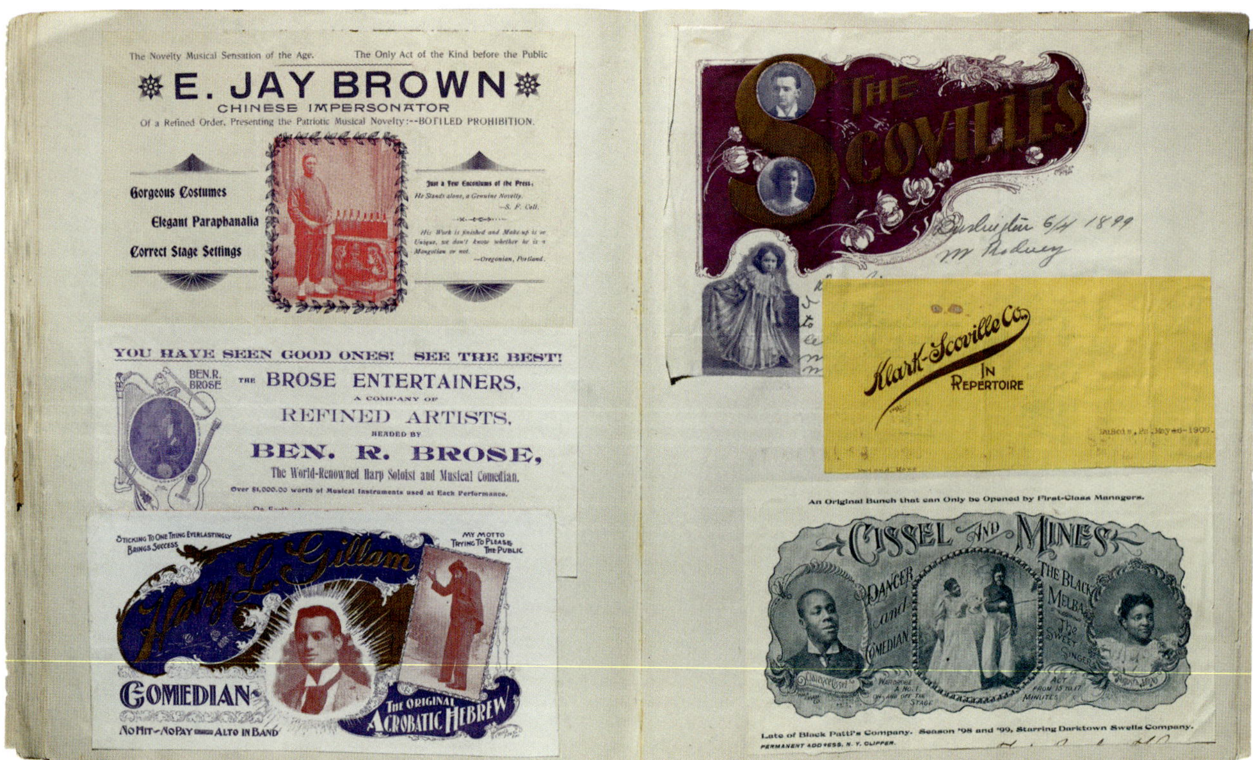

These pages from a scrapbook maintained by members of the George & Hart's Georgia Up To Date Minstrels troupe demonstrate the breadth and diversity of the acts vying for vaudeville stardom. Advances in transportation, communication, and print technology made it possible for vaudevillians to travel circuits around the country, creating a truly national entertainment culture.

comedians practiced could be understood and enjoyed by everyone in the audience, whether they spoke English or the language of their homeland, rich or poor, young or old. More innovative comedians, like the Marx Brothers, Eddie Cantor, or Frank Fay, brought the dizzying energy, multicultural cosmopolitanism, and modernist absurdism of urban living to the stage, presaging late twentieth-century observational comedy.

At a time of great demographic and social change, vaudeville comics also found humor in the dislocations and frustrations of modern American life, especially drawing on the experiences and confusions of immigration and migration. Crude ethnic caricature of Black, Irish, Chinese, Italian, German, and Jewish Americans created and reinforced harmful stereotypes, while also demonstrating familiar interactions, misunderstandings, and experiences. Mass entertainment created a shared experience for diverse Americans to engage in reciprocal cross-cultural exchange, examining and evaluating ideas about race, ethnicity, sexuality, gender, and morality. In the thousands of vaudeville theaters in nearly every town across the United States (at least two thousand by 1900), performers helped solidify Americans' understanding of themselves and each other, forging visions of community and citizenship.[25]

Broad, physical humor helped vaudeville comedians overcome not only the language barrier in their diverse, immigrant audiences, but also the lack of amplification in the dark and smoky theaters. With this "slap stick" sound effect device, even those in the cheap balcony seats could hear a character slap another, though they might not have clearly seen it.

Vaudeville's predecessors like variety theater, concert saloons, and burlesque were more bawdy, rowdy entertainments, appealing primarily to male audiences on the margins of polite society in urban commercial districts or boom towns on the frontier. In the 1870s, entertainment entrepreneur and performer Tony Pastor realized that a more genteel format, appealing to middle-class tastes and families, could bring in bigger audiences. In 1881, he opened what is often credited as the first vaudeville theater, his Tammany Hall Theater, also known as Pastor's, in the heart of New York City's fashionable Union Square neighborhood. Pastor introduced some of the biggest stars of the era, including Lillian Russell, May Irwin, and Edward Harrigan, and with his prohibitions of alcohol, smoking, and vulgarity onstage, he attracted an audience that included women, children, and people of all classes and backgrounds. Vaudeville became a distinct entertainment medium, with pretensions to more refined and morally upright amusement.

Theater owner Benjamin Franklin Keith was the first to popularize the French term *vaudeville* to refer to this high-class variety entertainment, referring either to satirical songs from the Val-de-Vire region or to the urban folk songs called *voix de ville* ("voice of the city").[26] He joined forces with impresario Edward Franklin Albee in the mid-1880s to create what became an entertainment empire: the Keith-Albee chain of theaters and a booking syndicate that dominated the nation's vaudeville circuits. Patrons at the opulent and clean Keith-Albee theaters (sometimes derided as "the Sunday School circuit") were guaranteed polite, moral entertainment enforced via censorship.[27] Contracts and backstage notices prohibited performers from using profanity or vulgar humor, and theater managers called out objectionable material with notes delivered in blue envelopes, warning those who "worked blue" to clean up their act, coining a phrase still with us today.[28] In reality, the enforcement of high-class vaudeville's standards of morality and decorum was more a marketing ploy than a genuine dedication to decency, as even owners like Keith and Albee understood that audiences enjoyed titillating and ribald entertainments. Boundary-transgressing performers like comic singers Eva Tanguay, Mae West, and Sophie Tucker were among the medium's biggest draws.[29]

Vaudeville was a product of its time, made possible, profitable, and popular by a raft of contemporary technological and social developments. The scale and scope of the variety entertainments required

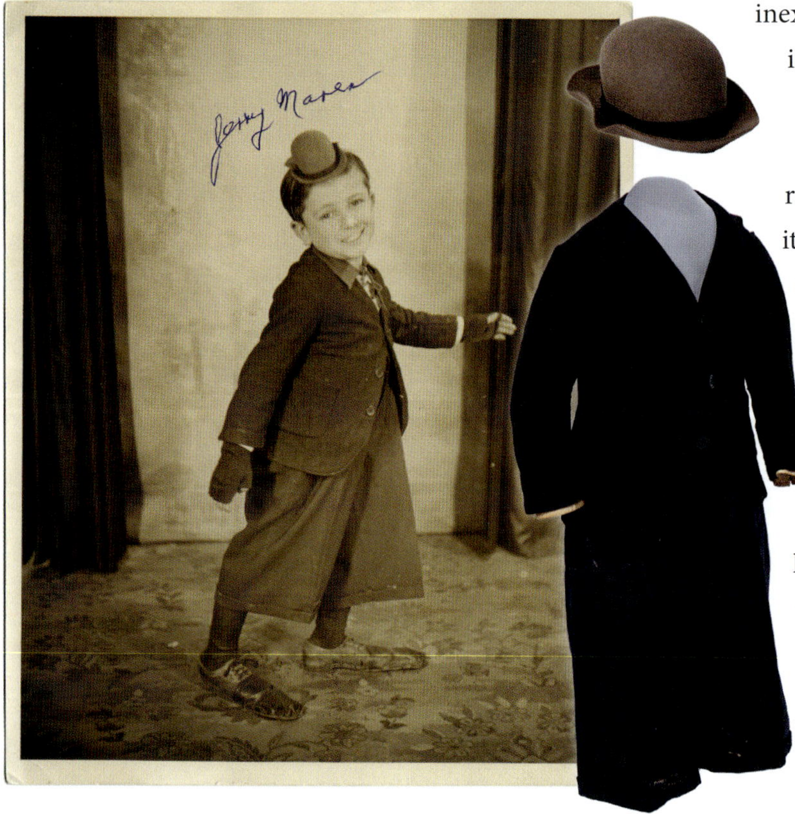

Jerry Maren was an actor and comedian who succeeded in show business despite, and in part because of, the pituitary dwarfism that stunted his growth. Shown here in the tramp/hobo costume he wore in his vaudeville act "Three Steps and a Half," Maren went on to appear in television and film—most notably, as a member of the Lollipop Guild in *The Wizard of Oz*.

inexpensive printed material for advertising, a nationwide network of trains for transportation, telegraph and telephone communication for booking, incorporation and efficient scheduling for profitability, the labor movement's promotion of the forty-hour work week and leisure time for its audience, and unprecedented immigration and migration within the United States for its labor, audience, and subject matter. Vaudeville circuits were among the first corporate chains, with standardized and coordinated product, identity, and business practices. Keith and Albee instituted the first continuous vaudeville theaters, running shows from morning to night, back-to-back; booked acts and plugged them into bills like interchangeable parts in an entertainment machine; and built a hierarchical, national organization that maximized profit and efficiency, while consolidating control and capital.[30]

Vaudeville ticket prices were low, with many theaters employing a ten-, twenty-, and thirty-cent tier for different seating areas, and the ubiquity of theaters by the mid-1890s made it a remarkably accessible and popular form of entertainment. However, audiences and circuits were segregated by race, with Black patrons limited to balcony seating in almost every major mainstream theater. The Theatre Owners Booking Association (TOBA, or "tough on Black Asses," as artists called it) ran the "Chitlin' Circuit" of all-Black shows for Black audiences. Performers like Moms Mabley, Dewey "Pigmeat" Markham, Lincoln Perry (Stepin Fetchit), and Sammy Davis Jr. got their start in these segregated theaters. Over time, a so-called Borscht Belt of venues and audiences for Jewish comedians also came to exist as a circuit based around resort hotels in the Northeast, especially in the Catskills. The Grand Ole Opry also became home base for a circuit of "hillbilly" entertainers that helped give birth to country and western music and a distinct rural and southern style of vaudeville humor.[31]

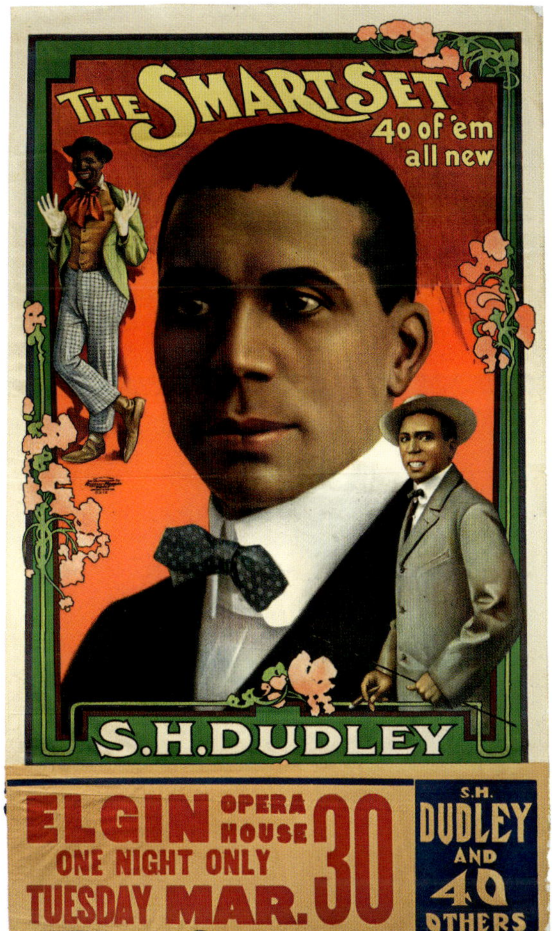

This poster advertises the 1908 vaudeville production *The Smart Set*, a vaudeville-style revue by S. H. Dudley's all-Black company of musical and comedy performers. Black vaudevillians navigated a complicated world of segregation and racial prejudice that limited opportunities, but a few enterprising performers like Dudley and Bert Williams persevered and succeeded.

Most vaudeville shows offered audiences a dozen or more acts in a bill, ranging from opener to closer over the course of one to two hours. Theater managers employed a brutal calculus in creating a bill, sentencing acts to spots that determined how audiences would receive them and making it clear how their performances were perceived. The opening act was the worst spot on the bill, often ignored as customers filed in to their seats. The "deuce spot" could be an opportunity for up-and-coming acts to try out before an audience settling in, but merely set up the big "flash acts" before and after intermission. This is where comics might be placed, especially those who worked in front of the curtain, to allow complicated sets to be changed, though sketch comedy could work here as well. Next to last was the best spot on the bill—stars could demand this. Getting the closing slot was so bad that it was called "playing to the haircuts"—a performer would see the backs of the audience's heads as they filed out—and managers might purposely book a bad act as closer to get the audience out before the next show.[32]

Comic acts varied from the broad, physical humor practiced by clowns in mismatched and ill-fitting clothes to the ethnic and racial caricature of blackface, Irish, Hebrew, Dutch, or Italian acts, or the modern, observational proto-stand-up comedy practiced by performers like Frank Fay. This style of comedy developed from the double duty comics sometimes had to perform, presenting their own acts and serving as masters of ceremony, helping to introduce and manage the crowd between acts. Serving this role, comedians often became standouts, recognized not only for their prepared material but for their offhanded, ad-libbed reactions to unforeseen moments onstage or in the audience. Some of the most famous and influential vaudeville comedians, like Will Rogers and Jack Benny, only accidentally became comics when their vaudeville acts (rope tricks and violin performance, respectively) went wrong, and their ad-libbed stage banter impressed the audience more than their "real" act.

Many, if not most, vaudeville performers came from underprivileged backgrounds, proving their mettle in the relatively meritocratic and egalitarian business while hoping for rags-to-riches success. Mirroring the diverse urban audiences to whom they played, among the thousands of vaudevillians were first- or second-generation European Jews, recent immigrants from Ireland or Italy, African Americans, and young strivers from the lower rungs of the economic ladder. Lured by visions of the glamor and earnings of some of the top stars, many vaudeville troupers believed that this was their best shot to make it big and were willing to put up with the long hours, grueling work conditions, interminable travel, and psychological stress of the circuit to pursue their dream. Few realized that dream of stardom, but for generations of vaudeville performers, the lifestyle had its benefits, and at least allowed them to eke out a living away from the factories and farms that employed most of their fellow Americans.

By the 1920s, vaudeville audiences began to dwindle as critics complained that the acts felt stale and new forms of electronic mass media

Nellie Burt wore this dress in a "flirtation act" she performed with husband Billy Gould in the 1890s. Vaudeville offered opportunities for female comedians to enter the business, but they often found themselves typecast in ditzy "dumb Dora" roles alongside eye-rolling straight men or sexualized and objectified in comic sketches.

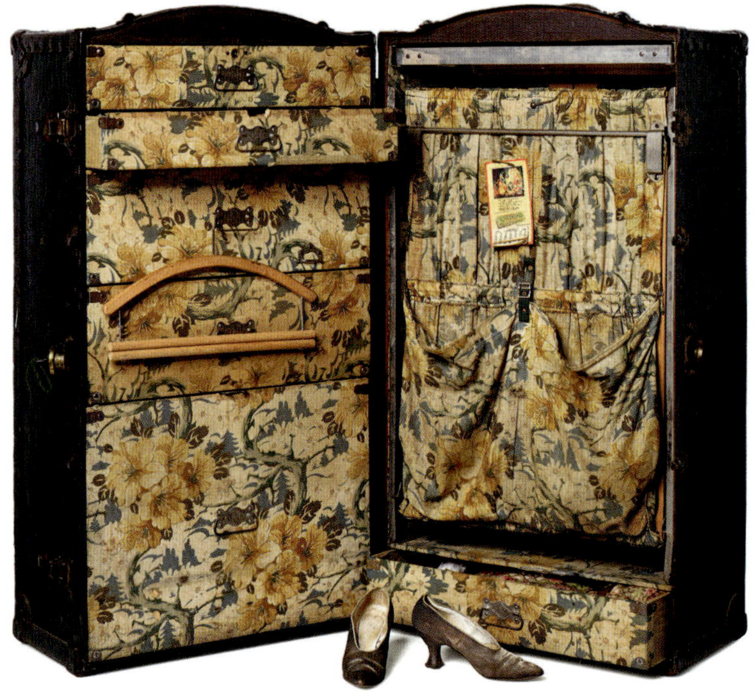

The Boudini Brothers, Phil and Dan (actual names Filippo and Domenico D'Agostino), were accordionists who worked the Orpheum circuit in the 1910s and 1920s. Phil left in 1917, and Dan's wife Adele Bernard joined the act in his stead. Their travel trunk, made to hold everything performers would need for their life on the road, is a marker of the vaudevillian's trade and lifestyle.

like sound recordings, motion pictures, radio, and eventually television began offering Americans a variety of entertainment in the comfort of their own homes. Though for decades vaudeville alumni would bemoan the death of the business, many comedians were happy for the opportunity to take their acts to radio, film, or television, as did Will Rogers, Bob Hope, George Burns and Gracie Allen, Al Jolson, Milton Berle, and hundreds of others. By World War II, most vaudeville theaters had closed, and performers had moved on to new formats, not only radio and movies but also more cosmopolitan and sophisticated nightclubs. Vaudeville had an enormous social impact: it helped immigrant audience members articulate and understand new identities as American citizens, lent a buoyant, egalitarian style to the nation's popular culture, and helped subvert and transform hegemonic Victorian morality and middle-class values.[33] In creating and solidifying American entertainment culture, it also planted the seeds for generations of comedians to come.

Ryan Lintelman

THE MARX BROTHERS: "WHATEVER IT IS, I'M AGAINST IT!"

A scene from the 1935 film *A Night at the Opera* succinctly encapsulates the Marx Brothers' signature brand of comic anarchy. After harried stagehand Tomasso (Harpo Marx) knocks out internationally renowned opera star Rudolfo Lassparri (Walter Woolf King) with a wooden mallet, Otis B. Driftwood (Groucho Marx) and Fiorello (Chico Marx) put their feet up on the unconscious tenor to negotiate a contract for up-and-coming Ricardo Baroni (Allan Jones) to replace him. In a surreal and absurd exchange, the men—Driftwood the sketchy business manager of a widowed philanthropist and Fiorello Baroni's scheming manager—discuss the confusing legal language ("The party of the first part shall be known in this contract as the party of the first part") and decide to tear off sections of the document they don't like. After a few minutes, they're left with a small shred of the original document and decide to debate its merits.

Fiorello: Hey, wait, wait. What does this say here, this thing here?

Driftwood: Oh, that? Oh, that's the usual clause that's in every contract. That just says, it says, 'if any of the parties participating in this contract are shown not to be in their right mind, the entire agreement is automatically nullified'.

Fiorello: Well, I don't know . . .

Driftwood: It's all right, that's in every contract. That's, that's what they call a sanity clause.

Fiorello: Ha-ha-ha-ha-ha! You can't fool me. There ain't no Sanity Clause!

Cartoonish violence, absurdist wordplay, literal shredding of symbols of authority, and defiant disregard for social elites: these were the hallmarks of the Marx Brothers' inimitable style of comedy over the course of their decades-long career. Their outrageous and combative skewering of social norms and authority made them populist heroes at the height of their popularity in the 1930s, but also with freethinking and antiestablishment Americans in the decades since. Through their mastery of both physical and verbal comedy, the Marx Brothers transformed the irreverent outsider humor of the Jewish, immigrant, working-class community where they were born into an indelible and universal form of

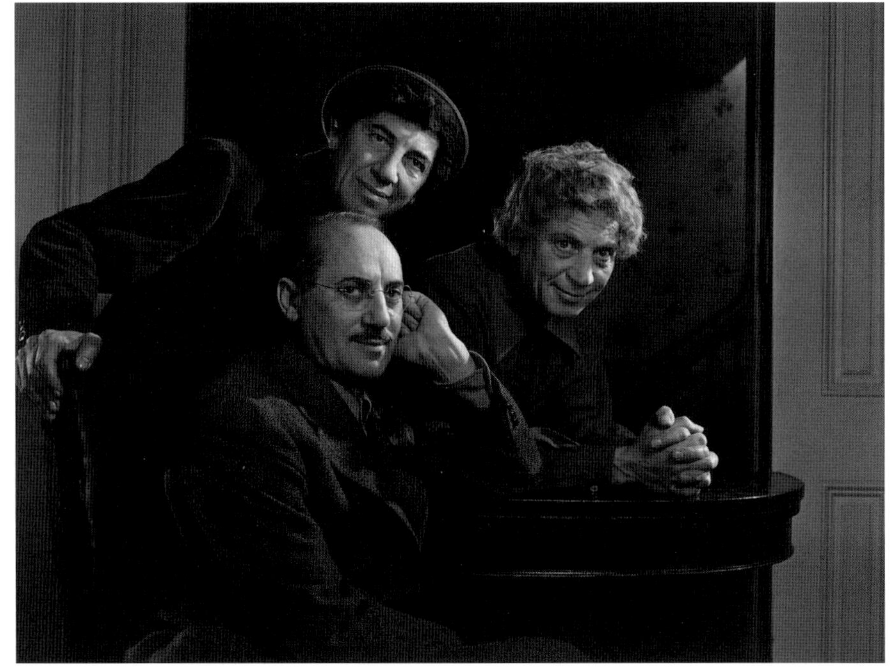

The Marx Brothers were among the most recognizable and popular comedians of the 1920s to 1940s, frequently photographed, quoted, and parodied themselves. This portrait of the brothers was taken in 1948 by Yousuf Karsh for an article in *Collier's* magazine. Karsh wrote, "I hope I have captured in my photograph the spontaneity that resulted from the three brothers' inability to be still for even one moment."

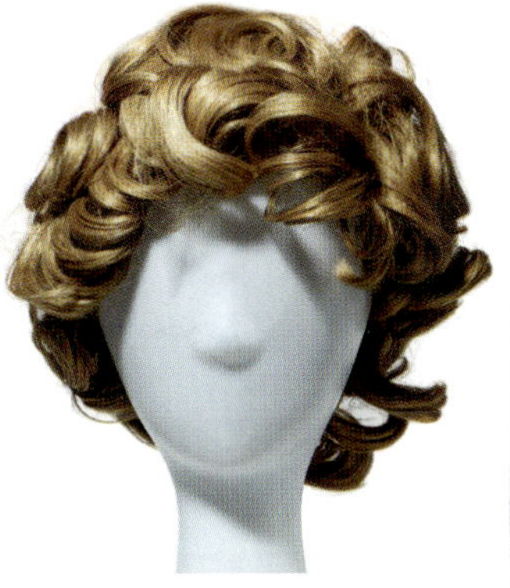

While their character personas and costumes originally drew on vaudeville stereotypes (Groucho a German, Chico an Italian, and Harpo an Irish immigrant), by the time they were starring in their own musical reviews on Broadway their act had evolved into a wholly novel form of comic anarchy and commentary on modern life. These costume pieces, a Harpo wig, and a suit Groucho wore in the film *Duck Soup*, were left to the Smithsonian Institution in Groucho's will.

comic catharsis at a moment when it felt like the wheels were coming off of Western civilization.

The Marx Brothers grew up looking at American society from the bottom up. Born to Alsatian and German Jewish immigrant parents in the working-class Yorkville neighborhood on New York's Upper East Side, brothers Leonard "Chico," Adolph "Harpo," Julius "Groucho," Milton "Gummo," and Herbert "Zeppo" Marx lived in a cramped tenement and were sent to work as children to support the family. As the boys were musically gifted, their mother drove them to begin performing in musical groups as teenagers; Minnie was the sister of vaudeville comedian Al Shean, giving the brothers a leg up as they broke into show business. According to legend, one night in Texas, the brothers' act was interrupted by news of a mule misbehaving outside, and as the audience filed out to take a look, young Julius's rapid-fire insults and irritated wisecracks not only brought them back but had them in stitches. He was soon performing under the name Groucho, and the other brothers took on their own stage names and personas as the act evolved into a vaudeville comedy routine.

Groucho wore an absurd greasepaint mustache and eyebrows that would later become a popular culture icon in the form of gag eyeglasses worn as a throwaway costume; he was also known for his omnipresent cigar and stooped, rapid stride. Most often cast as a high society pretender, Groucho would barely disguise his disdain for the elites he was trying to scam through witty wordplay. Chico, so named for his womanizing habit of chasing "chicks," was the vaudevillian caricature of a scheming, clever, yet outwardly naïve Italian immigrant, his heavily accented speech marked by malapropisms and misunderstandings. Harpo was a mute, impish, reality-bending clown in a curly blonde wig, battered top hat, and oversized trench coat, from which he often produced a dizzying array of impossible objects, including a cup of coffee. He would balance the character's childlike, animalistic, and sometimes terrifyingly wild impulsiveness with sweetness and grace, including demonstrations of his incredible talent at the harp. Brothers Gummo and Zeppo played straight men but eventually both dropped out to pursue other careers, unable to compete with the lunacy enacted by the other three.

By the early 1920s, the Marx Brothers were vaudeville headliners, earning critical praise for their mastery of wordplay, improvisation, and satirical jabs at social elites, hypocrisy, and modern American life. Their successful Broadway musical comedy revues *I'll Say She Is* (1924) and *The Cocoanuts* (1925) earned the brothers their first film role, a 1929 Paramount adaptation of the latter. Arriving on celluloid at the birth of sound film, they brought the best of vaudeville's witty verbal sparring to the silver screen, blazing the trail for followers like Mel Brooks, Woody Allen, and Albert Brooks. In the popular films that followed, the work the brothers are best known for, Groucho, Chico, and Harpo took relentless aim at rich and powerful elites: philanthropists, doctors, professors, diplomats, even performing artists and art collectors. Amid the social and economic failures of the Great Depression, audiences flocked to theaters to enjoy seeing these privileged people pulled into the anarchic world of the brothers' down-on-their luck characters, who usually end up getting the better of them. *Animal Crackers* (1930) skewered society pretentiousness, *Horse Feathers* (1932) satirized college and prohibition, *Duck Soup* (1933) mocked nationalism, war, and diplomacy.

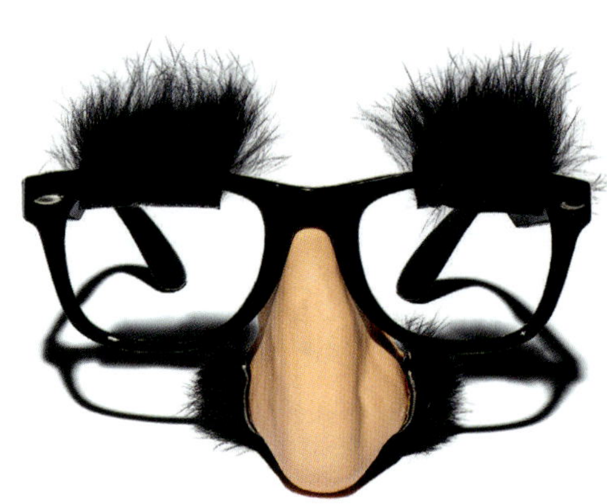

These Groucho Marx costume eyeglasses were worn by Alan Alda portraying Benjamin Franklin "Hawkeye" Pierce on the television series *M*A*S*H*. The sardonic surgeon's sharp wit and world-weary characterization were partially inspired by Groucho. Freethinking and countercultural Americans rediscovered the Marx Brothers' antiestablishment irreverence and cynicism in the 1960s and 1970s.

At the height of their popularity in the years before World War II, bigger-budget MGM films like *A Night at the Opera* (1935) and *A Day at the Races* (1937) allowed the brothers to bring their comic anarchy to other cherished elite pastimes, while *At the Circus* (1939), *Go West* (1940), and *The Big Store* (1941) further satirized American culture. Under major studio scrutiny, however, these films lacked the insolent edge and countercultural inventiveness that had defined the brothers' earlier work. Chico and Harpo faded into semiretirement by the late 1940s, while Groucho had a late career revival as a television personality, memorably hosting the comedy quiz show *You Bet Your Life* on radio and television from 1947 to 1961. By that decade, the Marx Brothers were being rediscovered as antiauthoritarian heroes. Young Americans disillusioned by postwar social conformity, military adventurism, and elite hypocrisy eagerly filled revival houses to see

Groucho, Chico, and Harpo thumb their noses at the starched shirts and fortunate sons of three decades prior.

Ryan Lintelman

LAUGHTER AT THE FRONT LINES: BOB HOPE AND THE USO

For half a century, perennial entertainer Bob Hope crisscrossed the globe bringing laughter and solace to deployed military troops in partnership with the United Service Organizations. Founded in 1941 under the auspices of President Franklin Roosevelt, the USO's enduring mission has been to buoy the morale of soldiers far from home. From Phyllis Diller to Redd Foxx to Robin Williams, few comedians have turned down the call to service, and more than two dozen have made the ultimate sacrifice, giving their lives to the cause. However, no one personified the spirit and mission of the USO as thoroughly as Bob Hope, who served a remarkable fifty-seven tours, from the battlefields of World War II through the Gulf War, weaving his life and work inseparably with a devotion to supporting America's troops.

Hope's storied career spanned every performance medium of the twentieth century. He sang, danced, and joked his way to the heights of stardom in vaudeville, on Broadway, on radio, on film, and on television during a century-long life that spanned from his 1903 birth in London to his 2003 death in Los Angeles. He performed professionally for eighty-five of those hundred years.

After an inauspicious start busking for change on streetcars, a young Hope plied his craft onstage as a vaudevillian and enjoyed a short but notable Broadway career that included a starring turn in Jerome Kern and Otto Harbach's *Roberta* (1933). He experimented with film shorts before making his mark in over fifty Hollywood features, including a string of seven wildly popular films costarring Bing Crosby, from 1940's *Road to Singapore* through 1962's *The Road to Hong Kong*. Hope was the affable host of radio's *Pepsodent Show*, which was among the defining programs of broadcasting's golden age. In the early 1950s, he was

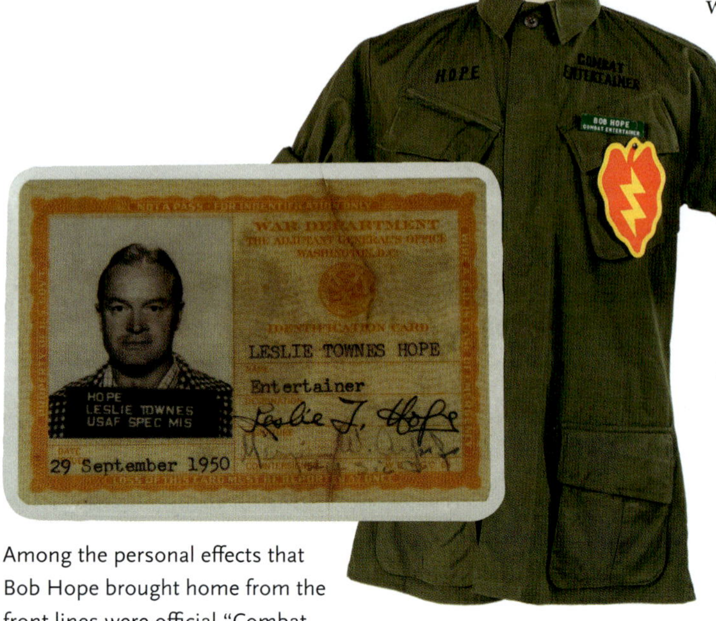

Among the personal effects that Bob Hope brought home from the front lines were official "Combat Entertainer" fatigues and identification cards that allowed him safe passage to perform in some of the most dangerous and remote outposts in American military history.

one of the first major stars to make the move to television, where he remained among the medium's most popular draws for half a century—raking in record-setting ratings with his beloved NBC specials and still-unmatched nineteen turns as host of the Academy Awards.

Hope was already a veteran performer and a household name when his first USO show was broadcast live on May 6, 1941, from an Army Air Force Base in Riverside, California, at the escalation of World War II. While the USO grew to become a pillar of the military's morale-boosting efforts, its origins were modest and not every performance was a highly produced affair; some of Hope's earliest USO shows were delivered from atop a ramshackle plank propped between two convoy vehicles. Nevertheless, the spirit-lifting impact of his humor was deeply felt, and military leaders quickly dubbed him a "secret weapon."

During the summer of 1944, one of the most violent seasons in global history, Hope logged over thirty thousand miles of travel and performed one hundred and fifty times as he hopped across the islands of the South Pacific on the front lines, in medical wards, and at remote military encampments under extremely trying conditions. Explosions along the tour route, or even adjacent to the stage, were not a rarity: the enemy was attuned to Hope's presence and power. With thousands of servicepeople gathered to watch these performances, they became highly strategic enemy targets, and show times and locations were often withheld until moments before Hope's arrival. Throughout the course of World War II, he would log over one million miles on six separate overseas tours, entertaining hundreds of thousands of soldiers.

On Christmas Day 1948, Hope—commissioned expressly by the Pentagon—entertained the troops supporting the historic Berlin Airlift, inaugurating what would become an annual ritual of leaving his own family for the holidays to entertain soldiers abroad. After only the briefest of respites, Hope resumed touring in Korea and Japan during the 1950s. In 1963, with America's involvement in Vietnam rapidly escalating, he prepared ambitious arrangements for a Christmas tour across Southeast Asia, planning to broadcast his journey on national television in a ninety-minute special from the Vietnamese warzone. The Pentagon forbade the trip, citing unsurvivable danger.

A year later, in 1964, Hope and his troupe successfully touched down in Vietnam, only to be greeted by a blast that leveled their accommodations and narrowly missed killing Hope himself. Although further attacks were a likelihood, they embarked on a historic course of performances to present the first of nine annual *Bob Hope Vietnam Christmas Show* broadcasts. These holiday specials were galvanizing moments for a broken world, as troops far from home enjoyed a brief respite from the horrors of war and their faraway families participated in the shared experience of watching Hope's performance from thousands of miles away.

So prolific was Hope's involvement in Vietnam that by 1966 a new military office devoted exclusively to Bob Hope tours was organized, with each performance requiring high security coordination and infrastructure planned up to a year in advance. Hope was a stalwart supporter of the troops even as a younger generation of anti-Vietnam activists back home balked at what seemed to be his blind patriotism. Hope's steadfast response was that he had no politics—only support for the servicepeople putting their lives on the line.

Hope's final USO tour, carried out at the age of eighty-seven, was to Bahrain and Saudi Arabia during 1990's Operation Desert Shield. Hope's legacy in comedy is uniquely entwined with the history of U.S. influence abroad. Hope was the recipient of thousands of humanitarian, political, and arts awards as well as honors bestowed by several presidents, including John F. Kennedy's Congressional Gold Medal in 1963, Lyndon B. Johnson's 1969 Presidential Medal of Freedom, and, Hope's self-stated proudest honor, being named an Honorary Veteran by Bill Clinton in 1997. He remains the only civilian ever to have received this distinction.

MARTHA RAYE AS "COLONEL MAGGIE"

World War II was a time of drastically shifting gender roles for the more than six million American women who entered the workforce when their husbands, brothers, and sons were deployed.

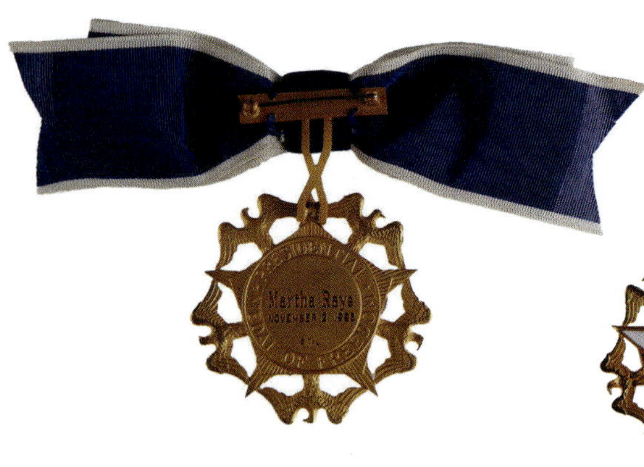

Martha Raye was awarded the Presidential Medal of Freedom, the nation's highest civilian honor, in 1993 by President Bill Clinton.

While many of these women labored in mechanical jobs as "Rosie the Riveters," the USO—at home and abroad—was largely staffed by women in both administrative and performance roles. Stars like Betty Grable, Judy Garland, Dinah Shore, and Marilyn Monroe logged overseas performances with the organization, but the most visible and devoted woman working in service to the USO was comedian Martha Raye—playfully called "Colonel Maggie" by the soldiers she supported.

Known for her uniquely expressive face and resonant belting voice, Raye was a musical comedy star who shipped out with one of the USO's very first service units in October 1942. The group traversed Europe and headed to North Africa, where Raye voluntarily stayed on alone to continue her service after the rest of the unit returned to the United States. She performed ninety-minute solo shows up to four times per day—for audiences of any size in locations of any type—and, between performances, supported medics in the hospital tents. A serious case of yellow fever and a Nazi bombing raid on her position were not enough to break her spirits.

At the escalation of the Vietnam War, Raye resumed her tireless dedication to the deployed troops, traveling with the USO or, if no tours were active, on her own dime as a solo act risking her personal safety in extraordinarily dangerous conditions. There was no location too remote and no hospital ward too dire for Raye's attentions. Among the many acts of service for which she is remembered, Colonel Maggie famously collected thousands of phone numbers and messages from soldiers and spent hours communicating with their loved ones upon her return to America. For the rest of her life, the door to Raye's Los Angeles home was always open to veterans, and she proudly donned her jungle fatigues and a green beret in public appearances.

Raye was bestowed the Presidential Medal of Freedom by Bill Clinton in 1993. Upon her passing the following year, her friend and peer in service Bob Hope remarked, "She was Florence Nightingale, Dear Abby, and the only singer who could be heard over the artillery fire." Colonel Maggie was interred at Fort Bragg with full military honors.

Laura LaPlaca

BLACKFACE MINSTRELSY

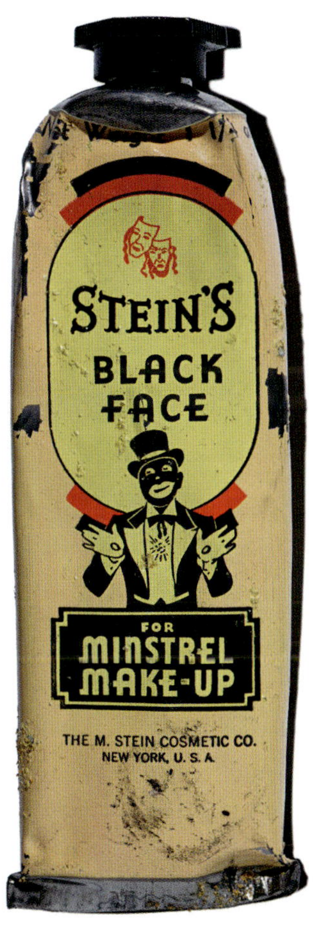

This tube of "Stein's Black Face for Minstrel Make-Up" illustrates how widespread and industrialized blackface minstrelsy had become by the early twentieth century. Performers from amateurs to professionals could purchase jet-black greasepaint off the shelf for their productions of racial caricature.

The first uniquely American form of entertainment performance, blackface minstrelsy dominated popular culture from its origins in the 1830s through the end of that century and endured as a mainstay onstage, on film, and even on radio through the 1940s. Its burnt cork and greasepaint stain everything from Mickey Mouse to motion picture sound and, most of all, American comedy. While explicit blackface performance has largely disappeared from mainstream entertainment in recent decades, performers have often drawn on its tropes and legacies for effect, and its influence is still ubiquitous, albeit unnoticed.

Blackface minstrelsy worked to both shape and distort understandings of African Americans, directly contributing to social prejudice, segregation, and enactment of Jim Crow laws. The entertainment genre functioned as a cultural tool for social and political control, creating and popularizing a limited view of Black ability, intelligence, community life, and self-governance that reduced and dehumanized the entire population, reinforcing white supremacist ideology.

Blackface minstrel shows mythologized the antebellum South as a utopian society of happy, childlike, musical, and emotional naïfs who entertained and served benevolent white masters and thereby received the benefits of paternal care, supervision, Christian salvation, and civilization. In the nineteenth century, as debates raged over Black freedom and citizenship, and into the twentieth century, with segregation and racist violence challenging Black Americans' full exercise of their citizenship, minstrelsy's reactionary nostalgia and malignant distortion of Black life had real consequences.

Minstrelsy has its roots in white urban theatrical entertainment, especially working-class variety theater. Around 1830, a performer named Thomas Dartmouth "Daddy" Rice created a new character for his act, Jim Crow. He claimed to base the shabbily dressed, ebullient, and comical persona on an African American man he met in Louisville who showed him an eccentric dance in which he'd "turn about, wheel about, and do just so," as outlined in the lyrics of the folk song "Jump Jim Crow" that Rice popularized. Wearing burnt cork in a grotesque imitation of Black skin tone, Rice portrayed Jim Crow as a dim-witted and buffoonish enslaved person. Jim Crow spoke in an exaggerated dialect, but was naturally nimble and

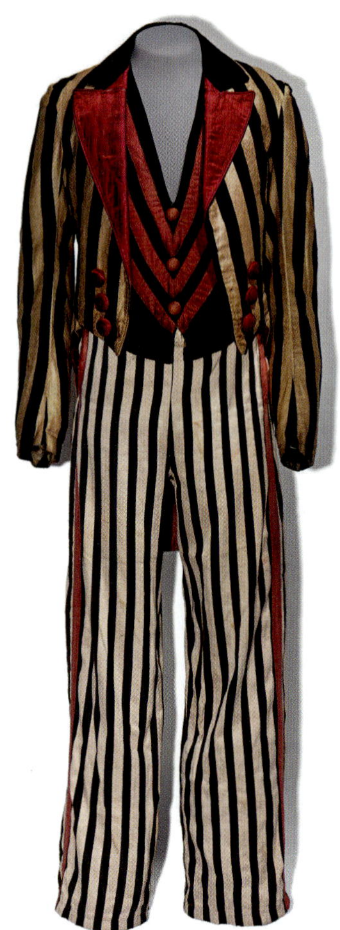

This minstrel costume, worn by a member of the itinerant Fogg, Finning, and Alger troupe around 1905, was a widely available model manufactured by Hooker and Howe theatrical costumers. The troupe played small-town theaters and opera houses from the Ohio River Valley to Oregon in the early years of the twentieth century.

musical. Rice's act became a success, inspiring competitors and ever larger and more sensational minstrel productions as blackface minstrelsy spread like wildfire across the nation in the coming years.

The growth of the entertainment industry, transportation networks, and inexpensive printing also helped fuel the popularity of minstrelsy, as performers appeared in venues all over the country, songwriters like Stephen Foster became famous writing minstrel music, and minstrel performance informed the emerging popular culture vernacular. In the years leading up to the Civil War, national politics were increasingly dominated by the slavery debate, and for many white Americans blackface minstrelsy satisfied their curiosity and fascination with Black culture and bodies while also reinforcing their beliefs about white superiority. Working-class men and immigrants were among the most enthusiastic audiences for early blackface minstrelsy. Historians have argued that minstrelsy's demeaning stereotyping of Black men in pageants of subordination and inferiority calmed their fears of labor competition and emasculation while contributing to the formation of a multiethnic white working-class identity.

Beginning in the 1840s, troupes of minstrel musicians and comics with names like the Virginia Minstrels and Ethiopian Serenaders toured the country and a regular show format began to emerge, with three parts. In the first act, the entire company would appear onstage, seated in chairs arranged in a semicircle with end men Mr. Tambo and Mr. Bones playing tambourine and rhythm bones and an interlocutor—the straight-man emcee—introducing the company and engaging in humorous banter, riddles, and wordplay. The second act, the olio, was the variety segment, very often including a mock stentorian stump speech, parody of a popular opera or musical number, or a "wench song," performed in drag. The third act was often a burlesque comic sketch or parody of Shakespeare or some other theatrical classic. Over the course of the nineteenth century, as these minstrel troupes grew ever larger and more complex, they might include sensational productions of *Uncle Tom's Cabin* or other popular works, and took on aspects of circus and vaudeville entertainment.

The standard aspects of blackface costume included dark black makeup, usually made from burnt cork mixed with grease, often accompanied by similarly stark red or white greasepaint makeup around the mouth creating the appearance of large lips; a wig made of curly black hair; clothing either rustic and distressed or urban and garish, often mismatched, ill-fitting, colorful, and patched. Minstrel comedy performance cemented stereotypes and validated white audiences' prejudices, suggesting Black

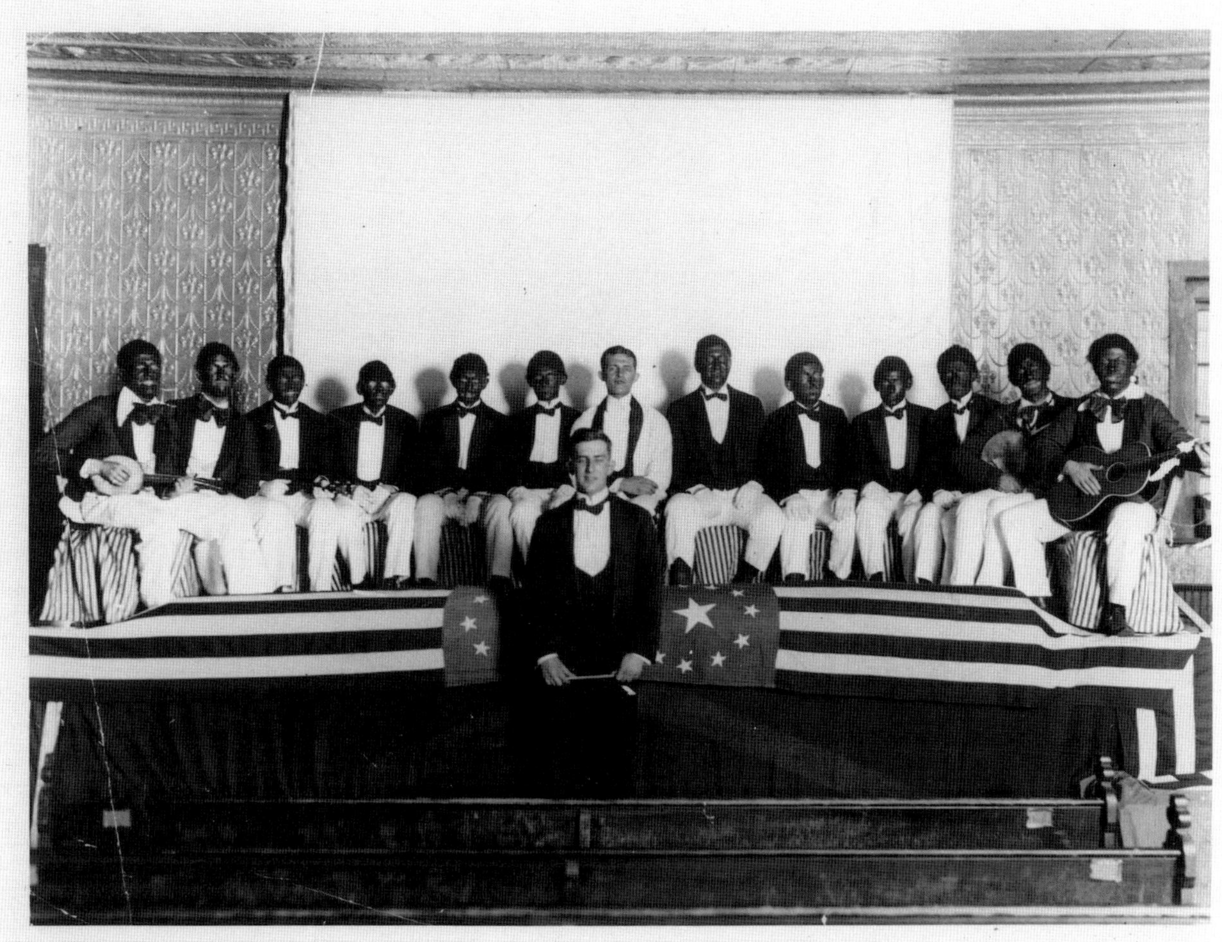

This photograph illustrates the traditional minstrel show lineup, with musicians arranged in a semicircle and an interlocutor—out of makeup—ready to engage the troupe in humorous banter.

Americans were simple, unintelligent, carefree, lazy, mischievous, immature, cowardly, superstitious, irresponsible, and happiest while engaged in useful labor, or at least singing and dancing. Stock characters included the plantation pickaninny, mammy, and loyal Uncle Tom types, but also urban "Jim Dandy" and "Zip Coon," caricatures of urban free men as arrogant and ostentatious, putting on airs by dressing well and acting as an urbane man about town though his speech was full of tellingly unintelligent malapropisms. The popular stump speech routine lampooned Black political participation, with pompous candidates or advocates for causes made to look ridiculous and ill-informed, reinforcing the notion that Black Americans weren't ready for or capable of full citizenship.

The dedicated minstrel show troupe and circuit began to decline in the decades following the Civil War, in part because of increased competition from the broader entertainment genres minstrelsy had inspired, especially vaudeville. Its influence lived on, however, with entertainers continuing to perform in blackface onstage, and even in film and radio. Singer and

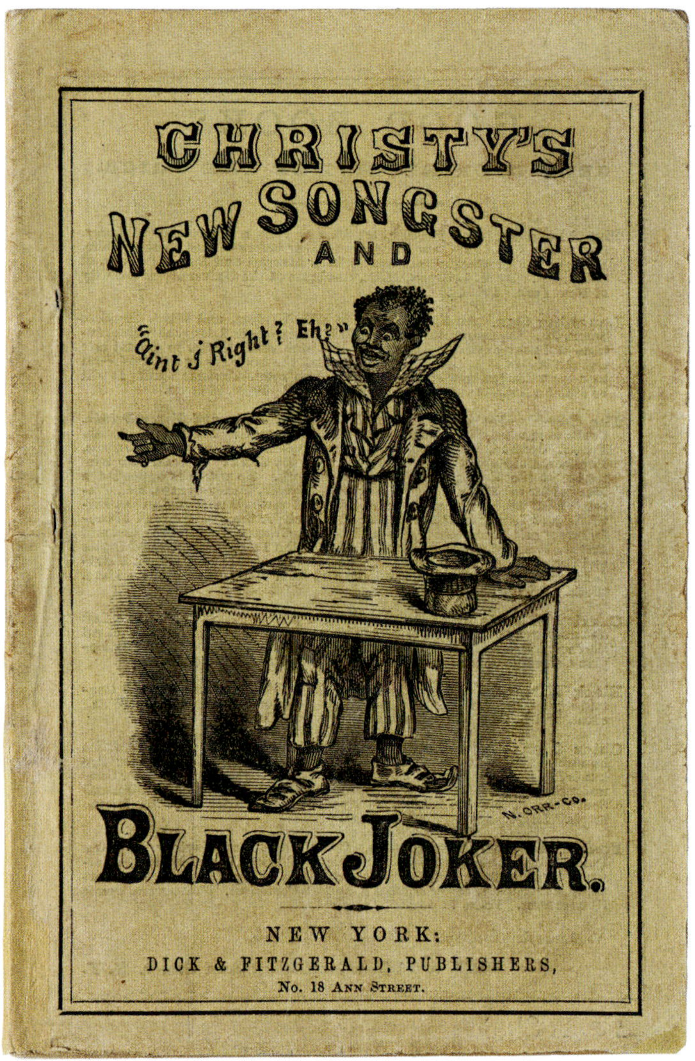

Songsters were inexpensive books of popular music available in the decades before the introduction of recorded music. Minstrel songsters and joke books like this one, connected to the Christy's Minstrels troupe, allowed Americans to stage their own minstrel shows at home. It purports to contain "all the most popular and original songs, choruses, stump speeches, witticisms, jokes, conundrums, etc."

comedian Al Jolson was particularly well-known for his performance of popular music in blackface, as he did in the groundbreaking sound film *The Jazz Singer* in 1927. Charles Correll and Freeman Gosden became the first superstars of scripted radio with their verbal blackface performance in *Amos 'n' Andy* from the 1920s through the 1950s. In films released as late as the 1950s, actors like Bing Crosby, Fred Astaire, Judy Garland, and even Shirley Temple continued to appear in blackface in sequences presenting the performance as a nostalgic and all-American entertainment.

Blackface minstrelsy is shameful, undeniably racist and harmful, but also complicated. Through white performers' appropriation and misrepresentation of Black culture, it became the essential bedrock of American popular culture, a source of inspiration and economic opportunity for generations. While some Black Americans, like Bert Williams, Sam Lucas, Billy Kersands, and Brooker and Clayton's Georgia Minstrels, actually performed minstrelsy in blackface makeup themselves, others have denounced the format since its genesis. Frederick Douglass was among the first, calling minstrel performers "the filthy scum of white society, who have stolen from us a complexion denied to them by nature, in which to make money, and pander to the corrupt taste of their white fellow-citizens."[34] Though most modern Americans would likely wholeheartedly agree with Douglass's assessment, modern blackface scholarship has wrestled with the endless variety of complex experiences, understandings, and legacies of aspects of blackface performance.

It might not sell out theaters anymore, but blackface minstrelsy is still with us. You'll find its influence in numerous essays throughout this book, and its tropes, style, and form undergird all modern comedy performance. Even its most contemptable aspect—the literal black face paint—hasn't yet been totally eradicated from our culture. Recent controversial examples of blackface performance in popular culture include Robert Downey Jr.'s overzealous method actor in *Tropic Thunder*, Sarah Silverman applying blackface makeup in an episode of her eponymous comedy program, Roger Sterling's party performance in *Mad Men*, the self-aware and stylized reappropriation of blackface tropes in Spike Lee's *Bamboozled* and the Broadway musical *Scottsboro Boys*, and ill-advised Halloween costumes worn on college campuses that capture headlines every year.

Ryan Lintelman

BROWNFACE AND BROWNVOICE

Most people living in the United States today can probably recall seeing costumes for sale that include sombreros, faux mustaches, and woven ponchos or colorful serapes. In recent years, public discourse has surged around cultural appropriation and the offensive costumes that perpetuate racist stereotypes of "foreign" cultures. But where do these images come from? Who spread the idea that it's funny to mock other cultures by slapping on a costume, painting yourself brown, pasting on facial hair, and parodying the accents of people whose first language is not English? Examining the origins, manifestations, and consequences of these practices provides insight into the complex racial dynamics and societal perceptions that shape the lives of racialized ethnic "others" in the United States—particularly those of Mexican heritage.

An offshoot of blackface minstrelsy, brownface—and brownvoice—are characterized by the misrepresentation of racialized ethnic "others" for comedic effect. These performances often rely on white performers darkening their skin tone as well as exaggerating their speech and mannerisms in dehumanizing ways. Brownface minstrel caricatures are appropriated from many different communities and lead to unflattering portrayals of people of Latinx (particularly Mexican), South Asian, Pacific, Middle Eastern, and Indigenous backgrounds. Since the nineteenth century, these performances have catered to the public's fascination with exotic cultures and the colonial narratives prevalent during an era of imperialistic expansion for the United States.

After the Treaty of Guadalupe Hidalgo was signed in 1848, the United States claimed vast Mexican territories from the West Coast to the Southwest. The treaty gave Mexican citizens one year to choose U.S. or Mexican citizenship, but many chose to remain on the land they had occupied for generations. As these formerly Mexican citizens came into increasing contact and conflict with Anglo-Americans, many encountered violence, dispossession, and discrimination. The practice of brownface minstrelsy was one way for the dominant culture to assert itself over these newly conquered peoples, whose claim to the lands predated the United States.

By the early twentieth century, Hollywood films and vaudeville stages prominently featured racial and ethnic minstrelsy. Just as blackface perpetuated anti-Black stereotypes and yellowface perpetuated anti-Asian ones, brownface perpetuated specific caricatures of Latinxs—most often represented as the stock characters of the Greaser and the Bandit. These caricatures entrenched racial prejudice by representing Mexicans (and Mexican Americans) as stupid, lazy, filthy, drunk, underhanded, and prone to criminal behavior, and helped solidify prejudice in the American imagination. In vignettes like a 1914 Ziegfeld Follies scene set on "The Border Line Between Texas and Mexico" or other imagined settings in the American Southwest, vaudeville comics like Frank Conroy and George La Maire performed stereotype-laden character acts where penniless Mexican peasants lazily drank and conversed with burros or signed up to fight alongside Pancho Villa.[35] Like the ahistorical white supremacist epic *The Birth of a Nation*, the D. W. Griffith–produced 1915 film *Martyrs of the Alamo* mythologized that famous battle by depicting virtuous white heroes defending civilization against hordes of evil, drunk, and rapacious Mexican bandits (mostly played by white actors in brownface makeup). Even as the popularity of blackface minstrelsy waned in the mid-twentieth century, the practice of brownface and brownvoice persisted, adapting to new comedic formats in radio, television, and the emergent popular art of animation.

This straw sombrero was worn by white actor Mel Blanc portraying "Sy, the Little Mexican" on Jack Benny's radio and television programs in the 1950s. The character, said to be from Tijuana, answered Benny's questions with a monosyllabic "Sí" or other variations of the word in a Mexican accent with a deadpan stare.

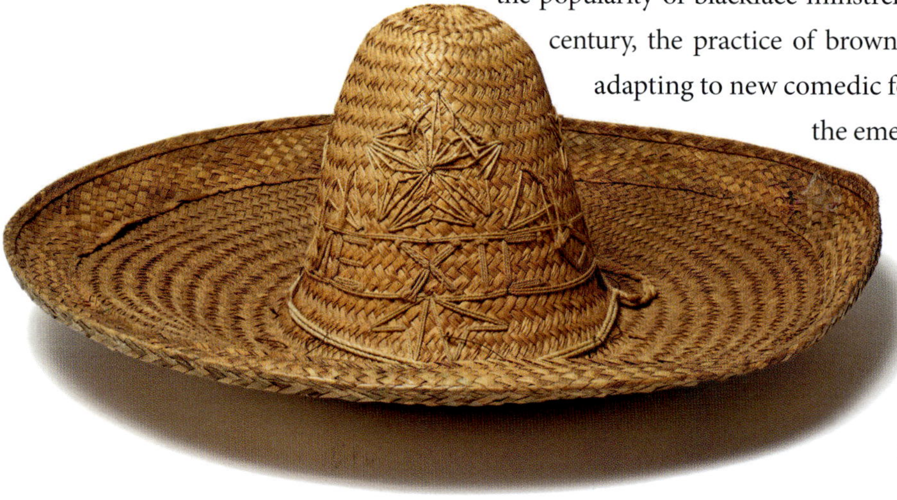

It is not difficult to encounter stereotyped caricatures of Mexicans and Mexican Americans even today as the practice has become normalized in the entertainment industry. Even some of the

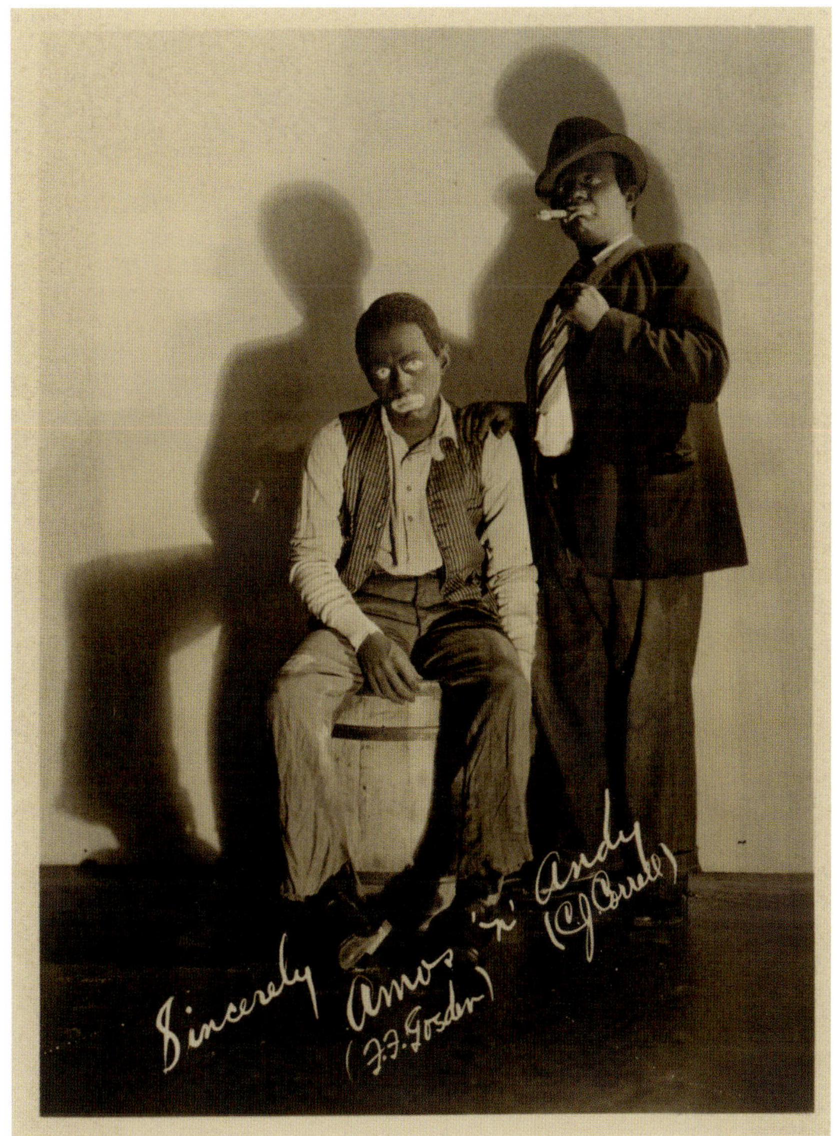

This 1935 publicity photograph shows Charles Correll and Freeman Gosden in character as Amos and Andy. The duo is shown in blackface, wearing wooly black wigs minstrels typically donned to imitate African American hair, as they did in the 1930 *Amos 'n' Andy* film *Check and Double Check*.

Company, attend meetings of the Mystic Knights of the Sea fraternal lodge, and try to keep out of trouble, usually resulting from lodge leader Kingfish's get-rich-quick schemes.

For fifteen minutes, six times a week, Gosden and Correll dominated the nation's attention. At the height of the *Amos 'n' Andy* craze, from 1929 to 1932, department stores would play the show over their PA systems and theaters would stop movies and play the show rather than risk customers heading home to catch it. Telephone operators noted a dramatic fall in call volume at show time. President Calvin Coolidge reportedly made it clear he wasn't to be disturbed when *Amos 'n' Andy* was on the air.[40] The show's dialogue was natural and realistic, with witty banter peppered with colloquialisms, slang, and wisecracks, and lent several

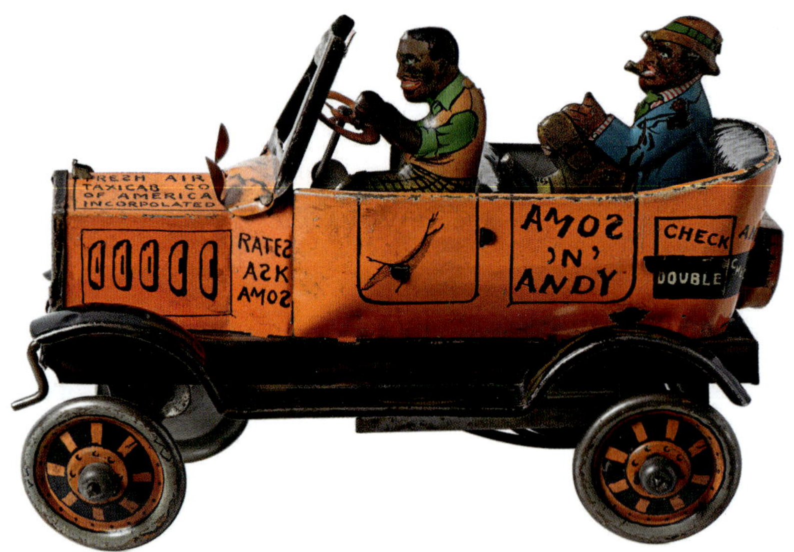

This toy taxi was made by the Louis Marx Company in 1930 as a merchandising tie-in to the film *Check and Double Check*, in an attempt to cash in on *Amos 'n' Andy* mania. The run-down jalopy bears the name of their "Fresh Air Taxi Co of America Incorpolated," with spelling errors, reversed letters, and poor penmanship representing the show's "aural blackface."

phrases to the vernacular, including "check and double-check," "holy mackerel," and "I'se regusted." *Amos 'n' Andy* even influenced politics, with Louisiana politician Huey Long appropriating the nickname "Kingfish" for himself in the lead-up to his mid-1930s presidential campaign to bolster his populist credentials.[41]

Correll and Gosden attracted up to forty million listeners every week and managed to keep it fresh and evolving, appearing in a 1930 motion picture adaptation, and making the change to a weekly half-hour radio series with a studio audience in 1943. In the 1950s, *Amos 'n' Andy* was adapted as a popular but ultimately short-lived television series, and finally reconfigured as a daily music radio program, *The Amos 'n' Andy Music Hall*, that last aired in 1960.

That made the series one of the last major, mainstream instances of blackface minstrelsy performance in a culture that was increasingly hostile to this form of racial caricature. In retrospect, radio seems like an odd medium for blackface performance, but in the 1920s racial and ethnic imitation was still an immensely popular genre of comedy. The purely aural form made *Amos 'n' Andy*'s racial ventriloquy easier on the air than on the stage since the white performers didn't have to mimic the appearance of Black people, only their voice, through caricatured dialect and inflection.[42] The creators had both begun their careers performing in blackface minstrel shows, and Gosden was a Virginian who claimed to have honed his racial mimicry through friendships with Black neighbors; at the beginning, neither Gosden nor Correll thought twice about the ethics of portraying Black characters laden with stereotypical traits in grotesquely exaggerated dialect.[43]

By the 1920s, white supremacist ideology and Jim Crow segregation were deeply entrenched, and despite the efforts of Black civil rights leaders and a few standout entertainers like Bert Williams, Black Americans were almost entirely represented in popular entertainment by white performers appropriating, mocking, and misconstruing their lives and culture, in blackface minstrelsy, vaudeville, music, and film. Unlike other aspects of contemporary life like politics and business where most white Americans might have preferred their absence, Black people were central to popular entertainment, tightly contained within prescribed roles and stereotypes that ranged from childlike, ignorant, sensual, musically talented, sentimental, foolish, or unthreatening comic relief. Gosden and Correll believed that their series was providing a positive benefit to the Black community and that their characters demonstrated humanity and reality rather than the grotesque caricature of traditional minstrelsy. In representing the modern, urban African American experience, they claimed, they were proving that there was more to the community than the images of simple, rural pickaninnies, loyal mammies, and criminal urban hustlers of contemporary popular culture.[44]

Indeed, *Amos 'n' Andy* encompassed a wide range of characters, storylines, and genres, appealing to a broad, national audience of all racial backgrounds. For instance, many early episodes explored the trials and frustrations of Amos and Andy adjusting to city life, gaining employment, building a new social network, and being swindled by city slickers. At a time of unprecedented migration and urbanization, this resonated with millions who had likewise moved from country to city for work or opportunity. Its diverse cast of characters included George "Kingfish" Stevens, the blustery and perpetually scheming leader of the Mystic Knights lodge, Amos's attractive and intelligent wife Ruby, and a host of supporting characters that included rare representations of Black ministers, medical professionals, journalists, teachers, businessmen, and law enforcement officers. Proponents of the show argued that its layered and complex depiction of a Black community compensated for its sometimes hackneyed and stereotypical depiction of its residents.

Some felt pride that Black characters—even portrayed by white performers—were the most popular and famous entertainers in the country. Where else, the argument went, could Americans of any color find a depiction of contemporary Black life in all its variety, from labor to romance to social organizations to politics, or even a popular entertainment program set in Harlem? *Amos 'n' Andy* represented aspects of the African American experience that had heretofore been totally absent in American popular culture, including the Great Migration (early episodes featured stories about their journey from rural Georgia to Chicago), romance and marriage (Amos's devotion to his wife Ruby, Andy's dating life), and social life (the fraternal hijinks of the members of the Mystic Knights of the Sea). White and Black listeners alike expressed their genuine affection for Amos and Andy and saw something of themselves in the characters, some argued, bolstering sympathy for Black Americans and broader acceptance of their humanity and citizenship.[45]

Other Black leaders and viewers, however, found the show's characterizations little changed from the stereotypes of the minstrel show and rejected the series as a white fantasy of Black life. In 1931, *Pittsburgh Courier* publisher Robert L. Vann launched a petition drive, with endorsements from other Black organizations, churches, and civil rights leaders, to protest *Amos 'n' Andy*'s harmful representation of Black Americans. The largest protest against a mass media product since *The Birth of a Nation* in 1915, the campaign delivered over 740,000 signatures to the Federal Radio Commission asking that *Amos 'n' Andy* be taken off the air. The FRC dismissed the petitions, show sponsor Pepsodent shook off the threats of a boycott, and the campaign did little damage to the series' popularity, even among Black listeners.[46]

Somewhat surprisingly, twenty years later the story played out differently. In 1951 the *Amos 'n' Andy* television series premiered, with Black actors Alvin Childress and Spencer Williams Jr., playing Amos and Andy, making it the first TV series to feature an all-Black cast. Gosden and Correll had wisely decided that times had changed and they would be unable to portray the characters in blackface on television, and early reviews celebrated the Black cast's success in reinventing the series for the screen. However, the very night of the debut episode, June 28, 1951, the NAACP was holding its annual national meeting in Atlanta, and under executive secretary Walter White, the group passed a unanimous resolution condemning *Amos 'n' Andy* for "[depicting] the Negro and other minority groups in a stereotyped and derogatory manner . . . [strengthening] the conclusion among uninformed or prejudiced people that Negroes and other minorities are inferior, lazy, dumb and dis-honest."[47]

NAACP executive Roy Wilkins, who had defended the radio series as a journalist during the protest campaign in 1930, now helped mobilize opposition to the show, arguing that "the visual impact is infinitely worse than the radio version . . . the television brings these people to life—they are no longer merely voices and they say to millions of white Americans who know nothing about Negroes, and to millions of white children who are learning about life, that this is the way Negroes are."[48] Though there were still supporters of *Amos 'n' Andy* and dialogue about the show's values within the Black community, this time the protest was more successful. Though the show was earning good ratings, main show sponsor Blatz Beer pulled its support and CBS decided to cancel the series in 1953.

Amos 'n' Andy proved that comedy has enormous power to shape an audience's conception of a community, from within or without. While paving the way for all scripted comedy to come, it also ignited a debate about race and representation that continues today.

Ryan Lintelman

PHYLLIS DILLER CRACKS THE COMEDY CEILING

Cigarette holder askew and fright wig aloft, Phyllis Diller rewrote every social script of her time to presage the coming of a new order for women in comedy—and in American cultural life. Before she became one of the most iconic voices in the history of stand-up and one of the savviest operators in the business of entertainment, Diller hailed from rural Lima, Ohio, and fashioned herself as a practical feminist whose vast and varied talents were put to use supporting five children. She achieved hard-won financial solvency via a self-made local broadcasting career in San Francisco and then, after finding a guiding light in the self-help tome *The Magic of Believing*, risked it all as she approached age forty to embark upon a second career as a stand-up—despite never having set foot in a nightclub, let alone on a stage. It was March 1955 when she debuted at San Francisco's Purple Onion. She was held over for eighty-nine weeks.

The comedy industry was not waiting with bated breath for someone like Phyllis Diller to arrive on the scene; she would have to succeed not only on the strength of her talent but also by building—and then selling—a new brand of entertainment that drew on her perspectives as a wife, a mother, and a woman in post–World War II

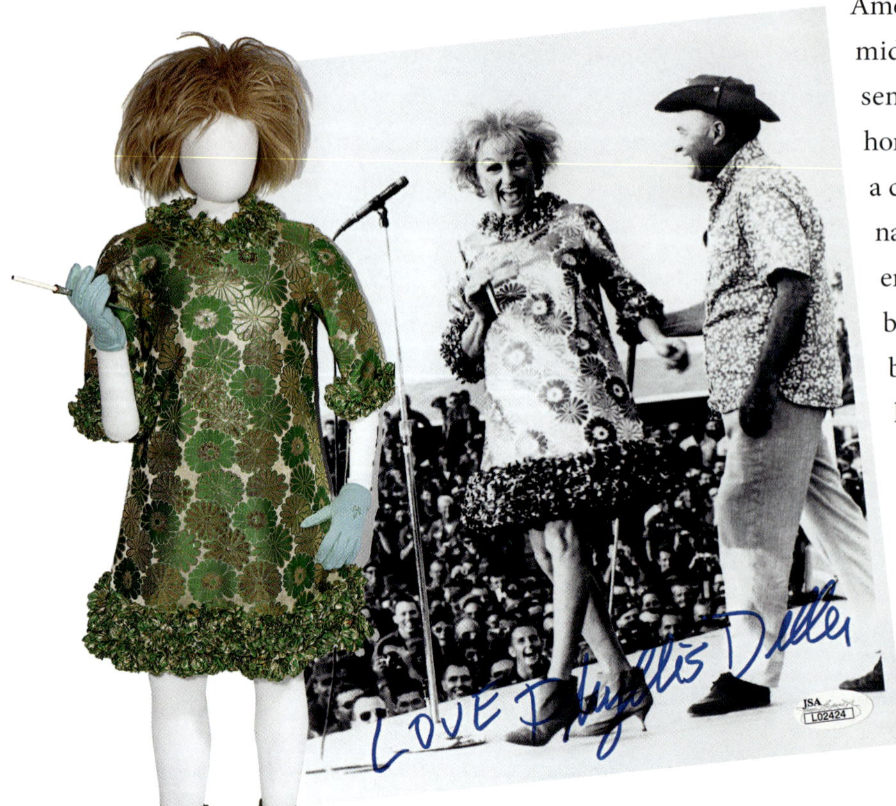

Phyllis Diller wore this green costume ensemble when she joined Bob Hope's USO Christmas tour in 1966.

America. Against the backdrop of a mid-century suburban idyll represented by television sitcoms and homemaking magazines catering to a commercialized American dream narrative, Diller spoke to her generation's domestic discontent—a bold and quite singular move before second-wave feminism had coalesced into a mainstream movement.

The *New York Times* would dub Diller "the ultimate domestic demon,"[49] a character that performed serial incompetency as a housekeeper, cook, and wife, and who histrionically flouted traditional standards of beauty. Her signature fashion involved masking a conventionally feminine shape with boxy structured dresses in clashing iridescent colors, and she referred to her own face as "not ugly, but dysplastic."[50] In her now-legendary "gag file," Diller logged over 52,000 one-liners like "I'm a method housekeeper—I have to be in the mood" and "I once wore a peek-a-boo blouse. People would peek and then they'd boo." She reversed a decades-long tradition of "take my wife—please!" jokes by assigning her lackadaisical husband the moniker "Fang" and berating his indifference. With a rat-a-tat-tat delivery timed with a stopwatch, Diller made it her goal to clock a joke every five seconds and punctuated her punchlines with bursts of inimitable cackling laughter. Diller's self-deprecating presentation was tactical on two fronts: By literally laughing at herself, she assuaged very real tensions around a woman assuming the powerful position of a stand-up—commanding attention alone on stage. And by performing the act of "failing at socially assigned roles," she welcomed her audience—especially the women in the audience—to a form of pleasurable release from the standards that defined them.[51]

Diller was hardly alone as a woman in comedy; she counted peers such as blue comedians Rusty Warren and Belle Barth, variety artists like Martha Raye and Imogene Coca, and musical comedy stars like Bea Lillie

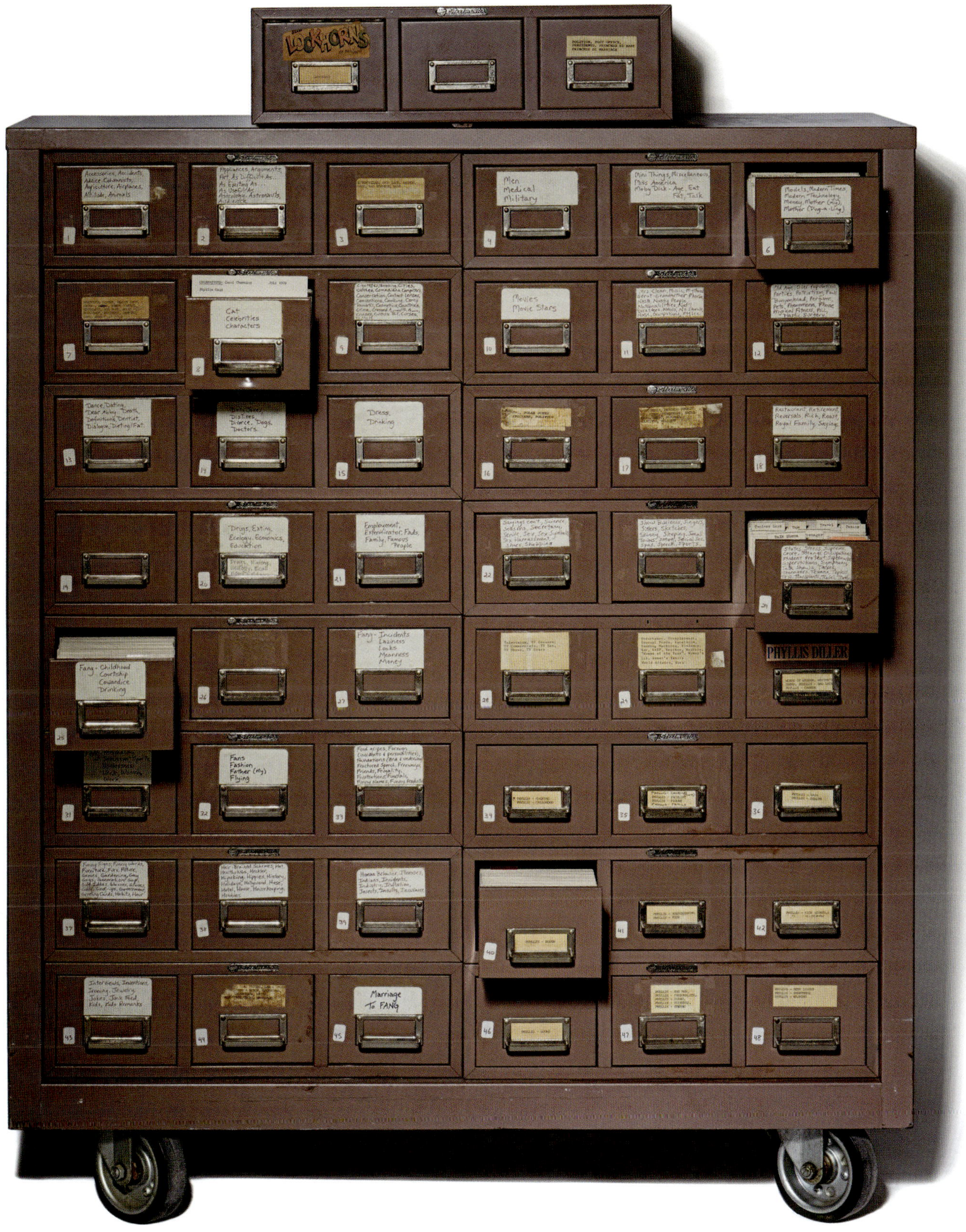

Phyllis Diller's forty-eight-drawer steel file cabinet contains more than fifty thousand typewritten gags arranged alphabetically by subject: Appliances, Beauty, Cooking, and so on.

and Minnie Pearl. The formidable stand-up Jean Carroll was leaving the scene as Diller burst upon it, Moms Mabley was a fixture on the touring circuits, and future innovators like Joan Rivers were waiting in the wings. A strong, active lineage of women was recontouring the art form, but Phyllis Diller accrued a level of industrial clout and creative influence that would forever alter the playing field. Her stance was confident, her gaze direct, her voice full—and her success was entirely undeniable by any metric.

One part of Diller's legacy involves the enormous acts of negotiation, advocacy, and sheer reputational *work* involved in racking up all the benchmarks of mainstream success for (mostly male) A-list stand-ups of the 1960s: bookings on *The Ed Sullivan Show*, gigs in Greenwich Village, a USO caravan at the height of the Vietnam War, playing Carnegie Hall. Diller did it all with aplomb. The other, less often acknowledged, part of her legacy involved leveraging that hard-won insider status to comment from *within* on the entertainment industry's terribly antiquated attitudes toward women. In one of her most audacious moments, Diller infiltrated that most storied of comedic boys' clubs when she snuck into the inner sanctum of the Friars Club dressed in drag, taking a seat at a ringside table during an X-rated roast.

After a career that spanned nearly fifty years, Diller retired from stand-up in her eighties. "I miss the laughter. It's as good as you can feel. A wonderful, wonderful happiness," she reflected, "and great power."[52]

Laura LaPlaca

THE COMEDY ALBUM BOOM

Until the advent of the televised stand-up special in the age of cable and streaming, comedy albums were the primary means for communities of fans to discover, repeatedly consume, and identify with the work of their favorite comedians. The rise of the comedy album in the 1960s demonstrated a massive commercial audience for recorded humor, and when comedians began to routinely rank on the *Billboard* charts and rack up Grammy wins, the viability of the new format was indisputable.

Though recorded comedy quickly became ubiquitous, the art of the album is a refined one: Not every performance, or performer, is suited to the format. An album can be an artist's defining work—a statement of purpose, a political dictum, or a rallying cry. The power of the format is in its intimacy, allowing a performer to speak directly into the ear of the listener and to manifest the all-important, and deeply personal, relationship between artist and audience that makes comedy such a potent expressive form.

INSIDE SHELLEY BERMAN

1959's *Inside Shelley Berman* was the first comedy album ever to "go gold" (selling at least half a million copies) and the first non-musical comedy performance to win a Grammy Award. It kickstarted what was to become the comedy album boom of the sixties and seventies. Berman was a pioneer of observational comedy who, with peers like Mort Sahl and Lenny Bruce, instilled a new authenticity, vulnerability, and topicality into the art form of stand-up. A seasoned stage actor and founding member of the famed Compass Players (which went on to become the Second City), Berman found his niche seated on a barstool in Chicago clubs like Mister Kelly's, pantomiming hilariously convoluted and anxiety-ridden one-sided telephone calls. A signature piece, "The Morning After the Night Before," was a mini-psychodrama about a hungover partygoer who learns that he'd run an epic course of destruction through his host's home the evening prior. It featured as a seven-minute centerpiece track on the album and vaulted Berman to nationwide stardom. The cadence, timing, and inflection of Berman's actorly delivery and the resonance of his well-trained voice enchanted audiences who flocked to purchase the recording, which stayed at number two on the *Billboard* charts for five weeks and spurred follow-up albums *Outside Shelley Berman* and *The Edge of Shelley Berman* (both of which also went gold). As a measure of how nascent the comedy album industry was at the time, Berman genuinely feared that he was endangering his career by recording his set: "I thought no one would want to see me anymore if they could just play it." After the album's debut, Berman arrived for a regularly scheduled club gig and witnessed a line around the block. "'I can buy two suits now,' I told my wife."[53]

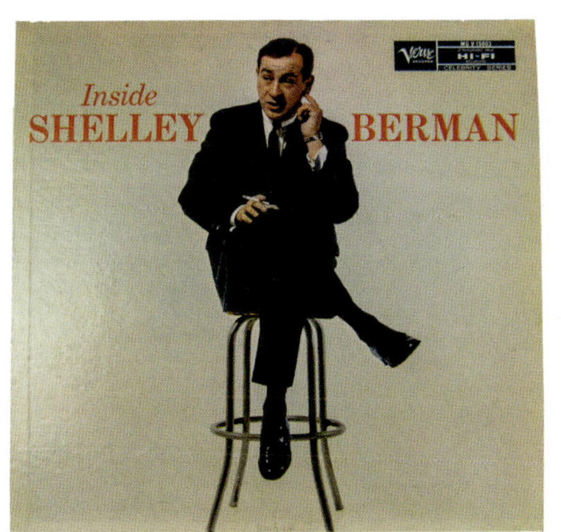

THE FIRST FAMILY

Before satirizing the American president became a routine part of entertainment culture, *The First Family* (1962) turned John F. Kennedy into comedy gold through impersonator Vaughn Meader's uncanny New England accent and bumbling sense of aloofness. During the height of America's obsession with the Kennedys' "Camelot," the album parodied the family's traditionalism, the First Lady's muted voice and penchant for redecorating, and the children's bedtime routines—gentle topics by today's standards, but enough at the time to ignite a flurry of hand-wringing.

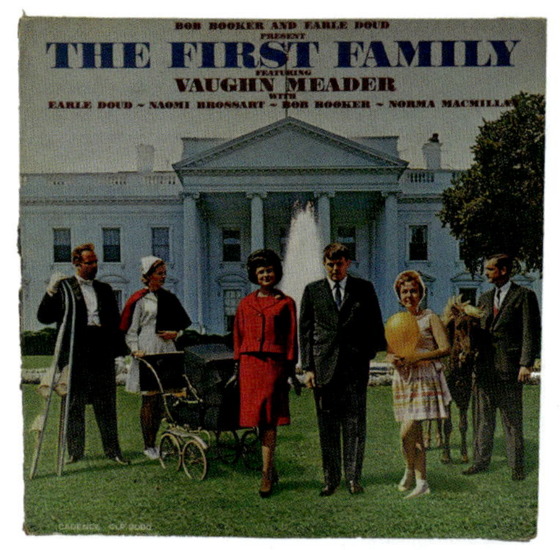

With the world suspended at a peak of Cold War paranoia, record executives recoiled at the thought of pressing the album, fearing that lampooning the American presidency might hand traitorous fodder to communists, or be an outright insult to the wildly popular commander in chief. Passed over by all the major labels, producers Bob Booker and Earl Doud signed with indie Cadence Records and ultimately proved that such fears were misplaced: the public went wild for the political parody, and Kennedy himself applauded the album, once addressing the Democratic National Committee by quipping, "Vaughn Meader was busy tonight, so I came myself."[54]

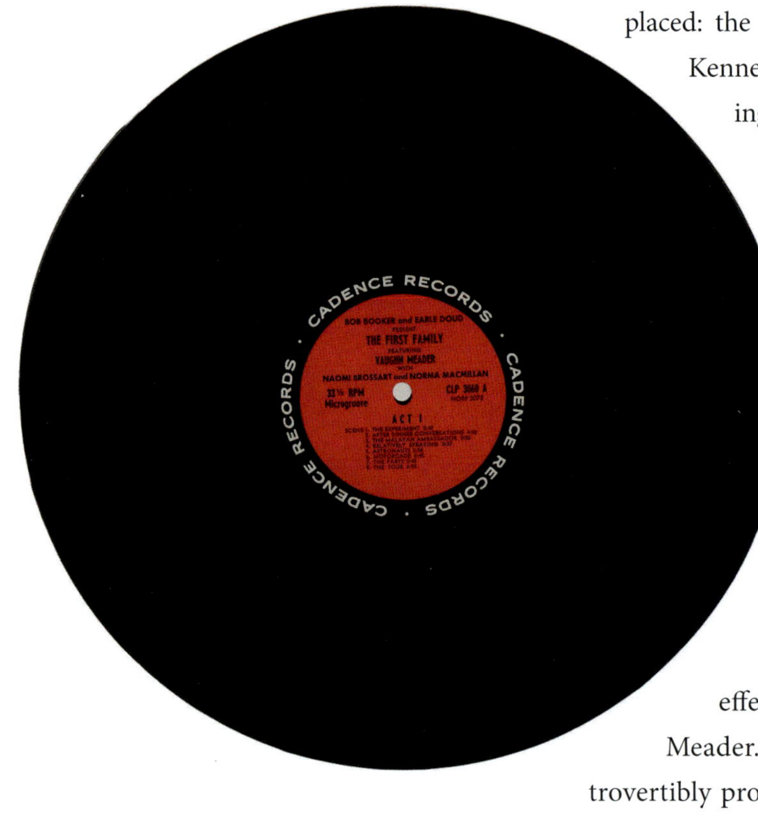

The First Family went on to become the fastest and best-selling album in the history of the recording industry to that date, selling more than one million copies per week during the first six weeks of its release. It won the Grammy for Album of the Year in 1963. Following the assassination of John F. Kennedy in November 1963, less than one year after the album's debut, *The First Family* was pulled from store shelves, effectively ending the meteoric career of Vaughn Meader. Yet the album's significance endured: it incontrovertibly proved the existence of a mainstream mass audience for sharp political humor.

A WILD AND CRAZY GUY

Steve Martin's 1978 megahit *A Wild and Crazy Guy* ushered in the era of the comedy superstar. Martin had been seeking out an audience for his esoteric style until he finally clicked at West Coast clubs like Pasadena's Ice House, LA's Troubadour, and San Francisco's Boarding House, where the countercultural music scene was flourishing. Making an impression with his goofy physicality, clumsy balloon animals, and tendency to call his crowds out into the streets for performances that invaded the urban public sphere, Martin's one-of-a-kind approach expanded the possibilities of what stand-up performance could be.

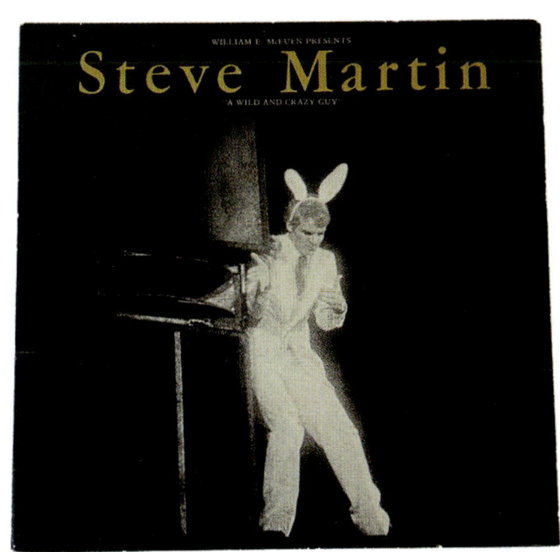

Breakout performances on early episodes of an iconoclastic new television show called *Saturday Night Live* made Martin a household name. As his popularity spiked, Martin began to sell out stadium-sized venues across the country and established stand-up comedy as a popular art form on par with rock music. His standing-room-only crowds drew comparison to the audiences who turned out for Rolling Stones concerts. *A Wild and Crazy Guy* registers this moment in comedy history quite literally: The first half of the album was recorded live before three hundred patrons at his homeroom club, the Boarding House, while the second half was recorded before a raucous crowd of ten thousand at the Red Rocks Amphitheatre. Crowd noise is a defining sound of the album, whose iconic cover features Martin silhouetted in his trademark white suit and bunny ears.

With the soundtrack of *Saturday Night Fever* lodged firmly at the top of the *Billboard* charts, *A Wild and Crazy Guy* never broke through to number one, but it did sell nearly one million copies in presales before going double platinum and winning the Grammy for Best Comedy Album.

LAFF OF THE PARTY

Redd Foxx's 1956 debut album *Laff of the Party* was X-rated, laced with profanities, and massively popular. It was sold under the counter as contraband, often wrapped in brown paper as record stores and their patrons made a charade of avoiding midcentury obscenity laws that banned explicit content. (Those laws, of course, made

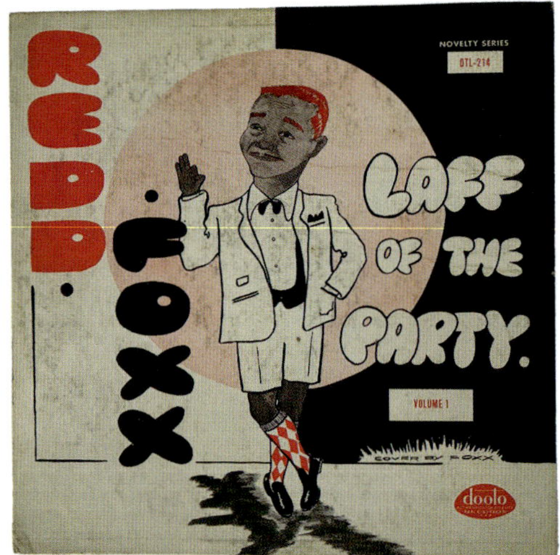

purchasing and listening to "blue" material all the more thrilling.) *Laff of the Party* spawned the release of more than thirty-five Redd Foxx records in the ensuing five years—all circulated as part of a growing comedy underground. With *The Ten Commandments* reigning as 1956's top-grossing film, *I Love Lucy* topping TV ratings, and *Billboard* charts dominated by Elvis Presley, mainstream popular culture was inattentive to demand for entertainment with more bite. Though raunchy recordings are as old as recorded sound itself, the late 1950s came to mark the peak of the "party record."

While Foxx would go on to phenomenal fame on TV's *Sanford and Son* in 1972, he had plied his craft for decades prior with a career crystallized in Harlem and launched on the Chitlin' Circuit. He seized upon an opportunity for widespread recognition when he was offered twenty-five dollars to capture his act with a reel-to-reel recorder placed in the back of a crowded club. The recording was cheaply made and hastily edited, filled with the sounds of clinking glasses and ambient crowd noise, but it had a candid "you-are-there" sound that appealed—even in an era that prized "high fidelity." Excluded from the airwaves and unadvertised via mainstream channels, *Laff of the Party* nevertheless ignited a firestorm, making good on the ostentatious promise emblazoned in its liner notes: "THE FUNNIEST MAN IN THE WORLD is what they say of Redd Foxx and in hearing the contents of this album you will agree."

2000 YEARS WITH CARL REINER & MEL BROOKS

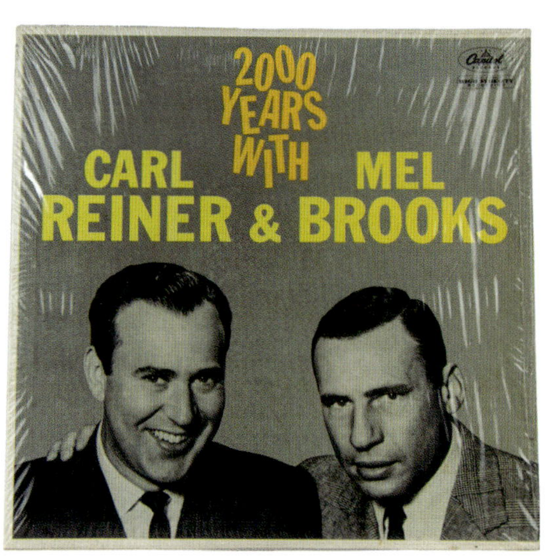

Carl Reiner and Mel Brooks met while working side by side in the pressure cooker of live television. It was inside the legendary *Your Show of Shows* writers' room that they first ad-libbed a mock interview with a 2,000-year-old man who had seen it all and lived to tell about it. Reiner played straight man to Brooks' "Jewish Methuselah," who'd been acquainted with everyone from Shakespeare to Paul Revere, riffing on meeting Jesus and the apostles "before they became a hit" and dating Joan of Arc. The character philosophized about world history through the lens of the Jewish immigrant experience and, remarkably, all of the

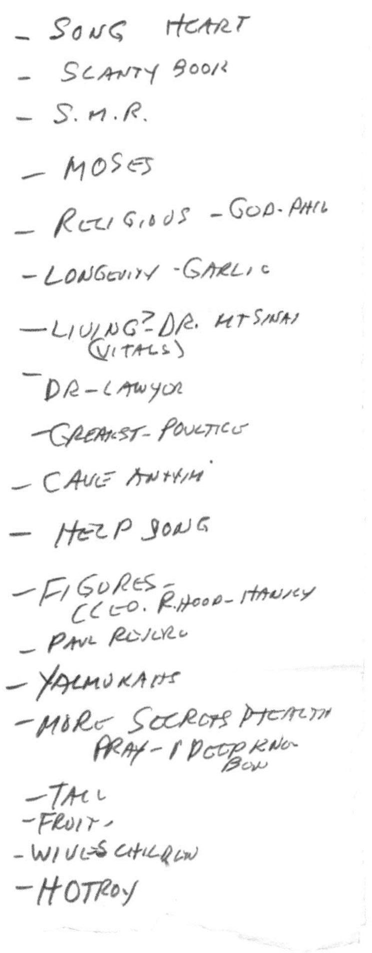

2,000-Year-Old Man's appearances—live or recorded—were unique and improvised at breakneck speed.

After performing the routine at Hollywood house parties, Reiner and Brooks were persuaded by Steve Allen to release a comedy album. Following a single ninety-minute recording session, *2000 Years with Carl Reiner and Mel Brooks* launched in 1960 and became a phenomenon, followed in short order by 1961's *2000 and One Years*. The albums reaffirmed Reiner's place as one of comedy's most popular personalities and introduced Brooks as a performer to national audiences for the first time (after years spent as a prolific writer and creative).

After a third album in 1963, *Carl Reiner and Mel Brooks at the Cannes Film Festival*, the two planned to retire the "2,000-Year-Old Man," as Reiner was busy helming *The Dick Van Dyke Show* and Brooks was trying his hand at film—ultimately winning an Academy Award for his first feature, *The Producers*. The character would prove to be far too beloved to shelve for good: A decade later, they recorded 1973's *2000 and Thirteen*, and twenty-five years after that, they shared a Grammy for 1997's *The 2000 Year Old Man in the Year 2000*. The Grammy marked the culmination of the adventures of "history's biggest know-it-all" and the pinnacle of one of comedy's most enduring collaborations. As Mel Brooks explained on the cusp of winning the award, "Carl's my best audience, and therefore he's my best friend."

Carl Reiner and Mel Brooks improvised their "2,000-Year-Old Man" routines using a loose methodology Reiner liked to call "writing with the mouth," or riffing to create a cohesive, but always unique, performance that surprised even the comics themselves. Reiner and Brooks tape-recorded their improvisations to study the rhythms that worked best, and prepared simple outlines, like this one, to guide live performances. However, Reiner's precise line of questioning was never known to Brooks, who delighted in shocking his partner with off-the-wall answers that sent them both into hysterics.

WHOOPI GOLDBERG: ORIGINAL BROADWAY SHOW RECORDING

In 1983, Whoopi Goldberg's one-woman show, originally titled *The Spook Show*, made waves as both an artistic tour de force and a galvanizing commentary on hard-hitting social issues like equity and representation. Goldberg—a virtuosic performer with a seemingly inexhaustible range—embodied a gallery of characters with palpable empathy and authenticity: from a wheelchair-bound woman who dreams of dancing to a young woman navigating the psychological and social traumas of abortion. As Goldberg would later reflect, "I've had lots of experiences with different kinds of people. I don't always like the people, but I accept their experience. I understand why they feel the way they feel."[55]

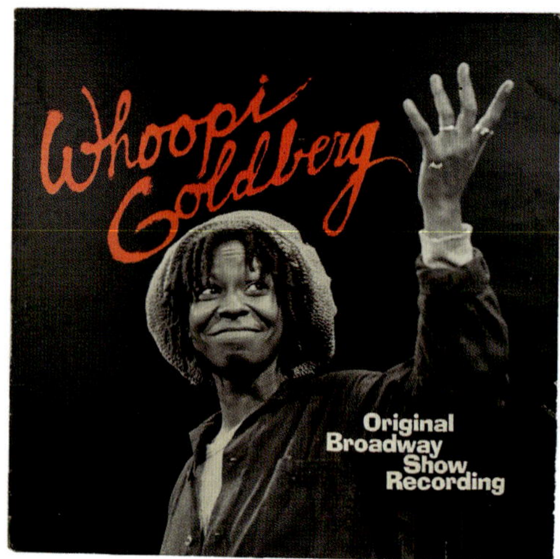

The show's genesis was in the challenging reality that Hollywood gatekeepers had left Goldberg little choice but to take the arc of her career into her own hands: she created for herself the complex, nuanced characters she knew she was capable of playing, but which a deeply entrenched entertainment industry refused to acknowledge or imagine.

Among those who reveled in Goldberg's *Spook Show*, and in the excitement that came with "discovering" a fresh comic talent, was noted comedian and director Mike Nichols, who approached Goldberg with an offer to help ferry her production to Broadway. Retitled simply *Whoopi Goldberg*, the show elicited buzz from every corner of the entertainment industry and launched Goldberg to notoriety. The *New York Times* boasted that "Miss Goldberg is not simply a stand-up comedian but a satirist with a cutting edge."[56] The show was broadcast on HBO, and its audio adaptation won the Grammy for Best Comedy Recording in 1986. Goldberg, of course, is now among the elite artists who have achieved "EGOT" status—winners of all four of the entertainment industry's most prestigious awards, the Emmy, Grammy, Oscar, and Tony.

CHILD OF THE 50S

Raised in the Bronx and steeped in the tone of the Borscht Belt comics, Klein honed his craft at the Yale Drama School and the Second City before ascending as a comedic mouthpiece for the baby boom generation. *Child of the 50s*, Klein's 1973 album reflecting on the cultural and political moment of his upbringing, was a sharp entry into the comedy canon at a moment when stand-up was being redefined and mainstreamed for growing audiences. The album established Klein as one of the most revered comic voices of the era, shaping the observational style of a generation of performers to follow, including Jay Leno, Bill Maher, and Jerry Seinfeld, who remembers that, for him, Klein was "the Beatles of comedy."[57]

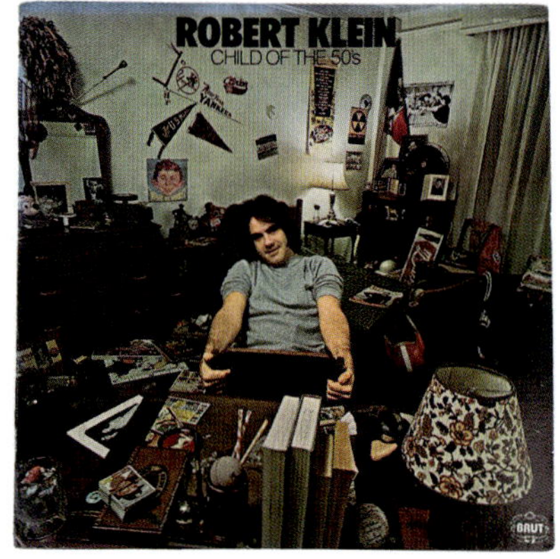

Child of the 50s is certainly something of a period piece to contemporary ears, with its musings on air raid drills, lunch ladies, and obnoxious television commercials, as well as Klein's clever musical interlude "Middle Class, Educated Blues." Nevertheless, it remains a masterclass in observational humor as Klein elevates the everyday and the mundane into relatable, resonant humor. With his ability to orchestrate complex admixtures of pop cultural references, social commentary, and generational in-jokes with a broad—and sometimes goofy—physicality, He drew a roadmap for stand-up in the latter part of the twentieth century. He described his own talent as "taking what everyone else sees and making it into coherent comedy."[58]

In 1975, Klein made history when he was selected by HBO as the first artist to perform a stand-up special on its air, inaugurating the cable network's long tradition of amplifying the work of comics for national audiences and cementing the televised special as a coveted career benchmark that persists to this day.

WATCH IT, SUCKER!

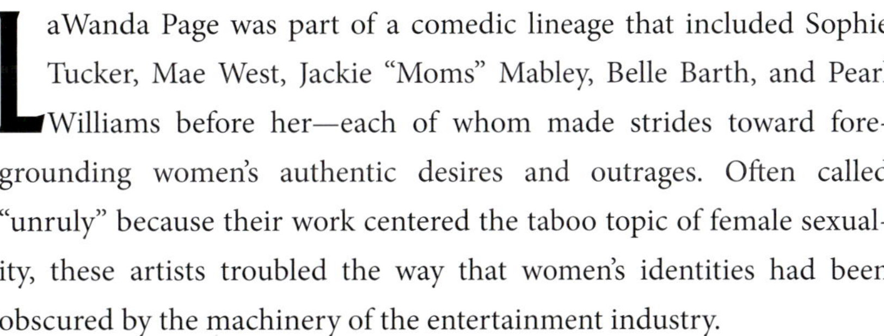

LaWanda Page was part of a comedic lineage that included Sophie Tucker, Mae West, Jackie "Moms" Mabley, Belle Barth, and Pearl Williams before her—each of whom made strides toward foregrounding women's authentic desires and outrages. Often called "unruly" because their work centered the taboo topic of female sexuality, these artists troubled the way that women's identities had been obscured by the machinery of the entertainment industry.

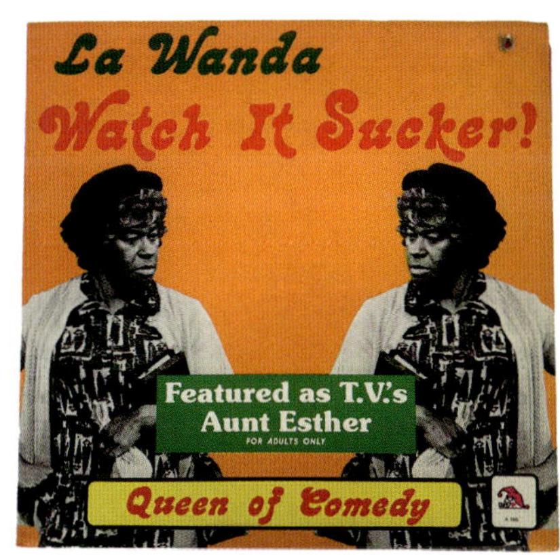

Page's comedic voice was forged on the Chitlin' Circuit, a string of southern performance venues that catered to Black audiences and that was notoriously helmed by exploitative theater owners and bookers. Despite its reputation for unsavoriness in business, the Chitlin' Circuit was also a space that was at a remove from the highly regulated (and censored) strictures of the larger circuits; a veritable comedic Renaissance fueled by Black artists and their audiences resulted.

Initially a burlesque dancer, Page transformed into a profane purveyor of the "blue humor" that was typically the domain of men. However, far from *merely* scandalizing her audiences, her work commented on how women were perceived by a culture that systematically devalued them and did so from inside institutions like the church and the family. By attacking these most sacred of spaces with no-holds-barred street humor, Page burst through acceptable codes of respectability. The work was captivating in its raunchiness, but laden with the lofty mission to reveal, and then dismantle, the systems that confined, overlooked, and silenced women like her.[59]

Her 1971 debut album, *Mutha' Is Half a Word*, introduced her work to a broadening audience, but it was after she was cast as the indefatigable Aunt Esther, foil to Redd Foxx's cantankerous Fred Sanford on TV's *Sanford and Son*, that Page became a household name. Though Aunt Esther's brand of comedy was a far cry from Page's stand-up humor, she still represented a woman audaciously commanding her own body, identity, and agency in a man's world. As the series skyrocketed in popularity, Aunt Esther's catchphrase "Watch It, Sucker!" entered the popular lexicon and became the title of Page's 1977 comedy album, which went gold and solidified her self-anointed role as the "Queen of Comedy."

Laura LaPlaca

THE BEVERLY HILLBILLIES AND THE OTHER AMERICA

Come and listen to a story 'bout a man named Jed
Poor mountaineer barely kept his family fed
Then one day he was shooting for some food,
And up through the ground come a bubbling crude

So begins "The Ballad of Jed Clampett," the most unusual hit single of 1962.[60] The bluegrass song by Lester Flatt and Earl Scruggs tells the story of the Clampett clan's accidental discovery of oil in their backwoods swamp, sale of the family homestead for untold millions, and move to Beverly (Hills, that is). The ritzy California suburb is home to swimming pools, movie stars, and—as fans of the television series *The Beverly Hillbillies* would learn—some of the greediest and most treacherous neighbors ever created for an American comedy program. Sure, the enormously popular CBS sitcom, which ran from 1962 to 1971, mined its unusual premise for comedy. But it also engaged viewers in conversations about wealth inequality and American values at a moment of socioeconomic reckoning, though its exclusively white lens on these issues minimized its impact and contributed to its cancellation.

Created by writer Paul Henning, the series drew on long-standing stereotypes and entertainment tropes to characterize the Clampetts as naïve, uncivilized yokels whose rags-to-riches journey leaves them vulnerable to the machinations of savvy urban folk who aim to take advantage of them. Jed (Buddy Ebsen), Granny (Irene Ryan), Jethro (Max Baer Jr.), and Elly May (Donna Douglas) are unsophisticated, but also unpretentious, caring, ethical, and responsible citizens. In contrast, their Beverly Hills neighbors are often exposed as vain, superficial, scheming, and unscrupulous. Buddy Ebsen demanded that Jed Clampett be written with dignity and wisdom, despite his lack of formal schooling, and he portrayed the character as an almost Lincolnesque backwoods sage.

The persistence of the yokel, rube, or hillbilly character in American entertainment—from the uncouth Jonathan in the influential early American play *The Contrast* (1787) to rural naïfs in the stories of Mark Twain and Will Rogers, the residents of Hooterville in the *Li'l Abner* comic strip, and trailer-park-dwelling Cletus in *The Simpsons*—speaks to the resilience of the trope despite enormous changes over the course of U.S. history. Rubes were a constant presence on the vaudeville stage from the 1870s to the 1920s, when rapid urbanization, industrialization, and technological innovation created drastic dislocations and disorientation in lifestyle, labor, and leisure in the United States. Depictions of country folk in the big city, including the Clampetts, derived their humor from their subjects' presumed unawareness of "modern" urban life and its contrast with their allegedly quaint mannerisms. Indeed, period commentators noted similarities between the uncouth Hillbillies humorously crashing polite Beverly Hills society and folksy Texan Lyndon Baines Johnson's coarse mode of operating within the refined Washington society of the Kennedy era. Like Johnson, the Clampetts were derided as nouveau riche, unschooled in the usual performances of wealth and consumption.

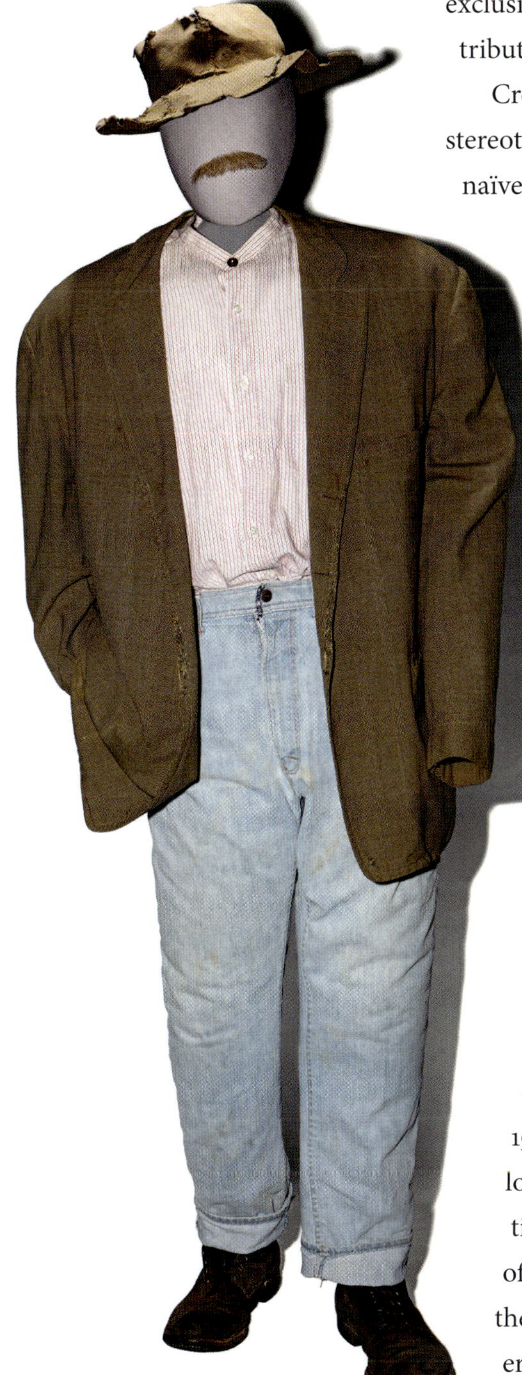

This costume of soiled and worn "Sunday Best" clothes was worn by Buddy Ebsen as Jed Clampett on *The Beverly Hillbillies.* The veteran actor and dancer insisted upon playing Jed with paternal dignity, making him an ideal straight man to the antics of the rest of the cast.

Yet the show's depiction of the dignity and morality of the rural poor, particularly in comparison to their wealthy neighbors, made a unique

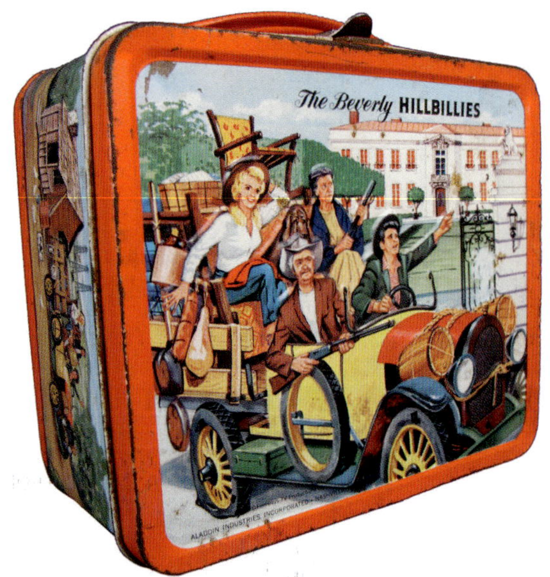

The fish-out-of-water sitcom was one of the most popular shows on television throughout its nine seasons on air, with especially high ratings in rural areas. This lunch box featuring scenes from the show testifies to both its cultural relevance and revival of vaudeville-style rube and rural humor.

statement in popular culture at a time when Johnson's "War on Poverty" drew national media attention to disadvantaged communities throughout Appalachia and the rural South. Inspired by Michael Harrington's best-selling book *The Other America*, the president visited communities in eastern Kentucky in 1964 in a well-publicized tour to cast light on the economic hardships faced by Americans in regions untouched by the nation's post–World War II prosperity. Harrington's point was that the rural poor were invisible in American life, and in some ways the Clampetts did as much as Johnson to change that.

Tellingly, though, *The Beverly Hillbillies* did not explicitly engage Johnson's policies. The Clampetts were not only yokels but rare ones who escaped poverty, embodying a rags-to-riches storyline as entrenched in the national psyche as rube characters themselves. Having made their fortune, they did not address economic inequality, and their critique focused not on how money is earned but rather on how it is spent, held, envied, and wasted. The Clampetts' banker and friend Milburn Drysdale (Raymond Bailey) is obsessed with their fortune and ways to exploit it; his wife Margaret (Harriet MacGibbon) represents the old money elite and cannot hide her disdain for the Clampetts' unsophisticated lifestyle and manner or the way they spend their money. Various guest stars and bit players constantly attempt to scam and steal from the good-natured and generous Clampetts, offering weekly indictments of American society's greed.

More importantly, despite informing conversations about socioeconomic inequality among whites, this most visible representation of the American South had nothing to say about racism or civil rights, even though the civil rights movement emerged during the show's run. In this omission, as well as the absence of any characters of color, *The Beverly Hillbillies* pandered to white viewers like many other contemporary shows and films. In his 1970 Black power anthem "The Revolution Will Not Be Televised," Gil Scott-Heron foretold that "Green Acres, The Beverly Hillbillies, and Hooterville [Petticoat] Junction will no longer be so damned relevant"—a prescient comment on the changing face of network television. CBS canceled *The Beverly Hillbillies* in 1971 alongside several other series in what was termed "the rural purge"—an attempt to redirect resources to programming that better represented a younger, more diverse, and more urban audience. Among the replacements in coming years were *Good Times*, *The Jeffersons*, and *All in the Family*, shows that more directly addressed contemporary conversations about race, politics, and inequality.

Ryan Lintelman

DON RICKLES, EQUAL OPPORTUNITY OFFENDER

During his long and distinguished career in insult comedy, Don Rickles earned the moniker "The Merchant of Venom," or, more sarcastically, "Mr. Warmth." For his millions of fans there was no greater thrill than to be picked out of the comedy club audience to be roasted by the most accomplished verbal abuser in the business. Rickles didn't invent insult comedy—Jack E. Leonard made the format famous on the comedy circuit in the forties and fifties—but he did perfect it. Defying the odds (and somehow avoiding bodily harm), Rickles endeared himself to some unlikely fans, including image-conscious celebrities and thorny mobsters. His memorable schtick included racial and ethnic humor that was increasingly outdated as his career reached into the first decades of the twenty-first century. Yet Rickles was able to carry it off, branding himself an equal opportunity offender, subjecting everyone to the same abuse (including himself and his fellow Jewish Americans), and assuring his audience of his ultimate affection with a rakish charm.

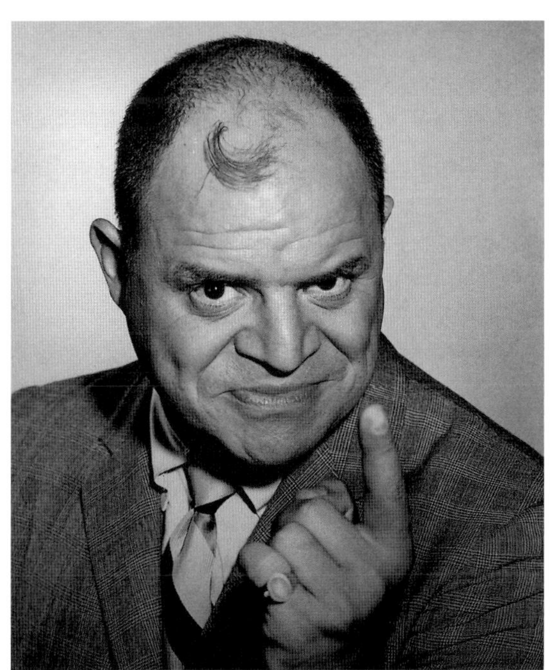

Rickles's insults were often raw, angry, and shockingly personal, but audiences loved him. His sarcastic, direct, and improvisational style inspired a generation of stand-up comedians, shock jocks, and increasingly, politicians.

Born to immigrant Eastern European Jewish parents in Queens in 1926, Donald Jay Rickles inherited his mother's exuberant, outgoing spirit and learned toughness on the streets. While serving in the navy in World War II, Rickles enjoyed entertaining his fellow seamen and decided to study at the American Academy of Dramatic Arts. He began working in television but, frustrated with the slow progress of his career, started doing

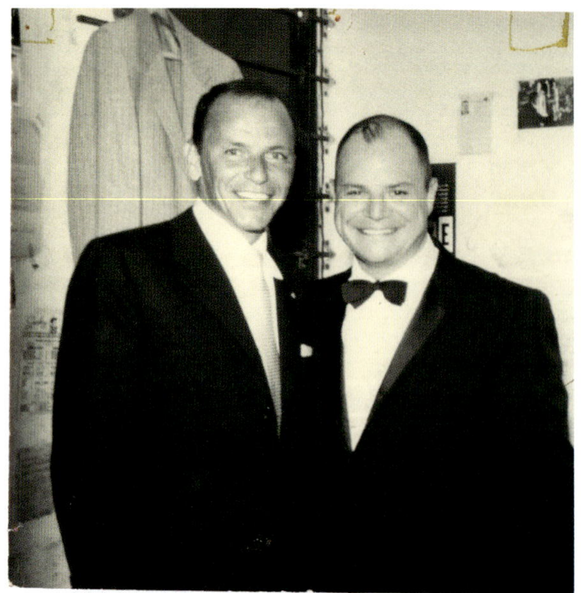

To Rickles' surprise and relief, otherwise thin-skinned celebrities usually took his jesting in stride, with frequent target Frank Sinatria becoming his friend and champion.

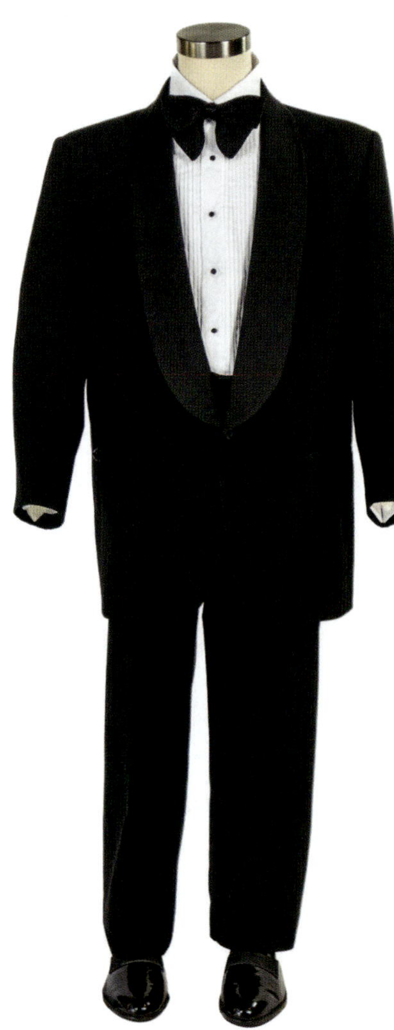

stand-up comedy, where he earned a reputation for his memorably cutting takedowns of hecklers. In time, he began making fun of not just the hecklers but the audience itself, picking victims from the crowd to tease for their appearance, behavior, or information he gleaned by asking them questions: Where are you from? What do you do? Why are you wearing that tie? With a ferocity and intensity he brought from his dramatic training, Rickles would harangue his victims for their ethnicity or race, sexual orientation, appearance, spouse, job, or anything else he could find to mock.

One of his happy victims was Frank Sinatra, whom Rickles savaged for his uneven acting career and rumored reputation for violence and organized crime connections. When he first noticed Sinatra in the audience at Los Angeles's Slate Brothers Club in 1957, he welcomed him, "Make yourself at home, Frank. Hit somebody!" To the crowd's surprise, Sinatra doubled over with laughter. Sinatra so enjoyed Rickles's ribbing that he became his champion, recommending and bringing celebrity friends to come see him, and helping him become a headliner in Las Vegas, where Rickles helped pioneer the big-time comedy scene. He developed an act of insult improvisation that he would perform for decades to come, striding onstage like a pugilistic matador to the Spanish bull fighting anthem "La Virgen de la Macarena," staring out into the audience with "his trademark expression of bulge-eyed irascibility," looking for victims.[61] Rickles also became a frequent and favorite guest of Johnny Carson on *The Tonight Show*, where he mocked the host and guests alike. He was well-known for his mastery of the celebrity roast, including memorable sets on the nationally broadcast *Dean Martin Celebrity Roast* specials in the seventies and eighties.

As audiences became increasingly uncomfortable with and hostile to ethnic jokes and racial caricature, Rickles carried on, undaunted. There was something about the audacity, parity, and diversity of his employment of stereotypes that made fans believe him when he said he was only kidding, frequently ending his act with a prayer to see "all bigots vanish from the earth." In an increasingly politically correct culture, Rickles's aggressive frankness, unabashed misanthropy, and

"I make fun of the president, why not? I make fun of everyone. That's America."
—Don Rickles at Ronald Reagan's second inaugural celebration, 1985

anachronistic style became a sort of postmodern and self-referential performance of entertainment history, gesturing to comedy's potential to unite audiences through a common experience. As one scholar has described it, through "sequential degradation," Rickles assured his audience of their equal value in a "community of laughter," asserting that while we're all different, we're also equal.[62]

Even if that means we're equally deserving of scorn.

Ryan Lintelman

TOOTSIE AND *9 TO 5*: WOMEN'S LIB AND MEN'S CRISIS

In the early 1980s, two of the most successful and influential comedy films of the decade tackled the changing gender dynamics and sexual politics of the workplace. *9 to 5* (1980) and *Tootsie* (1982) came from different perspectives, but both films found humor in the social and political forces transforming the nation's economy and culture, including the sexual revolution, feminism and women's liberation movement, and the rising number of women in the workforce. Both films have endured as classic comedies, racking up honors, being adapted as Broadway musicals, and posing questions that still resonate as culture war battles about gender and sexuality rage on.

Starring Jane Fonda, Lily Tomlin, and Dolly Parton, *9 to 5* featured the three women as colleagues at a generic corporate office who decide to take revenge on their "sexist, egotistical, lying, hypocritical bigot" of a boss, played by Dabney Coleman. Judy Bernly (Fonda) is a longtime housewife who finds a job at Consolidated Companies after her husband leaves her. Her manager is Violet Newstead (Tomlin), a competent and smart leader who trained and now serves as "right hand" for Vice President Franklin Hart (Coleman). Coleman sexually harasses his beautiful and underestimated secretary Doralee Rhodes (Parton); as a result, rumors spread that the two are having an affair, and Rhodes must endure her colleagues' scorn.

When Violet learns that she's been passed over for promotion in favor of a lesser-skilled man, the women find solace and solidarity together and fantasize about seeking revenge for their poor treatment in the office. In a madcap turn of events, the women end up kidnapping and blackmailing Hart once they discover he's been embezzling from Consolidated Companies. Afterward, the three take over leadership of the company in Coleman's absence and implement egalitarian and worker-friendly policies at the office, leading to enormous gains in productivity and happy endings for each of the women.

Fonda conceptualized the story of *9 to 5* herself, drawing inspiration from the 9to5 National Association of Working Women, which advocated for better working conditions for the millions of women entering the workforce in the 1970s, and produced it through her company IPC Films. The film had originally been intended as a drama, with Fonda conducting research on women's experiences with sexism and harassment in the corporate world; however, when Fonda decided that she wanted to work with Tomlin and that the film could speak to significant cultural issues while being lighthearted, she decided to rework the film as a screwball comedy from a female perspective.

While the film received mixed critical reviews at its release, it was extremely popular among filmgoers and developed a reputation as a cult classic. Over time, critics have reappraised *9 to 5* and now hail its social commentary as prescient; in 2018, one critic wrote, "Thirty-eight years on, this tale of misogyny, kidnap and rattling typewriters is a boldly progressive piece of film-making."[63] Indeed, it is still powerful for its identification and excoriation of the sexist and racist power structures that face women in white-collar work, including unequal pay, inflexible work schedules, lack of child care, implicit bias limiting career growth, and sexual objectification.

Dustin Hoffman wore this red sequined dress as Michael Dorsey / Dorothy Michaels in the film *Tootsie*. Men have worn drag for comedy performance for centuries, and Hoffman and director Sydney Pollack used it in this film to provoke a conversation about gender roles and expectations. In an increasingly conservative political climate, however, the film's poster makes it clear that Michael is "hopelessly straight."

Tootsie tells the story of talented but fussy actor Michael Dorsey (Dustin Hoffman), whose reputation for being difficult has kept him from getting work. When he decides to audition for a part in a soap opera dressed as a woman, in part to prove a point to his agent (portrayed by director Sydney Pollack), he gets the role that his actress girlfriend (Teri Garr) lost. Dorsey then must conceal his new job from her while learning to navigate a complex minefield of interpersonal relationships, sexual politics, and workplace harassment as a woman.

Meanwhile, his alter ego Dorothy Michaels becomes a television star, a pseudo-feminist icon, and the object of his costar Julie's (Jessica Lange) widower father's affections. The very aspects of Michael's personality that make him an insufferable man—his stubbornness, outspokenness, and creative perfectionism—make him a compelling and irresistible woman. And the lessons he learned about women's experiences and challenges while living as Dorothy Michaels make Michael a better person, ready to start a new relationship with Julie. As he says in the film's final scene, "I was a better man with you, as a woman, than I ever was with a woman, as a man."

The film's satirical exploration of contemporary conversations about gender, sexuality, feminism, show business, and women at work earned critical acclaim and commercial success. *Tootsie*'s script, by Larry Gelbart, Murray Schisgal, and a long-rumored slate of uncredited contributors including Elaine May and Barry Levinson, is often used to teach screenwriting; its well-developed structure, still-hilarious dialogue, and deft blending of social satire and screwball comedy make the script a model of movie writing craft. However, scholars have debated whether *Tootsie* was indeed as enlightened and progressive as many contemporary critics claimed, pointing to the caricatured version of sexism the film presents (all too easy for audience members to dismiss without soul searching) and the essential fact that it took a man experiencing sexism for it to become a major problem. "TOOTSIE's message is loud and clear," Deborah H. Holdstein wrote, "only because of a man can a woman achieve any modicum of greatness or rise from the mire of self-doubt and psychological trauma. Only through a man will a mass-audience 'feminist' message be taken seriously."[64]

Ryan Lintelman

ANDY BUMATAI AND LOCAL COMEDY IN HAWAI'I

Comedy doesn't exist in a vacuum—it comes out of a specific place, culture, and history. That's certainly the case with the local comedy scene in

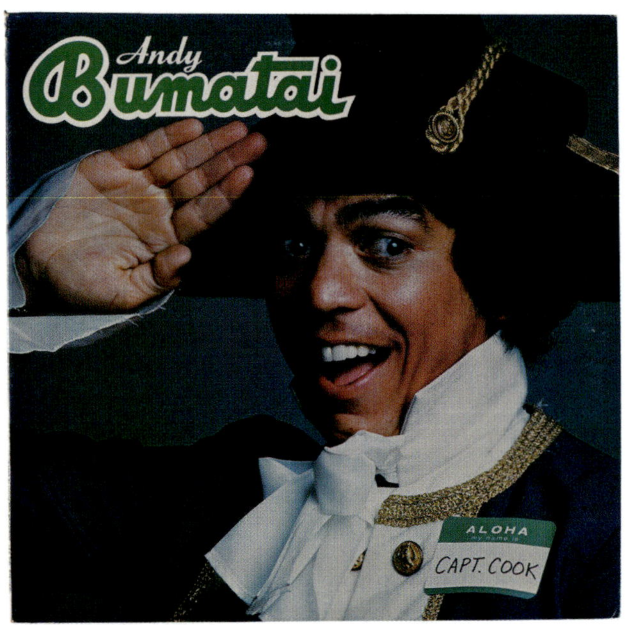

Andy Bumatai's third comedy album, *Aloha, My Name Is Captain Cook*, was released in 1980 and includes routines on topics ranging from Chinese names and being Filipino/Hawaiian to the contemporary comedy scene.

Hawai'i since the 1970s. Take, for example, this Andy Bumatai joke, which appeared in a Hawai'i tourist guide: "Hawaiian people have always had three important gods. Pele, god of fire. Lono, god of war. Dillingham, god of land."[65] A tourist wandering into a Waikiki comedy club on a Friday night might recognize the first two names, central to Hawaiian mythology. But unless you're actually from the islands, that third name—a family of white industrialists who added concrete and rail lines to Hawai'i's landscape—won't ring a bell. That's a deeply local reference to a family whose name appears on airfields and major streets. If you didn't work on one of their construction sites or help to refine their sugar for transport to the continent, most likely someone in your family or neighborhood did. Bumatai's joke is the essence of local comedy: it mines the particular to reveal something universal.

In Hawai'i, the terms "local" and "Hawaiian" are not synonyms. "Local" is about residency and belonging to the islands' mixed cultural environment. While Hawai'i is incredibly remote, it's been at the crossroads for empires and settlers. Native Hawaiians, or *kanaka maoli*, are the native people of the archipelago whose presence dates back five thousand years; it's a question not of residency but of genealogy. Hawaiian comedy that calls itself "local" works in this space—bridging immigrant histories, colonial legacies, and Indigenous presence.

A prominent, if not defining, feature of local Hawai'i comedy has been the playing up of ethnic stereotypes among the islands' various groups—e.g., Chinese, Japanese, Korean, Filipino, Puerto Rican, Portuguese, and Native Hawaiian—many of whom collided in plantations, industrial farms, and shipyards from the nineteenth century forward that were formally segregated by ethnicity and nationality. Even though housing may have been segregated, workers' lunch and social breaks were often shared spaces where not only the contact language of pidgin (or Hawai'i Creole English) but also a distinctive local culture emerged. Writer Darrell H. Y. Lum explained how, on the one hand, comedians often lean on pidgin and exaggerated ethnic stereotypes: "e.g., the big violent Samoan, the lazy Hawaiian, the oversexed Filipino with a heavy accent, the tightwad Chinese, the slant-eyed Japanese, etc."[66] On the other, Lum argued, pidgin itself is "a language of this place and of their lives and experience. Here is a language that allows them to say something. Something important."[67] Comedy often carries both sides at once: a way of poking fun, but also of claiming a voice.

Bumatai, and other artists, developed a vibrant culture involved in working out the definitions of what it means to be from and of this particular place—Hawaiʻi's 1970s cultural renaissance. His work was part of a creative moment that included Rap Reiplinger's comedy albums like *Poi Dog* and his work with the comedy troupe Boog Booga; the music of Jonathan Osorio; a reconnection to ancient voyaging skills with the Polynesian Voyaging Society; and the activism of groups like John Kelly Jr.'s Save Our Surf, to halt hotel and corporate development. Local comedy was just one of many cultural sites where identity was tested and performed.

Bumatai is of Native Hawaiian and Filipino heritage and began performing in the 1970s as a stand-up comedian, as a comic performer working in troupes, and as an actor. Bumatai's act consisted of "thickly ethnic local humor," entertaining his audiences with his "rubber faced" and "energetic" expressions, as well as the use of "ethnic and nostalgic vignettes" laced heavily with pidgin and local slang.[68] By the later 1970s, he was regularly headlining shows that drew mixed crowds; a 1979 show reportedly drew eight hundred audience members, half of whom identified as "haole" (a Native Hawaiian term for those who are not Hawaiian, usually referring to white persons). Bumatai began playing regularly to tourists in places like the Monarch Room at the Royal Hawaiian hotel and was featured prominently in travel guides to Hawaiʻi. In addition to the Polynesian Cultural Center (to this day, the most popular paid tourist attraction on Oahu), a tour of the Iolani Palace, snorkeling at Hanauma Bay, and grabbing shave ice at Matsumoto's on the North Shore, the comic's Waikiki show was listed as one of the star attractions in "The Best of Oahu."[69] In 1985, Bumatai was listed as one of "20 Filipinos Who Made Good"—including fellow performers like saxophonist Rene Paulo, jazz musician Gabe Baltazar, and actor Tia Carrere (née Althea Rae Duhinio Janairo).[70] As Bumatai's star continued to rise, the continent called. Throughout the 1980s Bumatai appeared on national TV, shared stages at the Improv, and landed a prime-time Showtime spot hosted by Pat Morita, a pioneering Japanese American comedian in his own right.

When Andy Bumatai cracked wise about Pele, Lono, and Dillingham, he delivered more than a punchline: he channeled the islands' history. His work is a record of who we are, how we live together, and what it means to belong to a place.

Theodore S. Gonzalves

"YEP, I'M GAY": *ELLEN* AND *WILL & GRACE*

Until the mid-1990s, sexual orientation had rarely been discussed or represented overtly in situation comedies, with a few exceptions in "special episodes" or over-the-top characters played for laughs. That all changed in 1997, when Ellen DeGeneres came out, both in real life and in character on her eponymous ABC sitcom. The following year, *Will & Grace* premiered on NBC, proudly featuring gay lead characters in conventional sitcom storylines, albeit about same-sex love and life. Though both shows were controversial, igniting culture war battles and debate about particular characters' portrayals within the gay community, *Ellen* and *Will & Grace* were landmarks for representation and normalization of homosexuality in American life, proving the power of comedy to influence conversations about identity and civil rights.

Stand-up comic Ellen DeGeneres parlayed a successful career on the comedy club circuit into a role on an ABC sitcom titled *These Friends of Mine*, which premiered in 1994. After a first-year refresh and renaming as *Ellen*, the show hit its stride as a *Friends*-like sitcom focused on the daily lives of a group of quirky urban professionals, and DeGeneres was heralded as a "female Seinfeld" for her hip, observational style of humor. But as the series ran on, it became clear that the tomboyish yet eminently likable lead wasn't interested in having her character engage in the usual romantic hijinks of the era's television comedies, leaving something missing from *Ellen*. "The problem was not that the writers weren't writing good scripts, it's that there was no center to the show," recalled producer Mark Driscoll. "Ellen whose character is 35 was an asexual character who hung out with friends, really exhibiting behavior more suited to 20-somethings."[71]

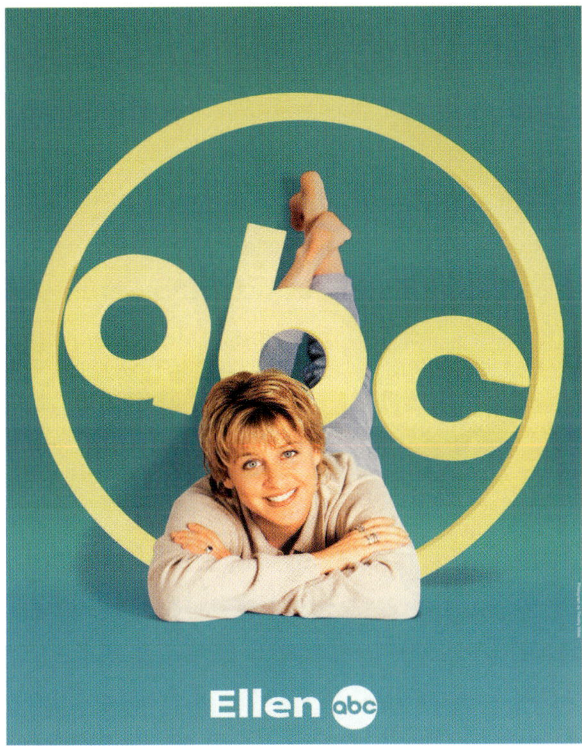

ABC canceled *Ellen* in 1998, the year after DeGeneres came out as lesbian on air. She and guest star Laura Dern, who played the woman who helped Ellen Morgan come to terms with her sexuality, have spoken about how they had trouble finding work after the controversial episode aired.

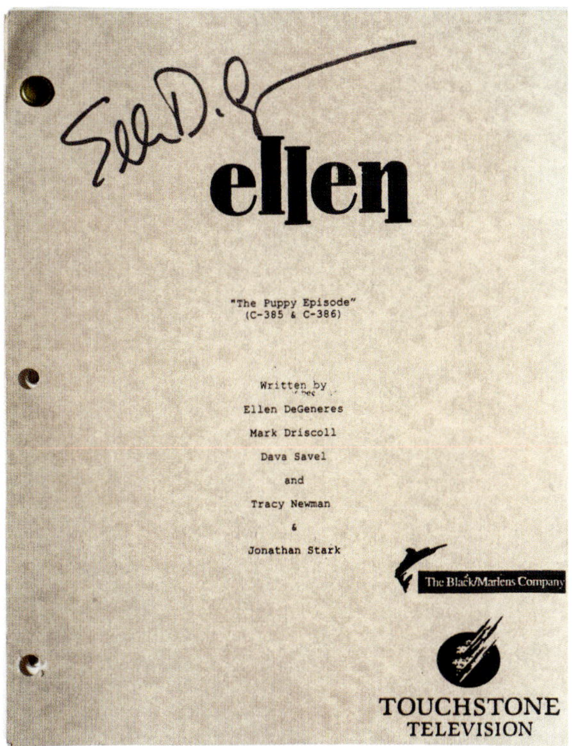

ellen

"The Puppy Episode"
(C-385 & C-386)

Written by
Ellen DeGeneres
Mark Driscoll
Dava Savel
and
Tracy Newman
&
Jonathan Stark

The Black/Marlens Company

TOUCHSTONE
TELEVISION

"The Puppy Episode" won an Emmy Award for Outstanding Writing for a Comedy Series, a Peabody Award, and a GLAAD Media Award for DeGeneres and her writers, Mark Driscoll, Tracy Newman, Dava Savel, and Jonathan Stark. It generated intense controversy in 1997 but has since been acclaimed as one of the most important sitcom episodes in television history.

The truth was, Ellen DeGeneres was gay. She wasn't out, but in a media and political environment that seemed increasingly hostile to and ignorant of gay lives and rights, she decided that the time had come to make her identity known. "I decided this was not going to be something that I was going to live the rest of my life being ashamed of," DeGeneres told Diane Sawyer in a *20/20* interview about her coming out. Meanwhile, *Ellen* was slumping in the ratings, and network executives began pushing for the main character to begin dating someone or, since she didn't seem interested in romance, at least get a puppy, in order to boost viewership. In the summer of 1996, DeGeneres and the show's writers began working with ABC on a plan to have her character come out as a lesbian. Amid the intense negotiations, the writers began writing the script for the episode that they now christened "The Puppy Episode," in part to keep it under wraps, but also to pay mocking tribute to the earlier suggestion.[72]

The lead-up to the premiere of the hour-long episode that aired April 30, 1997, was a media circus, in part because of advance media previews that played up the moment as an epochal event. DeGeneres appeared on the cover of *Time* magazine with the headline "Yep, I'm Gay." Gay and lesbian organizations across the country organized "Come Out with Ellen" parties for the episode premiere, while Reverend Jerry Falwell and televangelist Pat Robertson railed against "Ellen Degenerate's" "blatant attempt to promote homosexuality" and tried to organize a boycott. Sponsors Wendy's, Chrysler, and JCPenney did pull their advertising from the series, and an ABC affiliate in Birmingham, Alabama, refused to broadcast the episode, but it was still a ratings success.[73] Forty-two million people tuned in to the hour-long special episode, with millions of others seeing Ellen's dramatic real-life coming out on *Oprah* or reading about it in newspapers and tabloids.

In the years since, DeGeneres has earned praise for her bold move and advocacy for the LGBTQ community, paving the way for greater gay representation on television and helping to influence American public opinion on issues of gay rights. However, that wasn't enough to save *Ellen*, which quickly dropped in the ratings after the spectacular "Puppy Episode" and was canceled in 1998. DeGeneres has also been criticized by some scholars and activists for failing to fully seize the cultural moment, portraying a reductive and simplistic representation of the coming-out process and doing little to challenge mainstream biases against gay people. Social scientists, however, have largely found that *Ellen* and other popular portrayals of gay and lesbian characters on television are positively correlated with decreased prejudice and increased support for gay marriage and other civil rights among the broader public.[74]

Ellen certainly paved the way for *Will & Grace*, which aired on NBC from 1998 to 2005. Created by Max Mutchnick and David Kohan, the sitcom was one of the first network comedies to prominently feature out gay men in lead roles. Its central premise was the platonic friendship (and codependent "all but married" relationship) between roommates Will Truman (Eric McCormack) and Grace Adler (Debra Messing). The attractive, well-off pair of urban professionals share the joys and frustrations of their love lives. They would seem like a natural romantic couple on any other sitcom, and indeed are shown to have dated in college before Will realized he was gay; they've been best friends ever since. Jack McFarland (Sean Hayes) is Will's flamboyant and campy struggling actor friend, and wealthy socialite Karen Walker (Megan Mullally) is an ambivalently bisexual narcissist, rounding out the most queer-representative main cast on American television to that point.

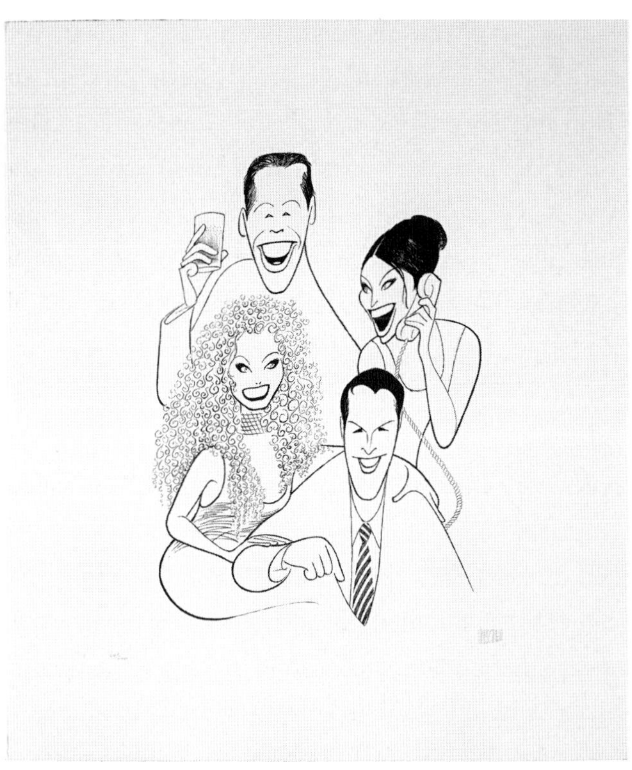

Legendary caricaturist Al Hirschfeld created this portrait of the *Will & Grace* cast in 2000, the year the show earned the Emmy Award for Outstanding Comedy Series. Though initially highly rated, the series slipped over time as it was criticized for seeming stale.

Gay author and critic Andrew Holleran found *Will & Grace*'s matter-of-fact representation and normalization of gay life almost unbelievable. "From the very start the show has seemed not merely gay, but hard-edged, LA circuit-queen gay," he wrote in a 2000 review, "Nothing of the gay content has been held back, nothing homogenized."[75] Will and Jack were not simply stereotypical or token gay characters but fully fleshed modern Americans who happened to be gay.

But *Will & Grace* was also cautious and somewhat conventional in its presentation of gay life, at least as represented by the well-off, straitlaced Will and superficially "wacky" Jack. Some critics suggested that the series was simply placing a gay veneer on existing stock sitcom characters, rather than delving deeply into the less mainstream and hetero-friendly aspects of American gay culture. For instance, the show seemed to go out of its way to avoid depicting homosexual affection to prevent alienating its audience, which became a metanarrative plot point in the season 2 episode "Acting Out." In the episode, the characters eagerly anticipate the "first ever prime time network kiss between two gay men" on their favorite sitcom *Along Came You* but are disappointed when it occurs off camera. When Jack and Will attempt to complain to NBC executives, they instead end up running into Al Roker filming a segment for *The Today Show* and decide to kiss on air, thereby taking the honor for themselves. While noteworthy, this kiss was more a political gesture than genuine romantic affection.[76]

Will "approaches asexual," *Los Angeles Times* critic Howard Rosenberg wrote in his 1998 review, "his gayness appearing to exist solely as a device to give him the moral authority to repeatedly ridicule the mincing manner of his bandanna-wearing homosexual friend, Jack, without being labeled homophobic."[77] Some gay activists, meanwhile, argued that Jack exhibited some of the most extreme stereotypes of the effeminate, swishy gay man; they feared that straight viewers liked Jack because he confirmed their suspicions about who gay men were. As one retrospective writer put it, "The frequency with which *Will & Grace* returned to the well of nelly—usually Jack flailing about—for its (predominantly mainstream and straight) audience had a touch of the minstrel to it."[78]

However, as with *Ellen*, scholars and critics alike have found that *Will & Grace* demonstrated that mainstream audiences would accept gay characters in television comedy programs and had an impact beyond the television screen. Edward Schiappa, a professor of comparative media studies at MIT, has studied what he calls the parasocial contact hypothesis, positing that exposure to gay characters on television programs is correlated with a reduction in sexual orientation prejudice, especially for those who have little other direct interpersonal contact with to homosexual people. In one landmark study, he used *Will & Grace* as the experimental test case and found that "increased viewing frequency and parasocial interaction were found to correlate with lower levels of sexual prejudice—a relationship that was most pronounced for those with the least amount of social contact with lesbians and gay men."[79]

When Vice President Joe Biden made headlines in 2012 by endorsing legal same-sex marriage, he credited the series with helping to change minds. "I think Will & Grace did more to educate the American public more than almost anything anybody has done so far," he told *Meet the Press* host David Gregory. "People fear that which is different. Now they're beginning to understand."[80] When Barack Obama awarded Ellen DeGeneres the Presidential Medal of Freedom in 2016, he also singled her out for praise for understanding the power of representation in entertainment. "It's easy to forget now when we've come so far, where now marriage is equal under the law, just how much courage was required for Ellen to come out on the most public of stages almost 20 years ago," Obama said. "Just how important it was. Not just to the LGBT community, but for all of us."[81]

Ryan Lintelman

2

Comedy Creates American Identity

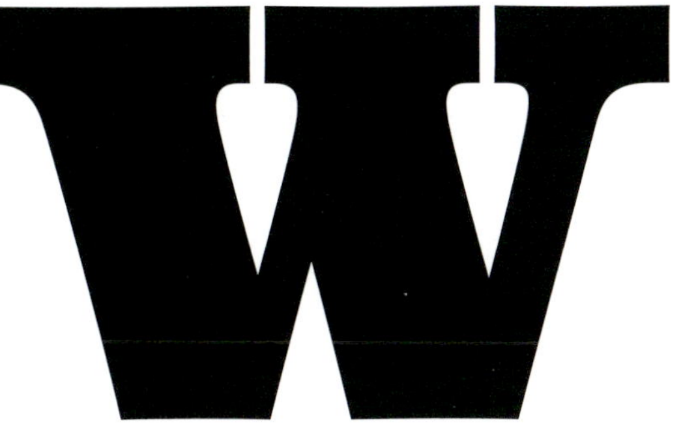

We don't often think of the Founding Fathers having a sense of humor. Benjamin Franklin enjoyed a good fart joke, yes. (See Franklin, "Fart Proudly" or "A Letter to a Royal Academy about Farting," 1781.) But George Washington? That archetype of serious statesmanship and gentlemanly propriety who frowns at us from the face of every one-dollar bill?

Believe it or not, a remarkable object has survived that proves the "Father of His Country" was also an early promoter of American comedy. Washington was a frequent theatergoer, and in 1790, while serving as president of the United States, he subscribed to the publication of the first American theatrical comedy, Royall Tyler's *The Contrast*.[1] Washington received two printed copies of the play, one of which remained in the library at Mount Vernon until his heirs sold it off after the Civil War. That copy, bearing Washington's signature on its title page, has survived to this day in the Silver Special Collections Library at the University of Vermont.[2]

Frontispiece illustration and title page of George Washington's copy of Royall Tyler's *The Contrast.*

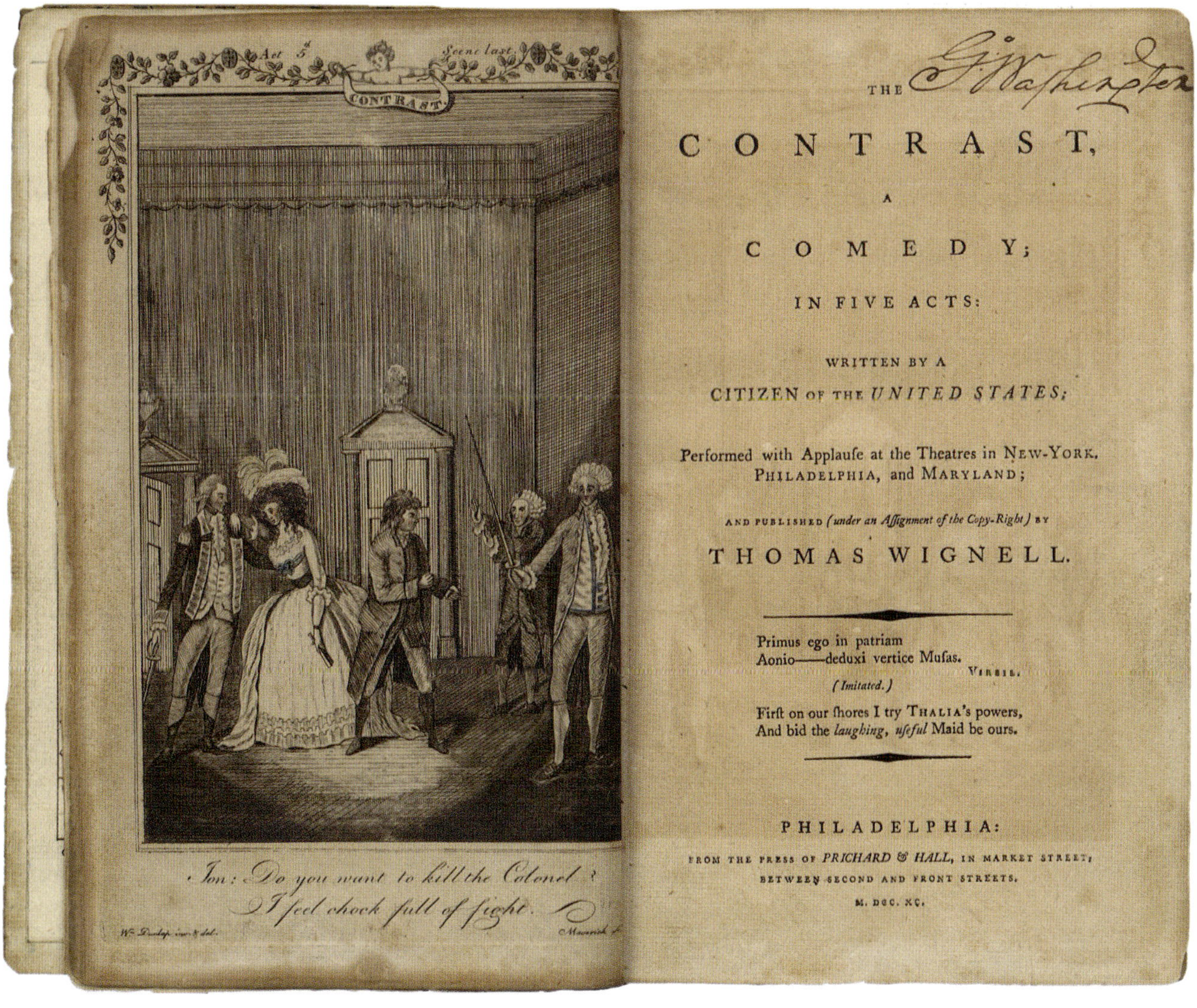

It's a fitting piece of comedy that must have seemed supremely relevant for the former commander in chief at a time when he was working to establish the United States as an independent nation. First staged in New York in 1787, *The Contrast* was the first professionally produced comedy performance by an American writer and a landmark in the emerging popular culture of the United States. The play, inspired by English Restoration comedies of manners like Richard Brinsley Sheridan's *The School for Scandal*, is a farce in which the nobly modest Revolutionary War hero Colonel Manly wins the heart of a virtuous and beautiful young woman over the foppish, cosmopolitan lothario and Anglophile Billy Dimple. The highlight of the play was the rendition of the popular comic song "Yankee Doodle" by Manly's servant Jonathan, making a mockery of effete dandies like Dimple in favor of the sturdy, homespun virtues Manly represented. The *contrast* in values and identity the play explored has been a constant source of inspiration for American entertainment in the centuries since, with the unpretentious naïf Jonathan presaging comic characters like Huckleberry Finn and Will Rogers, paragons of American virtue eschewing complicated, cosmopolitan entanglements.[3]

In the nearly two hundred fifty years since George Washington enjoyed *The Contrast*'s farcical take on American values, comedy has helped Americans create their idea of themselves and their nation, shaping their visions of patriotism, values and virtues, and shared culture. From Mark Twain to the Muppets, comedy performers have shaped national identity while adding insight to political discourse and historic developments.

Humorists like Twain and Will Rogers drew on regional storytelling traditions to celebrate the nation's democratic spirit and expanding global power while nudging their fellow Americans—especially politicians—to live up to its founding creed. Pioneering female comedians of the twentieth century, including Gracie Allen, Minnie Pearl, and Carol Burnett, picked up where their predecessors left off, using exaggeration, parody, and satire to celebrate the nation's creative culture while critiquing society's greed, materialism, and sexism. Comedians of color, like Bert Williams, Cheech Marin, Key and Peele, and Butterbeans and Susie, persevered despite prejudice and narrowed opportunities, using comedy to craft nuanced statements about a nation that was failing to deliver the justice, equality, and opportunity it promised.

Other comedians played with notions of American character. Silent clowns like Charlie Chaplin, Buster Keaton, and Harold Lloyd used the motion picture medium to embody character types—ne'er-do-well tramps, luckless losers, and striving go-getters—that functioned as fun-house mirrors for Americans to examine themselves and their values at a time of rapid social and demographic changes. Cartoon comedians like Mickey Mouse, Woody Woodpecker, and Bugs Bunny became heroic icons of plucky and mischievous underdogs overcoming the odds to fight injustice, making audiences smile amid the challenges of the Great Depression and World War II. Bob Newhart, Johnny Carson, and *Happy Days* shaped conversations about American culture and society in the postwar years, while *Saturday Night Live* and Jim Henson's Muppets mixed countercultural chaos with sly social critique. And misanthropic vaudeville, radio, and film comedian W. C. Fields examined American values with a weary cynicism that paved the way for comic skeptics from Nichols and May to Larry David and Jerry Seinfeld.

To bring the story full circle, let's consider comedy and the U.S. presidency. Elsewhere in this book you'll find examples that prove the president has always been fodder for humorous criticism, like Vaughn Meader's famous John F. Kennedy impression album *The First Family* or the Smothers Brothers' political jokes at the expense of Lyndon Baines Johnson. But the fake presidential campaign might be one of the most memorable ways comedians have commented on American values and politics over the years. Will Rogers may have started the trend, using his column in *Life* magazine to launch his bid for the nation's highest office as candidate of the Anti-Bunk Party, promising that if elected he would resign. "Our support will have to come from those who want nothing and have the assurance of getting it," he wrote.[4] Gracie Allen, running on the Surprise Party ticket, used the slogan "Down with Common Sense" and noted "everybody knows a woman is better than a man when it comes to introducing bills into the house."[5] W. C. Fields nominated himself for president in 1940 by publishing a parody campaign book, promising to break his campaign resolutions just as astutely as he broke New Year's resolutions.

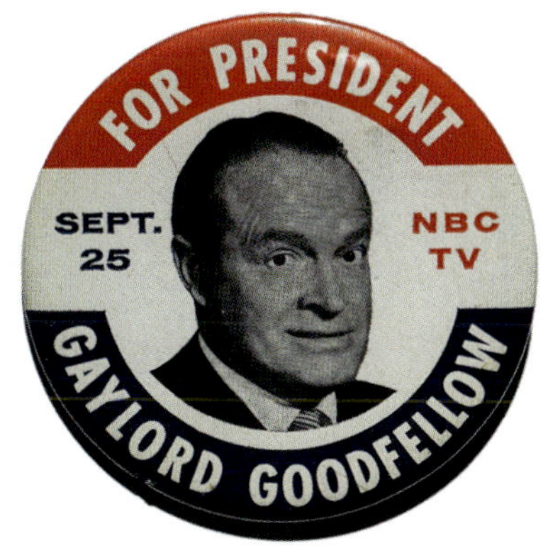

Comedians from Will Rogers to Stephen Colbert have waged farcical presidential campaigns to satirize American political culture. On a 1968 television special that aired in the middle of a tumultuous presidential campaign season, Bob Hope portrayed candidate Gaylord Goodfellow, who drops out of the race to become a ukulele-playing hippie, forcing his advisers to draft lookalike cab driver Irving (also played by Hope) to secretly take his place on the campaign trail.

More pointedly, in the 1960s comedian Dick Gregory used his semiserious presidential campaign to draw attention to progressive causes like civil rights and ending the Vietnam War. And perhaps the best-known comedy presidential candidate, Pat Paulsen, described himself as "just a common, ordinary, simple savior of America's destiny." The 1968 candidate of the Straight Talkin' American Government Party, or STAG Party, waged a wickedly satirical campaign with frequent appearances on *The Smothers Brothers Comedy Hour*, as you'll read more about in the essay on Paulsen in chapter 3. As even more recent comedy presidential campaigns by Roseanne Barr and Stephen Colbert have demonstrated, the concept still gets laughs. And as with comedy works dating back to *The Contrast*, Americans still find something irresistible about humor that takes aim at—and helps to define—American identity and values.

Introduction by Ryan Lintelman

MARK TWAIN, AMERICAN

Mark Twain forged an American style of literature that drew on vernacular and folk traditions unique to the United States. This 1873 portrait suggests his resolute and singular voice.

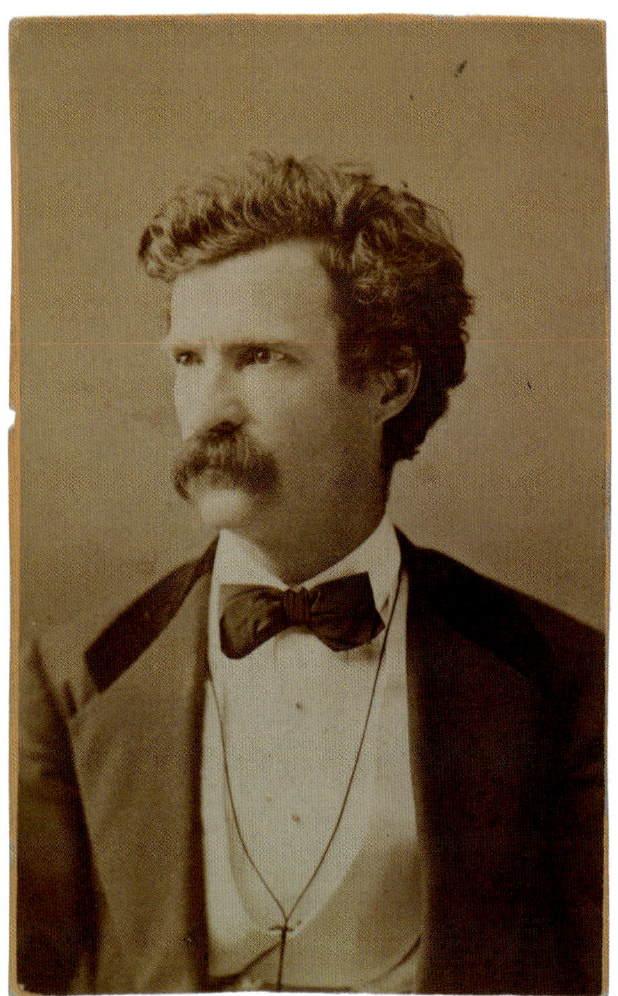

It's difficult to imagine American comedy, or American culture, without Mark Twain. There's a reason that the most prestigious award granted to comedians in the United States is named for him: the Mark Twain Prize for American Humor, presented annually by the John F. Kennedy Center for the Performing Arts. Twain was a writer of humorous short stories, novels, letters, and essays, a lecturer who paved the way for observational comedy, and an epoch-defining celebrity who used his fame to both defend and critique American values and culture. One biographer called Mark Twain "the man who found a voice for his country," and indeed his homespun, earthy wit was essential to an emerging national consciousness and identity as the nation developed and grew in the late nineteenth century.[6]

In this crucial period in American history, from the Civil War to the early 1900s, through its centennial, Reconstruction, and imperial Gilded Age, Twain earned a reputation as a compelling and oracular voice of conscience. His humor writing reminded Americans of their past, helped them understand their present, and warned them about the future. He helped Americans laugh again after the Civil War, mostly at themselves, as his stories poking fun at shared values and foibles helped reunite a fractured national culture. He explored

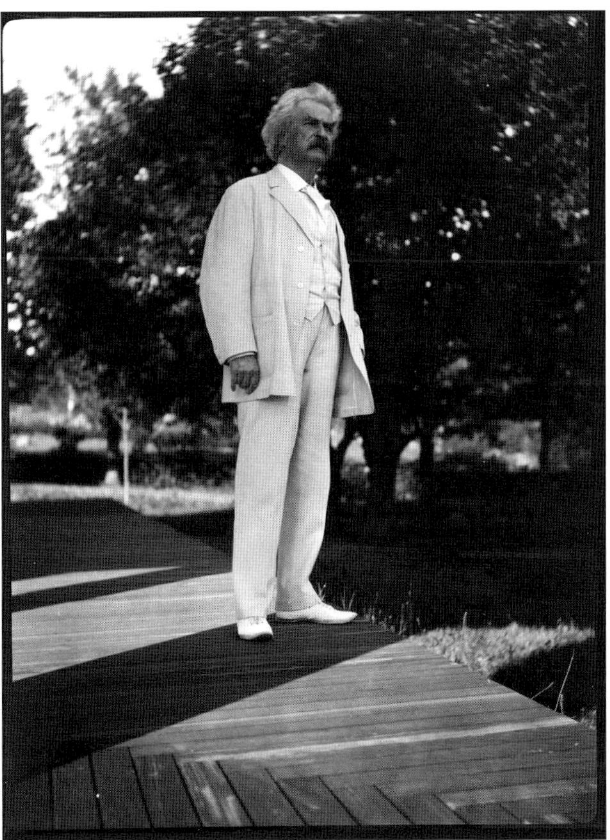

In his late career, including an 1890s world lecture tour, Twain took on the mantle of America's conscience. Aware of his image like a modern celebrity, he made a point of wearing a bright white suit that made him appear like "an avenging angel."

human nature, freedom, responsibility, race, religion, class, and greed in clear, precise, vernacular prose. His most enduring works are still studied, debated, and treasured today as landmarks of American literature and humor.

Samuel Clemens was born in the small town of Florida, Missouri, on November 30, 1835, but spent most of his childhood in nearby Hannibal, where in his teenage years he began apprenticing as a printer. Restless and ambitious, he began writing humorous letters and stories, even sending contributions to East Coast newspapers and earning his first byline in the Boston *Carpet-Bag* as a teenager in 1852. Always an inquisitive and tireless traveler, Clemens worked as an itinerant printer in St. Louis, Cincinnati, New York, and Philadelphia and visited Washington, D.C., Chicago, and New Orleans. Through his travels, Clemens soaked up regional stories, dialects, and perspectives, an education in the emerging culture of the young nation. But his most significant schooling took place on the Mississippi River, where he trained and worked as a steamboat pilot for four years. In those days before railroad supplanted the steamship, the river was the central artery of commerce, news, life, and culture in the American West, and the river boat life was filled with adventure, romance, and excitement.

By 1861, Mississippi River traffic dried up as the Civil War began, and Twain fled westward. He took up writing again, contributing to newspapers in the far western states, and adopted the pen name Mark Twain in 1863 while working in Nevada. On the river, "mark twain" meant two fathoms, a measurement of water depth suggesting safe navigation ahead, and perhaps his assumption of the name represented his hopes for a new direction in life. In any case, that's what came; he gained notice for his journalistic and humor writing, especially for a short story based on tales he heard in California mining camps. Twain's 1865 "Jim Smiley and His Jumping Frog" is better known by the title of Twain's first book, in which it was published, *The Celebrated Jumping Frog of Calaveras County*, but the folksy story gained national attention and launched his career.

He earned commissions from several newspapers to travel and return letters about his experiences, first to the Hawaiian Islands, then to the

Mediterranean and the Holy Land. These trips informed his travelogues *The Innocents Abroad* (1869), about the latter, and *Roughing It* (1872), a collection of stories about his journeys through the American West and Hawai'i. Readers loved these books for the pictures Twain painted with words of exciting and exotic places, but also for his witty, nearly subversive, commentary on history, culture, current events, and his fellow travelers. The books and popular lectures Twain gave based on his travels seemed to strike a chord with an American public seeking novelty, adventure, and expanded horizons following years of internal conflict and discord.

Twain's writing was refreshingly colloquial, homespun, and familiar, so different from the serious, self-consciously weighty prose of the northeastern writers who had so long dominated the nation's literature. Rather than emulating European styles and trends to appease critics, Twain embraced vernacular language and humor to deflate and disarm, weaving social commentary and anthropological observation alongside tall tales and comical anecdotes. While he both enjoyed and employed low-brow *bawdy* and *body* humor, he also wrote pointed satire, sophisticated even if the language was plain. Twain had no patience for pretentious, pompous, or "proper" people; he preferred writing about those with unexpected depth or duality, who were "both colorfully profane and profoundly innocent."[7] He created rich and uniquely American characters who represented the nation's sturdy traditional values as well as its restless, unorthodox spirit. His most famous and enduring novels, *The Adventures of Tom Sawyer* (1876) and *Adventures of Huckleberry Finn* (1884), are filled with such characters, celebrating the American spirit while also probing issues of humanity, morality, and conscience.

Over the course of his career, Twain wrote increasingly socially conscious work, drawing his fellow Americans' attention to the threats posed by greed, corruption, racist prejudice, and imperialism. He collaborated with writer Charles Dudley Warner on the satirical novel *The Gilded Age* (1873), coining the term that would become synonymous with this era's industrialization and corporate consolidation, political corruption, economic inequality, and conspicuous consumption. In *Tom Sawyer* and especially *Huckleberry Finn*, Twain spoke truth out of the mouths of babes, targeting adult prejudices, vanities, and vices with these family-friendly tales told from the perspectives of ornery youngsters. *The Prince and the Pauper* (1881) and *A Connecticut Yankee in King Arthur's Court* (1889) were spoofs of European class and aristocracy, closed-minded

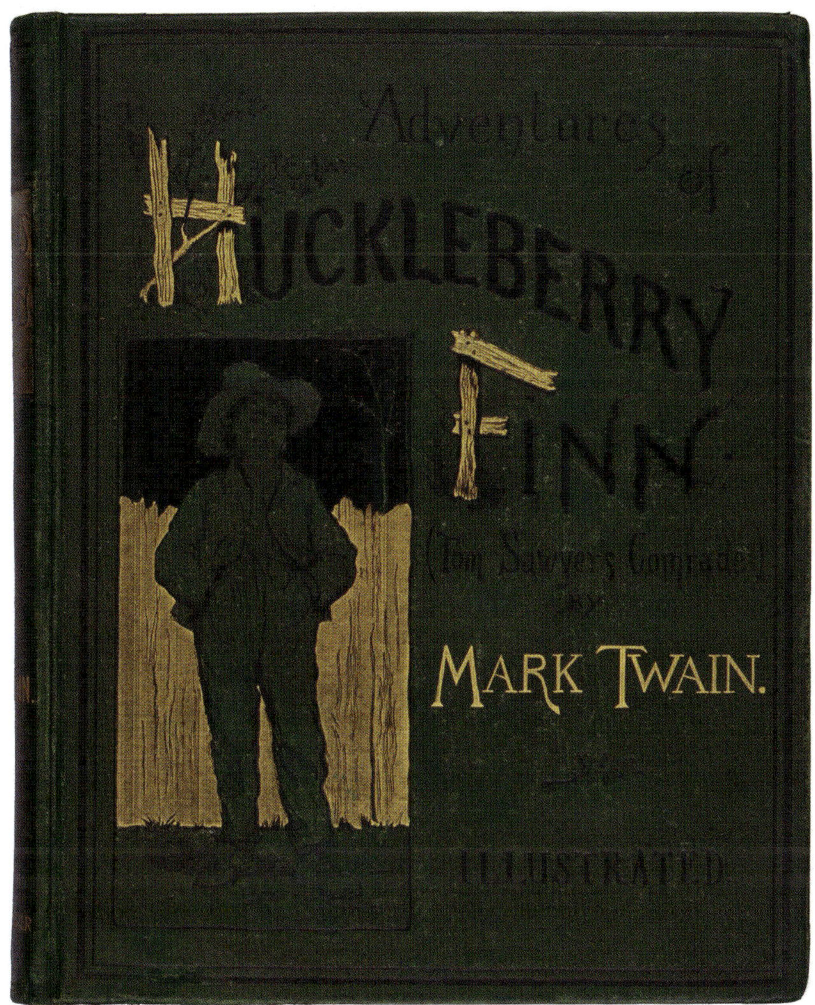

Adventures of Huckleberry Finn has endured as a classic of American literature for its colorful, action-packed story, colloquial humor, and slyly serious exploration of racist prejudice, social responsibility, and the meaning of civilization and freedom. Twain described it as "a book of mine where a sound heart and a deformed conscience come into collision and conscience suffers defeat."

culture, and religious mysticism. In his novel *Pudd'nhead Wilson* (1894), Twain tells an ironic and satirical tale of switched birth that highlights the absurdity of race and class essentialism. Twain understood the power of humor to educate, provoke, and liberate, helping Americans understand themselves and the rest of the world understand Americans.

At this moment of widespread anxiety about out-of-control urbanization, immigration, the closing of frontiers, labor unrest, and rapid technological change, one scholar wrote, "Twain reaffirmed the country's shared rural roots, its refugees and rogues, pillars and pretenders, with intimate knowledge and powerful familiarity."[8] He created an American style of literature that was direct and familiar in its language,

"Ours is the 'land of the free'—nobody denies that—nobody challenges it. (Maybe it is because we won't let other people testify.)"

—Mark Twain, **Roughing It**

contemporary and relevant in its subjects, and enduring in its themes. In his writing, he frequently returned to the river that so dominated his early years, not just for reasons of personal nostalgia, but because it represented adventure, romance, liberty, and freedom from the stifling responsibilities and constraints of modern life. His works, *Huckleberry Finn* in particular, beautifully express the fundamental tension between that yearning for freedom and disentanglement with the responsibilities to one's fellow humans and oneself. It's why the novel continues to resonate, and why students are still assigned to read it today. "All modern American literature comes from one book by Mark Twain called *Huckleberry Finn*," Ernest Hemingway wrote. "American writing comes from that. There was nothing before. There has been nothing as good since."[9]

Ryan Lintelman

WILL ROGERS, POET LARIAT

Will Rogers may be the most popular and influential comedian in American history who is least remembered today. While a few of his best-known catchphrases ("I never met a man I didn't like"; "All I know is what I read in the papers") and some vague image of a smiling cowboy holding a lariat persist in public memory, most Americans alive today do not grasp the cultural prominence, near-universal appeal, and power once held by the actor, author, and cultural commentator.

Beyond his untimely death in a 1935 plane crash in Alaska, Rogers's modern obscurity is also the flip side of the coin that made his career: he was the ultimate man of his times. He experienced a meteoric rise through the entertainment industry at the exact moment new broadcast media and momentous world events made his homespun, plainspoken, sincere humor irresistible to an American public yearning for authenticity and familiarity. At a time of rapid and disorienting technological, social, economic, and demographic change, the Oklahoma-born Rogers seemed like the definition of a real, decent, old-fashioned American who stood up for the little guy, knew right from wrong, and told it like it was. In his newspaper column and radio appearances, he became a popular and *populist* hero. His wry, genial, informal, self-effacing, "pointed yet

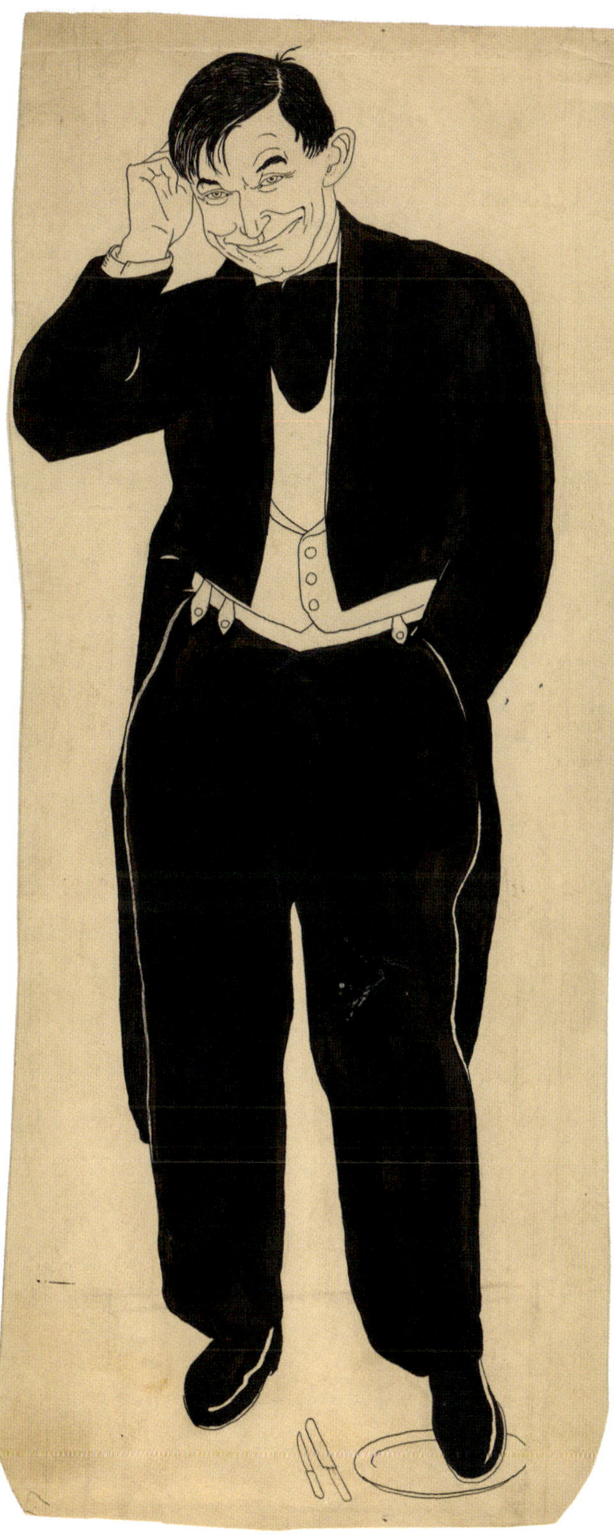

This drawing of Will Rogers by Walter Kinstler, made around 1923, shows the entertainer in formal wear rather than the more common depictions of him in cowboy garb of red flannel shirt, neckerchief, leather chaps, and boots with his rope lariat. Despite his folksy, homespun affect, Rogers became a powerful cultural commentator, hobnobbing with political and business elites.

never overheated" comic commentary on current events helped forge an American popular cultural vernacular and laid the ground for all observational and political comedy to follow.[10]

Will Rogers was born in Oologah, Indian Territory (now Oklahoma), on November 4, 1879. His father was a Confederate veteran, a Cherokee Indian, a politician active in tribal government, and a successful rancher, making Will the heir to a sizable estate. He was an indifferent student whose true interests were in ranching, riding, and roping, and he spent his formative years figuring out exactly how he could best put his boundless energy and ambition to use. His family and friends found him genial, talkative, good-hearted, modest, and witty, all characteristics that would define his public persona in years to come.

Young Rogers eschewed his father's advice to go into business to seek adventure, first trying ranching in Argentina before making his way to South Africa and Australia, where he found employment as a performer with Texas Jack's Wild West Circus. Inspired by Vicente Oropeza, a Mexican trick roper who performed with Buffalo Bill's Wild West at the 1893 World's Fair, Rogers took up the art and began billing himself "The Cherokee Kid—the Man Who Can Lasso the Tail off a Butterfly."[11]

Returning to the United States in time for the 1904 St. Louis Exposition, he performed there, then audaciously adapted his roping act for the relatively small vaudeville stage. Will, dressed in a cowboy's red shirt and buckskin trousers, would display fancy rope work and then lasso his assistant and horse Teddy in a dizzying variety of loops and nooses. He was also known for a trick known as a crinoline, in which he spun a giant lasso over the heads of the audience. By 1905, he was working the stage at some of New York's grandest vaudeville theaters, including Keith's

Union Square and Hammerstein's Victoria. From the beginning, Rogers employed stage banter, in part to explain his complicated rope tricks, but also because it made him feel more comfortable—"verbal defense against failure."[12] If he ever fumbled a trick, he'd complain, "I'm handicapped up here, 'cuz the manager won't let me swear when I miss," or stick a wad of chewing gum on the *W* in his name on the sign, drawing huge laughs.[13] Before long, his humorous, understated, self-effacing musings made him one of the most in-demand stars of the national Keith vaudeville circuit. In 1911, having reached the top of vaudeville's midlevel "dumb act" ladder, Rogers dropped the rope tricks and began appearing as a monologist, marketing his new act as "Will Rogers, the droll Oklahoma cowboy, in his new single offering, all alone, no horse."[14]

Now he won acclaim for his genuine, homespun charm and spontaneous improvisation—but that was just an act; in fact, the routine was scripted and rehearsed extensively. That worked well for the traveling vaudeville circuit, with new audiences to charm every night, but when Rogers began settling into a career in Broadway plays and revues in the mid-1910s, he had to up his game. At venues like Florenz Ziegfeld's Midnight Frolic, a tony garden nightclub on the rooftop above the New Amsterdam theater where his Follies played, the cosmopolitan audiences, peppered with repeat customers and critics, demanded fresh material every night. Ziegfeld, not known for his sense of humor, was said to have employed comic acts only to keep patrons occupied while the chorus girls changed outfits, but Rogers soon became the talk of the town, adding deft commentary on news and politics to his vaudeville act. His innovative ten-minute proto-stand-up act consisted of wry, folksy, seemingly extemporaneous musings on current events and jokes about famous figures. Rogers would single out celebrities in the audience for teasing patter, and this became a highlight of his performances, with the publicity provided by newspaper columnists in attendance a bonus for both the teased and teaser.

In May 1916, his star on the rise, Rogers even performed before President Woodrow Wilson at a Friars Club benefit in Baltimore. The humorist broke a long-standing show business taboo by directly ribbing him for recent failures and controversies like the Pancho Villa raid and his convoluted diplomacy and slow response to World War I. Wilson, though not known for his sense of humor, took the teasing in stride, telling Friars Club "Abbott" George M. Cohan, "I'd travel ten times that distance to listen to as wise a man as Will Rogers," and inviting the comedian for a private meeting after the show.[15]

Soon, Rogers began appearing in the *Ziegfeld Follies*, the vaudeville revue that made him the nation's most famous and well-paid comedian. In this famous production, Rogers appeared alongside Fanny Brice, Bert Williams, Ed Wynn, and his friends Eddie Cantor and W. C. Fields, a roster of some of the greatest entertainers of the era. It also cemented his reputation as "poet lariat," as critic Channing Pollock called him—the heir to Mark Twain as rural philosopher and national court jester whose commentary on modern life, skepticism of the powerful and mighty, and folksy embodiment of heartland American values made him one of the most popular and revered men of the early twentieth century.[16] By the early 1920s, Rogers had perfected his act and set rules for success: jokes must be brief enough for the audience's attention span, appear spontaneous, be based on fact, and be recent enough to have relevance. Breaking new ground for American humor, he believed that audiences would prefer relevant, pointed, and current humor to stock gags and slapstick. With an emerging political consciousness and power, he also believed that political humor for a popular audience was "diagnostic and therapeutic for a healthy democracy."[17]

At this new height of fame and adulation, Rogers was also remarkably productive, channeling his prodigious energy into writing, first just for his constantly evolving act, but then also for newspapers and magazines and books. He wrote two books in 1919: *Rogers-isms*, subtitled, *The Cowboy Philosopher on the Peace Conference* and *The Cowboy Philosopher on Prohibition*, testaments to his growing reputation as a comical commentator on current events. He also began a daily column, syndicated in over sixty newspapers across the United States from 1922 until his death, making him the most widely read and trusted columnist in the country. Like letters from a faithful friend, his colloquial writing, peppered with intentional misspellings, slang, and humorous malapropisms, struck a chord with an American public yearning for authentic, evenhanded, and direct reporting and commentary on world events. His intimate, self-deprecating, and commonsense missives took aim at hypocrisy, privilege, and corruption; he supported religious tolerance, freedom of speech, aviation, the abolition of child labor, and veterans' benefits and opposed Prohibition, imperialism, and welfare. At the height of Rogers's popularity, "his readers found his sensibility an irresistible way of filtering the news," one biographer wrote, and "many of them literally did not know what they thought about an issue or an event until they found out what Will Rogers had to say."[18]

He also appeared in sixty-eight films, first for Samuel Goldwyn, and later for comedy expert Hal Roach and Fox, for whom he became the studio's most bankable star. His film appearances were acclaimed for his naturalism and realism, his lack of training proving a boon in a film scene still dominated by exaggerated rhetorical gestures and stagy mugging. Most of his early films were wholesome western romances, in which he played a version of his good-natured, morally upright, and modest stage character, often in a fish-out-of-water situation; as Rogers put it, "I'm just an old country boy in a big town trying to get along."[19] Balancing skepticism and sentimentality, his movie performances resonated with American audiences trying to reconcile the massive demographic, social, economic, and cultural changes that made the modern, heterogeneous, cosmopolitan cities of the 1920s seem alien and threatening to traditional rural and regional values.

Rogers's folksy charm likewise made him a star in the emerging medium of radio, where his meandering storytelling and colloquial style marked him as a countercultural hero, aurally representing not only southern and western communities but also Native Americans who had precious little positive representation in mainstream popular culture.[20] He was therefore more naturally suited to talking pictures, where the innovative style of verbal humor he'd developed for the stage helped push the entire industry forward. Disregarding scripts still written in the formal, stilted language of silent intertitles, Rogers ad-libbed many of his lines, making the dialogue feel natural and fresh. His political consciousness also seeped into his film performances, with his 1930s movies focusing on community alliances and action that transcended lines of race, class, and gender, all while his increasingly progressive political commentary on the radio and in his columns earned him the name "Number One New Dealer."[21] Though Rogers publicly endorsed Franklin Delano Roosevelt and appeared with him on some memorable radio broadcasts, he still claimed not to have political ambitions himself, preferring to make his civic contributions as an outsider, keeping the system honest. Though he was sometimes mentioned as a presidential candidate, he wanted nothing to do with public office. "Everything is changing," he once wrote," people are taking their comedians seriously and the politicians as a joke, when it used to be visa versa [*sic*]."[22]

"When I die, my epitaph or whatever you call those signs on gravestones is going to read 'I joked about every prominent man of my time, but I never met a man I dident [sic] like.' I am so proud of that that I can hardly wait to die so it can be carved."
—Will Rogers, 1930

When Rogers died on August 15, 1935, near Point Barrow, Alaska, in a plane crash with pioneering aviator Wiley Post, he was at the height of his popularity and power. He had a radio series, wrote a daily newspaper column read by millions, and was one of the most successful and profitable actors in the American movie industry. He was mourned and celebrated as the most incisive political humorist of the era, a sagacious observer and oracular shaper of public opinion who proved that comedy could function as a public service.

Ryan Lintelman

BERT WILLIAMS: "FUNNIEST MAN I EVER SAW, AND THE SADDEST MAN I EVER KNEW"

Bahamian American Bert Williams was acclaimed as the greatest Black comedian of his generation, and perhaps the first universally known Black entertainer in American history. His fame, however, was achieved at great cost and compromise. At the height of Jim Crow segregation and entrenched white supremacist ideology, the light-skinned Williams performed in blackface, believing that the benefits of his more authentic and positive portrayal of African American life and humor outweighed the damaging effects of racial caricature. He rose to the heights of the entertainment industry, appearing in the *Ziegfeld Follies*, starring in the first Black musicals on Broadway, owning his own production company, and becoming the first major Black film star, but he struggled with alienation, shame, and prejudice that drove him to depression. In his groundbreaking yet fraught career, Bert Williams strived to use the tools available to him as a comedian to plead for Black humanity and pave the way for Black entertainers to come.

Born in Nassau in 1874, Williams moved to California with his family as a child and attended college at Stanford before deciding that the stage was calling him. Opportunities were few and fleeting for Black entertainers, but the handsome and charming Williams worked his way

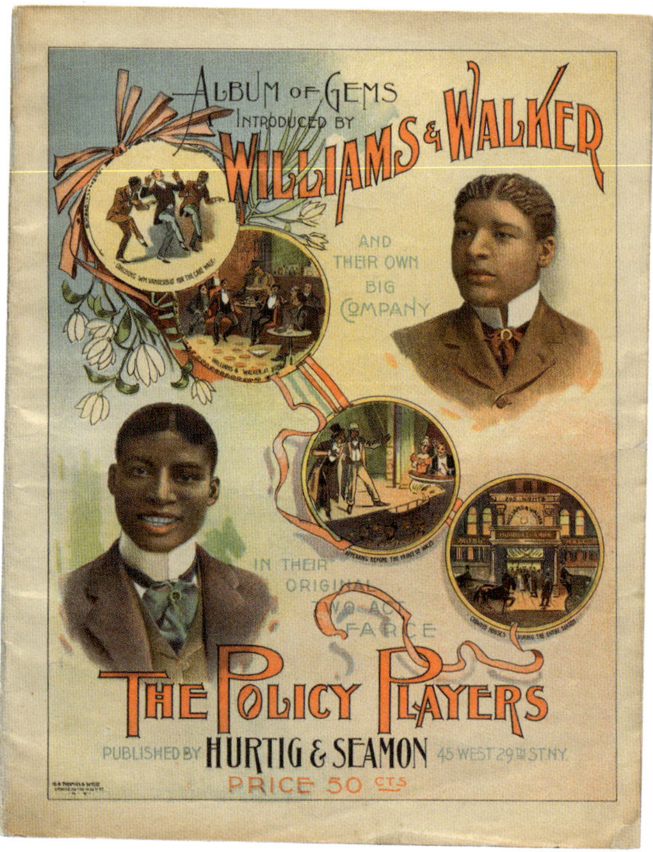

Williams and Walker were among the most successful Black entertainers of their generation, embracing the narrow roles and opportunities available to them in a segregated society while also performing enormously popular cultural forms like the cakewalk. Using blackface as a mask, Williams embodied W. E. B. Du Bois's concept of "double-consciousness," employing racial masquerade as a survival tactic.

through western medicine shows, concert saloons, and minstrel shows while honing his act as a singer and comic. While performing with Martin and Selig's Mastodon Minstrels in San Francisco, he met African American comedian George Walker, and before long the kindred spirits broke out on their own. In a devil's bargain, Williams and Walker found success working the gigs available to them, whether impersonating Africans in the Dahomey Village exhibit at the 1894 San Francisco Midwinter Exposition, wearing blackface makeup and kinky wigs as endmen in minstrel acts, or performing stereotypical and derogatory "coon songs."

By the time they were headlining major New York vaudeville houses in 1896, Williams and Walker had developed an immensely popular act, billing themselves "Two Real Coons," and combining comic skits, dance, and musical performance. They embodied two classic minstrel types, with Williams the dimwitted country bumpkin Jim Crow—oafish, gangly, and dressed in ill-fitting clothing—while Walker's well-dressed, strutting, smooth-talking straight man drew from minstrelsy's Zip Coon. The normally poised and dignified Williams wore blackface, dropped his West Indies English accent for a southern drawl, and moved in a hunched, shuffling, clumsy manner, displaying a mastery of physical humor. Over time, this evolved into his mournful, contemplative "Jonah Man," a resigned and put-upon everyman whom Williams portrayed with pantomime and pathos to humanize and elicit audience empathy for his character.

The duo's complicity in the proliferation of these harmful stereotypes was a complicated choice. Walker and Williams felt that their work could help correct the misrepresentations and stereotypes so prevalent in American society at the time. "We discovered an important fact . . . the one hope of the colored performer must be in making a radical departure from the old 'darky' style of singing and dancing," Walker said, "so we set ourselves the task of thinking along new lines."[23]

They claimed that they suppressed the more odious elements of the stock Black characters they portrayed, underplaying dialect, buffoonery, and dimwittedness, and playing up their intelligence and comic personalities, lending them realism and multidimensionality. Williams thought of the blackface mask as an essential and liberating costume, allowing him to immediately take on all the white audience's preconceptions about Black people, and then through this separate persona, play with their assumptions and prejudices, hopefully coaxing a greater empathy and pan-racial understanding through comic performance.[24] "When we picture the negro on the stage," Williams explained, "we think of him singing, laughing and cutting up. That seems to be his nature. But has it ever occurred to you that under his mask of smiles and this cloak of capers there is a hidden dire tragedy?"[25]

Walker and Williams helped popularize the cakewalk, a comic dance that perhaps best represents the complexity of their take on race and representation. Drawing inspiration from European and African dance styles, as well as a stylized dance that enslaved African Americans performed as a way of subversively mocking their enslavers, the cakewalk entailed well-dressed Black dancers strutting, shuffling, and prancing in outrageous and pretentious fashion. The energetic, high-stepping dance became a cultural sensation in the 1890s, performed by both Black and white entertainers in blackface. It was celebrated in the first Black Broadway musical, a production that Walker and Williams inspired their friends Paul Laurence Dunbar and Will Marion Cook to write, *Clorindy, or the Origin of the Cakewalk*.[26]

In 1902 Dunbar and Cook wrote a new musical, *In Dahomey: A Negro Musical Comedy*, specifically for Walker and Williams and an all-Black cast. The musical, which took satirical aim at the "back to Africa" movement, was a popular success on Broadway and toured nationally; Walker and Williams also took it to Buckingham Palace for a command performance for King Edward VII. In the first decade of the new century, Walker and Williams were the most popular and visible Black performers in the world, Broadway producers, best-selling recording artists, and vaudeville headliners.

"Bert Williams was the funniest man I ever saw and the saddest man I ever knew."
—W. C. Fields, 1923

When Walker died in 1911, Williams carried on a solo act, moving away from the coarser "coon" act toward a more subtle and studied form of humor that won him top billing on the high-class vaudeville circuit. A reserved and contemplative scholar in his personal life, Williams wrote and spoke about the history and future of Black entertainment as a force

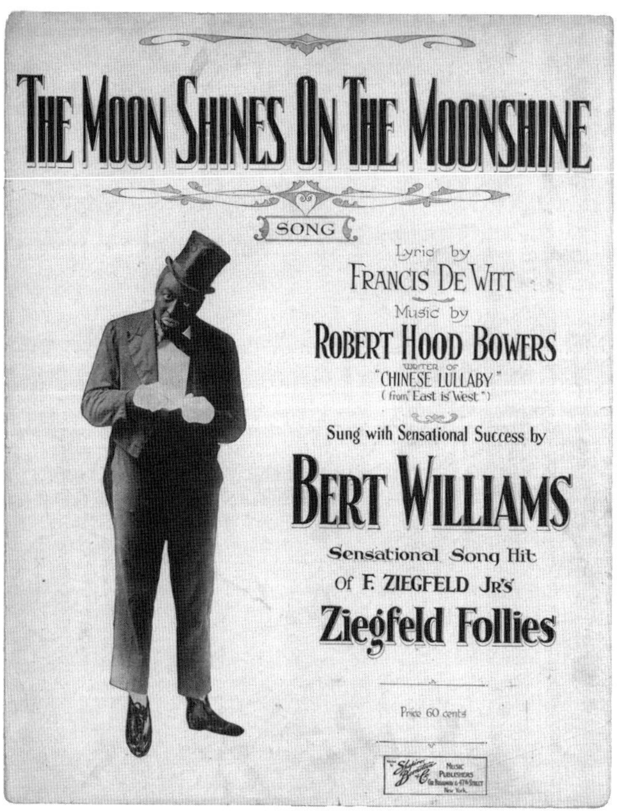

This song, among the most popular in the *Ziegfeld Follies* of 1919, laments the closure of liquor distilleries and breweries while celebrating the illicit production of moonshine "in the mountain tops, far from the eyes of cops." The song became a hit the same year that the Eighteenth Amendment, prohibiting the production and consumption of alcoholic beverages, was ratified into law. Williams recorded the anti-prohibition anthem for Columbia Records, and it sold over 250,000 copies, one of his best-selling releases and biggest hits of the era.

for social change, while advocating for greater and more dignified representation onstage and in the new film medium. Increasingly, however, racial prejudice began to limit his opportunities. Without Walker, Williams was almost always the sole Black performer on the bill for his vaudeville performances and often found himself alienated from jealous white colleagues. He made headlines in 1910 when hired for the nation's premier vaudeville revue, the *Ziegfeld Follies*, but some members of the cast threatened to quit rather than share the bill with Williams. The only Black member of the troupe, he nevertheless became the show's biggest draw over his eight years in the cast.

At the height of his fame as a vaudevillian, recording artist, and Broadway star, Williams also became the first Black film star, bringing his talents for physical comedy and unequaled celebrity to the silent screen. In popular films like *Darktown Jubilee* (1914) and *A Natural Born Gambler* (1916), Williams simply performed parts of his vaudeville act, like his famous poker pantomime, but he fought for greater representation, including a remarkable early Black film made for an interracial audience.

Surviving only in fragments, the 1914 Biograph production *Lime Kiln Club Field Day* provides a rare glimpse into contemporary Black middle-class life, with all the dignity and humanity that Williams strove for. In the film, Williams appears in blackface and a version of his Jonah Man costume performing a cakewalk, eating ice cream, riding a carousel, and charming an attractive and young Black actress while other well-dressed members of his troupe enjoy an outing at an amusement park. The film included a romantic kiss between Williams and costar Odessa Warren Grey that, according to one scholar, "would have been among the boldest expressions of racial progress in popular entertainment at the time—had it been seen." Ultimately, filmmakers decided that the moviegoing public wasn't ready for such a generous and positive representation of authentic African American life, especially after the blockbuster release of D. W. Griffith's white supremacist epic *The Birth of a Nation*, and so the film was never released.[27]

After Williams's death in 1922, W. E. B. Du Bois wrote a eulogy for his friend, expressing a reverence that spoke to the comedian's greatest hopes for his legacy. "When in the calm afterday of thought and struggle to racial peace we look back to pay tribute to those who helped most, we shall single out for highest praise those who made the world laugh . . . above all, Bert Williams. For this was not mere laughing: it was the smile that hovered above blood and tragedy; the light mask of happiness that hid breaking hearts and bitter souls. This is the top of bravery; the finest thing in service. May the world long honor the undying fame of Bert Williams as a great comedian, a great negro, a great man."[28]

Ryan Lintelman

THE CAROL BURNETT SHOW: SKETCH COMEDY, HER WAY

Television was in transition in 1967, with the medium's veteran talents tentatively making space for a new generation: *The Ed Sullivan Show*, nearing its twentieth anniversary on the air, was the lead-in for the revolutionary new *Smothers Brothers Comedy Hour*, narrowly beating it in the ratings; *Laugh-In* landed like a transmission from another planet, and Milton Berle, "Mr. Television" himself, attempted a ballyhooed comeback but was canceled halfway through the season.

Among TV comedy's new guard of superstars was Carol Burnett, who was a young-but-tested entertainer when she approached CBS to pitch a comedy variety show for which she would serve as both host and principal performer. Burnett had an Emmy award, a starring run on Broadway, and multiple prime-time TV specials behind her, but network bosses questioned her ability to carry a weekly prime-time hour, suggesting her talents might be best suited to a sitcom premise. (And they offered her one on the spot—the inauspiciously titled *Here's Agnes*.) When Burnett doubled down, she was told that hosting was "a man's game" and was summarily shown the door.[29] But she leveraged

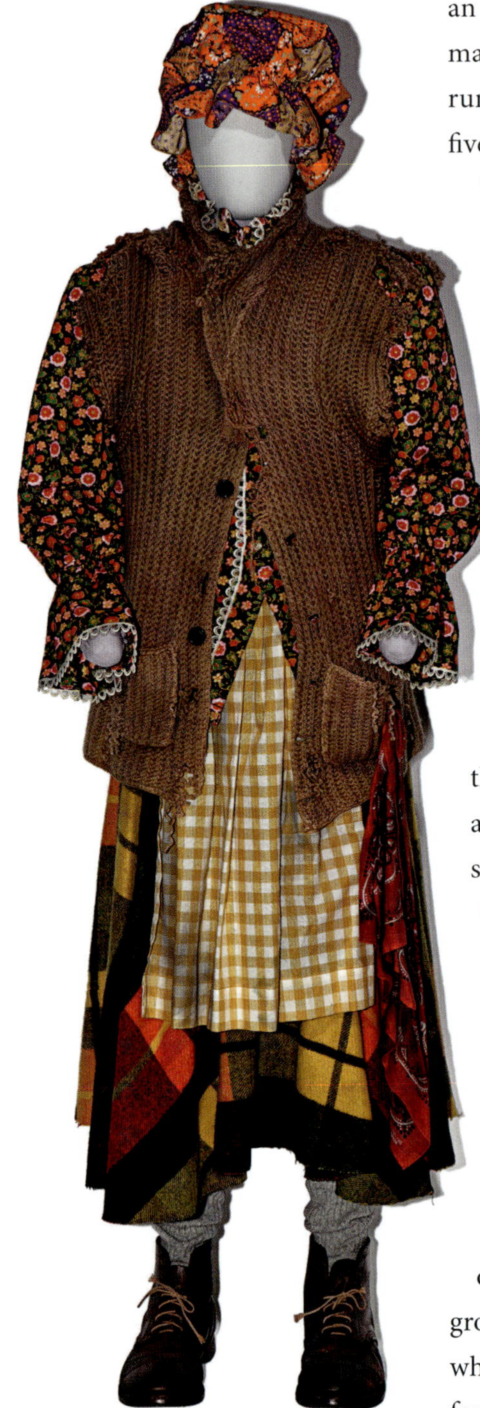

Carol Burnett's Charwoman was a melancholy housemaid that become her unofficial avatar and the icon of the long-running *Carol Burnett Show*. The series closed after eleven seasons with the charwoman's searing rendition of Burnett's theme, "I'm So Glad We Had This Time Together."

an extraordinary clause in her contract to force the issue and ultimately did debut in prime time that fall. *The Carol Burnett Show* would run for eleven years, garner seventy Emmy nominations and twenty-five wins, and average thirty million viewers each week.

The naysaying executives weren't wrong: Burnett did cut a revolutionary figure within a genre that had almost exclusively offered opportunities to men. With few exceptions, including Martha Raye, Dinah Shore, and Judy Garland, TV history was littered with affable male variety hosts. In 1967 alone, *The Andy Williams Show*, *The Garry Moore Show*, *The Danny Kaye Show*, *The Steve Allen Comedy Hour*, *The Dean Martin Show*, *The Red Skelton Show* and *The Jackie Gleason Show* were *some* of the offerings. Even as she mastered the craft of variety performance as it had been modeled by her mostly male forebears, Burnett would strike out on her own to emerge as a key architect of modern sketch comedy. *The Carol Burnett Show* could trace its ancestry to vaudeville theaters and music halls, but it was also an avant-garde entry in the canon of televised comedy as it reframed performance tropes from an earlier era for a future that would be more concerned with satire, social commentary, and anarchic humor than burlesque and pratfalls (which she, incidentally, also did very well).

Burnett opened every episode of her show with an invocation to "bump up the lights" so that she could establish a personal rapport with her studio audience—and, by extension, all of America. Outfitted in stunning couture designed by Bob Mackie, Burnett endearingly fielded questions off-the-cuff, often collapsing into fits of laughter or extending a warm hand to a fan bearing gifts, and established a mutual adoration society that had all the good feeling of a real interpersonal relationship. These cameo appearances grounded Burnett's star persona in an accessible, approachable guise, which was the prelude to an hour of wildly wide-ranging humor that found the comic actress inhabiting characters that spanned from a precocious child star to a slow-witted grandam, from a blackmailing Girl Scout to a deranged silent film vamp, and from an airheaded secretary to a heart-wrenchingly earnest charwoman.

By dint of Burnett's extraordinary versatility and performative stamina, she played a central role in just about every sketch the show put forth in its nearly three hundred episodes, as well as Broadway-quality production numbers that involved rigorous singing and dancing. Though certainly not to the exclusion of other themes, *The Carol Burnett Show* was, fundamentally, a showcase for humor by a woman, and about women, especially as it privileged send-ups of traditionally "feminine" media genres like soap operas and romance movies. Even without explicitly announcing itself as a feminist platform, the show consistently advanced a point of view that critiqued the drudgery of domestic confinement, the grotesquery of conventional standards of beauty, and the narrowness of the stories that are told about women. In an era when most comedy originated from a male subject position, this was a significant—and a liberatory—shift.

From recurring sketches like "As the Stomach Turns" (which heightened the narrative and aesthetic conventions of the soap opera genre to hilarious effect) to parodies of inane television commercials (Burnett plays a housewife violently overrun by advertising mascots who've come to life and invaded her kitchen), the show was far from subtle about its attitudes toward the coalescing second wave feminist movement. The most trenchant example of this was Burnett's magnum opus characterization, Eunice Higgins, a middle-aged woman trapped in an unhappy marriage who haunts her tacky Texas living room in a threadbare floral dress, suffering insults hurled by her overbearing mother, "Mama." Eunice's hopelessly unfulfilled ambitions were hardly hilarious at face value, but made for sophisticated black comedy when handled by Burnett. In a sense, "the undertow of female anger and disappointment" that propels these sketches makes them incredibly risky as fodder for comedy. Unlike movie parodies or soap operas, which offer histrionics that are easily mined for laughs, Eunice calls forth the relatable, and therefore utterly terrifying, "cruelties of everyday life."[30]

Carol Burnett's technical skill as a physical comedian and charisma as a television personality are apparent to anyone who sees her work. Her prowess as a leader and creative mind is less visible, but no less central to her success. Though she was not credited as a producer, writer, or director on-screen, it was Burnett's ultimate creative discretion that ensured the vibrancy, originality, and quality of the show that bore her name—as well as its endurance. As a consummate collaborator and cultivator of talent, she assembled, fostered, and then set free one of the greatest ensemble casts in comedy history: Vicki Lawrence, Lyle Waggoner, Harvey Korman, and Tim Conway. It is convenient to call their chemistry a kind of magic; in reality, the mood on the set, and the spirit of camaraderie that sharpened the edge of their work, was Burnett's to establish and maintain. Exceptional comedy is made in exceptional conditions, and the joy in their shared work spilled out through the TV screen in bursts of irrepressible laughter that became an integral part of the show's rhythm and tone, redolent of the excitement and unpredictability that characterized television's first generation of live variety programs like *Your Show of Shows*. Guest starring on *The Carol Burnett Show* became one of the most coveted gigs in Hollywood, because of the high caliber of the work, and because of the fun that was had.

Carol Burnett's *Went with the Wind* costume, designed by the legendary Bob Mackie, is a masterpiece of camp and creativity that nods to the grandeur of classic Hollywood fashion. The costume represents one of the most memorable and celebrated moments in TV comedy history.

The Carol Burnett Show would generate dozens of sketches that ascended to become "classic" cultural touchstones, and which continue to circulate as highwater marks in the history of American comedy. The most iconic among them is "Went with the Wind!," a parody of the 1939 film version of *Gone with the Wind* that includes a peerless sight gag: As "Starlett" O'Hara, Burnett descends a grand staircase in a gown quite literally made of window drapes, with the curtain rod still attached, naïvely intoning, "I saw it in the window and I couldn't resist." Tim Conway and Harvey Korman's uproariously funny "Dentist" sketch, which finds the duo immobilized by errant shots of Novocain, along with Burnett's blaring "Tarzan yell," have also forged permanent places in the echelons of television nostalgia. Most memorably of all, Burnett closed every episode of her show with a melancholic gesture of utmost gratitude, tugging at her ear in a private gesture of thanks to the beloved grandmother who raised her through a hardscrabble childhood in Depression-era Hollywood, as she sang the show's lilting theme song, "I'm So Glad We've Had This Time Together."

Laura LaPlaca

W. C. FIELDS, GENTLEMAN MISANTHROPE

W. C. Fields was a stage and screen comedian whose misanthropic persona and anarchic disruption of social norms and niceties shocked and thrilled Americans throughout the twentieth century. He worked his way from burlesque and vaudeville to Broadway and radio but is best remembered today for his 1930s films, where he usually portrayed a put-upon everyman navigating a host of indignities and insults. In his memorable drawl, he muttered a wistful, mumbling monologue of curses and wisecracks at the objects of his scorn, from his movie wives and children to ventriloquist dummy Charlie McCarthy. His wicked sense of humor and disregard for convention has made him an enduring symbol of comedy's countercultural potential.

Born William Claude Dukenfield in 1880, Fields ran away from home at the age of eleven after a troubled childhood, scraping together a living pool sharking and juggling. By the age of eighteen, he began working as an "eccentric juggler" under the stage name W. C. Fields in burlesque and vaudeville, where he honed his skills as a mime and physical comic. Like his contemporary Will Rogers, Fields learned that he could get big laughs from the audience intentionally fumbling and narrating his juggling or billiard tricks and began to develop a comic persona. He earned parts in popular Broadway revues, then six appearances in the prestigious annual *Ziegfeld Follies.* From there, he became a star in the long-running 1923 Broadway comedy *Poppy*, appeared in twelve silent and thirty-two sound movies, and frequently guest-starred on radio comedy programs before his death in 1946.

The character that W. C. Fields created was a politically incorrect antihero, a self-centered huckster, a cantankerous alcoholic, and a world-weary cynic who stood in visible opposition to nearly every social

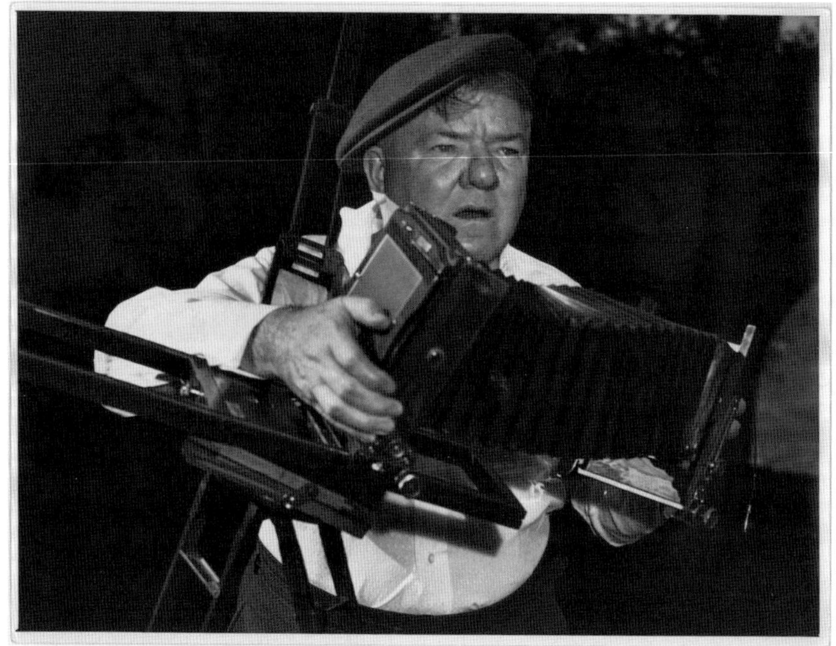

Celebrated Los Angeles photographer Will Connell visited his friend W. C. Fields at his home in Los Feliz one afternoon in the early 1940s. True to his reputation, Fields had been imbibing and improvised a comic scene he christened "the accordion player" with Connell's old-fashioned bellowed framing camera.

trend and polite norm of the era otherwise defined by Prohibition, optimism, and an energetic work ethic. He famously even hated children, dogs, and Christmas. His performances were marked by bemused indignation, frustrated slow burns, startled jumps, and sarcastic insults delivered out of the side of his mouth, comic techniques he delivered brilliantly onstage and especially on-screen; larger than life, in close-up or medium shots, he was funnier than ever.

There were actually two sides to the Fields character, which he sometimes even employed in the same film: the henpecked, harassed husband, and the conceited yet charming con man. Like the Yankee peddler and snake oil salesman character types from which he drew comic inspiration, Fields often employed inflated, grandiose language and dress while scamming guileless naïfs to get his way or make a quick buck. Fields's larceny could be small and petty, like moving all the meat to his side of a sandwich when forced to share with his bratty son in the 1934 film *It's a Gift*, or more substantial, like embezzling from a bank in 1940's *The Bank Dick*.

"In Fields's vision," one scholar wrote, "America is ultimately one gigantic con game, and he was determined to come out on the winning side, both in his life and in his art."[31] To some fans, his characters were underdog heroes to be celebrated. Disrespected, underemployed, trapped in loveless marriages and unfulfilling family lives, overweight, and unhealthy, they typically endured their trials and ended up besting the authority figures and disrespectful relations who kept him from

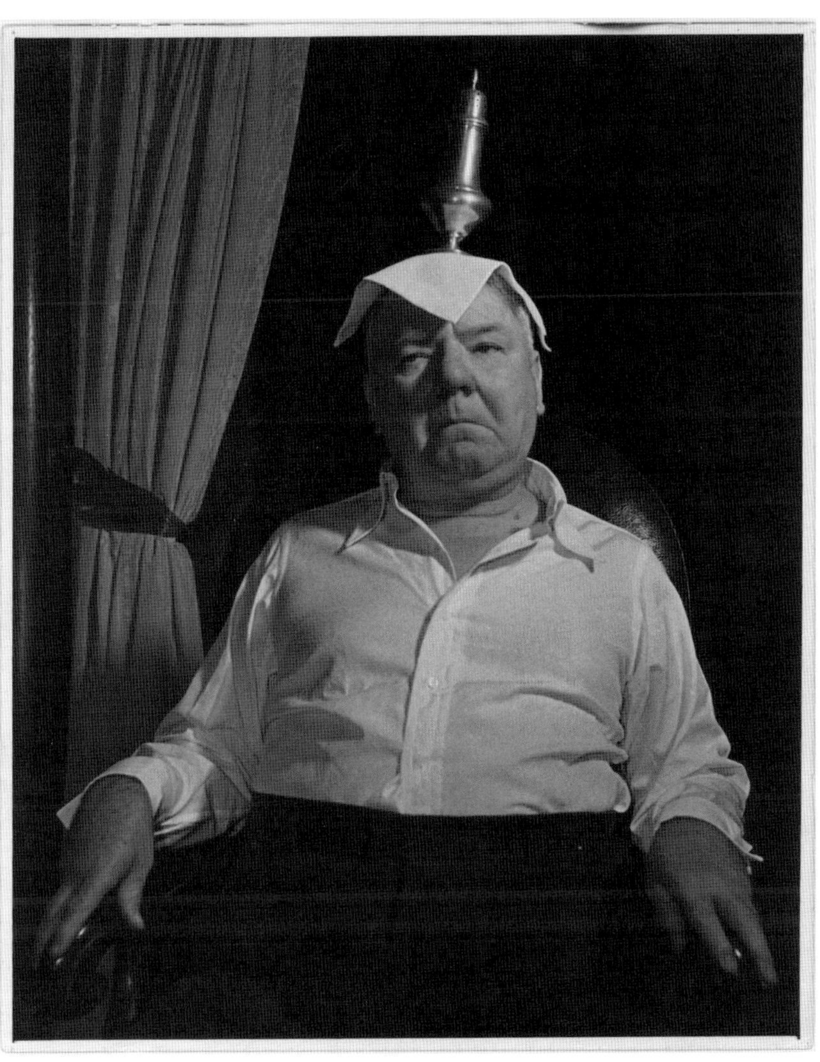

"W. C. Fields as Queen Victoria," photograph by Will Connell.

enjoying life. His later films, like *The Bank Dick*, were fantasies of restoration of paternal authority, social respect, and sudden financial gain. But there is also a gendered interpretation of his comedy, in which women are always either sexual objects or scolding, uncaring nags—perhaps Fields's misogyny resonated with American men who found it a comforting backlash against the emasculating forces of female empowerment in the early twentieth century.[32]

In retrospect, much of his humor reads as reactionary, especially in the context of the era's New Deal programs and dramatic social change. He promised "no such empty panaceas as a New Deal, or an Old Deal, or even a Re-Deal" in his 1940 book *Fields for President.* Fields's farcical presidential campaign had a proto-libertarian platform, primarily based on his hatred of the income tax, but also exhibiting a serious undercurrent, rejection of government corruption, surveillance, censorship, and arbitrary exercise of authority.[33] "Hell, I never vote for anybody," one

Fields biographer reported him saying one election day, "I always vote against."[34]

Fields's contrarian nihilism, perhaps most evident in the legendarily heavy drinking that eventually killed him, was countered only by his inexorable creative spirit that continues to influence comedians and freethinkers today. His films often exhibit a postmodern self-referential awareness of their absurdity and unreality, such as in 1933's *The Fatal Glass of Beer*, which ludicrously lampooned temperance reform drama with bizarre juxtapositions and a stilted staginess that confused both contemporary and modern viewers.[35] Indeed, the surreal and illogical worlds of his films almost border on cartoonish, with scenes like Fields jumping out of a plane without a parachute to catch a falling bottle of liquor in *Never Give a Sucker an Even Break* (1941), speaking to an interesting subjectivity and perhaps the hallucinatory drunkenness of many of his characters.

By the late 1960s, twenty years after his death, Fields had become a countercultural icon, appearing in surprising places as a symbol of rebellion against social and cultural norms. He was one of the celebrities chosen by members of the Beatles to appear in the crowd scene on the cover of their 1967 *Sgt. Pepper's Lonely Hearts Club Band*, and his likeness became popular as a subject of five and dime store stickers, college dorm posters, and other merchandise like battery testers (his bulbous nose lighting red if the battery held a charge). And he got nods from entertainers ranging from the surrealist comedy troupe Firesign Theatre to celebrity impressionist Rich Little as a nostalgic forebearer of their brands of transgressive humor.

His influence looms large over characters like Homer Simpson and the Dude from *The Big Lebowski*, not to mention comics like Norm Macdonald and Larry David. "Of all the great comedians," wrote film historian Arthur Knight, "none has ever been more openly hostile, more flagrantly misanthropic, more downright cantankerous."[36]

Ryan Lintelman

SILENT CLOWNS: CHAPLIN, KEATON, AND LLOYD

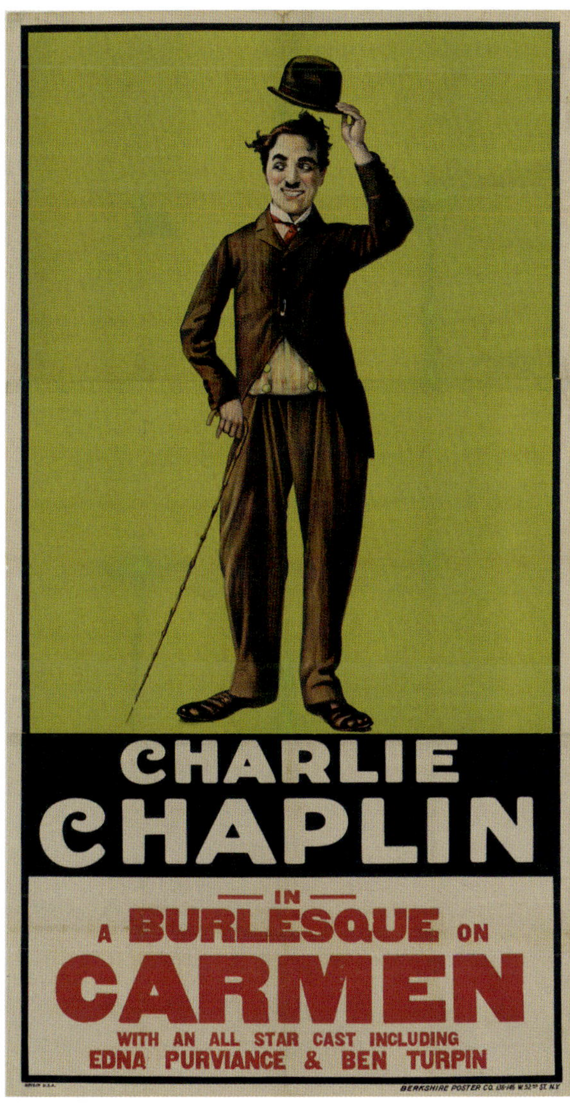

This poster for the 1915 Essanay Studios film *A Burlesque on Carmen* shows Chaplin in his iconic costume as the Tramp, with ill-fitting clothing, bowler hat, mustache, and cane. A master of pantomime, Chaplin made his thin, bendable bamboo cane an essential prop. He used it for balance, hooking unsuspecting bystanders, pulling women toward him, fidgeting, and, in one memorable scene, even pulling himself out of the splits by grabbing on to a chandelier.

In the first three decades of the twentieth century, silent cinema captured the nation's attention and transformed its popular culture. Never before had every American been able to experience the same entertainment performance at the same time, regardless of location, class, race, gender, or even language. In the thousands of movie theaters that spread across the country like wildfire, from frontier tents and small-town storefront nickelodeons to majestic movie palaces in major cities, people from all backgrounds saw the same images on the screen, cheered on the same larger-than-life heroes, and booed the same dastardly villains. Inexpensive, accessible, and sensational, moviegoing became a national pastime and instrument of social transformation. As the United States entered the new century, the movies created and propagated a shared popular culture, shaping Americans' concepts of success, beauty, patriotism, and morality.

Though audiences loved westerns, romances, melodrama, and adventure, the most popular and prolific genre of early film was comedy. At first, film comedians adapted the broad physical comedy, ethnic and racial stereotypes, and exaggerated actions and comic mugging of vaudeville and burlesque performance to the new medium. By the mid-1910s, however, they had developed a new vocabulary for film comedy that helped bring the genre in to its own. Three of the most popular and successful of the film comedians of the silent era, Charlie Chaplin, Buster Keaton, and Harold Lloyd, even transcended the specific constraints of silent cinema to earn recognition as enduring artistic auteurs. Each of these "silent clowns," as scholars have named them, moved beyond well-worn tropes to create novel characters that made them international stars. Though some of their work could resemble the anarchic disorder of the Keystone Kops style of slapstick, they each developed a more sophisticated form of physical comedy with acrobatic feats that sometimes verged into the surreal, bending time and space to their bidding. In the stories they developed and brought to life, they created situation-based comedy and played with concepts of morality, success, authority, work, and romance. Each also developed sympathetic and well-realized characters that became audience favorites. Americans cheered on these underdog everymen, Chaplin's Tramp, Keaton's stone-faced little guys, and Lloyd's "glasses character," in their struggles against unjust authority, bullies, and the frustrations of modern life.

CHARLIE CHAPLIN: THE TRAMP

Charlie Chaplin was the biggest star in the world in the late 1910s and early 1920s. His Tramp character realized the potential of silent cinema for universality, recognized and loved across borders and boundaries of class, race, and gender. The Tramp was a tragicomic underdog who faced the hostility of the world with upbeat pluck and self-assuredness despite his disadvantage. Dressed in tattered and ill-fitting clothes and usually depicted as financially insecure and transient, the Tramp nevertheless retained his sense of personal dignity, sauntering with a cane and bowler hat, demanding respect for himself and others, and showing a determination and resilient spirit that made him a hero of underprivileged people everywhere.

Chaplin was born in London in 1889 to two struggling entertainers, his father a comic singer in music halls and mother a musician and singer. Both parents battled alcoholism and poverty, and Chaplin and his brother Sidney spent their childhood in deprivation, with periods spent in homelessness, workhouses, and boarding schools. By 1898, Charlie was performing professionally, touring British music halls with troupes of performers who provided him with an education in the physical comedy he was to master. The broad, working-class humor of his fellow performers also inspired Chaplin, from the oddly dressed, "shabby genteel" characters including drunks and tramps to scenes set in lodging houses, restaurants, and pawn shops. He studied the clowns' pathos, way with props, comic movements, and acrobatic feats, not only pratfalls but also specialized gags like abruptly stopping or turning a corner while running, bits that would later become his trademarks.[37]

He arrived in the United States with Fred Karno's American Company in 1910, and after he toured in vaudeville for a few years, comedy

"Life is a tragedy when seen in close-up, but a comedy in long-shot."
—Charlie Chaplin

impresario Mack Sennett hired him to appear in films for his Keystone Studio. Sennett was the progenitor of the brand of silent comedy that survives as cliché today, with grotesque mugging, ridiculous costumes, madcap car chases, and exaggerated violence. Chaplin sought to distinguish himself by developing a unique character, and created the Tramp, first appearing in the 1914 short *Kid Auto Races in Venice*. Chaplin's character wore a tight coat, baggy trousers, ridiculously large shoes, bamboo cane, bowler hat, and small mustache, and he imbued the character with a nonchalant self-assuredness and mock formality at odds with his downtrodden appearance. The Tramp's waddling shuffle, twitching mustache, "cock a snoot" nose thumbing at authority, and skidding run around corners delighted audiences, and they flocked to theaters to see his prodigious output of film shorts.[38]

By 1916, Chaplin became an international star, one of the highest paid and most recognizable people in the world. In a phenomenon labeled "Chaplinitis," his popularity inspired other film actors to imitate him, companies to market merchandise based on his name and image, and unauthorized comic strips and lookalike contests across the country. Newspaper and movie magazine profiles played up the Englishman's humility, genius, and work ethic, painting a Horatio Alger–like picture of rags-to-riches meritocratic success, and branding him a true American. The Tramp character resonated with audiences who saw something of themselves in this lonely outsider just trying to get a leg up in a cruel world, especially when he stood up to unjust authorities or made some pompous bully look like a fool. The Tramp appeared in films that spoofed many Americans' lived experiences, from his penniless immigration story in *The Immigrant* (1917) to his life in the trenches as a doughboy in *Shoulder Arms* (1918).

In films like *A Dog's Life* (1918) and *The Kid* (1921), Chaplin moved beyond the simple structure of his earlier films to craft more complicated, sentimental stories that explored concepts like poverty and freedom. The Tramp became less anarchic and subversive than in some of his earlier films, with greater emphasis on his good nature and heart. Now directing his own pictures at his own studio, Chaplin moved into feature films that balanced comedy and tragedy, leveraging the popularity of the Tramp to produce comedic art films imbued with social commentary. *The Gold Rush* (1925), inspired by the Klondike Gold Rush and the starvation and cannibalism of the Donner Party, was the longest and most expensive comedy film made to date and included the memorable sequence where Chaplin performs a dance with dinner rolls on forks. *City Lights* (1930), an epic sentimental tale of love overcoming adversity, and *Modern Times* (1936), a satire on modern industry and capitalism, were even more ambitious and acclaimed. With the coming of sound, however, Chaplin decided to retire the Tramp, and in his later films he appeared (and spoke) as other characters, notably in *The Great Dictator* (1940), his prescient antiwar film released on the cusp of World War II.

Chaplin's Tramp was the most popular and influential of the silent clowns, becoming a global icon of cinema and comedy.

BUSTER KEATON: THE GREAT STONE FACE

Joseph "Buster" Keaton purportedly earned his nickname from magician Harry Houdini, who knew his parents from the vaudeville circuit they worked together. "The Three Keatons" were known for the knockabout act where father Joe threw his son across the stage, made easier by a luggage handle sewn into his clothes. After one particularly painful-looking fall down a flight of stairs that seemed not to phase young Joseph, Houdini is said to have remarked, "That was a real buster!" and the name stuck.

Throughout his lifetime in show business and his five decades in film, Buster Keaton proved himself the most accomplished and compelling physical comedian in American history. His acrobatic clowning,

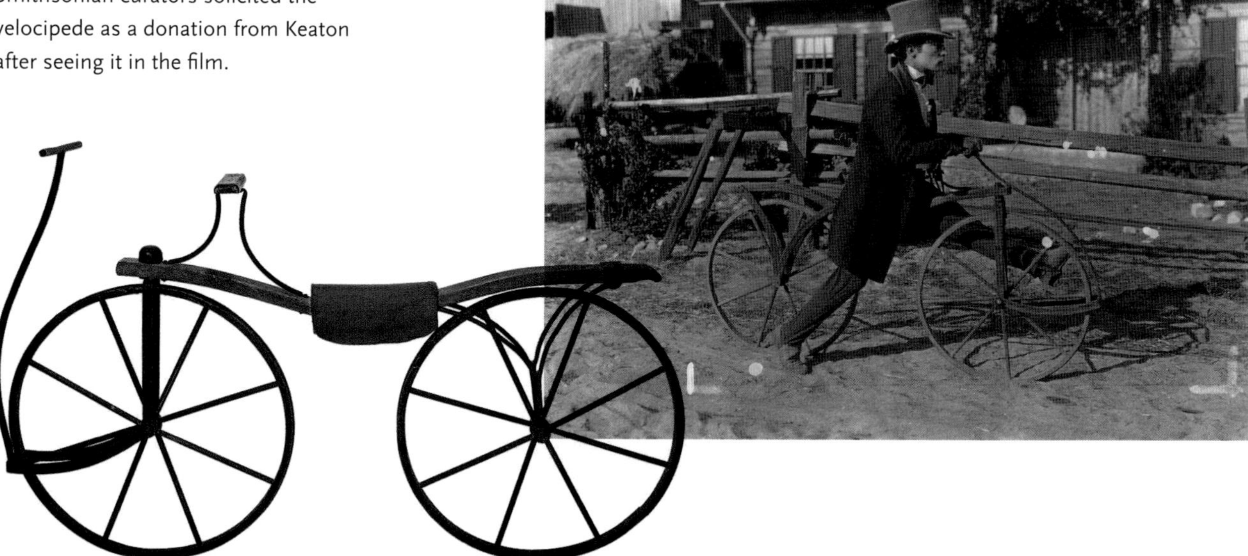

Buster Keaton used this velocipede, an early, pedalless bicycle, in the 1923 film *Our Hospitality*, his farce on the legendary Hatfield-McCoy feud. He was a stickler for historical authenticity and aficionado of transportation technology. Smithsonian curators solicited the velocipede as a donation from Keaton after seeing it in the film.

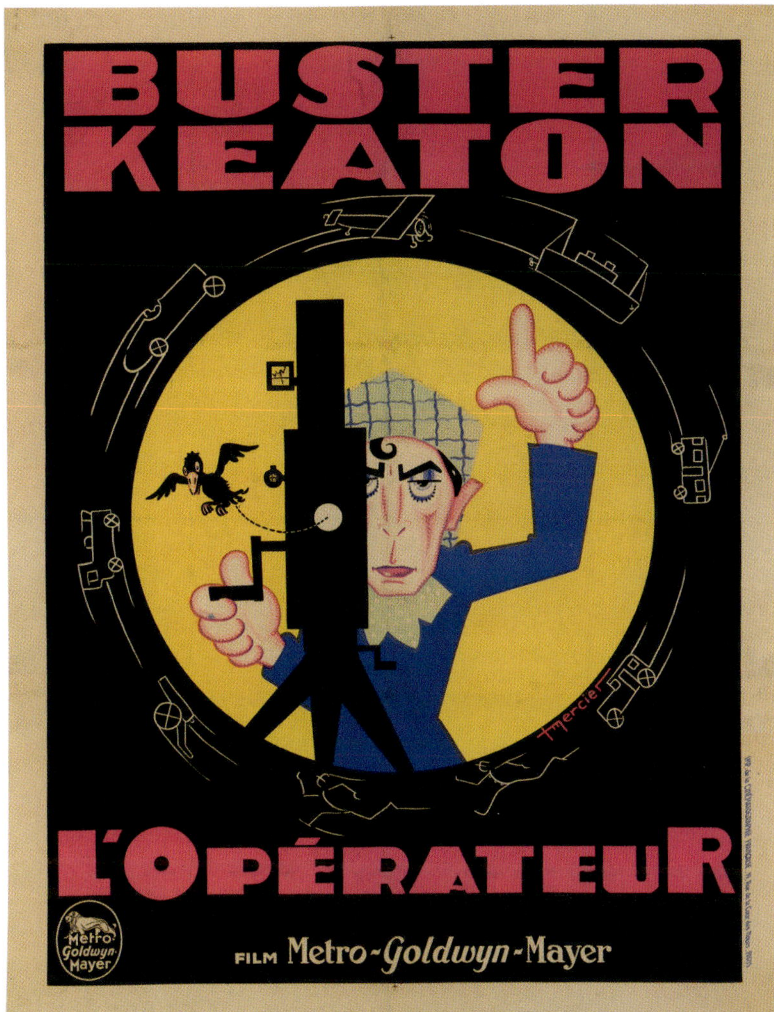

This poster for the French release of Buster Keaton's last great film, *The Cameraman* (1928), based on an illustration by Jean A. Mercier, speaks to the international popularity and universality of silent film comedy.

astounding stunts, and inventive visual imagination have inspired artists from Orson Welles and Salvador Dali to Jackie Chan and Johnny Knoxville. His film characters were all variations on the same type, a naïve and sensitive young man trying to make his way in a world that seems out to get him, just barely escaping pitfalls, bullies, and forces of nature through his remarkable agility or, in some cases, bending the rules of physics through surrealist camera trickery. His trademarks were his pork pie hat and the stoic "stone face" that set him apart from his demonstrative, mugging contemporaries. Keaton was anti-sentimental—his characters take the hits as they come, endure, adapt, and move on.

He was also a skilled filmmaker with a keen interest and appreciation for the technical side of the art. Keaton's cinematic imagination allowed him to do things that appeared unexpected, magical, and possible only on the silver screen, like painting a hook on the wall to hang his hat in *The High Sign* (1921), using multiple exposures allowing him to perform alongside himself onstage in *The Playhouse* (1921) or to escape from his own body and jump through the cinema screen into the movie action in *Sherlock, Jr.* (1924). In that film, he even found a way to spoof film editing, creating a meta-joke on the filmmaking process as his character endures the whim of the editor's cuts to different locations, placing Keaton's character on the side of a cliff, next to hungry lions, in the path of a coming train, and marooned on rocks at sea in quick succession.

If his film plots were often less original than the works of Chaplin or Lloyd, his gags were unrivaled, unsurpassed in scale, complexity, and skill of execution. In his solo debut, *One Week* (1920), Keaton plays a newlywed who receives a kit house as a wedding gift and sets about trying to build it with his wife, despite her former suitor's sabotage. The short film is densely packed with hilarious sight gags and surreal slapstick, culminating in a still-shocking final sequence in which the house is stuck on train tracks while being towed. Keaton's character and his wife look on in horror as a train roars toward the house but misses, as it's on a separate track. The couple breathes a sigh of relief just as a train comes from the opposite direction, smashing the house to pieces.

Keaton's stunts are also legendary, exhibiting the strength, precision, and agility he had practiced his whole life onstage. In one of the best-known and most imitated, from his film *Steamboat Bill, Jr.* (1928), Keaton's character is making his way through a town as a cyclone hits, and as he ponders his next move, an entire building façade falls on him. Keaton survives only because he is in the exact place of an open window as it lands. No trickery was involved in the staging of the gag; if he had been inches off his mark, the two-ton façade would have crushed him. He was a master of movement, with a fluidity of motion that verged on superhuman, as when he would reach out and grab hold of a speeding car to escape from pursuers or, straddling the running boards of two cars driving at full speed, end up sitting alongside the driver of a motorcycle that drove between them.

Keaton's magnum opus, *The General* (1926), was a Civil War epic that is essentially a feature-length chase sequence as his character, a railroad engineer, sneaks behind enemy lines to steal the titular locomotive and evade the Union soldiers trying to stop him. It offered Keaton an opportunity to fuse historical realism (he loved trains and all other transportation technology) with adventure and comedy. *The General*'s enormous budget also allowed him to indulge in excess, like hiring thousands of extras and staging the most expensive single scene in film to that point, when he blew up a railroad bridge and moving train. Unfortunately, that excess and the film's lackluster ticket sales led to tighter studio control. Without creative freedom, Keaton's work suffered and his professional challenges led to personal issues that, combined, kept him from ever again reaching the heights of his earlier 1920s output.

Facing down technology, from trains to cameras, in an attempt to maintain his dignity and autonomy, and bending the rules of time and space to his will, Keaton's films made farce of modernity.

"The more trouble you can get a man into, the more comedy you get out of him."

—Harold Lloyd

HAROLD LLOYD: THE GLASSES CHARACTER

Harold Lloyd is often the odd man out in discussions about the great comedians of silent film, with even a documentary about his life and career labeling him "The Third Genius." But his impact on American history was no less than that of the other two, Chaplin and Keaton, and the term "genius" certainly applies. Lloyd made more films—nearly two hundred—and had more consistent success with audiences, who identified with the earnest, striving, middle-class characters he portrayed. Lloyd's "glasses character" seemed to represent the zeitgeist of the 1920s United States, a resourceful go-getter who was set on getting the girl, making his fortune, and moving up in the world. In his best-known movies, so-called thrill comedies, Lloyd captivated and thrilled fans with high-stakes stunts hanging off the side of skyscrapers and out-of-control streetcars, making the modern city a comic character and creating unforgettable images that gave voice to contemporary anxieties about the pace of technological and social change.

Lloyd began his acting career with bit parts in Edison and Universal films in the early 1910s before he moved to his friend Hal Roach's new comedy film studio. There he developed Lonesome Luke, a near-copy of Chaplin's Tramp that nevertheless became a minor success in a series of mostly uninspired slapstick shorts. Yearning for something more personal, he fashioned a new character, notable for his horn-rimmed round glasses, first appearing in the 1917 film *Over the Fence*. Lloyd's "glasses

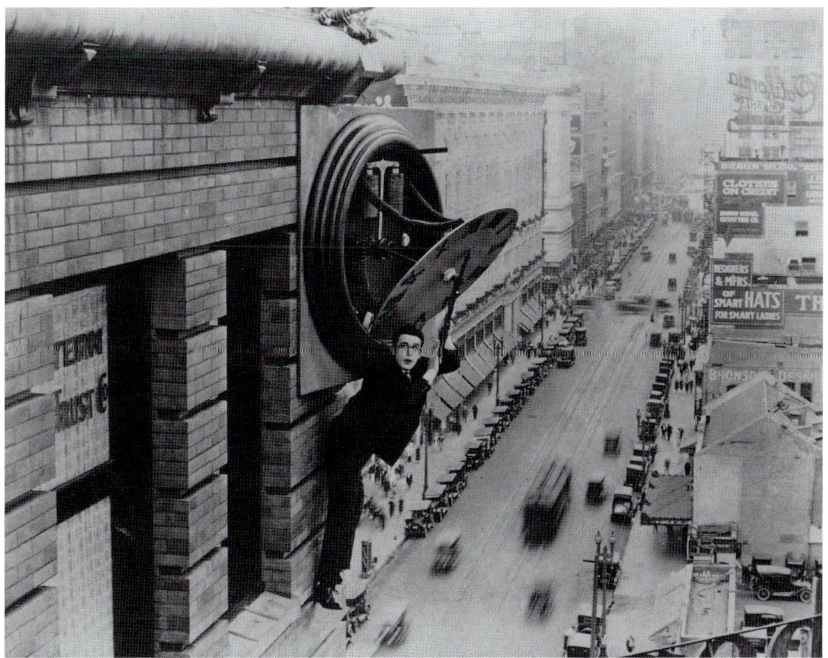

Harold Lloyd created some of the most indelible images of the silent film era with his death-defying stunts in thrill pictures like 1923's *Safety Last!*

character" was a man of the 1920s, an optimistic, eager to please, determined, yet frequently befuddled everyman / boy next door. He didn't wear a funny costume with ill-fitting clothing and a comical mustache; he dressed in a modern suit and tie, and maybe a straw boater. He was well-kempt and well-mannered. And in most every film, the glasses character finds himself in deep trouble, proves himself a hero, and earns a happy ending.

This formula worked well in Lloyd's 1910s shorts for Roach, but even better when he moved into longer features, where he could fully exploit the emotional complexity and audience sympathy for his characters. In 1922's *Grandma's Boy*, for instance, he plays a timid and cowardly young man who musters the courage to prove himself to his sweetheart after his grandmother gives him a magical amulet that once protected his grandfather from harm during the Civil War. The mysterious object is actually just her umbrella handle, and Lloyd's character realizes he had the courage within him all along. In his most successful film, *The Freshman* (1925), his ridiculously naïve and overeager college freshman joins the football team to become popular. He is the worst player on the team, but in the big game against a rival school everyone else is injured, and the coach is forced to put him on the field. Disaster is averted when Lloyd's battered and bumbling character miraculously scores the winning touchdown.

Today, Lloyd is best remembered for his spectacular and thrilling stunts in movies like *Never Weaken* (1921), *Safety Last!* (1923), and *Speedy* (1928). Stradling steel girders on a skyscraper under construction, hanging from the hands of a clock suspended stories above the sidewalk, or piloting a runaway trolley car careening through crowded city streets, Lloyd crafted images of modern urban anxiety that seemed almost pulled from the collective subconscious. In *Safety Last!*, Lloyd played a small-town boy in the city desperate to earn enough to marry his sweetheart from back home. He sells a department store on a publicity stunt: a "human fly" will climb up the side of the store building without support. However, at the last minute, the climber is detained, and Lloyd has to make the ascent himself, dealing with a barrage of obstacles and impediments. He was as skilled an acrobat as Chaplin and Keaton, and the stunts are even more impressive considering he lost his right thumb and index finger in an accident involving what he thought was a prop bomb in a photo studio in 1919. Throughout his career he wore a prosthesis concealed within a glove, barely visible as he tempts fate in these thrill films.

Though Lloyd continued working into the sound era, his best work was behind him. The glasses character didn't transition well to the new pace and vocabulary of sound comedy, but more crucially, he seemed out of step with the times in the 1930s. Lloyd's glasses character was the quintessential 1920s striver, showing contemporary American audiences what they thought they looked like, and promising a happy ending.

Ryan Lintelman

CARTOON COMEDY

Comedians are known for breaking the rules, but they usually must obey the laws of physics. That's not the case for animated characters, who take subversive humor to the next level by transgressing reality itself. The cartoon violence, anarchic mayhem, and irreverent buffoonery practiced by Mickey Mouse, Bugs Bunny, Woody Woodpecker, and other popular animated film characters in the thirties and forties went far beyond the antics of the zaniest performer on the vaudeville stage. Imaginative animators created indelible characters whose self-assured, mischievous, antiauthoritarian personas made them heroes to Americans facing confidence-shaking world events like the Great Depression and World War II. Animated comedy seemed to suggest that anyone

Though less well known today, Woody Woodpecker was just as popular as Mickey Mouse and Bugs Bunny in the 1940s and was the archetype of the screwball trickster animated character. These are original cels from the first Woody Woodpecker cartoon, the 1940 Andy Panda short *Knock Knock*, made by Walter Lantz.

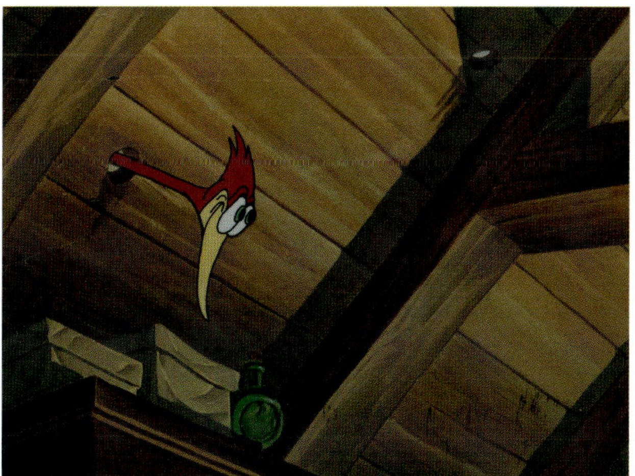

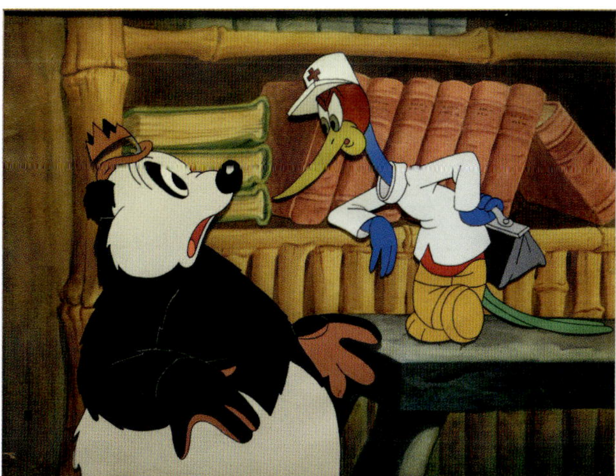

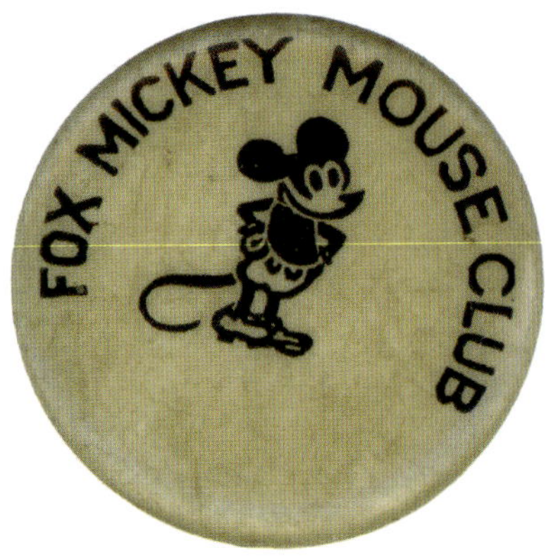

The first Mickey Mouse Club was organized in 1930 by the manager of the Fox Dome Theater in Ocean Park, California, who saw the potential to use the popular Mickey Mouse character to increase ticket sales. The clubs were designed to encourage brand loyalty, but also aspired to educate children in good citizenship "through inspirational, patriotic, and character building activities related to the Club."

could draw on a hidden reservoir of disruptive energy to conquer the challenges before them.

Animation has its roots in the experimental motion pictures that preceded the introduction of film, but really began to develop as a genre of cinema in the 1910s. Experimental animated films like cartoonist Windsor McCay's 1914 *Gertie the Dinosaur* used paper illustrations and cutouts to simulate movement. In the years that followed, innovative artists like John Bray and Max and Dave Fleischer used new technology and media like transparent celluloid "cels" to improve and simplify the animation process, making it more viable and profitable. The first animated star was Felix the Cat, created by Otto Messmer for Pat Sullivan Studios in 1919. The sensationally popular Felix film series demonstrated the possibilities of animation, with fantastic landscapes and settings, surreal visual effects, and a fully fleshed main character whose cunning, liberated, trickster attitude made him a popular culture icon. Felix was celebrated in song, made a mascot, adapted as a comic strip, and licensed for a bewildering array of merchandise and toys.

Naturally, Felix's success inspired competitors, and Walt Disney was the most successful of them all. The struggling animator believed that synchronized sound was the future of animation and made his 1928 film *Steamboat Willie* a showcase for the emerging technology. Though it was not technically Mickey Mouse's first screen appearance, the film's success kickstarted his rise to superstardom. Mickey was an anthropomorphic mouse with large, round black ears whose characterization as a plucky underdog drew inspiration from silent comedians like Charlie Chaplin, Buster Keaton, and Harold Lloyd. Mickey's characterization also drew inspiration from blackface minstrelsy, which lent Mickey the expressive features, white gloves on impossibly dark skin, and natural musicality he displays in early appearances, especially in his debut, where he performs the minstrel song "Turkey in the Straw / Old Zip Coon."[39]

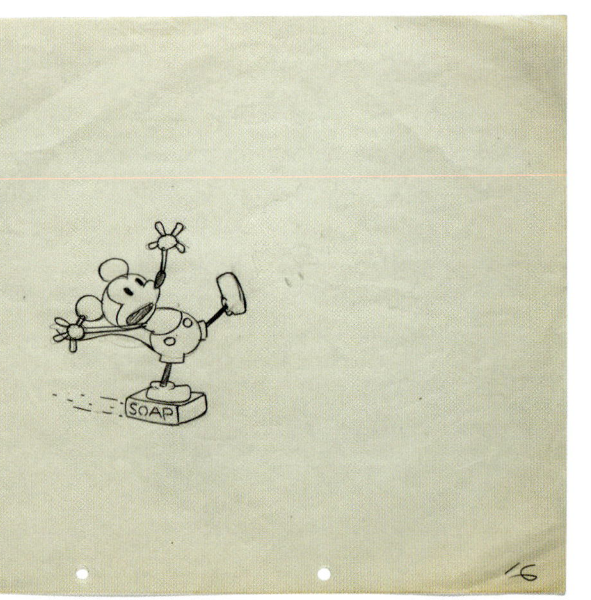

This drawing was made by Disney animation artist Ub Iwerks for the 1928 sound debut of Mickey Mouse, *Steamboat Willie*. Mickey Mouse seemed to represent the spirit of the 1930s United States with his scrappy determination and good humor.

Mickey became enormously popular as the star of Disney's animated comedy film shorts, surpassing Felix, who failed to make the transition to the sound era. In parodies and homages to other film genres, he was sometimes portrayed as a swashbuckling hero, sometimes a scrappy regular Joe frustrated in his romantic pursuit of Minnie Mouse, though over time they became dedicated sweethearts. As the series expanded through the early 1930s, he was also joined by his dog Pluto, his dim-witted but good-natured friend Goofy, and his sometimes-rival Donald Duck. Hundreds of Mickey Mouse Clubs sprang up across the country to cater to communities of mostly young fans as Disney increasingly positioned him as a role model. As other characters took on the mantle of the mischievous and juvenile prankster, Mickey was more often depicted as a humble and virtuous hero, thoughtful friend, and good citizen.

While Disney refocused on feature-length animation starting with *Snow White* in 1937, other studios continued to explore the comic potential of animation. The Fleischers adapted the spinach-eating strongman Popeye comic strip to film and created the flapper sex symbol Betty Boop. Walter Lanz introduced the madcap trickster Woody Woodpecker, and William Hanna and Joseph Barbera launched a series of Tom and Jerry cat and mouse cartoons. In 1930, a group of ex-Disney animators took their talents to Warner Brothers to help launch the animation shop there: the Warner Bros. *Looney Tunes* series melded music from the entertainment company's recording catalog with a sensational style of animation, especially after its transition to color. *Looney Tunes* filmmakers Chuck Jones and Tex Avery imbued the series with a modern, fast-paced style involving rapid-fire joke delivery, hip, colloquial dialogue and dialect, and irreverent, referential humor. The series developed a memorable slate of characters including Porky Pig, Daffy Duck, Elmer Fudd, and its biggest star, Bugs Bunny.

Bugs made his first appearance in *Porky's Hare Hunt* (1938) but was redesigned and given his unique Bronx/Brooklyn accent by Mel Blanc in the 1940 film *A Wild Hare*; he would go on to star in more than 160 Warner Brothers shorts between 1940 and 1964. If Mickey Mouse seemed to represent the spirit of the 1930s, Bugs Bunny became the American cartoon hero of the 1940s. He was also an underdog, but he possessed working-class

Bugs Bunny's clever, self-assured wise guy attitude made him a popular hero and American icon during World War II. Not one to pick a fight, Bugs is nevertheless willing to give as good as he gets, and in his *Looney Tunes* shorts, he took cartoon violence and madcap hijinks to new heights.

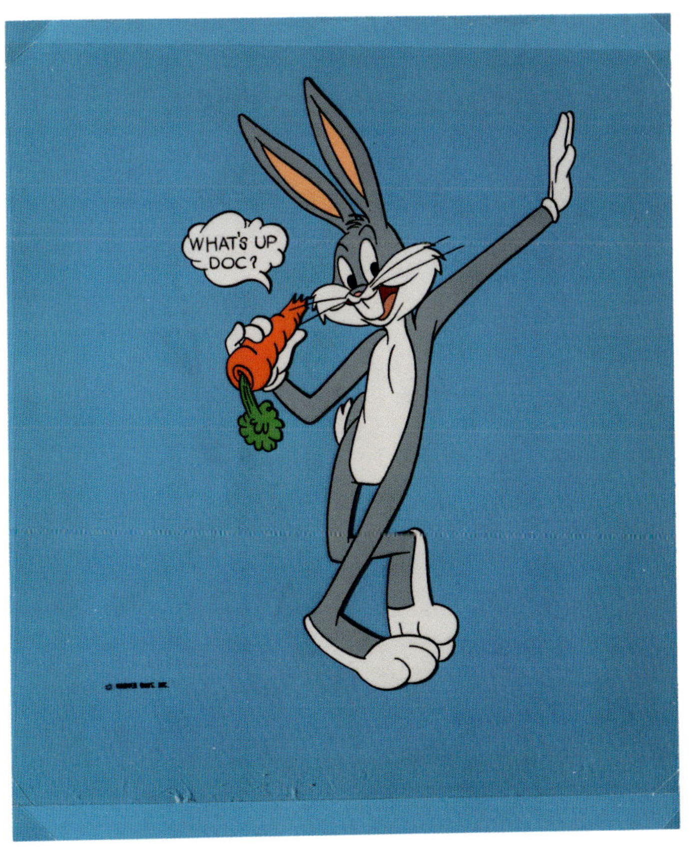

street smarts and attitude, with a cocky determination to stand up to bullies. Bugs never picked a fight but was always ready to defend himself, borrowing Groucho Marx's "of course you know this means war" as one of his catchphrases, making his schtick timely and relevant as the United States also made its stand in World War II.

Animators from both Disney and Warner Brothers created films depicting their characters contributing to the war effort. They sold war bonds in *The Thrifty Pig* (1941) and *Bugs Bunny Bond Rally* (1942), mocked the Axis powers in *Der Fuehrer's Face* (1943) and *Bugs Bunny Nips the Nips* (1944), and even showed characters enlisting in the armed services in *Donald Gets Drafted* (1942) and *Super-Rabbit* (1943). The U.S. Marines were so happy with Bugs' morale-raising film that they inducted the cartoon character as a private, even issuing dog tags. The wartime animated films capitalized on the popularity and reputation of these beloved comic characters for propaganda purposes, from military training films to cathartic and morale-boosting lampoon, even including racist representations of the nation's enemies, making some of these films difficult to see today.

After the war, these cartoon comedy characters remained popular, influencing youth culture with their subversive and irreverent humor, but the genre was threatened by changes in the movie industry. The labor-intensive animation process became less economically viable while many theaters began removing shorts from their screening schedules. The characters lived on in television, feature films, and merchandise, but the golden era of animated film shorts was over by the end of the 1950s.

Ryan Lintelman

COMEDY DUOS

The alchemy that makes a great comedy duo click is a rare and enigmatic force. Usually premised on an uneven relationship between countervailing comic types—the tall and the short, the smart and the dumb, the cool and the quirky—"double acts" have been a fixture of American comedy since the vaudeville era. From Laurel and Hardy to Burns and Allen to Bert and Ernie to Nichols and May, iconic and inseparable pairs have emerged as cultural touchstones generation after generation.

BURNS AND ALLEN

Vaudevillians George Burns and Gracie Allen first teamed up in 1922 as a banter act, with their onstage chemistry blossoming into a real-life marriage four years later. Though Burns initially fancied himself the comic force that would drive their boy-meets-girl act, audience reactions quickly made it clear that Allen was stronger at delivering the punchlines. He reformed himself into the consummate straight man. Though the real Gracie Allen was serious, shy, and elegant, the comic character she created was an uninhibited chatterbox and meddler, famous for an "illogical logic" that spun her into convoluted confusions and miscommunications. Though George, and the audience, saw the error of her ways, Gracie never did, always bending the laws of common sense to score the upper hand. While she played what was traditionally called a "Dumb Dora" role, part of the act's charm was that Gracie always held on to her agency and triumphed as the one in control of the narrative.

Burns and Allen cemented their place in vaudeville's comedic pantheon and, following the collapse of the stage circuits, went on to become popular and enduring broadcast personalities. They reinvented themselves several times over to stay ahead of rapidly advancing

Radio script for *The George Burns and Gracie Allen Show*, February 3, 1949.

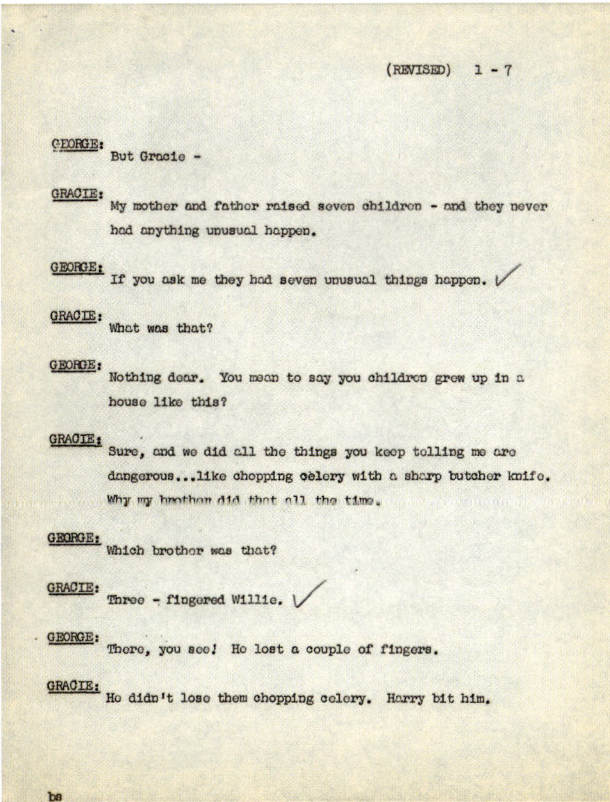

(REVISED) 1 - 7

GEORGE: But Gracie -

GRACIE: My mother and father raised seven children - and they never had anything unusual happen.

GEORGE: If you ask me they had seven unusual things happen.

GRACIE: What was that?

GEORGE: Nothing dear. You mean to say you children grew up in a house like this?

GRACIE: Sure, and we did all the things you keep telling me are dangerous...like chopping celery with a sharp butcher knife. Why my brother did that all the time.

GEORGE: Which brother was that?

GRACIE: Three - fingered Willie.

GEORGE: There, you see! He lost a couple of fingers.

GRACIE: He didn't lose them chopping celery. Harry bit him.

bo

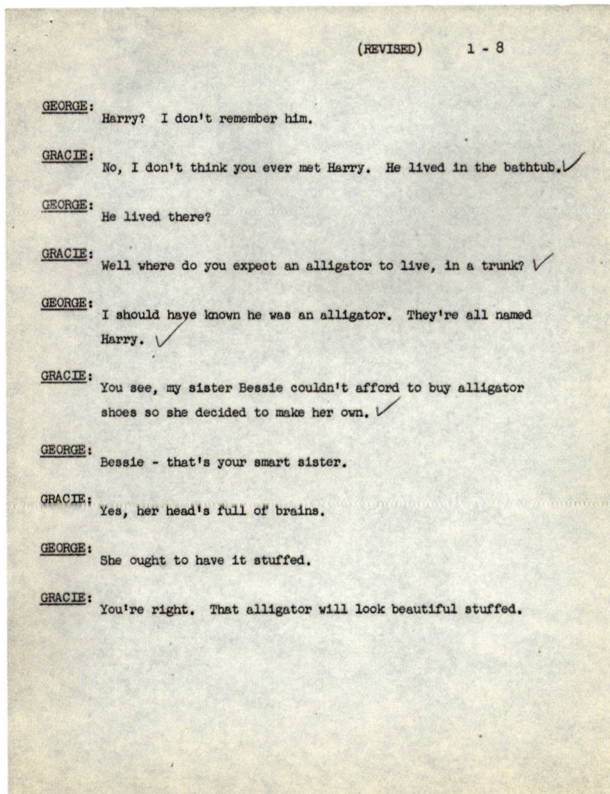

(REVISED) 1 - 8

GEORGE: Harry? I don't remember him.

GRACIE: No, I don't think you ever met Harry. He lived in the bathtub.

GEORGE: He lived there?

GRACIE: Well where do you expect an alligator to live, in a trunk?

GEORGE: I should have known he was an alligator. They're all named Harry.

GRACIE: You see, my sister Bessie couldn't afford to buy alligator shoes so she decided to make her own.

GEORGE: Bessie - that's your smart sister.

GRACIE: Yes, her head's full of brains.

GEORGE: She ought to have it stuffed.

GRACIE: You're right. That alligator will look beautiful stuffed.

entertainment technologies, even as many of their peers failed to innovate so swiftly. Radio's *George Burns and Gracie Allen Show* was a genre-defining entry in the canon of great American sitcoms, entertaining forty million listeners per week at the height of its popularity. In TV's earliest years, Burns and Allen boldly approached the new medium with a spirited experimentalism, carrying their radio show over to a visual format with a stylistically, technologically, and narratively unique approach that still feels fresh, and unusual, today. Gracie Allen's retirement from television in 1958 marked the duo's final bow, but Burns went on to enjoy a lengthy career as an elder statesman of comedy, relishing a second wave of stardom in the seventies and eighties.

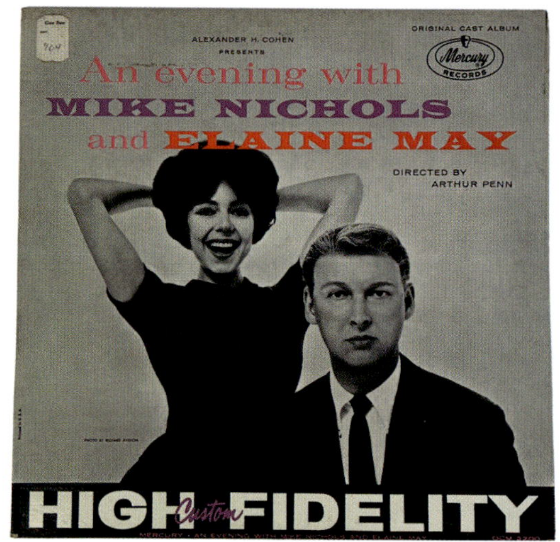

NICHOLS AND MAY

Mike Nichols and Elaine May first crossed paths on the campus of the University of Chicago in the 1950s, a hotbed of hipster artistic revolution. As members of the fabled Compass Players, a foundational improvisational troupe, their unlikely and unusual rapport crystallized. Their double act capitalized on the same strain of neurotic observational comedy that propelled peers like Lenny Bruce and Shelley Berman to renown and was concerned with unraveling and satirizing the pretensions of the cultural intelligentsia—a job they did from the "inside" as members of the educated liberal elite. Far from repeating "take my wife" jokes, their act cited Dostoevsky, Tennessee Williams, and *Oedipus Rex*, lending a new sophistication to stage comedy.

Nichols and May played a fundamental role in establishing the art of improv, but theirs was not a replicable format; a certain alchemy was in play when they sparred together. The act was one of juxtapositions, like all great comedy duos, extending to their varying approaches to the craft: where May famously followed the flow wherever it might take her, Nichols was a precise editor—already with the eye of a future director.

They broke away from Compass to make waves in nightclubs and on the Broadway stage in the landmark show *An Evening with Mike Nichols and Elaine May*, where the rigors of performing over three hundred nightly performances mandated an armature of preplanned beats from within which improvisations could emerge. To totally eliminate the challenge and potential of improvisation would have been anathema to both artists' philosophies, not to mention that Nichols's spontaneous breaking up on stage when May lobbed an unexpected bit his way was a crucial part of the act's charm. ("Elaine could crack me up by changing one digit in a phone number," Nichols would recall.)[40] The recording of the Broadway show won the Grammy for Best Comedy Performance, and all three of their albums landed on the *Billboard* charts.

Given the outsize influence of their work, which has been cited as a catalyst for countless comedians who followed, it's stunning that Nichols and May truly enjoyed only about four years of mainstream exposure as a duo before ending their partnership at its peak. One of their final outings was a command performance for President John F. Kennedy's 1962 birthday celebration alongside the likes of Marilyn Monroe, Ella Fitzgerald, and Maria Callas. Both Nichols and May went on to fantastically successful solo careers in the arenas of film and theater, including groundbreaking writing, directing, and producing achievements.

MARTIN AND LEWIS

Dean Martin and Jerry Lewis flamed fast as America's top comedy duo for exactly ten years, from their first outing on July 25, 1946, at Atlantic City's 500 Club to their dramatic farewell performance on July 25, 1956, at New York's Copacabana. Their partnership, and their comedy, proceeded at a breathless pace.

Martin and Lewis's first pairing was the result of sheer happenstance: Jerry Lewis volunteered Dean Martin, then no more than an acquaintance, as a replacement for an absentee singer. Their premiere performance was so weak and stilted that management forewarned of a contract termination. They hastily tossed out the stale script and improvised, with Lewis donning a busboy's uniform and bungling Martin's crooning routine to enormous response from the surprised audience, who delighted in the pandemonium. Indeed, pandemonium would become the hallmark of their style, which was a comic affront to the elegance of the venues in which they played, including the tony Copacabana, where their reputations were solidified and they alighted as the talk of the entertainment world.

Jerry Lewis's comedic style was kinetic—a torrent of sheer momentum; Dean Martin's was staid—though he, too, broke up and gawked and succumbed to the utter goofiness of it all, his was an art of restraint.

At the peak of their fame, Lewis was in his early twenties and Martin was in his early thirties, hardly the seasoned "hoofers" who typically dominated cultural conversations about comedy in the first half of the twentieth century. They were friends on- and offstage, and the chemistry and pure fun shone through. By 1950, they not only had risen to the highest echelons of nightclub performance but also were the number-one box office draw in America (they would costar in sixteen feature films from 1949 to 1956), were headliners of an eponymous radio show, and appeared on some of the earliest commercial television broadcasts (including the first episode of Ed Sullivan's show). Their humor was especially well matched to the new medium of television, and the duo was welcomed into millions of American homes in the 1950s as frequent hosts of NBC's popular *Colgate Comedy Hour.*

Ten years into one of the swiftest career trajectories in comedy history, a complex of bruised egos, burnout, and youthful aplomb disintegrated Martin and Lewis's partnership. Barely able to speak to one another, the duo begrudgingly fulfilled an obligation to perform once more at the Copa to a press enraptured by their dramatic falling out. Following their farewell, both artists went on to arguably greater success as solo acts. Dean Martin became a popular recording artist, the host of his own ratings-smash *Dean Martin Show*, and a member of the era-defining Rat Pack. Jerry Lewis peaked as Paramount's highest-earning film star in a string of films he helmed both on- and off-camera, including pop-cultural staples like *The Bellboy* and *The Nutty Professor.*

BUTTERBEANS AND SUSIE

Butterbeans and Susie—Jodie and Susie Edwards—were among the most successful musical comedy duos of the twentieth century, performing from 1917 (the year of their marriage) until 1963 (the year of Susie's death). The act was a sensation as part of the TOBA (Theatre Owners Booking Association) circuit that played to primarily Black audiences, with a 1925 issue of *Billboard* reporting a street blockade to accommodate dense crowds gathered to greet them at a Macon, Georgia, theater.[41]

Butterbeans and Susie performed a variation on a classic vaudevillian domestic bickering routine—a battle of the sexes in which the stately, elegant, and ever-confident Susie would vie against the bumbling, hotheaded Butterbeans, who was attired in a trademark outfit of too-tight

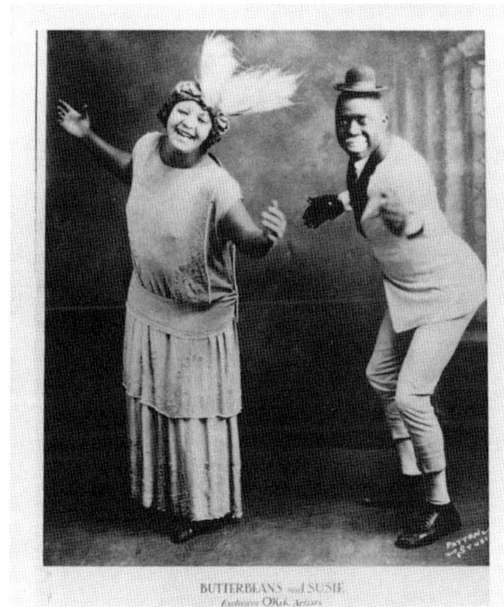

pants, oversized shoes, and a tiny bowler hat that underscored the virtuosic physicality of his humor. The act was liberally laced with innuendo and off-color humor that pushed the bounds of acceptability—but delighted audiences. During their peak popularity in the decade of the 1920s, Butterbeans and Susie released dozens of recordings with Okeh Records, though some of the bits that made them most famous onstage "transgress[ed] even the more elastic limits of good taste" and were too risqué for the label.[42]

By the early 1960s, Butterbeans and Susie had endured long enough that they were plying their vaudevillian act at the Apollo Theater alongside the day's hottest Motown artists. Their longevity in the arena of comedy performance was a unique bridge between opposing eras in entertainment history, introducing a complex duality for audiences who recognized that while they demanded deep respect as pioneering comedic artists, they also drew on tropes from a bygone era that was rife with racial stereotyping. Among their many legacies in entertainment was a fealty to fellow performers: Butterbeans and Susie cultivated the early career of Jackie "Moms" Mabley and supported Lincoln Perry, also known as Stepin Fetchit, through his waning days.

BOB AND RAY

The early 1950s marked an inflection point for the broadcasting industry, as television ascended and spurred a great exodus of radio comics to the new visual medium. Seemingly immovable forces like Jack Benny, Bob Hope, and George Burns and Gracie Allen, whose voices had flooded millions of American living rooms throughout the Depression and World War II years, abandoned the sound medium, forcing a dramatic reorganization of broadcast comedy's genres, styles, and modes of consumption. In the gaping void they left behind, a new guard of esoteric talents stepped in to fill airtime. Without mandates to command the staggering ratings or sponsorship deals that television's newly minted superstars enjoyed, the upstart radio comics were free to be subversive, take risks, and appeal to niche audiences. As in radio's earliest days, the airwaves were once again a playground for inventive, experimental comics who thrived outside the mainstream.

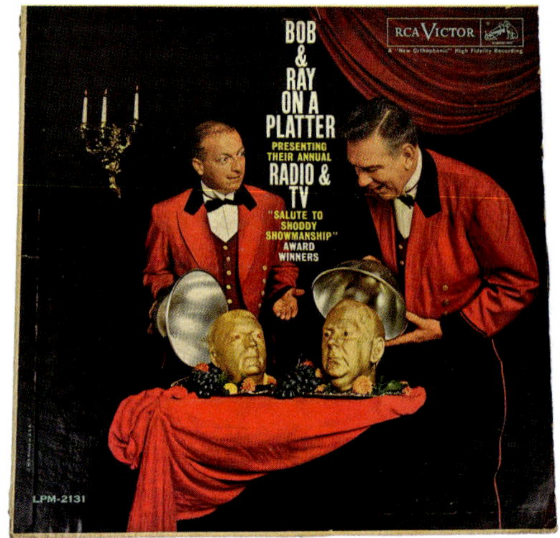

It was in this atmosphere that Bob Elliott and Ray Goulding began a legendary partnership. *Matinee with Bob and Ray* began as a quite humble fifteen-minute weekday spot with reach across most of New England. (Years later, when asked why Bob received first billing, Ray explained that *Matinob with Ray and Bob* didn't have quite the same ring to it.) The show captured an extremely loyal fan base and grew exponentially, picked up by networks with wider reach until the duo became a nationwide phenomenon with a cult following.

The Bob and Ray style was dry, sometimes deadpan, and premised on marathon-like ad-libs and riffs as their program evolved into a long-form, multihour staple in the evening drive-time hours. They used the medium to its full potential, incorporating flourishing sound effects with a playfulness that was a tongue-in-cheek throwback to the so-called golden age of radio and lampooning familiar broadcast genres like overborne soap operas, ecstatic sportscasts, droll quiz shows, droning farm reports, and especially the inane and endless commercials that clogged the airwaves ("Mushies! The Cereal that gets soggy even without adding milk!").

The show assumed a variety of titles, forms, and durations over its remarkable four decades on the air, but generally consisted of Bob and Ray presiding as the hosts of a self-referential and only quasi-serious radio program. In the mode of *The Jack Benny Show* or a classic backstage musical, which incorporated production elements right into the narrative, Bob and Ray voiced a sprawling cast of cartoonish characters that comprised the show-within-a-show's "production staff." Perennial favorites included incompetent reporter Wally Ballou, bumbling stagehand Pop Beloved, and the fan-favorite happy housewife Mary Margaret McGoon.

Bob and Ray fandom was reignited when the duo hit National Public Radio's airwaves in the 1980s. They worked together until Ray's passing in 1990, when Bob retired the act that was, for all intents and purposes, impossible to reprise without his partner. During the second of the pair's three Peabody Award ceremonies, the committee explained that not only was their material "fresh, original, imaginative, and terribly funny," but *Bob and Ray* had, somewhat ingeniously, found a way to persist as "the lone magnificent palm tree" in a "vast, dreary" radio desert.

STILLER AND MEARA

Jerry Stiller and Anne Meara emerged as one of the most enduring and culturally significant comedic partnerships of the sixties and seventies. Across more than a dozen appearances on Johnny Carson's *Tonight Show* and over thirty-six on *The Ed Sullivan Show*, the pair became a beloved and consistent presence in living rooms across the country. More than an iconic double act, Stiller and Meara were real-life spouses who brought their offstage personas to bear on their comedy. At surface level, theirs was a humor of physical juxtaposition: Meara a tall redhead with a clear-eyed earnestness, Stiller shorter and stockier with a rumpled volatility. More significantly, though, their humor often navigated the fraught terrain of their interfaith marriage—a subject largely taboo in mainstream entertainment of the period.

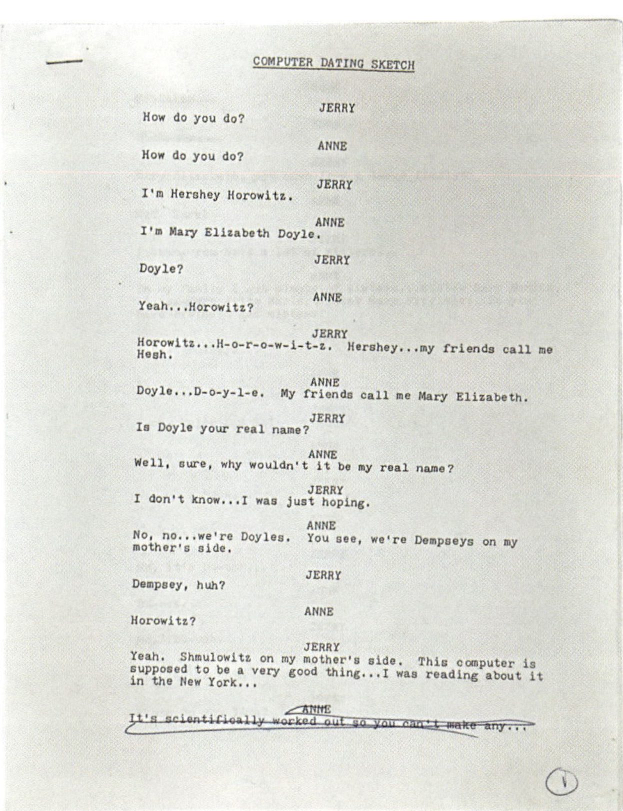

COMPUTER DATING SKETCH

JERRY
How do you do?

ANNE
How do you do?

JERRY
I'm Hershey Horowitz.

ANNE
I'm Mary Elizabeth Doyle.

JERRY
Doyle?

ANNE
Yeah...Horowitz?

JERRY
Horowitz...H-o-r-o-w-i-t-z. Hershey...my friends call me Hesh.

ANNE
Doyle...D-o-y-l-e. My friends call me Mary Elizabeth.

JERRY
Is Doyle your real name?

ANNE
Well, sure, why wouldn't it be my real name?

JERRY
I don't know...I was just hoping.

ANNE
No, no...we're Doyles. You see, we're Dempseys on my mother's side.

JERRY
Dempsey, huh?

ANNE
Horowitz?

JERRY
Yeah. Shmulowitz on my mother's side. This computer is supposed to be a very good thing...I was reading about it in the New York...

~~ANNE~~
~~It's scientifically worked out so you can't make any...~~

1

Stiller and Meara's "Computer Dating Routine" centered their real-life interfaith relationship at a moment when many found the topic taboo.

Stiller and Meara's defining characters were Hershey Horowitz and Mary Elizabeth Doyle, a Jewish boy and a Catholic girl improbably matched by a "computer dating machine" despite all outward appearances of total incompatibility. In one classic exchange, Mary Elizabeth explains that "they're having a dance tonight at my sodality." "What's that?" Hershey asks. "It's a girls' organization in my parish." "You mean like Hadassah?" "What's that?" "It's a girls' organization in my parish." Such bits—still structurally sharp, but not quite stinging by today's standards—were not without risk in the 1960s. Few in comedy—or in public discourse at all—had broached the subject with any nuance. In fact, CBS's ill-fated sitcom treatment of the topic, *Bridget Loves Bernie*, was pulled from its airwaves due to vitriolic viewer complaints around the same time as Stiller and Meara were at a peak of popularity, functioning as lone voices in a cultural climate that was hostile to less savvy, less sophisticated, or less funny variations on the theme.

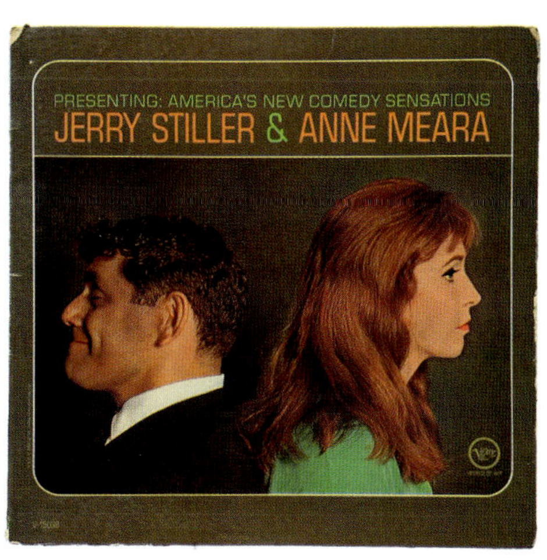

Actors with serious theatrical chops and roots in the storied Compass Players improvisational group (which became the Second City), Stiller and Meara were consummate performers who each carved out *two* careers—as a double act and as respected, in-demand solo talents who experienced career renaissances after making it big as a couple: Anne's turn on *Archie Bunker's Place* earned her two Emmy nominations, and Jerry's "Frank Costanza" on *Seinfeld* is among the most beloved characters in TV history, immortalized as the creator of "Festivus"—an absurd wintertime holiday for "the rest of us." Into their eighties, the couple starred in a weekly web series riffing hilariously on everyday life (and produced by their son, Ben Stiller) until their act broke up after sixty-two years, ended only upon the occasion of Meara's death in 2015.

PATSY KELLY AND THELMA TODD

Between 1933 and 1935, Patsy Kelly and Thelma Todd starred in 21 two-reelers released by the influential Hal Roach Studios—an early Hollywood laugh factory whose output, including the Laurel and Hardy and *Our Gang* films, defined the art of film comedy. Enterprising Hal Roach saw the phenomenal success of Stan Laurel and Oliver Hardy and concocted a gender-swapped copycat act, which ultimately evolved into an original short subject series with comic chops that were all its own.

Initially pairing Thelma Todd—a silver screen ingenue with two Marx Brothers features already on her résumé—and ZaSu Pitts—a veteran of the silent film era, Roach replaced Pitts with Patsy Kelly following a volatile contract dispute. Kelly was a vaudeville "hoofer" with years of stage experience and a perfect foil for Todd. The two "played themselves" in the films, a juxtaposed elegant blonde and sparky brunette: one demure and the other wisecracking, one poised and the other raring for a fight. Todd and Kelly were equally proficient comedians despite their differing performative styles, appearances, and voices—Todd's muted eloquence was a counterpoint to Kelly's brash streetwise sound (of the "Pipe down!," "Hiya, Toots!" variety). Despite what could have been a low-hanging impulse to pit the women against one another, the duo was crafted as a true buddy act: two against the world, not one against the other.

With titles like *Beauty and the Bus*, *Maid in Hollywood*, *I'll Be Suing You*, *Three Chumps Ahead*, and *Bum Voyage*, the films were riotous slapstick romps, rife with misunderstandings, pratfalls, and mugging. "The girls" were streetwise and self-sufficient, usually fashioned as working-class strivers wrapped up in trouble of their own designing. They strode confidently through their world, undeterred in the face of authority and unconcerned with polite comportment. Wacky storylines found them exhibiting considerable comedic talents at large and small scales, from tripping on roller skates to lavishly choreographed car chase scenes. Though their partnership was wildly successful, it was also tragically brief: Thelma Todd died, under still mysterious circumstances, at the age of twenty-nine. Though Patsy Kelly was paired with others in attempts to keep the act going, the alchemy was never again achieved.

LAUREL AND HARDY

Perhaps the most iconic double act in entertainment history, Stan Laurel and Oliver Hardy's pairing was a perfect harmonic expression. In more than one hundred film comedies crafted between 1927 and 1950, Laurel—the innocent Briton with his bemused smile—played opposite Hardy—the stocky Georgian with a perpetual twinkle in his eye. They cut a dashing figure that remains a part of American entertainment iconography to this day: one taller, one shorter; one fatter, one thinner; both outfitted in unmistakable derby hats.

While slapstick devices like pie fights and pratfalls had been a staple for decades in music hall, vaudeville, and earlier film comedy, Laurel and Hardy pushed these gags to their limits and elevated knockabout humor to an art. Their *Battle of the Century* (1927), for example, involved dozens of extras lobbing thousands of fruit pies across a set the size of a city block, and *Liberty* (1929) finds the pair dangling from I-beams at the top of an unfinished skyscraper while wearing one another's pants. The *New York Times* described their work as a sort of "galloping bedlam."[43] Their Sisyphean film *The Music Box* (1932), which finds the pair endlessly lugging a piano up and down a hill, won the Academy Award for Best Short Comedy in 1932. Significantly, Laurel and Hardy not only made a successful transition from silent films to "talkies," but embraced the addition of sound in the oppositional timbres of their voices (the prim English accent and the southern drawl) and the popularization of Hardy's catchphrase, "Well, here's another nice mess you've gotten me into."

Even in light of the enormously challenging technical labor involved in orchestrating their comedy—from feats of camerawork and prop building to intricate stunt work and complex choreographies of comedic timing—Laurel and Hardy connected with their audiences at an intimate, human level. Their real-life camaraderie, with its up and downs, reached audiences in the simplest of moments, like the delightful soft-shoe performance in *Way Out West* (1937) that has become symbolic of not only one of comedy's great partnerships but also a shared cultural nostalgia for early twentieth-century entertainment. Indeed, Laurel and Hardy's style exuded a level of polish and dignity that would seem at odds with slapstick sensibilities. Their genius lay in this juxtaposition.

ABBOTT AND COSTELLO

Bud Abbott and Lou Costello's partnership made them archetypal figures in the annals of comedy history—their very personas synonymous with the genre of burlesque humor. Their partnership was accidental: Costello's regular straight man fell sick, and Abbott filled in on a whim. Lightning struck, and the two went on to become among the most popular entertainers of the twentieth century, and of the American World War II era in particular. Of their nearly forty feature films, the three that made them superstars debuted in 1941, on the cusp of the U.S. declaration of war on Japan: *Buck Privates*, *In the Navy*, and *Keep 'Em Flying* were massive moneymakers, as was a 1942 war bond tour helmed by the duo.

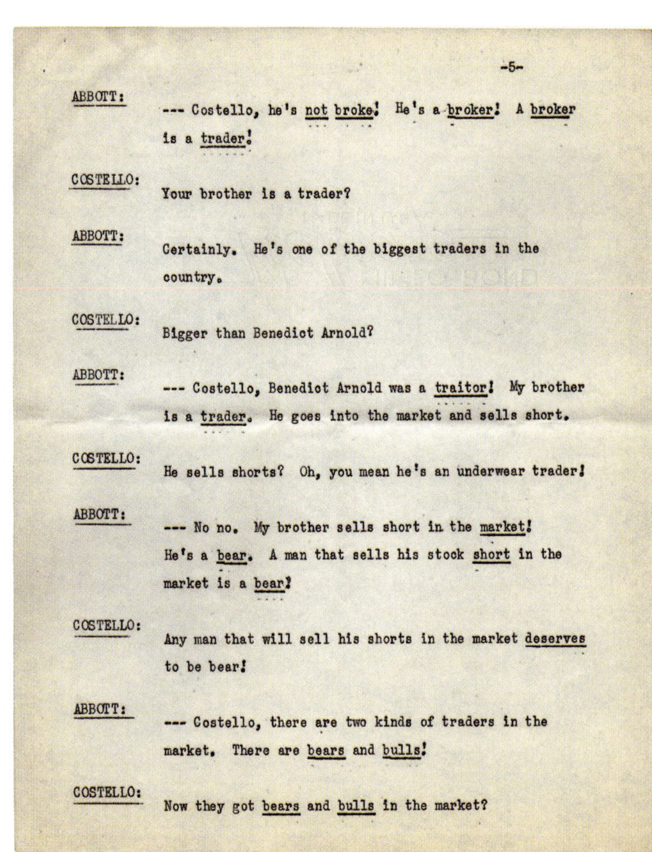

-5-

ABBOTT: --- Costello, he's not broke! He's a broker! A broker is a trader!

COSTELLO: Your brother is a trader?

ABBOTT: Certainly. He's one of the biggest traders in the country.

COSTELLO: Bigger than Benedict Arnold?

ABBOTT: --- Costello, Benedict Arnold was a traitor! My brother is a trader. He goes into the market and sells short.

COSTELLO: He sells shorts? Oh, you mean he's an underwear trader!

ABBOTT: --- No no. My brother sells short in the market! He's a bear. A man that sells his stock short in the market is a bear!

COSTELLO: Any man that will sell his shorts in the market deserves to be bear!

ABBOTT: --- Costello, there are two kinds of traders in the market. There are bears and bulls!

COSTELLO: Now they got bears and bulls in the market?

Radio script for *The Abbott and Costello Show*, March 27, 1947.

The pair's career resurged in the postwar years with a series of monster horror spoofs, including the classic *Abbott and Costello Meet Frankenstein* (1948). An eponymous radio show and stint in the early 1950s as rotating hosts of TV's *Colgate Comedy Hour* (duties they shared with Martin and Lewis, among others) made their humor part of daily life for millions of Americans during the golden age of broadcasting. Their own televised *Abbott and Costello Show* was popular when it debuted in 1952 but went on to even greater acclaim when it emerged as a stalwart syndication darling decades later, introducing a new generation to the snappy, knockabout humor of a bygone era.

Abbott and Costello's most enduring contribution is "Who's on First?," an endlessly quotable wordplay and patter bit about baseball with an apparently ceaseless afterlife. They first performed the bit on vaudeville stages, before repeating variations—that spanned from one minute to nearly ten minutes in length—on the radio, on television, and in films to constant calls for encore. The true origins of "Who's on First?" are murky, as is the case for most of the so-called stock routines of vaudeville. Though Abbott and Costello refined the concept far beyond the reach of most comedians, it is likely a variation on a subgenre of sketches with similar misconstruals of language, like "Who Died?"—involving a man with the surname "Who." As in almost all of their work, Abbott and Costello's particular genius was reinterpreting and re-enlivening vestiges of vaudeville and burlesque humor for new media contexts and new audiences. Significantly for historians of comedy, their body of work was an instrumental vehicle for transposing beloved routines from the vaudeville stage to electronic media, constituting one of our most important records of that fleeting earlier moment in entertainment history.

This derby hat was worn by Lou Costello in television appearances on the *Colgate Comedy Hour* in the 1950s and 1960s.

BERT AND ERNIE

Hailing from the basement apartment at 123 Sesame Street, Bert and Ernie have been a beloved fixture of American popular culture since 1969, when they debuted in the original pilot for the genre-defining children's educational program. Jim Henson's performance of the affable Ernie opposite Frank Oz's adorably neurotic Bert drew immediate and apt comparison to Oscar Madison and Felix Unger of Neil Simon's *The Odd Couple*, a prominent part of the zeitgeist of the 1960s.

Intended to teach children that even the best of friends could have different personalities, appearances, and interests, Bert and Ernie were a lesson in opposites: Bert's jaunty unibrow, tuft of tousled hair, and lanky foam body adorned in vertical stripes mismatched Ernie's loose open grin, slightly crossed eyes, and stocky body outfitted in horizontal stripes. While Ernie devoted himself to the pursuits of a practical jokester, shared endless bubble baths with his iconic "Rubber Duckie," and stayed up all night counting sheep or playing his saxophone, Bert preferred to studiously arrange his paper clip collection, observe pigeons, and devour books like *Boring Stories* and *The History of Oatmeal.*

These original Bert and Ernie puppets, created by Jim Henson, appeared in the pilot episodes and 1969 premier of *Sesame Street*.

The two have been embraced by the LGBTQ+ community and—even though *Sesame Street* hasn't fully authorized this subtextual reading—they have become culturally prominent symbols of the queer rights movement. Their resonance was perhaps most clearly expressed when they poignantly graced the cover of the *New Yorker* following 2013's landmark Supreme Court decision on same-sex marriage.

It's been estimated that the antics of Bert, Ernie, and their neighbors on *Sesame Street*, spanning nearly five thousand episodes across fifty years, have been witnessed by an astonishing 95 percent of all Americans.

Laura LaPlaca

UNDER THE STRAW HAT: MINNIE PEARL AND HER COMEDY COMMUNITY

"Howww-DEEEEE!! I'm just so proud to be here!"

In character as the homespun comic Minnie Pearl, Sarah Ophelia Colley Cannon greeted exuberant audiences with this refrain from the stage and over the radio and television airwaves throughout her extraordinary fifty-year career. Best known as a longtime cast member of Nashville's immensely popular live country music program on WSM radio station's *Grand Ole Opry*, she regaled her audiences with quaint yet uproarious stand-up routines about her family and neighbors living in her mythical tiny Tennessee hamlet of Grinder's Switch.

While Cannon first felt ambivalent, if not disappointed, that she could only find professional success by embracing the long-standing comic tradition of the country "rube," she determined never to bring indignity to the role, nor make it a caricature of her largely rural audiences. They came from places like Grinder's Switch, and while many were migrating to cities or otherwise feeling unsettled by the changes wrought by a rapidly urbanizing twentieth-century modern life, they

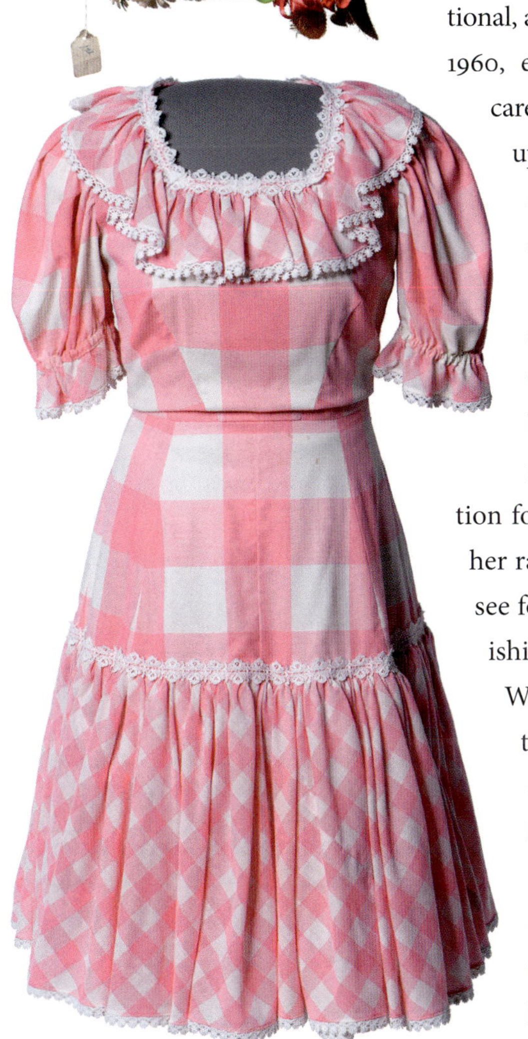

Costume worn by Sarah Cannon in character as Minnie Pearl, complete with her iconic hat.

knew that they could turn on the radio every Saturday night to hear Pearl's stories and immediately feel at home.

Cannon's reach as a woman comic was unprecedented, unconventional, and underestimated. As author Shawn Levy put it, "from 1940 until 1960, even with Moms Mabley and Jean Carroll forging significant careers . . . Minnie [Pearl] was the most famous woman doing standup in the nation, even if she mainly worked in Tennessee and the big shots in the media industries of New York and Hollywood hadn't even heard of her."[44]

Pearl's fictitious hometown of Grinder's Switch was named after a railroad line switch that lay just a few miles from the small town of Centerville, Tennessee, where Cannon (née Colley) was born in 1912. Her parents ran a successful lumber business and filled their home's library with books that inspired her imagination for lands and big cities far from home. Sarah became known for her rambunctious sense of humor and soon yearned to leave Tennessee for good to become a professional actress in New York. After finishing school, she secured a job as a traveling play director for the Wayne P. Sewell Company, which sent directors to small towns throughout the South to organize and direct plays featuring local casts, with half of the proceeds going to the company, the other half to a local host organization or charity drive.

Cannon was on her way, and though the Great Depression delayed her dreams of New York stardom, her work and travels throughout the South provided rich experience of a different kind: she became familiar with the challenges, circumstances, humor, and hopes of thousands of rural people suffering during that period. In 1936 one poor but remarkably generous woman took her in during a blizzard in Cullman, Alabama, and changed her life. The woman's warmheartedness and folksy mannerisms and expressions inspired Colley to create a new character for the stage: Minnie Pearl. In a comedy routine she began to perform at local events in the South, she portrayed Pearl as the high-spirited, homespun country girl with down-home humor and self-deprecating charm.

WSM executives got wind of Colley's popular act, and in November 1940 she was invited to perform stand-up monologues on the *Grand Ole Opry*, in character as Minnie Pearl. Appearing onstage before the Opry's live audience and broadcasting on the air through WSM's powerful antennae, and eventually the NBC radio network, Cannon's comic

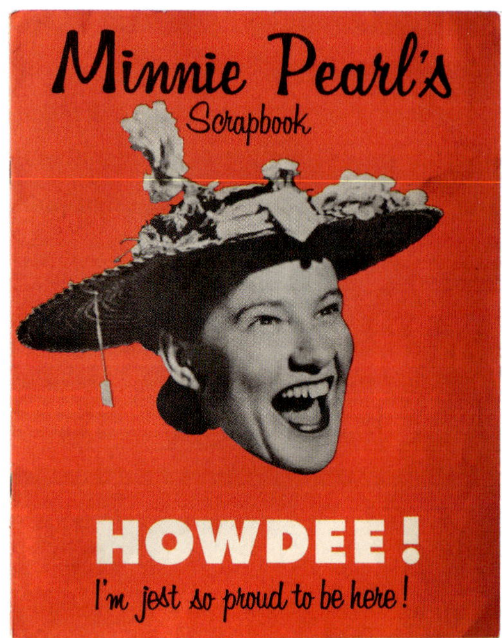

Souvenir book for Minnie Pearl's fans, around 1959.

character immediately ingratiated herself to hundreds of thousands of regular listeners from the Northeast to the Rocky Mountains. Even while ignored or unheard by audiences indifferent to rural humor or "hillbilly" music, as country music was then branded, Pearl quickly became one of the best-known comic characters in the United States.

Listeners across the country loved Pearl's raucous and gregarious personality, her colloquial humor, and her commentary on rural southern life, seemingly preserving and affirming the values of this isolated yet neighborly, swiftly fading lifestyle. During the thirties and forties, advances in agricultural mechanization, along with long-standing economic and other hardships, dispersed thousands of rural families—who composed the bulk of the audience for the *Grand Ole Opry*—to big cities throughout the country. Radio offered them a sense of community during a period marked by migration to unfamiliar places, economic hardship, and, after the attack on Pearl Harbor, war and loss.

As *Washington Post* writer David Von Drehle lamented after Cannon's passing in 1996, "For all us hicks, my wife reminds me, she was our aunt come to visit. And it's true—to the generation that left the dirt farms and coal mines and railroad towns that made America, and to their children and children's children, Pearl was an echo of those good people for whom a pretty bonnet and a clean heart were the makings of an Easter parade . . . and she reassured her [radio] listeners that the new electronic world still had a place for them."[45] Always self-deprecating, Pearl's character made fun of herself before anyone else, inviting audiences to consider her as the mythical town's unmarried spinster always on the hunt for a man, while resigned that he'll likely never be caught. She created a town's worth of kooky family members and neighbors such as Uncle Nabob and Aunt Ambrosia, Lem Teppin, and Buster Owens. She all too eagerly shared the gossip of Grinder's Switch while spinning yarns and one-liners: "Uncle Nabob only takes a nip when he's nervous—and it's not his fault he's such a nervous wreck." Everyone in Grinder's Switch was fair game during her monologues, and even when offstage, Pearl fans could keep up with the townsfolk through a regular subscription to Cannon's newspaper, the *Grinder's Switch Gazette*. She kept thousands of subscribers updated on the latest gossip ("Miss Pansy Perdy was put out because didn't win the Beauty Contest prize. In fact, she was put out before it started"); commentary on her family ("Brother's just naturally a slow-movin' feller. You wouldn't call him lazy, but he just gets started late and finishes up later"); on local romance, through Miss Carrie Snoots' "Courtin' Corner" column; and during the World War II, on the latest from the front, through dispatches from her enlisted cousin Elmer.

Cannon's career flourished in the decades following her first appearance on the Opry. She performed on several traveling shows of country artists, performed for hundreds of thousands of soldiers and support personnel on USO tours all over the world during and after World War II, and performed on a multitude of radio and television programs through the 1980s, including as a founding star on the highly popular syndicated television series *Hee Haw*. Sarah Cannon was paid handsomely for performing for thousands of one-off events throughout the country, from Rotarian conventions and store openings to at least two rallies for the outspoken segregationist George Wallace during his 1956 and 1962 Alabama gubernatorial campaigns.

Indeed, although her character Minnie Pearl steadfastly avoided politics and social commentary during her stand-up routines, Sarah and her manager-husband Henry Cannon saw no reason to turn down Wallace's large financial offer for her appearances, no doubt as they assumed that many in her *Grand Ole Opry* audience subscribed to his views. Thus while Pearl's comedy was extraordinarily impactful in helping to create a sense of community and national belonging for a widely dispersed and transitory audience claiming rural roots, Cannon's political and social commitments as a conventional southern white woman of her day rarely seemed to stray far from home, with a couple of notable exceptions: later in life she became outspoken in support of annual mammograms for women during a time when her peers felt such matters inappropriate for public conversation, and during the eighties she was one of only a handful of country stars who publicly embraced the cause to raise funds on behalf of AIDS patients.

Just three years before Sarah Cannon passed away, she and her husband donated several key objects from her career to the National Museum of American History. At every public appearance the character Minnie Pearl wore a typically plain and homemade dress to comically signal her out-of-step fashion, on the one hand, while also conveying to the audience that she had nothing to hide or to be ashamed of: after all, Pearl wore her "best dress" for trips to town on Saturdays, no matter how modest it might appear. Along with the dress and a pair of simple black shoes, she always donned what soon became one of the most iconic straw hats in history—Pearl's hat—famously topped with fake flowers and tethered to an ever-hanging $1.98 price tag. She was proud to wear a store-bought hat, but so eager to wear it that she forgot to remove the tag; or perhaps she wondered if someday she might need return it to the shop in Grinder's Switch. Sarah Cannon once said, "The price tag on my hat seems to be symbolic of all human frailty." The Cannons also donated three early acetate recordings of her stand-up routines on the *Opry* and several issues of the *Grinder's Switch Gazette*, which, together with her fifty years of Saturday night comic performances on the *Opry*, ensured audiences would keep up on the latest gossip from their favorite, nonexistent, hometown.

John W. Troutman

LATE-NIGHT TV TAKES AMERICA'S PULSE

Late-night talk shows have offered a reliable mix of crowd-pleasing humor and hot-button sociopolitical commentary for over seven decades, serving as a megaphone for America's shifting moods. The genre is almost as old as television itself, with CBS's *Faye Emerson Show* debuting in 1949. Initially available only in East Coast markets, as many early offerings were, the show went nationwide in 1950. "I purposely chose to go on in the late evening," Emerson recalled, "even though I was told no one would be around to watch me. I think I was proved right."

Emerson was a Hollywood star and outspoken political voice, comfortable sparring with elite power brokers and cultural changemakers. Her show welcomed personalities as renowned, and as eclectic, as Édith Piaf and Frank Lloyd Wright—each greeted with Emerson's sharp and informed interview style as she "hosted" her "guests" on a living-room-like stage. She shied away from no topic, openly discussing pressing issues like the Korean War, nuclear armament, and gender parity at a moment when many TV personalities dodged reputational risks by avoiding political statements altogether.[46] Emerson's story has been largely forgotten. As would become a recurring pattern in TV history, women who carved out and proved the viability of certain dayparts or formats often saw their successes handed over to more "marketable" male counterparts.

It was NBC's short-lived *Broadway Open House*, debuting in 1950, that most clearly cast the mold for late-night's enduring tone and format, including the placement of a comedian at the helm—a role originally filled by a rotating slate of veteran comics including Jerry Lester and Morey Amsterdam. In 1953, the *Knickerbocker Beer Show*, led by the avuncular and off-beat Steve Allen, skyrocketed in popularity; it was rechristened *Tonight!* in 1954. Allen, referring to the program's 105-minute runtime, opened his first episode by quipping "this show is going to go on forever!" The remark inadvertently heralded one of the most venerable and long-running franchises in entertainment history.

Allen was followed as host by Jack Paar, who cemented the now-familiar late-night recipe of opening monologue, quirky sidekick, and celebrity interviews. Paar was a firebrand, making headlines for his clashes with NBC executives—most famously when he stormed off the set mid-monologue in 1960 over a censorship dispute, returning weeks later with the line, "As I was saying before I was interrupted. . . ." Paar also turned late-night into a significant political platform. In 1960, both John F. Kennedy and Richard M. Nixon appeared on his show, becoming the first major presidential candidates to tap into the genre's reach. Though Nixon plodded through, much as he did during the infamous Kennedy-Nixon debates that same year (which many say cost him the election), Kennedy immediately grasped the right blend of humor and relatability that the genre demanded. When Paar ventured to ask "a tough question," Kennedy smirkingly volleyed back, "Whether I am a Democrat or a Republican?"

In 1962, Paar exited and *The Tonight Show Starring Johnny Carson* debuted. Carson perfected the formula: his topical monologues skewered politicians across seven presidential administrations; he interviewed thousands of celebrities and kickstarted hundreds of careers; and he delighted audiences with his portrayal of recurring kooky characters like "Carnac the Magnificent" and "Aunt Blabby." With a style that appeared effortless, casual, and authentic, Carson ascended as "the King of Late Night," helming TV's most profitable show and hitting peak popularity in the seventies, with the *Tonight Show*'s rainbow curtain, plaid suits, and haze of cigarette smoke defining an era.

Carson was among the most important cultural gatekeepers of the twentieth century—in any medium. *The Tonight Show* became the most coveted booking in the country, and for comedians in particular, a gig on Carson's

The Tonight Show's rainbow curtain has become one of the most recognizable icons of American pop culture, and was the familiar backdrop against which millions of Americans spent thousands of nights together with Johnny.

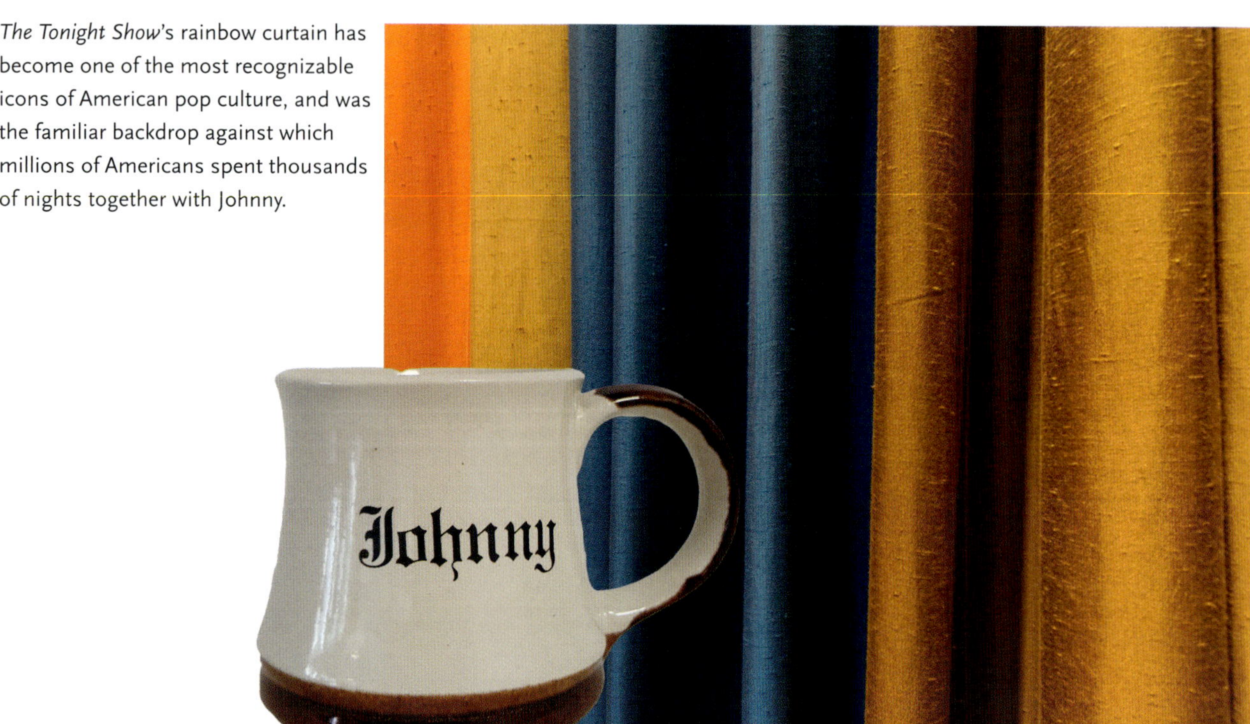

CARSON MONOLOGUE 6/11/87 HG & LK

(AFTER OPENING APPLAUSE)
DO YOU KNOW HOW MANY TIMES I'VE WALKED OUT HERE FROM BEHIND THE CURTAIN IN 25 YEARS? I SHOULD BE PAID BY THE MILE.

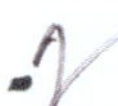
YOU SOUND LIKE A GOOD GROUP. WHAT DO YOU SAY WE GO TO THE BAR ACROSS THE STREET AND WATCH THE LAKERS-CELTIC GAME?

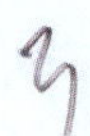
ANYBODY HERE FROM BOSTON? ANYBODY HERE FROM LOS ANGELES?

THIS IS THE MONOLOGUE. I'D LIKE TO PAY TRIBUTE TO THE LITTLE PEOPLE BEHIND THE SCENES WHO MAKE THE MONOLOGUE POSSIBLE...ALL THOSE CLOWNS IN THE WHITE HOUSE.

TODAY IS JUNE 11...I THOUGHT YOU SHOULD KNOW. THAT INFORMATION ALWAYS COMES IN HANDY WHEN YOUR WIFE SAYS...DON'T YO KNOW WHAT DAY THIS IS??

Johnny Carson's topical nightly monologues tracked the pulse of the nation during his reign as "The King of Late Night." Carson's writers delivered an array of up-to-the-minute jokes to the host each evening, from which he carefully curated and arranged his performances.

stage was a career-changing opportunity. Comedian Byron Allen once said: "Comedians have two birthdays: The day they were born, and the day they did *The Tonight Show with Johnny Carson*." Keenen Ivory Wayans called it "the dream on top of the dream" to be invited to sit on Carson's couch—a stamp of approval from Johnny, and a comic's ticket to overnight acclaim.

The 1980s were a time of transformation for television. The brand-new Fox network's debut offering would be *The Late Show Starring Joan Rivers*—a history-making entry in the canon of late-night. Rivers had herself been anointed by Carson after a flawless stand-up set on his stage in 1965. After announcing on the air that Rivers was "going to be a star," Carson handpicked her as the *Tonight Show*'s permanent "guest host"—filling in on the not-infrequent evenings when he missed the show. After garnering ratings that sometimes topped Carson's, she was courted by Fox, but her show faltered—hampered by limited national reach, slow audience adoption of a fourth network, and creative disputes. Carson, feeling betrayed, never spoke to her again.

After finding success as a temporary host in the slot vacated by Rivers, Arsenio Hall landed his own late-night entry in

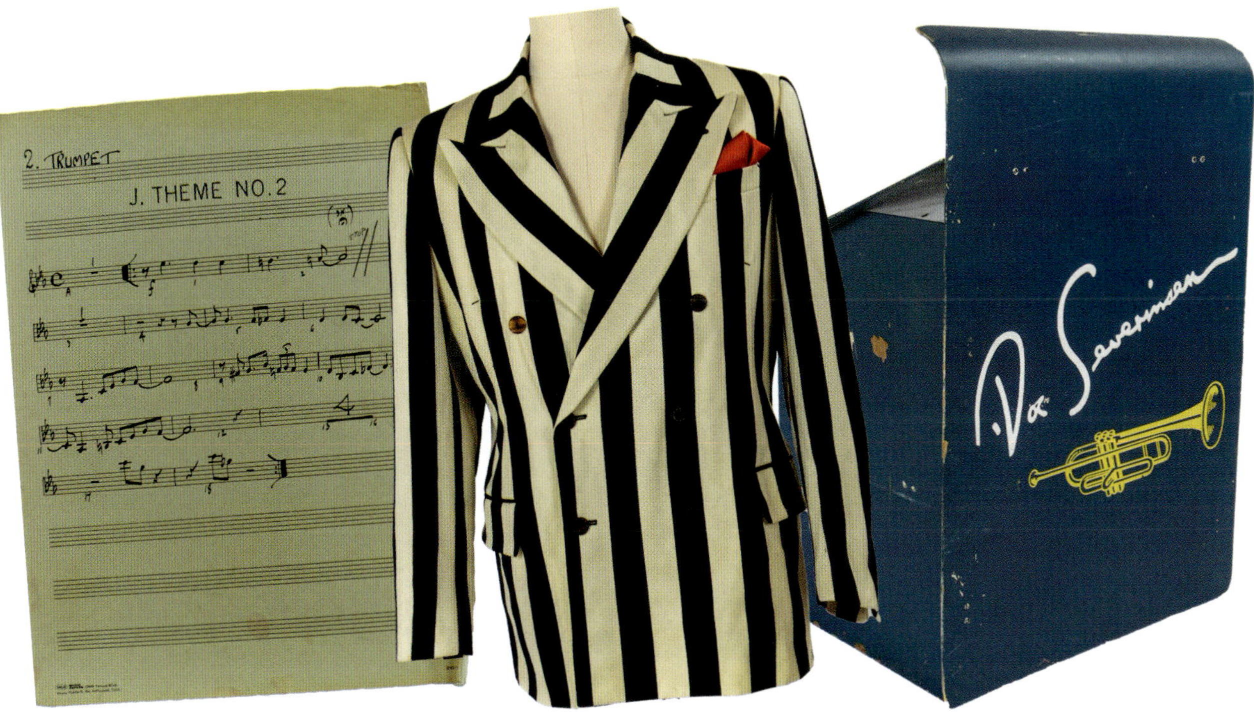

Late-night shows have been as popular for their sociopolitical commentary and comedy as they have been for their musical components—from trending visiting artists to familiar house bands, like that of the affable Doc Severinsen who served as *The Tonight Show*'s beloved resident bandleader under Johnny Carson.

1989. *The Arsenio Hall Show* was a cultural touchstone that defined the early 1990s and targeted the so-called MTV generation with its upbeat atmosphere and lineup of guests that included younger talents with wide-reaching fan bases, like Eddie Murphy, Paula Abdul, and George Lopez. Hall quickly slotted into second place in the ratings race, just behind Carson—who was rumored to be on the verge of retirement. Hall's show not only tapped into an underserved youth demographic that late-night had begun to leave behind, but also established itself as essential viewing. Presidential hopeful Bill Clinton famously chose to appear on the show to shore up support for his candidacy, playing a now-iconic rendition of "Heartbreak Hotel" on his saxophone, and Los Angeles Mayor Tom Bradley used the platform to call for peace in his embattled city during 1992's historic riots.

Meanwhile, *Late Night with David Letterman*'s offbeat style was also appealing to a youthful demographic as it shook up late-night's hold on a largely middle-aged and conservative-leaning core audience. Merrill Markoe, the show's cocreator, brought a sensibility that she called "smart yet stupid" to television with goofy bits that included casting sixty-foot hand shadows on the side of the Exxon Building or interviewing oddball guests like a man who flew at fifteen thousand feet in a lawn chair.[47] Letterman's

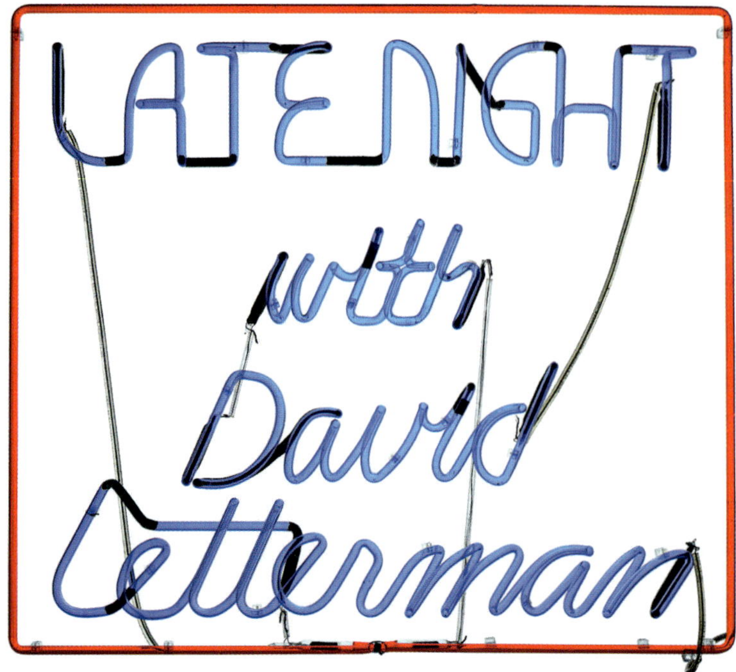

This neon sign appeared in the title sequence of NBC's *Late Night with David Letterman*, a show whose ironic style challenged late-night conventions and influenced generations of comedians.

anxious everyman persona was in stark contrast to the slick confidence of a Carson or Paar, and his show seriously challenged NBC's domination of the late-night hours for the first time in TV history.

Johnny Carson's 1992 departure from *The Tonight Show* upended the late-night hierarchy. While many presumed that Letterman would fill his seat, the network anointed Jay Leno, who was quickly branded "The Most Popular Regular Guy in America."[48] *Late Night with Conan O'Brien* debuted in 1993 and, though initially met with skepticism, evolved into a laboratory for absurdist comedy that laid the groundwork for a broader stylistic experimentation later expanded by cable ventures—from HBO's *The Chris Rock Show* to E!'s *Chelsea Lately*—which collectively destabilized the traditional boundaries of late-night.

By 2013, Jimmy Kimmel had moved into the 11:30 P.M. slot on ABC, and soon after Jimmy Fallon revitalized *The Tonight Show* with a high-energy, variety-driven approach, symbolically restoring the franchise to its historic home at 30 Rockefeller Plaza—the hallowed ground where Carson once held court. Thanks in large part to the influence of Jon Stewart and *The Daily Show*, the axis of late-night has largely shifted to satirical political commentary. *Late Night with Seth Meyers* and *The Late Show with Stephen Colbert*, which debuted in 2014 and 2015, respectively, both hit a stride during the 2016 presidential campaign and presidency of Donald Trump, during which late-night became more germane than ever to American politics. Today, the format is under revision yet again, with polarizing social issues, market saturation, shifting viewing habits, and the breakneck evolution of digital platforms forcing hosts to interrogate the formula they've inherited, vying, like their predecessors before them, for relevancy in an ever-changing media climate.

Laura LaPlaca

SITCOMS FORGE FAMILY IDEALS

The domestic sitcom is among the most enduring entertainment genres in American history, with a genesis in comic strips and feature film serials, a flowering during radio's golden age, and an unassailable place on every network's primetime roster since the dawn of television. With great durability comes formulaic narrative tropes, stock characters, and, yes, predictable patterns of canned laughter. But a genre that has insinuated itself so thoroughly into the collective consciousness also carries with it vital ideological functions. More than any other cultural form, and generation over generation for more than a century, the domestic sitcom has been the primary site for articulating ever-evolving definitions of what it means to be an American family.

Sitcoms have led us through sweeping social change. By holding up a mirror that reflects the limitations and potentials of their respective moments—from the throes of the Depression through the struggles of the civil rights era and into the turn of the twenty-first century—they have modeled our best (and worst) selves and helped us rehearse new ways of forging community and kinship. Domestic sitcoms, and the way that they caricature our familial roles, aren't just funny. They allow us to explore and sometimes challenge elemental aspects of human experience: parenthood, coming of age, marriage, and the transmission of cultural values across generations.

THE GOLDBERGS

While we often associate family comedies with idealized black-and-white depictions of suburban life in post–World War II sitcoms, the genre was a ubiquitous part of popular culture during the depths of the Great Depression. Widespread financial insolvency and profound fears about global unrest left people cleaving to the shared cultural bulwark that was the home. It was at this moment that the aspirational fiction of the "American dream"—complete with its symbolic "dream house"—took hold as a defining cultural mythology. In the face of major social dislocations, as millions of immigrants were busied with forging new family groups and rebuilding fractured communities, comedy about domestic life was much more than merely an escapist diversion during hard times; it was a vital tool for negotiating America's changing social fabric. Phenomenally popular series like *The Goldbergs* offered audiences a script for navigating the complex realities of assimilation, community building, and economic survival. They also offered a life-affirming form of collective release, locating their humor in comeuppance with camaraderie that spoke defiantly to the power imbalances of the time.

The Goldbergs debuted in 1929 as the semiautobiographical brainchild of Gertrude Berg, a phenomenally talented broadcasting pioneer who also produced, starred in, and wrote the series. The show was a staple of Americans' entertainment diet for seventeen years on the radio and another seven years on television. Airing initially in fifteen-minute slots the show combined elements of situation comedy and soap opera to weave story arcs about the lives of a multigenerational Jewish immigrant family in a bustling tenement house in the Bronx. The show was lauded for its realism and relatability for viewers of all backgrounds, who found common cause and empathy with Berg's intimate, authentic tone. The series was at times lighthearted, touching, and didactic, with a focus on fostering cultural tolerance and a capacity for channeling matters of enormous import during divisive times: a 1939 episode, for example, dealt with the aftermath of a rock hurled through the Goldbergs' window during Passover Seder. The show reached peak popularity in the 1930s, a period that found Americans turning to the new popular culture of broadcasting to navigate rapidly evolving ways of life and forms of community. In the hands of a fearless, sensitive, and principled creator like Berg, situation comedy had real power to intervene in shaping the lived experience of everyday Americans on a mass scale.

I DREAM OF JEANNIE

I Dream of Jeannie worked at the intersection of two apparently dichotomous trends in the TV industry of the 1960s: a weird and wild vogue for magical beings (talking horses, monster families, flying nuns) and a mandate to capture more progressive, youthful, and highly educated demographics of viewers by addressing issues of social relevancy. At a moment when *The Donna Reed Show* and *The Adventures of Ozzie and Harriet* were still presenting housewives representative of post–World War II conservativism, the publication of Betty Friedan's *Feminine*

Never mind that it was really a painted glass bourbon decanter, the groovy genie's bottle that Major Tony Nelson found on a desert island in the South Pacific represented pure magic for the TV viewers that made *I Dream of Jeannie* a hit for the NBC network from 1965 to 1970, and for generations that would discover it in rerun syndication.

Mystique, which catalyzed the second-wave feminist movement, was a clarion call to America's cultural gatekeepers: popular media had to evolve past a single-minded definition of womanhood or risk alienating a generation of consumers. What would develop was a gradual and limited effort to depict women outside traditional marriages and nuclear family structures.

I Dream of Jeannie's protagonist was a cunning, confident, and hypersexualized imp that burst forth in puffs of chromatic pink smoke to shake up the life of her straitlaced "Master," a NASA astronaut (a sheer distillation of 1960s masculinity and rationality). The only way to suppress her superpowers was to contain her in a bottle, a not-so-subtle allegory for the raging national conversation about women's domestic containment that characterized the sociopolitical climate of the era. The premise was not unproblematic, nor was the show's saturation with exoticizing and colonialist views of the East. However, *I Dream of Jeannie* did present something bold for its moment: a conspicuously unmarried couple sharing a home and a life—for four seasons. In its fifth and final season, a doomed and dreaded wedding episode sounded the show's death knell, an unwanted ultimatum from network executives who would see no other acceptable resolution to the couple's verboten relationship.

JULIA

During TV's first decades, the sitcom landscape was marred by the structured absence of racial, regional, and class identifiers. Networks put forth "lowest common denominator" programming that pandered to a middle American consensus ideology preferred by advertisers seeking buy-in from white middle-class consumers. Perhaps *Julia* was destined to become a lightning rod, then, when it premiered in the fall of 1968 as the first sitcom representing a Black family since the highly problematic *Beulah* and *Amos 'n' Andy* had left the airwaves fifteen years earlier. Starring Diahann Carroll as Julia Baker, a war-widowed nurse raising a young son, the show shot to the top of the ratings on NBC. But

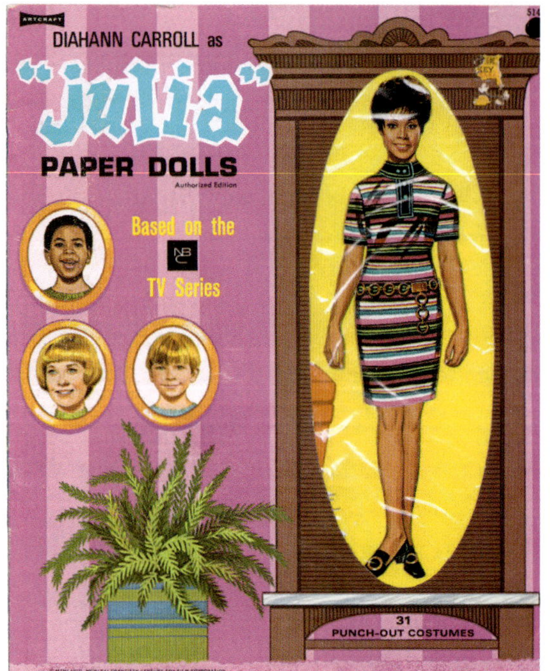

blunt popularity belied criticisms from cultural leaders who found *Julia* to be a scourge that failed to reflect the lived experiences of most Black families. A star vehicle for a Black actress in primetime, with the real potential to mark a step forward for TV comedy, it presented no real route to engagement with the civil rights era that was its undeniable backdrop. It seemed the series was irredeemably troubled by the Bakers' chic antiseptic lifestyle, a white supporting cast prone to dashing off racist asides for laughs, and a naïve premise suggesting that Julia had skirted the specter of institutionalized racism simply by working hard to carve out her own piece of the American dream.

Such criticisms, while merited, applied crushing pressure to the series and its star, who found herself required to justify the show's very existence in the public arena. Citing her own intrepid efforts to work within challenging limitations to improve the series' tone, Carroll upheld the value of the incremental, but very real, progress that the show had made by breaking the color line in prime time. It was ultimately an impossible weight to bear, and Carroll left the show at the close of its third season. *New York Times* TV critic Jack Gould pegged Julia as "tepid escapism" upon its debut, but cautioned that "its advent is not to be altogether underestimated."[49] Indeed, the series has persisted as a precedent-setting, if imperfect, entry in the sitcom canon that catalyzed vital, and still ongoing, discourse around the stakes of representation on television.

CHEERS

For eleven years from 1982 to 1993, America tuned into a Boston watering hole called *Cheers*, presided over by former Red Sox pitcher Sam Malone and a motley crew of wait staff and regulars who found family in one another despite their differences. *Cheers* was a second home where, as the theme song intoned, "everybody knows your name" and the welcoming Naugahyde barstools were burnished with nostalgia. The series was a top ten show for eight of eleven seasons, alternately reflecting and defining the zeitgeist of 1980s America as it tracked alongside the culture wars wrought by President Ronald Reagan's two-term tenure. With a series architecture undergirded by layers of class and gender dynamics, the show was a site for enacting widening socioeconomic rifts that characterized the latter decades of the American twentieth century.

Cheers' ensemble cast was an exercise in contrasts that produced a type of finely wrought comedy stemming from both colliding worldviews and unlikely allegiances. With some characters exemplifying the newly coined term "yuppie" and others representing the principled working class, the sitcom was ultimately a study in social mobility. While its characters grappled with distinctly modern issues, the show's format was, in many ways, a callback to an earlier generation of sitcoms that centered the workplace or the public sphere, notably including radio's quintessential bar comedy *Duffy's Tavern*, which was not incidentally created by Abe Burrows, father of *Cheers* creator James Burrows. *Cheers*' extraordinary durability presaged the coming of a slew of surrogate family palcoms like *Seinfeld* and *Friends* and workplace comedies like *The Office* and *It's Always Sunny in Philadelphia*.

Anchored by the sartorial marker of his Red Sox jacket, *Cheers*'s Sam Malone put forward a version of American masculinity that reflected the complexities and contradictions of 1980s social expectations and changing gender norms.

THE GOLDEN GIRLS

The Golden Girls was highly acclaimed during its first run from 1985 to 1992 but may be even more popular these four decades later. Helmed by a formidable ensemble cast of veteran comedic talents that included Bea Arthur, Betty White, Rue McClanahan, and Estelle Getty, the series was, and remains, notable for centering the lives of older women setting out on their second, or third, acts. Dorothy, Rose, Blanche, and Sophia—their names now the subject of countless internet memes and personality quizlets—built an almost familial attachment as roommates in a fabulously comported Miami home brimming with rattan, shoulder pads, and cheesecake. *The Golden Girls* was noted then, as

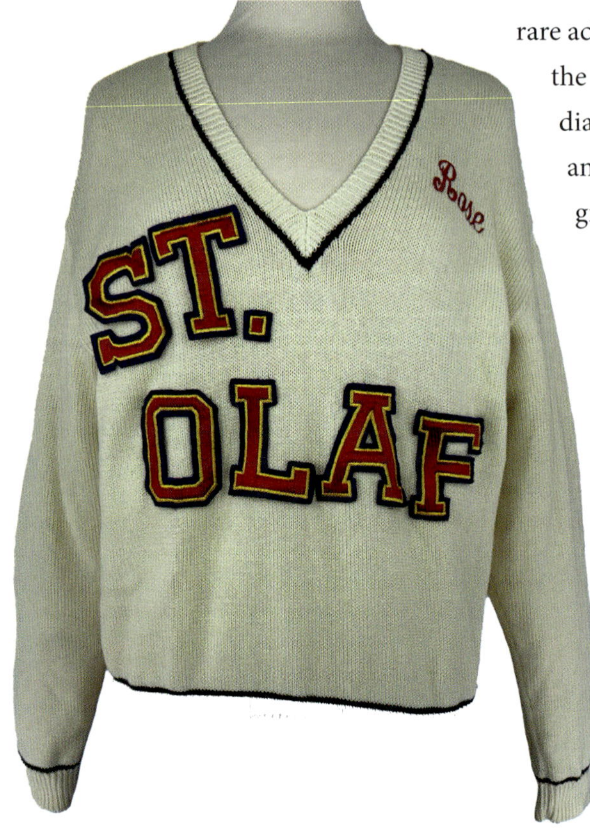

Betty White portrayed Rose Nylund from the fictional town of St. Olaf, Minnesota on *The Golden Girls*—a sitcom that centered sharp, relevant storytelling about aging, social issues, and finding community.

now, for its smart writing (punctuated by devastating one-liners) and virtuosic comedic performances (all four lead actors received Emmys—a rare achievement). But part of its continued resonance stems from the show's facility with harnessing comedy's power to foster dialogue and empathy around issues of national importance—and doing so with a directness that few other television programs, of any genre, had matched before.

Aside from its consistent, and important, treatment of aging and related issues like menopause, ageism, and mortality, *The Golden Girls* addressed a constellation of dynamic social issues that included homelessness, addiction, suicide, reproductive rights, and antisemitism. Premiering during the fall of 1985, three days before President Ronald Reagan publicly acknowledged the AIDS tragedy for the first time, *The Golden Girls* put forth a clear and confident stance on matters impacting LGBTQ people, reflecting the attitudes of its creative team and all four leading actors, who were each lifelong allies of the community. Even when the show was not explicitly taking a stand, its overriding message is a powerful one that rings true with countless fans on a deeply felt level: it is possible to forge bonds with chosen family members who support and enrich one another—even, and especially, when biological ties, societal structures, or traditional family groups fail to sustain us.

Laura LaPlaca

FAMILIAS FROM THE BARRIO: THE 1970S LATINX FAMILY IN THE NETWORK ERA

The idea that Latinxs value family above all else is entrenched in most people's understanding of the fastest-growing demographic in the United States. Latinx families—often close-knit, multigenerational, and including extended relatives—were a natural launching point for diversifying situational comedies (sitcoms) on television. These sitcoms kept the framework familiar enough to American viewers by focusing on one "family" while exposing the average American to the concept of "Hispanic" identity—added to the U.S. census only in 1970. Early Latinx family sitcoms were characterized by the trials and tribulations of working-class ethnic families coping with life in the United States, portraying a range of characters who were either struggling to assimilate or already fully assimilated into mainstream American culture.

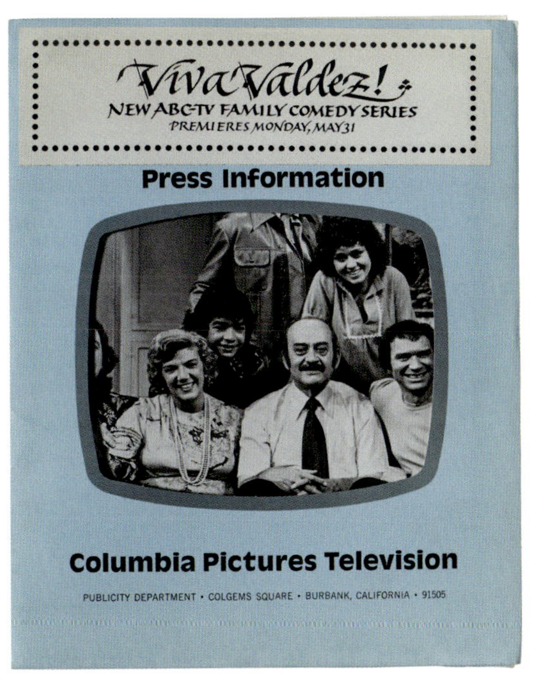

Viva Valdez was a briefly lived sitcom that aired on ABC from May 31 to September 6, 1976. Created by Bernard Rothman, Jack Wohl, and Stan Jacobson, the show told the story of the Mexican American Valdez family of East Los Angeles, California.

Historically, prime-time television, identified by peak viewing times on weeknights from eight to eleven o'clock, has entertained audiences with sitcoms centered on traditional, nuclear white family structures with culturally conservative American values. By the 1970s, networks were under pressure to create roles and storylines that centered people of color. Network studios bent to public demands and simultaneously capitalized on them as advertisers sought to reach new demographics.[50] With the early success of several African American family sitcoms, the major networks greenlit new productions focusing in on Latinxs—some series like the dramedy *Popi* flopped, whereas NBC's *Chico and the Man* was deemed a hit.

Airing on ABC in 1976, *Viva Valdez* was the first Latinx family sitcom nationally broadcast and featured a nuclear Mexican American family living in East Los Angeles. The Valdez family consists of proud plumber and family patriarch Luis Valdez, his wife Sophia, and their grown children Victor, Ernesto, Connie, and Pepe, along with their Mexican cousin Jerry

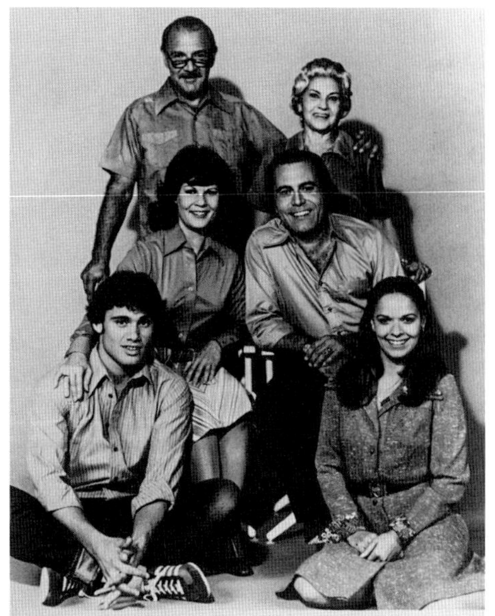

¿Qué Pasa, USA? was the first bilingual sitcom in American history. It was created by Manuel "Cookie" Mendoza and written by Luis Santeiro, filmed at PBS member station WPBT in Miami, Florida, and aired on PBS nationwide from 1977 to 1980. The program followed the lives of the Cuban American Peña family in Little Havana, Miami, Florida, representing the joys and frustrations of daily life in this community, including code-switching, intergenerational conflict, and cultural pride versus acculturation to American norms.

Ramirez. The show's punchlines relied on generic family dynamics and tropes like the lighthearted bickering between out-of-touch parents, while the young adults in the family reject tradition (but not too much). If you removed the sprinkling of "Hispanic" props, stereotypical references, and bilingual interjections by the actors, it could have been a show about any nonethnic American family. The show lacked cultural specificity. After all, the all-white production team was "a group of Canadians . . . with some New Yorkers,"[51] including producers Bernie Rothman, Jack Wohl, and Stan Jacobson and Alan Rafkin as director. While it was the first show to attempt a fair and honest portrayal of a Mexican family, it nonetheless suffered from a "cultural gap between the scripters and the actors."[52]

A first for prime-time television, the show included a majority-Latinx cast including Mexican actor Rodolfo Hoyos Jr., Mexican-Argentinian American actress Carmen Zapata, Dominican-born Lincoln Peralta known professionally as James Victor, actress Lisa Mordente of Puerto Rican descent, and Mexican actor Jorge Cervera Jr., among others. Despite progress in casting Latinxs in Latinx roles, there was a startling lack of Mexican Americans from East LA cast for a series focused on a family with that background. Networks could not grasp that Latinx communities and identities were not interchangeable, and ethnic experiences are distinct depending on their identity, history, and geography. Despite assigning Carmen Zapata to "in-house consultant" on Mexican American culture, the creative team felt little needed to be changed because to them Jewish ethnic experiences could easily translate into Latinx ethnic experiences.

After twelve episodes, *Viva Valdez* was canceled due to the low ratings—unsurprising considering the inadequate promotion by the networks. The show's early cancellation established an unfortunate pattern for subsequent Latinx-focused series, in which the majority would not survive past their first season. Television's first foray into Latinx family sitcoms missed the mark.

When the Public Broadcasting Service (PBS) received sponsorship from the U.S. Office of Education Emergency School Assistance Act, they initiated production of PBS's first sitcom series, *¿Qué pasa, USA?* The goal was to use television programming to minimize inequalities in the post–civil rights era, while improving "inter-ethnic and intra-ethnic relations."[53] That thirty-nine-episode sitcom remains one of the most significant pieces of Latino television history. It was the first bilingual sitcom produced in the United States.

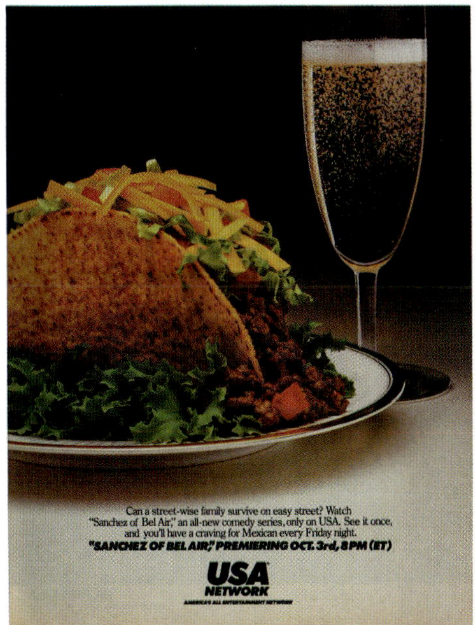

Sanchez of Bel Air was a sitcom created by Dave Hackel and April Kelly that aired on the USA Network from October 3 to December 26, 1986. The show was a loose adaptation of *The Beverly Hillbillies'* concept of a family's dramatic change in fortune, following the Sanchez family's move to the Bel Air neighborhood of Los Angeles, California. The series was criticized for its inattention to Hispanic culture, with few Latinos on its writing staff.

Produced by and targeted toward Miami's Cuban community, the show follows the multigenerational Peña family as they navigate life as Cubans *en exilio* in the United States living in the Little Havana barrio. The Peña family is made up of Spanish-speaking maternal grandparents, Antonio and Adela; sort-of-bilingual parents Pepe and Juana; and their English-dominant bilingual teenagers Joe and Carmen. Each generation is struggling through the cultural and linguistic barriers experienced by immigrants in different ways, demonstrating how age factors deeply into acculturation. Diasporic identity is a central theme of the show as it decoded aspects of Cuban and American culture in the context of a relatable working-class family. Although the show initially aired only in Florida, after its 1977 season it was broadcast nationally on PBS. By the time it was cancelled in 1980 due to contract disputes with the head writer Luis Santeiro, the show had reached almost a million viewers.

The show frequently positions language as one of the key sites of comedic misunderstandings. In contrast to other shows that privilege English and set up the joke to bring attention to the "ignorance" of non-native speakers with heavy accents, *¿Qué pasa, USA?* reverses that long-standing trope. The show finds humor in the linguistic interactions between people who have varying degrees of Spanish and English proficiency and rely on Spanglish (a blend of Spanish and English) to better communicate with each other. While the show ultimately reinforces the importance of English-speaking skills, its representation of older Spanish-speaking family members (and the cultural isolation that they experience as immigrants) is a rarity on U.S. television.

¿Qué pasa, USA?'s successful portrayal of the realities of life in Miami's Cuban community in the 1970s demonstrates the potential that exists for Latinx-focused television to be comedic without being condescending. Given that many Latinx characters and storylines fail to communicate real Latinx lived experiences, this sitcom stands as proof that storytelling by and about a particular community leads to more accurate and authentic depictions that resonate with viewers.

Prime-time television did not take any cues from public television. By the 1980s, new Latinx-focused series like USA's *Sanchez of Bel Air* and ABC's *Condo* suffered the same fate as *Viva Valdez*. What can you expect with advertisements that ask, "Can a street-wise family make it on easy street?" alongside a hard-shell taco that would make anyone familiar with authentic Mexican cuisine cringe. They were flat representations of a

Mexican American family with little authenticity to the true experiences of Mexican Americans, particularly those living in the East Los Angeles barrio. It is only as new Latinx storytellers have risen in recent years that we have begun to see nuanced and complex portrayals of Latinxs on television—even if many still struggle to make it past a couple of seasons.

Ashley Oliva Mayor

BOB NEWHART: JUST ANOTHER SLIGHTLY AMUSING ACCOUNTANT

The most celebrated and influential comics are often rebellious outsiders, lobbing bombs at authority and speaking truth to power. So how did mild-mannered, middle-class midwesterner Bob Newhart, perhaps the ultimate *insider* comic, become one of the most successful comedians of his generation? Maybe it was the stammer.

Born George Robert Newhart in Oak Park, Illinois, on September 5, 1929, Newhart had an unlikely journey to comic stardom. He served in the U.S. Army during the Korean War, briefly attended Loyola University Chicago School of Law, and held a series of white-collar jobs, from accountant to copywriter. As a lark, in 1958 he and friend Ed Gallagher began to develop a comedy routine based on the concept of absurd phone conversations. The duo recorded a demo of their act and sent it to local radio stations but had little success, and soon Gallagher took a job in New York, leaving Newhart on his own. However, WCFL radio disc jockey Dan Sorkin, a fan, learned that Warner Bros. Records was seeking new talent for its fledgling comedy line and helped Newhart get his material in front of the record company's executives.[54]

When A&R director George Avakian first heard a demo tape of Bob Newhart's act, he decided they had to record this fresh new comic talent right away. When he called Bob and asked where he was playing, he got a shock: he'd actually never worked a nightclub before; this comedy thing was just a fun side project. Undaunted, Avakian booked

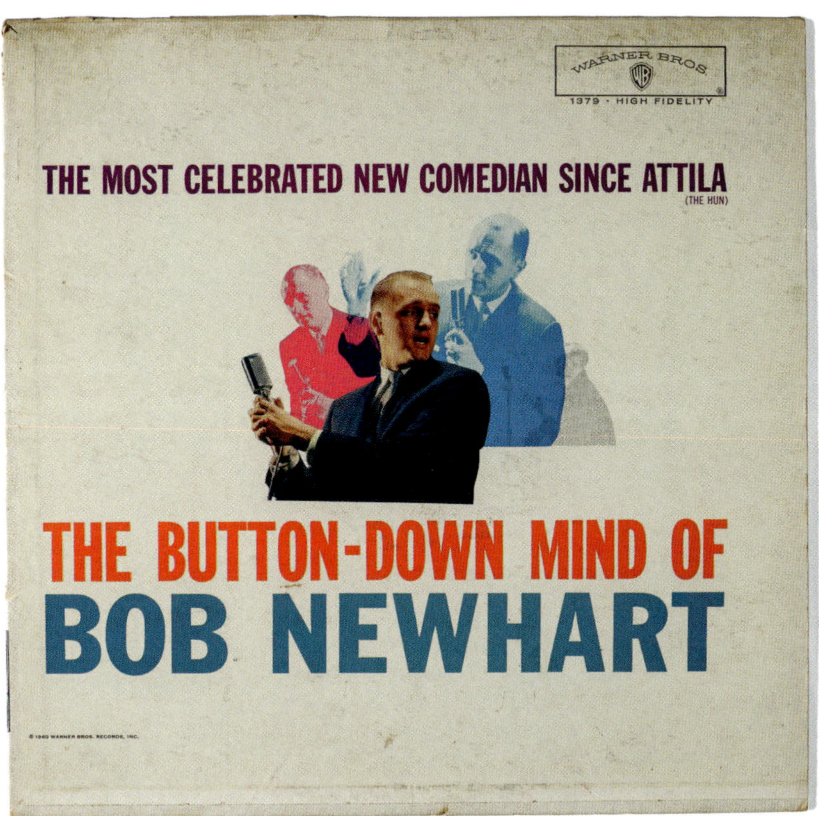

The newly professional comedian would become the first to win the Grammy Award for Best Album, beating Harry Belafonte, Nat King Cole, and Frank Sinatra in 1961.

him at Houston's Tidelands Club and sent engineers to record and produce a comedy record. At first, Newhart had only three routines, but the crowd went wild, roaring for more. "Which one would you like to hear again?" he asked.[55]

No one could have anticipated how successful the album would be. *The Button-Down Mind of Bob Newhart* became the first comedy LP ever to hit number one on the *Billboard* charts, won a remarkable three Grammys, including 1961 Album of the Year, and launched a career that lasted six decades. Newhart became a fixture on film and television, including two acclaimed and long-running sitcoms, *The Bob Newhart Show* (1972–1978) and *Newhart* (1982–1990), and continued to play small roles and make guest appearances into his nineties.

"I've been told to speed up my delivery when I perform. But if I lose the stammer, I'm just another slightly amusing accountant."
—Bob Newhart

So what was it about Bob Newhart? Eschewing the more aggressive and controversial style of "sick comic" contemporaries like Lenny Bruce and Mort Sahl, Newhart's deadpan, stammering, straight-man persona allowed him to subtly excoriate social mores, crassness and greed, hypocrisy, and the absurdities of modern American life.

One of the routines that Newhart brought to the stage in Houston was an imaginary conversation between Abraham Lincoln and a slick press

MAY 8,1959

I WAS THINKING THE OTHER DAY, SUPPOSING THAT LINCOLN HAD NOT BEEN A GREAT PRESIDENT, BUT INSTEAD JUST A GOOD PRESIDENT, IT MIGHT WELL HAVE ALTERED THE COURSE OF OUR NATION'S HISTORY, UNLESS LINCOLN HAD ONE THING THAT WE HAVE TODAY AND THAT IS THE SCIENCE OF AD- VERTSING. I THINK THE FOLLOWING SCENE MIGHT AHVE TAKEN PLACE BETWEEN LINCOLN AND HIS ADVERTISING MANAGER JUST BEFORE GETTYBURGH.

HI THERE ABE SWEETHEART, HOW'S EVERYTHING GOING? HOW'S THE WEATHER DOWN THERE KID? OH THAT'S WONDERFUL...HERE, A LITTLE DRIZZLEDOO... WELL WHAT ARE YOU GOING TO DO? RIGHT ... WELL THEY BRING MAY FLOWERS, THEY SAY...(LAUGHS) LISTEN ABE, I GOT YOUR NOTE... WHAT'S THE PROBLEM?... YOU'RE THINKING OF WHAT? THINKING OF SHAVING IT OFF... YOU'RE KIDDING ME AREN'T YOU ABE... DON'T YOU SEE ABE, IT'S PART OF THE IMAGE... YEAH, ALONG WITH THE STOVEPIPE HAT AND THE SHAWL, DON'T YOU SEE THAT ABE... YOU'RE GOING TO HAVE TO TRUST US ON SOMETHING LIKE THIS ABE, SWEETHEART... WELL I KNOW IT ITCHES...BUT I MEAN, WHAT WOULD YOU RATHER BE AN ATTORNEY IN ILLINOIS OR A PRESIDENT WITH AN ITCHY BEARD... IT'S THAT SIMPLE KID DON'T YOU SEE THAT... ABE LEAVE IT ON WILL YA?... NOW WHAT'S THE PROBLEM WITH GRANT... YEAH, YOU'RE GETTING A LOT OF COMPLAINTS IN THE MAIL ABOUT GRANT'S DRINKING? WELL ABE I DON'T SEE THE RPOBLEM, I MEAN YOU KNEW HE WAS A LUSH WHEN YOU APPOINTED HIM... YEAH, YOU'RE GAG WRITERS ARE HERE... BUT WHY... YOU THINK YOU OUGHT TO COME BACK WITH SOMETHING FUNNY THE NEXT TIME THEY ASK... AN ANECEDOTE ABOUT A TOWN DRUNK YOU ONCE KNEW OR SOMETHING LIKE THAT?... WELL ABE, YOU KNOW IT JUST ISN'T THAT EASY TO COME WITH ANECEDOTES... WELL I'LL GET THEM STARTED ON IT, BUT I CAN'T PROMISE ANYTHING... LISTEN ABE YOU GOT THE SPEECH ALL RIGHT... GOOD...NOW AB E YOU HAVEN'T CHANGED THE SPEECH, HAVE YOU?... ABE LISTEN, WHY DO YOU CHANGE THE SPEECHES, YOU KNOW YOU'RE NO WRITER... JUST A COUPLE OF MINOR CHANGES... OKAY LET'S HEAR 'EM... YOU WHAT? YOU TYPED IT... ABE HOW MANY TIMES WE HAVE TO TELL YOU ON THE BACKS OF ENVELOPES ... I KNOW IT'S HARDER TO READ THAT WAY ABE BUT DON'T YOUSEE, IT LOOKS AD LIBBED THAT WAY. LIKE YOU WROTE IT ON THE TRAIN COMMING DOWN...LOOK ABE MEMORIZE IT AND THEN PUT IT ON THE BACKS OF THE ENVELOPES WILLL YOU... WE'RE GETTING A LOT OF PLAY IN THE PRESSON THAT HOW ARE THE ENVELOPES HOLDING OUT, KID... YOU SURE YOU GOT ENOUGH... NOW WHAT ELSE? YOU CHANGED FOUR SCORE AND SEVEN TO WHAT?

This original typescript for Newhart's "Abe Lincoln vs. Madison Avenue" routine was among those hurriedly assembled for the recording that would be released as *The Button-Down Mind of Bob Newhart.*

agent advisor. As with many of his comedy routines, in "Abe Lincoln vs. Madison Avenue," Newhart's genial, halting, square delivery obscured a sly, subversive, and quietly revolutionary form of satire. In talking through Lincoln's upcoming Gettysburg Address, the ad man advises the sixteenth president on his image ("Abe, would you leave the beard on?"), suggests jokes and merchandising tie-ins, and bats down Lincoln's speech revisions. The advisor's insincere platitudes, prioritization of style over substance, and obsession with focus group testing poke fun at the popular perception of the advertising world's asinine commercialism. His frustration with Lincoln's earnest and thoughtful intelligence, out of its historical context, reads like relatable frustration with a coworker who just doesn't get the point of a collaborative project. Meanwhile, the sketch's irreverent and ahistorical representation of Lincoln's dithering deflates the mythology around the venerated leader. The routine even ends with the publicist suggesting that Lincoln "take in a play," suggesting he may have been responsible for the president's assassination at Ford's Theatre. Newhart wrote that he was inspired to write the monologue by a 1957 study of the advertising world, *The Hidden Persuaders*, "which talked about the danger of PR men creating images in presidential campaigns to the degree that you were voting for a personality rather than a leader's ideology."[56]

Other early Newhart routines imagined conversations with the Wright brothers, Abner Doubleday trying to explain the rules of baseball to an incredulous newcomer, and a camera rehearsal for Nikita Khrushchev's visit to the United States. In an era of conformity, patriotism, and respectability, Newhart took a deviant, countercultural aim at some of the nation's proudest myths and cultural heritage. Each of these monologues was delivered in Newhart's trademark deadpan style, with stammers, pregnant pauses, forced laughter, and surprised reactions making his characters both believable and relatable, and guiding the audience's imagination to involve them in the performance.

Like a wolf in sheep's clothing, respectable everyman Bob Newhart snuck into the heart of mainstream America, held a mirror up to its frailties, vanities, and absurdities, and helped unbutton some minds.

Ryan Lintelman

HAPPY DAYS AND THE NOSTALGIA BOOM

In the mid-1970s, Americans were feeling nostalgic. Exhausted from a turbulent era marked by political assassinations, an unpopular war, earthshaking liberation movements, civic revolt, and government scandals, audiences sought refuge in the not-so-distant past of the midcentury. The flagship for this emotional retreat was the television program *Happy Days* (1974–1984), not only a hit sitcom set in the 1950s and early 1960s but one that reflected and reaffirmed that era's popular cultural presentation of a simpler, more homogenous America centered around the values of the white, middle-class nuclear family. The escapist sitcom offered a soothing vision of consensus and social cohesion free from the complications and political conflicts of the 1970s.

To millions of Americans weary of contemporary problems, *Happy Days* presented a comfortable, if idealized, vision of the recent past, as depicted in the illustrations on this lunch box.

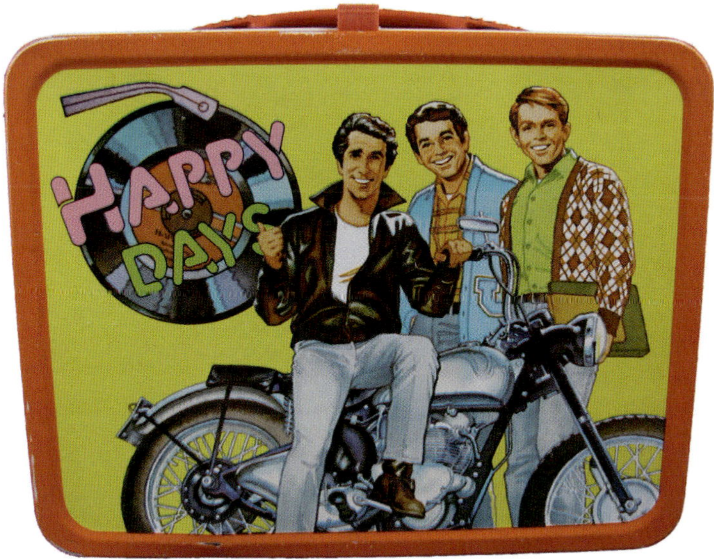

Created by producer Garry Marshall, *Happy Days* seemed like a direct rebuke of the contemporary social realism and political consciousness of television series like *The Jeffersons*, *Maude*, and *All in the Family*, which it replaced as the number-one show in the Nielsen ratings in 1976–1977. The series featured former *Andy Griffith Show* child star and future A-list movie director Ron Howard as Richie Cunningham, an average

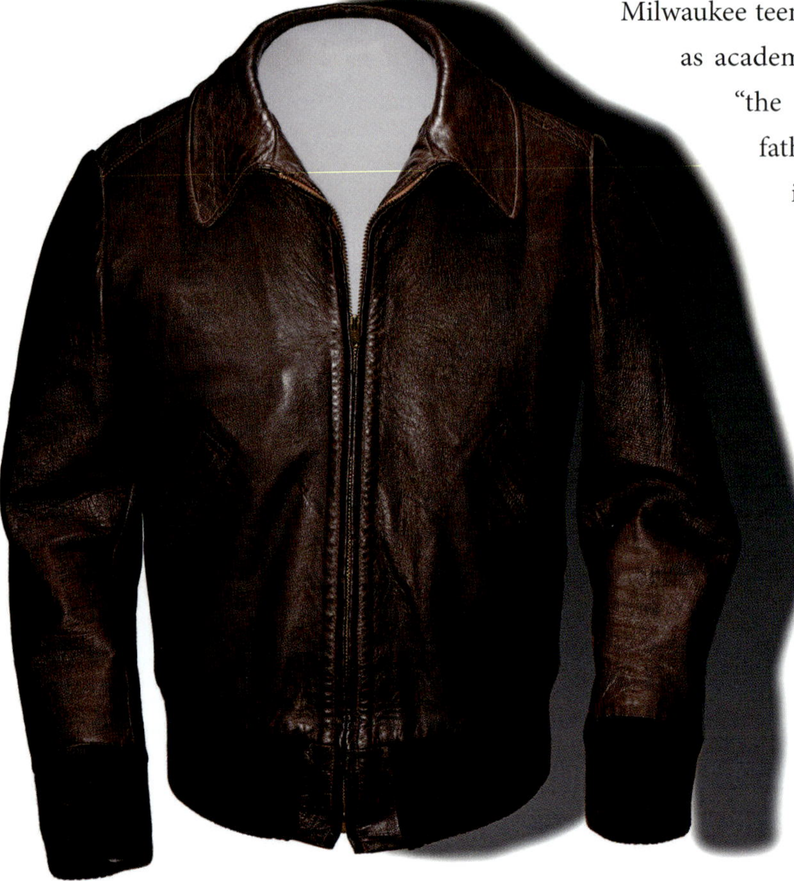

Milwaukee teen with typical adolescent concerns such as academic success and "necking" with girls at "the point." Living with archetypal fifties father Howard (Tom Bosley), mother Marion (Marion Ross), and younger sister Joanie (Erin Moran), Richie hangs out at Arnold's Drive-In with his nerdy buddies Ralph Malph (Donny Most) and "Potsie" Weber (Anson Williams) talking about girls, cars, and rock music.

However, as the show developed, audiences gravitated toward Henry Winkler's character, Arthur "Fonzie" Fonzarelli, making this side character the true star of the show. Known for his confident catchphrase "Ayyy!" and cocky two thumbs-up mugging, the Fonz was good in a fight, was successful with the ladies, and possessed near-miraculous powers such as the ability to start a jukebox by pounding it with his fist. For millions of fans, the biker with a heart of gold became synonymous with being "cool" and a true pop-culture icon. However, in the genial spirit of *Happy Days*, even Fonzie, presented as a leather-jacketed ruffian, was a mild and nonthreatening interpretation of rebellious fifties youth. Over the course of the series, this would-be rebel without a cause earns his high school diploma, becomes a teacher, tones down his womanizing ways, and even adopts an orphan, performing the very normalization and domestication that his character type was first supposed to challenge.[57]

The epitome of cool, Henry Winkler wore this leather jacket as Arthur Fonzarelli on *Happy Days*. Originally intended as a side character, "the Fonz" instead became the show's most popular. He shared characteristics with some of the other macho, ethnic, working-class white heroes of the era like Rocky Balboa, John Travolta's Vinnie Barbarino on *Welcome Back, Kotter*, or Tony Manero in *Saturday Night Fever*.

With viewers eager to spend their time in the *Happy Days* of the idealized past, network executives used the successful show as a launchpad for numerous spin-offs, including *Laverne & Shirley*, *Mork & Mindy*, and *Joanie Loves Chachi*. However, as *Happy Days* progressed, it strayed far from its original premise, literally "jumping the shark" in an infamous episode that inspired the modern phrase for programs that have outlived their narratives.

Happy Days did not last far into the eighties, but the nostalgia boom it started continued on in popular family comedies such as *Family Ties* and *Growing Pains*, shows that entertained Reagan-era Americans with midcentury visions of the "traditional," white, middle-class family.

Eric Jentsch

SATURDAY NIGHT LIVE AND TV'S COMEDY REBELLION

At the moment of *Saturday Night Live*'s electrifying emergence in 1975, NBC's weekend programming consisted largely of reruns of Johnny Carson's *Tonight Show* and endlessly recirculated old movies. Mainstream TV was fixated on "dealing with the problems of another generation—divorce, Valium, crabgrass, adultery."[58] For the pioneering sketch show's creators, *Saturday Night*—as it was initially called—would be a bold rebellion against this stagnation, suffused with the attitude and the edge of an underground comedy scene that had emerged far outside the high tower fortified by the three-network oligopoly. Over the course of more than fifty years, *Saturday Night Live* would go on to reinvent itself again and again in the face of dramatic industrial and cultural shifts, defending its claims to avant-gardism even as the revolutionary new comedy show coalesced into a stalwart institution itself.

Saturday Night Live's closest televisual ancestors were *Laugh-In* and *The Smothers Brothers Comedy Hour*, whose controversial cancellation about five years prior had opened up a conspicuous content vacuum for young, liberal audiences. The show's creator/producer, Lorne Michaels, had worked on high-profile comedy variety projects including *Laugh-In*, Lily Tomlin's innovative TV specials, and the short-lived *Beautiful Phyllis Diller Show*. But most of *SNL*'s original creative team hailed from outside the broadcasting industry proper, with roots in the improv scene, humor magazine editorial staffs, or early video groups making guerrilla films with handheld camcorders. While *Saturday Night Live* would not entirely reinvent the variety show (one of American entertainment's most

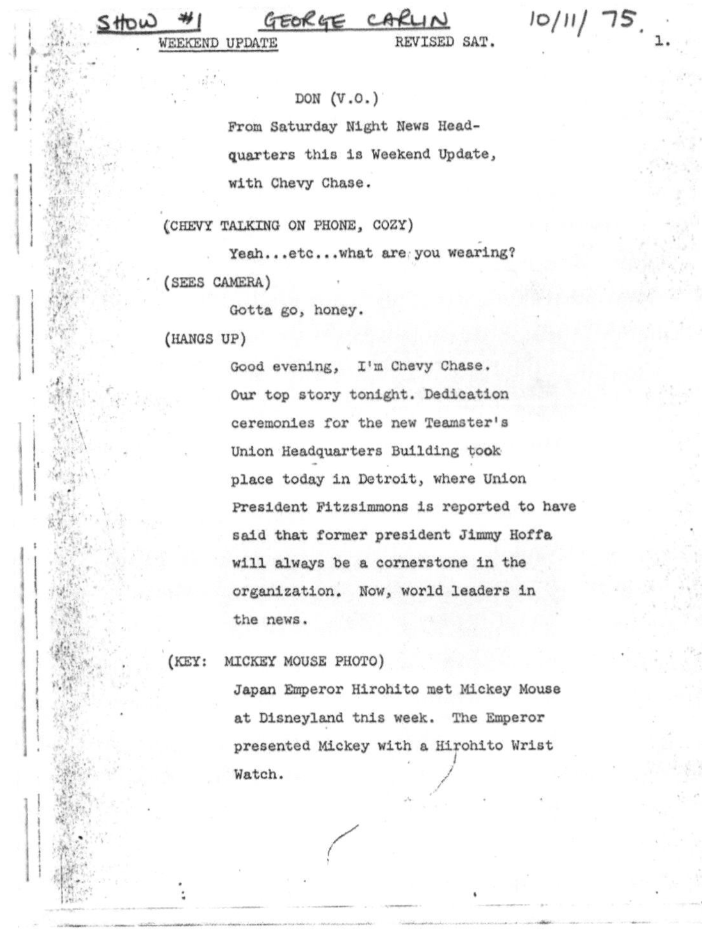

SHOW #1 GEORGE CARLIN 10/11/75.

WEEKEND UPDATE REVISED SAT. 1.

DON (V.O.)

From Saturday Night News Headquarters this is Weekend Update, with Chevy Chase.

(CHEVY TALKING ON PHONE, COZY)

Yeah...etc...what are you wearing?

(SEES CAMERA)

Gotta go, honey.

(HANGS UP)

Good evening, I'm Chevy Chase. Our top story tonight. Dedication ceremonies for the new Teamster's Union Headquarters Building took place today in Detroit, where Union President Fitzsimmons is reported to have said that former president Jimmy Hoffa will always be a cornerstone in the organization. Now, world leaders in the news.

(KEY: MICKEY MOUSE PHOTO)

Japan Emperor Hirohito met Mickey Mouse at Disneyland this week. The Emperor presented Mickey with a Hirohito Wrist Watch.

Saturday Night Live's very first "Weekend Update," October 11, 1975.

traditional forms), it did supercharge and modernize the genre with its youthful, countercultural bent and experimental attitude.

In its first iteration, the show included a crowd of Jim Henson puppets and short films by Albert Brooks, as well as sketches performed by a repertory company, the Not Ready for Primetime Players, that included Dan Aykroyd, John Belushi, Chevy Chase, Jane Curtin, Garrett Morris, Laraine Newman, and Gilda Radner among them, with head writer Michael O'Donoghue. George Carlin hosted the premiere episode on October 11, 1975, which also included the earliest iteration of *SNL*'s longest continually running sketch, "Weekend Update."

From that first episode on, *Saturday Night Live*'s history has become mythology, replete with tales about creative geniuses hitting artistic peaks, larger-than-life personalities clashing and crashing, incendiary behind-the-scenes shake-ups, and epic redemptions. Its storied Studio 8H has become hallowed ground in comedy, variously considered an incubator for the greatest talents of the past half century (from Gilda Radner to Eddie Murphy to Will Ferrell to Amy Poehler) and a pressure cooker that requires cutthroat lobbying for preciously guarded airtime. Of course, the show's most popular sketches have had enormous longevity and become a durable part of our shared cultural consciousness, from "The Church Lady," "The Californians," and "Debbie Downer" to "More Cowbell," "Black Jeopardy," and "Lazy Sunday." The most beloved have reemerged as spin-off films, including *The Blues Brothers*, *Coneheads*, and *Wayne's World*. To host the show is to reach a certain pinnacle of cultural relevance, with the coveted gig having been occupied by a who's who of Hollywood power brokers, including a running list of elite "Five-Timers" (with at least five hosting gigs on their résumés) that includes, among others, Tom Hanks, Steve Martin, Dwayne Johnson, Melissa McCarthy, and Kristen Wiig. The youngest host was a seven-year-old Drew Barrymore, while the distinction of the oldest goes

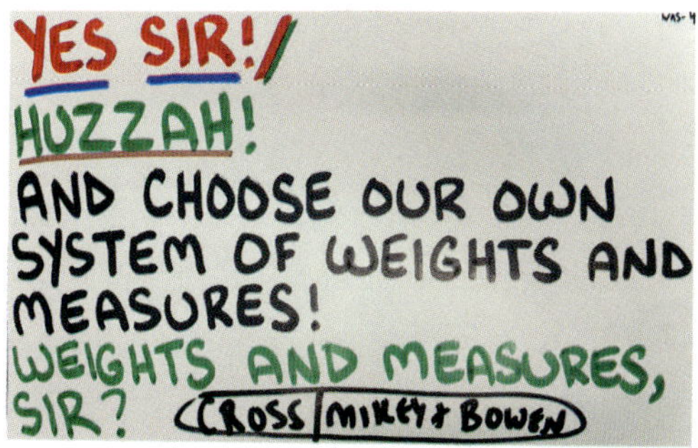

Even in a world of digital teleprompters, *Saturday Night Live* relies on handwritten cue cards. To accommodate the frenetic pace of production, which plays out across just a few long days and one nail-biting Saturday night, over 1,000 cards per week are rewritten constantly by a team of ten—sometimes up until the commercial break just before a sketch airs live. The cue cards displayed here were used during production of "Washington's Dream," a fan-favorite sketch that has logged well over 20 million views on YouTube since it debuted on the October 28, 2023 episode of SNL, hosted by Nate Bargatze.

to Betty White at a vibrant eighty-eight—a performance for which she won an Emmy.

Saturday Night Live is both an undeniable popular cultural touchstone and an institution with an uneven record that reflects, to a large extent, the broader patterns of exclusion that have troubled the entire arc of American entertainment history. For all its complexities, it may be that *Saturday Night Live*'s most enduring challenge has been to walk a tightrope as it makes claims toward edginess while falling squarely within standards of acceptability for network television's national audience. Every one of the show's nearly one thousand episodes is a snapshot of our popular culture as it reckons (imperfectly) with a moment in time.

This is never more apparent than when *Saturday Night Live* delves into politics, with some statisticians citing an "*SNL* effect" with real impacts on the viability of individual candidacies. While political impressions like Will Ferrell's George W. Bush and Tina Fey's Sarah Palin made headlines in the new millennium, Dan Aykroyd's Jimmy Carter, Jane Curtin's Nancy Reagan, and Dana Carvey's George H. W. Bush were also lightning rods in their moment. The tradition dates to Chevy Chase's relatively innocent mockery of President Gerald Ford's clumsiness, which Ford received good-naturedly when he set a precedent by appearing in a 1976 cameo on the show, signaling the value of *SNL* as a platform for politicians to connect with constituencies on a humorous, human level. Senators John McCain and Hillary Clinton, as well as Presidents Barack Obama and Donald Trump, have followed suit in more recent years. The show has never shied away from hard-hitting sociopolitical issues, and functions as a platform for the airing of perspectives on matters of global importance. It was *SNL*'s season opener three weeks after the attacks of September 11, 2001, that galvanized the nation and functioned as a vital form of catharsis, and the show has also treated issues ranging from the fall of the Berlin Wall to Three Mile Island, the Iran-Contra Affair, and Hurricane Katrina—topics that most other entertainment programs have stayed away from addressing.

Saturday Night Live's story is one of continual reinvention. Outside of very-long-running soap operas, *SNL* is one of vanishingly few shows on network television to have survived the coming of cable and streaming media. Its format has been remarkably consistent: a host's opening monologue, sketches, pretaped segments, and a musical guest. Based on one of the oldest and most regimented genres in entertainment history, the comedy-variety show, its format harkens back to the turn of the twentieth century but is also perfectly suited to the internet age, with bite-size sketches serving as ready-made fodder for social media circulation.

Laura LaPlaca

CHEECH MARIN'S *BORN IN EAST LA*

Hardly anyone would have predicted that Richard Anthony "Cheech" Marin, with a career LAPD cop as a father, would become a stoner comedy legend. Marin went from being a Chicano youth on the path to priesthood to embracing the late sixties counterculture and dodging the Vietnam War draft by moving to Canada. While in Canada, Marin met Tommy Chong, and the comedic duo Cheech and Chong was born. As a duo, Marin and Chong chronicled their misadventures as cannabis enthusiasts through stand-up routines, skits, songs, and films. Their 1978 feature film *Up in Smoke* cemented their status as counterculture icons. Between film projects and stand-up gigs, the duo also recorded and released several comedy albums. Among them was the 1985 comedy album *Get Out of My Room*, which featured the single "Born in East LA" as the opening track.

The "Born in East LA" song was a parody of Bruce Springsteen's popular 1984 hit "Born in the U.S.A." As Marin tells it, he came up with the song while he was sitting at his kitchen table reading an *LA Times* article about a local kid who was caught in an immigration raid and mistakenly deported to Mexico despite being a U.S. citizen. As he read the article, Springsteen's "Born in the U.S.A." came on the radio and inspired the parody of the song. The song—and its accompanying music video—appeared often on MTV, helping the song peak at number forty-eight on the *Billboard* Hot 100 chart. Soon after the song's release, Cheech and Chong parted ways to pursue independent projects. Marin decided to expand the "Born in East LA" story further by writing, directing, and acting in the *Born in East LA* movie.

The 1987 comedy film follows a Chicano mechanic named Rudy Robles—played by Marin—as he is caught without suitable identification during an immigration raid at a toy factory in downtown Los Angeles. Robles is detained and later deported to Tijuana, where he struggles to find his way back across the border by hook or by crook. At the time of the film's production, President Ronald Reagan signed into law the Immigration Reform and Control Act. The law made it illegal for businesses to knowingly hire undocumented workers. *Born in East LA* deceptively wove social commentary of U.S. immigration policy into a comedy film. Drawing from Marin's experiences questioning his own identity as a Chicano, Mexican American, and Los Angeles native, the film "critiques the notion that Chicanos are foreigners, not 'real' Americans, and so must carry documentation to prove their citizenship."[59]

This groundbreaking film brought issues of identity, immigration, citizenship, and belonging to the fore—forcing audiences to think and question even as they laughed. In the film, Marin as Rudy Robles endures an interview with an immigration officer who questions his identity, his citizenship claim, and why his English is so good. The paradox of the film is that Robles is a third-generation Chicano born and raised in East LA who can barely speak Spanish, yet the U.S. immigration officers want to send him "back where he came from." The immigration officers think Robles, profiled as a "bean in a beanbag," belongs in Mexico because he looks Mexican. For many Chicanx and Latinx people living in the United States, this is a reality that they must regularly contend with. After all, what does it mean to look or sound like you belong in the United States?

Another of *Born in East LA*'s iconic scenes shows Rudy Robles leading a mass border crossing of Mexicans into the United States. This scene played on the anxieties of unchecked "illegal" immigration that were the justification for the militarization of the border and the criminalization of undocumented people (particularly workers) throughout the eighties and nineties. As immigration and migration from Latin America surged toward the end of the twentieth century, the political discourse positioned migration as a problem to be solved. *Born in East LA* complicated this problem by subverting the "illegal" narrative and underscoring the entrenched racism and prejudice that exists in the U.S. immigration system. Cheech Marin transformed Hollywood's "slapstick, one-dimensional Chicano characters" by using humor to "expose the stereotype as racist."[60]

Comedian Paul Rodriguez (who also played a supporting role in the film as Robles's cousin Javier) called *Born in East LA* the litmus test of being Chicano, pointing to the film's popularity within the Chicanx community. Marin's film exposes the identity crisis that comes along with being "ni de aquí, ni de allá" (not from here nor from there), even for those Mexican Americans and Chicanxs whose presence predates the Treaty of Guadalupe Hidalgo.

Ashley Oliva Mayor

THE MUPPETS TAKE AMERICAN HISTORY

The original Kermit puppet, made by Henson in 1955 from his mother's wool coat, a ping-pong ball, and a pair of jeans. Kermit has appeared in most Muppet productions from *Sam and Friends* (1955) to the most recent movie *Muppets Most Wanted* (2014) and series *Muppets Now* (2020).

In the spring of 1955, nineteen-year-old Jim Henson stitched together pieces of his mother's green felt coat, painted two halves of a ping-pong ball with crossed black eyes, and created a puppet he simply called Kermit. Little did he know that this scrappy sock puppet would go on to become one of the most recognizable and best-loved characters in American history. Through television series, films, theme park attractions, video games, and social media, the Muppets conquered American culture with their signature brand of madcap, irreverent humor. Henson's boundless creativity and absurdist sensibility made his Muppets a popular sensation at a time of great cultural change; their expressions of optimism, tolerance, and belief in the power of friendship has made an enduring impression on American history.

Born in Leland, Mississippi, Henson spent his formative years in the Maryland suburbs of Washington, D.C., where his father worked for the federal government. An imaginative and creative young man, Jim loved comics (especially Walt Kelly's zany character ensemble

Pogo) and television, where he was drawn to the silly, subversive humor of Sid Caesar and the visually experimental antics of Ernie Kovacs. Determined to work in the exciting new medium, Jim studied set design, took classes in visual arts at the University of Maryland, and even joined a puppetry club, which led to his first job in television—as a puppeteer. After a brief stint on local daytime variety shows, Jim was offered a show of his own: *Sam and Friends* premiered on Washington's NBC affiliate WRC in 1955.[61]

For *Sam and Friends*, Henson and his partner Jane Nebel (soon to become his wife) created a coterie of fantastic and funny-looking puppets with names like Mushmellon, Icky Gunk, Professor Madcliffe, Yorick, and, most memorably, Kermit. The puppets were soft, simple, and flexible, and operated by hand and rod rather than strings, making them expressive, emotive, and reactive as earlier puppets and marionettes had been too wooden to accomplish. He called them Muppets—either a portmanteau of "marionette" and "puppet" or a play on "moppet," an archaic word describing an endearing youngster. *Sam and Friends* sketches were inventive yet simple—puppets would lip sync and clown to popular songs, parody genre film and television, or engage in banter and special effects tricks that owed a great debt to Ernie Kovacs's broadcast experimentation. Henson intuitively understood that television allowed a new kind of closeness with the audience; by using monitors on set puppeteers saw exactly what the viewer would see, allowing them to interact freely without the traditional theater proscenium arch and

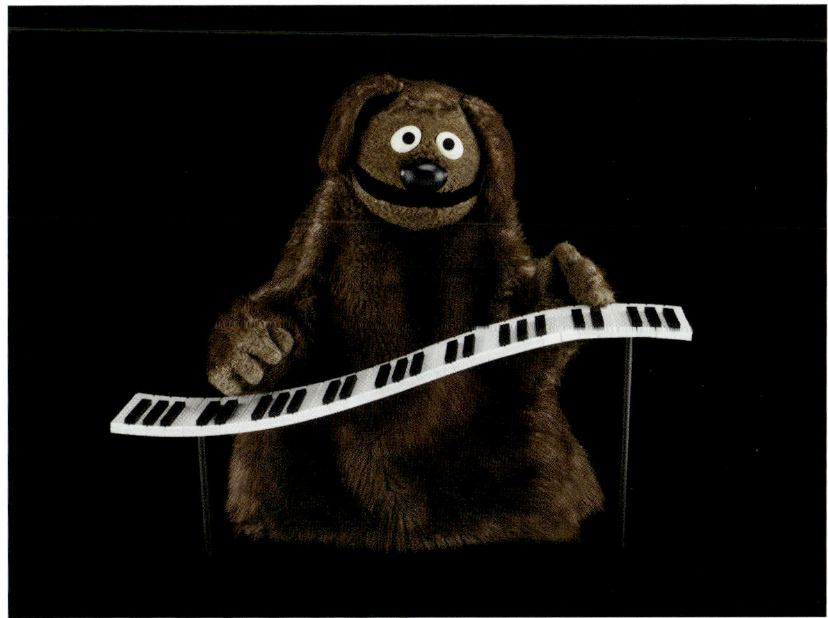

Originally designed in 1962 for a series of commercials for Purina Dog Chow, Rowlf became the first national Muppet star with his regular appearances on *The Jimmy Dean Show*. This is one of the first two Rowlf puppets, made by Muppet builder Don Sahlin from puppet fleece expertly stitched to hide seams and with large eyes and nose positioned in a characteristic "magic triangle" that was essential to the Muppet look.

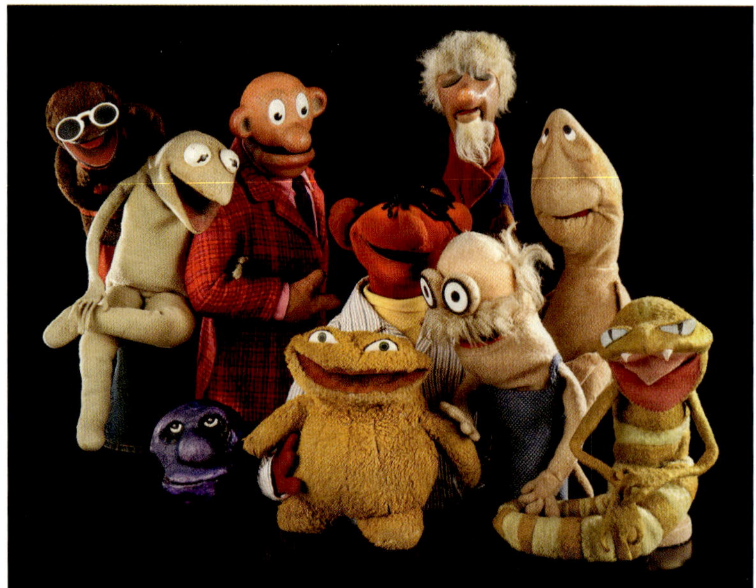

Sam and Friends was the first Muppet production, a five-minute show that aired on the NBC station WRC-TV in Washington, D.C., from 1955 to 1961. The series featured a cast of hand puppets created by Jim Henson and his future wife Jane Nebel; Kermit, Sam, Harry the Hipster, and the rest of the madcap characters lip-synched to popular songs, acted in surreal comedy sketches, and changed the face of American puppetry.

stage that separated the audience from the action.[62]

Before long, the Muppets were appearing on *Ed Sullivan* and *The Tonight Show* and gaining national exposure. The gravelly voiced, genial dog Muppet Rowlf so impressed country musician Jimmy Dean that he made him a wisecracking sidekick on his eponymous variety show (1963–1966). Henson conquered the advertising world as well, creating memorable and enormously popular spokespuppets for Wilkins Coffee and LaChoy Foods for television commercials with the gleefully anarchic humor of *Sam and Friends*. In the coffee ads, when Wontkins announces that he doesn't drink Wilkins Coffee, Henson delighted in finding creative ways for Wilkins to blow him up, drown him, or unleash ravenous creatures to devour the hapless abstainer. The human-sized LaChoy Dragon extolled the virtues of the dragon fire-cooked (actually steamed) packaged Chinese food while clumsily destroying supermarket displays with his flailing tail.[63] This kind of marketing was part of a cultural revolution in advertising in the sixties—a move away from the serious,

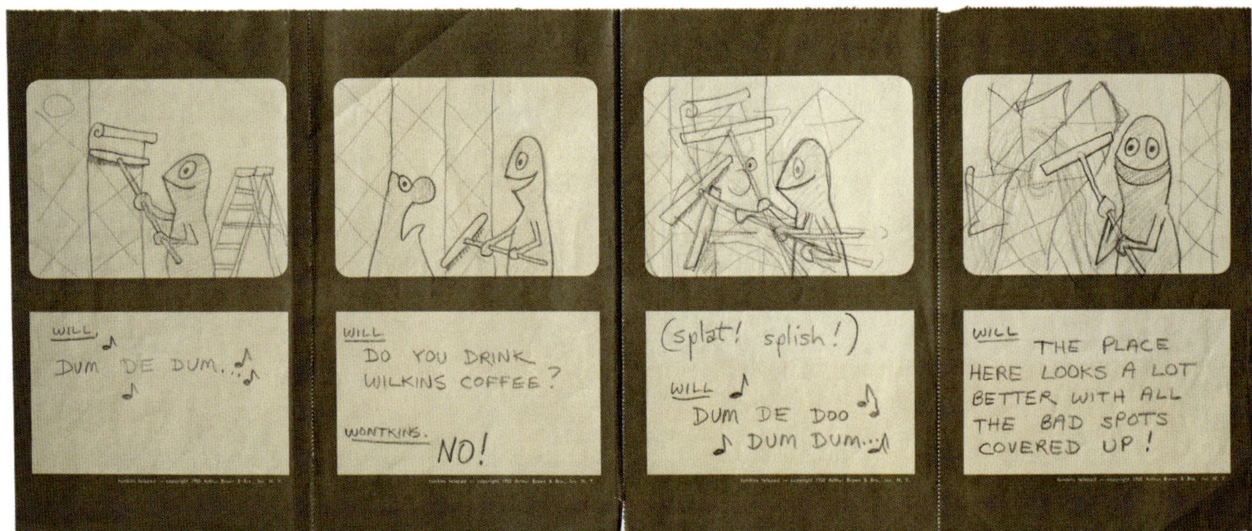

Jim Henson helped revolutionize advertising in the 1960s, making television commercials infused with his hip and absurd sense of humor. Muppet characters like Wilkins and Wontkins, shown in this hand-drawn storyboard, engaged in violent physical humor, often poking fun at the product they were selling and the concept of advertising itself.

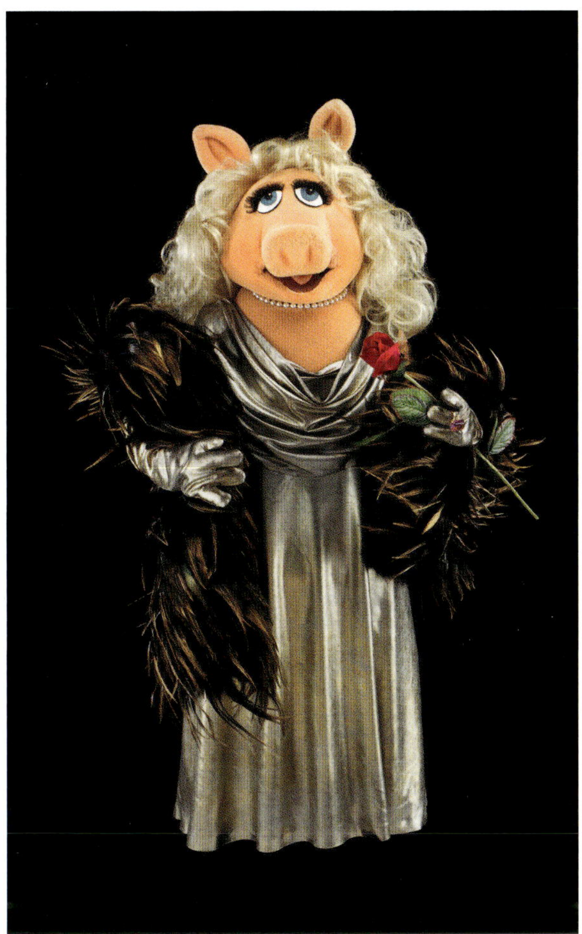

The glamorous and self-possessed diva Miss Piggy quickly became one of the most popular Muppets after taking a starring role in *The Muppet Show* and *Muppet Movie*. Though she was performed by a man, Frank Oz, Piggy's independence and ambition have made her a feminist icon—Gloria Steinem presented her with the Sackler Center First Award from the Elizabeth A. Sackler Center for Feminist Art at the Brooklyn Museum in 2015.

direct pitch to a more hip and freewheeling commercial world of the late twentieth century. "Till then, [advertising] agencies believed that the hard sell was the only way to get their message over on television. We took a very different approach," Henson said of his advertising career. "We tried to sell things by making people laugh."[64]

Those captivating commercials brought Henson to the attention of Joan Ganz Cooney, a producer whose Children's Television Workshop was developing a new children's series with an ambitious agenda. *Sesame Street* (1969–present) would harness the enormous reach of the medium and the tools of the advertising world to use television to teach as well as entertain. Henson created Muppet characters aligned with the developmental and educational aims of the show: Big Bird shows it's okay to ask questions, Oscar the Grouch prompts lessons about conflict and tolerance, and mismatched roommates Bert and Ernie demonstrate friendship and understanding. The Muppets were a key factor in *Sesame Street*'s success, and the show's research staff found that children paid more attention to the program when Muppets were on-screen alongside the human cast.[65] The sense of scale and grounding that humans introduced to sketches by comparison to the often fuzzy and strange creatures surrounding them was key to the humor of these interactions and one of the things that distinguished the Muppets from other forms of puppetry.

The Muppet Show (1976–1981) brought Henson's creatures to an even wider audience, becoming an international hit. An homage to vaudeville, the series was set in an old theater with the Muppet cast shown working with human guest stars behind the scenes and onstage to put on a variety show. The characters created or repurposed for the show have become the core cast of Muppet films, television shows, and other forms of media in the years since: brash diva Miss Piggy, struggling bear comedian Fozzie, eccentric performance artist Gonzo, as well as Rowlf and myriad others. In the middle of all the madness was Kermit, everyman ringmaster desperately trying to ensure the show would go on. The show drew inspiration from countercultural comedy of the era including *Laugh-In* and *The Smothers Brothers Comedy Hour*, presenting comedy sketches, performances to popular songs, and rapid-fire jokes in "a universe of generally benign absurdity."[66] Miss Piggy became the breakout star, her aggressive pursuit of stardom, nontraditional relationship with romantic partner Kermit, and self-possessed independence making her a third-wave feminist icon.[67] Indeed, the topsy-turvy world of *The Muppet Show* was all about transgression and subversion of norms, with fourth-wall-breaking jokes, drag performance on- and offstage, and romance across species lines. The diverse cast of misfits and oddballs find community and equality in the shared dream of entertaining others.[68]

The Muppet Movie (1979) was the first of several films to star the puppet troupe but was perhaps the best distillation of the spirit and comic sensibility of Henson's creations. The story loosely mirrored Henson's life trajectory through Kermit's journey, leaving the swamps of the American South to follow his dream to work in entertainment, picking up friends and overcoming adversity along the way. True to the Muppet sensibility, the film is full of surreal humor, unbound optimism, countercultural resistance to conformity, and meta-commentary on the movies themselves. At the film's climax, Kermit faces down an assassin hired by the fried frog leg magnate determined to make him a spokesman for his fast-food chain (it's a long story) and gives a speech that's close to mission statement for the Muppets: "I've got a dream, too. But it's about singing and dancing and making people happy. That's the kind of dream that gets better the more people you share it with. And, well . . . I've found a whole bunch of friends who have the same dream. And it kind of makes us like a family."[69]

Henson created a batch of iconic Muppet characters for the groundbreaking children's television series *Sesame Street* (1969–present) to help teach kids the values of diversity and inclusion. The cookie-obsessed blue monster, classically mismatched roommates, and misanthropic trash can dweller all look and think differently but are still valued members of the neighborhood, prompting lessons in tolerance and understanding.

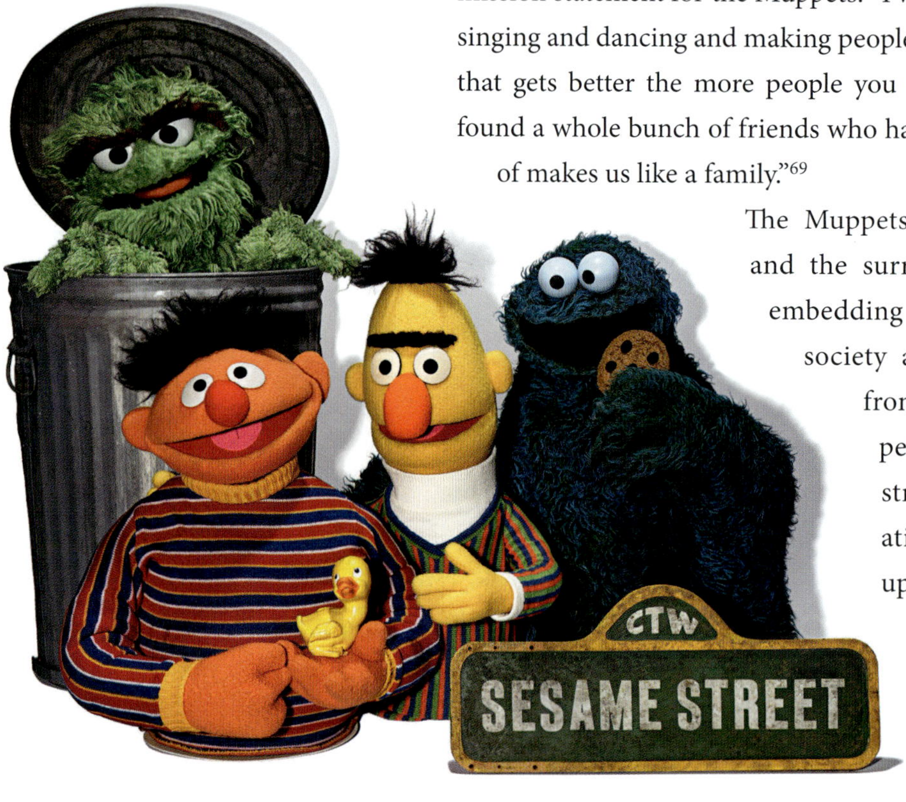

The Muppets celebrate absurdity, silliness, and the surreality of life, often implicitly embedding commentary on contemporary society and culture. In each iteration from *Sam and Friends* to the Muppets' recent YouTube videos and streaming series, Henson's creations have used humor to blow up (sometimes quite literally) the selfish, greedy, and closed-minded aspects of American society, celebrating the power of friendship, imagination, and determination to chase dreams to build a better world.[70] The Henson family made a gift of historically significant Muppets, including *Sam and Friends*, *Sesame Street*, and *The Muppet Show* puppets, to the National Museum of American History in 2013. Among these, one object stands above all: the one that started it all, the original Kermit puppet, handmade by Jim Henson over sixty-five years ago.

Ryan Lintelman

"DO WHAT YOU WANT TO DO": *IN LIVING COLOR*

In Living Color debuted on Sunday, April 15, 1990, in a 9:30 P.M. time slot just following the upstart Fox network's smash hit shows *The Simpsons* and *Married . . . with Children*. Five months later, the sketch series won the Emmy for Outstanding Variety, Music or Comedy Series, triumphing in a crowded field of nominees that included *Saturday Night Live*, *The Tracey Ullman Show*, *Late Night with David Letterman*, and *The Arsenio Hall Show*. With creator-producer-writer Keenen Ivory Wayans also presiding as the show's host, *In Living Color* was a powerful platform for giving voice to the Black experience, but also a proving ground for sketch comedy's unique ability to speak multivocally about social issues while being incorporated into the mainstream cultural zeitgeist. Even as *In Living Color* creatively leveraged a newfound flexibility of form and content offered by cable TV, its production offices became the site of vitriolic clashes between artists and executives deadlocked in censorship brawls that constantly threatened to compromise the show's integrity.

When Fox approached him with an offer to create a TV series, Keenen Ivory Wayans was known primarily as a cinematic auteur with two searing satirical films (*Hollywood Shuffle* and *I'm Gonna Git You Sucka*) recently having debuted to popular and critical acclaim. After years of paying his dues as a writer, producer, and stand-up comedian, it was not a given that Wayans would embrace a pivot to television, but the

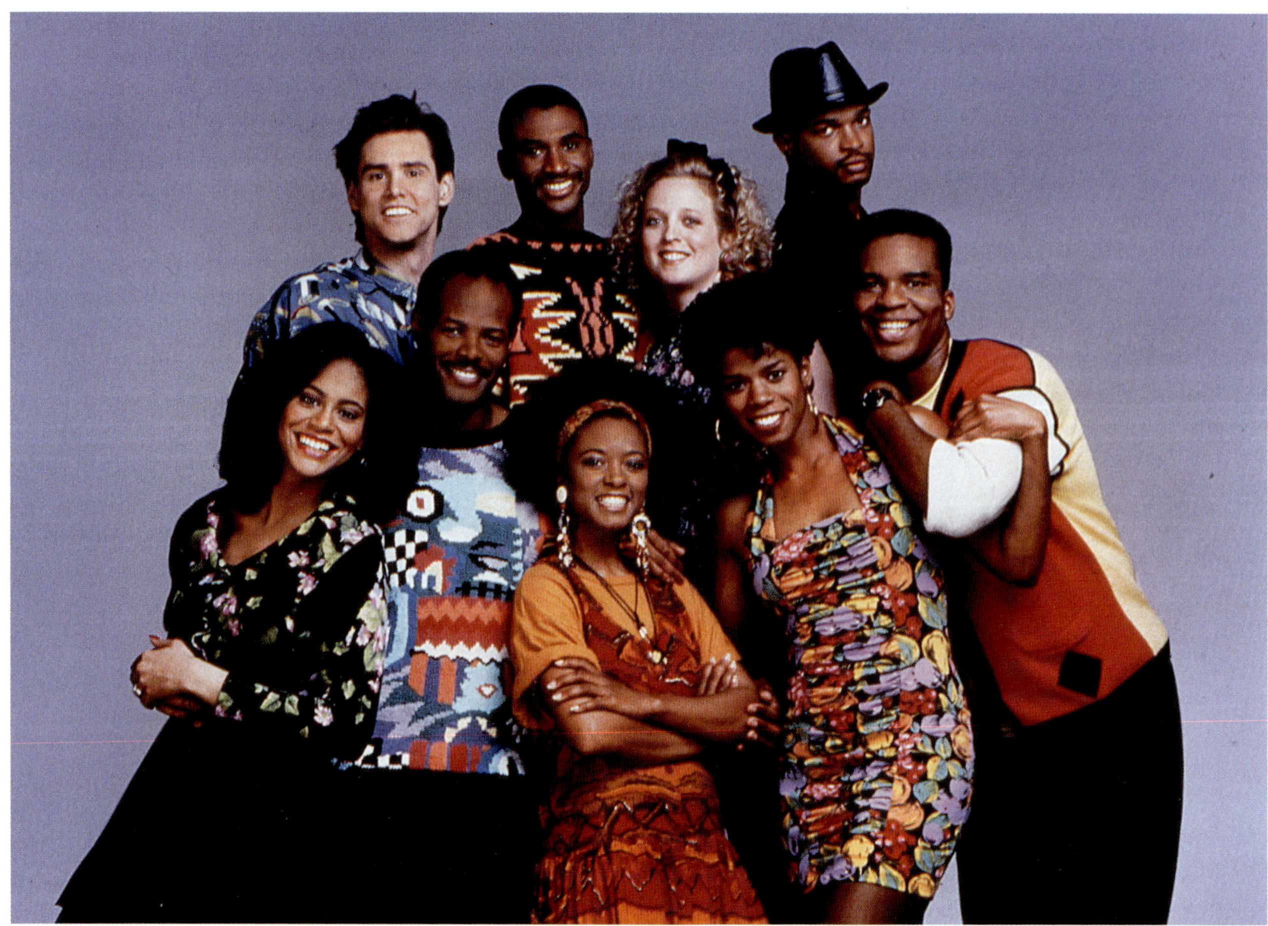

new cable network's promise of total creative freedom was ultimately too good to refuse. Network television's historical failure to respect the artistic visions of Black comedians was all too well-known: the 1970s had seen multiple high-profile battles waged by talents with considerable industry clout, most notoriously witnessed when Richard Pryor's show was sent to an early cancellation after only four episodes, but also as multihyphenate artists like Flip Wilson and Redd Foxx took principled stances about the authorship of their work, including—and especially—when their shows won in the ratings. It was clear that the new Fox network's goal was to disrupt TV's status quo, and so Wayans ably answered the call.

The sketch show's title was a throwback to a retro network tagline ("Brought to you in living color"), but was also a reference to Hollywood's history of systemic exclusion. *In Living Color*'s original repertory company would feature a deep bench of talents, including Wayans's siblings Damon, Shawn, and Kim, as well as David Alan Grier, Tommy Davidson, Jim Carrey, T'Keyah Crystal Keymáh, Kim Coles, and Kelly

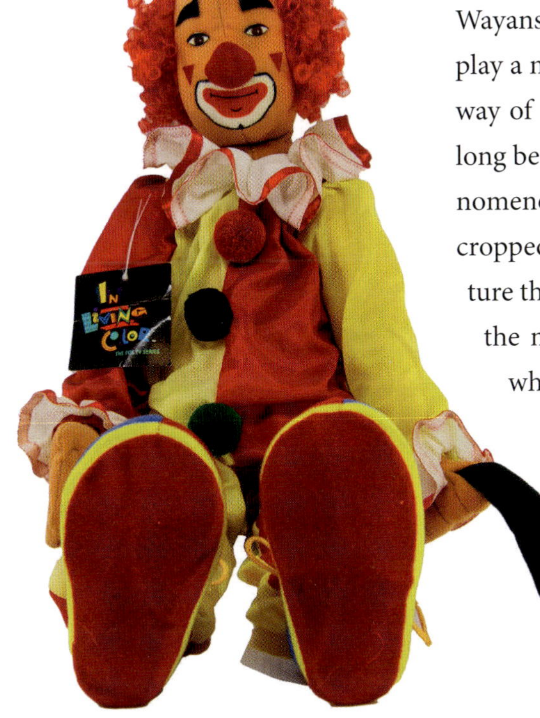

Homey the Clown, embodied here as a commercially produced collectible, voiced frustrations about poverty, racism, and systemic inequality through comedy—becoming a cultural symbol of resistance.

Coffield. (Later additions to the cast would include Jamie Foxx, Marlon Wayans, Ali Wentworth, and Steve Park, among others.) And it would play a major role in the mainstreaming of hip-hop culture, primarily by way of its troupe of Fly Girls, led by Rosie Perez. Though dancers had long been a staple of variety television, the Fly Girls were a cultural phenomenon; donning street couture like designer combat boots and cropped jackets, they brought deep connections to New York club culture that furnished the show with an authentic tone that was keyed into the most innovative musicians and artists of the moment, many of whom (like Queen Latifah and Public Enemy) appeared on *In Living Color*'s stage. For most Americans, and certainly for most of middle America, *In Living Color* was the avenue by which nineties street culture melded into popular culture.

From the very first episode, *In Living Color* possessed the core elements that would define its vibrant, energetic, edgy brand: the electric theme song that exhorted viewers to "do what you want to do," the Fly Girls, and anarchic, self-reflexive sketches like "Homeboy Shopping Network" and "Men on Film." The show was an immediate ratings boon for Fox, not only because it drew large numbers in general but because it performed phenomenally well with a desirable eighteen- to thirty-four-year-old demographic. The younger generation, an audience share that had been notoriously challenging to capture, latched on to recurring characters like Kim Wayans's Lil' Magic, Jim Carrey's Fire Marshal Bill, and Damon Wayans's Homey the Clown, whose catchphrase—"Homey don't play that"—became part of the lexicon of the nineties. *In Living Color*'s humor was often broad and playful, and many of the scenarios were adapted from the Wayans siblings' lively childhood games. But the content of the show's more biting sociopolitical commentaries, even if they were called "amiably lethal" by contemporaneous critics, sounded alarm bells for Fox executives.[71]

Only seven episodes into the series, it was already outwardly apparent that censorship issues were plaguing the creative team: "It's not very difficult to sense some of the behind-the-scenes wars that are undoubtedly being waged about content and the extent of permissiveness regarding language and sensitive subjects. Doing what you want to do still has its limits on commercial television."[72] Wayans and his team, wearied of justifying their creative decisions to no avail, developed strategies for subverting standards and practices, writing intentionally inflammatory material to distract the censors or heightening the seditiousness of first

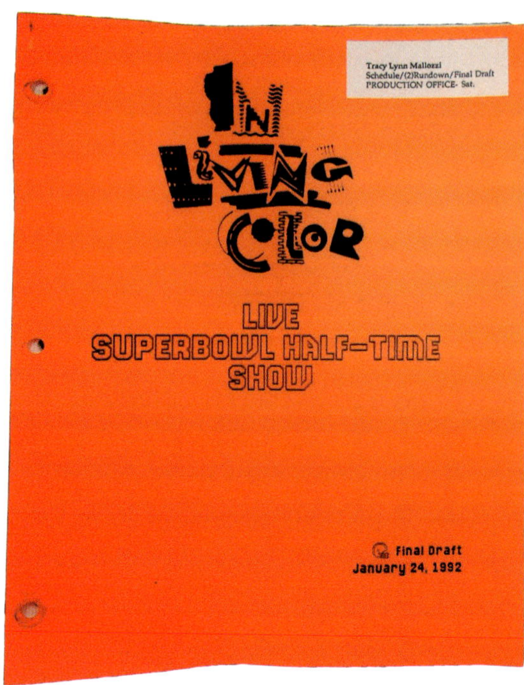

Tracy Lynn Mallozzi
Schedule/(2)Rundown/Final Draft
PRODUCTION OFFICE- Sat.

IN LIVING COLOR

LIVE
SUPERBOWL HALF-TIME
SHOW

Final Draft
January 24, 1992

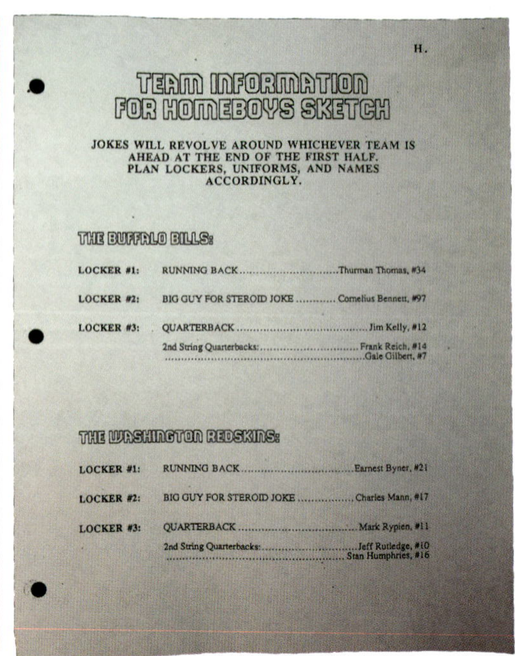

H.

TEAM INFORMATION
FOR HOMEBOYS SKETCH

JOKES WILL REVOLVE AROUND WHICHEVER TEAM IS AHEAD AT THE END OF THE FIRST HALF. PLAN LOCKERS, UNIFORMS, AND NAMES ACCORDINGLY.

THE BUFFALO BILLS:

LOCKER #1: RUNNING BACK..........Thurman Thomas, #34

LOCKER #2: BIG GUY FOR STEROID JOKE..........Cornelius Bennett, #97

LOCKER #3: QUARTERBACK..........Jim Kelly, #12
2nd String Quarterbacks:..........Frank Reich, #14
..........Gale Gilbert, #7

THE WASHINGTON REDSKINS:

LOCKER #1: RUNNING BACK..........Earnest Byner, #21

LOCKER #2: BIG GUY FOR STEROID JOKE..........Charles Mann, #17

LOCKER #3: QUARTERBACK..........Mark Rypien, #11
2nd String Quarterbacks:..........Jeff Rutledge, #10
..........Stan Humphries, #16

In 1992, the *In Living Color* creative team produced a live "Super Bowl Halftime Party" that drew nearly 25 million viewers away from the game. Featuring football-themed comedy sketches delivered in the show's signature no-holds-barred style, the special revealed a growing demand for edgier, more contemporary entertainment among mainstream audiences. Its unexpected ratings success shook up the TV industry . . . and prompted the NFL to book Michael Jackson for its halftime show the following year.

drafts so that they could pretend to compromise it back to its originally intended tone. Regime changes at Fox, the departure of frustrated core cast members—namely, Damon Wayans—and the entrenchment of censors who more aggressively attempted to seize creative oversight ultimately drowned *In Living Color*'s vitality and resonance in layers of red tape. By the time the show entered its fourth season, Wayans had reached a point of resignation, and *In Living Color*, while occasionally recapturing some of its original brilliance, had been diluted almost beyond recognition.

Laura LaPlaca

WHAT'S THE DEAL WITH *SEINFELD*?

Kramer's girlfriend is a "low talker," and Jerry doesn't want to ask her to repeat everything she's saying at dinner, so he decides to politely nod his head. He doesn't realize that he's agreed to wear a new shirt she designed in an appearance on *The Today Show*, or that the outrageous shirt has puffy sleeves, ruffles, and prominent pearl buttons. By the time he realizes his mistake it's too late: the shirt is selling well based on his upcoming appearance and he's forced to wear it, even though he thinks it makes him look like a pirate. Host Bryant Gumbel agrees, mocking Jerry, who fesses up he thinks it's the stupidest shirt he's ever seen, leading the low talker to loudly curse him on air. "THAT I heard," Jerry says.[73]

"The Puffy Shirt" was one of the most memorable but also one of the most archetypal episodes of *Seinfeld*, the "show about nothing" that captured the zeitgeist of 1990s American urban life. Creators Jerry Seinfeld and Larry David mined the minutiae of everyday social interactions, personal frustrations, and city living for comic gold. Manhattanites Jerry, his ex-girlfriend Elaine Benes (Julia Louis-Dreyfus), friend George Costanza (Jason Alexander), and apartment neighbor Cosmo Kramer (Michael Richards) broke the mold for sitcom protagonists. The misanthropic characters were selfish and egotistical, uncommitted to family or romantic partners, ambivalent about community, and frequently scheming, with their chief concerns—dating, money, and maintaining appearances—often driving them to make socially unacceptable or morally reprehensible decisions. Yet this modern comedy of manners became one of the most successful and influential sitcoms in television history, offering viewers a cathartic exploration, if not excoriation, of the rapidly changing social mores and cultural milieu of urban, middle-class American life.

"It's a puffy shirt. I feel ridiculous in it and I think it's the stupidest shirt I've ever seen, to be perfectly honest with you." Jerry Seinfeld wore this shirt in one of the most memorable episodes of the ultimate "water cooler show," creating a new cultural vernacular for the 1990s.

The series had an inauspicious start, the product of NBC's interest in fledgling stand-up comedian Jerry Seinfeld, who often shared the stage at New York comedy club Catch a Rising Star with fellow observational comic Larry David. The duo developed a pitch for a series exploring the absurdity of the mundane, a group of thirtysomething friends in New York who more than resembled themselves (Jerry being Jerry, George Costanza embodying the darker parts of David's personality, and

"But I don't want to be a pirate!"
—Jerry Seinfeld

Kramer named for David's real-life neighbor) navigating modern American life. Plotlines would be pulled from the writers' life experiences, though dialed up and exaggerated. The show would break the mold of the traditional sitcom, with dark, cynical characters unmoored from suburban family life, edgy sarcastic humor, and a subversive lack of feel-good wrap-ups. Larry David's rules for the show were "no hugging, no learning." And each episode's divergent plotlines had to dovetail into a single explosive ending.[74]

NBC executives were perplexed by the show. Network president Brandon Tartikoff reportedly asked, "Who will want to see Jews wandering around New York acting neurotic?"[75] It was unusual in almost every way, from its opening—with Seinfeld making a few observational jokes in a comedy club while the series' bass slap theme song meandered—to its location shots and single-camera format. But critics got the appeal of the show before NBC did: "Like real life, but with better dialogue," Kit Boss wrote in the *Seattle Times*.[76] *Seinfeld* was a modest ratings success until its fourth season, when viewership boomed with a number of now-iconic episodes like "The Bubble Boy," "The Junior Mint," and "The Contest," the latter a censor-baiting story about the main characters competing to outlast each other as "master of my domain."[77]

As the keystone of NBC's "Must See TV" Thursday night lineup, *Seinfeld* became the archetype of the "water cooler show," each episode provoking conversations the next day about the latest Kramer scheme, George humiliation, Elaine date, or Jerry turn of phrase. Indeed, *Seinfeld* might be most remarkable for its contributions to the American cultural vernacular, with the show's catchphrases instantly becoming common parlance, as with "master of your domain," "yadda, yadda, yadda," and "no soup for you!" But the show also probed the meaning and power of words, especially amid the heated debate about political correctness in the early 1990s, which inspired the episode "The Cigar Store Indian," in which Jerry is foiled in his romantic pursuit of American Indian Winona by his frequent and inadvertent use of phrases she finds offensive, "ticket scalper," "making a reservation," and "Indian giver" among them.[78]

The 1993 episode "The Outing" earned a GLAAD Media Award for Outstanding Comedy Episode for its storyline involving a reporter misunderstanding Jerry and George to be in a gay relationship. While attempting to deny the misconception without appearing homophobic, the two condition their denials with "not that there's anything wrong with that," coining a new catchphrase that seemed to perfectly capture straight

"No hugging, no learning."
—Larry David's rules for* Seinfeld *writers

liberals' cautious and lukewarm support for the LGBTQ community. The episode was a rare depiction of homosexuality as a matter of fact, rather than the butt of the joke, on network television at that time; the joke was instead on the discomfort experienced by these purported allies.[79]

Despite its characters' misanthropy, civility usually triumphs over the characters' basest impulses in the end, especially as illustrated in the 1998 series finale, which sees Jerry, Elaine, George, and Kramer imprisoned for their callous disregard of a robbery in progress, not to mention the litany of past abuses they're subjected to having read into public record during the court trial by character witnesses including the "Soup Nazi," the low talker, and Babu Bhatt.[80] As Kramer tells Jerry in the episode "The Face Painter," "Good manners are the glue of society."[81]

Ryan Lintelman

3

Comedy PROVOKES CONVERSATIONS

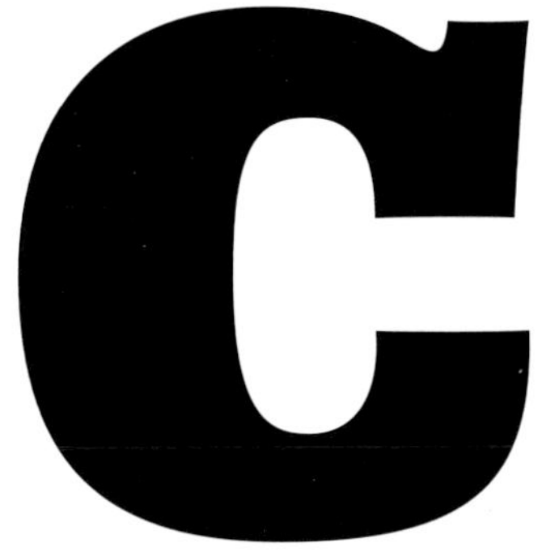

omedy can make us uncomfortable, laughter often signals shock, and jokes can be formidable weapons. In the hands of bold artists like Lenny Bruce, Richard Pryor, or Joan Rivers, well-crafted punchlines have been gateways to disarming, honest, culture-shifting conversations. In this chapter, we're thinking through comedy's vital historical role in provoking public discourse about matters of national importance: our right to freedom of speech, the structural inequities wrought by racism, the subjection of women by a patriarchal society, the true costs of human conflict. It's heavy stuff, distilled by comedians with unique powers of observation, and the unbridled courage to speak truth to power.

We'll introduce you to a lineage of truth-tellers and change makers who have shaped the very fabric of our society, from the turn of the twentieth century to the present day. It was 1927, for example, when Mae West, the wisecracking bombshell of stage and screen, was arrested by the New York Police Department's Vice Squad. The cause: her audacious new play *Sex*, which drew huge crowds and sparked debates about the representation of women in popular media. Most concerning for hand-wringing morality police was how West's work furnished people with social scripts for examining their own sexual agency—a topic almost never broached in the public sphere at the time. A quarter century later, in 1952, Lucille Ball challenged prevailing taboos when news of her pregnancy sent shockwaves through the network that aired her phenomenally popular sitcom *I Love Lucy*. The show narrowly escaped cancellation before Ball leveraged her considerable influence to incorporate her pregnancy into prime-time programming—an unprecedented move in an era when married couples were forbidden from sharing a bed on the air. An episode that culminated in the birth of Lucy's son shattered all ratings records, helping to normalize the portrayal of women's bodies, and their lived experiences, on mainstream TV.

Comedians have long been at the vanguard in exposing the ideological machinations of American news media and government bodies. At the close of the tumultuous sixties, as the Vietnam War raged and the fight for civil rights unfurled, *The Smothers Brothers Comedy Hour* was yanked from the airwaves after its stars' outspoken antiwar stance and trenchant critique of government hypocrisy rendered them cultural lightning rods. CBS fired the comedy duo under pressure from advertisers and political groups, but Tommy and Dick Smothers, who had given voice to a generation of disaffected youth, sued the network and won, catalyzing national discourse about the limits of censorship and the power of television to shape public opinion. In the early twenty-first century, *The Daily Show* with Jon Stewart assumed this mantle, speaking urgently to activate a new generation of young people who had grown weary of traditional news media. The show drew on humor to ignite critical engagement with urgent issues ranging from climate change to global human rights atrocities.

The craft of stand-up comedy has been one of the most effective and flexible platforms for communicating and critiquing American identity politics, in large part because it is an art form that was forged from the ashes of vaudeville, with its melting pot of perspectives and experiences. Moms Mabley, who honed her craft on the Chitlin' Circuit in the 1930s, was a key architect of the form who gained widespread recognition by using humor to speak about and across profound divisions in a deeply segregated America. In landmark appearances at venues like Harlem's Apollo Theater and Carnegie Hall, Mabley's sharp, candid humor struck at the heart of entrenched issues like systemic racism, gender inequity, and sexism. Into the later twentieth century, stand-ups like Charlie Hill brought mainstream visibility to marginalized voices. Hill's 1977 breakout performance on *The Tonight Show* stage cast light on the enduringly unjust legacies of colonialism, generational poverty, and historical trauma in Native communities—issues that were often misrepresented within, or entirely absent from, the national discourse.

Throughout these pages you'll explore how comedy has played an important role in driving the cultural conversations that inform the American experience, often emerging in force during moments of upheaval. In times of crisis or profound reckoning, comedians offer frameworks for organizing and understanding our world. Their work reveals nuances that might otherwise remain opaque to us, and they help us make sense of our messy, contested, ever-evolving social order. At an even more basic—and therefore perhaps more profound—level, comedy offers us a shared space for confronting our deepest divisions. It's an inherently communal art that forces our common vulnerabilities to the surface in a form of collective catharsis.

Introduction by Laura LaPlaca

MAE WEST: "AS HOT AN ISSUE AS HITLER"

When Mae West swaggered on to stages and screens with a shockingly frank, confident, and outrageous take on female sexuality and its power, she put the final nail in the coffin of Victorian morality and decorum. Though she first gained notoriety for the censor-baiting Broadway plays she wrote in the 1920s, it was her 1930s film career that made her the biggest star in the world, for a time the film industry's highest paid actor and a potent provocateur. At a time of great social and cultural upheaval, West modeled a strikingly modern form of liberated, powerful womanhood with a saucy, sexually voracious comic persona that made her, in the words of a *Variety* reporter in 1933, "as hot an issue as Hitler."[1]

Growing up in Brooklyn in the early 1900s, Mary Jane West was fascinated by beautiful and confident women of the vaudeville stage and began performing at the age of sixteen. Working the burlesque and vaudeville circuits through the 1910s, West began to develop a unique stage persona that combined the nonconformist audacity of female impersonators like Julian Eltinge, the subversive wordplay and irreverent humor of Bert Williams, the salacious swagger of musicians like Eva Tanguay and Mamie Smith, and the stylish opulence of actress Lillian Russell and the *Ziegfeld Follies*. West earned a reputation as a "freak performer" with her sexually suggestive dances, rapid-fire delivery of double-entendre-laden bawdy banter, and irreverent impersonations. She was also an avid explorer and student of the entertainment innovation catalyzing at the margins of urban American life in the 1910s and 1920s. She befriended queer performers and attended drag balls, frequented jazz venues, integrated the hot new music into her act, and sought out Black dance instructors who taught her "the shimmy," a titillating and risqué dance she was credited for introducing to Broadway.[2]

Like many comedians who followed, West found pushing social boundaries almost a calling and began writing plays whose titles, like *Sex*, *The Drag*, *Pleasure Man*, and *The Wicked Age*, betray their frank and sexually transgressive content. "I became a writer by the accident of needing material and having no place to get it," West later recalled in her autobiography.[3] Her characters were prostitutes, pimps, corrupt cops,

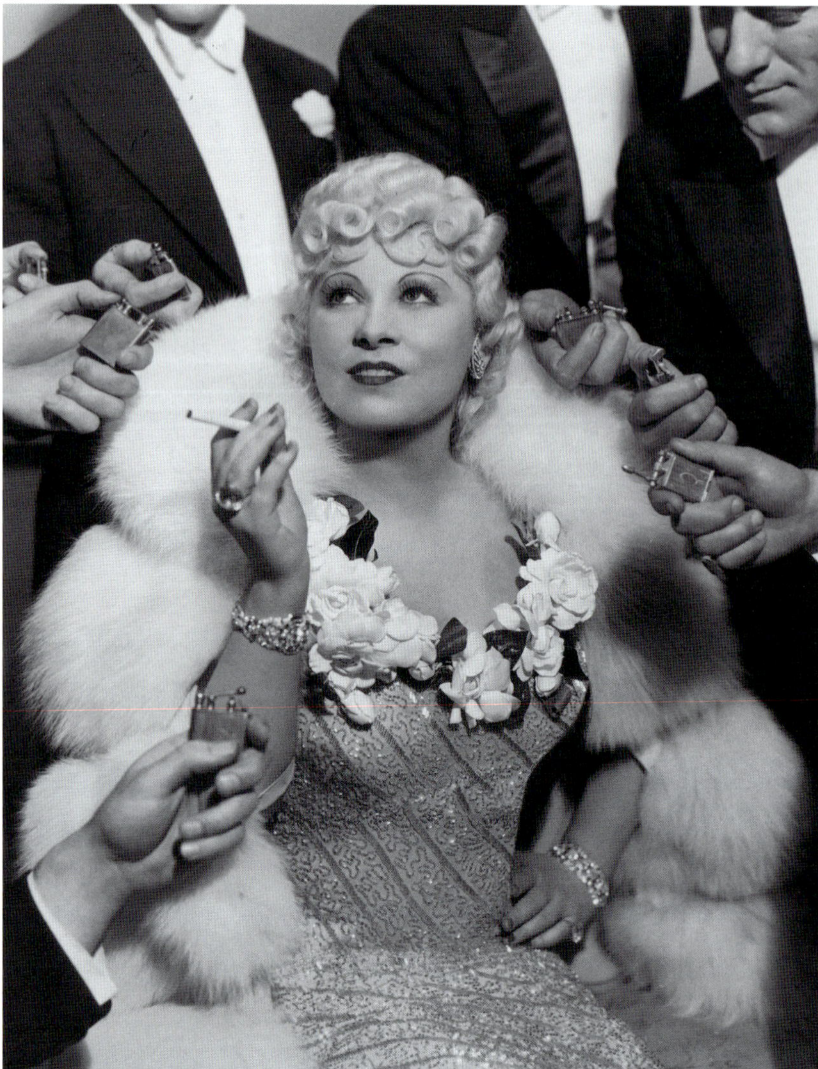

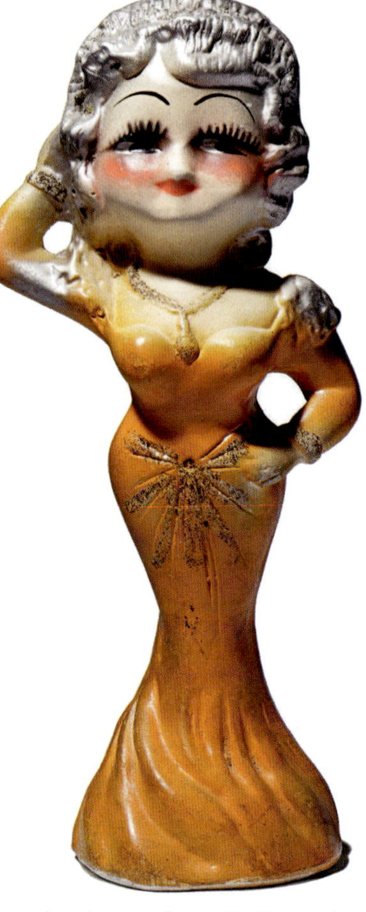

In a comedy career that spanned the 1920s to the 1970s, Mae West courted controversy and created an image of sexually liberated femininity that changed American culture. This 1930s chalkware figurine caricaturing West's curvaceous image—likely a carnival game prize—and 1935 portrait by C. Kenneth Lobben are testaments to her cultural ubiquity and power.

madams, drag performers, and the upper-crust "slummers" who traveled downtown to take in the underworld after dark. These plays explored taboo subjects, elevated the lives of marginalized people, and with a liberal and protofeminist audacity, dared to suggest that women should have agency over their bodies and pleasure.

In the 1926 play *Sex* West wrote the lead for herself, the prototype for the kind of role she'd play for the rest of her career. Margy was a self-possessed prostitute with a heart of gold whose liberated sexuality gave her freedom as well as power over men. In a subversion of the traditional morality play that made this setting and this kind of character acceptable on the legitimate Broadway stage, West's Margy lives a wicked life, faces a crisis, but doesn't quite vow to change her ways in the end. Critics savaged *Sex* ("the nastiest thing ever disclosed on a New York stage," one wrote), and the theater was raided by New York City police, earning West an eight-day prison sentence for staging an indecent performance and "corrupting the morals of youth and others."[4] Never one to waste a scandal, West took full advantage of the publicity the arrest generated, with tabloid coverage making her a household name, and ticket sales for *Sex* soared, encouraging her to continue to test censors and the public in her most famous play, *Diamond Lil*.

Set in a Bowery brothel in the 1890s, *Diamond Lil* featured West in the title role, again a self-assured and independent sex worker who flouts paternalist authority, even seeking to seduce a Salvation Army captain (actually an undercover federal agent investigating criminal activity). Mocking normative morality, reform movements, and male sexual hypocrisy, *Diamond Lil* was in many ways West's most provocative play, but it was enormously successful, its social criticism draped in gay nineties nostalgia, winking wordplay, and self-aware, campy humor.[5]

By 1932, West's Broadway success made her too big a star for Hollywood to ignore. Although the film industry's self-censoring Hays Office was enforcing the new production code, the financial burdens of the Great Depression and heavy debt from the conversion to sound production left the studios in desperate need of new, sensational draws. Paramount signed West to adapt *Diamond Lil* for the screen, but due to its notoriety it had to be produced under a different title (*She Done Him Wrong*), with a renamed lead character (Lady Lou) and a heavily edited script, emphasizing its comedic elements. With a young Cary Grant cast as West's romantic partner, the film grossed $2.2 million, one of the most profitable blockbusters of the year, earned an Academy Award nomination for Best Picture, and immediately made Mae West one of the biggest movie stars in the world.[6]

By 1934, West was the highest paid actor in the United States, reportedly making only slightly less than notoriously wealthy publisher, William Randolph Hearst. Paramount created a separate Mae West production unit and turned out six follow-up films in rapid succession after *She Done Him Wrong*, each following the Mae West formula. The films were successful across the country, perhaps saving Paramount from bankruptcy, and setting new records for return engagements. West became a quotable, universally recognizable icon, making frequent guest appearances on radio programs, providing fodder for tabloids and fan magazines, and being immortalized in cartoon caricatures and merchandise (and unlicensed homages in

"Why don't you come up some time and see me?"
—She Done Him Wrong *(Paramount, 1933)*

"When I'm good I'm very good. But when I'm bad I'm better."
—I'm No Angel *(Paramount, 1933)*

unrelated but shapely objects like life preservers and gasoline pumps).[7] She took full advantage of her popularity, daring the censors to challenge her bawdy and irreverent dialogue, making a point of casting Black entertainers in key roles in her films and crafting a larger-than-life public image.

But her major movie stardom was short-lived. By the late 1930s, more cosmopolitan screwball comedies, dance musicals, and romantic comedies were beginning to dominate the box office, and West's lower-class, gay nineties, vaudeville-tinted act was beginning to feel stale as audience tastes changed and increased censorship took the edge off her humor. Her once-transgressive, campy comic sensibility matured into self-parody. Despite an audacious late-career comeback, West never again dominated the headlines, but she remained a household name, a byword for the kind of transgressive comic characters she was famous for portraying.

Indeed, her influence still permeates American society and culture, inspiring generations of trailblazing female comedians and creators, memorable lines like "come up and see me sometime" joining the cultural vernacular despite the modern obscurity of the source material, and her persona providing perennial fodder for drag performance. In fact, some scholars have identified her greatest accomplishment as the mere creation of her iconic comedic persona, a harbinger of modern celebrity.[8] In retrospect, her plays and films were stinging critiques of American class and race prejudice, sexual repression and double standards, and society's stifling treatment of women, all skillfully concealed in crowd-pleasing humor and song. Mae West demonstrated that the most disruptive and challenging social commentary could be made palatable with a spoonful of comedic sugar.

Ryan Lintelman

LENNY BRUCE: "DON'T LOCK UP THESE WORDS"

Lenny Bruce was an iconoclastic social commentator who mobilized the art of stand-up comedy to rouse discourse about freedom of expression in America. Though his work resonated with many, it was an affront to

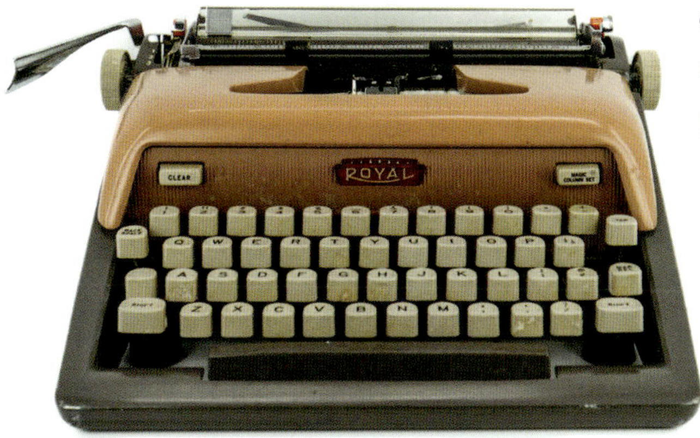

Bruce was a prolific and serious author who, in addition to developing his stand-up sets, wrote newspaper columns, essays, and an autobiography titled *How to Talk Dirty and Influence People* on this Royal typewriter.

others—specifically, vice squads, government agents, religious leaders, and other self-proclaimed guardians of public decency intent on stifling "deviant" sociopolitical speech. Like contemporaneous rebel artists in other realms of creative practice—from abstract expressionist painting to method acting to jazz music—Bruce infused his work with deeply personal ideas and ethics, establishing comedy as a form of self-expression in addition to a form of entertainment. His body of work upset conservative artistic traditions and served as a pressure valve for a constrained, repressed culture that was emerging from the long decades of the forties and fifties. More than merely a raconteur, Bruce was among the first to indisputably demonstrate comedy's power to incite hard-hitting conversations about cultural, social, and political issues of national importance.

Bruce's confessional style did not emerge in a vacuum. Along with peers like Mort Sahl and Dick Gregory, he was part of a new wave of so-called sick comics who sent stand-up in a cerebral, topical direction that many considered designed to stoke controversy. The frameworks of Bruce's routines were not revolutionary in and of themselves—in fact, many were reminiscent of the work of Godfrey Cambridge, Bob Newhart, and Shelley Berman, incorporating one-sided telephone conversations or long-form meandering anecdotes. Bruce's "Religions, Inc." bit is a classic involving a phone call to Pope John XXIII: "Johnny! What's shakin', baby? When you coming to the Coast? I'll get you the *Sullivan* show the nineteenth. It's good television. Wear the big ring." However, Lenny Bruce's approach to the language of stand-up comedy was all his own, contributing indelibly to the evolution of the art form's tones, rhythms, and attitudes. Verboten words like "motherfucker" and "shit" entered the mainstream comic lexicon for the first time, as did "jive" talk, which Bruce wove seamlessly with Yiddishisms that referenced not only his own cultural milieu but also the stylings of Catskills comedy. With street words like "cat," "dig this," and "wow, man" colliding with "putz," "shtup," and "schmuck," Bruce's work came to represent a "radical head-on collision of old and new comedy."[9] Although such a creative and cavalier approach to language was hardly uncommon within burlesque houses and bars, the anarchical attitudes of the underground were shocking when they emerged on nightclub stages before "respectable" audiences.

Eschewing all pretentions toward good taste as it was policed by the cultural gatekeepers who would censor his work, Bruce attacked hypocrisy and complacency in any form. Some, including a young George Carlin, flocked to see him perform and were inspired by Bruce's fervor; others recoiled and marked him a dangerous force. Following a 1961 arrest in San Francisco for using explicit language onstage, Lenny Bruce was repeatedly hauled off stages to prison cells in a highly publicized scrimmage with the authorities. He took to wearing a trench coat onstage, loaded with the personal possessions (like a toothbrush) that he would need to spend his requisite night in jail. Though he was hardly the first comedian to risk prosecution for his art (Sophie Tucker and Mae West, for example, preceded Bruce with lengthy arrest records and indecency charges), Bruce's situation galvanized the public at a crucial turning point in American history, and the media attention that ensued made him an artistic martyr.

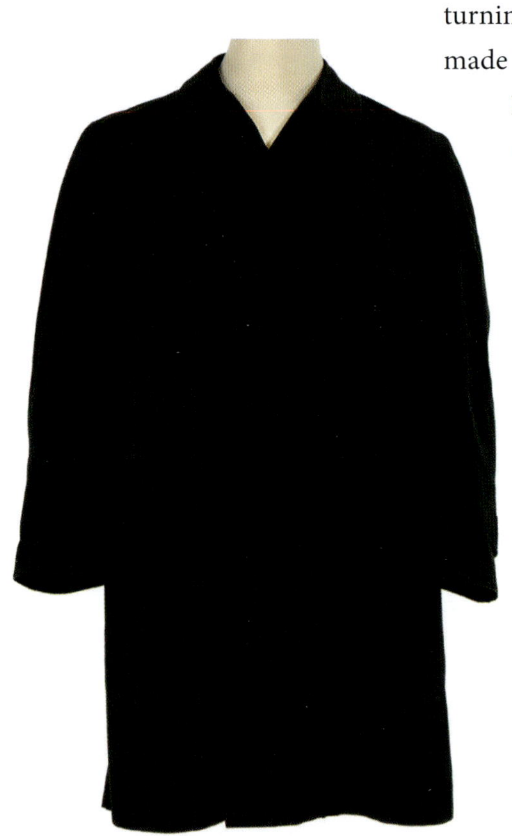

As he was more and more frequently hauled off of nightclub stages in handcuffs, bound for a night in a jail cell, Lenny Bruce took to wearing this trench coat onstage, loading his pockets with the personal items he wouldn't have time to retrieve when police dragged him straight to a waiting squad car.

In 1964, moments before striding onstage at Greenwich Village's Café Au Go Go, Bruce was arrested yet again. The case, to be titled *The People v. Lenny Bruce*, went to trial and evolved into a history-making test of the First Amendment as Bruce was indicted by a grand jury for violation of New York Penal Code 1140, prohibiting "obscene, indecent, immoral, and impure" entertainment that would "tend to the corruption of the morals of youth and others." During the hotly publicized trial, an undercover agent testified with a stilted recitation of excerpts from Bruce's act that he had scribbled surreptitiously while hiding in the crowded nightclub, prompting Bruce to point out the injustice of a comic's work being judged based on the "bad timing" and "garbled language" of a cop butchering his act. Bruce defended himself with a petition signed by luminaries as various as Paul Newman, Bob Dylan, Susan Sontag, Allen Ginsberg, Elizabeth Taylor, and Norman Mailer, asserting that all artists should be permitted to perform without harassment. Bruce passionately pleaded with the judges, "Don't lock up these words. That's what you're doing: taking away my words." In a recess, Bruce was hospitalized for chest pain in the midst of a flurry of impassioned testimonies. Ninety-nine days later, the court announced its verdict: Bruce's act was found "patently offensive" and lacking in "social importance." He was sentenced to four months in a workhouse. Before his appeal of the conviction could be considered, Bruce had died of a morphine overdose.

In many ways, Lenny Bruce's death was the cost of protecting the integrity of his life's work. With a career that lasted only about one decade, he nevertheless emerged as a sort of comedic folk hero of mythical proportion. In 2003, his legend was further cemented when New York governor George Pataki granted the first posthumous pardon in the state's history, upholding Bruce's story as poignantly, and morbidly, symbolic of America's promise to protect First Amendment rights.

Laura LaPlaca

RUSTY WARREN AND WOMEN'S SEXUALITY: TOO TABOO FOR YOU

Sex was her subject, and sex is what kept her off the airwaves when censors attempted to stifle her decades-long career. Rusty Warren, her stage name a reference to her naturally red hair and the street she grew up on, was one of the most successful nightclub comedians in the history of the art form, with seven of her comedy albums "going gold" to represent a multimillion-selling body of work, achieved *despite* being relegated by her risqué humor to comedy's underground. Indeed, Warren built her brand around being banned, and it was against the backdrop of the sexual revolution of the 1960s and the beginnings of second-wave feminism that she emerged as a voice for women who had never before felt that they could speak on "taboo" topics like their own sexuality.

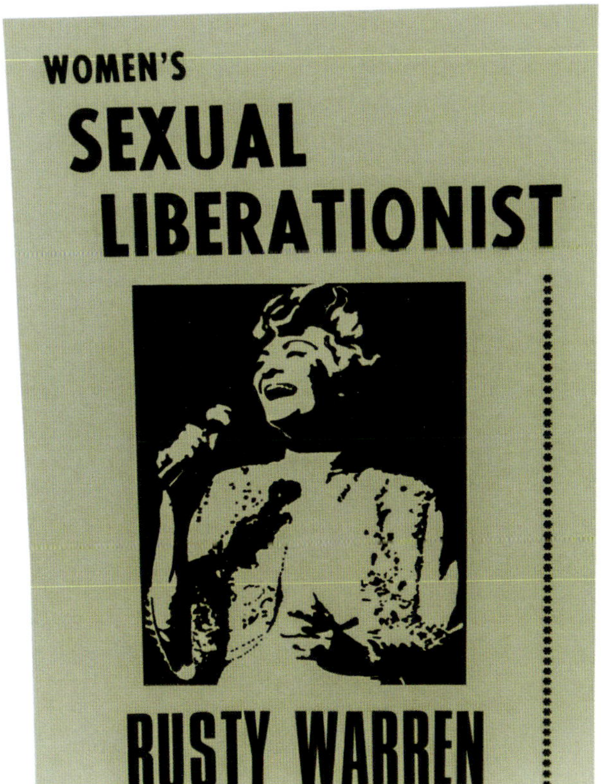

WOMEN'S SEXUAL LIBERATIONIST

RUSTY WARREN

Hailing from New England, Warren—also known as Ilene Goldman—was classically trained on the piano from her time at the New England Conservatory of Music in Boston. Having excelled among her peers, she was afforded the opportunity to perform under Boston Pops Orchestra conductor Arthur

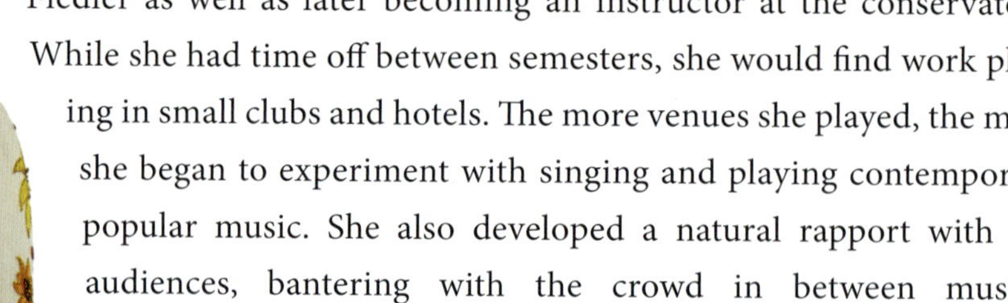

Fiedler as well as later becoming an instructor at the conservatory. While she had time off between semesters, she would find work playing in small clubs and hotels. The more venues she played, the more she began to experiment with singing and playing contemporary popular music. She also developed a natural rapport with her audiences, bantering with the crowd in between musical numbers.

Influenced greatly by Nan Blakstone and Sophie Tucker—early twentieth-century American singers and comedians skillful in the use of double entendre, and proponents of using their powerful voices to focus on cultural and societal topics typically considered off-limits, especially for women—Warren stood on the shoulders of these earlier entertainers as she slowly began developing her own original material. It was Blakstone who told her to "always mean what you say," a notion that Warren latched onto as she began including more observational comedy in her routines.[10] But this was a world where women rarely felt heard, and Tucker made sure she encouraged the up-and-coming nightclub entertainer to "present a strong delivery, with punch, and always have the courage to say what you want to. So few women know how to."[11] Warren used the launch pad provided to her by these daring women to push the boundaries of comedy and sexual innuendo further in the very male-dominated arena of so-called blue humor.

In 1955, Stanford Zucker, a music agent who also recorded Blakstone, saw Warren perform in Chicago and knew there was something special happening when she took the stage. He booked her shows on the West Coast, including at a venue called the Pomp Room in Phoenix—a booking that was the catalyst of her career. Not only did Warren's Pomp Room gig turn into an eight-month residency, but it also became the site where she recorded her first comedy album, *Songs for Sinners*, released in 1959.

Following her huge success on the West Coast and the release of her first album, Warren found herself performing around the country, working on new material that came in the form of an interactive "march" involving her audience. In what was dubbed the "Knockers Up March," Warren would encourage the ladies of the room to "march with their boobs held high" while she performed her song. This "march" was an outlet for the women of the audience to reclaim their sexuality, allowing them

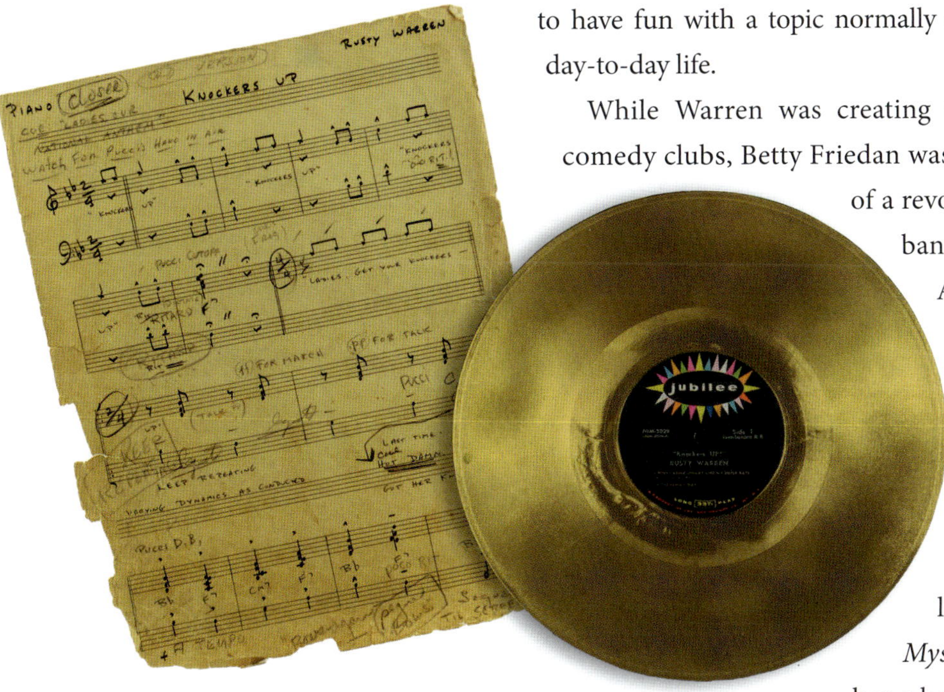

Rusty Warren saw her comedy career skyrocket with the debut of *Knockers Up!* which brought forward-thinking concepts around women's sexuality to the forefront in an era of American history experiencing heightened social change related to sexual liberation. This original hand annotated sheet music for the song, and the accompanying gold record, underscore how Warren's words challenged societal taboos and became catalysts for change.

to have fun with a topic normally off-limits for discussion in day-to-day life.

While Warren was creating this sexual revolution in comedy clubs, Betty Friedan was forming her own version of a revolution for the same suburban housewives of 1960s America. For five years, Friedan conducted interviews with white middle-class women who were grappling with their roles as housewives. Her findings would later be published as *The Feminine Mystique*, instantly making her a household name among millions of women, just as Warren herself was becoming a rising star. What would be later considered an early feminist anthem and precursor to the sexual revolution of the era, "Knockers Up!" was such a huge hit with audiences that in 1960 it was used as the title for Warren's second comedy album, which landed Warren her first million seller and served as incontrovertible evidence that audiences—composed mainly of women—were hearing and internalizing her message.

While Los Angeles County Sheriff's officers conducted covert raids on warehouses to destroy copies of the album, *Knockers Up!* made *Billboard*'s Top 10 Bestselling Albums overall for two years in a row, demonstrating that despite not having her material played on mainstream airwaves, the American public was responding in a big way to Warren's "salacious" recordings focused on sexual liberation, equity, and women's rights.[12] *Knockers Up!* and her subsequent three albums, aptly titled *Sin-sational*, *Rusty Warren Bounces Back*, and *Rusty Warren in Orbit*, were so popular with her audiences that Warren was awarded the National Association of Record Merchandisers' "Best Selling Comedy Recording Artist of the Year Award for 1962"—outperforming the likes of Allan Sherman's 1962 *My Son, the Folk Singer* with the hit track "Hello Muddah, Hello Fadduh" and Vaughn Meader's uncanny impersonation of then-President John F. Kennedy on *The First Family* comedy album that went on to win the Grammy for Album of the Year.[13]

Due to the perceived naughtiness of her albums—and without the benefit of radio play or television appearances—Warren still managed to sell more than two million albums in less than two years. Though she developed a reputation for trafficking in obscenity, she would often emphasize that she never deigned to using "those four-letter words" to get her point across. She was doing nothing more than frankly discussing sex, romance, and marriage from the point of view of a modern woman. Given the droves of both men and women filling the clubs where she performed, Warren's work was clearly providing a coveted space for audiences to experience a sort of release from societal chains that kept people tightlipped and ashamed about their sexuality.

Many of those who felt these societal chains were women, who up to this point rarely felt emboldened to speak freely about, or even acknowledge, their own desires and sexual pleasures. Warren's goal for her performances was to spark authentic conversations about sexuality at home, while also showing an uptight America that it was taking itself too seriously when it came to matters of intimacy and pleasure. With the success of *Knockers Up!*, a fan club dubbed the "Knockers Up Club" spawned—a marketing gimmick handed down to Warren by Tucker, who explained the power of marshaling an audience that, in this case, was made up mostly of housewives who followed Warren religiously, often traveling long distances in groups to see her perform.

Ironically, offstage and in her personal life, Warren found herself navigating another type of societal repression: she would never announce to her audiences that her own preference was for women. The sixties were not kind or safe for anyone existing outside of heteronormative romantic relationships, particularly for those who were in show business. It was quite common for entertainers prior to the twenty-first century to keep their true sexual orientation hidden out of fear of societal backlash and for personal safety, let alone a fear of their careers being stripped from them. The first gay rights demonstrations in Philadelphia and Washington, D.C., in the sixties and the riots at Stonewall in 1969 caused significant shifts in LGBTQ activism. During such an uncertain time, Warren managed her public persona quite skillfully and was afforded the ability to retain some modicum of privacy and anonymity—safeguarding her reputation among audiences who may or may not have been receptive to her private life.[14] However, Warren never shied away from supporting the LGBTQ+ community and would spend the rest of her life speaking freely about topics like pornography, legalized prostitution, censorship, and obscenity until she passed away in 2021. In her own words, "Love has no gender . . . today love can be anything. Two men can touch each other, two women may touch each other, a man and a woman may touch each other. It doesn't matter where it's at."[15]

Ashley Senske

MOMS MABLEY WAS "THE FUNNIEST WOMAN IN THE WORLD"

Jackie "Moms" Mabley's story tracks an arc from the most challenging of upbringings in an 1890s Blue Ridge Mountain town to the stage at Carnegie Hall, as she honed the turn-of-the-century craft of monology into the distinctly modern art form of stand-up.

Donning the signature housedress, clodhopper shoes, and floppy hat that defined the matronly, truth-telling character of "Moms," Mabley built, and then sustained, a half-century career that began in the depths of Jim Crow in the 1920s and found her ascending as one of the most outspoken voices of the civil rights era. The social, political, and cultural changes wrought during her lifetime were enormous, not to mention the sweeping progression of the media and entertainment industries that she helped to innovate. The grandmotherly persona she affected was a highly strategic, and highly successful, means of stealthily asserting herself at a moment in the history of American entertainment that was hostile, if not completely inaccessible, to voices questioning the status quo. Her apparently harmless, endearing character worked as a kind of ingenious subterfuge, a loophole that allowed Mabley to broach utterly taboo topics while softening the edge, but not the urgency, of her message.

Born Loretta Aiken before adopting a stage name, Mabley fled a childhood that was characterized by sexual violence and family tragedy

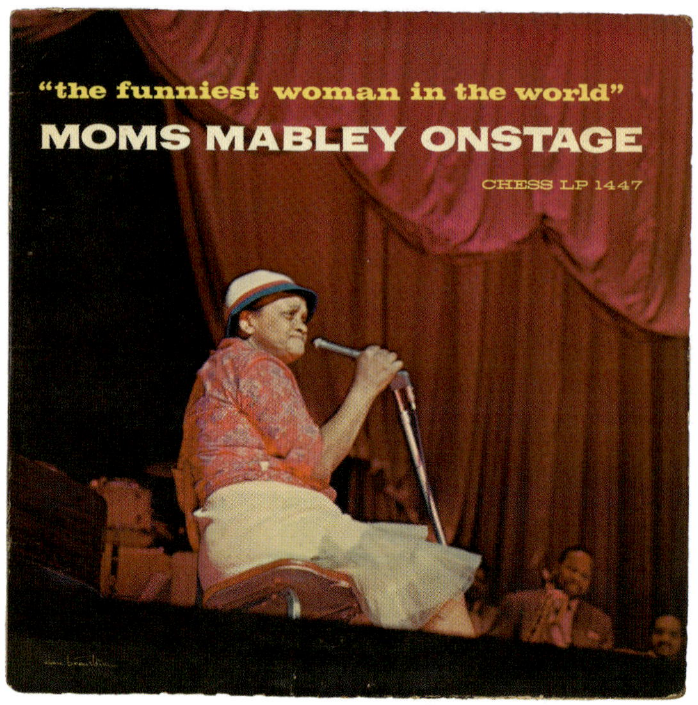

to embark upon a risky, uncertain future as an entertainer. She evolved her act on the Chitlin' Circuit, a string of vaudeville venues serving Black audiences that was one of the most important talent incubators in American cultural history as well as one of the most exploitative. Mabley's was a rare solo act by a woman, who were typically limited to the roles of dancers, singers, or comic foils for men. A supportive boost from Jodie and Susie Edwards, the couple behind the immensely popular double act known as Butterbeans and Susie, ferried Mabley to Harlem during its storied Renaissance, a period of artistic flowering and creative collaboration that marked an apogee of American cultural production helmed by Black innovators. Mabley was a fixture at venues like the Cotton Club and, later, the historic Apollo Theater, where she headlined alongside other generational talents like Louis Armstrong and Duke Ellington.

The grand circuits of variety entertainment struggled, and ultimately collapsed, with the widespread adoption of radio and television into family homes. It was not a given that performers who came to prominence on the stage would successfully make the transition to electronic media, and most faded into obscurity. Mabley adapted, innovated, and excelled. She appeared in films (1948's *Killer Diller* and *Boarding House Blues* among them), but made her mark most lastingly as one of the first artists to leverage recorded sound as a vehicle to mainstream recognition as a comedian. Mabley's albums were not only popular but also wildly original and in their way established a blueprint for what it would mean to build a commercially viable comedy brand.

For generations, the nomadic life of the vaudevillian had allowed comedians to perfect and then repeat the same routines for months, or years, on end. Albums changed the calculus when they promised to distribute material to a mass audience for repeated replay. At a moment when many other comics were wringing their hands about the risks inherent in committing their limited work to the recorded medium, Mabley was seizing an opportunity: she saw a way toward sharing

"Moms" with an audience that was not limited by a regressive entertainment culture that had left her work familiar to (and beloved by) the Black community but largely unknown to white audiences. The first record she cut, 1960's *Moms Mabley Onstage: The Funniest Woman in the World*, went gold. Eight follow-up albums were released in the ensuing three years, and for the rest of the decade Mabley logged a place in the *Billboard* Top 100 each year.

For an artist with a thinner repertoire, a less honed voice, or a less savvy business acumen, this deft approach would have been impossible to execute. Mabley was one of few comedians to successfully "crossover" in the 1960s, a colloquial term for addressing a body of work to audiences beyond the Black community. As scholar Bambi Haggins has explained in her own extensive treatment of Mabley's influence, crossover "adds a problematic twist to the already Byzantine task faced by the African American comic: to be funny, accessible, and topical while retaining his or her *authentic* black voice."[16] Mabley was a fifty-year veteran of show business before she ever appeared on network TV, but logged some of the most fruitful years of her career—at least as measured in mainstream name recognition and financial remuneration—in her seventies. Her work connected with a broad-based new generation of viewers, including audiences of countercultural programming like *The Smothers Brothers Comedy Hour*, *Laugh-In*, and *The Flip Wilson Show*, who embraced her no-nonsense takes on issues of civil rights and the way that she transparently addressed social issues at the intersection of race, gender, and sexuality. "Moms opened a door," comic Whoopi Goldberg would explain in her 2013 documentary tributing Mabley's legacy, for comedians "to stand up and be funny . . . to talk about things as they saw them."[17]

Laura LaPlaca

LUCILLE BALL AND "LUCY RICARDO"

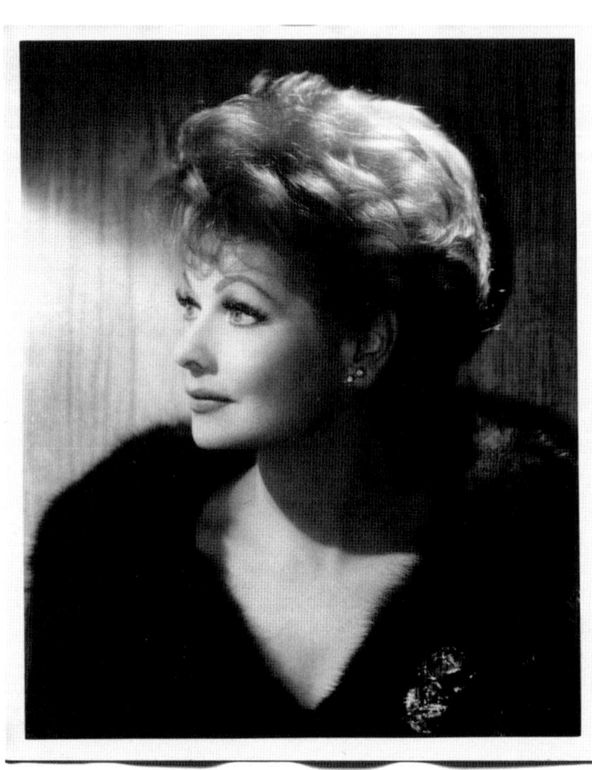

Lucy Ricardo, the zany sitcom housewife who has become part of the symbolic register of Americana, has always been inseparable from her creator Lucille Ball, an incomparable comedic artist, business leader, and changemaker. When *I Love Lucy* premiered on October 15, 1951, TV was rapidly transforming American culture, and situation comedies were among the medium's most popular offerings. Sitcoms were well matched to the historical moment, as they beamed representations of domestic life right into the family home, alternately reflecting, forging, and challenging new definitions of family structure and gender identity at a moment of widespread societal reorganization. Regarded then, as now, for its peerless comedic performances and expert story crafting, *I Love Lucy*'s unprecedented popularity not only made its titular character an avatar for postwar American womanhood but made its star one of the most significant power brokers of the twentieth century.

At *I Love Lucy*'s inception, Lucille Ball was a Hollywood veteran of nearly twenty years with almost a hundred film credits to her name and the star of radio's *My Favorite Husband*—a sitcom in which she played Liz Cugat, the spirited wife of a bank executive, who was a close ancestor of Lucy Ricardo. Network executives had taken note of the alchemy that happened when Ball performed before live audiences: her palette of nuanced expressions and facility for physical comedy were being squandered in an audio-only format. The creative team behind *My Favorite Husband*, including producer Jess Oppenheimer and writers Bob Carroll Jr. and Madelyn Pugh, readied themselves for a move to television, but Ball, at age forty and with her first child on the way, put forth stipulations: the new show must be produced close to home and must costar her real-life husband, Desi Arnaz—an actor and bandleader who had risen

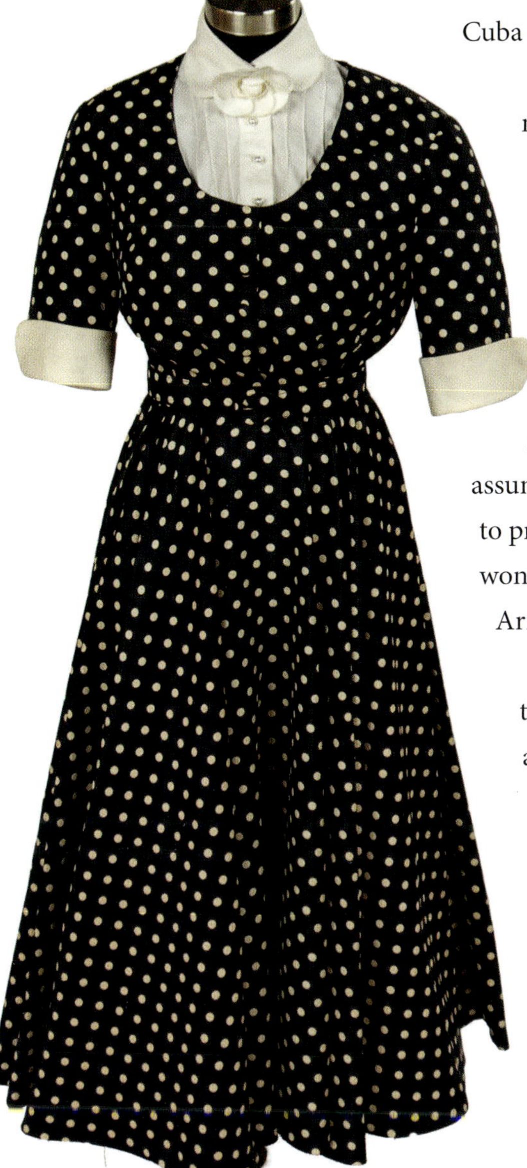

Conceived by Oscar-winning costume designer Elois Jenssen, Lucille Ball's polka dot dress recalls her role as the star of *I Love Lucy* and her lasting impact as a groundbreaking comedian, savvy studio executive, and style icon who redefined women's roles.

to renown after transplanting the Afro-Caribbean music of his native Cuba to the United States.

It was an audacious move to suggest that CBS—a formidable media empire—concede to such demands. Producing a weekly series three thousand miles from the young TV industry's center in New York City was seemingly impossible, and the network balked at the idea of representing an intermarriage on its airwaves, viewing it as a risky proposition. Ball and Arnaz were inured to the naysaying: each of their stories had been forged in defiance to those who would underestimate them. They renegotiated with the network, agreeing to assume financial risks and handle the significant logistical hurdles to production, making an unflinching bet on themselves. And they won: *I Love Lucy* leapt to the head of the ratings race, and Ball and Arnaz were among TV's first self-made millionaires.

Part of the alchemy that made *I Love Lucy* chime with its historical moment involved the emergence of the "Lucy" character against the backdrop of the American midcentury—an era when consensus ideologies were tightly organized around defining women as domestic subjects. It was Lucy Ricardo's unceasing charge to escape the confinement of her home, to skirt the controlling impulses of her husband, and to find fulfillment in a career of her own. She schemed and dreamed incessantly, and up against odds that would have halted anyone with realistic convictions; but audiences didn't love Lucy because she was *realistic*—she was fiercely, powerfully, excitingly *aspirational*.

When the world conspired to shut her out, Lucy's reaction was to find a way in: enter through the window, wear a disguise, outfox the gatekeeper. The character was a trickster figure who triumphs over forces more potent and powerful by finding loopholes. In *I Love Lucy*'s case, this meant manipulating social scripts that limited women's access to agency, power, and self-actualization in the 1950s—and these social scripts often involved controlling and confining the female body. Lucy Ricardo's trademark red updo, red lips, neat string of pearls, and cinched polka dot dresses exemplified contemporaneous standards of beauty, and she was adept at strategically emphasizing aspects of her femininity or sexuality to exploit the weaknesses of men who would try to contain her. The athleticism of Ball's humor required that her wardrobe marry postwar politesse with activewear, and the Lucy character broke ground

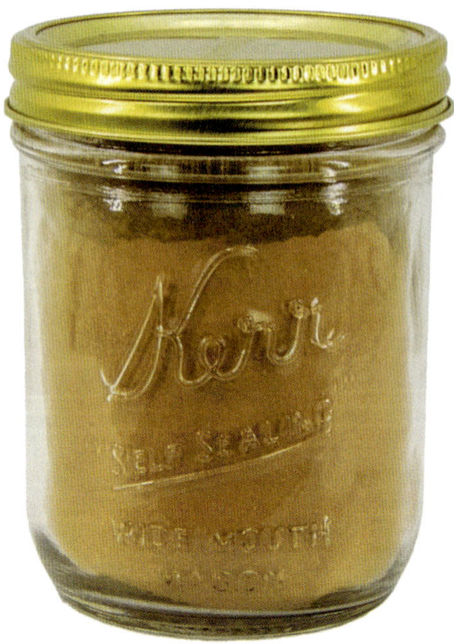

Lucille Ball's iconic red hair not only defined her own star persona but became part of the fabric of midcentury American popular culture. Beginning during her years as an ingenue at MGM Studios during the coming of Technicolor technology, Ball used an imported henna rinse to achieve her signature "apricot" color.

on television by wearing pants. She also used menswear as a tool that allowed her to take on a tactical type of gender fluidity, and cross-dressing to infiltrate male-dominated spaces like poker games or stag parties was a staple in her repertoire of tricks.

As was the case more generally at the midcentury, women's sexuality was highly controlled and filtered through a male gaze. Sitcom housewives were not permitted to share beds with their husbands or to voice desires of their own, but they were subjected to the fetishized surveillance of both the men in their story worlds and the audiences watching at home. In this context, when news of Lucille Ball's real-life pregnancy reached the network, it was an assumption that America's top-rated show would be canceled or put on hiatus; pregnant women could not be represented on the air. Ball and Arnaz rejected the premise that women's real lives had to be erased to appease moral grandstanders, and they once again defied a skeptical network by crafting a multiepisode story arc about pregnancy, childbirth, and motherhood that passed the muster of hardline censors and religious leaders. It was an enormously visible and vulnerable moment for Lucille Ball, made a historic one when, on January 19, 1953, she gave birth to her real son on the same day as an *I Love Lucy* episode titled "Lucy Goes to the Hospital" aired in prime time. It shattered the ratings records to become the most watched half hour of television to that point in the medium's history, outstripping even the inauguration of President Eisenhower and the coronation of Queen Elizabeth. America's ecstatic response to the birth was both a watershed moment in TV history and a prelude for how popular culture would play a role in the emergent feminist movement, in terms of proving how mainstream audiences were not only interested in but drawn to storytelling about the substance of women's lives.

Lucy Ricardo was not alone in her scheming and subterfuge, often working in cahoots with her best friend, neighbor, and foil Ethel Mertz, played by Vivian Vance. This supportive female friendship was the emotional anchor and the comedic engine of the series. Lucy and Ethel worked as a well-oiled buddy act, staking out together against the vagaries of their marriages and in pursuit of their deferred dreams. It was Ethel's friendship that girded Lucy against an often-unforgiving world. After Lucy Ricardo and Ethel Mertz took their last bows in 1960, the story of their friendship carried forward across a new series called *The Lucy Show*. This series reincarnated the Lucy character, largely intact, as

Lucy Carmichael, a widow with a divorced best friend played by Vance. It is not often enough acknowledged how significant this was: Vance was the first divorced recurring character on TV, and the show was groundbreaking for representing two women making it on their own—before a younger generation of creatives like Marlo Thomas and Mary Tyler Moore used the sitcom format to push an explicitly feminist message further.

The Lucy Show was hugely popular and was in second place in the ratings when Lucille Ball ended it to embark upon production of *Here's Lucy*, which would once again present a version of Lucy, this time called Lucy Carter, as a widow raising two children played by her real-life daughter and son, Lucie and Desi Arnaz Jr. The Lucy character made a final resurgence in *Life with Lucy*, which found Lucy Barker as a widowed grandmother who inherited an interest in a hardware store. All five sitcoms that presented the Lucy character, from 1948's debut of *My Favorite Husband* through the conclusion of *Life with Lucy* in 1986, were conceived and written by the team of Bob Carroll Jr. and Madelyn Pugh, who were Lucille Ball's most significant—if unseen—creative collaborators.

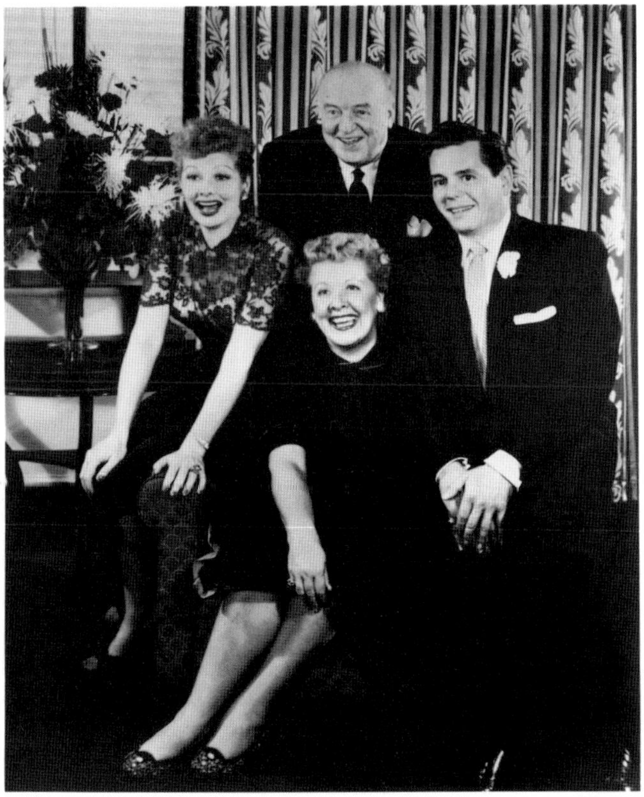

The cast of *I Love Lucy:* Lucille Ball, Desi Arnaz, Vivian Vance, and William Frawley.

In the hands of an artist with less skill or less life experience facing down obstacles to her own self-actualization, the Lucy character might have been one-dimensional: a cartoonish vehicle for slapstick untethered to any sense of humanity or pathos. But Ball treated Lucy's unruliness with a deliberate, measured progression that made even the most outlandish situations appear relatable and true. She had an intuitive command of her physicality that, when paired with rigorous rehearsal, produced performances that still stand as high watermarks in the history of comedy. Yet while Lucy schemed and dreamed to little avail for almost forty years, never really breaking free (the sitcom format, after all, demands constant renewal week over week), Lucille Ball herself was achieving something very different. Behind the scenes, she was parlaying her considerable experience and industrial clout into an ascendancy as one of the most visible executives in Hollywood.

Lucille Ball assumed the presidency of Desilu Productions in 1962. Initially founded with Desi Arnaz to produce *I Love Lucy*, the company had grown to become the largest and most prolific independent producer of television. As one of vanishingly few women in leadership in the entertainment industry, and one of the only women to helm a publicly traded company of any type, Ball faced intense scrutiny. She was charged with navigating some of the most dynamic years in broadcast history: the coming of color, stereo sound, and portable cameras reorganized production practices at every level; the advent of chroma key opened a door to special effects that would power the enormous popularity of new genres like science fiction; and the launch of the first satellites portended the rise of television as a truly global medium. Many of the studios and creatives who had steered television's first decade backed away from the table. Ball stepped forward and took big risks, including approving production of new series like *Star Trek* and *Mission: Impossible*. At the same time, she continued to carry the company on her own shoulders by starring weekly in *The Lucy Show*—a series that ranked in TV's top ten for all six of its seasons and garnered Ball two Emmy Awards. It was the commercial success of *The Lucy Show* that provided Desilu with the financial stability it needed to survive its period of transition, making Ball's dual role—as studio head and star performer—not just remarkable, but indispensable.

In a world that refused to really acknowledge her authority and acumen off-screen during her lifetime, Ball quietly, persistently ferried the company into the black and made a historic sale to Paramount after years of hard-won success. Always a savvy and careful broker of her own image, Ball formed Lucille Ball Productions in the aftermath to produce her own projects, including *Here's Lucy*, going forward—never content to allow a conglomerate to own the brand she had so carefully forged. When asked in her later years how the world might commemorate her considerable achievements, Ball rejected the idea that a monument to "Lucy" needed to exist. Instead, she envisioned the establishment of a place that celebrates comedy itself as a vital, vibrant art form with a storied history. In furtherance of her wishes, the National Comedy Center opened its doors in Ball's hometown of Jamestown, New York, in 2018 with a mission to educate the public about comedy's impacts and preserve its heritage for future generations.

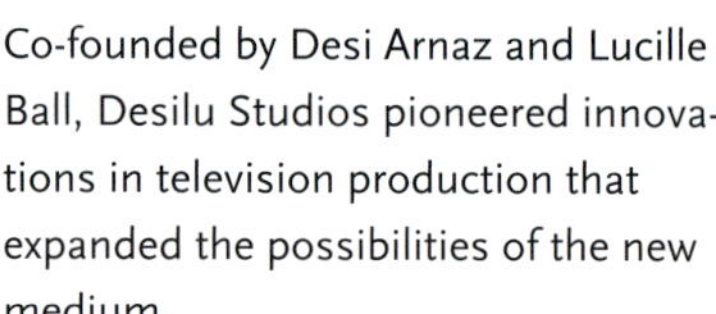

Co-founded by Desi Arnaz and Lucille Ball, Desilu Studios pioneered innovations in television production that expanded the possibilities of the new medium.

Laura LaPlaca

S'PLAINING RICKY RICARDO

"Luucyyyy! I'm home!" It's one of the most memorable catchphrases in television history (though ironically, uttered only once!), and most likely, when you read it, you imagined it delivered in the Cuban-accented English of Desi Arnaz. In *I Love Lucy*, Ricky Ricardo (Arnaz) is a talented Cuban bandleader and husband to the troublesome and charismatic Lucy Ricardo (played by Lucille Ball). The sitcom tells the story of the happily married Ricardos, whose domestic bliss is constantly threatened by a fundamental tension: Lucy wants to be a famous entertainer, but while Ricky supports the family through show business, he dreams of normalcy.[18] The series was television's first monster hit—seen every Monday night in ten million American homes and credited by historians as cementing the sitcom format. For many, Ricky Ricardo became the quintessential Cuban, a testament to the power of television comedy to shape Americans' vision of cultural difference and the assimilationist experience.

It's remarkable that the series, centered on an intermarriage, was produced at all. When Lucille Ball was given the opportunity to take her hit radio show *My Favorite Husband* and adapt it for TV, she fought for Arnaz to be cast as her husband in the show. The networks and sponsors were skeptical that a relationship between a redheaded all-American girl like Ball and a Cuban bandleader with a heavy accent like Arnaz would be believable to audiences. Despite being married for almost a decade by then, they had to prove that their relationship would appeal to mainstream American viewers. When Arnaz and Ball tested the act out on the road, the response from the audience was overwhelmingly positive, compelling CBS chief executive William Paley to greenlight the show, which premiered in 1951.

I Love Lucy ran for nine years and was nominated for twenty-three Emmy awards. The show made Lucille Ball and Desi Arnaz household names. The series' success lies in how it "distorts, exaggerates, and makes vastly amusing every little incident, foible, and idiosyncrasy of married life," columnists Jack and Madeline Sher wrote.[19] The postwar 1950s brought forth enormous pressure to conform to societal norms—from traditional family values, strict gender roles, and American cultural supremacy to the rise of consumerism, suburbanization, and the middle-class "American dream." *I Love Lucy*'s Ricky Ricardo simultaneously

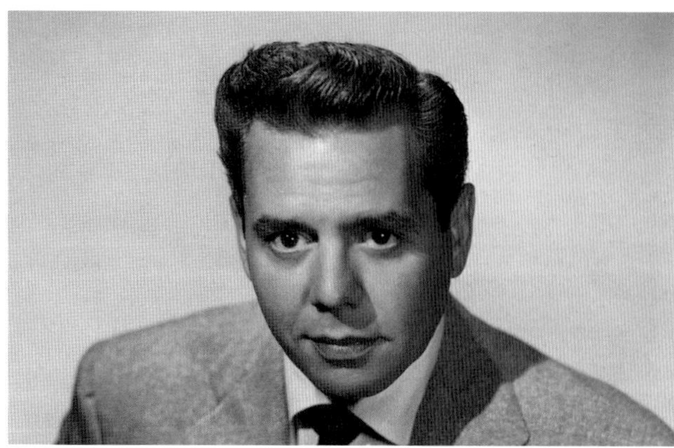

Desi—Desiderio Alberto Arnaz y de Acha III—was born in Santiago de Cuba in 1917 to a wealthy and politically connected Cuban family. The family was forced to flee the country during the Cuban Revolution of 1933, resettling in Miami, where Desi began performing as a drummer and singer. He caught the attention of bandleader Xavier Cugat, who helped make him a star.

embraced and challenged the conformity of the 1950s. On one hand, the character of Ricky Ricardo embodied the ideals of a middle-class husband—he was the breadwinner and the patriarchal head of the family. On the other, Arnaz's character was a fast-talking ethnic foreigner who managed to marry a white wife as American as apple pie.

The complexities of Arnaz's portrayal of Ricky Ricardo did not end there. Ricky Ricardo—and Arnaz by extension—was exoticized, sexualized, and othered in ways that made his presence palatable and acceptable to white Anglo audiences. Despite resisting stereotypes that most often plagued Mexicans in Hollywood, Ricky Ricardo ultimately renewed the "Latin lover" stereotype with his suave masculine appeal, passionate temperament, and seductive foreignness. In this instance, instead of being a momentary love interest for the female lead, he was the one that she settled down with.

As historian Louis A. Pérez Jr. has written, Ricky Ricardo "easily reinforced the dominant images: rumba band leader, heavily accented English, excitable, always seeming to be slightly out of place."[20] The scripted show was performed in front of a studio audience, so "dialogue and production cues were deliberately and skillfully engineered in ways meant to cause a humorous response" from the primarily English monolinguals present.[21] Any of Ricky Ricardo's "Spanish utterances [were] shot through with anglicisms so that the monolingual viewer [could] understand what he was saying,"[22] or the indecipherable English communications were intended to create comedic misunderstandings. The first season of the television series established the pattern of Lucy making fun of Ricky's English for big and reliable audience laughs, a trope that continued throughout the series. Indeed, Arnaz's popularity as Ricky Ricardo set a linguistic standard for newer interpretations of the exotic "Latin" foreigner. The *Los Angeles Times* published a piece that labeled Arnaz's pronunciations as "an entirely new language" and called it the "Arnaz-ization of the American language." Lucy's "Cuban Dreamboat" didn't hide or fake his accent for audiences—Arnaz himself truly spoke a heavily accented English: "Above all, Ricky is the sound of his voice, a distinguishing trait made all the more evident by the fact that he is a singer."[23] Arnaz built his career deftly navigating—sometimes

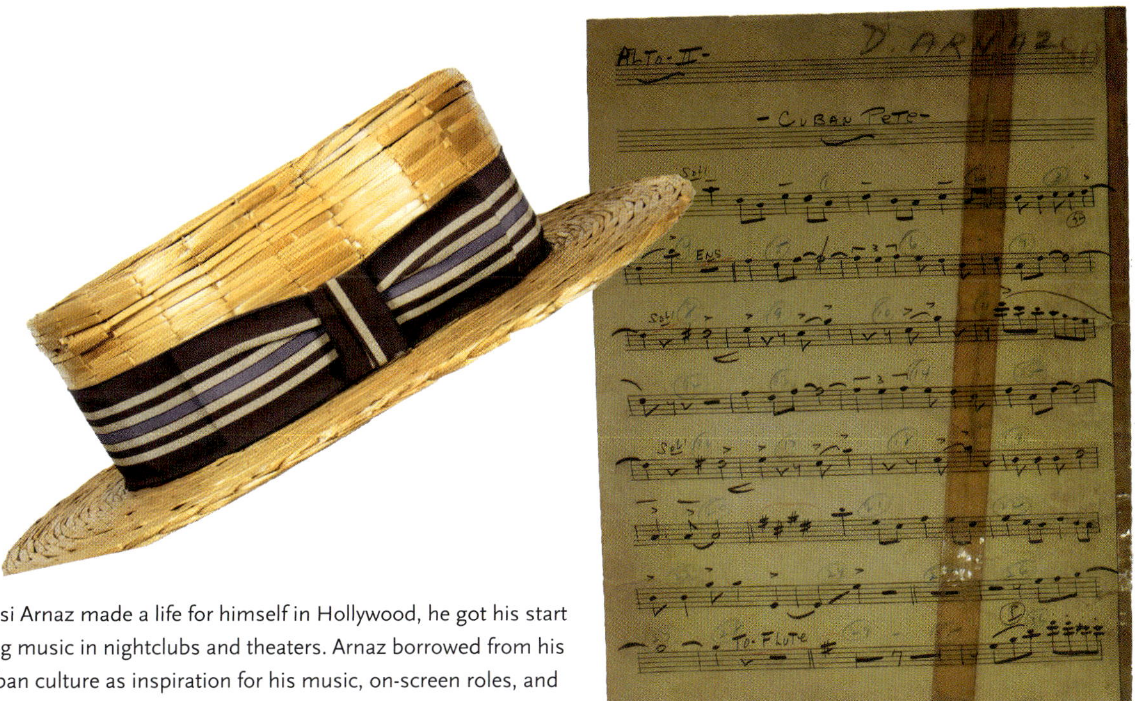

Before Desi Arnaz made a life for himself in Hollywood, he got his start performing music in nightclubs and theaters. Arnaz borrowed from his native Cuban culture as inspiration for his music, on-screen roles, and performance routines. During a particularly disastrous performance, Arnaz—desperate to salvage the gig—grabbed a conga drum and directed the band to improvise with a basic rhythm while dancing in a line. This stroke of genius set in motion one of the most popular dance crazes of the 1940s—the conga line, inspired by the *comparsas* of the Carnival celebrations in Arnaz's hometown of Santiago de Cuba. In the 1946 film *Cuban Pete*, Arnaz plays the role of a Cuban bandleader persuaded to leave Cuba and travel to New York for an opportunity to appear on an American radio program. His musical number from *Cuban Pete* was later reprised on the *I Love Lucy* show. That same year, Arnaz released his own version of Cuban singer Miguelito Valdes's "Babalú"—which became a hit and his signature song on the *I Love Lucy* show.

meeting and sometimes subverting—English-speaking Americans' expectations and cultural stereotypes about Spanish speakers. In his pre-television career as a successful bandleader he helped popularize Latin music in America, blending Afro-Caribbean traditions with a big band sound. In Arnaz's frequent musical performances on *I Love Lucy*, he brought that music and Latinx vocals to a wide national audience that, in the immediate postwar era, consisted of millions of Americans who had rarely—or perhaps never—welcomed foreign-language speech or music into the intimate space of the family home. Arnaz used humor and music to offer Anglo Americans a vision of Latinx culture that was exciting, rhythmic, sensual, and, most of all, appealing, even if it often affirmed and played into enduring and simplistic stereotypes.

The passion that characterized Ricky Ricardo as a "Latin lover" and a passionate musical performer, known for an extremely strenuous style of conga drum playing, also positioned him as quick-tempered and high-strung. A 1952 *New York Times* article described Arnaz's character as "volatile," while other articles emphasized that he was "an emotional Latin." Ricky Ricardo became the male version of the Latina/Mexican spitfire stereotype, cementing the notion of the hotheaded Latino. Since the show did not subtitle anything spoken in Spanish, Ricky Ricardo's Spanish monologues were employed solely for comedic effect, with a singular interpretive phrase like "She's nuts!" occasionally placed on-screen. Yet at times Arnaz as Ricardo used his hot-tempered tirades in Spanish on the show to express himself openly in a way that English speakers wouldn't understand but that Spanish speakers could relate to. Confusion and exasperation are often the dominant sentiments in many of Ricky's rants, more so than anger or condemnation toward Lucy's antics.

Arnaz was not the first, nor the last, Latinx entertainer to chart a tenuous course through the murky waters of cultural and ethnic stereotypes on the way to stardom. But he may have been the most successful. While Arnaz performed on-screen as Ricky Ricardo, behind the scenes he was building one of the most influential television empires in Hollywood history—to that point and since. With Ball, he founded Desilu Studios and oversaw its operations, including the development of technical innovations—most famously the three-camera method of filming sitcoms live in front of a studio audience on 35-millimeter film, a standard production practice still used today. Arnaz's public persona circulated not just as "Ricky Ricardo" but as Hollywood's sole—and terrifically successful—Spanish-speaking studio executive.

Through continuous reruns, generations of Americans have watched Ricky love Lucy and laughed at the pair's wacky antics. Despite the show's groundbreaking popularity, Arnaz was the only lead actor on the series who never won an Emmy for his role. Even without recognition from the Television Academy, Desi Arnaz became the most visible and influential Latino in Hollywood during the mid-twentieth century. He was far from merely a TV husband—he was a refugee who navigated, and then reshaped, Hollywood during a moment of extraordinary xenophobia when the industry was steeped in stereotype—when it was open to Latinxs at all. Decades later, Desi still matters, and Latinxs in Hollywood (and the rest of the United States) are still reckoning with questions that shaped his own approaches to comedy and to celebrity: How much of one's authentic culture and personal identity should be leveraged, or erased, in pursuit of mainstream success in a fraught American entertainment landscape?

"Those people there in the audience—they tell you what's good and what isn't."
—Desi Arnaz on* Late Night with David Letterman*, May 23, 1983

Ashley Oliva Mayor

"CAN WE TALK" ABOUT JOAN RIVERS?

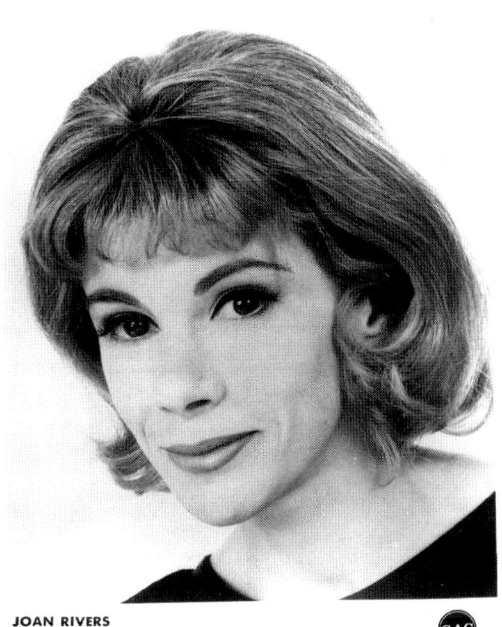
JOAN RIVERS

For the 1960s, Joan Rivers was a girl behaving badly—speaking the unspeakable, exposing the rigged game stacked against her, and refusing to shrink into the polite invisibility expected of women. She brought a sound, a look, and a perspective unlike anything stand-up had seen, and became the first comedian to directly address the intimate and unspoken realities of women's lives. By the close of a seven-decade career, she was respected not only for her craftsmanship but also for her unwavering insistence on claiming space within an industry that was at times dismissive and hostile.

Joan Molinsky was not an overnight success. She graduated from Barnard College and dabbled in theater before setting upon a career in stand-up comedy, plying her craft in obscurity for more than ten years during an era when opportunities for women in comedy were few and narrowly defined. She played every room that would book her—dive bars, strip clubs, social lodges—meticulously refining her craft and building the armor she needed to survive the sharp edges of a comic's grueling existence. Those lean years fueled her hard-won transformation into Joan Rivers—an audacious force in a little black dress.

On February 17, 1965, after a breakout set on Johnny Carson's *Tonight Show*, Joan Rivers emerged as a household name. With her confessional "over-the-back-fence" style, punctuated with a signature "Can we talk?," she broke the silence around the double standards that governed women's lives: the drudgery of domesticity, the traps of marriage, and the relentless pressure to be pretty. She laughed at her own insecurities and, in doing so, exploded cultural anxieties around sex, marriage, aging, and taboo subjects like divorce and abortion.

Rivers's career was built tactically, often in defiance of an entertainment industry that was intent on boxing her in. While establishing herself as one of the most bankable headlining acts in the nation, and maintaining a breathless pace on the road, she was also the creative force behind Broadway's *Fun City* (a play about women's liberation) and TV's *The Girl Most*

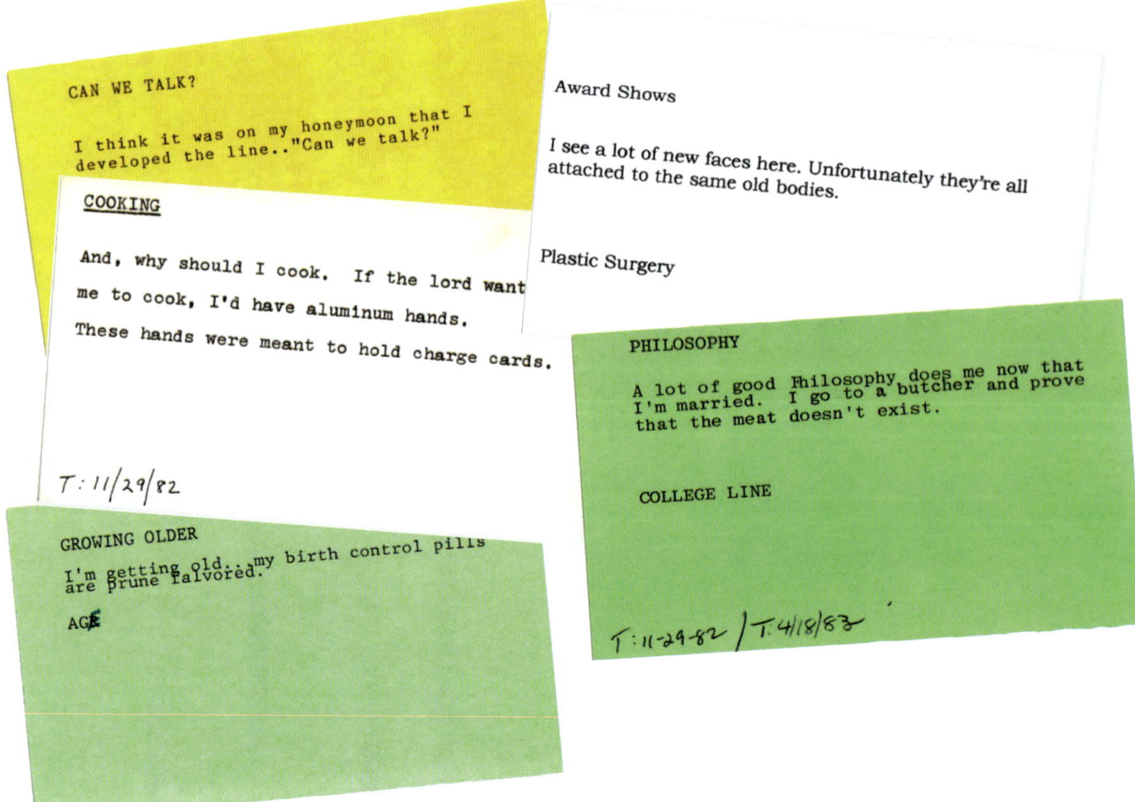

Likely To . . . (a record-setting dark comedy about a girl struggling with traditional standards of beauty). She became one of the first women ever to both write and direct a comedy feature—*Rabbit Test*, a cult classic about a man (Billy Crystal) becoming pregnant. When she booked dates on America's widest platforms, she used them to put her authentic self on display in vulnerable ways: In 1968, she appeared nine months pregnant on *The Ed Sullivan Show*—a watershed cultural moment at a time when the word "pregnant" was still illicit on TV.

Rivers was such a frequent and in-demand presence on *The Tonight Show* stage that Carson ultimately named her his permanent guest host—a role she filled nearly two hundred times. When it became clear to her that she wouldn't inherit the desk upon Johnny's rumored retirement, she launched *The Late Show Starring Joan Rivers* on the fledgling Fox network, making history as the first woman to helm a major late-night show. Rivers's skill as an interviewer was distinct—spontaneous, direct, intimate, and often more revealing than that of her detached, affable male peers. Yet the show was short-lived, hampered by tepid network support and a public professional fallout with Carson, who viewed her move as a betrayal. Decades later, even with hosts like Wanda Sykes, Chelsea Handler, and

Taylor Tomlinson following in her footsteps, no major network has yet chosen a woman to lead its flagship late-night show.

Just as Rivers suffered the devastating break with Fox, her husband and closest collaborator died by suicide. Then aged fifty-four, she found herself a single mother, indebted and—in her estimation—"un-hireable." She set about rebuilding her career from a new vantage. She developed a daytime talk show and won an Emmy; she wrote a Broadway play (*Sally Marr*) and received a Tony nomination for her performance as its star; she accelerated the pace of her career as a touring headliner with dates at premier venues around the world; and she founded the wildly successful Joan Rivers Worldwide fashion brand. "My alternate career," she once said, "has been pulling myself up from rock bottom."

In later years, Rivers's comedy sharpened in bite and precision. Though some labeled her too caustic for their taste, Rivers believed, deeply, that humor was a salve and a leveler—a way of diffusing enormous pain (including her own) and connecting to others in empathy. No one was "safe" from her barbs, least of all herself. Public figures from Dolly Parton, Yoko Ono, and Liz Taylor to Jacqueline Kennedy Onassis, the queen of England, and President Barack Obama were the recipients of Rivers's humor, and most considered it a badge of honor. She often reminded critics that "punching up" at the powerful was not cruelty but catharsis—a release valve for a culture obsessed with status.

In a world of fleeting fame, Rivers evolved as quickly as the entertainment industry itself—if she wasn't the one driving it forward. In the 1990s, alongside her daughter Melissa Rivers, she reimagined contemporary awards-show coverage with E!'s *Live from the Red Carpet*, where she coined the phrase "Who are you wearing?" and planted herself, once again, at the red-hot center of Hollywood and pop culture. She made early forays into reality TV, web series, and social media, crafting a stunning second act that helped to set a tone for the postmodern metatextuality and ironic confessionalism of the reality TV age.

On February 17, 2014—forty-nine years to the day after her first appearance on Carson's stage—Rivers's story came full circle when she was a guest on the premiere episode of *The Tonight Show Starring Jimmy Fallon*. Months later, she passed away suddenly, leaving behind one of comedy's most daring and original bodies of work. In 2023, Joan Rivers's legendary joke file was accessioned into the collections of the National Comedy Center. The meticulously alphabetized and cross-referenced file, which the *New York Times* called a "crown jewel of comedy," includes

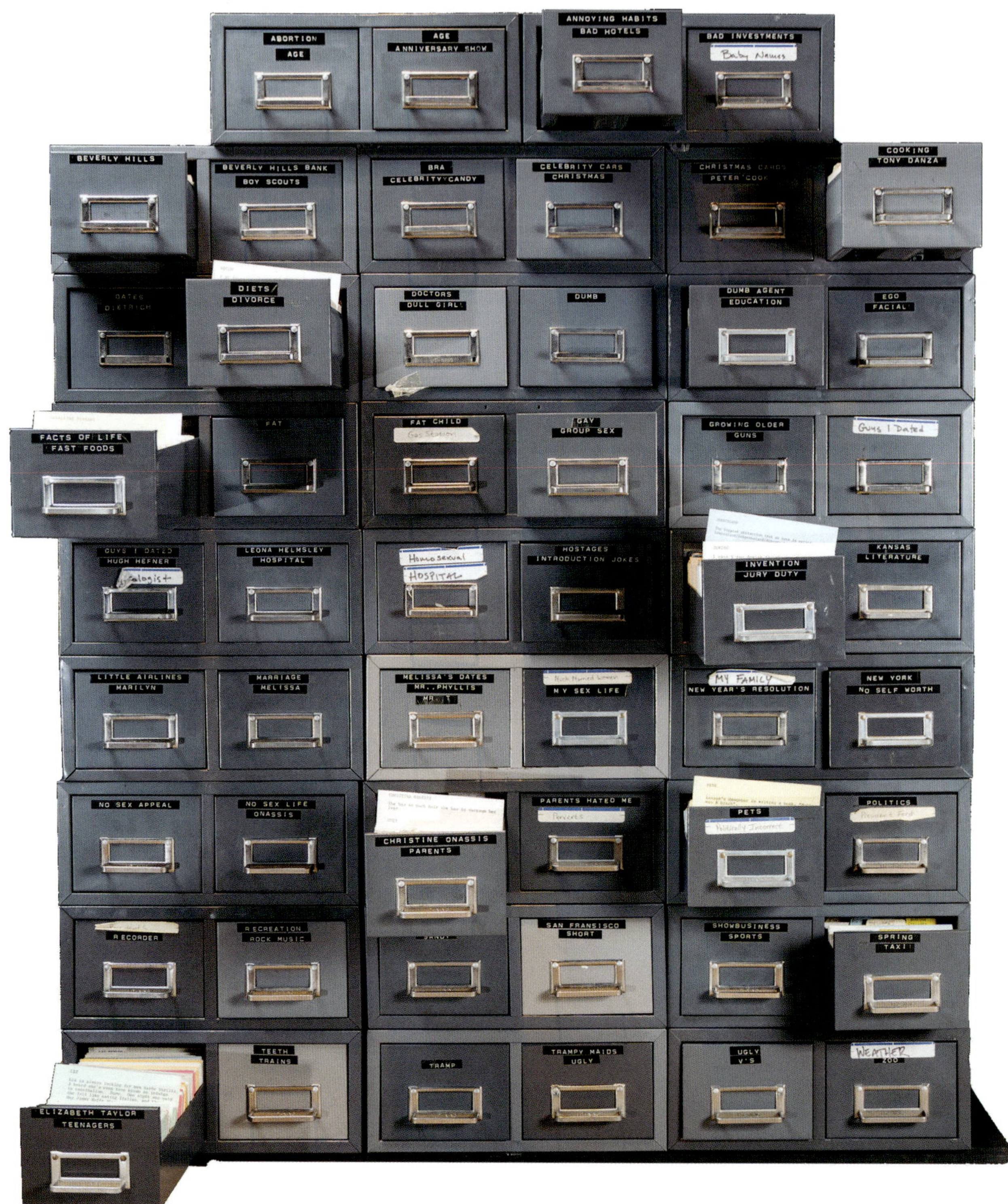
ABORTION
AGE
AGE
ANNIVERSARY SHOW
ANNOYING HABITS
BAD HOTELS
BAD INVESTMENTS
Baby Names
BEVERLY HILLS
BEVERLY HILLS BANK
BOY SCOUTS
BRA
CELEBRITY CANDY
CELEBRITY CARS
CHRISTMAS
CHRISTMAS CARDS
PETER COOK
COOKING
TONY DANZA
DATES
DIETRICH
DIETS/
DIVORCE
DOCTORS
DULL GIRL
DUMB
DUMB AGENT
EDUCATION
EGO
FACIAL
FACTS OF LIFE
FAST FOODS
FAT
FAT CHILD
GAY
GROUP SEX
GROWING OLDER
GUNS
Guys I Dated
GUYS I DATED
HUGH HEFNER
LEONA HELMSLEY
HOSPITAL
Homosexual
HOSPITAL
HOSTAGES
INTRODUCTION JOKES
INVENTION
JURY DUTY
KANSAS
LITERATURE
LITTLE AIRLINES
MARILYN
MARRIAGE
MELISSA
MELISSA'S DATES
MR. PHYLLIS
MY SEX LIFE
MY FAMILY
NEW YEAR'S RESOLUTION
NEW YORK
NO SELF WORTH
NO SEX APPEAL
NO SEX LIFE
ONASSIS
CHRISTINE ONASSIS
PARENTS
PARENTS HATED ME
PETS
POLITICS
RECORDER
RECREATION
ROCK MUSIC
SAN FRANSISCO
SHORT
SHOWBUSINESS
SPORTS
SPRING
TAXI
TEETH
TRAINS
TRAMP
TRAMPY MAIDS
UGLY
UGLY
V'S
WEATHER
ZOO
ELIZABETH TAYLOR
TEENAGERS

nearly 70,000 original jokes ranging across hundreds of subject areas: 390 jokes on NEW YORK, 538 on GUYS I DATED, 989 on POLITICS, and 1,434 on AGING among them. It is a time capsule of the American twentieth century as filtered through the comic sensibility of one of its most unflinching witnesses. Like its creator, the jokes it contains are uninhibited, unapologetic, and very funny.

Laura LaPlaca

COUNTERCULTURE TV: *THE SMOTHERS BROTHERS COMEDY HOUR* AND *LAUGH-IN*

By the 1960s, television was a primary source of world news and political discourse for most Americans. Highly respected anchors like Walter Cronkite and David Brinkley were voices of journalistic integrity who galvanized the nation. At the same time, the baby boom generation—raised on broadcast media and composing nearly half of the total U.S. population—was fomenting a so-called crisis of authority that would challenge the power of America's increasingly institutionalized, bureaucratic, and conservative institutions—including the television networks.

It was television that showed the world vivid footage of officers quashing rallies on college campuses, violent scenes at the 1968 Democratic National Convention, fire hoses at civil rights marches, draft cards and bras being burned, and the assassination of President Kennedy. Nevertheless, most network fare was divorced from these realities, operating in an escapist world of fantasy that was far removed from the real sociopolitical temperature of the nation. TV comedy's first generation of innovators—Jack Benny, Lucille Ball, Milton Berle—had made an indelible mark on the trajectory of the art form and were still drawing top ratings on the airwaves, but a new vanguard was emerging to push boundaries in ways that comedic artists before them hadn't—or couldn't.

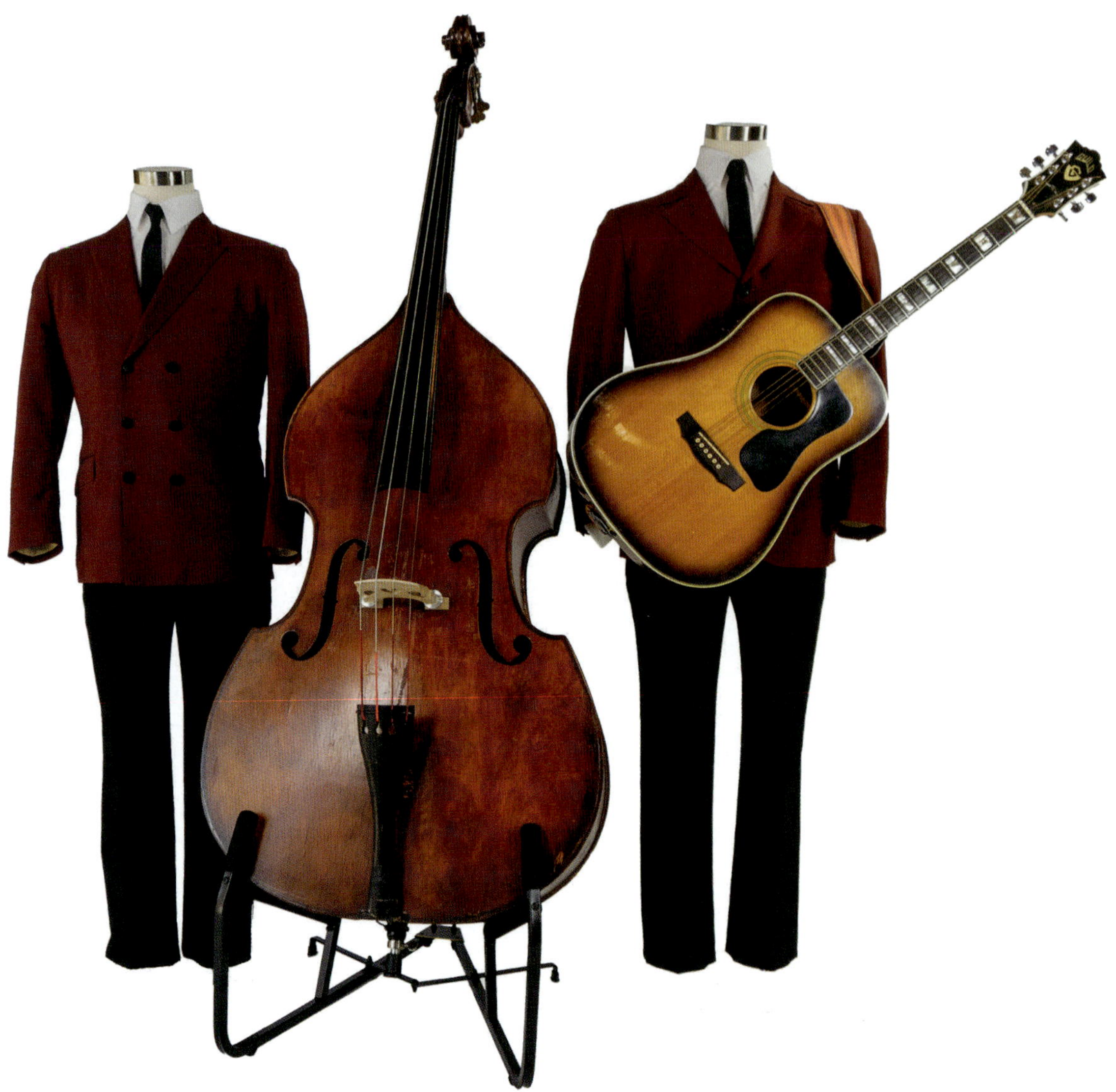

The Smothers Brothers' matching suits and clean-cut look allowed them to bridge the so-called generation gap. Though they began their careers as folk singers, with Tommy on guitar and Dick on bass, they ascended to become unwitting martyrs to the cause of freedom of speech.

The Smothers Brothers came up as part of Northern California's folk music scene in the late 1950s. Known initially for their musical performances (Tommy on guitar and Dick on bass), they developed a classic sibling rivalry act with Dick as the unflappable straight man to Tommy's naïve comic foil. A career-making thirty-six-week gig at San Francisco's Purple Onion launched the brothers to renown at an auspicious sociopolitical moment. Though their deceptively simple comic formula appeared straightlaced and was laden with jokes of the "mom always liked you best" variety, their work came to distill, with shocking clarity, what really mattered to a generation of disaffected youth. Indeed, the Smothers Brothers were to be among the era's most important mouthpieces for liberal American politics and, ultimately, unwitting martyrs to the cause of the First Amendment.

In the grand tradition of variety shows that preceded it, *The Smothers Brothers Comedy Hour* on the CBS network consisted of musical numbers, guest star appearances, and direct-to-camera bits by its hosts. With their matching suits, crisp haircuts, and mild-mannered demeanors, the brothers were poised to work both sides of the proverbial "generation gap"—appealing at once to an older demographic of television viewers and their own youthful cohort of baby boomer peers. The show walked this line with intention: guest stars included established broadcast legends like Danny Thomas, George Burns, and Jimmy Durante as well as emerging rock artists like Buffalo Springfield, The Who, and Jefferson Airplane; the writers' room included veterans Hal Goldman and Al Gordon (with credits dating back to *The Jack Benny Show* of broadcasting's golden age) as well as innovative new voices like Steve Martin, Rob Reiner, and Bob Einstein. All of America tuned in to a "something-for-everyone" admixture of humor, music, and—increasingly—social commentary.

Indeed, the straightforwardness of *The Smothers Brothers Comedy Hour* formula concealed a biting sociopolitical agenda that ended up taking television's gatekeepers by surprise. Ingeniously mobilizing the televisual medium's own immediacy and directness, Tommy and Dick loaded their show with comic allusions to drug culture, feminism, draft dodging, civil rights abuses, government corruption, education reform, and American colonialism abroad—among myriad other topics that were energizing a rising youth movement. Most of the time, these references were so ingeniously integrated into the show's humor that they flew over the heads of censors, speaking in a sort of double-talk to audience members who were part of the counterculture. The network found itself scrambling to rein in the Smothers Brothers' infiltration of the airwaves at the same time as audiences were turning to the show with increasing interest as a counterpoint to the mainstream news media.

THE WHITE HOUSE
WASHINGTON

November 9, 1968

Dear Messrs. Smothers:

I am very grateful for your kind and thoughtful letter.

To be genuinely funny at a time when the world is in crisis is a task that would tax the talents of a genius; to be consistently fair when standards of fair play are constantly questioned demands the wisdom of a saint.

It is part of the price of leadership of this great and free nation to be the target of clever satirists. You have given the gift of laughter to our people. May we never grow so somber or self-important that we fail to appreciate the humor in our lives.

If ever an Emmy is awarded for graciousness, I will cast my vote for you.

Sincerely,

Messrs. Tom and
Dick Smothers
7800 Beverly Boulevard
Los Angeles, California 90036

President Lyndon B. Johnson graciously accepted a letter from the Smothers Brothers expressing their antiwar stance, reflecting an upstanding attitude toward the art and impact of comedy as a form of cultural expression. His successor, Richard Nixon, would not be as gracious.

With the dawning of the new year in 1968, the nation faced a sociopolitical crisis of grand proportions. Particularly in the weeks following the Tet Offensive, it had become clear to many Americans that their fellow citizens were fighting, and dying, in a war with unclear motives. More than half of all Americans considered the conflict in Vietnam to be a fool's errand. In February, Tommy Smothers invited folk singer Pete Seeger, who had been blacklisted from television due to his leftist political views, to perform his antiwar song "Waist Deep in the Big Muddy" on *The Smothers Brothers Comedy Hour*. The song was based on a photograph of troops slogging through Vietnam's Mekong Delta and was an allusion to President Johnson's misguided wartime leadership. CBS removed the song before broadcast, prompting the irate Smothers Brothers to launch a campaign informing the American public of what they believed to be a violation of the First Amendment. CBS responded to the public outcry by allowing Seeger to return to the show to perform the controversial piece, inadvertently amplifying its audience in the wake of the media frenzy that had ensued.

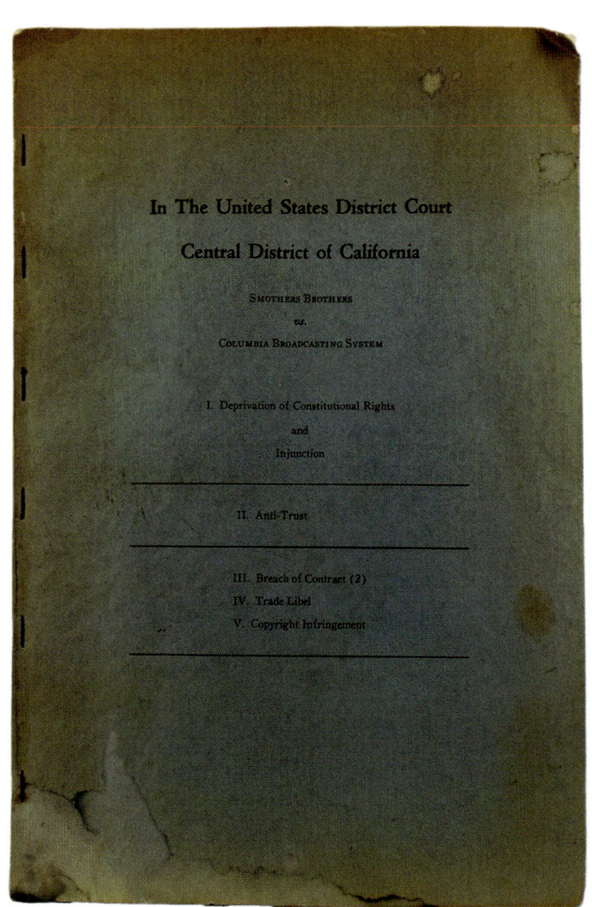

In The United States District Court

Central District of California

SMOTHERS BROTHERS

vs.

COLUMBIA BROADCASTING SYSTEM

I. Deprivation of Constitutional Rights

and

Injunction

II. Anti-Trust

III. Breach of Contract (2)

IV. Trade Libel

V. Copyright Infringement

Though the Smothers Brothers were fired by CBS at the pinnacle of their fame and influence, they ultimately won a breach of contract suit in a California district court, proving that they had been erroneously yanked from the airwaves.

The Smothers Brothers didn't adjust their stance on the war. It seemed, instead, that a new seriousness of purpose had entered their work. Though they seemed to delight in the provocations, they were also willing martyrs for a cause—with a lot to lose. What they said on the airwaves was heard and felt by millions, and they ensured that what they *couldn't* say was made "no less meaningful".[24] One especially biting episode opened with the show's writers silently passing along a copy of a *Smothers Brother Comedy Hour* script and ripping out pages until nothing was left; the Beatles' George Harrison made a cameo on the show, speaking for his generation when he turned to Tommy and boldly said, "Whether you can say it or not, keep trying to say it"; and when the president imposed a travel ban to foreign countries, Tommy stared into the camera lens and shouted, "Okay, all you guys in Vietnam, come on home!" In September 1968, as the Smothers Brothers' ongoing and highly public battle with their censors continued to rage, the network cut a performance of "Don't Stop the Carnival" by Harry Belafonte, which the activist and musician had sung before a video canvas of violent footage from the 1968 Democratic National Convention. Tommy and Dick's moral and ethical stand for freedom of speech had reached an inflection point.

Increasingly forced into constraining, narrow lanes that neutralized the urgency of their message (and challenged their integrity as artists), the Smothers Brothers metamorphosized from folk-singing comics into some of the most powerful defenders of the First Amendment in American history. *The Smothers Brothers Comedy Hour* was targeted by the network, by the media, and by the president. While Johnson had tolerated—and perhaps even understood—the brothers' humor, Watergate reporters later confirmed that Nixon's campaign funds had been used to investigate the Smothers Brothers as dangerous agents. Being part of Nixon's enemy list was, Tommy would later quip, "kind of a badge of honor."

Finally, CBS conspired to remove *The Smothers Brothers Comedy Hour* from its airwaves—even as it tracked impressive ratings and ranked among the network's most popular offerings. Alleging that Tommy and Dick had broken the terms of their contract by delivering an episode late, they fired the Smothers Brothers, citing breach of contract. A year later, the brothers were vindicated when a U.S. district court ruled in *Tom Smothers et al. v. Columbia Broadcasting System* that it had been CBS that actually violated the contract terms. They received a financial payout but were illegitimately wrested from the peak of their fame and influence at a crucial moment for their audiences, and for the nation.

Though they went on to perform together for another half century, the Smothers Brothers never fully recovered from the fight they waged; the industry held them at arm's length—too volatile to touch. Finally, in 2008, before an audience of his peers, Tommy Smothers was honored with a special Emmy Award for having served as head writer of *The Smothers Brothers Comedy Hour.* As all of Hollywood greeted him with a long-overdue standing ovation, Tommy dedicated the award to all those "who refuse to be silenced."

Across the dial on the NBC network, another boundary-pushing sketch comedy show was making waves. Beloved for its mod aesthetic and hyper pace, *Laugh-In*—created and produced by George Schlatter—was a weekly party on TV that awakened the nation as it used comedy to speak truth to power during the turbulent sixties. The number-one show in America during the height of the countercultural movement, *Laugh-In* was a hodgepodge of burlesque sketches, musical numbers, non sequiturs, slapstick gags, one-liners, and kaleidoscopic visual effects that was unlike anything ever seen—before or since—on the airwaves. The show launched powerful comedic voices like Lily Tomlin and influenced generations of future sketch shows like *In Living Color* and *Saturday Night Live.*

Laugh-In's first episode opened with hosts Dan Rowan and Dick Martin laying bare the show's ethos: "Good evening, ladies and gentlemen, and welcome to television's first 'Laugh-In.' Now, for the past few years, we have all been hearing an awful lot about the various 'ins.' There have been be-ins, love-ins, and sleep-ins. This is a laugh-in and a laugh-in is a frame of mind." If the avant-garde series raised some eyebrows when it debuted in 1968, it quickly shot to the top of the ratings, beating out seemingly immovable stalwarts like *Gunsmoke* and *The Lucy Show* and altering the landscape of TV forever.

The *New York Times* described *Laugh-In* at the peak of its popularity as "hilarious, brash, peppery, irreverent, satirical, repetitious, risqué, topical, and in borderline taste—it is primarily and always fast, fast, fast! And in this it is contemporary. It's attuned to the time. It's hectic, electric; McLuhanism applied."[25] *Laugh-In* was, indeed, a uniquely televisual spectacle that toyed with TV's lo-fi aesthetic and rapid flow in ways that exposed techniques like editing and sound design as visible ingredients in the show's structure. More significantly, it was designed expressly for an audience raised on a media-saturated cultural diet, with its zooms, blackouts, and pratfalls punctuating a symphony of modernist pop cultural allusions. Producer George Schlatter called its fast, segmented style, which consisted of a remarkable 250 cuts per hour, a form of "comedy verité."

Perhaps because *Laugh-In* judiciously lobbed zingers across both sides of the political aisle, it was never subject to the level of censorship faced by *The Smothers Brothers Comedy Hour*, though some theorize that the show simply moved too fast and was so laced with suggestiveness that censors struggled to decipher it. One way that *Laugh-In* circumvented the censors was by inventing nonsense words and phrases that bordered on innuendo, like "You bet your sweet bippy" and "ring my chimes." A recurring sketch that parodied the soap opera genre was all about the Farkel Family—an extended clan of relatives who spoke almost exclusively using words that started with the letter F. The show's infamous Flying Fickle Finger of Fate was a not-so-subtle gesture of disapproval to individuals and organizations who had badly blundered in the week's news—the Public Health Service, for example, was awarded the finger when it spent taxpayer dollars on a bogus medical survey "proving" that citizens with more money were generally happier than those living in poverty.

FLYING FICKLE FINGER OF FATE

Dan Rowan and Dick Martin presented the Flying Fickle Finger of Fate Award weekly as a tongue-in-cheek acknowledgment of the individuals, institutions, and government agencies that had made the news recently for especially egregious missteps, botches, and scandals.

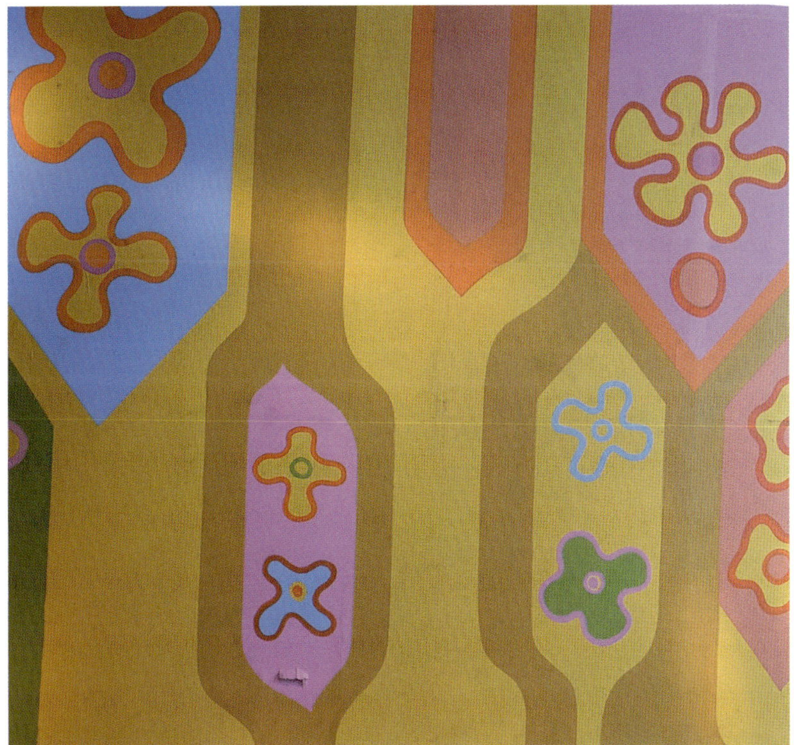

Though *Laugh-In* tackled serious subject matter and presented biting commentaries, it was also a celebration of silliness. The show's signature "joke wall," a segment of which can be seen here, was an iconic backdrop for a psychedelic age.

"*Laugh-In* Looks at the News" was one of the show's most influential weekly segments, going on to inspire *Saturday Night Live*'s "Weekend Update" and the tone of many of today's satirical late-night news programs. The sketch featured Dan Rowan and Dick Martin presenting "News of the Present," "News of the Past," and "News of the Future" with pointed criticism of government agencies, celebrities, institutions, and other power brokers who were shaping the course of the late sixties—one of the most politically troubled epochs in world history. At the same time as *Laugh-In* delved into serious and impactful commentaries that challenged the status quo, it also traded in a pure playfulness that was nothing short of silly. Its signature conceit was its joke wall—a psychedelic façade with geometric porthole doors through which cast members and guest stars alike, balanced precariously on a concealed scaffolding, would emerge to deliver corny one-liners and knock-knock jokes in a loose and improvisational style as the show's credits rolled.

With a versatile ensemble cast that was bolstered by recurring characters like Ruth Buzzi's spinster character "Gladys Ormphby," Arte Johnson's "Wolfgang the German Soldier," and Judy Carne's "Sock It to Me Girl," *Laugh-In* was an incubator for comedy talents—not least of all a culture-shifting stand-up named Lily Tomlin, a future Academy Award winner named Goldie Hawn, and a promising young writer named Lorne Michaels. It was also a showcase for a who's who of twentieth-century Hollywood, with a guest starring gig on the show becoming a coveted invitation: Cher, Orson Welles, Kirk Douglas, Milton Berle, Hugh Hefner, Rock Hudson, Richard Nixon, Vincent Price, Lena Horne, Carol Channing, and Liberace all appeared on the show, as did semi-regular guests like Pigmeat Markham, Sammy Davis Jr., Phyllis Diller, Flip Wilson, and Henny Youngman.

Laugh-In garnered thirty-one Emmy nominations during its run, including consecutive wins for Outstanding Musical or Variety Series in

1968 and 1969. As a key part of the cultural landscape of the sixties and seventies, the show set the tone for a generation and altered the way that the medium of television was regarded as both an artistic canvas for sociopolitical expression and a forum for airing differing perspectives on challenging issues.

PAT PAULSEN

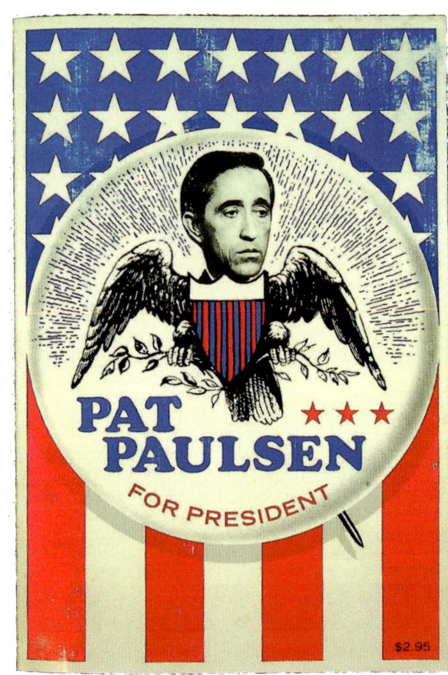

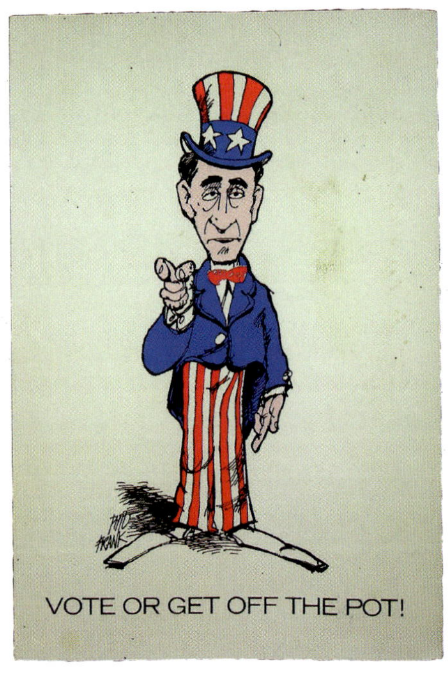

In the spring of 1968, comic Pat Paulsen leveraged the platform of *The Smothers Brothers Comedy Hour* to launch a run for the presidency under the banner of the "Straight Talking American Government" (or STAG) Party. Campaigning on the premise that "issues have no place in politics," Paulsen, with his deadpan facial expressions and double-talking speech pattern, announced his candidacy with a ringing promise: "Will I solve our economic problems? Will I ease the causes of racial tension? Will I bring a peaceful end to Vietnam? Sure, why not?"

Paulsen's campaign became one of the most popular, and salient, sketches to emerge from *The Smothers Brothers Comedy Hour*, including a classic bit where Paulsen's face was shown via split screen—so that he could answer political questions two-faced, literally speaking out of both sides of his mouth. The bit extended to in-person stump speeches at rallies across the country, where he liberally lied and attacked real candidates who, in most cases, played along sportingly—Senator Robert F. Kennedy even pledged his personal support for Paulsen's phony campaign.

Paulsen ran for office five times, appearing on official presidential election ballots until 1996, promising in his last Democratic National Convention appearance, "If elected, I will win!" Paulsen's run is part of a long lineage of comedic political campaigns that have satirized the ironies, deceits, and histrionics spilling out of Washington during election season. From Dan Rice's bombastic Civil War–era candidacy to Will Rogers's run on the eve of the Great Depression, from Gracie Allen's 1940 formation of the "Surprise Party" on the radio to Stephen Colbert's 2008 campaign launched on cable TV, comedians have fashioned themselves as preposterous politicians to suggest that the real joke might have been the dysfunction of the American electoral system itself.

LILY TOMLIN

Laugh-In's Lily Tomlin parlayed her national exposure on the hit TV show to become one of the most outspoken comedic voices of her generation. Tomlin honed her craft as part of the emergent comedy club scene but differentiated herself with a unique approach to stand-up that relied heavily on deeply embodied character work. After being hired by *Laugh-In* creator George Schlatter to replace an exiting cast member, Tomlin became a breakout star on the series, portraying a roster of memorable characters of her own creation, including the pint-sized know-it-all Edith Ann, who lisped words of wisdom from her perch on a gigantic rocking chair, and the irascible phone operator Ernestine, who became a household name along with catchphrases like "Is this the party to whom I am speaking?" By the end of the decade, she was featured on the cover of *Time* magazine and hailed as "America's New Queen of Comedy."

Lily Tomlin embodied a range of comic characters on TV's *Laugh-In*, including Ernestine the phone operator who was known for her nasal-voiced non sequiturs and an iconic curly up-do.

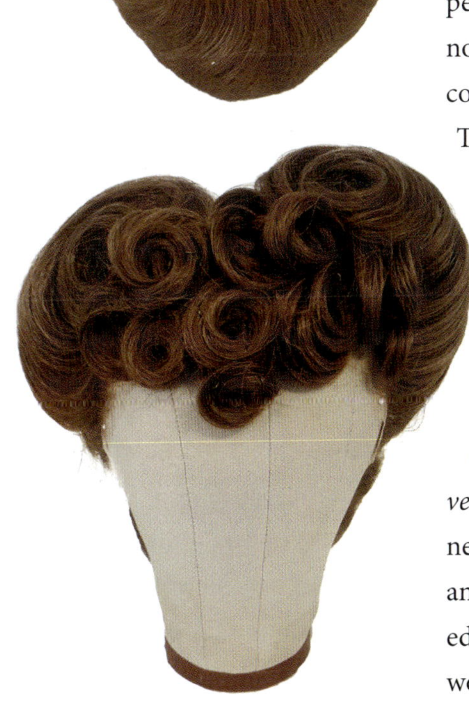

At *Laugh-In*'s conclusion, Tomlin reprised her role as Ernestine for *This Is a Recording*, a Grammy-winning comedy album that smashed *Billboard* records, and debuted on Broadway in the Tony-winning play *Appearing Nitely*—a solo show cocreated with her partner, Jane Wagner. *Appearing Nitely* was an inheritor of the traditions of stand-up comedy, monology, and the expressionist movement in the theater, but it defied categorization. Instead, it opened up new performative possibilities for comedians who were increasingly seeking not only to get laughs but to communicate deep truths about the human condition. Alone on a blank stage, with no sets, props, or costumes, Tomlin inhabited fifteen distinct characters—sometimes more than one at a time—blurring distinctions between age, race, gender, ability, and sexuality with a fluidity that was both profoundly funny and profoundly moving. When asked about the motivations behind her character work, Tomlin bluntly explained, "I feel I'm being politically active when I perform."[26]

Appearing Nitely was followed up by Tomlin's personal magnum opus in 1985, when *The Search for Signs of Intelligent Life in the Universe* debuted on Broadway to enormous acclaim. Also written by Wagner and showcasing Tomlin's masterful ability to wholly inhabit diverse and idiosyncratic characters, the show cemented Tomlin's place in comedy history and earned her another Tony. Like her earlier work, the one-woman show was a bold and forward-looking statement about identity and difference—and, more particularly, about the many and various ways that it was possible to inhabit and express one's womanhood. At a moment when identity politics were under severe revision in the United States, Tomlin's use of comedy performance to crack open rigid definitions of selfhood and demonstrate the folly of "othering" those with differences was an artistic, cultural, and social watershed.

Laura LaPlaca

RICHARD PRYOR: OUTRAGEOUS AUTHENTICITY

It's one of the most shocking and provocative sketches to ever air on *Saturday Night Live*, laying bare the long-simmering racial tension and righteous anger felt by Black Americans tired of the never-ending struggle for civil rights and equality.

The "Word Association" sketch, which aired in the series' first season in 1975, features the Black comedian Richard Pryor as an applicant for a job, with the white comedian Chevy Chase playing the interviewer. He asks Pryor's character to take a psychological test, a word association exercise where he will throw out random words to see what comes to the applicant's mind. Though it starts innocently ("Dog?" "Tree." "Fast?" "Slow."), the test soon escalates into racial slurs, with an incredulous Pryor turning to anger as he matches Chase's insults with his own ("Spearchucker?" "White Trash!" "Jungle bunny?" "Honky!"). When Chase says the N-word, Pryor's demeanor turns deadly serious, with eyes flinching ominously, as he responds, "*Dead* honky!" Chase's persona suddenly changes too, as the interviewer attempts to clear the open hostility by offering Pryor not only the job but a substantial salary ("You'll be the highest paid janitor in America!") but also a few weeks' leave, as long as Pryor won't hurt him.[27]

Brilliant, irreverent, aggressive, vulnerable, socially conscious, and profane, Richard Pryor was one of the most influential and significant

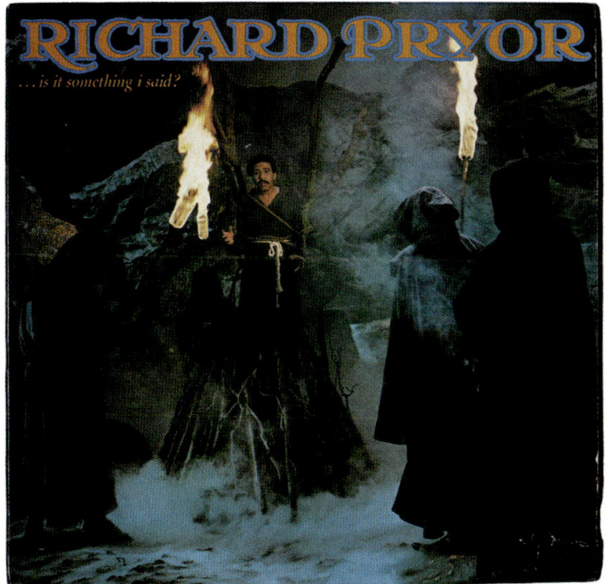

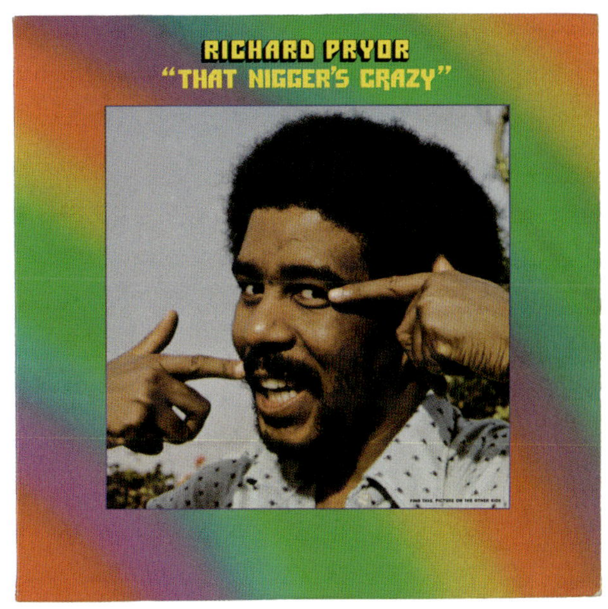

In his revolutionary stand-up performances, especially those captured on film and on vinyl like these records, Richard Pryor's transgressive social commentary generated controversy and critical acclaim. Pryor earned three Grammy Awards in a row for Best Comedy Album, for *That N[-----]'s Crazy* (1975), *. . . Is It Something I Said?* (1976), and *Bicentennial N[-----]* (1977), then two more for *Rev. Du Rite* (1982) and *Richard Pryor: Live on the Sunset Strip* (1983).

comedians of the twentieth century. The groundbreaking Black comic tackled race, politics, gender, and sexuality in shockingly frank terms, holding a mirror to the absurdities, hypocrisies, and prejudices of modern American life. In his raw and wildly improvisational stand-up performances, Pryor combined an explosive mixture of countercultural transgression and provocative rhetoric. He also brought a new sensibility and perspective to television and film comedy, as both a writer and a performer. At a critical cultural moment, Richard Pryor brought the Black vernacular comic voice into national consciousness, provoking and shaping conversations about society, politics, and identity.

Born in Peoria, Illinois, in 1940, Pryor was raised by his grandmother in the brothels she operated, surrounded by prostitutes, pimps, hustlers, and alcoholics. In later years he spoke about feeling abandoned and lonely as a child; he found refuge in his imagination and his seemingly natural ability to make others laugh. After spending a stint in the army mostly incarcerated for his part in beating a racist white soldier, Pryor became a stand-up comic in New York City in the early 1960s. His middlebrow, buttoned-down, observational style was a conscious imitation of Bill Cosby, who had recently become the most popular Black comedian in America by largely ignoring race in his act, sticking to universal and nonthreatening topics for the white audiences who flocked to his appearances.

Pryor's career took off, with appearances on *The Ed Sullivan Show* and *The Tonight Show Starring Johnny Carson*, a record deal, and performances in Las Vegas. It was at Vegas's Aladdin Hotel where Pryor had a career-altering epiphany in 1967. As he recounted in his autobiography, *Pryor Convictions and Other Life Sentences*, he had grown increasingly weary of his safe and derivative comic persona, and walking out on stage to see Dean Martin in the audience that night, he imagined what he must look and sound like onstage. "I imagined what I looked like and got disgusted," Pryor recalled. "I grasped for clarity as if it was oxygen. The fog rolled in. In a burst of inspiration I finally spoke to the sold-out crowd: 'What the fuck am I doing here?' and walked off stage."[28] Soon, Pryor moved to Berkeley, California, where he mingled with a crowd of Black intellectuals and countercultural artists and began honing a new act, inspired by the era's ethnic pride and civil rights movements. He decided he would no longer hide his Black, working-class roots, moving to better embrace the Black vernacular humor he'd grown up with.

His first album, *Richard Pryor*, released in 1968, inaugurated his more freewheeling and aggressive style of comedy as well as his more pointed take on Black identity in a racist society. The cover photo satirically depicted Pryor as an African tribesman in loincloth and jewelry, holding a bow and arrow in front of a cave, with a National Geographic–like yellow line and oak cluster border. In this and the six other wildly successful comedy records he released over the 1970s, his routines included characters drawn from the Black community of his youth, like street preachers, winos and junkies, and Mudbone, an elderly storyteller who embodied the Black folk humor tradition. Pryor also employed raw and sometimes shockingly intimate observations and stories drawn from his own life, and a brash new stream-of-consciousness style and voice, including use of the N-word. In his autobiography, Pryor called it "the most humiliating, disgraceful, ugly, and nasty word ever used in the context of black people," but by 1968 he had decided to use it frequently in his act, "over and over again like a preacher singing hallelujah," to take the sting out of the word, "as if saying it over and over again would numb me and everybody else to its wretchedness."[29] Pryor's new style was more militant and aggressive than Black comic forebears like Flip Wilson, Redd Foxx, and Dick Gregory, and without being explicitly political, still represented a new social consciousness, a mission to call out and excoriate hypocrisy and prejudice.

Pryor performed this controversial new style in comedy clubs that catered to Black audiences, such as the Apollo Theater in Harlem, but also integrated venues where he gained a following with young people of all backgrounds. He wrote for television, including an Emmy Award–winning 1973 Lily Tomlin special and shows like *Sanford and Son* and *The Flip Wilson Show*, and became the first Black host of *Saturday Night Live*. He even helmed his own variety show, *The Richard Pryor Show*, which premiered on NBC in 1977, but lasted only four episodes. Pryor courted conflict with the network from the start, insisting on a title sequence for the first episode where he appeared completely naked but neutered, lacking genitals altogether, while insisting he had "given up absolutely nothing" to network censors. Pryor quit the show, claiming that NBC was unfairly restraining his creativity; he was to have greater success in movies.

Over the course of the 1970s, Pryor became the most popular and successful Black film star in the world, appearing in films like *Lady Sings the Blues* (1972), a series of four interracial buddy films with Gene Wilder including *Silver Streak* (1976), and blaxploitation-era comedies like *Uptown Saturday Night* (1974), *Car Wash* (1976), and *Which Way Is Up?* (1977). Pryor pioneered the filmed stand-up comedy special, getting theatrical releases for *Richard Pryor: Live in Concert* in 1979 and *Live on the Sunset Strip* in 1982. He cowrote *Blazing Saddles* (1974) with Mel Brooks, but the studio wouldn't insure him so he couldn't appear as the costar with Gene Wilder, as planned—that role went to Cleavon Little instead. The casting change was also due to Pryor's increasing reputation for erratic behavior, copious drug use, and tumultuous personal life, which always threatened to derail his burgeoning career. He suffered a heart attack at the age of thirty-six and nearly died in 1980 when he was badly burned in an infamous fire, possibly a suicide attempt, reportedly involving high-proof rum, freebase cocaine, and a bout of drug-induced psychosis.

But Pryor survived and rebuilt his career with well-received stand-up specials, tours, and film appearances. After a trip to Kenya in 1979, Pryor swore he would never again use the N-word in his stand-up routine, and stuck to his word. He saw a generation of comedians who revered him as the creator of modern Black American comedy build careers in his wake, including Eddie Murphy, Whoopi Goldberg, and Chris Rock. He was the first comedian to receive the Mark Twain Prize for American Humor, in 1998, by which time he had scaled back his career due to multiple sclerosis that had severely limited his mobility. He died in 2005.

Ryan Lintelman

LAND BACK!: CHARLIE HILL AND THE POWER OF INDIGENOUS REPRESENTATION

When the Smithsonian's National Museum of the American Indian opened in Washington, D.C., in 2004, comedian Charlie Hill was the emcee for the First Americans Festival on the National Mall. As a stand-up performer since the 1970s, Hill effortlessly dove into his tried-and-true routines and crowd work while introducing musical acts such as Mary Youngblood and Lila Downs.[30] More than eighty thousand people came to the National Mall for the museum's opening day, and there was no one else who could handle that crowd and keep the festivities rolling.

Hill was a comedian whose career included many "firsts." He was the first Native American comedian to perform on national television. His credits included *The Mike Douglas Show*, *The Tonight Show Starring Johnny Carson*, the *Late Show with David Letterman*, and *The Tonight Show with Jay Leno*. Hill was among the famed Comedy Store regulars in the 1970s with David Letterman, Jimmie "J. J." Walker, and Robin Williams. There were no other Native comedians performing across North America. Hill was a complete original; his comedy merged the Native American experience and viewpoint with biting

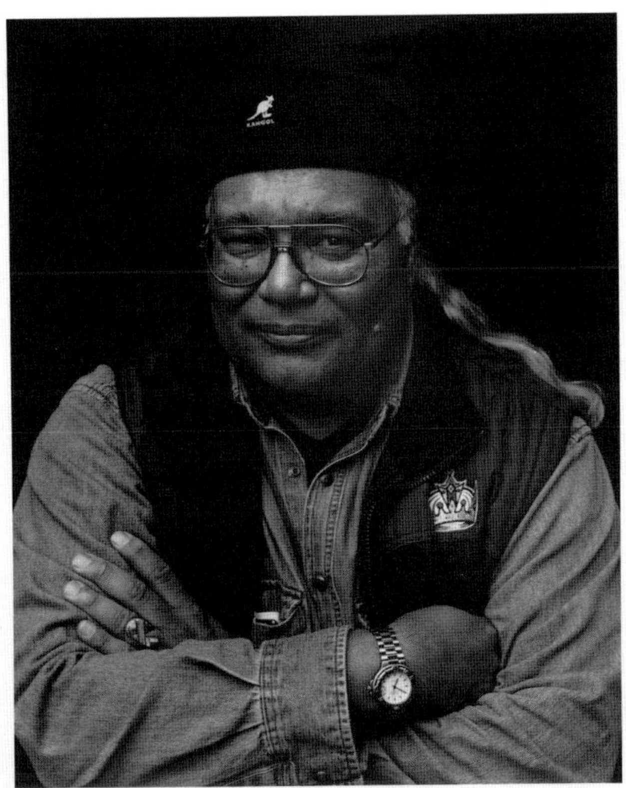
Portrait of Charlie Hill, ca. 2000s.

and truthful social commentary on U.S. history, politics, and pop culture. He performed for Native and non-Native audiences and never shied away from confronting stereotypes or exposing American myths.

Born in Detroit, Michigan, in 1951, Hill was a citizen of the Oneida Nation of Wisconsin and of Mohawk and Cree heritage. He was born into a family of strong leaders and community activists. Hill's grandmother, Lily Rosa Minoka Hill (Mohawk), was the second Native woman to earn a medical degree, and she operated a private practice, first in Pennsylvania and later on the Oneida reservation.[31] His father, Norbert Hill Sr., was one of the founders of the Great Lakes Inter-tribal Council and held many elected positions in Oneida government and intertribal organizations. Norbert married Eileen Johnson (Cree), and they had six children, with Charlie being the fourth.

In 1962, the Hill family moved to the Oneida reservation, and Hill recalled the influence of the television sitcoms and late-night talk shows that his family watched together on his career. As retold in Kliph Nesteroff's book on Native Americans and comedy, *We Had a Little Real Estate Problem*, Hill recalled, "My mom would be watching Jack Paar . . . I thought, 'How do I get in there? How do I learn how to do that?'"[32] When comedian Dick Gregory appeared on *Tonight Starring Jack Paar* and landed a biting joke on his visit to Minnesota and observing the horrible treatment of Native people there, it unlocked a possibility that Hill never knew existed. He saw that observational comedy could expose injustices and advance social justice.

Hill did not pursue stand-up comedy immediately after high school. He attended the University of Wisconsin–Madison, where he majored in speech and drama. Then he worked in theater in New York, Seattle, and Europe before trying for open mic nights in Los Angeles in 1974. After rotating through various clubs, Hill then earned an audition with Mitzi Shore at the Comedy Store. The conversation quickly turned to Shore and Hill's shared memories of being Wisconsinites, and he received a spot. Hill experienced some pushback for his material about

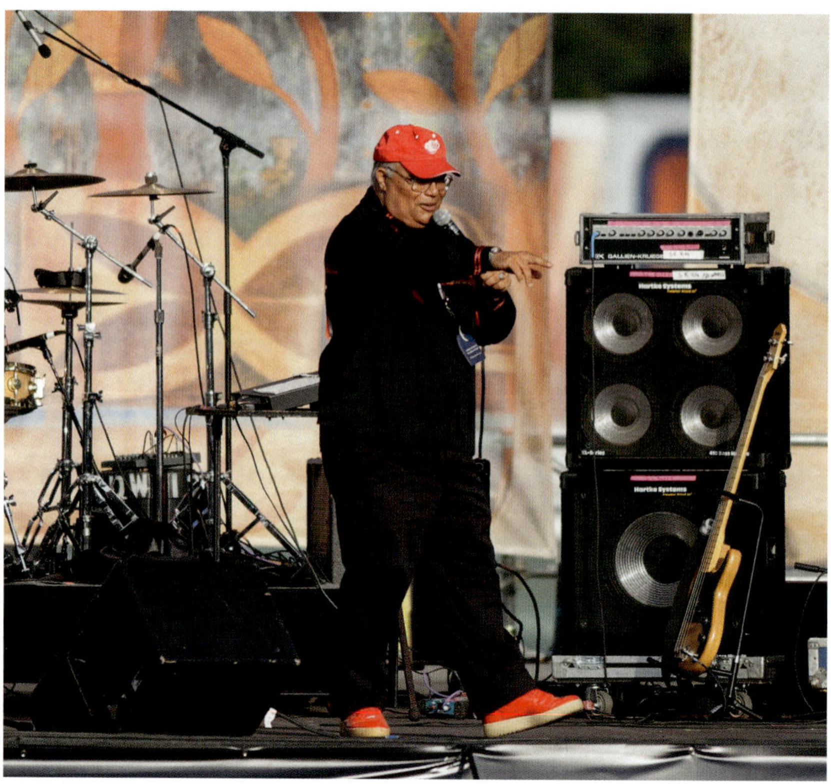

Comedian Charlie Hill onstage during the Smithsonian's First Americans Festival in Washington, D.C.

being Native American, but he remembered that "Mitzi always let me do whatever I wanted onstage."[33]

In 1975, Hill met Richard Pryor through the Comedy Store, and Pryor appreciated Hill's witty comedic style and fearlessness around racial discourse. Pryor promised to get Hill on television, and on October 20, 1977, Hill performed a five-minute set on *The Richard Pryor Show*, a short-lived comedy variety show on NBC. Hill began with a few throwaway jokes but then launched into his main routine: "Shekoli. I'm Oneida. I'm from Wisconsin. It's part of the Iroquois Nation. My people are from Wisconsin. We used to be from New York. *We had a little real estate problem*."[34] The punchline brought a roar of laughter and applause from the audience. Hill knew that he was speaking to a non-Native audience who wouldn't be familiar with his Native nation or history. The setup to the punchline established the dramatic geographical distance between the Oneida's original homeland of New York State and the present-day reservation in Wisconsin. Of course, the forced removal of the Oneida was more than a mere real estate transaction, but the audience would understand that Native people had been robbed of their land and the enormous monetary value of New York property. Hill also included "shekoli" or "hello" in the

"A redneck told me to go back where I came from, so I put a tipi in his backyard."
—Charlie Hill

Oneida language. He understood the power of using his Indigenous language on national television and the pride from other Oneidas for the shoutout.

Hill's performance on *The Richard Pryor Show* was a comedy first—it marked the first time a Native American comedian performed on national television. Originally the show's writers wanted Hill to act in a demeaning sketch, but he refused, and Pryor agreed to a stand-up spot on the show. They also wanted Pryor to dress as George Armstrong Custer with arrows in his back and have Hill jump out from behind a rock, but Hill protested. Unfortunately, the southwestern backdrop and rock remained.

During that set on the Pryor show, Hill constructed jokes through analogies, a comedic formula he perfected throughout his career. Hill started with, "Like the Pilgrims, they weren't my forefathers," and then landed the punchline, "Pilgrims came to this land four hundred years ago as illegal aliens." Hill made the audience realize the Native people do not view the Pilgrims as forefathers and that Native people predate the Pilgrims and other European "discoveries" of America. For Native people, the immigrants or "illegal aliens" are the Pilgrims. Hill effectively infused a Native perspective on American history and brought it to current-day discussions of immigration.

After appearing on Pryor, Hill became an in-demand comic, with appearances on *The Mike Douglas Show*, *The Tonight Show Starring Johnny Carson*, the *Late Night* (and *Show*) *with David Letterman*, and *The Tonight Show with Jay Leno*. Hill never shifted his comedy away from the topical and socially aware routines that originally drew him in; he continued to talk about politicians, religion, and world events. Hill and Letterman met at the Comedy Store, and they traveled together to gigs throughout Southern California; when Letterman debuted his late-night show, he invited Hill to perform a few times. During an appearance on Letterman in the early 2000s, Hill talked about the Iraq War and brought up the conditions of the Iraqi civilians who were losing their land, homes, and resources. He finished with, "They're gonna have to build casinos!" Again, through an analogy, Hill hoped the audience could understand the devastation of war on everyday people and that Native nations turned to gaming enterprises as a way to gain economic independence and rebuild nationhood.

Hill adapted his routines for Native and non-Native audiences. Along with the comedy clubs in cities across North America, he would perform for Native organizations, conferences, and Native comedy specials. He commented, "It was almost like talking two different languages when you'd play to each crowd . . . I learned how to do it in both worlds."[35] On New Year's Eve in 2009, Laugh Out Loud Comedy presented an all-Native comedy special that aired on Showtime. Hill acted as the emcee and led with a parody to the song "This Land Is Your Land," thereby becoming, "This Land Is My Land." He continued with, "We are doing pretty good with our casinos, folks. Someday we are going to buy our land back . . . from the Japanese."[36] Cheers from the Native audience erupted when he mentioned "buy[ing] *our* land back." Then he flipped the script by adding "from the Japanese," which brought more groans and laughter. Hill knew that the audience would not expect the surprise ending. Especially with Native audiences, Hill inserted more information about his personal life and spoke about pan-Native experiences. He would mention his wife, Lenora Hatathlie Hill, being from the Navajo Nation, and how proud he was that his children, Nabahe, Diné Nizhoni, Nanabah, and Nasbah, spoke the Navajo language.

Along with his Native community and family, Hill also had a community of comedians as friends. When Bobby Lee spoke with fellow comedian Marc Maron on the *Tiger Belly Podcast*, Lee fondly remembered Hill as "a kind man" and Maron called him "one of the original guys" along with sharing other funny memories about him.[37] Hill passed away in 2013 at the age of sixty-two after battling lymphoma. Before his death, there was a benefit held at Hollywood's Laugh Factory featuring his comedian friends Jay Leno, Roseanne Barr, and Paul Rodriguez, among others.[38] On his late-night show, Letterman, along with Jeff Altman, took the time to mention Hill's passing and commented that Letterman "never heard anyone say a bad thing about Charlie Hill." While Hill would be amazed to see the number of Native actors in media and the presence of majority-Native writing rooms on streaming shows like *Reservation Dogs* and *Rutherford Falls*, Hill offered that possibility. Through comedy, Hill provided an insight on Native American identity, history, and worldview that was severely lacking in television and movies of his time.

Anya Montiel

ALL IN THE FAMILY AND THE "LOVEABLE BIGOT"

The premiere of *All in the Family*, on January 12, 1971, marked a turning point in television history. Before that night, the family, rural, and fantasy sitcoms that composed the majority of the television comedy landscape had only lightly or indirectly touched on contemporary political and social issues. More politically conscious, polemic, or transgressive comedy, like *The Smothers Brothers Comedy Hour*, faced network censorship, viewer and affiliate indignation, and cancelation. *All in the Family*, however, changed the game, bringing divisive political issues and significant social satire into American living rooms in prime time. A critical and popular success, the "relevance sitcom" opened the door for other shows that probed contemporary issues and political debates and opened a new front in the culture war.

As soon as producers Norman Lear and Bud Yorkin saw the British sitcom *Till Death Us Do Part*, which focused on a working-class family

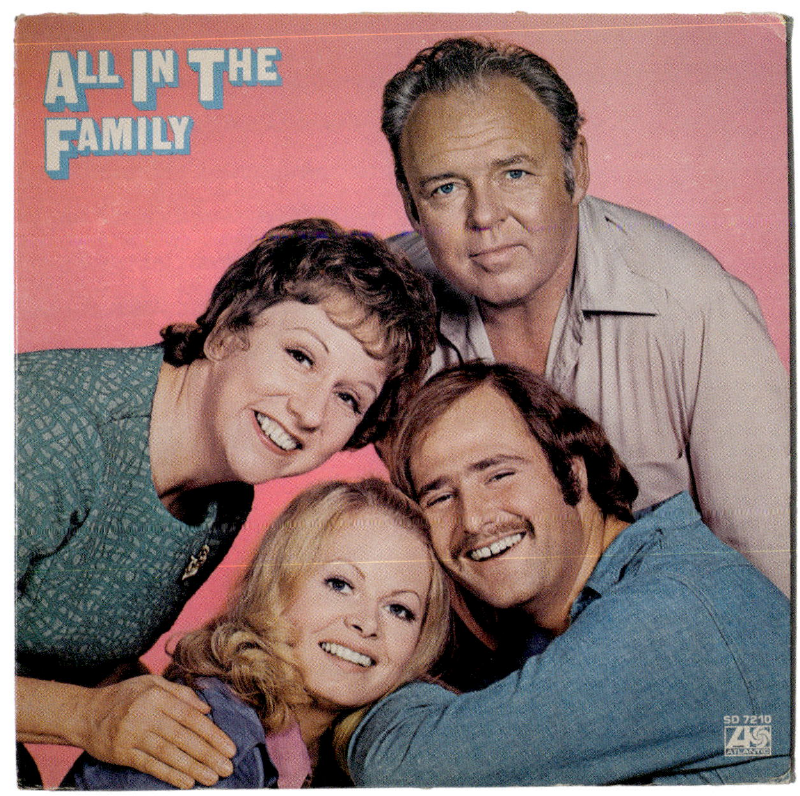

All in the Family's theme song, the subtly satirical and nostalgic earworm "Those Were the Days," was written for the production by Lee Adams and Charles Strouse. The song was released along with recorded audio of some scenes from the series as the 1971 *All in the Family* album, which became a best-seller.

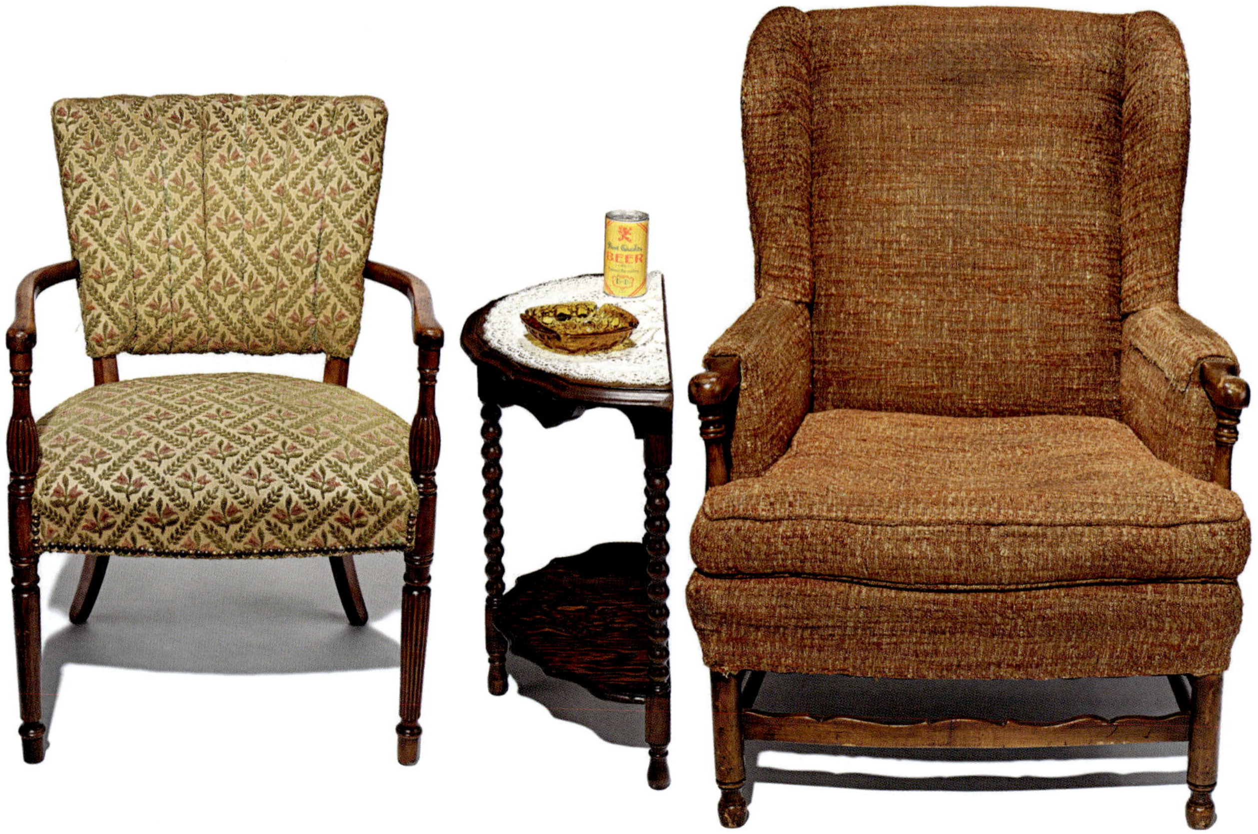

Norman Lear donated the Bunkers' living room furniture set to the National Museum of History and Technology (now the National Museum of American History) in 1978, and the props have been visitor favorites ever since. Lear had the show's set designers dress the Bunker house set in drab, sepia-toned furniture, props, and textiles to make viewers feel as if they were looking at an old family photo album.

grappling with the social changes and political tumult of the 1960s, they sought to adapt the series for the United States. They produced a pilot episode titled "Justice for All" that was rejected by ABC. Then another, "Those Were the Days," that was also rejected. Too controversial, the network said. CBS finally picked up the show, now titled *All in the Family*, but was so worried about audience backlash that it subjected it to a year of focus group testing and, when it finally consented to airing the series as a midseason replacement, insisted the series' first episode be introduced with what we would recognize today as a trigger warning. A title card read, "WARNING: The program you are about to see is ALL IN THE FAMILY. It seeks to throw a humorous spotlight on our frailties, prejudices, and concerns. By making them a source of laughter, we hope to show—in a mature fashion—just how absurd they are."[39] Though the series would prove popular—number one in the ratings by the end of its first full season—the caution was warranted.

Set in Queens, New York, *All in the Family* followed the working-class Bunker family: Archie (Carroll O'Connor), a blue-collar World War II veteran and outspoken conservative; Edith (Jean Stapleton), kindhearted wife and mother; Gloria (Sally Struthers), their college-aged liberal feminist daughter; and Michael "Meathead" Stivic (Rob Reiner), Gloria's husband and a politically progressive graduate student. In the Bunkers' living room and at the kitchen table, Archie frequently butted heads with Mike and Gloria, demonstrating the contemporary "generation gap" as well as his intolerance and ignorance on issues of race, ethnicity, religion, sexuality, and civil, women's, and LGBTQ rights.

Archie was the archetype of the era's so-called silent majority, the kind of former New Deal Democrat who, threatened by the liberation movements of the 1960s, sickened by opposition to the Vietnam War, and forgotten in a deindustrializing economy, now gravitated toward the grievance-based conservative populism of George Wallace and Richard Nixon. Archie was a bigot, using racist, homophobic, and anti-semitic slurs and reducing to stereotypes people from any background different than his own as a white, Anglo-Saxon Protestant, including his Polish American son-in-law. He also demeaned and disrespected women, even his own daughter, for her advocacy for "women's lib," and his wife, whom he derided as a "dingbat."

"No bum that can't speak poifect English outhta stay in this country—oughta be de-exported the hell outta here!"

—Archie Bunker (Carroll O'Connor)

But Archie wasn't the heel; rather, he was the hero of the show. The problem was that Archie was "too damned lovable . . . ignorant but never mean-spirited," and often near-sympathetically rendered as pitifully disposed by the modern world.[40] In one episode, for instance, when Mike complains to Edith that Archie won't give him a break, she explains, "Archie yells at you because Archie is jealous of you. . . . You're going to college, and you've got your whole life ahead of you. Archie had to quit school to support his family. He ain't never going to be nothin' more than he is right now. But you, you've got a chance to be anything you want to be. . . . So the next time Archie's yelling at you, try to be a little more understanding."[41]

In an interview with *Variety*, Lear called Archie a "lovable bigot," and the name stuck. "There is no reason bigots shouldn't have a hero, too, and if they are going to have a hero, thank heavens he's a fool, like Archie Bunker," Lear said and ignited a debate about the meaning and reception of Archie Bunker that continues to this day.[42] Civil rights leader Whitney Young suspected that "while the show tries to satirize bigotry, it only succeeds in spreading the poison and making it—by repetition—more respectable."[43] Some viewers certainly tuned in because of the sheer shock value of hearing racial slurs on television, or because they thought Archie represented them, unafraid to speak the truth of the dispossessed and forgotten conservative viewpoint. Perhaps Archie was just as popular among liberal viewers as conservatives, functioning as "a sacrificial lamb for an angry, frightened, would-be progressive America" to project their fears and frustrations about the reactionary turn in contemporary politics. In true sitcom fashion, Archie always grudgingly learns his lesson in the end, over time becoming a more tolerant and enlightened character, perhaps suggesting that all would be well in the civic sphere as well, as long as we could all continue to learn to get along.[44]

Supporting characters introduced as foils to Archie including Black neighbors George and Louise Jefferson (Sherman Hemsley and Isabel Sanford), their son Lionel (Mike Evans), and Edith's stridently progressive cousin Maude (Bea Arthur). These characters not only served to humanize and teach Archie lessons but also proved popular enough to warrant their own Lear-helmed spinoff series, *The Jeffersons* (1975–1985) and *Maude* (1972–1978). Special guest stars, too, made a mockery of Archie's prejudices, including Sammy Davis Jr. appearing as himself in the season 2 episode "Sammy's Visit." Davis plants a friendly kiss on Archie's cheek while posing for a photo, prompting what has been called the longest sustained moment of laughter by a television studio audience.

All in the Family certainly pushed the bounds of propriety for primetime television, as the network had feared, but any backlash from viewers or advertisers was balanced by high ratings (it was the top-rated show on American television for five of its nine seasons), critical acclaim (it earned twenty-two Emmy awards), and its undoubtable cultural relevance. Among the topics the series explored were draft dodging and the Vietnam War, racism and the Ku Klux Klan, homosexuality and transgender identity, protest and the limits of free speech, affirmative action, crime, women's rights, and antisemitism. Mike struggled with impotence, Gloria suffered a miscarriage, Edith endured menopause and fought off a rapist home intruder, and Archie resisted temptation to infidelity over the course of its nine seasons. These episodes didn't often have a strong point of view about most of these issues, but the very fact that they were being discussed, and people of marginalized identities represented, was the real significance of the series.[45] If anything, the moral judgment is the unspoken reality that the younger generation, the mainstream future of the nation, is the progressive voice of conscience. Archie's bigotry, the show seems to suggest, is going to die out.

In a recent review of twenty-four contemporary empirical studies of *All in the Family*'s effects on viewers' opinions on race, Christina von Hodenberg concluded that the show may have failed to change the views of the most bigoted fans but, in lampooning Archie's racism, helped accelerate a broader decline in racially prejudiced attitudes among the American public.[46]

If the groundbreaking representation of these issues and identities had no other effect, it at least unnerved President Richard Nixon. The series' fifth episode, "Judging Books by Covers," was a landmark in LGBTQ representation on television, in which Archie airs his homophobic views regarding a colorful friend of Mike's before learning that his own macho ex-football player friend Steve is *actually* gay. This may have been the first ever gay character in a network sitcom and was at least the first ever portrayed in such a matter-of-fact, normal way, representing the diversity of the gay community. In a White House conversation recorded May 13, 1971 (made public as part of the so-called Watergate tapes), Nixon ranted about *All in the Family*'s "glorification of homosexuality," warning that such leniency in popular entertainment could lead to the downfall of the republic.[47] Meanwhile, Wisconsin Democratic Senator William Proxmire praised the series as having "done more to diminish prejudice and bias, by getting people to laugh at the prejudices we hold, than almost any other action that has taken place in the last 10 years."[48]

All in the Family was one of the most popular and influential television programs of the twentieth century. If judged only by the number of contemporary newspaper and magazine articles probing its provocative appeal, the countless scholarly appraisals of its significance, or the seven spin-off series it generated, it's impossible to dispute its impact on American culture.

Ryan Lintelman

MOVING ON UP: *GOOD TIMES* AND *THE JEFFERSONS*

In 1999, President Bill Clinton awarded the National Medal of Arts to Norman Lear for his work as the producer, screenwriter, developer, and creator of over one hundred television sitcoms that have aired in prime

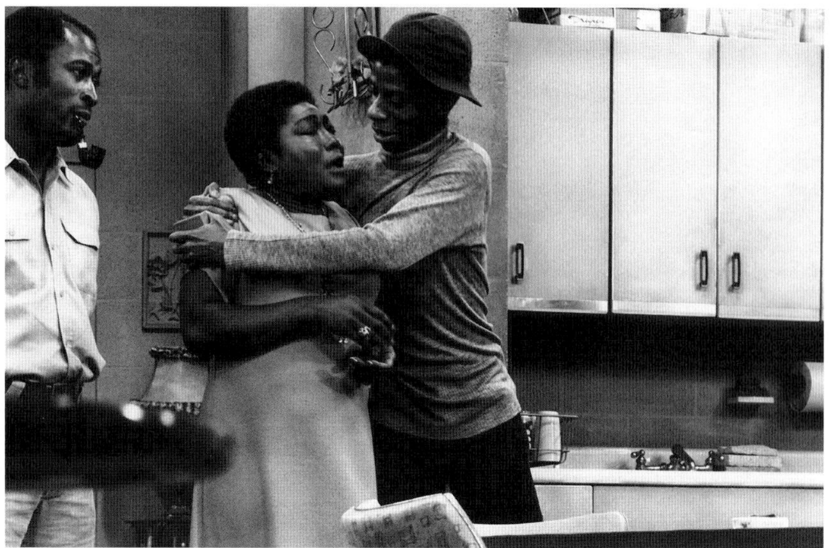

In this photo from the set of *Good Times*, James Evans (John Amos) looks on as J. J. (Jimmie Walker) tries to smooth things over with his mother, Florida (Esther Rolle).

time and in syndication since 1959. Recognizing Lear's pioneering work that created the template for the bold language and storylines introduced to American television in the 1970s and 1980s, Clinton noted that Lear "has held up a mirror to American society and changed the way we look at it."[49] In the 1970s with hits such as *All in the Family*, *Maude*, and *Sanford and Son*, Lear produced programming that showcased this formula, reaching homes across the country with television that blended comedy and drama to address the subjects and conversations relevant to the politically, racially, and economically diverse American family.

By 1974, Lear executive produced his fourth hit show, *Good Times*, which utilized characters from Lear's *Maude* but was the creation of screenwriter Eric Monte, who wrote the motion picture *Cooley High*, and writer/actor Mike Evans, who also portrayed Lionel in the Jeffersons for thirty-four episodes. Unlike previous Black-themed television programs like *Julia*'s story about a single parent and her son or the comedy *Sanford and Son*, *Good Times* was the first sitcom on television with a storyline featuring a two-parent Black household. *Good Times* was initially developed along traditional sitcom lines, focusing on the joys and struggles of the Evans family, a hardworking and proud family living in a high-rise public housing apartment in Chicago with the storyline modeled loosely on the life experiences of Monte, who grew up in Chicago's North Side in the Cabrini-Green projects in the 1950s. During its run from 1974 to 1979, *Good Times* began as a ratings hit in large part due to the breakout success of actor/comedian Jimmie Walker's portrayal of J. J., the eldest Evans son and his uniquely delivered signature catchphrase, "Dy-no-mite!" While the ratings climbed and J. J., along with his iconic bucket hat and catchphrase, became a marketed, household name, *Good Times* faced internal controversies as John Amos, who portrayed the Evans patriarch, James Evans, spoke critically about the direction of the series. In a 2022 interview he reflected, "When you allow other people to perpetuate your imagery, they will do so out

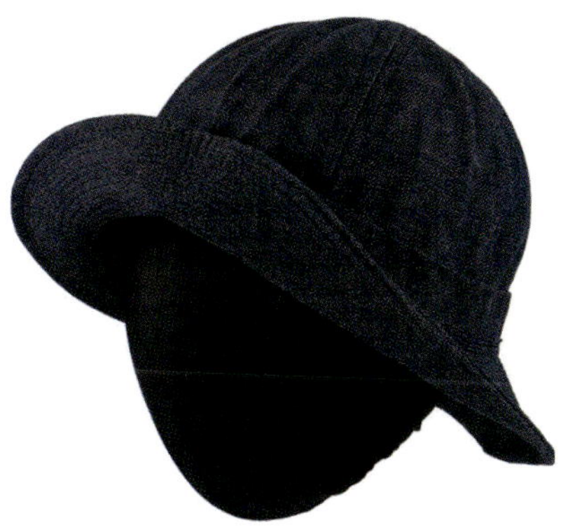

Actor, comedian Jimmie Walker wore this denim bucket hat with a quilted brim as James "J. J." Evans Jr. on the television show "Good Times."

of their own perceptions and minds, and it's not always an accurate view."[50] Esther Rolle, who portrayed matriarch Florida Evans, shared a similar perspective and in 1975 stated in *Ebony*, "They have made J. J. more stupid and enlarged his role. Negative images have been slipped in on us through the character."[51]

While the show maintained much of its popularity in its initial seasons, reaching 25 percent of American households during its first full season, the criticism over its portrayals reached Lear after he was visited by three members of the Black Panther Party, who voiced issues with *Good Times* and the portrayal of Black characters in his show. According to Lear, the group remarked, "Every time you see a Black man on the tube, he is dirt poor, wears shit clothes, can't afford nothing."[52] This exchange led to Lear codeveloping the idea for *The Jeffersons* and the catchphrase for the series, "moving on up."

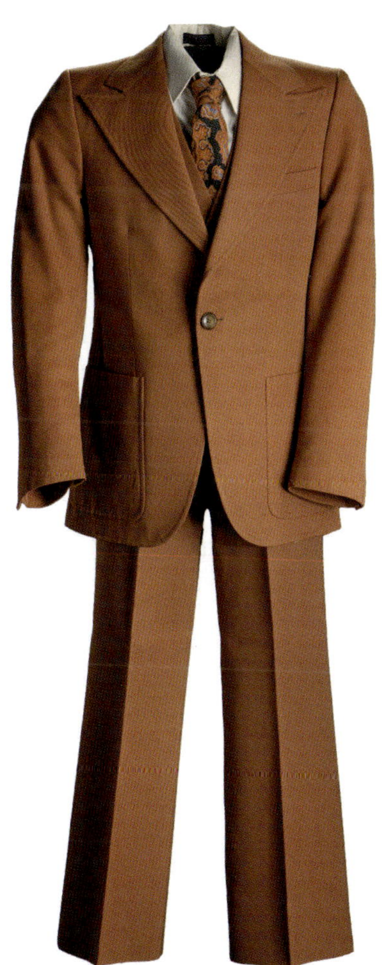

Sherman Hemsley wore this suit in his role as George Jefferson on the television show *The Jeffersons*.

Based on characters introduced in *All in the Family*, *The Jeffersons* became the second longest running series with a predominantly Black cast in television history, with 253 episodes aired over its 1975 to 1985 run. The show presented a radically different vision of the Black family, with the famous theme song narrating the upward mobility of George and Louise "Weezy" Jefferson "moving on up to a deluxe apartment in the sky." Developing the character of George Jefferson initially as an African American, ideological counterweight to Archie Bunker, both conservative-aligned characters blended rudeness and bigotry with loving and nurturing traits, while George Jefferson was written as a self-made, independent, and successful business owner. Like *Good Times*, *The Jeffersons* explored complex social themes, including racism, interracial relationships, alcoholism, illiteracy, sexual abuse, and more while using racial slurs as punchlines to confront America's racism and expose the hypocrisy of bigotry. Lear remarked, "I thought America was ready," as both shows introduced a new landscape for Black characters and storylines in American television.[53]

Kevin Strait

GEORGE CARLIN AND THE SEVEN WORDS

George Carlin was a comedic renegade whose art ranged from philosophical reflection to political outrage. As the indignant voice of the counterculture, he reinvented stand-up comedy as a form of social criticism, using his platform to counteract the platitudes spewed by politicians, advertisers, religious leaders, and others who conventionalized American thought. His landmark work led to robust cultural debates—including a Supreme Court ruling—that centered issues of censorship, obscenity, and freedom of speech during the tumultuous 1970s in America. As Carlin himself once put it, stand-up was not only his way

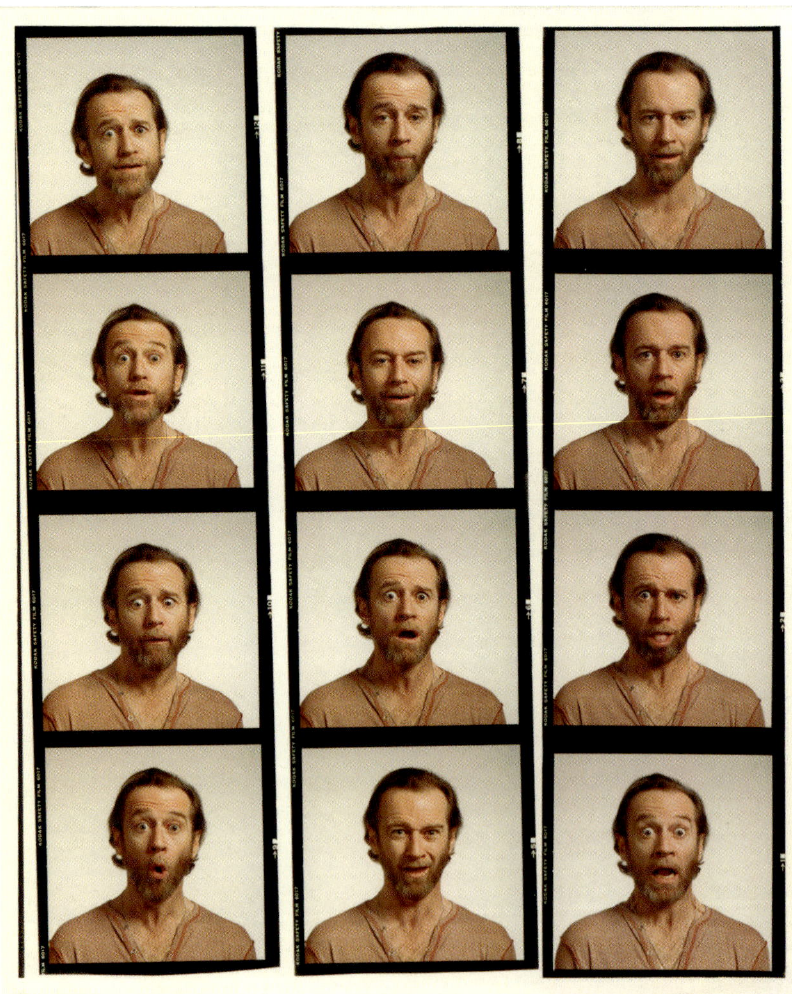

of life, his business, and his art, but his means of social and political "survival."

"Every day I take a lot of notes. And the notes go into files in various categories. They can be a sentence, a word, an idea, two things that connect or contrast, an afterthought, a neat phrase. It's an incessant process. I review a file and I get excited: 'This shit's going to be GOOD! Can't wait till they hear THIS!'"
—George Carlin, "Last Words," 2009

George Carlin was born in New York City in 1937 and grew up on West 121st Street, where he and his younger brother were raised by their mother, Mary. From an early age, he was attentive to the rhythms, sounds, and meanings of words, marveling at a perfectly placed adjective in a newspaper article that his mother read aloud at the breakfast table or the virtuosic wordplay of his boyhood idol, the tongue-twisting comedian Danny Kaye. Though his fascination with language did not result in stellar academic performance (Carlin was expelled from school), it would go on to become the core of his artistic achievement as a stand-up comedian, whose style involved a cadenced, melodious delivery that was not unlike spoken word poetry. George Carlin was also attentive, as a teenager and young adult, to the work of comedians who graced his mother's television screen—a rare commodity in his neighborhood in the early 1950s. Perhaps drawn in by his own rebellious streak, Carlin admired the slapstick antics of the Marx Brothers and Jerry Lewis, whose humor upended social mores, and, in the later 1950s, was galvanized by the "sick" comedy of revolutionary stand-up comedians like Lenny Bruce and Mort Sahl, who were often banned from the airwaves.

After a brief stint in the Air Force, Carlin found his first calling as a radio disc jockey. While working in Fort Worth, Texas, in the late 1950s, he met fellow DJ Jack Burns and the two developed a coffeehouse comedy act. The pair found success plying their beatnik style and moved together to Los Angeles, where their album, *Burns and Carlin at the Playboy Club Tonight*, was released before they amicably went their separate ways in the early 1960s.

THEM, LOOK AT THEM BY POINT POINT, AND
SUBJECT THEM TO CLOSE
SCRUTINY, AND THAT IS WHAT
I ENJOY DOING. DOESN'T MEAN I THINK
I'M SOLELY RIGHT – IT JUST MEANS
I THINK IT IS IMPORTANT TO
LOOK AT THESE THINGS A
LITTLE MORE CLOSELY
BELIEFS
POINTS OF VIEW
BEDROCK PRINCIPLES

During this transitional moment in his career, Carlin honed his craft as a solo performer on some of the most demanding stages in American entertainment—in Hollywood and around the country. He developed crowd pleasing characters like "The Hippie-Dippie Weather Man" and "The Wonderful Wino," and was crafting a unique (if not yet fully formed) ability to toggle between silliness and high intellectualism, between light humor and rebellious insouciance, and between punning wordplay and linguistic rigor. Carlin became a favorite of

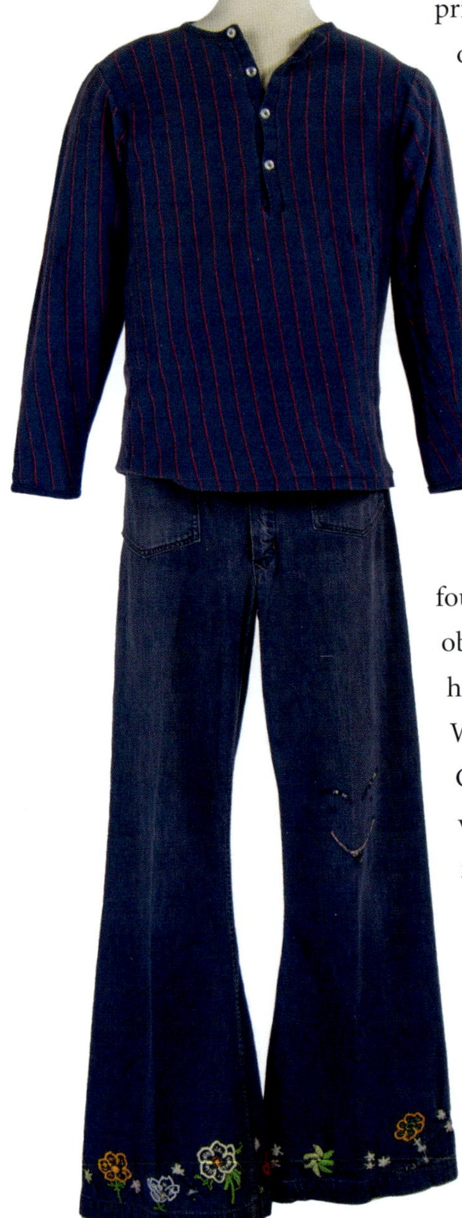

George Carlin's *FM & AM* marked a turning point in the artist's life and work, as he transformed himself from a straitlaced stand-up into a comedic renegade, with his long hair and bell bottoms signaling allegiance with his countercultural generation.

prime-time television hosts like Jack Paar and Johnny Carson, for both of whom he frequently guest-hosted at the helm of *The Tonight Show*. Carlin himself referred to this period of his career as his "Pre-Beard" years, characterized by delivering clean comedy—while donning a suit and tie—to what was then called a "lowest common denominator" audience of middle-class and middle-aged conservative-leaning adults.

Even as he excelled and rose through the ranks, Carlin was witnessing his activist generation rise as a political force to be reckoned with, and he was experiencing—at close range—the enormous power and potential of comedy to threaten, dismantle, and alter the status quo. In what might be among the most important moments in comedy history, a young George Carlin found himself present at one of Lenny Bruce's incredibly contentious obscenity arrests, where the comedian was removed from the stage in handcuffs for volleying supposedly incendiary language and ideas. When officers requested identification from members of the audience, Carlin refused; he was ferried to jail alongside Bruce in a shared police vehicle. The experience was formative. Around the same time, Carlin met and married Brenda Hosbrook—a Playboy Club waitress who became an essential partner in her husband's career. It was Brenda who finessed the pivotal press kit that marked Carlin's transition from a "straight" comic to a countercultural lightning rod.

The new "Post-Beard" George Carlin, as he described himself, temporarily retreated to small, hip comedy clubs like New York's Bitter End to refine his voice and sharpen his tone, signaling with his long hair, T-shirts, and denim jeans that he was speaking to the concerns and ideals of America's liberal youth. Using his newfound comic voice to communicate intelligently, forcefully, and courageously about issues like race relations, drugs, religion, war, and civil liberties, Carlin reemerged and came to encompass the outrage of a generation. His Grammy-winning album *FM & AM* memorialized the change: The "AM" tracks were more docile, a mocking throwback to his former self recorded in monoaural sound; the "FM" tracks were aggressive and challenging, the inauguration of a new sensibility recorded in full stereo.

Carlin's 1972 album *Class Clown* catapulted him to notoriety. The album lambasted the Vietnam War, religious doctrine, and conservative cultural values and became a landmark in both the history of comedy and the history of freedom of speech for its treatment of taboo subject

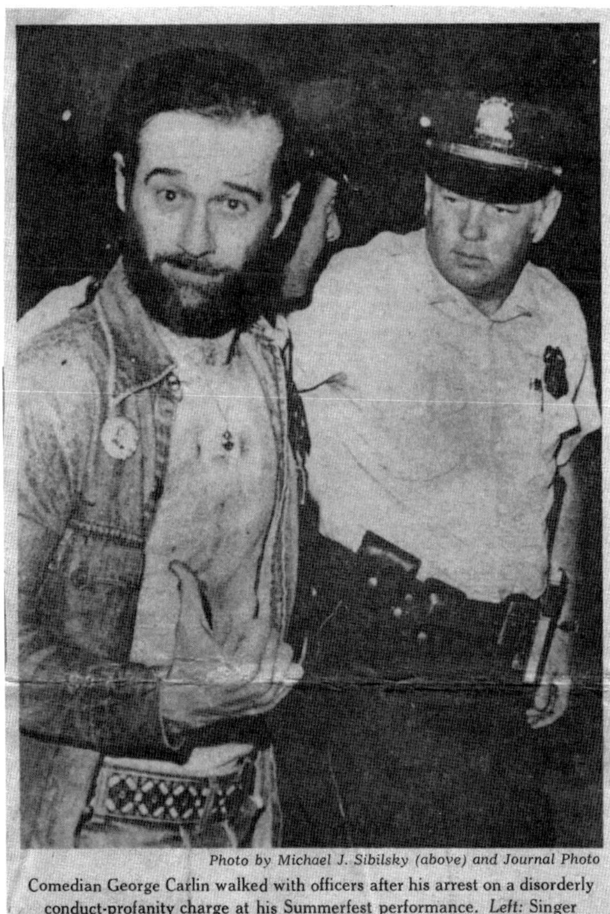

In the midst of performing his "Seven Dirty Words" routine before a live audience of thirty-five thousand, Carlin was arrested for violation of obscenity laws. The nation erupted in debates about freedom of speech, and Carlin was not sure yet if he was to be a hero or a martyr.

matter. Carlin dedicated the album to Lenny Bruce, writing in the liner notes that it was Bruce who "took all the risks." The album's final track, "Seven Words You Can Never Say on Television," explored the power of language, and the perils of censorship, by brilliantly disarming the explosive words "shit, piss, fuck, cunt, cocksucker, mother fucker, and tits"—which had been deemed off-limits by the broadcasting industry and the government agencies that oversaw it. The track, like all of the routines on the album, is delivered with Carlin's characteristically blunt and acerbic tone, recited in rhythm like a mantra or a bit of poetry in rapid-fire blasts of perfectly placed syllables.

While performing the "Seven Dirty Words" routine before a live audience of thirty-five thousand in the summer of 1972 in Milwaukee, Carlin was forcibly removed from the stage by police and arrested in violation of obscenity laws. The nation erupted in debates about freedom of speech and the regulation of artists, and Carlin—not sure yet if he was to be a hero or a martyr—sent a copy of *Class Clown* to his hotly anticipated court trial, remaining conspicuously absent from the courtroom himself. The judge, who was observed chuckling on the bench as the album played, dismissed the case, citing Carlin's First Amendment protections and setting a precedent for generations of courageous, and sometimes controversial, comedians who would follow in his wake.

The following year, Carlin built upon his "Seven Dirty Words" routine with an expanded "Filthy Words" track on the album *Occupation: Foole*. This track was broadcast on the radio to the consternation of a concerned parent, who alerted the Federal Communications Commission after inadvertently exposing his son to Carlin's "obscene" language during a car ride. The case was elevated to the Supreme Court in 1978, when they ultimately ruled, five to four, that Carlin's material was "indecent but not obscene," and so subject to regulation, if not outright censorship. The FCC, the court ruled, could prohibit the broadcasting of "indecent" material during the daytime, when children were most apt to be listening in. The case

triggered prolonged conversation about the role that the government should play in censoring comedy—a conversation that has informed the way that contemporary comic artists, who frequently delve into sensitive subject matter, approach their art and understand their freedoms of expression today. Carlin's 1977 album *On the Road* contained one of the first industry-applied rating labels, marked "R" for "Recommended Adult Listening."

Across his five-decade career, Carlin released twenty comedy albums and performed fourteen critically acclaimed HBO specials, each of which elevated stand-up comedy to new heights of complexity, artistry, and cultural resonance. His material evolved at a rapid pace, keeping up with—or, more accurately, just ahead of—the changing tenor of American politics. Carlin's album tracks railed against "Reagan's Gang, Church People and American Values" and philosophized about "Rockets and Penises in the Persian Gulf"; he complained about "Assholes," "Parents of Honor Students," and "Gun Enthusiasts," he lectured about "Capital Punishment," "Abortion," and "Free-Floating Hostility," and he reminded us that "Some People Are Stupid." In the 1990s, Carlin again evolved to become a sort of "elder statesmen" of comedy, adopting an almost philosophical outlook that used comedy as a vehicle for expressing his deep-seated concerns about the very fabric of American life. His final album, the Grammy-winning *It's Bad for Ya*, ended with a series of stand-up bits that doubled as rallying cries with eerily resonant echoes: "No One Questions Things," "God Bless America," "You Have No Rights."

Carlin died of heart failure in 2008, at the age of seventy-one, four days after being announced as the winner of the coveted Mark Twain Prize for American Humor. The award was conferred posthumously as the comedy community mourned the loss of one of its greatest champions.

GEORGE CARLIN'S JOKE FILE

George Carlin devised and maintained a massive, meticulous filing system to manage his creative output. In his distinctive all-caps handwriting, often with a stark black or red felt pen, he hastily recorded words, phrases, or ideas on thousands of tiny paper scraps—usually hurriedly torn from sheets of hotel stationary while touring the

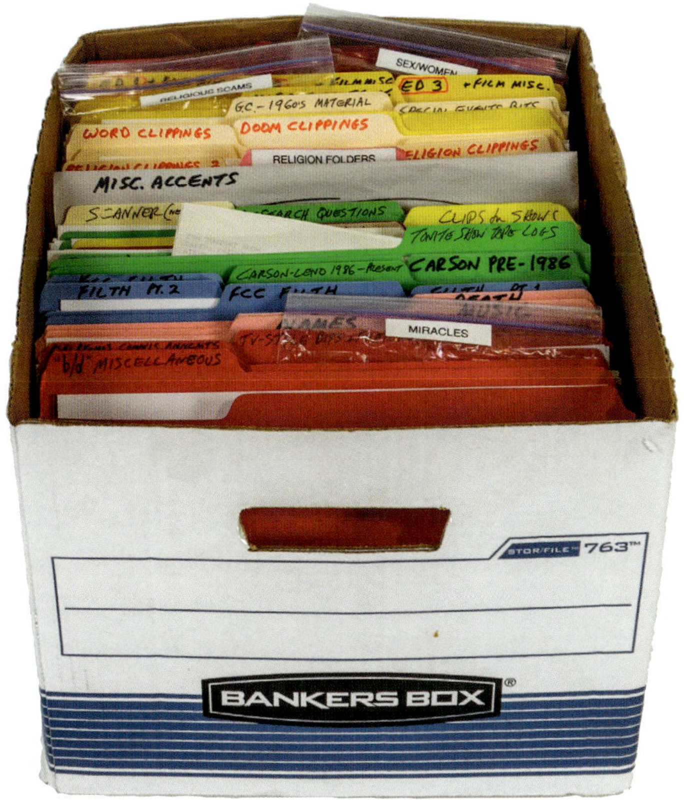

nation with his stand-up shows. These notes were scrawled quickly, and sometimes almost illegibly, out of fear of losing a fleeting inspiration that had been sparked by the minutiae of everyday life: the news, an overheard turn of phrase, statistics, advertising jargon, or unusual names. The scraps of paper were then sorted and arranged alphabetically into dozens of categories indicated by adhering label maker stickers to Ziploc sandwich bags: "Americans," "Death," "Euphemisms," "Fullashit," "Lingo," "Oddball Facts," "Race," "War & Peace." Once enough scraps had found their way into a Ziploc, Carlin dumped them out and rearranged them physically to craft a polished stand-up routine on that topic. Consisting of some twenty-five thousand individual notes that are now held in the National Comedy Center's archives, this extraordinary residue of a singular creative mind offers a unique and intimate glimpse into the artistic process of one of comedy's most prolific and influential figures.

Laura LaPlaca

*M*A*S*H*: BINDING UP THE WOUNDS

An exhibition titled "*M*A*S*H*: Binding Up the Wounds" opened at the National Museum of American History in July 1983. The exhibit, displaying thousands of original props, costumes, and other objects used in the production of the television series that had ended its eleven-season run that year, quickly set new records for attendance, with over a million visitors requesting timed passes. The exhibit's title had a double meaning: the doctors and nurses on the show literally bound up the wounds of the casualties passing through the front-line Korean War hospital each episode, but the series was also widely credited with helping Americans bind the civic wounds caused by the fierce debate about the Vietnam War.[54]

A television adaptation of the 1970 Robert Altman film of the same name, itself an adaptation of Richard Hooker's 1968 book *MASH: A Novel About Three Army Doctors*, the series debuted on CBS in September 1972. Though it first earned poor ratings, the show eventually gained an audience, becoming one of the most popular and successful sitcoms of all time.

Combining aspects of television medical drama, military comedy, and the workplace sitcom, *M*A*S*H* was a unique and remarkable television series. The dark comedy focused on a group of doctors and nurses in the 4077th Mobile Army Surgical Hospital during the Korean War. Doctors "Hawkeye" Pierce (Alan Alda) and "Trapper John" McIntyre (Wayne Rogers) butt heads with the by-the-book yet incompetent Majors Frank Burns (Larry Linville) and Margaret Houlihan (Loretta Swit), with comic relief provided by supporting characters including company clerk "Radar" O'Reilly

Alan Alda portrayed antiwar, pleasure-seeking Benjamin Franklin "Hawkeye" Pierce, chief surgeon of the 4077th M*A*S*H unit. He wore this Hawaiian shirt in the pilot episode and others throughout the series' run, often with a martini in hand.

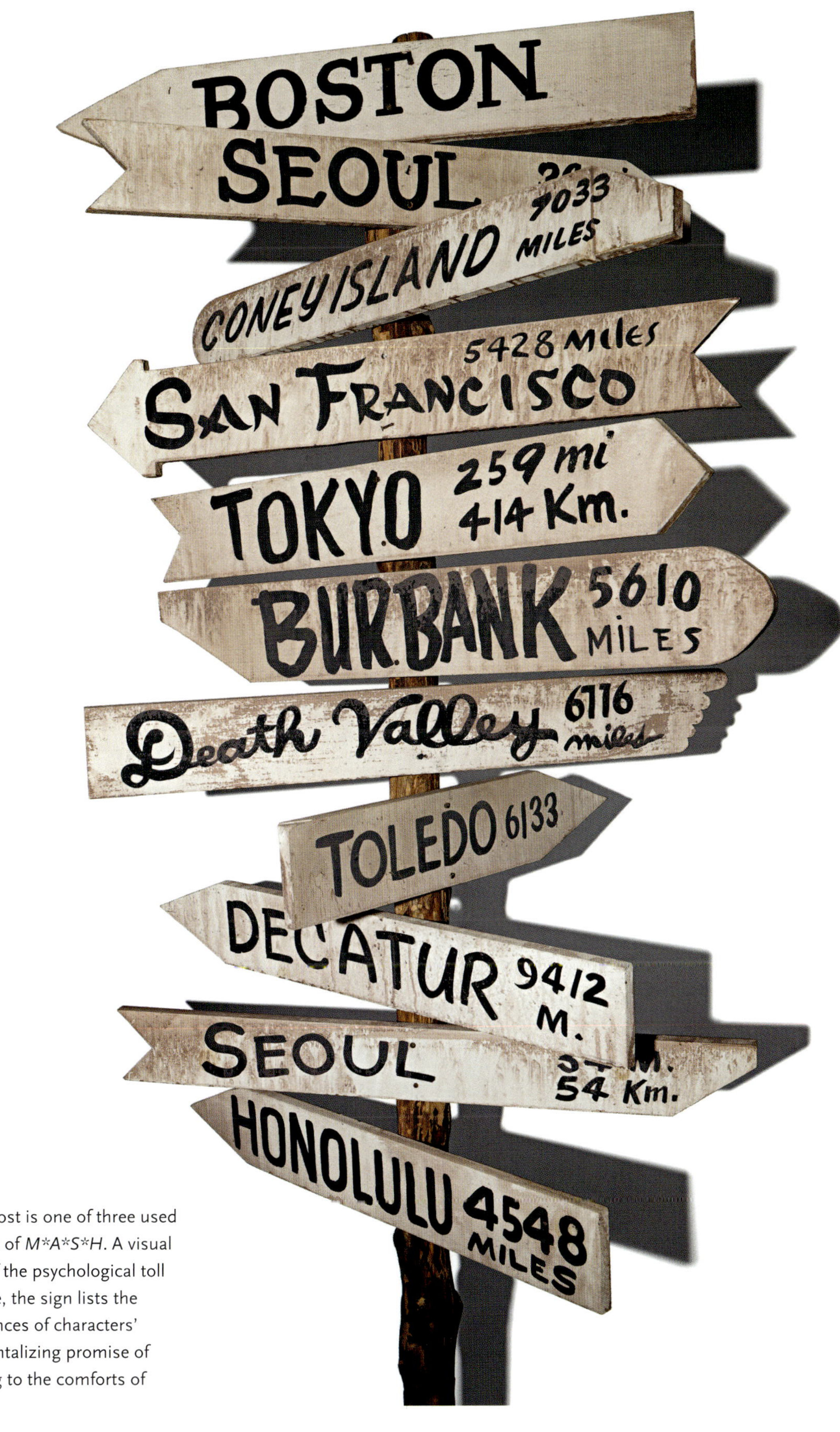

This iconic signpost is one of three used in the production of *M*A*S*H*. A visual representation of the psychological toll of military service, the sign lists the names and distances of characters' hometowns, a tantalizing promise of one day returning to the comforts of home and family.

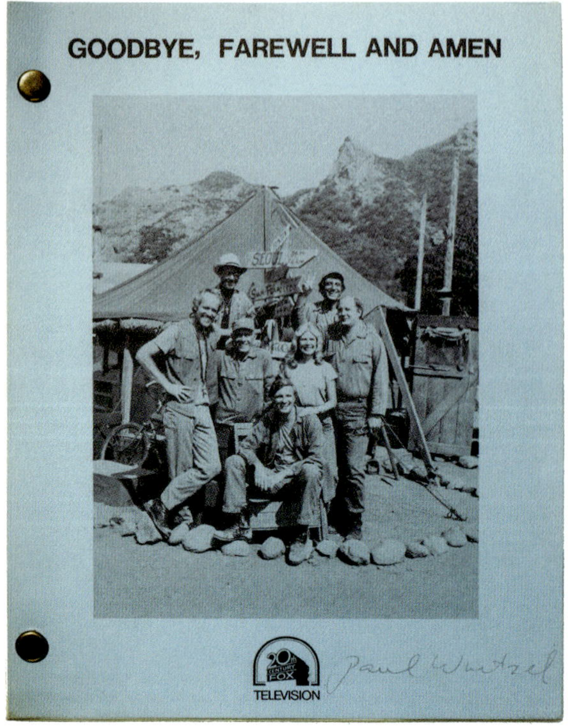

One hundred twenty-five million Americans watched the two-and-a-half-hour series finale of *M*A*S*H*, "Goodbye, Farewell, and Amen," on February 28, 1983, making it the largest audience for any single television episode in history. *Variety* estimated that 77 percent of all television sets in use in the United States were tuned in to CBS that night.

(Gary Burghoff), Father Francis Mulcahy (William Christopher), and Corporal Maxwell Q. Klinger (Jamie Farr), known for wearing women's clothing in an attempt to earn a psychiatric discharge.

Series cocreator and lead writer Larry Gelbart wanted to create a new kind of comedy series; inspired by Norman Lear's sociopolitical commentary in shows like *All in the Family* as well as the haunting Johnny Mandel theme song "Suicide Is Painless," Gelbart wanted *M*A*S*H* to be both provocative and moving, "comedy written in a minor key."[55] The series was celebrated for its realism, with period costumes and props and great attention to medical and military detail, its emotional resonance, its groundbreaking pseudo-documentary experimentation, and its memorable and beloved characters. As symbolized by the show's iconic signpost, *M*A*S*H* demonstrated war's broad and unforgiving impact on Americans from all walks of life and from coast to coast. Characters hailed from diverse hometowns including Ottumwa, Iowa (Radar), Crabapple Cove, Maine (Hawkeye), Mill Valley, California (B. J. Honeycutt), Boston's Beacon Hill (Charles Emerson Winchester III), and Toledo, Ohio (Klinger).

It also delved, like no television series had before, into war's psychological toll on its participants, demonstrating the traumatic experiences of doctors treating grievously wounded soldiers in the aftermath of battle. Unusual for a television sitcom of the era, sequences set in the hospital operating room—and sometimes, entire episodes—were shown without laugh tracks. Patients died, in some cases because the doctors were overwhelmed by the number of casualties flooding the hospital. In one episode, a main character is even killed in a military accident. *M*A*S*H* also depicted the attempts doctors and staff of the 4077th made to cope with the stress and trauma they faced, using drinking, womanizing, gambling, and gallows humor to try to stay sane.

Throughout the series run, *M*A*S*H* reflected the breakdown of civic consensus about the Cold War and the use of military force to project U.S. power. The most militaristic and moralistic characters, especially Frank Burns with his sense of purpose in defeating global communism, are frequent targets of derision and practical jokes, drawing large laughs for his ideological commitment to the war. The purgatory-like existence of the drafted civilians who make up most of the cast, stranded and struggling to

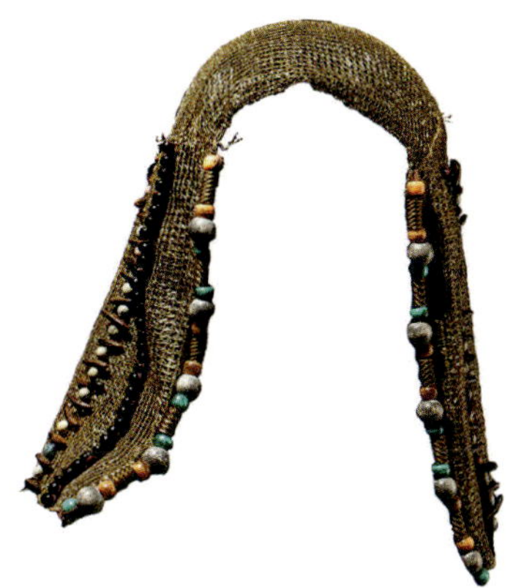

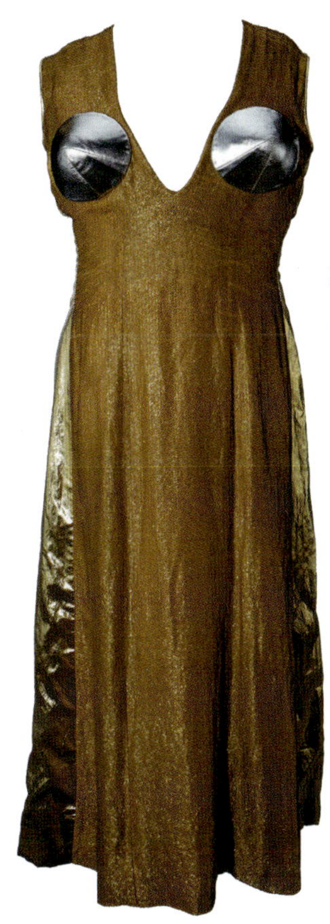

Max Klinger, portrayed by Jamie Farr, memorably hoped to earn a Section 8 psychiatric discharge from the Army by dressing in women's clothing. Farr was costumed in repurposed pieces from the 20th Century Fox wardrobe department, including a gold lamé gown previously worn by Ginger Rogers that helped complete this Queen of the Nile ensemble he wore in the season 8 episode "April Fools."

keep up with an endless stream of casualties in an unseen, stalemated war, spoke to the futility and absurdity of all wars, but especially the one in Vietnam, which ended during the series run. With nightly news broadcast reporting casualty numbers and airing graphic footage from the front lines, and the raging political debate about its justness, the Vietnam War was the first "living-room war," waged as much at home as overseas. In its tragicomic and sometimes dramatic depiction of war and its effects, *M*A*S*H* influenced debates and minds about American military involvement around the world.[56]

As with other seventies sitcoms that dealt with weighty social and political topics, *M*A*S*H* tempered its serious subject matter with a lovable cast, broad comedy, and mostly indirect messaging. Some scholars have in fact criticized the series for its pacification of public memory of war, rather than inspiring opposition to military intervention. Even writer Larry Gelbart worried that the series made war seem routine and acceptable, especially in its later years. He left the series after four seasons after receiving fan mail praising *M*A*S*H* for making war look fun, propagating the idea that "given the right buddies, and the right CO, and the right kind of sense of humor, you can muddle through."[57]

Ryan Lintelman

CHICO AND THE MAN: A FOOT IN THE DOOR FOR LA RAZA

With his enthusiastic exclamations of "Loo-king Good!," the television character Chico Rodriguez was written as a good-humored, optimistic, and hardworking Chicano youth. The character of Ed Brown was his

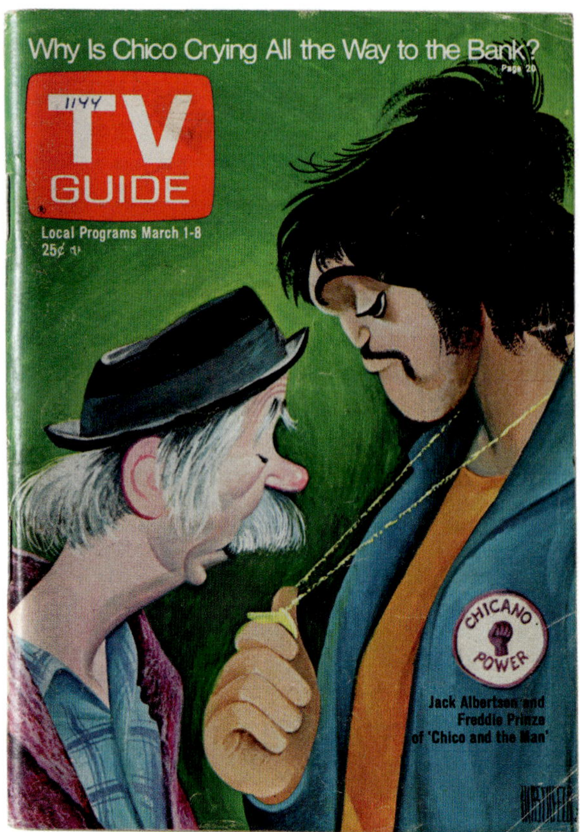

The Al Hirschfeld illustration on the cover of this 1975 issue of *TV Guide* features illustrations of stars Jack Albertson and Freddie Prinze. Prinze's energetic and upbeat Chico Rodriguez answered the racist and cynical comments spewed by Albertson's Ed Brown with pride and aplomb, softening the character's prejudice over the course of the series. The illustration features Chico wearing a "Chicano Power" patch, underscoring how the show transformed the Chicano movement into domestic comedy.

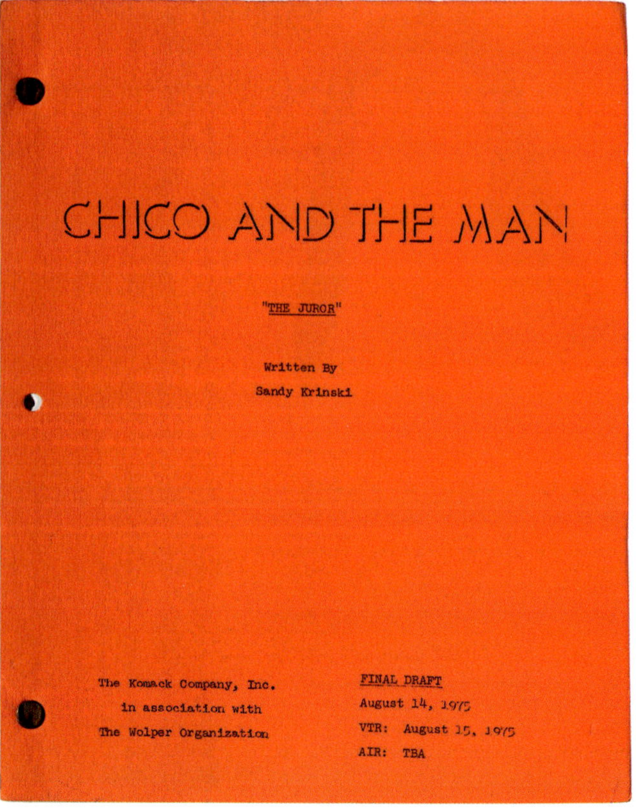
CHICO AND THE MAN

"THE JUROR"

Written By
Sandy Krinski

The Komack Company, Inc.
in association with
The Wolper Organization

FINAL DRAFT
August 14, 1975
VTR: August 15, 1975
AIR: TBA

This script was used for "The Juror," season 2, episode 13 of *Chico and The Man*, written by James Komack and Sandy Krinski. The episode follows Chico's experience serving on jury duty and features many tongue-in-cheek jokes about the justice system, representing the series' comic take on social and political issues.

exact opposite, a cantankerous old man filled with ingrained prejudice and grieving the loss of his wife. The television sitcom series *Chico and the Man* follows Chico (Freddie Prinze) and Ed (Jack Albertson) as they work together in Ed's run-down East LA garage. Over time, Chico begins to soften Brown's misanthropy and bigotry, becoming a surrogate son to the grumpy widower. Chico's character was a refreshing departure from stereotypical depictions of Mexican Americans as lazy louts or dangerous criminals. It presented a breakthrough in terms of visibility for the Latinx community, with a Chicano character in a leading role.

Chico and the Man aired from 1974 to 1978 and was notable as the first American television series set in a Mexican American neighborhood.

The series was created by veteran producer James Komack and was based on his observation of the humor of Cheech Marin and Tommy Chong, popular comedians who turned down his offer to appear in the show. The 1970s spurred network interest in ethnically and racially diverse comedies, albeit in interpretations still crafted by majority-white or entirely white writing rooms. The series directly influenced perceptions of the Latinx community and informed conversations about community identity, poverty, and ethnic/racial discrimination in the United States in the seventies and eighties. As a prime-time series, "Chico presented a mediated fantasy space that appealed to utopian possibilities . . . providing the opportunity to interrogate cultural signs of Otherness or Chicano-ness in comparison to whiteness."[58]

Amid its widespread success, the series did generate some controversy in its original run, particularly from the Chicano community. Despite introducing mainstream viewers to "barrio life," the show was plagued by inauthentic representations of Chicanxs and relied on stereotypical understandings of the Chicanx community. The main character of Chico, played by Puerto Rican Hungarian Freddie Prinze, drew criticism from *Movimiento* activists—including the Teatro Nacional de Aztlán, a network of Chicana/o theater groups—when the show premiered. Moreover, "prime-time sitcoms were home to a high-stakes culture war over who told the story of race in the post–civil rights era."[59] Ray Andrade—the singular Chicano voice in the production—expressed his concerns over these issues, while simultaneously being paraded publicly in defense of the show's storytelling, which caused many in the community to consider him a sellout. The show responded by adapting Chico's background and making the formerly Chicano character, part-Puerto Rican Hungarian. While *Chico and the Man* promoted the notion of an ethno-racial utopia and the resolution of racial conflict, it also "risked silencing marginalized voices" through the casting of a non-Chicano lead.[60] If the early success and later decline of *Chico and the Man* indicates anything, it is that the hopeful vision of ethno-racial reconciliation crumbled as the 1970s progressed.

The show simultaneously paved the way for Latinxs on television, while also bringing to light the failure of ethno-racial depictions shaped and defined by white producers and writers. Without dismissing its flaws, *Chico and the Man* offered a mechanism for Chicanxs to claim space in the entertainment industry by advocating for media industry reforms that would provide more opportunity for Chicanx and Latinx actors, writers, and producers. Its successes and failures reflect the ongoing struggle for authentic and nuanced portrayals of Latinxs in the media.

Ashley Oliva Mayor

"YOU'RE GONNA MAKE IT AFTER ALL": SITCOMS AND THE SINGLE GIRL

The Mary Tyler Moore Show (1970–1977) has emerged as the favored artifact of television's feminist awakening, with its folksy theme song serving as sort of a popular cultural anthem for multiple generations of women. But Mary Richards was far from the first single working woman to "make it on her own" on TV. Indeed, television's first decade was replete with popular sitcoms starring single girls, from Marie Wilson in *My Friend Irma* and Eve Arden in *Our Miss Brooks* to Elena Verdugo in *Meet Millie* and Ann Sothern in *Private Secretary.* As is often the case in the history of broadcasting, or any art form, the sitcom genre was co-opted as soon as it proved its reach and economic viability and was made to participate in the ideological work of upholding suburban nuclear family life.

By the close of the 1950s, TV land was almost totally vacant of young, urban career women, but the 1960s did see the stealthy reemergence of independent women in a few guises. Sitcoms about widowed mothers embarking on "second acts" found footing, including *The Doris Day Show*, *The Lucy Show*, and *Julia*. Costarring characters carried backstories with feminist overtones, like *The Dick Van Dyke Show*'s Sally Rogers—a single career woman, albeit one obsessed with finding a husband—and *The Lucy Show*'s Vivian Bagley—prime-time TV's first divorcée. So-called supernatural sitcoms like *Bewitched* and *I Dream of Jeannie* reinserted women's agency into the suburban home by assigning their protagonists absurdist, campy—and therefore essentially nonthreatening—"powers" that disrupted heteronormative gender roles and domestic social scripts.

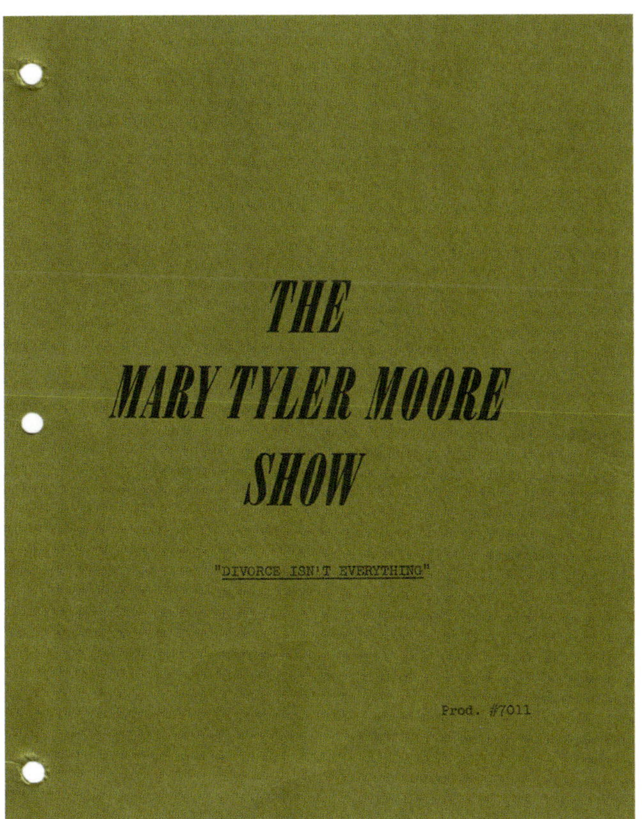
THE
MARY TYLER MOORE
SHOW

"DIVORCE ISN'T EVERYTHING"

Prod. #7011

Original script for *The Mary Tyler Moore Show*, "Divorce Isn't Everything," October 10, 1970.

Despite the TV industry's essentially conservative posture and imperatives to prioritize "least objectionable programming" (that appealed to the broadest swaths of the American public), the sitcom genre ultimately had to contend with a shifting culture. Early sixties landmarks like the FDA's approval of "the pill," the passage of the Equal Pay Act, and the publication of watershed literary works like Helen Gurley Brown's *Sex and the Single Girl* and Betty Friedan's *Feminine Mystique* were undeniably changing the lived experience of American women, and popular culture that refused to acknowledge the rising tide of mainstream liberal feminism was increasingly out of touch. In 1964, in fact, Friedan voiced these issues directly in *TV Guide*, when she asked, "What does it do to women or girls . . . to see no image at all of a self-respecting woman who thinks or does or aims or dreams large dreams or is capable of taking even small actions to shape her own life or her future or her society?"[61]

Onto this scene burst Marlo Thomas in 1966's *That Girl*, a series about a single young woman working, dating, and growing up on her own in New York City. Thomas was a rising star noted for her Hollywood pedigree (the daughter of comedian and producer Danny Thomas) but was also a formidable intellect and activist who was adamant that she would not merely play "the wife of somebody, or the secretary of somebody, or the daughter of somebody."[62] *That Girl* announced itself unequivocally as a show that would represent a changing social and political landscape for women, perhaps most resoundingly in its iconic opening credit sequence that superimposed its star's face upon the skyline of New York City before she is shown gleefully and assertively navigating the maze of the towering city on her own. Indeed, *That Girl*'s most salient contributions to TV history might be aesthetic: from its title sequence to its vibrant set and costume designs, the show put forth a sort of visual blueprint for a feminist lifestyle. Marlo Thomas as Ann Marie, an aspiring actress, had an impossibly chic wardrobe and a stylish bachelorette pad that appeared in stark contrast to the A-line dresses and chintz curtains that adorned sitcom neighborhoods of an earlier era.

Even if *That Girl* was a revolutionary entry in the television canon, it was, to be sure, a historically specific construction that reflected mainstream liberal feminist discourse of its era—and, more specifically, discourses that described the experience of white, upper-middle-class women. That construction was then filtered through the gauntlet of network television production, which meant that every message the show espoused was highly negotiated. For example, the very first episode finds Ann bumping into Donald, her future fiancé, in a traditional meet cute, immediately establishing a series-long tension between her newfound independence and a fundamental dependency on a long-term relationship, even if Ann and Donald are never actually married.

In 1970, as *That Girl* was entering its fifth season, Mary Tyler Moore (carrying significant creative clout after her costarring turn on *The Dick Van Dyke Show*) formed MTM Enterprises, the independent company that would produce her own eponymous sitcom. *The Mary Tyler Moore Show* chronicled the life of Mary Richards, a young woman who has fled an ill-fated long-term relationship, moved solo to a new city, rented a studio apartment with her own money, and landed a job previously held by a man (albeit after an awkward conversation about equal pay with her new boss). As Mary reinvents herself, her network of neighbors and coworkers coheres into a chosen family. The show marked "television's first serious concession to a changed world where middle-class daughters leave home, earn their living, and remain single."[63]

The Mary Tyler Moore Show was anchored in a must-see programming block along with *All in the Family*, *M*A*S*H*, and *The Bob Newhart Show*—three other so-called relevancy programs that tackled hot-button topics along axes of race, class, gender, and political affiliation, even, and especially, when that resulted in their content being hotly adjudicated in the press and around the watercooler. Collectively, these series emerged as a byproduct of a grand programming strategy that saw all three networks moving away from measuring total audience shares and instead cultivating narrower demographics of high-value viewers with spending power to be sold to advertisers. The most coveted of all the emergent demographic groups was women aged eighteen to forty-nine.

Assuredly, part of the reason for *The Mary Tyler Moore Show*'s more sensitive, realistic appeal to this demographic had to do with the presence of key creatives like Treva Silverman, Gail Parent, Barbara Gallagher, and Sybil Adelman in its writers' room, which was among the first to truly incorporate a multiplicity of women's voices. The result was a more nuanced and self-aware protagonist, and the creation of deep and complicated female friends for her to support, affirm, and turn to. Mary is part of a sisterhood with her neighbor, Rhoda, a Jewish New Yorker with an artistic streak who is beset with relationship problems. The pair occupy apartments in a home owned by Phyllis, their landlady and sometime friend, who is struggling with a strained marriage and a rebellious teenage daughter. The three women move in and out of one another's daily lives, listening, affirming, comforting, conspiring. Their relationship is the heart of the series, and it expands *The Mary Tyler Moore Show*'s feminist message by multiplying the ways in which women might organize their lives and tune their aspirations. As was the case for *That Girl*'s Ann Marie, Mary Richards does find herself recast in the role of the pseudo-daughter and -wife as various plotlines demand (particularly as it involves her lovable curmudgeon of a boss, Lou Grant), but Mary's happiness and self-worth are never tied to a committed romantic relationship. The series was ultimately the first in TV history to tell a story about a woman for whom strong friendships and meaningful work "could form the center of a satisfying life."[64]

By the mid-1970s, television boasted a number of series invested in feminist consciousness raising, including *One Day at a Time* (a divorced mother striking out on her own), *Maude* (a middle-aged "freedom fighter" undeterred by taboo topics like menopause and abortion), and even *Wonder Woman*. The 1980s saw the coming of *Kate and Allie* (two divorced moms pooling resources) and *Murphy Brown* (a career woman having a child on her own at age forty-two), as well as the ascendance of sitcom supermoms like *The Cosby Show*'s Clair Huxtable and *Family Ties*'s Elyse Keaton, who found ways to "have it all"—respected in their white-collar fields, present for their children and spouses, composed and flawlessly put together. In the early nineties, *Living Single* showcased the lives of four ambitious young Black women in New York City five years before *Sex and the City*'s own foursome would stretch the inheritance of the single girl sitcom to meet cable's demand for blue-chip dramas. The past decade has witnessed a resurgence of sitcoms, like *Insecure*, *Girls*, *The Mindy Project*, *2 Broke Girls*, and *Broad City*, that are adapting the tenets of this genre for a new generation.

Laura LaPlaca

Manhattan newspaper columnist Carrie Bradshaw, played by Sarah Jessica Parker, used this laptop to record her observations on modern relationships in HBO's *Sex and the City*.

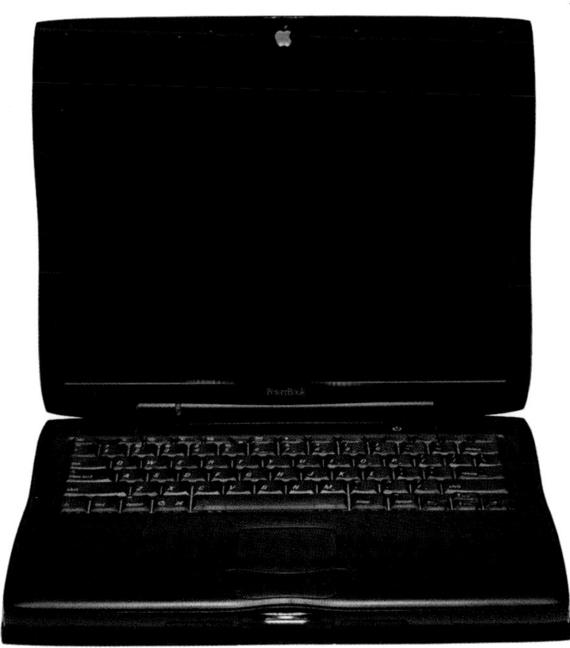

THE DAILY SHOW AND THE LIMITS OF SATIRE

Has comedy replaced the nightly news? Or is the nightly news actually a comedy performance? These questions have been posed by *The Daily Show* nightly since its premiere on Comedy Central in 1996, and particularly stridently by its host Jon Stewart in his tenure from 1999 to 2015.

In those years, even before Donald Trump made "fake news" a campaign issue and political rallying cry, the ratings- and revenue-driven fusion of entertainment and information was both the satirical target of Stewart's comical diatribes and the reason for his success. According to a poll by Pew Research, 12 percent of Americans got their news from *The Daily Show* in 2014, roughly the same reach as the national newspaper *USA Today*.[65] With twenty-four-hour cable news networks increasingly dominated by sensational headlines, political spin and posturing, and ideologically extreme commentary, respondents in a 2009 *Time* magazine poll named Stewart the most trusted newscaster on television.[66] Critics called him a spiritual successor to Walter Cronkite, and U.S. senator and 2008 presidential candidate John McCain compared Stewart to Will Rogers and Mark Twain. Some even suggested he should run for president.[67] Meanwhile, commentators argued that "infotainment" programs like *The Daily Show* contributed to the same worrisome fusion of entertainment and news and decline of trust in journalism as cable news was creating.

"When you go to the zoo and you see a monkey throwing poop, you go, 'that's what monkeys do, what are you gonna do?' But what I wish the media would do more frequently is say 'bad monkey.'"
—Jon Stewart, September 29, 2004, on Charlie Rose

When *The Daily Show* premiered on Comedy Central July 22, 1996, it was hosted by former ESPN anchor and comedian Craig Kilborn. Series creators Madeleine Smithberg and Lizz Winstead wanted to combine the satirical commentary of Bill Maher's *Politically Incorrect*, the format of cable and evening news programs, and the style and audience of late-night comedy shows into something new for television, a news parody series. The program focused more on popular culture and character humor during Kilborn's tenure, but once Jon Stewart took over, the show sharpened its satire, taking aim at political hypocrisy, government dysfunction, and media malpractice.

As host, Stewart played the role of the outraged straight man, queuing up footage drawn from network and cable news and unleashing tirades of exasperated commentary on the absurdities and disgraces of

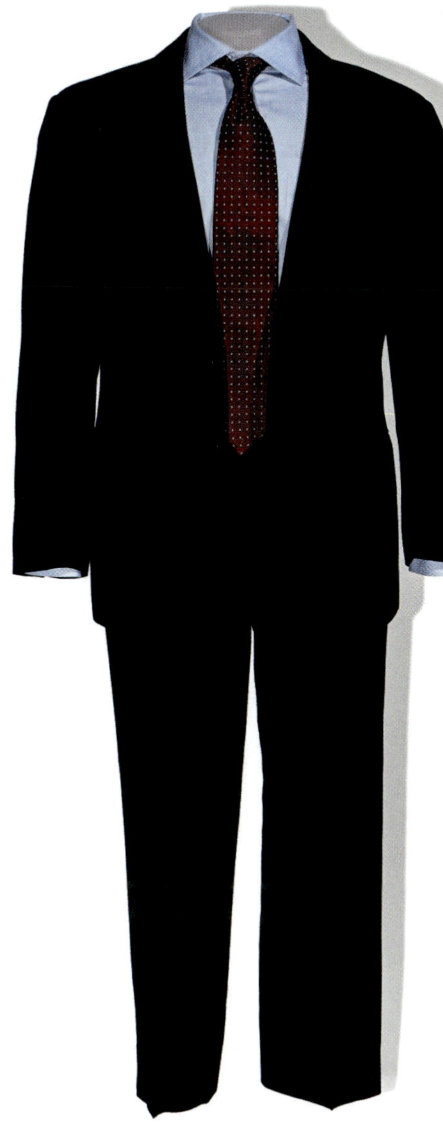

Jon Stewart wore this suit when he interviewed President Barack Obama on *The Daily Show* on October 27, 2010. Obama appeared on the program seven times during Stewart's tenure, attempting to make inroads with young voters and enduring teasing and tough interview questions from the host.

the daily news and political class from his anchor's desk. Correspondents introduced filmed reports that included mockumentary-style interviews with newsmakers and ordinary Americans as well as in-studio segments to discuss current events and debates. Coverage of the Iraq War in segments titled "Mess O'Potamia" and presidential campaign coverage titled "Indecision 20[XX]" have been particularly popular and well-remembered. The show boosted the careers of correspondents Steve Carell, John Oliver, Samantha Bee, Hasan Minhaj, and Larry Wilmore. Long-tenured correspondent Stephen Colbert, known for his segments "Even Stephven," "This Week in God," and "The Jobbing of America," so perfectly parodied the Fox News style of conspiratorial right-wing commentator that he got his own spinoff series, *The Colbert Report* (2005–2014), lampooning Bill O'Reilly and Glenn Beck.

Stewart's earnest and well-informed performance of skeptical outrage, his excoriation of self-interested public leaders, and his advocacy for the vulnerable—such as, in later years, his advocacy on behalf of September 11 first responders with chronic illnesses—made him a hero to viewers, who skewed younger and more liberal than other news programs. *Daily Show* cast and creative talent have claimed that the show has no political agenda beyond expositing hypocrisy and holding elected officials and media to account, but conservative critics have called for more fair and balanced coverage, especially given the series' demonstrable power to shape political debate and inform viewers. Politicians certainly recognized the show's potential. In the run-up to the 2008 election, political candidates appeared on *The Daily Show* twenty-one times.[68] Of young voters, 46 percent reported their vote was informed by what they learned from "comedy programs such as *Saturday Night Live* or *The Daily Show with Jon Stewart*."[69]

Though *Daily Show* ratings have dropped since Stewart's original tenure ended (he returned to the host chair in guest appearances beginning in 2024), they are still high for cable and news programs, especially among eighteen- to thirty-four-year-old viewers, and the series has won twenty-three Primetime Emmy Awards and three Peabody Awards. When Stewart organized a "Rally to Restore Sanity" and Colbert announced his mocking counterdemonstration, the "March to Keep Fear Alive," held on the National Mall in Washington D.C., in October 2010, a quarter million people attended. But what effect has

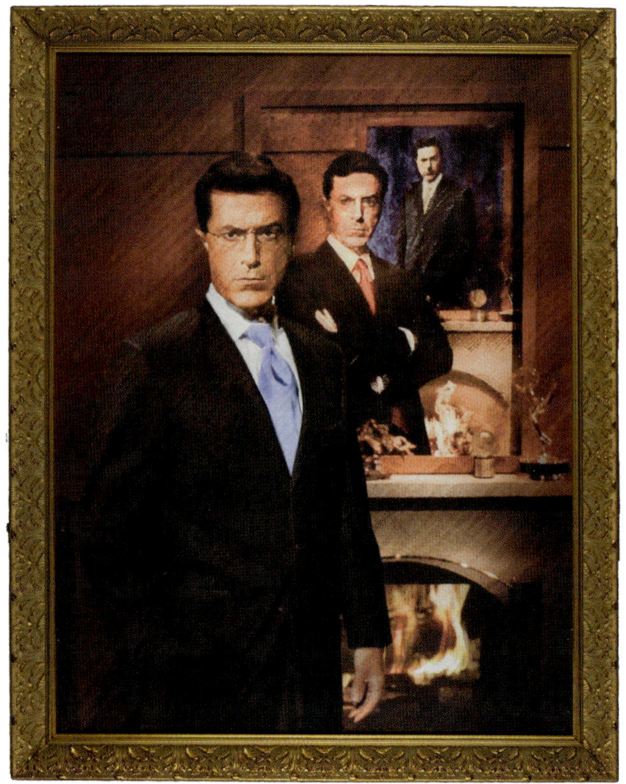

This recursive portrait of Stephen Colbert was created as a prop for his satirical Comedy Central series *The Colbert Report*, representing the mock formality of the show and its host. Colbert's parody of conservative media's conspiratorial style, emotional alarmism, and deceitful fact spinning took aim at Fox News hosts like Bill O'Reilly and Glenn Beck.

the show had on the body politic? In a 2006 study, researchers found that young *Daily Show* viewers were more informed but also more cynical about politics, perhaps contributing to wider distrust of institutions and civic disengagement.[70] Other scholars counter that the series has been beneficial, not only for informing otherwise disengaged viewers of political and world news in a digestible format, but also for teaching media literacy in an age of disinformation and mistrust.[71]

Skepticism is warranted, but it's hard to argue with the premise that *The Daily Show* has been the most successful and significant satirical news program of all time.

Ryan Lintelman

4

Comedy

BREAKS THE MOLD

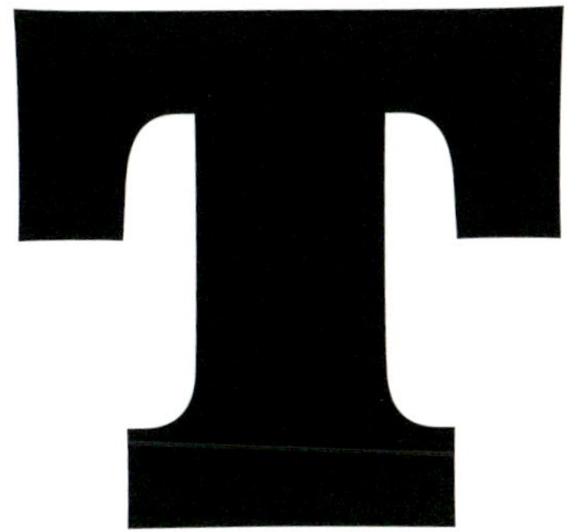he internet meme is both old as time and something new. In one sense, it's a familiar comedy form. Like Roman graffiti, Shakespearean comedy, or newspaper political cartoons, memes offer commentary on contemporary events using a common vernacular of images, characters, and phrases. But in the uniquely democratic and novelty-chasing United States, memes have taken on a new cultural power in recent years. The internet has created a global community to consume and distribute these images, while software and mobile technology have made creating them easier than ever. As Jim Deutsch writes in this chapter, meme images combined with gallows humor have helped Americans deal with traumatic events from the 1918 influenza epidemic to the 2020s COVID-19 pandemic.

In the same vein, presidents of the United States have been fodder for political humor since the nation's founding, when newspaper cartoonists and writers mocked Thomas Jefferson as a "brandy-soaked anarchist" and poked fun at John Adams's pomposity. However, the internet has changed the way that citizens generate and interact with political humor. Barack Obama has been called the "first meme president," every aspect of his personality and administration referenced and remixed in an endless stream of comedy images and videos.[1] You may remember a few of them: a photo of Obama on the phone looking unbothered in cartoon sunglasses titled "DEAL WITH IT." A line drawing of Obama in a

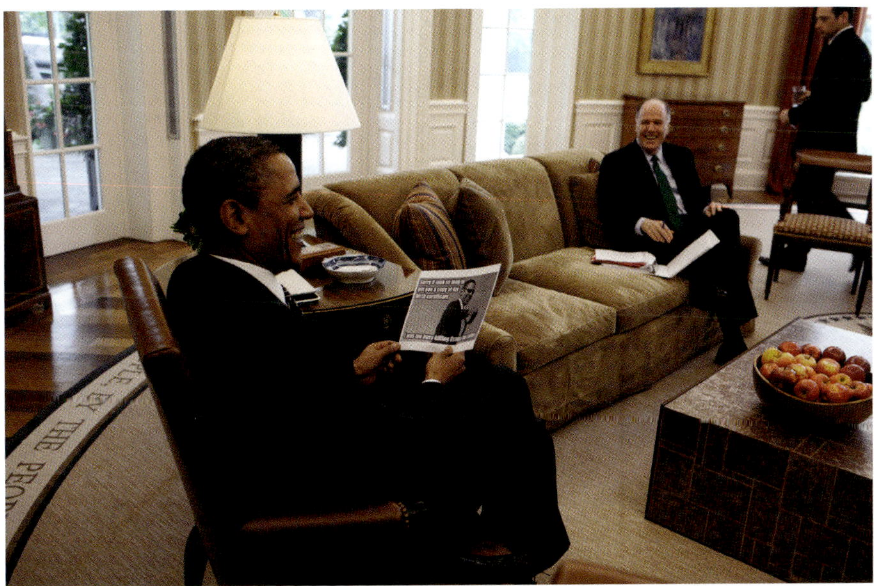

This photograph, dated May 2, 2011, shows President Barack Obama in the Oval Office with National Security Advisor Tom Donilon, enjoying a printed-out meme circulating the day after the raid that resulted in Osama bin Laden's death.

tuxedo looking impressed. "Thanks, Obama" as a catchphrase for any slight annoyance. Obama even addressed his memetic presidency in a video for digital media company ATTN: posted November 15, 2021, "I'm Barack Obama, and I was a viral meme." The video asserted memes served a vital democratic function, giving individuals a voice for political commentary and critique.

The meme presidency came full circle when, in October 2023, a *Washington Post* Freedom of Information Act request uncovered a photograph of the president enjoying a meme hot off the press. Referencing some Republicans' insistence that Obama release his birth certificate to prove his citizenship, the photo shows the president in the Oval Office laughing while holding a printed photo of himself with the stylized meme caption "Sorry it took so long to get you a copy of my birth certificate / I was too busy killing Osama bin Laden." The photo is dated May 2, 2011, the day after a Navy SEALs raid that resulted in bin Laden's death.

Fundamentally, comedy requires improvisation, creativity, transgression, and the courage to test limits and cross lines of social decorum, politesse, and conventional wisdom. When a comedian engages an audience—viewers, readers, listeners, or even critics—they open a conversation about what a shared community has experienced, believes, and holds dear. The comedian holds some part of their experience or culture up to scrutiny and, looking at it in a new and humorous light, explores new possibilities in a uniquely liberative space. Social convention is suspended in the service of entertainment.

It's not just comedy content that's innovative; it's also the medium. Americans' hunger for entertainment has driven comedians to create new performance styles, venues, and formats. Out of a melting pot of diverse cultural influences, senses of humor, and contemporary conversations, comedians forged unique and robust forms of comedy rooted in the American experience. Composers and librettists adapted European light opera to create the Broadway musical comedy, which has provided a platform for personal expression and subversive satire for generations of American audiences. Puppeteers and ventriloquists brought their impish alter egos and zany characters to unexpected places, including radio and television, proving that dummies can get away with ribald and transgressive commentary their human performers wouldn't dare to speak. Combining aspects of burlesque, vaudeville, and nightclubs, comedy clubs became vibrant venues for stand-up and improv comedians who challenged cultural norms, provoking controversy and conversation.

Comedians have been quick to adopt new communications media and find new opportunities to take the stage. As broadcast radio became a national phenomenon in the 1930s, Jack Benny was among the most innovative of the wave of vaudeville comics taking to the airwaves. In his eponymous radio program, perhaps the first "show about nothing," Benny helped formulate and formalize the situation comedy, with its memorable characters, catchphrases, and serial storytelling. A generation later, in the 1950s, Imogene Coca and Sid Caesar combined the best of radio and vaudeville comedy to create the television sketch/variety show, in the groundbreaking *Your Show of Shows*. Meanwhile, Ernie Kovacs brought his improvisational and inventive mind to the medium, creating memorable experimental effects and breaking the fourth wall, opening new frontiers in visual humor. In the sixties and seventies, the comedy record boom offered innovative performers a new platform to push the envelope, from the stag records of Redd Foxx and Rusty Warren to the groundbreaking social commentary of George Carlin and Richard Pryor and the oddball stylings of Allan Sherman, Stan Freberg, and Weird Al Yankovic.

While Bill Nye was taking a break from his career as a mechanical engineer to perform stand-up comedy in Seattle in the late 1980s, he developed an enthusiastically geeky Science Guy persona, using humor to educate. In 1993, after the federal Children's Television Act required stations to air a number of hours of educational television, Nye brought the act to national television with *Bill Nye the Science Guy*, adapting his comedy act to teach a generation of Americans about science, nature, and climate with a hip, quirky comic style.

Lab coat worn by Bill Nye on the educational television series *Bill Nye the Science Guy*, 1993–1998.

The internet age has opened a new world of possibilities for comedy, lowering the barrier to entry for any aspiring comedian to express themselves and provoke their audience in pursuit of laughter. In the 1990s, *America's Funniest Home Videos* paved the way, providing a platform for homemade comedy content to reach a national audience, and social media like YouTube has made this user-generated content ubiquitous in modern American life. Web series like Felicia Day's *The Guild* (2007–2013) have proved the viability of this media format while also representing the benefits for broader representation when more Americans can participate. Shows like *The Guild* and *The Big Bang Theory* (2007–2019) brought nerdy subcultural humor into the mainstream. Meanwhile, new generations of comic talent like Margaret Cho, Gabriel Iglesias, Cristela Alonzo, and Felipe Esparza have fought for a more inclusive American comedy scene by taking advantage of new media and platforms to advance their careers, despite systemic challenges and barriers. Like the Harlem Globetrotters, Harvey Fierstein, and Culture Clash, to name just a few pioneers who came before them, they recognize the liberative potential of comedy as novelty, the tip of the spear to bring about social and cultural change.

Introduction by Ryan Lintelman

EDGAR BERGEN AND CHARLIE MCCARTHY: EGO AND ID

One of the first superstars of American broadcast radio was perhaps the most unlikely: a ventriloquist dummy. Edgar Bergen was a canny vaudeville entertainer who used Charlie McCarthy as a projection of his id—an uninhibited, mischievous, and often raunchy partner who mocked social convention and morality. The duo starred in a series of top-rated radio programs from 1937 through 1956, with additional appearances on film, on television, and in a comic book making them household names. Bergen acted as the straight man and father figure balancing McCarthy's precocious and transgressive humorous banter. Despite being portrayed as a child, McCarthy was known for roasting celebrity guests and pursuing women, frequently flirting in provocative double entendre and libidinous innuendo that would have faced censorship if spoken by a human character. Bergen was among the first to recognize that electronic media enhanced the traditional shield of comedy performance, allowing performers to challenge social norms in new, extreme ways, while protecting themselves from the fallout.

Edgar Berggren (he dropped the extra "gr" for his stage name) was the son of Swedish immigrants who taught himself ventriloquism while working odd jobs to support his family following his father's death. In 1922, Bergen asked Chicago-area woodcarver Theodore Mack to make a dummy, based on a sketch of an impish young Irish neighbor who sold newspapers, and named him Charlie McCarthy. Working amateur nights in Chicago, and then taking the act to the vaudeville stage, Bergen found that he could get away with more suggestive, subversive, or even insulting humor when he said it in the voice of the bratty, self-centered Charlie rather than his own. Elegant attire and a modicum of class, too, enhanced the comic dissonance between the duo's appearance and Charlie's boundary-testing humor. Bergen first dressed McCarthy in his signature tuxedo, monocle, and top hat for a performance at the Rainbow Room of the Waldorf Astoria in New York City, and it was to become a signature of the act.

In 1936, the duo made their radio debut as guest stars on the *Rudy Vallee Radio Show* and the following year began starring in their own radio show, *The Chase and Sanborn Hour* (sponsored by Standard Brands' Chase and Sanborn Coffee), which aired on Sunday evenings on the NBC network. The series became a hit and maintained its high ratings for over a decade. Each episode saw Bergen and McCarthy engage in a rapid-fire dialogue, usually revolving around Bergen scolding the youngster for some transgression like truancy or chasing a girl. A celebrity guest would then spar with McCarthy; comedian W. C. Fields was a particular favorite, and their exchanges of insults became legendary. While Fields might call Charlie a "woodpecker's pin-up boy" or threaten to throw him into the fireplace, McCarthy would counter that the famously dipsomaniac Fields could be used as an alcohol lamp, or that "pink elephants take aspirin to get rid of W. C. Fields."[2]

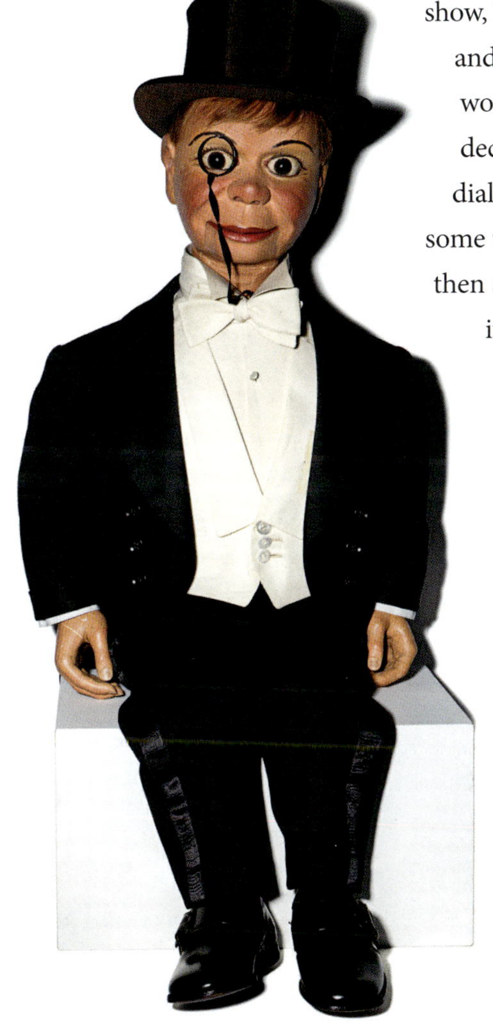

This is the original Charlie McCarthy dummy, donated to the Smithsonian Institution just after Edgar Bergen's death in 1978. McCarthy's strange combination of adolescent humor and gentlemanly dress made for an ironic and unpredictable radio comedy act.

In one of the most notable episodes in the history of the show, guest Mae West appeared with featured player Don Ameche in a 1937 sketch parodying the biblical Garden of Eden. Twenty-three million listeners heard West engage in innuendo-laden banter with Ameche, and later in the episode, with McCarthy, whom she invited to come home and "let you play in my woodpile."[3] Culturally conservative critics, especially those writing for Catholic publications, erupted in opposition to the episode, encouraging a letter-writing campaign that flooded the Federal Communications Commission with complaints. The Catholic Legion of Decency had long set their sights on West as a representative of degeneracy in popular culture and took this opportunity to drum up the largest opposition to broadcast indecency that had ever been waged, taking the radio industry by surprise. Show sponsor Chase and Sanborn Coffee expressed regret and apology through their advertising agency, J. Walter Thompson, as did NBC, and the FCC scrambled to redefine its standards of indecent or obscene content. Meanwhile, anticensorship forces rallied to argue that the federal government was

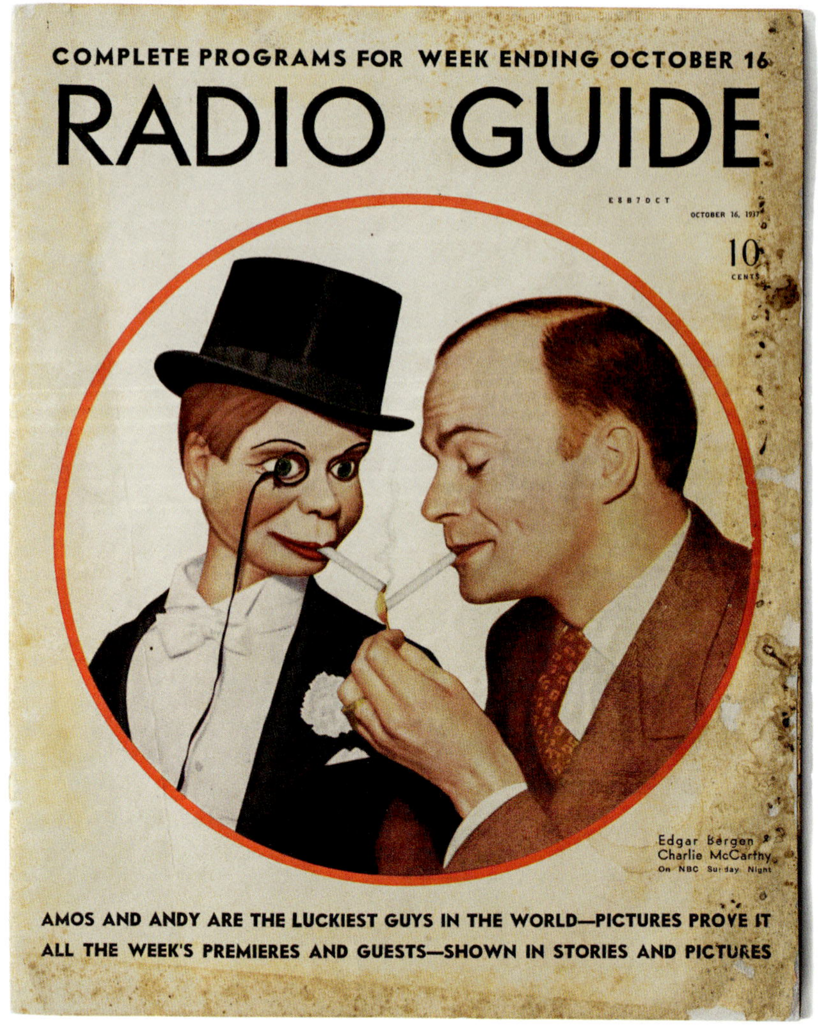

This *Radio Guide* magazine with its portrait of Bergen and McCarthy speaks to their enormous popularity in the mid-1930s. Bergen always seemed taken aback when McCarthy made cheeky jokes, and speaking as himself, admonished the puppet. The duo gave voice to tension between the pull to conform to straitlaced social norms and the desire to break the rules.

overreaching in its redoubled attempts to limit free speech on the radio. Meanwhile, the vast majority of radio listeners reported little interest in the scandal, and Bergen and McCarthy's *Chase and Sanborn Hour* endured on the air for another decade.[4]

Bergen and McCarthy proved to be popular film stars as well, making fourteen motion pictures and receiving an Academy Award for special achievement in 1938. The award statuette even featured a moveable mouth like Charlie's. During World War II, they toured military hospitals in the United States and made numerous appearances overseas, traveling with the USO and broadcasting from Army, Navy, and Marine bases during and after the war. With the declining popularity of radio, they made the transition to television with an NBC show, *Do You Trust Your Wife?* (NBC, 1958–1959), and continued to perform in nightclub and television appearances, with a notable final cameo in 1979's *The Muppet Movie*.

Bergen was known for his showmanship, exceptional humor, and a daring irreverence, opening the door for more transgressive comedians to use new media to challenge social mores.

Ryan Lintelman

JACK BENNY AND THE ORIGINAL "SHOW ABOUT NOTHING"

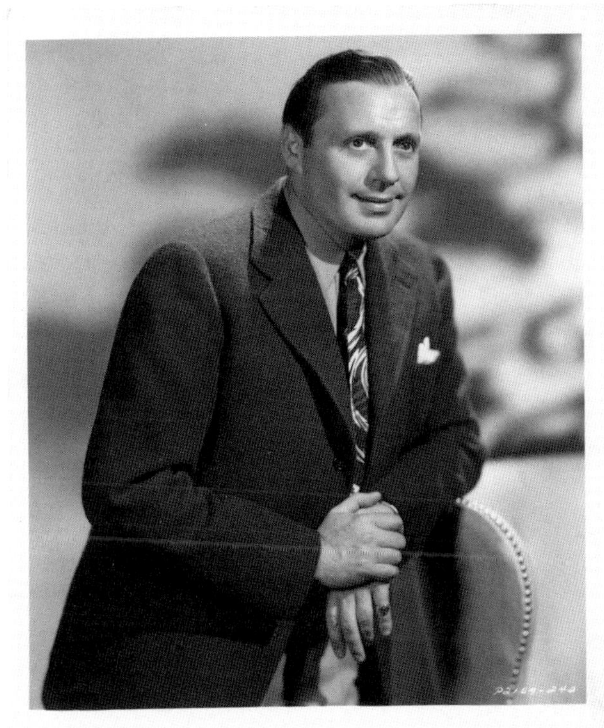

Unassuming violinist Benjamin Kubelsky, better known by his stage name Jack Benny.

Comedian Jack Benny negotiated the explosion of mass media in the twentieth century to become one of America's most popular and groundbreaking entertainers. Successful as vaudevillian, movie star, and television lead, Benny is best remembered for his long-running radio broadcast, considered by many a high point of the medium's "golden age." *The Jack Benny Show*'s many innovations helped forge the format of modern situation comedy, making it one of the most influential cultural programs in American history.

Born Benjamin Kubelsky, Benny, the son of Jewish immigrants, grew up in Waukegan, Illinois. As a teen, the aspiring entertainer learned violin, playing at local community functions before bringing his skills to vaudeville. On the road over the years, Benny developed his comedy, creating characters, participating in routines, and working his way up as an efficient master of ceremonies. In 1927 he married New York hosiery clerk Sadie Marks, who as "Mary Livingstone" would become a vital component of Benny's comedy and a national celebrity in her own right.

At this moment, radio was revolutionizing entertainment in America. Long seen as an experimental hobby, radio quickly became big business by the early 1930s, as national broadcast networks formed to deliver news and entertainment and the percentage of American households owning a radio set jumped from around 31 percent in 1929 to over 60 percent in 1932.[5]

Audiences no longer needed to attend theaters or cinemas to experience the latest in music, comedy, and drama. Without the need to purchase tickets, or even leave the house, mass entertainment quickly became an essential component of daily life. Connected to national audiences in real time, advertisers and performers had the ability to directly speak to millions.

However, success in the new medium had significant challenges. New content had to be continually produced to fill the seemingly limitless hours of airtime. In 1932, NBC hired Benny to host *The Canada Dry Program*, which, initially, greatly resembled other programs of the period, offering heavy doses of band music interposed with moments of comic levity provided by comedians, mostly drawn from the vaudeville stage. Entertainers such as Benny, who had traditionally developed jokes and routines over time, honing their act before successions of fresh audiences, now had to generate new, untested material multiple times a week. Furthermore, they could no longer rely on visual clues such as facial expressions to connect with audiences, forcing performers and their writers to develop narratives reliant solely on dialog and auditory clues.

Faced with these significant challenges, Benny and his lead writer Harry Conn developed a program that could sustain the rigors of such a heavy production schedule, while also utilizing the possibilities offered by radio's seemingly unlimited imaginative world. In so doing, they created one of the most successful comedy programs of all time, popularizing tropes and idioms that would become ingrained into the mainstream of American broadcast entertainment.

Performed before a live audience, *The Jack Benny Program* used the concept of a tight-knit family of performers, led by Benny, and their humorous interactions on and off the stage. This concept brilliantly allowed for an abundance of comedic possibilities while seamlessly incorporating musical numbers, sponsor messages, and metanarratives.

The unique structure and style of the program they created made *The Jack Benny Show* one of the medium's biggest successes, its popularity with audiences surviving numerous sponsorship and network changes as well as the loss of Conn, who was partially responsible for the program's distinctive brand of humor. Lasting until 1954, the program attracted audiences in the tens of millions, making Benny and his cast some of the most recognized performers in the nation.

Perhaps Benny's most inspired idea was to fabricate a persona that, unlike most of his comedic on-air peers, was the target of much of the show's humor, constantly suffering blows to his ego from myriad failures and insulting wisecracks. On the show, Benny portrayed a pompous, effete, and miserly middle-class American who, insecure about his age and untalented as a performer, encouraged the derision of others, drawing humor from these all-too-human foibles.

Much of the ribbing done at Benny's expense was done by his castmates, who in the context of the program were also the comedian's friends, employees, and neighbors. Spreading the jokes around this found family of personal and professional acquaintances not only provided *The Jack Benny Show*'s writers with plenty of opportunities to poke fun at the show's star, but also helped the show develop an intimacy and rapport with audiences who enjoyed the perceived closeness of the company of characters.

Benny's "found family" included announcer Don Wilson, young singer Dennis Day, and bandleader (and future voice of Baloo in Walt Disney's adaptation of *The Jungle Book*) Phil Harris. Benny and Harris famously developed a well-publicized public feud that lasted even when Harris was given his own namesake radio program. However, it was Benny's companion (and real-life spouse) Mary Livingstone and his African American valet, Rochester, played by actor Eddie Anderson, that produced the program's most subversive humor.

Although they shared names, *The Jack Benny Show*'s "Mary Livingstone" was very different from the actresses who portrayed her. Presented not as a wife or as a love interest, the scripted Livingstone was presented as Benny's best friend and constant companion. This independence set Livingstone apart from other on-air portrayals of women of the time, challenging traditional societal norms regarding women's roles, especially in relationships outside of the traditional family structure.

On a program that helped popularize humor based on witty comebacks and sharp put-downs, many of the harshest insults thrown Benny's way were provided by Livingstone. Presented as an equal member of Benny's gang, Livingstone's outspokenness, wit, and autonomy not only set her apart from other women on radio but also provided a perfect comedic foil to Benny's cowardly and pompous persona. Audiences loved the character, and Livingstone became one of radio's most popular performers.

Eddie Anderson's "Rochester" also provided transgressive humor that challenged stereotypes and upended patriarchal relationships. Benny's African American valet shocked listeners by daring to tease, one-up, and embarrass his white employer. Introduced in an early episode of

The Jack Benny Show in a small role of a Pullman porter, Anderson's gravel-voiced performance delighted listeners, leading to the creation of Rochester, Benny's full-time chauffer and attendant.

The character was championed by many for providing an alternative to the limited and stereotypical roles typically available to African Americans in film and radio. While drawing the ire of racist whites, Rochester soon became one of the program's breakout characters, with Anderson becoming the highest paid African American performer in the country and the recipient of much praise by the Black community.

However, the groundbreaking aspects of Anderson's character were often undermined by Benny and his writers' continued reliance on tired and formulaic and ugly racial tropes for humor. Already safely placed in a subservient position, Rochester was also presented as being a lazy gambler, overly interested in women and drink. By relying on such tired and pernicious cliches, *The Jack Benny Show* was criticized by many for maintaining harmful and derogatory impressions of Black culture. These criticisms became more prominent as younger generations of intellectuals confronted racial inequities in American life.

In both challenging and affirming racial stereotypes, *The Jack Benny Show* put Anderson in a difficult position within the entertainment community and hurt the actor's legacy as one of the most prominent Black actors in American history. Yet it can be said that with both Rochester and Mary Livingstone, *The Jack Benny Show* helped pave the way for new and more diverse representations of nonwhite male characters in American entertainment.

Another unexpected target for humor on *The Jack Benny Show* was the program's sponsors. Unlike today, where paid advertisements from numerous parties are inserted into program "breaks," most radio productions were underwritten by a single advertiser, with some shows, such as Benny's, smoothly incorporating the advertising within the context of the broadcast.

After having some difficulty pleasing sponsors with his mild and sarcastic tone, Benny struck gold with Post's struggling Jell-O brand gelatin product, finding numerous opportunities to gently poke fun at the product while incorporating the brand in skits and witty asides. Jell-O sales skyrocketed alongside the popularity of *The Jack Benny Show*. This break from the conventional heavy-handed presentation of products revolutionized advertising, revealing that consumers could be attracted by making a broadcast's promotional obligations part of the fun.

In ways both mild and manic, Benny adhered to and transgressed audience expectations and social norms to create comedy that delighted midcentury audiences, but also led to criticism of the performer from both sides of the political spectrum. He boldly blazed new ground in radio comedy and helped pave the way for situation comedies to come.

Eric Jentsch

ERNIE KOVACS: ELECTRONIC COMIC

At his peak, Ernie Kovacs was producing, directing, designing, and hosting twelve hours of live television programming per week, and introducing the American public to a new type of bold, irreverent humor for a mass-mediated age. While many artists approached the new medium of television with trepidation, Kovacs's innovative spirit was undaunted—and, in fact, propelled—by the spontaneity, experimentation, and chaos that characterized the early TV industry.

Perhaps the first artist to embrace television as a truly creative medium—as something more than "radio with pictures"—Kovacs dismantled TV's conventions as quickly as they emerged. More significantly, in an era characterized by inane advertising babble and cookie-cutter sitcoms and Westerns, he rejected the idea that audiences were passive media consumers, asking his viewers to share in his conception of television as an electronic playground.

Kovacs began his career as a radio DJ during the early 1940s. He ascended through the ranks of local and regional television during the medium's infancy and, in less than seven years, vaulted from hosting a local daytime show in Philadelphia to gracing the cover of *Life* magazine as a host of the original *Tonight Show*. He created several iterations of his eponymous *Ernie Kovacs Show* and a lauded string of ABC specials, which are masterworks in the canon of comedy history. While critics bemoaned the fact that television comedy had rapidly grown stale, stilted, and oversaturated with recycled vaudeville acts, they elevated

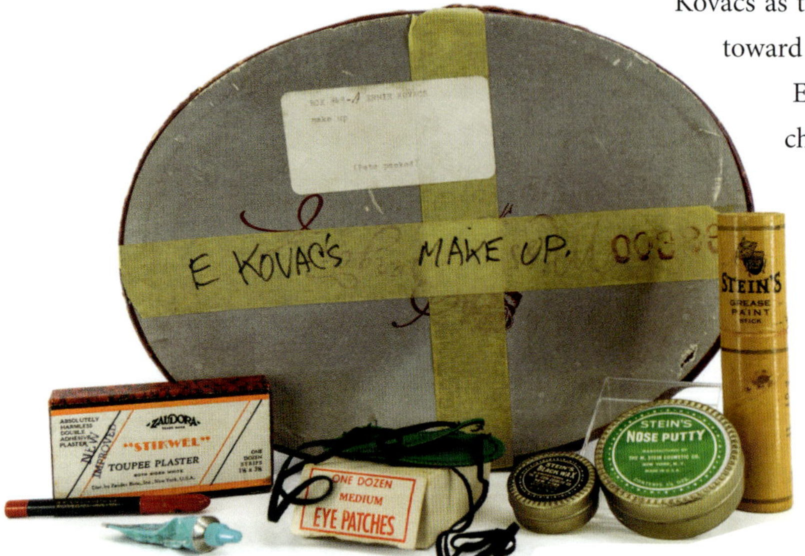

Ernie Kovacs had a remarkable ability to "put on" and "take off" an array of comic personas. His well-used make-up kit includes a range of mustaches, face paints, and adhesives for attaching putty noses, eyebrows, and hairpieces.

Kovacs as the savior who would usher the art form toward a modern future.

Ernie Kovacs's early life was rife with challenges. A child of Hungarian immigrants in Trenton, New Jersey, he weathered extreme poverty during the height of the Great Depression and endured a life-threatening bout of pneumonia that left him condemned to a sanitarium. To endure the endless days of convalescence, he entertained himself by playfully cutting and splicing his own X-rays, to the surprise of unsuspecting doctors. Despite these beginnings—or perhaps because of them—he would become known for his great zest for life. With an ever-present cigar in his hand and a poker game always in progress, he welcomed a revolving door of famous friends (like Billy Wilder, Dean Martin, and Edward G. Robinson) into his eccentrically appointed Hollywood home. His extravagant lifestyle was matched only by his insatiable work ethic.

His success in television was born not only from an innate comedic sensibility but from a herculean stamina and a discriminating taste. Kovacs is among few artists in TV history to have taken control of every aspect of production—from writing and directing to sound design and set decoration—a remarkable feat made almost unbelievable in light of the extreme technical and financial limitations that characterized the industry during its first decade.

Perhaps most fascinated with electronic effects and the potential of toying with television technology, Kovacs was constantly creating and refining invisibility illusions, superimpositions, rotations, mirror effects, and other tricks of the eye. Always working on a shoestring budget, he used everyday objects to achieve spectacular results. In one instance, he affixed two nested soup cans and an internal mirror to a camera lens in order to invert and rotate an image live on the air. In another, he appeared to "smoke" underwater by releasing a mouthful of milk while submerged in a tank. Perhaps the most celebrated trick in Kovacs's repertoire, the "tilted table" sequence, was the centerpiece of his iconic 1961 "Silent Show," which was performed with no dialogue. The confounding effect was ingeniously achieved by tilting both the set and the camera at identical eighteen-degree angles, so that objects appeared to shift and move in a physically impossible manner. Sometimes, Kovacs took simpler approaches to disrupting televisual norms, like filling a stray minute of airtime by simply staring into the camera lens and counting to sixty.

Fortunately, or unfortunately, Kovacs had an infamous disregard for monetary restraint or technical roadblocks, once using an entire week's production budget to execute a single four-second sight gag involving a car falling through the floor. No gag was too complicated or too far out of reach. "Syncopated Office" (1961) is a case in point: an elaborate choreography of animate office supplies, synced precisely to a symphonic soundtrack and interacting like a zany Rube Goldberg machine. The soundstage was outfitted with an array of spring-loaded parts, trap doors, and concealed levers before the complex "dance" was shot in one remarkable afternoon based on an imaginative, and foreboding, seven-page memo that Kovacs delivered to his crew: "TO ALL CONCERNED: AND BELIEVE ME YOU SHOULD BE, BECAUSE I AM: The following is going to be either the downfall of us technically or at the least, mentally. I don't know how the ## you're going to get this done by Sunday-but 'rots of ruck.'"

Among Kovacs's most beloved recurring sketches were appearances by "The Nairobi Trio," a group of musicians wearing ape masks and mechanically pounding drums in the manner of a wind-up music box. Kovacs played the center ape, with his ever-present cigar alight, while the other players rotated anonymously—allegedly including cameo turns by stars including Jack Lemmon and Frank Sinatra.

In addition to assuming full creative control behind the scenes, Kovacs was a virtuosic physical comedian. Often starting with a simple costume piece—like a pair of novelty glasses, a rubber ape mask, or a fake mustache—he built up a roster of recurring characters with outlandish accents, mannerisms, and motivations: Miklos Molnar, the sarcastic, irritable, and incompetent host of a Hungarian cooking show; Matzoh Heppelwhite, a boozy traveling showman with a repertoire of cheap tricks; Superclod, a buffoonish, low-budget hero with a vision problem; Wolfgang von Sauerbraten, the German "Disk Chöckey"; and Percy Dovetonsils, the lisping, martini-drinking "poet laureate."

At the height of acclaim and peak of creativity, Ernie Kovacs was killed in a car accident in Beverly Hills on January 13, 1962. His epitaph reads, "Nothing in Moderation." The shape of TV humor's trajectory had Kovacs not been prematurely killed stands as one of American comedy's great unanswerable questions. Ultimately, none of TV's genres could contain his forward-looking creativity. His work was more irreverent than that of his most daring peers. Years ahead of his time, Kovacs's innovative spirit would go on to inflect and inspire generations of comedy creators and seminal series like *Laugh-In*, *Saturday Night Live*, *The Muppet Show*, *Monty Python's Flying Circus*, and *SCTV*.

Laura LaPlaca

YOUR SHOW OF SHOWS AND THE BIRTH OF TELEVISION COMEDY

Over the course of a few years, from about 1948 to 1954, television went from being a futuristic novelty to the most important and exciting entertainment medium in American life. At the center of that burst of innovative creative energy was Sid Caesar, who helped create the vocabulary and style of television comedy with his variety series *Your Show of Shows*. With his costar Imogene Coca and a crack team of legendary writing talent, Caesar combined aspects of vaudeville, radio, and Borscht Belt humor to invent modern sketch comedy.

Caesar was the son of Polish Jewish immigrants, born in Yonkers, New York, in 1922. He learned to make people laugh working at his family's restaurant, then in the Borscht Belt resorts of the Catskills. When he was drafted into the Coast Guard during World War II, he put his skills to use creating a musical comedy revue that proved so popular he was asked to join a national tour and film production. He was working in nightclubs and as one of the stars of the 1948 Broadway revue *Make Mine Manhattan* when an offer came for him to work in television. Milton Berle had recently become the biggest star in the medium with his variety show *Texaco Star Theater*, and now NBC recruited Caesar to add a similar comedy program for its Saturday night lineup.

Caesar's producer Max Liebman was the Lorne Michaels of his era, or as Caesar called him, the "Ziegfeld of the borscht belt."[6] He had discovered comic actor Danny Kaye, produced vaudeville and Broadway shows, and now set to work helping Caesar create his television series. The *Admiral Broadway Revue* premiered in 1949 to immediate success. It was so successful, in fact, that it lasted only nineteen weeks, canceled after its sponsor, appliance manufacturer Admiral, couldn't keep up with demand for television sets and decided to drop its support.[7]

In 1950, the series was back, rechristened *Your Show of Shows.* The ninety-minute comedy-variety show aired live on Saturday nights on NBC from 1950 to 1954. Each episode would feature a celebrity guest, a combination of comedy sketches and musical performances, and a monologue by Caesar. Cast members included Carl Reiner, Howard Morris, and costar Imogene Coca, whose comedy chops more than matched Caesar's. Liebman recruited the brightest young comedy of the era for the show's writers' room, including Mel Brooks, Neil Simon, and Mel Tolkin. Notably, the writers' room also included pioneering female comedy writers Lucille Kallen and Selma Diamond; both would serve as inspiration for Sally Rogers, the female comedy writer portrayed by Rose Marie on *The Dick Van Dyke Show*. Liebman and Caesar wanted *Your Show of Shows* to be something new: sophisticated yet silly, irreverent yet relatable, and above all, the funniest show ever broadcast.

Critics and the public seemed to agree that they had achieved their goals. *Your Show of Shows* earned top ten ratings, numerous Emmy Awards, and near-universal acclaim. The shows were more sketch comedy based than anything that television had produced before, and paved the way for *Laugh-In*, *Saturday Night Live*, and other sketch series to come. The sketches were "sharper, edgier, more sophisticated than the other variety shows, by far," admirer David Steinberg recalled.[8] The writers and performers mostly eschewed broad slapstick, one-liners, and even specific drawn-from-the-headlines punchlines in favor of sketches that drew humor from human behavior, popular culture parodies, and character-driven routines. Among the most popular characters were Caesar's professor, a pompous and befuddled "expert" whose interviews by roving reporter Carl Reiner invariably involve him trying to evade questions and disguise his ignorance, and "The

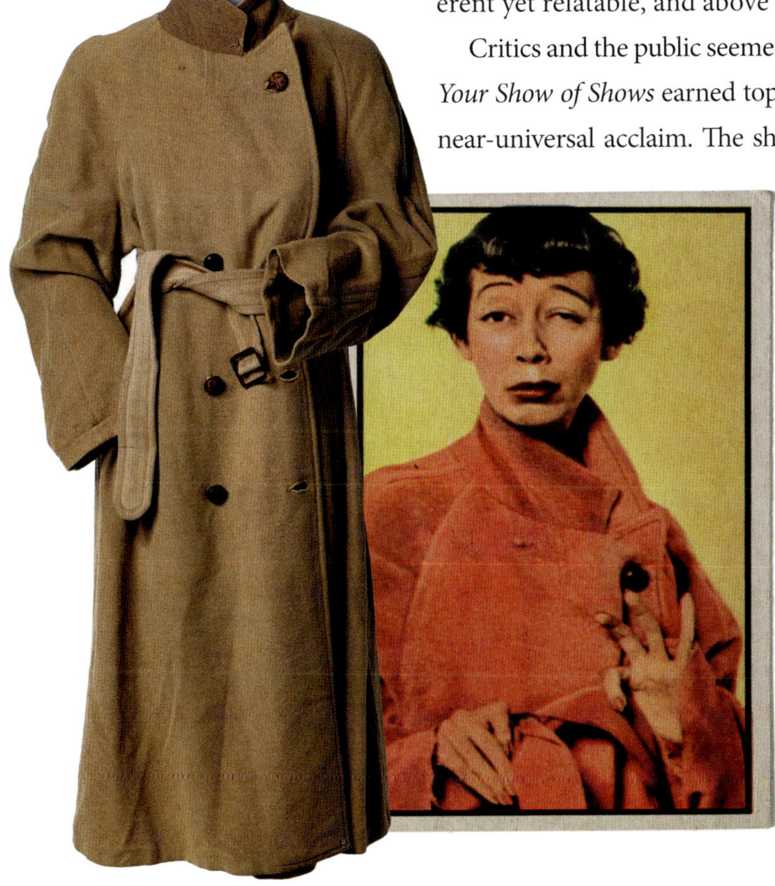

One of Imogene Coca's most memorable sketches involved her "modest stripper" act, wherein she performed a silly and seductive striptease in a camelhair trench coat before slinking behind the stage curtain. Extending an arm and dropping the coat seductively, she would then reappear wearing a second trench coat.

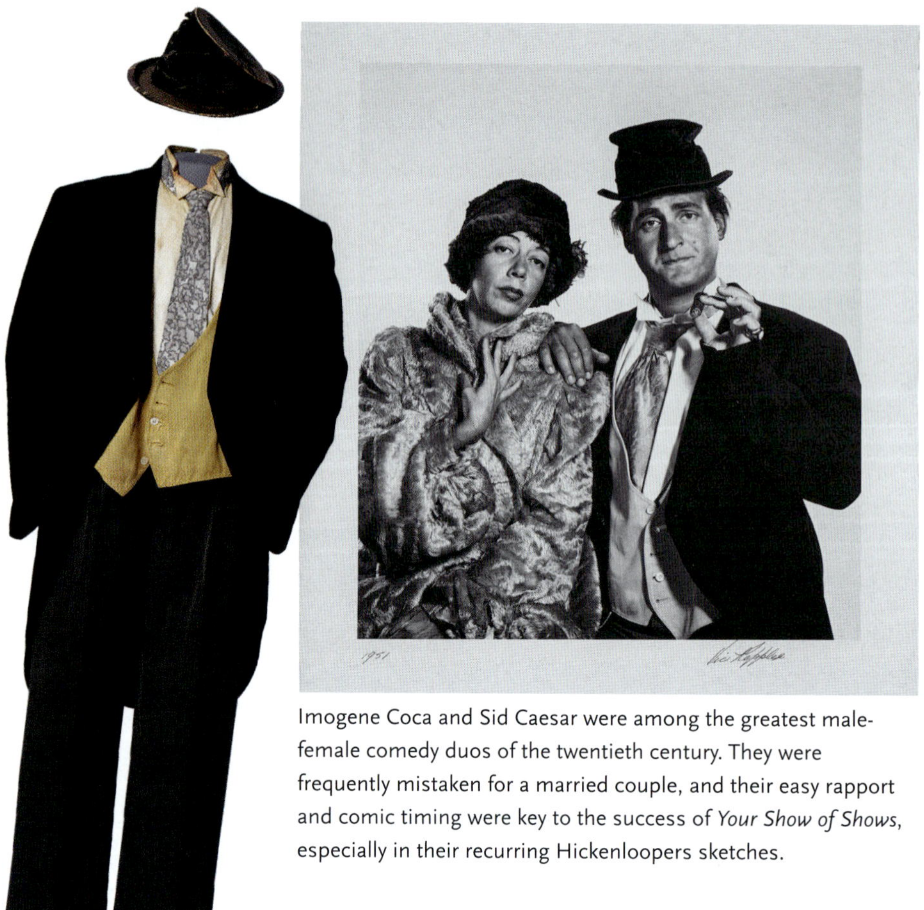

Imogene Coca and Sid Caesar were among the greatest male-female comedy duos of the twentieth century. They were frequently mistaken for a married couple, and their easy rapport and comic timing were key to the success of *Your Show of Shows*, especially in their recurring Hickenloopers sketches.

Caesar's professor character changed names depending on the area of expertise for which roving reporter Carl Reiner was interviewing him, from memory expert "Lapse Von Memory" to physician "Hugo von Gezundheit," archeologist "Ludwig von Fossil," and sleep expert "Sigmund von Sedative." The routine satirized the 1950s news media's obsession with European experts, some of whom, like rocket scientist "Wernher von Braun," had collaborated with the Nazi regime.

Hickenloopers," with Caesar and Coca as a bickering married couple, their middle-class, suburban milieu creating the mold for the family television sitcom.

The show's success certainly depended on the skills of the actors—Caesar and Coca in particular—but perhaps even more on the brilliance and eccentricity of the writers, who created the show's unique comic style. "We never wrote for the public," Mel Brooks remembered, "we wrote for us, and we prayed to God that the public would get it. That's the only way things are good."[9] That meant seemingly niche experiences and cultural references were fodder for parody, from orchestral performance to foreign movies. A pitiless spoof of the television series *This Is Your Life* with Caesar as a lachrymose dope and Howard Morris cast as his effusive "Uncle Goopy" garnered "what is probably the longest and loudest burst of laughter—genuine laughter, neither piped in nor prompted—in the history of television," one writer estimated.[10] This style of pop culture parody was so new and so effective that it generated controversy and even a lawsuit, as when Caesar and Coca parodied *From Here to Eternity* with a nearly twenty-minute-long sequence

("From Here to Obscurity"), including a famously wet love scene on the beach, and Columbia Pictures sued NBC for damages.[11]

Your Show of Shows' humor was more intellectual and cosmopolitan than shows that would follow, as television's audience broadened from its higher income, East Coast urban origins with national networks and increased television ownership. Network executives feared that spoofs of foreign movies and Yiddish-inflected dialect humor wouldn't play as well in the Mountain West as it did in Manhattan, and began to favor more formulaic situation comedies to the "spontaneous, bawdy, urban, and ethnic" comedy practiced by Caesar and Milton Berle.[12] In 1954, NBC canceled *Your Show of Shows*; Caesar and Coca were asked to break up the act and helm their own separate series. *The Imogene Coca Show* lasted only one year, while *Caesar's Hour* ran another four with new writers Woody Allen and Larry Gelbart keeping the humor fresh.

For decades, *Your Show of Shows* was considered lost, as its kinescope recordings had been mostly wiped and reused for other purposes. Rather than in reruns, it lived on in legend and in the prodigious output of its writing alumni. Some of them even created works about their time on *Your Show of Shows*: Carl Reiner based *The Dick Van Dyke Show* on his experience writing for Caesar, Mel Brooks produced the 1982 movie *My Favorite Year* with its fictionalized Stan "King" Kaiser and the writers of his *Comedy Cavalcade*, and Neil Simon's play *Laughter on the 23rd Floor* was a loving tribute to the show and its writers' room. Now available again to watch in clips on YouTube, a format in which its sketches hold up remarkably well, *Your Show of Shows* continues to shine as the brilliant prototype for modern sketch comedy.

Ryan Lintelman

BROADWAY: CRUCIBLE OF COMEDY

Broadway theater has been a laboratory for American comedy, a robust and durable cultural form in which writers and performers have created indelible works of topical humor, sending up society and culture in productions that wrangle with the joys and frustrations of modern life.

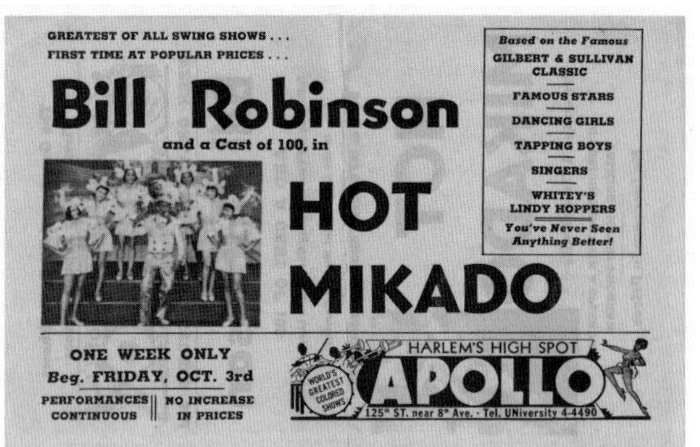

Black entertainers have found opportunities for employment and self-expression in Broadway theater for generations, though before the 1970s roles were limited and often stereotypical. The 1939 *Hot Mikado* was one of two all-Black cast adaptations of Gilbert and Sullivan's *The Mikado*, produced in the late 1930s and starring celebrated dancer Bill "Bojangles" Robinson.

The first mass entertainment medium to take root in the United States, theater was essential to creating a common culture from the nation's earliest days. American theater evolved as the country grew in population and diversity, its own development mirroring the urbanization, industrialization, and migration that shaped the nation in the nineteenth century. Shaped by immigrant (Jewish and Irish Americans in particular), migrant (like Black southerners who moved to urban areas during the Great Migration), and marginalized people (including LGBTQ+ Americans and young women), theater has a history of celebrating diverse perspectives and identities while encouraging understanding and empathy.

For performers, the Broadway stage has been a relatively meritocratic, though grueling, form of self-expression, community representation, and employment. For audiences, theatrical comedy has entertained, provided catharsis, fostered a sense of belonging, and opened eyes to new perspectives and ideas about the world around them. The most successful Broadway comedies shape and reflect contemporary conversations about American values, identity, sexuality, gender, race, morality, and class.

Broadway is a metonym for the nation's popular theater, which has ebbed and flowed in regional and local popularity over time but has, since at least the mid-nineteenth century, been centered on New York City's theater district, where most plays have their longest and most visible productions.

Early American theaters were democratic, open to all classes, and mostly urban, with most productions being dramatic adaptations of Shakespearean or other British or European works. Over time, as the United States and its cities grew, theatergoing became a frequent leisure activity for many people in the country, and the nation's playwrights and performers began to create a unique form of theater that reflected American concerns, culture, and current events, especially in comedic forms.

The 1787 comic play *The Contrast* by Royall Tyler was the first professionally produced comedy performance by an American writer, a landmark in the emerging popular culture of the United States. The play, inspired by English Restoration comedies like Richard Brinsley Sheridan's *The School for Scandal*, is a comedy of manners in which the nobly modest Revolutionary War hero Colonel Manly wins the heart of a virtuous and beautiful young woman over the foppish, cosmopolitan lothario

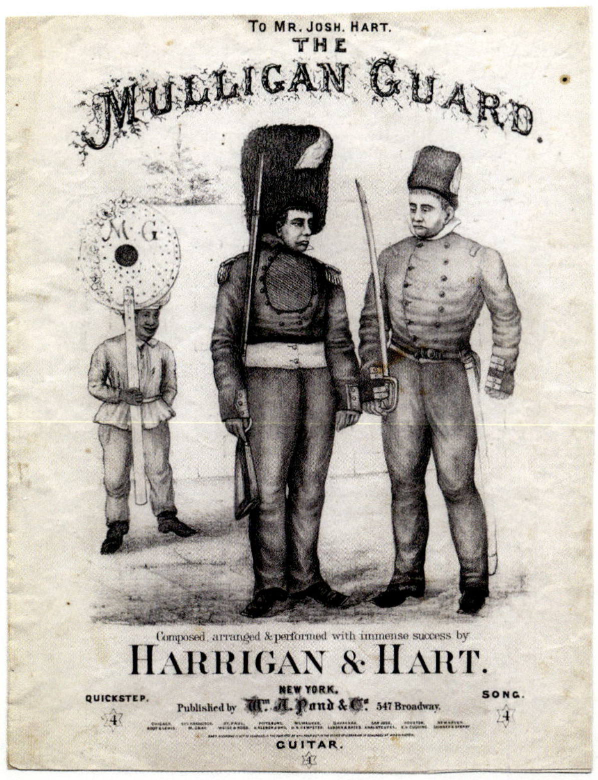

Edward Harrigan and Tony Hart were two of the nineteenth century's most significant comedy playwrights and performers. Their Mulligan Guard shows, popular sensations from 1878 to 1884, were musical farces that poked fun at working-class Irish New Yorkers and their neighborhood militias. These topical, contemporary, sensational shows paved the way for the American musical comedy.

and Anglophile Billy Dimple. The highlight of the play was the rendition of the comic song "Yankee Doodle" by Manly's servant Jonathan, making a mockery of effete dandies like Dimple in favor of the sturdy, homespun virtues Manly represented. The *contrast* in values and identity the play explored has been a constant source of inspiration for American entertainment in the centuries since, with the unpretentious, salt-of-the-earth Jonathan presaging comic characters like Huckleberry Finn and Will Rogers, paragons of American virtue eschewing complicated, cosmopolitan entanglements.[13]

In the nineteenth century, working-class men in cities and on the frontier enjoyed comedy sketches and songs in concert saloons, burlesque, and variety theater, while vaudeville brought legitimacy and standardization to variety theater performance for more integrated audiences. At the same time, New York theatrical comedy began to mature and take new forms. Full-length comedy plays, sometimes called burlesque musicals or farce comedies, began appearing in the 1880s. The long-running *Adonis* (1884) told the story of a sculpture of the handsome mythological lover magically brought to life. His sculptor, his owner, and nearly every other woman he encounters fall in love with him, hounding him through the countryside and numerous costume changes before he convinces the gods to turn him back into stone.[14] This kind of play with gender stereotypes and sexuality would be a staple of theatrical comedy for years to come, especially as the women's rights movement gained political clout and power in the coming decades.

European light opera like Gilbert and Sullivan's *H.M.S. Pinafore*, *The Pirates of Penzance*, and *The Mikado* took the United States by storm in the late nineteenth century and influenced playwrights and composers to create a new uniquely American form of comic theater, the Broadway musical. Spectacular stage productions like *The Black Crook* (1866) and the musical farces of Harrigan and Hart, the matchmaking comedy *A Trip to Chinatown* (1891), and the Tin Pan Alley musical revues of the 1910s and 1920s led the way, but most historians agree that the first modern American musical was 1927's *Show Boat*. It set the conventions of the genre, with a well-integrated book and score, a plot concerning

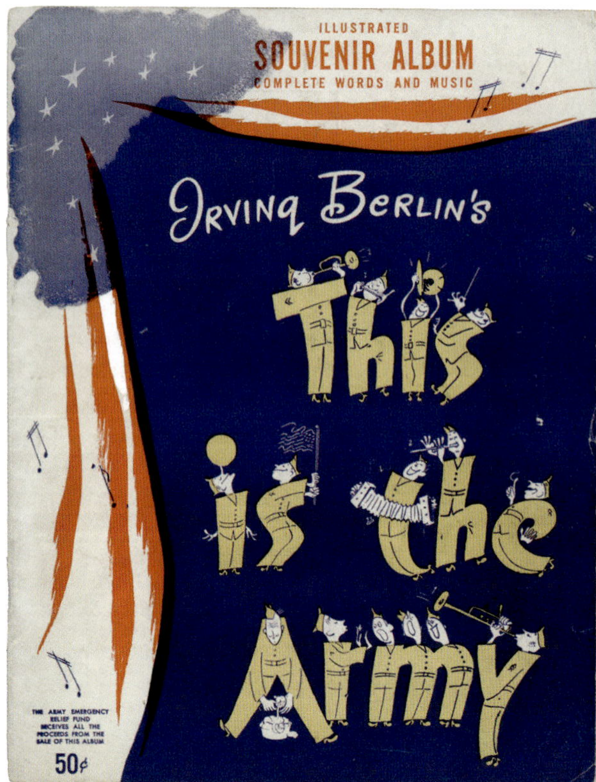

Some Broadway comedies satirized the government and political system, while others, like Irving Berlin's 1942 hit *This Is the Army*, were patriotic works supporting the U.S. armed forces during World War II. Russian-born Jewish American Berlin based the musical on his World War I revue *Yip Yip Yaphank* (1917) and insisted on a racially integrated cast and a stridently patriotic production and that proceeds be pledged to the Army Emergency Relief Fund.

contemporary American themes, fully fleshed-out characters, and a combination of comedy, choreography, and popular music.

With music and lyrics by George and Ira Gershwin, Cole Porter, Jerome Kern, Irving Berlin, and Richard Rogers and Lorenz Hart, books by George S. Kauffman and Oscar Hammerstein II, and performances by Al Jolson, Eddie Cantor, Marilyn Miller, and George M. Cohan, who could do it all, musical comedies captured the zeitgeist of the 1920s. Of the dozens of musical comedy hits of the twenties and thirties, few are remembered or revived today, in part because they so aptly spoke to contemporary changes in social mores, manners, courtship, and popular culture. At a time of unprecedented prosperity and fast-moving technological and social change, "Cinderella musicals" celebrated rags-to-riches stories of financial and social rise, "leisure-time musicals" championed the good life, and "backstage musicals" even applauded popular theater itself as a modern marvel.[15] Youthful, optimistic, sensational, romantic, patriotic, and filled with vernacular wordplay and slang, the Broadway musical defined the Jazz Age as television would define the baby boom generation.

Nonmusical Broadway comedy also continued to influence American culture and conversations about political and social change, with hits like *Lightnin'* (1918), *Abie's Irish Rose* (1922), and *Life with Father* (1939) provoking discussion of divorce, ethnic identity, and family values in the modern age. The Marx Brothers brought anarchic energy to the stage in their madcap and subversive shows *I'll Say She Is* (1924), *The Cocoanuts* (1925), and *Animal Crackers* (1928). Vaudeville comedians Ole Olsen and Chic Johnson went one step further with their zany and fast-paced revue *Hellzapoppin'* (1938), which seemed to capture the anxious and absurdist spirit of the age. The show began with newsreel footage showing Hitler giving a speech in Yiddish, Mussolini speaking in blackface dialect, and Franklin Delano Roosevelt speaking in gibberish before Olsen and Johnson burst through the screen, introducing comic sketches constantly interrupted by subversive and surreal bits like a florist wandering the aisles trying to deliver a potted plant that grew larger with each appearance, a man in a monkey costume chasing a young woman throughout the theater, and dozens of other over-the-top gags that changed from week to week.[16]

At the zenith of Broadway theater's cultural power, from the 1930s to the 1960s, many of the most popular musicals emphasized music, drama, and dance while sidelining comedy in an effort to stress the artistic merit of the form against critical dismissal of middlebrow entertainment. Playwrights like George S. Kaufman and Moss Hart found that political and social satire had uneven success, leading Kaufman to famously quip "satire is what closes on Saturday night." However, writers and performers still found ample opportunity to use comedy to disarm and provoke audiences to consider current events and debates in a new light.

Of Thee I Sing (1931) skewered the posturing and pretentions of modern politics, while *Born Yesterday* (1946) explored government corruption, corporate greed, and the shameful lack of opportunities for women to seek education and employment. Black-cast musicals like *Cabin in the Sky* (1940) and *Carmen Jones* (1943), as well as *Flower Drum Song* (1958), set in San Francisco's Chinatown, and *Fiddler on the Roof* (1964), adapted from Sholem Aleichem's stories about Jewish life amid the turn-of-the-century pogroms of Imperial Russia, reflected a more inclusive vision of American life and ethnic backgrounds. *Mister Roberts* (1948), *South Pacific* (1949), and *Teahouse of the August Moon* (1953), all set in the Pacific around World War II, explore the limits of American cultural imperialism.

Harry Goz and Zero Mostel wore this costume in the role of Tevye in *Fiddler on the Roof* beginning in 1964. The groundbreaking musical was an homage to Jewish resilience in the face of oppression, a huge success (the first Broadway musical to run for more than three thousand performances), and a landmark in theatrical representation and exploration of Jewish identity.

Stage comedy interrogated the era's stifling conformity, traditional family life, and changing conceptions of romance and marriage. *You Can't Take It with You* (1936) and *Harvey* (1944) were escapist odes to eccentricity and social nonconformity, *The Seven Year Itch* (1952) was a farce about infidelity, and *Bye Bye Birdie* (1960) asked "what's the matter with kids today?" Prolific playwright Neil Simon wrote comedies of middle-class malaise, while *How to Succeed in Business Without Really Trying* (1961) made a mockery of American corporate life and work ethic. Increasingly, Broadway shows of the period frequently celebrated proudly transgressive characters who overcome adversity and refuse to play by society's rules, whether burlesque performers as in *Gypsy* (1959), an eccentric aunt in *Mame* (1966), or the son of God as in *Jesus Christ Superstar* (1971).

Broadway theater stumbled in cultural relevance and power from the 1970s on, especially its comedies, as Stephen Sondheim's new style of musical drama and spectacular megamusicals dominated theaters while ticket sales stalled, cities faced demographic and crime challenges, and television

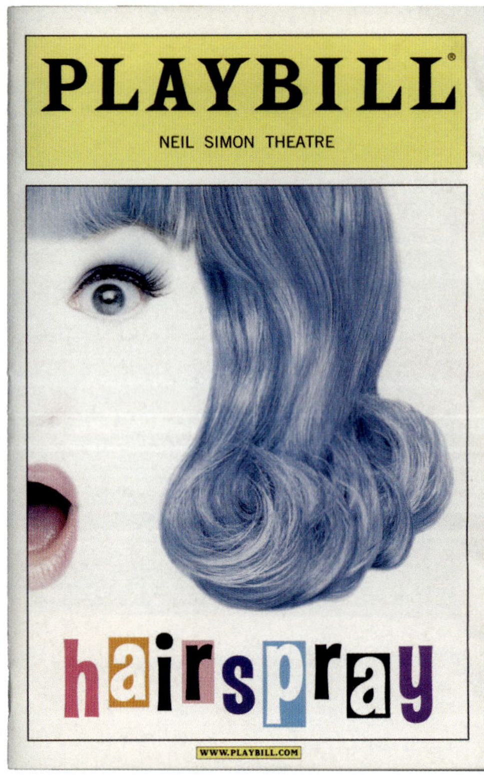

Adapted from the 1988 John Waters film, *Hairspray* opened on Broadway in 2002. The popular musical is representative of two recent Broadway trends, stories about nonconformists who challenge the status quo (in this case, Tracy Turnblad's brave stance against racism and fat shaming) and adaptations of existing entertainment properties.

offered nightly comedy in the comfort of one's living room. Nostalgic shows like the 1950s-set *Grease* (1972) and 1930s-set *Annie* (1977) presaged the jukebox musicals and film adaptations that worked like comfort food to help Broadway survive, while off-Broadway creative talent like Harvey Fierstein brought new perspectives and social relevance in shows like *La Cage Aux Folles* (1983).

All this paved the way for today's Broadway scene, with a combination of comic plays and musical comedies that lean heavily toward existing intellectual property, such as *The Producers* (2001), *Hairspray* (2002), and *Wicked* (2003), but still has room for creative new works that offer satirical commentary on modern society, such as *Urinetown* (2001), *Avenue Q* (2003), and *The Book of Mormon* (2011). With more entertainment options dividing the average American's attention like never before, the twenty-first-century theater retains a prominence and significance earned through its long history and centrality to the nation's cultural life. Its ability to provoke conversations and shape identities stands as a testament to this unique form of comedy performance.

AVENUE Q

Everyone's a little bit racist, sometimes.
Doesn't mean we go around committing hate crimes.
Look around and you will find,
No one's really color-blind.
Maybe it's a fact we all should face.
Everyone makes judgments . . .
Based on race. —"Everyone's a Little Bit Racist"

Avenue Q had one of the most audacious premises for a musical comedy in American history when it opened on Broadway in 2003: What if the puppet monsters, diverse human cast, and celebrity guest stars who taught basic skills on *Sesame Street* could be adapted for adults, to help grown-ups navigate the modern world? What if instead of using songs to teach numbers and reading skills, the puppets sang about racism, homosexuality, pornography, unemployment, and schadenfreude?

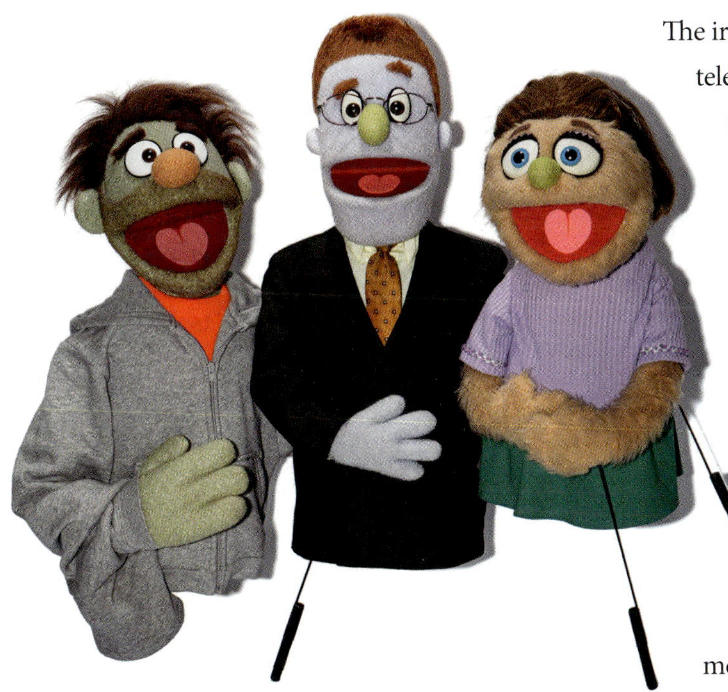

Nicky and Rod are parodies of *Sesame Street*'s Bert and Ernie, mismatched roommates who addressed the latter duo's long-rumored sexuality in a memorable song, "If You Were Gay"—Nicky assures him, "that'd be okay!" Meanwhile, twentysomething Kate Monster, who bears a resemblance to *Sesame Street*'s Prairie Dawn, struggles with her career, dating, and racism.

The irreverent, shocking, yet loving parody of children's television and its sunny, optimistic outlook was a monster hit, earning Tony Awards for Best Musical, Book, and Score, garnering critical acclaim, and running for over fifteen years on and off Broadway as well as in numerous international and even high school productions. Created by composers Robert Lopez and Jeff Marx, who wrote the music and lyrics, along with book writer Jeff Whitty and puppeteer Rick Lyon, *Avenue Q* tells the story of several residents of the eponymous avenue in New York City as they grapple with issues faced by young urban adults, including employment, housing, racial discrimination, sexuality, and identity. Through their interactions with each other, many of the characters learn more about themselves and the world around them, celebrating their revelations in song.

Drawing on the style and characteristics of Jim Henson's Muppets, especially as they are used in *Sesame Street*, *Avenue Q* plays on the audience's expectations and subverts that series' tame tone with adult themes and humor. Indeed, the show's central premise is its contrast with *Sesame Street*, as it humorously explores the gulf between innocent childhood and difficult adult problems. The show is notable for its use of visible puppeteers, requiring suspension of disbelief from the audience, as the puppet characters interact without acknowledging the puppeteers. *Avenue Q* proved that the Broadway musical—especially in its most comedic form—was still a provocative and powerful forum for conversations about contemporary events and debates.

KINKY BOOTS

One of the most popular and acclaimed musicals of the twenty-first century, *Kinky Boots* celebrates diversity and inclusion, self-acceptance, and love in an adaptation of a story drawn from the headlines. In true Broadway style, the show celebrates the story of a marginalized community, speaks to contemporary concerns like gender identity and the decline

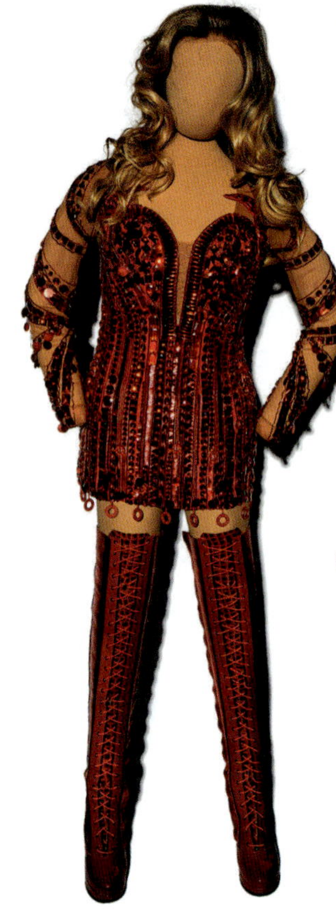

Actors Billy Porter and Eric LaJuan Summers wore parts of this costume in the role of Lola in *Kinky Boots* in its run at the Al Hirschfeld Theatre in 2016–2017. "Look to the heel young man," advised Lola. "The sex is in the heel."

of manufacturing, and combines stirring pop music with a modern comedy of manners.

Based on the 2005 British film of the same name, itself an adaptation of a 1999 episode of the BBC2 documentary series *Trouble at the Top*, *Kinky Boots* tells the story of Charlie Price, an English shoe company executive who faces the prospect of having to close his family's factory due to rising costs and declining profits. When drag queen Lola enters his life, she convinces him to manufacture women's boots made for men, an idea that could save the company. In order to do so, however, Charlie must introduce Lola to his closed-minded employees and defend her against their prejudiced preconceptions. Charlie and Lola both navigate complicated relationships with their fathers and the factory workers come to accept Lola for who she is.

Broadway producer Daryl Roth recruited Harvey Fierstein to write the book and pop musician Cyndi Lauper to write the music for the show, which opened on Broadway on April 4, 2013, and ran for six years and 2,505 performances. The show won a season-high six Tony Awards out of thirteen nominations in 2013, including Best Musical, Best Original Score, and Best Choreography, and has gone on to be a popular choice for touring and international productions. Critics lauded the musical for presenting a positive depiction of a drag performer in a public discourse increasingly marked by reactionary conflict and misunderstanding about gender and performance.

ABIE'S IRISH ROSE: MIXED MARRIAGE MIRTH

Abie's Irish Rose was an enormously popular comic play that spoke to contemporary cultural anxieties about immigration, assimilation, and ethnic identity. Written by Anne Nichols, the farce tells the story of Jewish Abraham Levy and Irish Rosemary Murphy, a couple navigating familial and societal prejudice while marrying and raising a family in contemporary New York City. The lead characters' audacious and escalating lies to hide their relationship from their bigoted fathers culminate in an absurd climax of multiple marriages and religious reconciliation.

Nichols was remarkably successful as a playwright and sole female producer on Broadway; when other producers turned down this seemingly

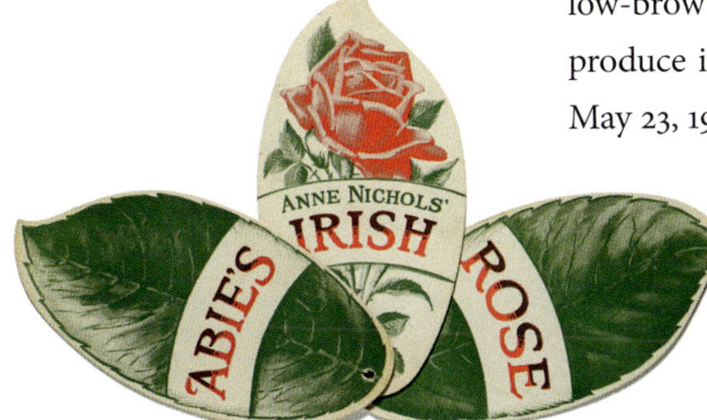

This fan-style trade card advertises the original Broadway run of *Abie's Irish Rose* at the Republic Theatre. Advertising was key to the show's success. In 1924, an enormous life-sized diorama of the play's wedding scene was built within a reproduction of the theater proscenium in a Jewish neighborhood in the Bronx.

low-brow ethnic play, she pawned her jewels and mortgaged her house to produce it herself, in "a historic case of chutzpah." The show premiered May 23, 1922, at the Fulton Theatre and ran for 2,327 performances before closing at the Republic in 1927, making it the longest running comedy in Broadway history. *Abie's Irish Rose* was seen by an estimated eleven million audience members in its Broadway and six national touring productions and was adapted for film in 1928 and again in 1946, adapted as a weekly radio show in the 1940s, and revived on Broadway in 1937 and 1954.[17]

The show's comical plot spoke to the complexities of modern urban life, exploring the freedoms and opportunities of pluralism while also confirming the comforts and benefits of traditional family values. The Jewish and Irish characters were certainly informed by the ethnic caricature long popular on the vaudeville stage, but Nichols softened and modernized the stock characterization, writing a play that made ethnic and religious prejudice seem ridiculous, rather than relying on stereotypes for humor. The show's biggest applause lines were those that celebrated multiethnic harmony, with the families and their rabbis and priests finding common ground and coming to embrace the "melting pot" this blended family represented. Theater scholars have suggested that Jewish Americans made *Abie* a success because its plot reflected the community's experience as families increasingly left urban ghettoes for the middle class and forged new identities as "mainstream" Americans. In a blow to the era's hegemonic ideology of racial hierarchy, Nichols suggested through this comic comedy of errors that race and ethnicity were mutable, social constructions that could change over time, combine, or perhaps not really exist at all.[18]

Despite its popular success, critics savaged the play for its hackneyed formula and sentimental plot. In the pages of *Life* magazine, critic Robert Benchley made his distaste for the production abundantly clear, writing, "People laugh at this every night, which explains why a democracy can never be a success," and "America's favorite comedy. God forbid."[19] Others, however, credited the play with democratizing American theater. Alexander Wolcott, long a critic of the show by reputation, finally saw it himself in 1924 to satisfy his curiosity and found that he understood its appeal: it spoke to people who were not traditionally theatergoers. "In short," he wrote, "Abie's Irish Rose has not only pleased its public. It has created its public."[20]

Ryan Lintelman

NEIL SIMON CAPTURES MIDDLE-CLASS MALAISE

Neil Simon was one of the most influential and prolific playwrights of the twentieth century, celebrated for bringing a new comic sensibility to the postwar stage. During his five-decade career, Simon wrote or cowrote forty-nine Broadway plays, earning four Tony Awards, the Pulitzer Prize for Drama, and popular acclaim for his perceptive explorations of modern, middle-class American life. His most successful plays, including *Barefoot in the Park* (1963), *The Odd Couple* (1965), and *Lost in Yonkers* (1991), focused on the mundane: young adulthood, marital problems and divorce, and family dysfunction. He made his specific milieu—well-educated, New York Jewish men in crisis, or as critic John Lahr called them, "stranded bourgeois souls"—seem universal.[21] Simon crafted comedies that were really dramas with comic moments, filled with complex, fully realized characters, realistic relationships, and memorable dialogue that resonated with theatergoers like nothing before.

Simon began his career in the 1950s alongside Carl Reiner, Mel Brooks, Woody Allen, and Larry Gelbart in the television writers' rooms for Sid Caesar and Phil Silvers. He and his peers were at the vanguard of a new American style of comedy. Like the most innovative stand-up and broadcast comedians of the era, Simon's comedy relied less on jokes and punch lines than on comical observations and revelations about the absurdities and frustrations of daily life. Frequent collaborator Mike Nichols said that the key to Simon's humor was "recognizability": hilarity teased out of the ordinary and universal.[22]

Simon wore these iconic horn-rimmed glasses and used this electronic typewriter in his New York City apartment in his final few decades, writing plays, scripts, and books including *Brighton Beach Memoirs*, *Biloxi Blues*, and *Lost in Yonkers*.

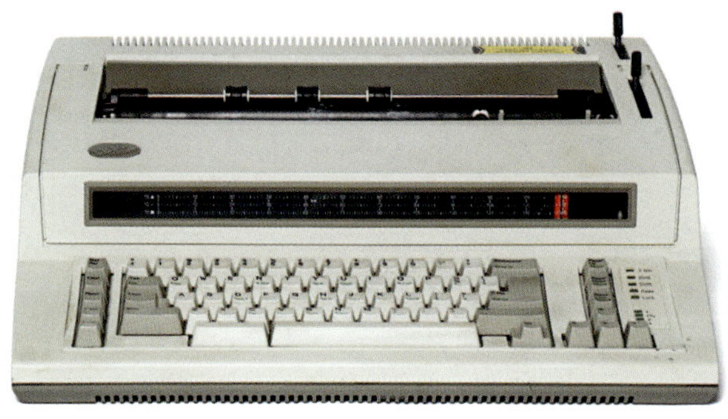

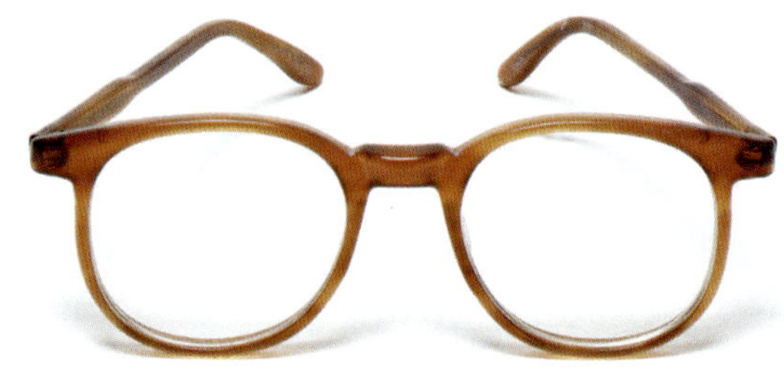

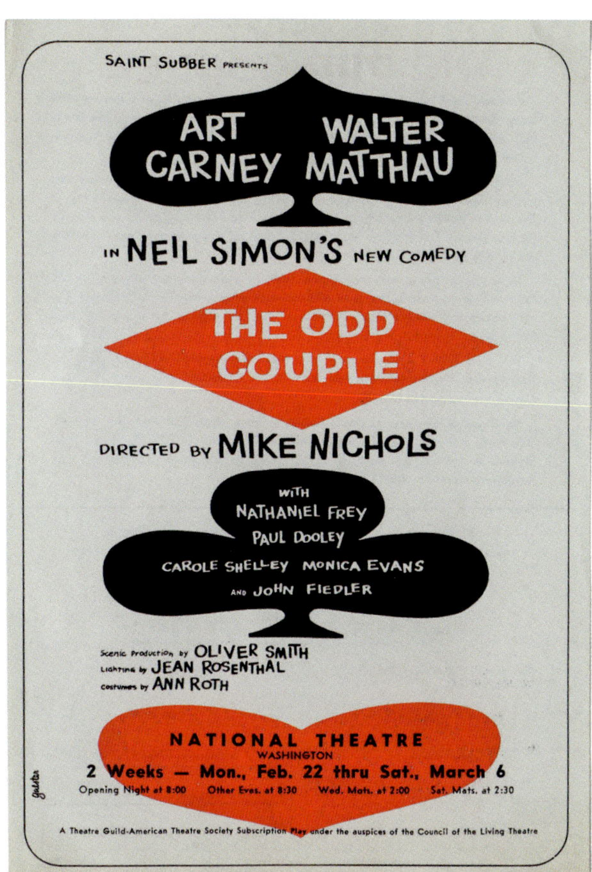

This flyer advertised the 1965 pre-Broadway engagement of Neil Simon's play *The Odd Couple* at the National Theatre in Washington, D.C. The production was the second of four Simon plays directed by Mike Nichols, ran for 964 performances on Broadway, and was adapted as a 1967 film and television series that aired from 1970 to 1975.

Simon's writing drew heavily on his life and experiences, referenced psychology and analysis, and dealt frankly with contemporary social mores and issues, though he claimed that his work was not political. "I don't write social and political plays, because I've always thought the family was the microcosm of what goes on in the world," he said in a 1992 interview.[23] But through his characters' dilemmas—the word he defined as his chief comic weapon—Simon engaged his audiences in conversations about weighty issues, for instance, the sexual revolution (*Last of the Red Hot Lovers*), alcoholism (*The Gingerbread Lady*), divorce and suicide (*The Odd Couple*), and masculinity in crisis (*The Prisoner of Second Avenue*).

Simon earned his greatest critical acclaim for the late-career semiautobiographical works that perhaps best represented the mixture of humor and pathos that was his signature: *Brighton Beach Memoirs* (1983), *Biloxi Blues* (1985), *Broadway Bound* (1986), and *Lost in Yonkers* (1991). In these and other works of "nostalgic ethnicity," Simon chronicled not only his American life, but also a sort of archetypal male Jewish American life journey, from "intellectually overdeveloped, sexually underdeveloped adolescent (1983's *Brighton Beach Memoirs* and its successors; [to] idiosyncratic, self-pitying, self-martyring, neurotic adult (Felix Unger in 1968's *The Odd Couple*; the description is Simon's, of how he wrote the character Jewish); [to] wise-cracking, crotchety senior citizen (1975's *The Sunshine Boys*)."[24] Along with *Laughter on the 23rd Floor* (1993), his theatrical memoir of his time writing for Sid Caesar, Simon staked a claim for Jewish Americans in a popular culture that was increasingly obsessed with canonizing and mythologizing twentieth-century lives and stories of ethnic acculturation.

So successful that he set records for the most combined Tony (seventeen) and Oscar (four) Award nominations as well as for the most plays running simultaneously on Broadway (four, in the late 1960s), Neil Simon had unrivaled power to shape the zeitgeist at the zenith of the theater's cultural power.

Ryan Lintelman

LYRICAL LAUGHTER

From vaudeville stages to viral videos, the fusion of music and comedy has engaged audiences throughout the history of American entertainment. Musical comedians—or comedic musicians?—have long harnessed the interplay between melody, rhythm, and carefully timed punchlines not only to amuse, but also to critique and comment. Across decades and mediums, the form has been endlessly adaptable and always popular.

ALLAN SHERMAN

Allan Sherman's landmark novelty song, "Hello Muddah, Hello Faddah (A Letter from Camp)," set to the tune of Ponchielli's *Dance of the Hours*, debuted in 1963 as a track on the third of his wildly popular musical parody LPs. The album, *My Son, the Nut*, smashed sales records, selling half a million copies in its debut month and becoming an unlikely sensation at a moment when the *Billboard* charts were dominated by artists like Ray Charles, Johnny Cash, and Elvis Presley. Based on actual letters sent by Sherman's son, the song chronicles a miserable day at sleepaway camp filled with ever-escalating dangers—like alligators, malaria, and being marooned in the woods. The song enjoyed constant radio airplay, and sustained its popularity as Sherman made frequent appearances on late-night and variety television, ultimately performing the tune as a headliner at Carnegie Hall. "Hello Muddah, Hello Faddah" was awarded the Grammy for Best Comedy Performance in 1964.

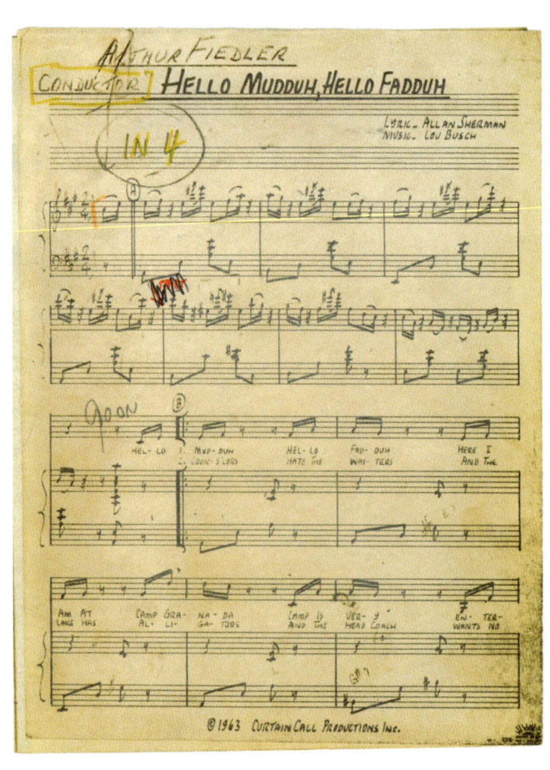

Far more than merely a novelty artist, Sherman was a seasoned comedy writer and a key player in the mainstreaming of humor based on the Jewish experience in the post–World War II era. Though he didn't typically employ overt Yiddishisms (like peers in parody music such as Mickey Katz), Sherman conceptualized his body of work as an answer to the rhetorical question, "What would happen if Jewish people wrote all the songs? (Which, in fact, they do.)"[25] Songs like "Harvey and Sheila" (to the tune of "Havah Nagila"), "Al 'N Yetta" ("Alouette"), and "Seventy-Six Sol Cohens" ("Seventy-Six Trombones") were about the Jewish American experience, but transcended cultural barriers with their mix of contemporary pop-cultural references, folk music, and everyday foibles that were relatable to a growing class of middle-class suburbanites of all backgrounds. The eight albums that he released between 1962 and 1967 demonstrated the popularity—and marketability—of cross-cultural humor in an era when American "melting pot" ideals were giving way to "hyphenated" identities that allowed for, and celebrated, difference.[26]

STAN FREBERG

Stan Freberg grew up fascinated with short-form cartoons and the radio comedy of childhood heroes Henry Morgan and Fred Allen—formats already fading with the rise of television in the 1950s. He managed to nose his way into Warner Brothers' animation studio and find voiceover work alongside the legendary Mel Blanc, and in 1957 landed radio placement with *The Stan Freberg Show*—a valiant but late entry into a medium whose audience had all but defected to TV. Undeterred, Freberg parlayed his love for sound comedy into a new career as a parody musician, poking fun at the machinery of American entertainment media and the audiences who devoured it.

Freberg quickly made a name for himself and built a cult following of disciples who called themselves "Frebies"; they made him one of the most successful artists on the Capitol Records label. His work was at once playful and biting, meticulously produced and wildly inventive—often with Freberg himself juggling performance, musical direction, and orchestration of voice actors, musicians, and sound effect artists. The variety of his approach was seemingly inexhaustible, from slapstick pop send-ups (like a rendition of "Heartbreak Hotel" in which Elvis rips his pants) to hard-hitting comedic takes on Cold War paranoia and McCarthyism. Dr. Demento—the great promoter of parody music—would go

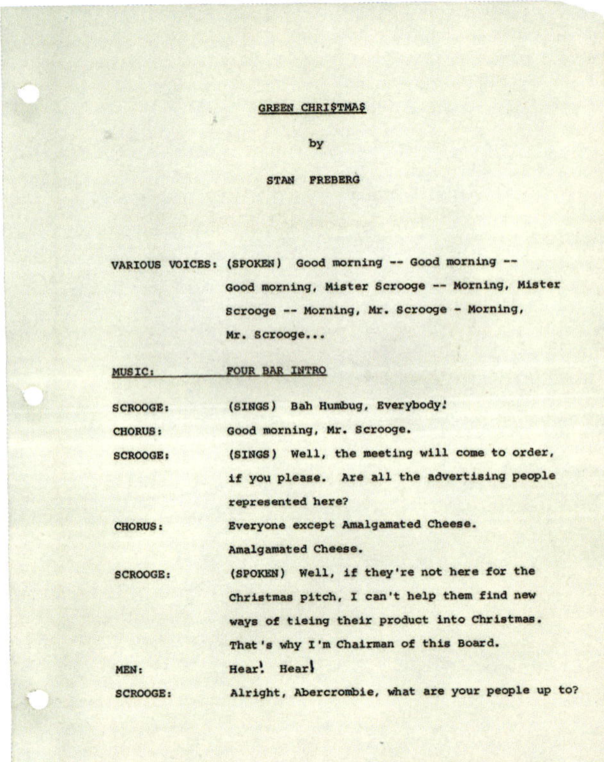

GREEN CHRITMA

by

STAN FREBERG

VARIOUS VOICES: (SPOKEN) Good morning -- Good morning -- Good morning, Mister Scrooge -- Morning, Mister Scrooge -- Morning, Mr. Scrooge - Morning, Mr. Scrooge...

MUSIC: FOUR BAR INTRO

SCROOGE: (SINGS) Bah Humbug, Everybody!

CHORUS: Good morning, Mr. Scrooge.

SCROOGE: (SINGS) Well, the meeting will come to order, if you please. Are all the advertising people represented here?

CHORUS: Everyone except Amalgamated Cheese. Amalgamated Cheese.

SCROOGE: (SPOKEN) Well, if they're not here for the Christmas pitch, I can't help them find new ways of tieing their product into Christmas. That's why I'm Chairman of this Board.

MEN: Hear! Hear!

SCROOGE: Alright, Abercrombie, what are your people up to?

GREEN CHRITMA 2

ABERCROMBIE: Ah, same thing as every year. Fifty thousand billboards showing Santa Claus pausing to refresh himself with our product.

SCROOGE: Hm, hm -- well -- I think the public has come to expect that and, er --

ABERCROMBIE: That's right - it's become tradition.

SCROOGE: Fine. Fine. You there, Crass. I suppose your company is running the usual magazine ads showing cartons of your cigarettes peeking out of the top of Santa's sack?

CRASS: Better than that! This year we have him smoking one!

SCROOGE: Uh-hum...

CRASS: Yes, we got Santa a little more rugged, too... Both sleeves rolled up and a tattoo on each arm. One of them says, "Merry Christmas".

SCROOGE: Er...What does the other one say?

CRASS: "Less Tars".

SCROOGE: Great stuff!

CRATCHETT: Er...but, Mr. Scrooge! --

SCROOGE: Who are you?

CRATCHETT: Er...Bob Cratchett, sir. I've got a little spice company over in East Orange, New Jersey. Do I have to tie my product into Christmas?

SCROOGE: What do you mean?

CRATCHETT: Well, I was just going to send cards out showing the Three Wise Men following the Star of Bethlehem.

on to call Freberg the most direct spiritual ancestor of satirical juggernauts like *National Lampoon* and *Saturday Night Live.*[27]

Although it may seem a light touch by contemporary standards, Freberg's most controversial work was "Green Chritma," a seven-minute track that took aim at the commercialization of the religious holiday. The piece recasts Ebenezer Scrooge as an ad-man and ends with a rendition of "Jingle Bells" in duet with a chorus of cash registers. Despite hesitation from Capitol Records, which rang its hands over attacking *both* corporate power players and religious institutions at the height of the conservative 1950s, "Green Chritma" was released in 1958 and became a surprise bestseller. The piece was nominated for two awards at the first-ever Grammy ceremony and, ironically, prompted Freberg's second, equally influential, career in advertising. The same corporations he had relentlessly mocked in the song flocked to hire him to create humorous campaigns for their products, leading to the formation of the ad corporation Freberg, Ltd. (But Not Very), whose motto was *Ars Gratia Pecuniae*—art for money's sake.

MARK RUSSELL

Political satirist Mark Russell skewered Washington's power brokers for six decades from behind his star-spangled piano. He kickstarted his career in the lounge of DC's famed Shoreham Hotel, where he honed his craft before the toughest possible audience—government insiders, including the likes of the notoriously humorless Senator Joseph R. McCarthy and then–Vice President Richard M. Nixon. Later, Russell reached national audiences with a string of beloved PBS comedy specials that captivated a devout following—even, and perhaps especially, among the political cognoscenti. Always snappily attired in a patriotic bow tie and suit, Russell cut a charismatic and imminently loveable figure as he launched fearlessly funny bombs across both sides of the political aisle. Crooning bespoke parody tunes for ten presidents—from Eisenhower to Trump—and catching a fair share of senators, congresspeople, and cabinet members in the crossfire, Russell was an institution in Washington and in comedy well before the likes of the *Daily Show* or *The Onion* mainstreamed political satire and humor ripped from the headlines.

Russell was a prolific lyrical mind, authoring thousands of songs in a series of meticulous lined notebooks, logging at least one completed lyric per day for most of his working life. Collectively, the notebooks are an up-to-the-minute tome chronicling American history. Whenever he was asked if he had any writers, Russell always playfully quipped "Oh, yes—100 in the Senate and 435 in the House of Representatives." Most of his songs borrowed familiar tunes, like "Bail to the Chief" (written for Richard M. Nixon), "Everything's Coming Up Rodham" (for Hillary Clinton), or "Rock Around Iraq Tonight" (for George W. Bush). "A Candidate Political," to the tune of Gilbert and Sullivan's "Modern Major General," encapsulates his equal-opportunity critiques of political jockeying and hypocrisy of all stripes with its jab at double-talking politicians who aim to please without any real convictions: "On both sides of a question I can speak with brash impunity / And I can sing a different song and please each damn community. / I plan to sing what pleases every different kind of resident / Until I count enough of them to vote for me as President. / In short because I bear in mind that winning's very critical / I am the very model of a candidate political."

Mark Russell was a Washington D.C. institution and a perennial presence on public television as he volleyed with politicians on both sides of the aisle from his star-spangled piano, always wearing a signature bow tie.

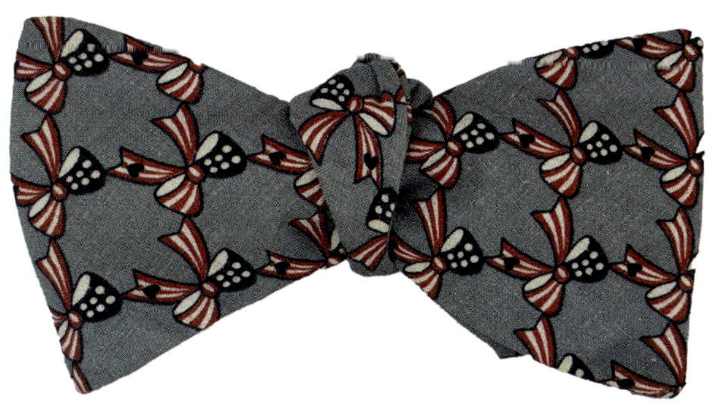

WEIRD AL YANKOVIC

The door-to-door salesman who furnished six-year-old Alfred Yankovic with accordion lessons was surely unaware that he'd inspire one of the most prolific, beloved, and original voices in comedy. From his bedroom in suburban LA, Yankovic devoured the humor of Spike Jones, Allan Sherman, and *MAD* magazine and surreptitiously tuned in to Southern California's quirky cult-favorite parody music program, *The Dr. Demento Show.* By the age of sixteen, his own homemade cassette recording of "Belvedere Cruisin'"—a tune about his family car—landed time on Demento's airwaves and marked the first entry in a repertoire of parody songs that would ultimately number well over 150. Weird Al Yankovic (the "Weird" was the redemption of a mean-spirited college nickname) went on to become the rare parody artist who broke the mold of the one-hit wonder, landing a Top 40 hit in every decade since he burst on the scene in the 1980s.

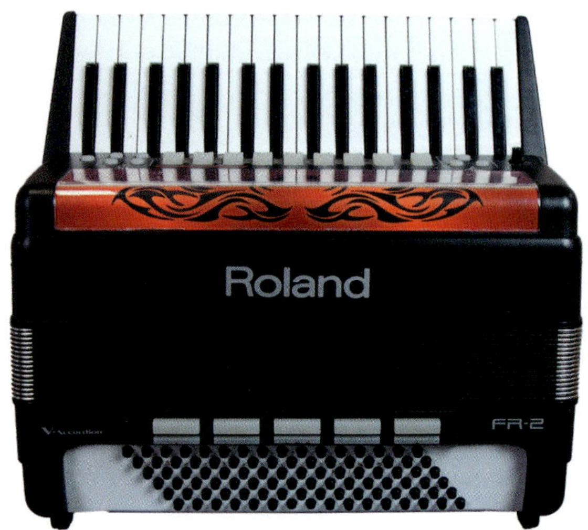

Weird Al Yankovic evolved the art of comedy music for the MTV era as both the writer and performer of generation-defining parody songs played on his iconic accordion.

Weird Al's ascendence was matched to its moment, as the music industry shifted its focus from radio play and album sales to the visual medium of television. "My Bologna," a spoof of the Knack's hugely popular "My Sharona," landed him his first recording contract, but it was music videos airing on the nascent MTV network—especially "Ricky" (a parody of Toni Basil's "Mickey") and "Eat It" (a shot-for-shot reinterpretation of Michael Jackson's "Beat It")—that made him a common cultural touchstone for a generation. When "Eat It" won the Grammy for Best Comedy Song of 1984, the Hawaiian-shirt-wearing accordion player came to the attention of mainstream consumers and significantly broadened the audience base for parody music. Thirty years after breaking through, Weird Al has more recently innovated in the arena of web comedy: his fourteenth album, *Mandatory Fun*, was his first to claim the top position on the *Billboard* charts, largely due to an incredibly savvy viral music video campaign orchestrated online in advance of the album debut.

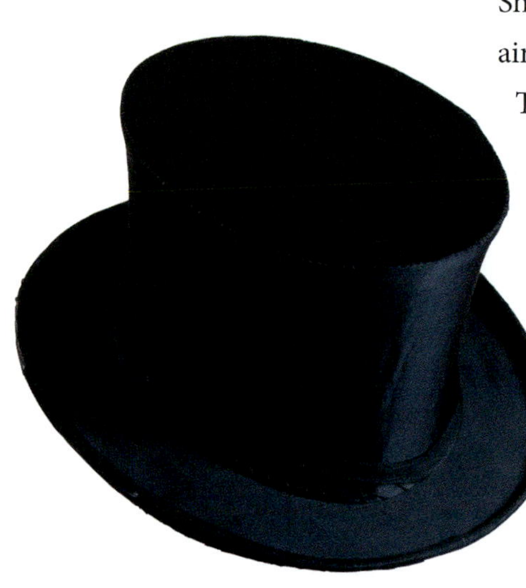
Top hat-wearing Dr. Demento, a figure on LA's radio waves, is known as parody music's biggest champion and promoter, and was a key figure in Weird Al Yankovic's rise to prominence.

Yankovic's wildly original work is steeped in a postmodern, endlessly referential sensibility that lands with listeners—and then holds up—because it is as well crafted as it is enjoyable. "Like a Surgeon," "Amish

Paradise," and "Tacky" are delightfully silly novelties that are simply fun to hear, but they are also intricate musical constructions with smart, surprising lyrics, of which Yankovic is the sole author. Most of the songs locate their humor in juxtaposition between the tone, content, and style of the original track and the parody track, as far from source texts like Madonna's "Like a Virgin," Coolio's "Gangsta's Paradise," and Pharrell Williams's "Happy," respectively, as they could possibly be. While works of parody can often cause offense (or spur litigation), being parodied by Weird Al has become a coveted badge of honor.

RUTH WALLIS

Ruth Wallis, aka "The Queen of the Party Song," earned her fame in the 1940s and 1950s as the writer, producer, and performer of innuendo-laced novelty songs that appealed to audiences seeking alternatives to the otherwise straitlaced sounds of the era. After forging a career in lounges and cocktail bars, Wallis became a fixture in Las Vegas and the founder of her own label, Wallis Original Recordings. Like many "blue" artists of the era, and women in particular, Wallis's work was heavily policed: banned from the airwaves, physically seized in censorship raids, and barred from mainstream circulation. The risqué, satirical songs, rife with double entendres, were a threat to conservative sensibilities, and though consumers found their way around restrictions (to the tune of more than a quarter million albums sold in the case of her most successful releases), the stifling effect of media censorship certainly limited the reach of Wallis's work.

Though her songs were far from X-rated by contemporary standards, they did tackle verboten subject matter, like cross-dressing ("He'd Rather Be a Girl"), infidelity ("The Pistol Song, Drill 'em All"), and homosexuality. A 1956 tune, for example, tells the story of a married couple who end their relationship when she learns that he is gay: "We have decided it cannot be / I'm not for him and he's not for me / He can do what he wants and I'll do what I can / But the both of us / Have gotta get a man." Lyrics like these were daring, but coyer than they were truly incendiary. Wallis's trademark was "The Dinghy Song," which playfully recapitulated the story of Davey, a sailor with "the cutest little dinghy in the Navy."

Wallis's work was "rediscovered" in the early 2000s and compiled as the off-Broadway cult hit "Boobs! The Musical: The World According to Ruth Wallis," which ran for nearly three hundred performances.

VICTOR BORGE

Victor Borge, "The Clown Prince of Denmark," was raised in an Ashkenazi Jewish family of musicians in Copenhagen and revealed his own prodigious talent for piano at an early age. He built a reputation as a classical concert pianist, increasingly incorporating an authentic, and endearing, sense of humor into a wildly successful touring act. As the Germans advanced through Europe at the outbreak of World War II, Borge boldly laced his performances with anti-Nazi jokes until the occupation of his native Denmark in 1940 necessitated evacuation aboard an American army transport ship.

Though he spoke no English, Borge quickly established himself as a fixture on top radio comedies and landed his own *Victor Borge Show* by 1945. The program deflated the "stuffiness" of the Western classical oeuvre with a quirky combination of the cultivated, the quotidian, and the avant-garde: Borge used the "Minute Waltz" as an ersatz egg timer, performed his "Unstarted Symphony" (dead air), and recited "Phonetic Punctuation"—in which he read aloud while assigning histrionic sound effects to each punctuation mark. The core of the show involved the performance of medleys that were humorous for being harmonically compatible but contextually assonant—like a robust rendition of "Moonlight Sonata" that devolved into a plunking out of "Happy Birthday to You."

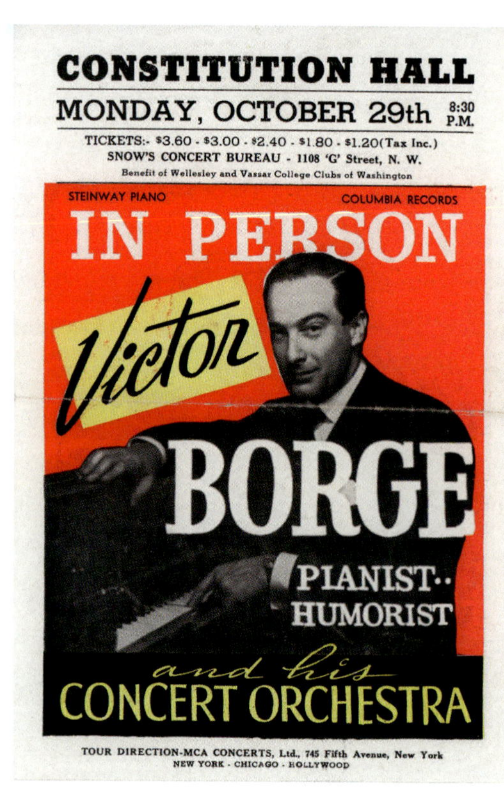

It was Borge's 1953 one-man show, *Comedy in Music*, that marked his arrival as one of the leading comic voices of the mid-twentieth century. Slated for a two-week Broadway run, *Comedy in Music* was extended for nearly nine hundred performances. The show incorporated physical comedy bits that would become staples of Borge's touring performances for decades, like playing upside-down sheet music, slamming his hands in the piano lid, and sliding off the bench when his performances became too impassioned—a hazard that was addressed by putting on a seat belt. Some of Borge's performances were so packed with sight gags and pratfalls that they hardly included piano playing at all.

Comedy in Music required an extraordinarily economical performance style that consisted of nothing but the artist alone onstage with his piano, often improvising (verbally and musically) at a formidable pace. The theatrical program for the evening listed nineteen musical numbers: "1. Frankly 2. We 3. Don't 4. Know 5. What 6. Mr. Borge 7. Will 8. Do 9. But 10. We're 11. Sure 12. He'll 13. Keep 14. Us 15. Posted 16. From 17. Time 18. To 19. Time." As the liner notes for the live recording of the show explained, "As a musician, he can, if he will, supply the audience with a beautifully articulated *Clair de Lune* or Chopin polanaise. The chances are that he will prefer not to, however."

Borge's popularity was relentless, and he maintained a decades-long career as an internationally touring concert pianist and comedian. He died at the age of ninety-one the day after a performance in his native Denmark—with a roster of show dates scheduled two years out.

Laura LaPlaca

COMEDY CLUBS

Early stand-up comedians honed their craft on the nightclub circuit at spots like the Blue Angel and the Bon Soir, or in Catskills resorts like the Concord and Grossinger's, but by the 1960s comedy clubs were a common sight in cities across America. The rise of the clubs was a prerequisite to the mainstreaming of stand-up as an art form. The creative alchemy of honing a joke requires a stage and an audience, of course, but also the freedom to fail—repeatedly. Clubs are gyms for comedians: rooms where stand-ups "work out" material, log hours on their feet, and stumble en route to perfecting a set. "You can't practice on the *Tonight Show*," comic David Brenner once said. Clubs are the "place where you can be bad, and that's how you get to be good."[28]

Overnight success as a stand-up is elusive, if not impossible. Anyone dedicating themselves to the craft faces down a probable decade of hardscrabble existence, bouncing from one club gig to the next as they "pay their dues." Every successful stand-up has a ferocious work ethic and a wealth of road tales; and with no guarantee of success, the long grind is not for the faint of heart. In this type of environment, clubs are gathering places and sacred spaces for the comedy community, which—though dispersed, itinerant, and sometimes cutthroat—is a network built on a unique shared experience.

Every club has its own history, vibe, and reputation, and the club scene itself has tracked a dramatic boom-and-bust evolution across the second half of the twentieth century. In the early 1950s, stand-up comedy inserted itself into nightclubs and bars that were already host to musical acts and cabaret performances. In San Francisco, Mort Sahl made the hungry i his homeroom, and Jorie Remus and Phyllis Diller were among the comics to launch careers at the Purple Onion. Nipsey Russell MCed at Harlem's Baby Grand, Bob Newhart broke through at Chicago's Mister Kelly's, and LA's Slate Brothers club launched an unknown Don Rickles. These venues demonstrated the viability of selling live comedy as a main attraction, with comedians increasingly appearing as headlining acts on mixed bills that included musicians, singers, and dancers.

The early 1960s saw the opening of Pips and the Improv in New York, two foundational clubs that, in many ways, heralded the arrival of the comedy club as a singular category of entertainment venue. The Improv, with its now-iconic interior brick wall, originated as an intimate fifty-seat room for the Broadway set that became favored by comedic innovators like Richard Pryor, Robert Klein, and Lily Tomlin before it evolved into a formidable chain of clubs across America. San Francisco remained a center for stand-up with breakout talents like Robin Williams and Steve Martin finding their footing at the Holy City Zoo and the Boarding House, and the array of clubs in Los Angeles sprawled to include venues like Redd Foxx's club in Beverly Hills and Pasadena's Ice House.

LA's Comedy Store opened its doors in 1972, only months before the relocation of Johnny Carson's *Tonight Show* from New York to Burbank—shifting the center of gravity for comedians eager to break through on television. Head spinning-moments like Freddie Prinze's meteoric rise from the Store to *The Tonight Show* to sitcom stardom in a matter of weeks in 1973 were clarion calls to comics seeking a fast track to national airtime. Across the country, New York's Catch a Rising Star launched a generation of talents that included Jerry Seinfeld, Andy Kaufman, and Richard Belzer—the club's emcee.

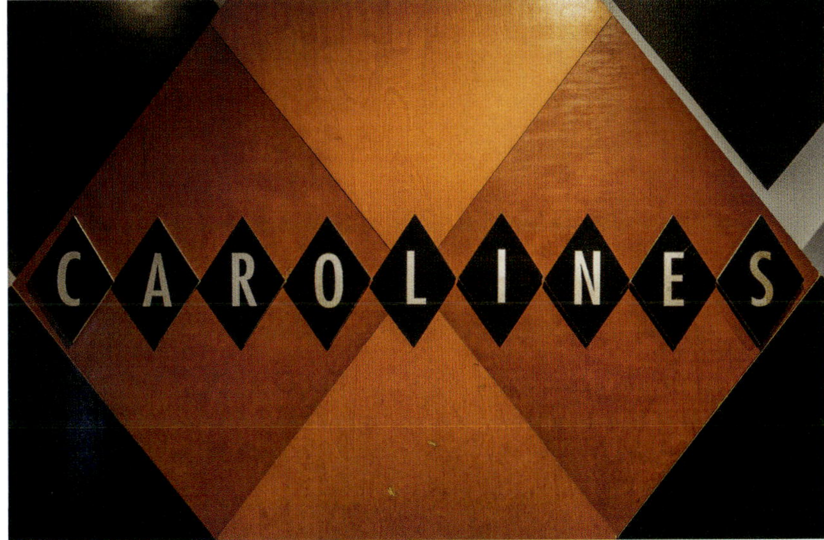

Carolines on Broadway opened its iconic harlequined doors in 1992, after a decade of operations in New York's Chelsea and South Street Seaport neighborhoods. The presence of the respected club contributed to the resurgence of the once-derelict Times Square and planted stand-up comedy right at the heart of Manhattan. Made a household name by way of *Caroline's Comedy Hour*—a six-season televised stand-up showcase—the club was a haunt for an array of comics from Robin Williams, Jerry Seinfeld, and Dick Gregory to Bo Burnham, Tracy Morgan, and Jeff Ross. The club's final show was performed on December 31, 2022 and headlined by Dave Attell, who closed his set by acknowledging founder Caroline Hirsch as a "force."

The cable era of the 1980s and 1990s saw the repackaging of the club experience for television, with shows like *An Evening at the Improv*, *Caroline's Comedy Hour*, and *Def Comedy Jam* bringing stand-up into American homes. Though widened exposure allowed a bigger tent for comedic styles and voices, it also meant an accelerated commercialization of the art form and, ultimately, an end to the rapid proliferation of physical clubs across the country. Like all live entertainment venues, comedy clubs struggled through the COVID-19 pandemic (and some were shuttered for good), but stand-up found a way, popping up in parking lots, in public parks, and, increasingly, via livestreaming. Though these approaches filled a gap temporarily, their limitations reminded comics and audiences alike that there really is no venue for comedy that is more intimate, immediate, or pure than a club.

Laura LaPlaca

THE DICK VAN DYKE SHOW: SITCOMS STEP FORWARD

The Dick Van Dyke Show is a cherished object of nostalgia, a love song to the craft of comedy, and one of the most important artistic expressions to emerge on the cusp of Kennedy's New Frontier. The show debuted in the fall of 1961, in the immediate wake of FCC Chairman Newton Minow's now-infamous "Vast Wasteland" speech, which announced the debasement of American television. As if in direct rebuttal to Mr. Minow's pronouncements about the state of the art, the show promptly transcended every perceived limit of the sitcom form to prove the mettle of mainstream TV comedy as a cultural force. *The Dick Van Dyke Show* would go on to hold a pivotal and prized place in the broad arc of comedy history, significant both for the ways that it built upon earlier comedic traditions honed in vaudeville, radio, and variety television, and for the ways in which it presaged the politically and civically engaged comedy of the 1970s "era of relevance."

After a lauded tenure as Sid Caesar's second banana and a fixture in the legendary *Your Show of Shows* writers' room, Carl Reiner was an in-demand Hollywood multihyphenate by the close of television's first decade. A litany of emotionally and psychologically vacant sitcom pitches left Reiner craving a creative outlet with more heart. Reiner's wife and muse, Estelle, urged him to write the show he was looking for: "I don't have the right words," he demurred. "But you have the right *feelings*," she countered. One evening, while commuting from Caesar's Manhattan

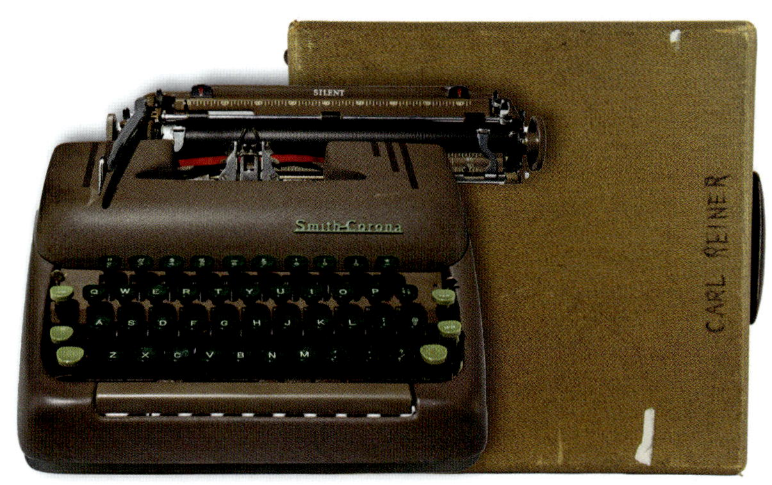

Using this typewriter, Reiner wrote the first thirteen episodes of *Head of the Family*, which later became *The Dick Van Dyke Show*, while vacationing on Fire Island with his family. This typewriter case, which bears Reiner's inscribed name, contained a sealed manila envelope of the original thirteen drafts that are now preserved in the National Comedy Center's archive.

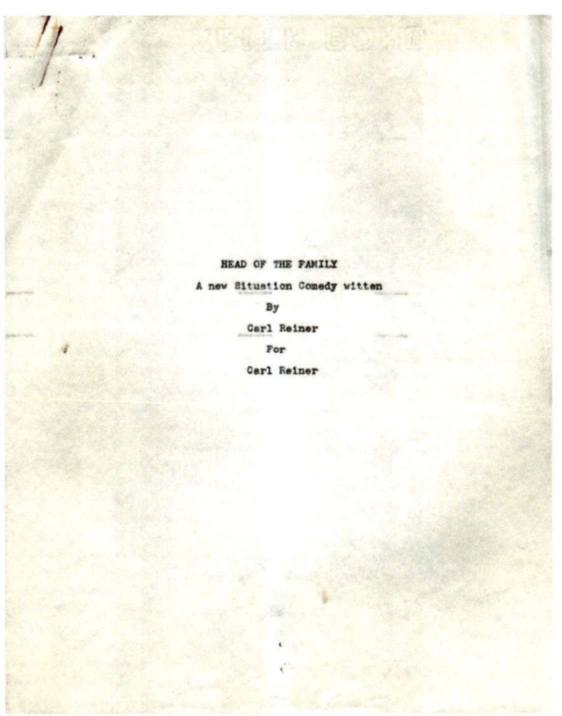
HEAD OF THE FAMILY
A new Situation Comedy witten
By
Carl Reiner
For
Carl Reiner

The original script for *Head of the Family*, "written by Carl Reiner for Carl Reiner," evolved into the sitcom classic *The Dick Van Dyke Show*.

offices to his family's home in suburban New Rochelle, Reiner resolved to authentically "examine the piece of ground that I stand on and nobody else stands on." His show would be about a comedy writer commuting from Manhattan to New Rochelle, discovering how to balance fulfilling creative work and an enriching family life while navigating the changing social climate of the 1960s. He would play himself and title the project *Head of the Family.* Sequestered with his typewriter on Fire Island, Reiner forged his first thirteen scripts in an uninterrupted burst of inspiration, applying a litmus test to every scene: "Take away the jokes and the story still works." His work would be truthful first, and funny second.

The 1960 *Head of the Family* pilot starring Carl Reiner in an exploration of life as a first-generation Jewish family man assimilating to the professional middle class was not picked up by a sponsor. The thirteen finished scripts stayed sealed in an envelope on a closet shelf for over a year as Reiner's disappointment mounted, until producer Sheldon Leonard approached him with an idea, famously quipping, "We'll get another actor to play you!" Reiner, with characteristic humility, later admitted that *Head of the Family*'s failure was ultimately the gateway to a different triumph: shepherding one of the greatest creative teams in comedy history through the 158-episode run of a TV classic. Though he forfeited the leading role, Reiner would remain the show's beating heart and pen an extraordinary fifty-four of the first sixty episodes on his own, leaving a deep narrative and stylistic imprint on every aspect of the series. Ahead of his time, he emerged as a foundational figure in the tradition of the TV comedy auteur—Larry David, Issa Rae, Tina Fey, and Donald Glover now among them—who have crafted comedy based on their authentic and singular points of view.

The rechristened *Dick Van Dyke Show* tracked the everyday life of Rob Petrie, an ex-GI making his way as a family man in the suburbs while pursuing a career as head writer for the fictional comedy-variety program *The Alan Brady Show.* While earlier sitcoms like *The Jack Benny Show*, *I Love Lucy*, and *Make Room for Daddy* were also structured around self-referential show-within-a-show premises, Reiner's format lent far more substance to Rob Petrie's professional life. The workplace scenes were showpieces: high-energy, fast-paced, and simply fun to watch, they were celebrations of the joy of creative production and of the art form of comedy writing. In this sense, *The Dick Van Dyke Show* not only laid a foundation for plenty of workplace sitcoms that would follow in its wake but worked as a testament and tribute to the great minds behind great TV humor. At a moment when television was still considered the depleted cultural stepchild of film, this was a rarity—and a revelation for a generation of future writers whose experience watching the show would spark their own careers in comedy.

The writers' room, where Rob spent about half of every episode, was populated by rounded characters—fellow writers Buddy Sorrell and Sally Rogers (Morey Amsterdam and Rose Marie), huffish producer Mel Cooley (Richard Deacon), and the egomaniacal Alan Brady (Carl Reiner himself in cameo). Morey Amsterdam and Rose Marie boasted some of the most robust credentials in show business and were, in many ways, the source energizing *The Dick Van Dyke Show* as a comedy powerhouse. Buddy and Sally were quippers, zingers, and—frequently—showstoppers. But they were also complex characters embodied with pathos that deepened the show's treatment of human themes: Buddy was an urban Jewish man in an unsatisfying marriage without children, who often sought refuge at work; Sally was a single career woman of unrelenting talents, who nevertheless struggled with her self-worth as she navigated a keenly felt pressure to land a husband. These characters introduced a stark contrast to Rob Petrie's more traditional version of nuclear family life and reflected Reiner's goal to infuse his work with realism and empathy as his characters disrupted the ideological strictures of the sitcom formula.

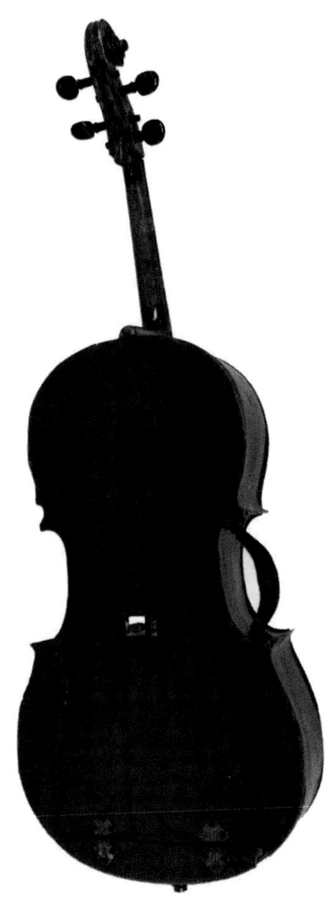

This trick cello, with a secret interior compartment for stowing comedy props, belonged to Morey Amsterdam, the quick-witted mind behind Buddy Sorrell on *The Dick Van Dyke Show*. Known as a 'human joke machine,' Amsterdam's rapid-fire humor, mastery of timing, and improvisational skill made him a standout performer during television's first decades, with his considerable musical talent enriching his performances.

While Dick Van Dyke's Rob Petrie won audiences over with his innate charisma and easy manner on screen, newcomer Mary Tyler Moore was a breakout star—and a lightning rod—in her role as his wife, Laura. A novice with a preternatural talent waiting to be molded, she found herself in league with some of the most brilliant minds in comedy—and rising to their level. Moore's growing confidence as a comedian emboldened Reiner, who layered her character with complexities unimaginable in the hands of a less adept actress. Moore's version of a sitcom housewife was intelligent, ambitious, stylish, and savvy, and she captivated audiences who were craving an update to the variously scatterbrained, demure, or deferential representations that had dominated 1950s TV offerings. Before long, the press had fashioned her as an icon of modern American womanhood; TV land's Jackie Kennedy.

This hair bow was worn by pioneering performer Rose Marie throughout her life and in her role as Sally Rogers on *The Dick Van Dyke Show*. Her confident, intelligent, and very funny interpretation of the role energized a generation of women, inspiring some of them to pursue careers in comedy.

Reiner was intent that his version of sitcom marriage would be a picture of mutual respect, and of mutual attraction. Rob and Laura Petrie would make household decisions together, raise their child together, share mutual interests, and find one another attractive. A consummate collaborator, Reiner listened when Moore embraced the opportunity to portray Laura in the mold of her own lived experience as a young wife and mother. It was a somewhat innocent moment when she suggested that Laura Petrie wear form-fitting capri pants instead of A-line dresses ("I decided to play the part honestly. I wear pants at home, all my friends wear pants at home"),[29] but that decision rocked the conservative media establishment with a vitriol that is almost unbelievable from a contemporary vantage. The show's sponsor intervened, barring the pants from air after allegedly receiving letters from distraught viewers until Reiner promised that the pants would appear in only one scene per episode. The wardrobe choice became symbolic of the widening generation gap, the rising tide of mainstream feminism, and changing morality codes on network television.

The Dick Van Dyke Show's presentation of an equitable marriage was not beyond reproach, but the way the series brought issues of gender roles to light—even when they were imperfectly resolved or unresolved (a daring narrative innovation for sitcoms of the era)—was a marker of major progress in broadcast comedy's journey toward "relevancy." Episodes dealt head-on with issues of gender equity, finding Laura sometimes cast as smarter, more talented, or physically stronger than her husband—and dealing with Rob's resultant crises of masculinity. Even if Laura's ambitions were often curtailed as each script returned to a neat ideological containment prior to the following week's episode, the show allowed hard truths like gender disparity, domestic malaise, and the pressures of middle-class striving to bubble to the surface and explode. Laura Petrie never rejected her status as a suburban housewife, but she weighed her options and allowed all America to bear witness to that uneasiness. *The Dick Van Dyke Show* was also significant in the way that it presented a spectrum of available roles for women, ranging from Laura's modern housewife to Sally's single career woman, and punctuated by Millie Helper, the Petries' next-door neighbor who was a throwback to the zany sitcom housewives of an earlier moment. None of these women were wholly

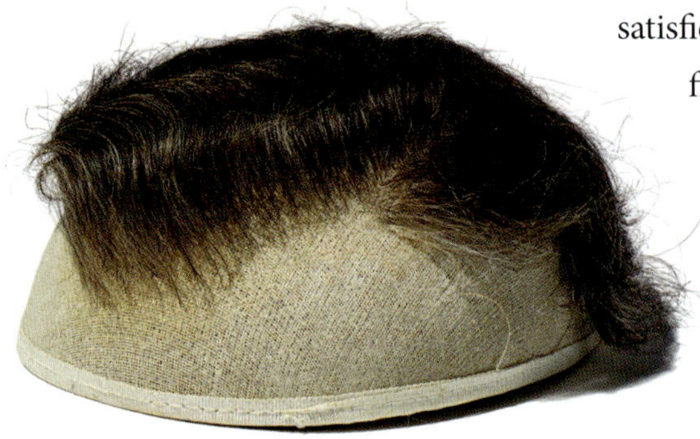

Carl Reiner famously donned this toupee when appearing in cameo as the vain Alan Brady, employer of *The Dick Van Dyke Show's* Rob Petrie. It become one of the show's central sight gags and the subject of a classic episode, "Coast to Coast Big Mouth," in which Laura inadvertently announces to the entire country that Alan Brady is bald.

satisfied with their position in life, each expressing overlapping unfulfilled desires that condensed the era's unsettled pre-feminist longings.

Reiner's remarkable ability to make his audiences think about social and political issues while in the throes of a laugh set his show apart and pushed the medium of television toward a more sophisticated engagement with the issues confronting real Americans—including gender issues, but also the climate of a country mired in sociopolitical unrest. Though the show wasn't laced with period-specific humor (and has therefore aged remarkably well) it did become a historical interlocutor at significant moments in the history of the American civil rights era. For example, in 1963's "That's My Boy??," which aired one month after the March on Washington and stands among the series' most memorable episodes, Rob becomes convinced that his wife has come home from the hospital with the wrong baby. The big reveal—when the couple that Rob thinks might be his son's true parents walk through his front door and are revealed to be Black—is a subversive surprise with Rob serving as the butt of the joke. The episode was as artistically daring as it was socially daring, with essentially the entire twenty-three-minute script building to a single punchline—that is, some say, the greatest sight gag in TV history.

The Dick Van Dyke Show stood apart at the moment of its airing as a smart, sophisticated program aimed at smart, sophisticated audiences, and proved the viability of sitcoms with social agendas. Even after it had racked up twenty-five Emmy nominations and secured an apparently perennial place on the "Greatest of All Time" lists, the show's purest legacy was in its irrefutable *quality*: "Hasn't TV got more than enough where that one came from?," one critic wrote on the occasion of the series finale. "No, gentle reader, it hasn't. It hasn't got any at all. *The Dick Van Dyke Show* was very special. Not because it was funnier, more regularly than most, but because it was lovingly fashioned every week of its long life with honest, painstaking craftsmanship."[30]

Laura LaPlaca

"STEPPING OFF THE CLIFF": THE ART OF IMPROVISATION

Though the history of improvisation can be traced as far back as ancient Roman farces and sixteenth-century *commedia dell'arte*, modern improv has its roots in early twentieth-century pedagogical movements that centered collaborative, experiential group learning through play. The innovative educator and acting coach Viola Spolin codified these so-called Theater Games in her canonical text *Improvisation for the Theater*, which underpinned the formation of the first organized improvisational troupe in the United States—Chicago's Compass Players, which was helmed by her son, Paul Sills, and David Shepherd, an impresario with dreams of creating a "people's theater." The Compass Players was to become the fountainhead from which a long and varied tradition of improvisational comedy would flow.

Sharing a cultural zeitgeist with method acting, abstract expressionist painting, Modern dance, and experimental music, the Compass Players emerged at a moment when American art was invested in spontaneous, honest, and instinctual human expression. The group was founded with a distinctly proletarian attitude, but ultimately played to audiences composed of a coffeehouse crowd drawn from the intelligentsia of their University of Chicago community. Their art was novel, somewhat shocking, and revelatory for those who experienced it in person; As one journalist put it, "You can practically feel their brain waves screaming helter-skelter toward one another, hoping for that mystical collision that will produce a miracle: a laugh that's true."[31]

The Compass Players was composed of a stunning array of talents that included Shelley Berman, Ted Flicker, Barbara Harris, Mike Nichols, and Elaine May. Nichols and May had an innate chemistry and a shared sense of rigor when it came to improvisational technique. Like Shelley Berman, who broke out of the Compass Players with a history-making comedy album, they transcended their ensemble. They adapted and perfected techniques honed during their time at the Compass Players to launch an unorthodox Broadway sensation: *An Evening with Mike Nichols and Elaine May* was performed over three hundred times—each with a totally different ending. The widespread success of the show proved improv's marketability and broad appeal.

By 1959, Paul Sills had moved on to form the Second City, enlisting Spolin to create the first formalized improvisational coursework for training new talents. The Second City still maintains a storied reputation as a breeding ground for comic talent, having launched the careers of icons from John Belushi and Dan Aykroyd to Tina Fey and Stephen Colbert. Initially emerging against a backdrop of avant-garde experimentation in the realms of performance art and the "happenings" of the 1960s, the Second City became a hub for innovation in comedy, championed by improv's self-styled "guru," Del Close. Close would go to inspire a broad lineage of improv troupes, from the Committee to the Upright Citizens Brigade, centering his belief that improv's purest function was to connect with oneself and others: "Don't let [the audience] make you buy the lie that what you're doing is for laughter. Where do the really best laughs come from? Terrific *connections* made intellectually, or terrific *revelations* made emotionally."[32]

Improvisation is both a form of hilarious entertainment and a creative tool. Often sparked by a game or audience suggestion, the format requires "making it up as you go" and giving up control—or, as Close liked to intone, "stepping off the cliff." Though the art of improv, by definition, places very little constraint on its practitioners, one rule unites every performer: In order to propel a scene forward, improvisors are bound to "completely commit to the reality they create for each other without a moment's hesitation."[33] In the parlance of the craft, to respond with a "Yes, and. . . ." Perhaps the most significant development in the evolution of the craft since Spolin recorded her first improv games has been "the Harold," a framework for creating long-form improvisations perfected by Del Close in collaboration with Charna Halpern. The Harold begins with free association and evolves into a sophisticated performance based on pattern recognition and deep trust in the collective mind of the ensemble, with each player building on and referring to the contributions of the others. Close and Halpern went on to open the ImprovOlympic Theater, a site devoted to teaching the Harold, which became a playground for a new generation of artists including Amy Poehler and Chris Farley.

Improv is more popular than ever and, increasingly, the basis for much of the entertainment we consume. Not only are disciples of Spolin, May, and Close running organizations like the Brave New Workshop, ComedySportz, and the Annoyance Theatre, but improv has become ubiquitous as a tool for creating TV, film, and Internet comedy of all formats, from sketch shows like *Inside Amy Schumer* and *Key & Peele*, to films like *This Is Spinal Tap* and *Caddyshack*, to hit sitcoms like *Curb Your Enthusiasm* and *The Office.*

THE GROUNDLINGS

In the early 1970s, improv veteran Gary Austin assembled a cohort of comics in Los Angeles to informally workshop material. As the performers gelled in the process of finessing monologues and character bits, they inadvertently discovered an unserved appetite for improv in Southern California. By 1974, the once-ragtag group had christened themselves the Groundlings, in reference to the commoners who crowded and jostled at the foot of Elizabethan stages in Shakespeare's *Hamlet.* The organization would always maintain a plebian attitude, with the members of its company acting as a self-governing democratic unit responsible for steering the nonprofit theater's creative direction.

Although the first official performance by the Groundlings was in a basement with a thirty-seat capacity, the *LA Times* was already reporting that "this could be the start of something big." Indeed, it was not long after their formation that the group emerged as a showcase for powerful comedy gatekeepers, including Lorne Michaels of *Saturday Night Live.* Laraine Newman would become the first in a long line of Groundlings to make the move to *SNL*, followed by the likes of Phil Hartman, Will Ferrell, Ana Gasteyer, Maya Rudolph, Kristen Wiig, and Heidi Gardner. By the late 1970s, the troupe had established a permanent home on Melrose Avenue (the Groundlings Theatre remains a fixture in LA's landscape) and a school that has, across five decades, trained tens of thousands of students, including Conan O'Brien and Jimmy Fallon.

Breakout talents like Kathy Griffin, Lisa Kudrow, and Jennifer Coolidge cemented the theater's reputation as a comedy incubator, and hugely successful properties piloted by alums—like the box office smash *Bridesmaids* (written by Wiig with Rudolph and Melissa McCarthy in the cast)—have kept the organization in the public eye for over fifty years since its founding. Perhaps the most surprising superstar to emerge from the Groundlings stage has been Paul Reubens, who parlayed a character invented during an improv show into the pop culture icon Pee-wee Herman.

THE LIVING PREMISE

The Living Premise debuted in June 1963 as a Greenwich Village–based improvisational cabaret helmed by Ted Flicker, an alumnus of the Compass Players who advanced the idea that true "integration" was achievable via the art of improvisation, which elevated honest and automatic thought. The troupe consisted of an "integrated company" of five performers, three of whom were Black: Godfrey Cambridge, Al Freeman Jr., Diana Sands, Jo Ann LeCompte, and Calvin Ander. Preceded by Flicker's earlier troupe, the Premise (which had launched the careers of George Segal and Buck Henry), the Living Premise's goal was to confront audiences with challenging, often controversial, "profundities and problems of integration."[34]

Based on a series of "group therapy" sessions held by the cast members with director Joan Darling, who summed up the show's raison d'être as simply to "tell the truth,"[35] the show consisted of partly improvised sketches with titles like "The Emasculation of Militant Negro Organizations by White Northern Liberals," as well as a segment of free-form dialogue with audience members. To set a tone, the opening scene found Black actress Diana Sands locked in an embrace with white actor Calvin Ander, as Al Freeman Jr. quipped, "We just did that little bit of nonsense to let you know that we're going to touch each other." *Ebony* called the show "vigorous, irreverent and occasionally shocking,"[36] and some percentage of the audience inevitably fled from the theater in outrage at each performance—a fact that the creative team was proud of.[37]

The Living Premise dissolved after 192 performances but stands as one of the most daring sociocultural experiments in comedy history. Its most celebrated cast member, Godfrey Cambridge, would go on to more mainstream success as a stand-up, employing a similar strain of satirical, confrontational humor.

THE UPRIGHT CITIZENS BRIGADE

With the teachings of improv sage Del Close as their lodestar, a group of guerrilla improvisors helmed by Matt Besser, Ian Roberts, Matt Walsh, and Amy Poehler rose to become the Upright Citizens Brigade, a comedy force in 1990s Chicago. With a membership

The founders of UCB: Matt Walsh, Matt Besser, Ian Roberts, and Amy Poehler.

that included an eclectic roster of sketch and improv artists like Adam McKay, Ali Farahnakian, and Horatio Sanz, the UCB ethos was scrappy and collaborative, held together by a tight creative fellowship devoted to performing improv anywhere and anytime they could.

By 1996, UCB had relocated to New York City, chasing greater visibility in the entertainment world. Though improv had a long and storied history in Chicago and was emergent in Los Angeles with troupes like the Groundlings having made a name for themselves, New York's improv scene was still raw and grassroots. The UCB Theater in Chelsea became the first permanent stage for long-form improv in the city.

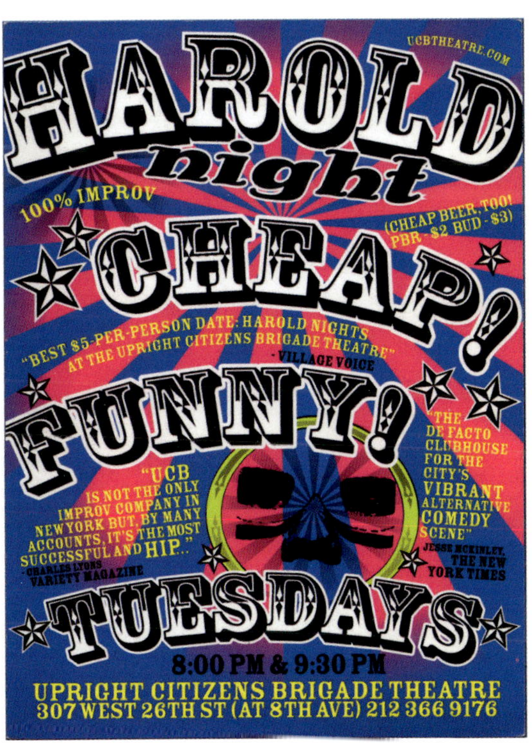

Centering the principles of the Harold and offering low-cost tickets for improv performances seven nights a week, UCB was a vital gateway for artists and audiences who became steeped in the form via the theater's innovative programming schedule, classes, and public "happenings." In 1998, the so-called UCB Four landed a game-changing Comedy Central contract that brought their work to an expanded national audience.

Ultimately evolving into a comedy empire that spanned theaters on both coasts, several touring troupes, and a training center that educated thousands of students each year, UCB became a launchpad for talents that went on to create, develop, and star in primetime sitcoms, blockbuster films, and TV comedy institutions like *Saturday Night Live* and *The Daily Show*.

Laura LaPlaca

ANDY KAUFMAN, "SONG AND DANCE MAN"

Andy Kaufman's approach to comedy integrated character work, performance art, and provocation. His performances as "Elvis Presley" reflected a fascination with popular culture and a career-long interest in deliberately challenging the expectations of his audiences.

Refusing to identify as a "comedian," Andy Kaufman fashioned himself as a self-described "song and dance man," though his audiences saw something most akin to performance art when they witnessed his intricate hoaxes and offbeat reinterpretations of stand-up comedy. Kaufman found a unique—and still unreplicated—route to success that involved a total willingness to flout convention. His goal seemed not merely to amuse or delight, but to thwart expectations and undermine traditional interactions between entertainers and their audiences. Though his body of work ranged widely across different formats, styles, and venues—from Greenwich Village stand-up sets to a hit sitcom, and from *Saturday Night Live* to Carnegie Hall—Kaufman's essential artistic premise was always to leave us unsure of where the "show" began and where it ended, ensuring that "nobody could see past the edges."[38]

Even as a young child, Kaufman fashioned himself as an entertainer. But it was at comedy clubs like the Bitter End, the Improv, and Catch a Rising Star that his one-of-a-kind brand of iconoclastic humor broke through. He achieved national exposure via prominent (and freewheeling) placements on Johnny Carson's *Tonight Show* and the very first episode of *Saturday Night Live* in 1975. The character that launched his career was the anti-charismatic "Foreign Man" from the fictional nation of Caspiar, who bumbles his way through a weak, muted, impossibly introverted stand-up set before unexpectedly exploding into a buoyant impression of Elvis Presley or a lip-synched rendition of the theme song for the Saturday morning cartoon *Mighty Mouse Playhouse*. As he shuffled offstage with a sheepish "Tank you veddy much," audiences alternately laughed or looked on in confusion. The character evolved to become Latka Gravas, a mechanic at the

Sunshine Cab Company on TV's *Taxi.* Though Kaufman was initially hesitant to take a role on a prime-time sitcom, it made him a household name in the early 1980s.

Being enigmatic advanced his legend, but Kaufman's process was a rigorous, serious one that involved a lifelong transcendental meditation practice. Fully inhabiting his characters was a strenuous endeavor that involved a level of focus achievable only after retreating into deep states of trance. The fullest expression of this particular art of embodied character work was Kaufman's transformation into the abrasive, tuxedo-clad, chain-smoking lounge singer "Tony Clifton." The vulgar, narcissistic character emerged for days on end, stalking clubs—or the set of *Taxi*—without the slightest cracks in a visage composed of full-facial prosthetics. The intermittent appearance of Clifton challenged and amazed those in Kaufman's circles, marking a total erasure of the artist's true identity.

Kaufman's career was spiked with a string of weird, shocking, notorious, and elaborately choreographed moments. In 1979 he graced the stage at Carnegie Hall, escorting his "grandmother" to a special seat from where she watched the performance. When the show concluded, she ripped off a mask and revealed herself to be fellow comedian Robin Williams—and then Kaufman invited the entire assembled audience of three thousand to enjoy a late-night snack of milk and cookies. A veteran of fourteen episodes of *Saturday Night Live,* Kaufman ran a live poll of the show's viewers during which the audience elected to "Dump Andy," banning him from appearing in future episodes. Across the dial on the competing sketch series *Fridays*, he broke the fourth wall mid-sketch to grapple with cast member Michael Richards. Perhaps unsurprisingly, Kaufman embraced the artifice of the sport of wrestling and crowned himself the "Inter-Gender Wrestling Champion of the World," offering to fight any woman who thought she could pin him in a match. An incendiary brawl in front of ten thousand spectators with wrestler Jerry "The King" Lawler, who supposedly took umbrage to Kaufman's making light of his profession, made headlines when Kaufman supposedly wound up in the hospital—and again when the two reignited the conflict in an absurd and violent exchange on *Late Night with David Letterman.* In spite of being a well-compensated prime-time sitcom star, Kaufman took a minimum-wage job as a busboy at Jerry's Famous Deli, a Los Angeles institution where he could be seen night after night slogging dirty dishes. After suddenly succumbing to cancer at age thirty-five, unfounded rumors circulated

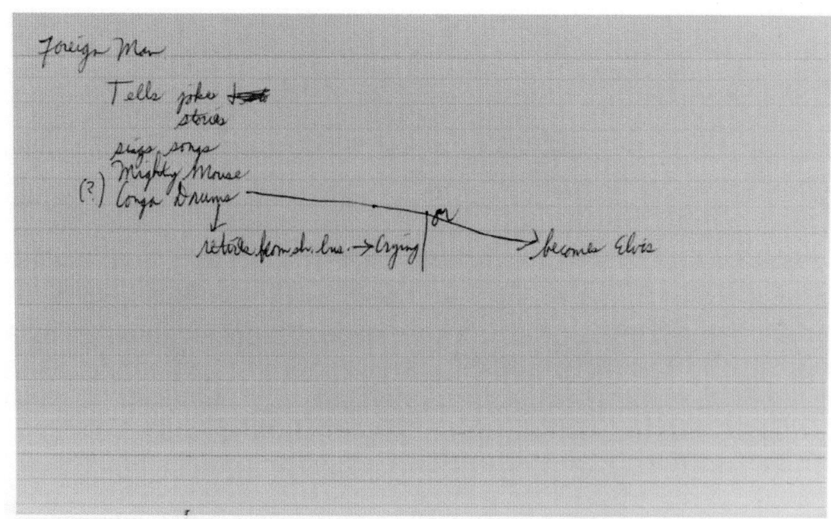

This notecard contains Andy Kaufman's handwritten notes about his *Foreign Man* character, an awkward persona whose slow speech and offbeat humor subverted the conventions of stand-up comedy. The character was central to Kaufman's exploration of discomfort as a deliberate element of performance and emerged from a meticulous, disciplined creative practice.

that Kaufman had orchestrated his most elaborate bit of performance art yet: staging his own death.

Interest in the groundbreaking body of work that Andy Kaufman left behind has never waned, and a steady stream of analysts, scholars, and acolytes have attempted to uncover the motivations behind his art. We can ask, uncertainly, which beats in Kaufman's journey are put-ons and where the authentic Andy might be glimpsed, but the engine that powers the legend is its deeply embedded, impossibly circuitous, lack of resolution. It was, perhaps, a telling moment when, at a 1971 gathering helmed by Maharishi Mahesh Yogi, Kaufman tentatively approached a microphone and asked whether entertainers have any place in a world of total enlightenment.

Laura LaPlaca

THE SIMPSONS: "DON'T HAVE A COW, MAN!"

"I'm Bart Simpson, who the hell are you?"

T-shirts with images of the spiky-haired animated character speaking this or a number of other catchphrases ("Don't have a cow, man!" "Eat my shorts!") were selling at a rate of one million per week in 1990, according to some estimates, as *The Simpsons* became a cultural phenomenon and ratings hit in its first season on the air.[39] For those born after the series' 1989 premiere, it's difficult to imagine a world before *The Simpsons* or to understand that the cartoon family was once the most controversial on television. Yet only a few years into its record-breaking thirty-plus-year run, *The Simpsons* was front-page news, getting kids thrown into detention, being denounced by the president of the United States, and opening a new front in the culture war.

The Simpsons was the first adult animated series to air on prime-time TV in thirty years (since *The Flintstones* in 1960), adapted from a series of animated segments on Fox's fledgling sketch comedy series *The Tracey Ullman Show* by alternative comics artist Matt Groening. After gaining favorable reviews, the show was picked up as a prime-time series by Fox, which brought on television veterans James L. Brooks and Sam Simon to adapt the idea for a family sitcom. Unlike the mild, saccharine family situation comedies of the era, *The Simpsons* broke the mold with its self-aware, cynical, and subversive sense of humor, its broad and deep cultural references, and its depiction of a somewhat dysfunctional, albeit traditional and well-meaning, American family.

An immediate critical and popular success, *The Simpsons* also generated controversy for its irreverent take on family, community, religion, and work life. *The Simpsons* in fact aired opposite and soon bested top-rated sitcom *The Cosby Show*, a juxtaposition that contemporary critics drew attention to. "'*The Cosby Show*,' it's been said, embodies the optimism and materialism of the '80s, whereas the Simpsons personify the sadder but wiser pragmatism of the '90s," *Washington Post* reviewer Tom Shales wrote.[40] Critics charged that parents Homer and Marge failed to adequately discipline Bart for his misbehavior, and his foul-mouthed, antiauthority attitude made him a poor role model. Bart was described as "Dennis the Menace for the 90s," a punk, prankster, smart-ass, and jester-like wit who delighted in subverting authority in all its forms, from his teachers to parents.[41] The show's creative talent had unique artistic freedom due to its success on the struggling Fox network, which allowed for transgression of the unspoken rules of family television. But its subversive, irreverent style was not anarchic; instead, it was an attempt to present a more realistic vision of family life. Cocreator James L. Brooks said, "I do think it's important for us that Bart does badly in school. There are students like that.

Shirts like this were bestsellers around 1990, when *The Simpsons* was among the most-watched programs on American television and riding a wave of merchandise sales and cultural import. These shirts lent wearers a punk sensibility, social clout, and popularity, but they could get them in trouble at school.

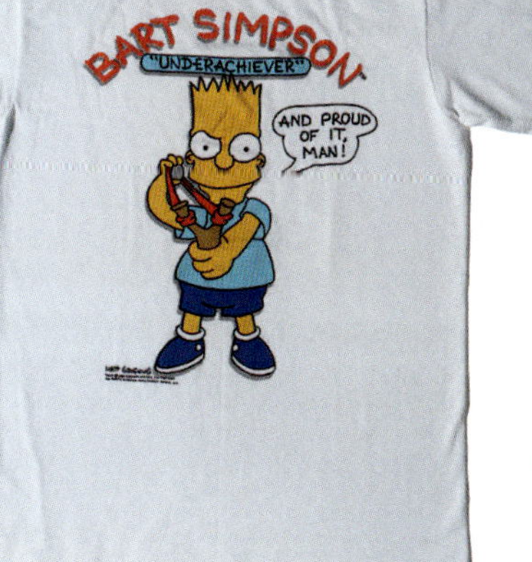

Besides, I'm very wary of television where everybody is supposed to be a role model. You don't run across that many role models in real life. Why should television be full of them?"[42]

However, in the increasingly heated political debate over popular culture that earned the still-relevant moniker "the culture wars," these explanations did little to quiet critics' claims that shows like *The Simpsons* were contributing to moral corruption and social decay. On a tour of a Pittsburgh drug-treatment center in May 1990, White House drug czar William J. Bennett saw a poster of Bart and told recovering addicts they shouldn't follow Bart's lead as an underachiever: "You guys aren't watching *The Simpsons*, are you? That's not going to help you any."[43] President George H. W. Bush, too, made headlines speaking out against the series' representation of family life, telling a 1992 National Religious Broadcasters' convention in Washington, DC, "We are going to keep on trying to strengthen the American family, to make American families a lot more like the Waltons and a lot less like the Simpsons."[44]

In 1990, Bart made the cover of *Time*, *Newsweek*, and *Rolling Stone*, and an estimated fifteen million Bart shirts were sold.[45] The shirts played up Bart's rude and aggressive attitude, making him a popular antiauthoritarian figure and the shirts symbolic signifiers of cool for young people. Unlicensed "bootleg" shirts also became popular, with depictions of Bart as distinctly African American, with brown skin, wearing sneakers, gold chains, and sweat suits then popular among rap music fans, his distinctive flat-top hairstyle augmented with shaved "tracks," quoting rap lyrics, playing basketball, or even celebrating South African leader Nelson Mandela. Soon, Bart shirts, especially those with profanity, rude phrases, or the "underachiever" label, were being banned in schools across the country, prompting some retailers to stop selling them amid public outcry.[46]

The controversy was short-lived, however, as *The Simpsons* remained popular and became increasingly baked into American popular culture and everyday life. Other television shows like *Married . . . with Children*, *Beavis and Butt-Head*, *Roseanne*, and *South Park* began taking more of the culture wars heat. Even staunch conservatives began to realize that the intact, churchgoing, middle-class, nuclear family with its working father and homemaker mother living in a suburban single-family home actually aligned well with the vision of American family life culture warriors were fighting to protect. In a 2000 *National Review* column, Jonah Goldberg wrote that *The Simpsons* was "possibly the most intelligent, funny, and even politically satisfying TV show ever," praising its even-handed satire, skewering conservative and liberal American hypocrisy and dysfunction alike. He noted that the series in fact represented "the best conservative principles: the primacy of family, skepticism about political authority, distrust of abstractions." Indeed, "the residents of Springfield are more religious than almost any other cast on television today. Springfield residents, pray and attend church every Sunday."[47] In 1999, *Time* magazine named *The Simpsons* the best television series of all time and Bart one of the hundred most influential people of the twentieth century: "Dazzlingly intelligent and unapologetically vulgar, *The Simpsons* have surpassed the humor, topicality and yes, humanity of past TV greats."[48]

Ryan Lintelman

HARI KONDABOLU AND *THE PROBLEM WITH APU*

You can say that the Apu character on *The Simpsons* is "just a cartoon" and tell people who have a problem with the stereotype—like comedian Hari Kondabolu—to just get over it. And, in a way, you would be right. It is a cartoon. But that's like saying *The Simpsons* is "just a TV show."

The show's characters have become iconic. You can reference them by their first names—or even by quirky grunts and catchphrases—and audiences throughout the world know instantly what you mean. *The Simpsons* has been a cultural touchstone for American humor for over thirty years. And as one of the most prominent South Asian characters on primetime television in the United States, Apu represents how racial caricature lives on in the twenty-first century, powerfully shaping our understanding of ourselves and each other.

Kondabolu's 2017 documentary *The Problem with Apu* guides viewers through some straightforward premises that challenge our understanding of popular culture and its power. Perhaps the hardest to confront is that all humor has a context. Even if you claim Apu is "just a cartoon," that stance is never neutral; it might operate within the limited universe of the show itself, or within your peer group. But when you begin to think beyond that, the context becomes more important especially for

South Asian Americans like Kondabolu who are both fans of the show and troubled by Apu.

Apu Nahasapeemapetilon, voiced by actor Hank Azaria from 1990 to 2017, embodied a bundle of South Asian stereotypes. Apu is an Indian immigrant to the United States, and like many real-life immigrants, despite holding an advanced degree, he works in the service sector, an owner of a convenience store, the fictional Kwik-E-Mart. Apu's voice is performed by a white man affecting a caricaturized Indian accent, with stilted pronunciation and grammar. With his wife Manjula, with whom he was forced by his parents into an arranged marriage, Apu raises eight children, all crowded in a small home.

Kondabolu's documentary raises the questions of choice: What kind of "choice" is it when your choices are slim to none? What kind of culture is it if members of the Desi (referring to the people and cultures of South Asia and its global diaspora) community rarely see the fullness of their lives reflected on-screen—except through someone else's stale and predictable stereotypes?

When what you know about who you are is narrowed into a tight space, the outcomes aren't surprising. One of the worst consequences involves internalizing those stereotypes, accepting the insults of others as your personal truth. Another is living in a culture that not only accepts but demands that your world can be defined only within that tight but legible space.

In a revealing episode of NPR's *Code Switch*, Azaria conceded that Apu was more than "just a cartoon" and that representations in the ether can have dire consequences on the ground: "I helped to create a pretty marginalizing, dehumanizing stereotype. . . . I read a little news blurb where a guy was attacked. It was actually a Middle Eastern guy who was attacked in his store and was called Apu *while he was being attacked*. . . . Apu had become a slur."

For Kondabolu, raising these questions was never about provocation for its own sake. With the release of *The Problem with Apu*, he received death threats. Yet his intent was simple: to have a conversation. "That's ultimately what the goal is," he told *Code Switch*. "You have this thing that you feel hurt by in some way or frustrated by, and you have a conversation with the person that you feel contributed to that. . . . I'm not trying to make you uncomfortable for the sake of being uncomfortable. I'm just sharing a reality with you."[49]

Theodore S. Gonzalves

MARGARET CHO: ALL-AMERICAN GIRL

Whenever the definitive history of Asian American comedy is written, *All-American Girl* will stand as a benchmark—not only as the first time a majority-Asian American cast played for laughs in prime time on television, but also as a case study in how the American entertainment industry failed to embrace, or fully recognize, its brilliance, its potential, and its impact.

Comedian, writer, and activist Margaret Cho is a second-generation Korean American born and raised in San Francisco. Her parents, who immigrated to the United States in 1964, owned a bookstore in the heart of the city's LGBTQ community, a place where a dizzying mix of lifestyles and cultures intertwined. Like many port cities, San Francisco is a place of contradictions built on vibrant cultures, ideas, and lifestyles that have energized, anchored, and attracted residents from all over the world. It has also seen some of the most shocking examples of violence in the nation's history—from targeting Chinese for exclusion in the late 1800s to the 1978 political assassination of Harvey Milk, the first openly gay man to be elected a city supervisor in San Francisco. The environment shaped Cho's sensibility—irreverent, boundary-crossing, and attuned to issues of race, gender, and sexuality in ways that few comedians before her had dared to be.

Cho's early career echoed thc hardscrabble path of countless other comics—working out routines in small clubs for indifferent audiences. But, from the start, her stand-up was both raunchy and incisive, blending personal narrative with sharp political critique. At the time, and still, seeing an Asian American woman command the stage as a stand-up comedian was incredibly rare. In the early 1990s, Cho broke further into comedy's mainstream than anyone else in the Asian American community before her. In 1994, one of the three legacy networks, ABC, offered her an 8:00 P.M. time slot—a chance to create and star in a prime-time television series.

The show's premise *loosely* followed the arc of Cho's life, but in practice reduced her story to a tired formula: The writing played on the simple fact of her Asianness and emptied out all of the dynamism of her actual

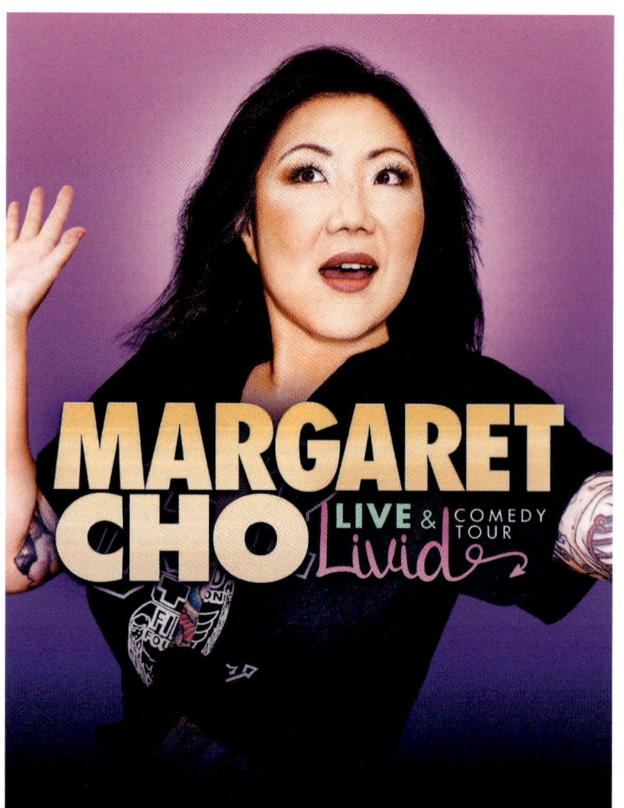

Promotional photo of comedian and actor Margaret Cho from her 2023 Live and Livid Comedy Tour. In a statement announcing the tour, Cho promised fans, "I will be radiating rage about homophobia, sexism, racism and the fight to stay alive in a culture that is killing us daily."

life. Absent was the outspoken girl who refused gender stereotypes and who was expelled from school for low marks; erased was the city's vibrant counterculture and the diverse crossroads of communities that patronized and worked in her family's bookstore. Instead of mining comedic insights from the truth of those experiences, the members of *All-American Girl*'s writing room flattened her experience and centered the well-worn trope of immigrant-born tradition versus U.S.-born rebellion; in other words, Hollywood failed Margaret Cho.

You certainly could not blame the talents of the actors on the show. Cho was supported by an outstanding cast that had a wealth of acting experiences, notably Jodi Long (the first Asian American actress to win an Emmy), union activist and veteran actor Clyde Kusatsu, the Emmy-nominated actor/comedian Amy Hill, and the Tony Award–winning actor BD Wong, who originated the Song Liling character in David Henry Hwang's *M. Butterfly*. But members of the Asian American community had a lot to say about the casting of non-Korean actors in roles specifically written as a Korean American family, as well as the cultural insensitivity of the scripting: "Chinese, Japanese, and Koreans were lumped together—their traditions mixed into a mishmash that grated on Koreans."[50] Understandable, given the lack of visibility of Korean Americans on either the big or small screen in the early 1990s.

But perhaps the most troubling aspect of the show had to do with how producers chose to reshape Cho herself. Cho has shared painful details about the production in her memoir and in her own comedy special, *I'm the One That I Want*. "The network has a problem with you," producer Gail Berman told her. "They are concerned about the fullness of your face. You need to lose weight."[51] Enter a physical trainer to come to her to home for four-hour workouts, six days a week, to help her lose thirty pounds in two weeks. Her kidneys crashed. She continued with diet pills and laxatives. From the stress, insecurity, and sheer exhaustion, how could she not ask simple questions like, "How do you keep going when someone tells you there is something wrong with your face?"[52]

Again, the assumptions being made—about Cho's body, about the show's premise and execution—not only were damaging to her health but also revealed how specific decision-makers in an industry were so ill-equipped to find comedy in the uniqueness of her experiences. Cho recalls the producers' lazy thinking:

> An Asian consultant was hired, mostly to help actors with their accents and to determine the Feng Shui on the set. It was all the more insulting because the actors didn't need any help, and "authenticity" was never the problem. It was insensitivity. The idea that there is one defining, "authentic" Asian American experience ignores the vast diversity of which we are capable. It discounts the fact that there can be many truths, and holds us in a racial spider-web. We were accused of being racist because we did not ring true as an "authentic" Asian American family, when the real racism lies in the expectation of one.[53]

It's tempting to think that perhaps Cho could have pushed back, been more assertive, and fought for more accurate and authentic representation, but the cards were stacked against her, and in fact, Cho has been on a lifelong journey of self-discovery. She didn't know this growing up, but Margaret Cho's family line stretches back to the thirteenth century. In her long line are members of royal families. Closer to her own time, there are joke tellers like her father. And then there are women like her mother, Young Hie, who challenged marriage and religious traditions, and her great-grandmother, who offers her an example of "compassion, protection, defiance, and laughter."[54] On the TV show *Finding Your Roots*, Henry Louis Gates Jr. asked Cho if knowing about her distinguished ancestors from centuries past would have helped her growing up. "Oh, it would have helped tremendously," Cho replied. "When I was going to school, it seemed like other kids could respond to history in a way that was personal, and I never could, because it was so much about other people and other experiences that were not mine. It would have been very powerful to have a sense of history." Cho paid a serious personal price, but also changed the conversation. Her work has transformed many of those wounds into material that blends vulnerability and rage into a revolutionary kind of laughter. She has made visible the pressures put on Asian American performers and refused to accept Hollywood's failed imagination of who she can be.

Today, Margaret Cho's influence is hard to miss. She's everywhere: stand-up specials, podcasts, TV and film appearances, and a hero to generations of comedians who recognize her as a pathbreaker. "Not only do I have a voice," Cho insists, "I have an indignant voice."[55] That indignation has made Margaret Cho a cultural force.

Theodore S. Gonzalves

NEW DIRECTIONS IN LATINX COMEDY

In recent years, new Latinx comedians have emerged to expand the landscape of Latinidad (Latinx identity) and move beyond the mainstream notions of what it means to be Latinx. From bilingual immigrant comics who perform in Spanish to Afro-Latinx comics, the U.S. comedy scene is catching up to the complexities of intersectional identities found in the Latinx community. This new generation of comedians carries forward a strong legacy of breaking barriers. From stand-up stages to social media streaming, Latinx comedians are redefining what Latinx comedy looks and sounds like—while gaining long-overdue visibility and fulfilling a legacy that earlier generations of comedians fought for but were often denied due to systemic barriers and industry bias.

Sketch comedy in the United States has its roots in vaudeville and the tent show circuits of the late nineteenth century. By the early twentieth century, Latinx performers like Rodolfo "Don Fito" García, Beatriz "La Chata Noloesca" Escalona Pérez, Leonardo "Lalo" García Astol, and Romualdo "Cachipuchi" Tirado were building careers in Spanish-language vaudeville and revues and laying the groundwork for a rich comedic tradition in Latinx communities.[56] As the Hollywood film industry took off, actors like Mario Moreno as Cantinflas and Pedro Gonzalez Gonzalez paved the way on-screen for future Latinx comic actors, even as their characters relied heavily on parody that exaggerated their cultural backgrounds at the expense of reinforcing many negative stereotypes of Latinx people as foolish, lazy, and uneducated. Moreno's Cantinflas character in Mexico challenged the status quo with quick-witted comedy that took aim at wealthy elites, but the U.S. version of Cantinflas fell flat as American studios devalued Moreno's talent and characterized his misadventures in stereotypical ways. After the American film *Pepe* flopped, Moreno returned to Mexico where he could have a larger role in the scripting and development of his films. Cantinflas's social satire, working-class character, and clever wordplay inspired many Chicano performers and playwrights in the sixties and seventies as the Chicano movement gained ground. Among them were Luis Valdez's Teatro Campesino and the satirical comedy troupe Culture Clash. Founded by José Antonio Burciaga, Marga Gómez, Monica Palacios, Richard Montoya, Ric Salinas, and Herbert Siguenza in 1984 at the Galería de la Raza in San Francisco's Mission District, the Culture Clash troupe used its theater performances to draw attention to the social and political conditions of the Chicanx (and broader Latinx) community. Their comedy was by, about, and for Latinxs and took aim at the "diversity and adversity" experienced by Latinxs. Through their use of satire, they radically exposed the injustices of multiethnic U.S. society. Sketch comedy series like *MADtv* and *Saturday Night Live* have also offered a platform for new Latinx comic actors like Pablo Francisco, Johnny Sanchez, Jill-Michele Meleán, Nelson Ascencio, Anjelah Johnson, Michelle Ortiz, Horatio Sanz, Melissa Anne Villaseñor, and Marcello Hernandez.

Stand-up has long been a space where comedians of color could launch their careers and test how to make their material appeal to a wide audience without relying on dehumanizing stereotypes. Entertainers like Cheech Marin, Paul Rodriguez, George Lopez, and John Leguizamo, among others, got their start in comedy clubs and

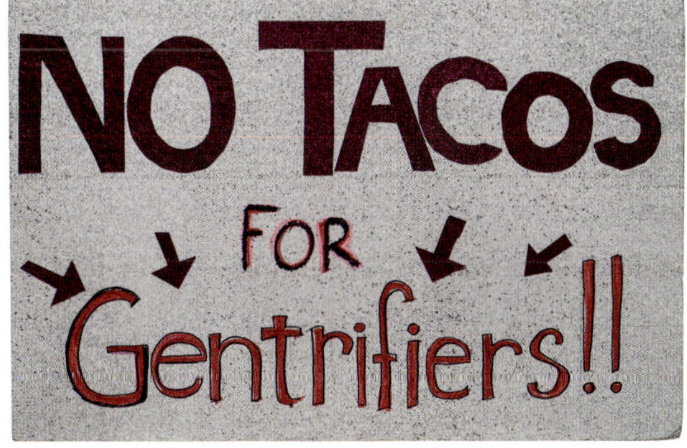

Gentefied, a comedy-drama series created by Marvin Lemus and Linda Yvette Chávez that ran for two seasons streaming on Netflix from 2020 to 2021, explored the Morales family's struggles to support and save their family taco shop, undocumented immigrant grandfather, and community in the face of gentrification in Los Angeles's majority-Latinx Boyle Heights neighborhood. The series title combines the English word "gentrified" and the Spanish word "gente," meaning people or community, in a nod to its investigation of the effects of socioeconomic and demographic change on traditionally Latinx communities in the United States in the early twenty-first century.

on the nightclub circuit. Stand-up comedy provided a space for these comedians (often Mexican American) to explore their own identities as a "minority" group in the United States in a relatable way. Historically, the most visible Latinx comedians were featured in productions like the *Latin Kings of Comedy*, yet today we see comedians like Gabriel Iglesias, Cristela Alonzo, Felipe Esparza, Ian Lara, Aida Rodriguez, and Gina Brillon headlining their own wildly popular stand-up comedy specials.

The digital media age has revolutionized the way that Americans consume entertainment, and the industry is adapting as a result. Historically, broadcast and cable networks saw huge risks in green-lighting productions that might not be successful with mainstream audiences—read palatable to white audiences. This presented an obstacle for many comedians of color who had to prove their commercial success before being granted opportunities from major networks for lead roles in television series or comedy specials. But in the age of streaming (and significant demographic shifts in the United States), previously marginalized stories and experiences are moving to the fore more often, yet the margin for success is much higher. Despite the critical acclaim of streaming series like *Gentefied*, *Mr. Iglesias*, and *Los Espookys*, these series struggle to achieve unrealistically high standards of "success" even while they attract niche and dedicated audiences. Too often, the result is cancellation by streaming services that are quick to move on to the next thing.

According to Nielson's 2020 special report on Latinx connectivity, 98 percent of Latinx people in the United States own a smartphone, and they use social media at higher rates than the general U.S. population. Latinx comedians are using social media as a tool to gain greater visibility by reaching diverse and more geographically distant Latinx communities. Most of these content creators are taking their comedy directly to audiences—with little to no help from the traditional entertainment industry. Some, like Julissa Calderon, Jenny Lorenzo, Joanna Hausmann, and Gadiel Del Orbe, are formerly BuzzFeed or Flama content creators, while others like LeJuan James, Mimi Davila, and Laura Di Lorenzo got their start using platforms like Vine and YouTube. Still other Latinx comedians record their stand-up club routines and share them on social media—transforming local comedy scenes into national/international phenomena. Social media is a space where Latinx comedy creators can experiment with new material, explore multiple (and conflicting) facets of Latinidad, and work outside the industry to bring laughs to the increasing number of Latinxs using their smartphone to consume entertainment.

With every new generation of comedians, the creative landscape shifts and adapts to changing technologies, modern relevance, cultural nuance, and the increasing competition in a media-rich world. Latinx comedians and comic actors of the past broke barriers to step into the spotlight even in typecast and stereotyped roles. This new wave of Latinx comedic talent is reshaping mainstream narratives by embracing multilingual and multicultural humor that resonates far beyond their own communities. By leveraging new digital media platforms, these comedians are experimenting with new and old forms of comedy, while reaching audiences and attaining visibility on a global scale.

Ashley Oliva Mayor

TRAUMEDY: FOLK HUMOR IN TIMES OF CRISIS

"Disasters breed jokes" is the opening sentence in one of the seminal articles by folklorist Alan Dundes on the folk humor—much of it undeniably in poor taste—that emerges in the wake of traumas and tragedies.[57] Survivors of events as diverse as nuclear-reactor accidents, spaceflight accidents, global epidemics, and global pandemics share jokes, which may seem utterly tasteless, if not also blatantly offensive. According to Dundes, this sort of humor in the face of crisis is inevitable: "Jokes themselves are neither good nor evil. They are simply reflections of the fears of a people or of individuals at a given instant in time."[58] What follows are some examples of the folk humor and jokes that have emerged and spread in response to national (if not also international) traumas from the late 1970s to the early 2020s—a genre labeled "traumedy."

Much of the humor that emerges in times of crises and disasters is certifiably folklore, which the American Folklore Society broadly defines as "our cultural DNA [which] includes the art, stories, knowledge, and practices of a people."[59] Although there is some overlap between the expressions of popular culture and folk culture, popular culture typically originates in forms of popular corporate media—such as television, cinema, and pop music—while folk culture emerges more informally and

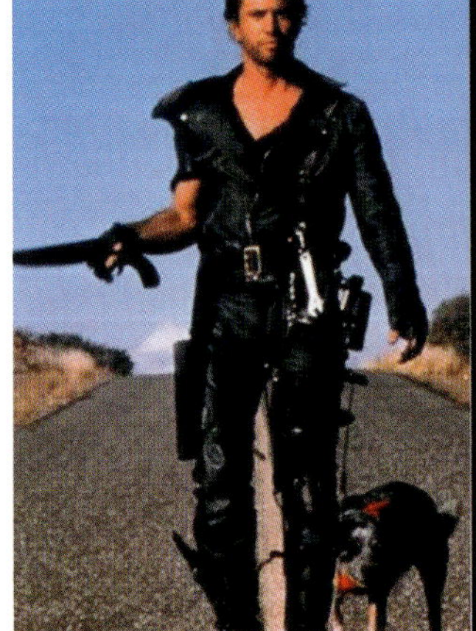

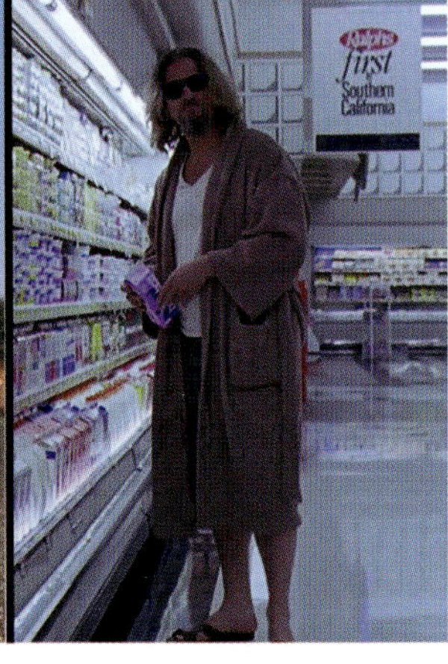

Many of the Internet memes during the coronavirus pandemic were deliberately self-deprecating. One fantasy may have been a rugged action hero, striding purposefully through a postapocalyptic wasteland like Mel Gibson in *The Road Warrior* (1981), but the reality for many was closer to a quintessential slacker, such as Jeff Bridges in *The Big Lebowski* (1998).

unofficially from an amorphous array of folk groups, which form via attributes of age, ethnicity, gender, geographic region, kinship, occupation, race, and religion, or combinations thereof. Whereas popular culture changes quickly over time, with a new number-one hit arising weekly or monthly, folk culture tends to endure for longer periods of time. The patterns of folk architecture, folk art, folk humor, folk song, folk speech, and so on become traditional, even as they adapt to new circumstances at what Dundes called "a given instant in time."

Folklorists often seek cross-cultural similarities in the humor of disaster, which underscore the traditional patterns that persist and endure among the folk. Not surprisingly, the nuclear disasters at Three Mile Island outside Harrisburg, Pennsylvania, in March 1979 and at Chornobyl, Ukraine, in April 1986 have inspired some of the same jokes. For example, roughly three weeks after the accident at Three Mile Island, folklorist Yvonne Milspaw heard the following joke: "What's the five-day forecast for Harrisburg? Two days, with temperatures to reach 3000°."[60] Nearly identical jokes (albeit with Celsius rather than Fahrenheit measurements) spread in Ukraine some seven years later: "What is the weather forecast in Kiev's region? There will be changeable cloudiness and a moderate eastern breeze. Temperature will be no more than 1500C."[61]

These sorts of jokes, which inhabitants of the affected regions shared with each other, reflect not only what Dundes called "the fears of a people or of individuals," but also what may be termed "gallows humor"—that is, "a type of humor that arises in a type of precarious or dangerous situation."[62] According to a sociologist who analyzed the jokes told in Czechoslovakia in 1939, following the Nazi occupation of the country, gallows humor serves as "a psychological escape . . . [and] psychological compensation," which allows the victims of a calamity to "persuade themselves as well as others that their present suffering is only temporary, that it will soon be all over, that once again they will live as they used to live before they were crushed."[63] Joking about an exaggerated weather forecast at a time when nuclear reactors are melting down, and the future is terrifyingly uncertain, seems akin to joking from the precipice of an executioner's gallows.

Moreover, folklorists have also collected a significant number of disaster jokes in which the tellers themselves may not be immediate victims, but rather may be more-distant observers of the event. In this category are the many morbid jokes about HIV/AIDS that Dundes collected and analyzed. To cite some of the milder examples, "Did you hear about the homosexual who finally decided to come 'out of the closet'? He told his parents he had bad news and good news: 'The bad news is I'm gay, the good news is I'm dying.'" Or, "What's the difference between Staten Island and Rock Hudson? The first is a ferry terminal, the second a terminal fairy." At the time of these jokes in the mid-1980s, the tellers (not gay themselves) believed that HIV/AIDS affected mainly gay men. That being said, Dundes notes that the morbid jokes about AIDS reflect fears of "two topics, both taboo: . . . homosexuality and a deadly disease," and both that "many Americans are uncomfortable talking openly about." By sharing these jokes, the tellers not only air their "private fears about contracting AIDS (and about possible connections with homosexuality)," but also are able to "distance [themselves] from the disease and from homosexuality."[64]

Another example of disaster jokes told from a distance are those that followed the explosion in January 1986 of the space shuttle *Challenger*, which killed all seven astronauts on board. Almost immediately across the United States arose dozens of morbid jokes, which initially shocked many with their insensitivity to the tragedy. To cite some of the milder examples, "What does NASA stand for? Need another seven astronauts." And "Why do they drink Coke at NASA? They can't get 7-Up."[65] Roger Simon, a columnist for the *Los Angeles Times*, was so terribly disturbed by the *Challenger* jokes that he sought explanations. Psychologists told Simon that "we joke about the truly horrible as a way of distancing ourselves from it, as a way of isolating ourselves from tragedy. By joking about it, we make it unreal." However, Simon also went on to speculate, "But maybe we joke about such things for a different reason. Maybe we do it to satisfy some deep, dark urge within us to speak the unspeakable, to push against the limits of decency."[66]

Agreeing in part with Simon's explanations is folklorist Willie Smyth, who drew upon theoretical perspectives from Sigmund Freud, Mary Douglas, Christopher Lasch, and others. Smyth observes that the *Challenger* sick "jokes may function to discharge the psychic energy connected with these topics by providing a channel through which the anxiety attached to a thought of catastrophic event may be diverted." More specifically—and

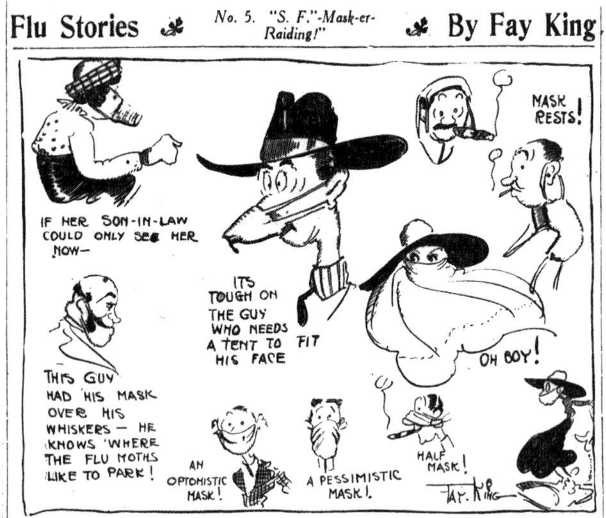

Roughly one hundred years before the coronavirus pandemic, newspaper cartoonist Fay King (one of few women in that profession at the time) used the influenza pandemic of 1918–1919 to poke fun at some of the ways in which San Franciscans wore their protective masks in public.

related to a universal fear of death among human beings—Smyth regards the *Challenger* jokes as "an expressive genre through which one is encouraged to defuse, by means of laughter or groans, anxieties about and consequent hostility toward thoughts of death and dismemberment."[67] Even though almost all tellers of the *Challenger* jokes had no direct connections to spaceflight and thus had little reason to fear dying in that particular way, a more general fear of death may have triggered their joking.

The coronavirus pandemic, at its height in the early 2020s, brought front and center the human fears and anxieties about death, enabling thousands of jokes to spread among individuals who—like almost everyone worldwide—were susceptible to a disease that could be alarmingly fatal. As a result, coronavirus jokes serve not only as a type of gallows humor (like the jokes about Three Mile Island and Chornobyl) but also as a way of distancing ourselves from the tragedy and defusing our anxieties through humor (like the jokes about HIV/AIDS and the *Challenger*).

Much contemporary humor is "meta," which reflects a multilayered awareness of one's environment. Accordingly, much of the humor about the coronavirus pandemic displays a self-awareness that registers as self-deprecating or making fun of ourselves. For instance, many of the most widely spread internet memes ridiculed our pretensions—what we might tell our grandchildren about our imaginary heroic activities fighting a deadly disease versus what actually happened. In the case of several widely spread memes, the visual humor contrasts, "What I had always pictured myself wearing during the Apocalypse" (illustrated by a photo of either black-leather-clad Mel Gibson as Mad Max in *The Road Warrior* or black-leather-clad Carrie-Anne Moss as Trinity in *The Matrix*) with "What actually happened" (illustrated by a photo of shaggy-bathrobe-clad Jeff Bridges as the Dude in *The Big Lebowski* or a photo of a cat in a terry-cloth robe with a plate of cookies). Facing a potential apocalypse in the form of a global pandemic, we make light of the situation by mocking our fantasies and ourselves.

Because all forms of folklore serve multiple functions, the folk humor of disaster defies any one interpretation of how it functions. However, it seems clear that during moments of national trauma, the dark humor expressed through morbid jokes and memes may function in part as cathartic salves to psychological wounds. Like all folklore, the folk humor of disaster serves not only to entertain or amuse, but also more importantly to maintain the stability, solidarity, cohesiveness, and continuity of folk groups and communities within the larger mass culture.

James I. Deutsch

HARLEM GLOBETROTTERS: CLOWN PRINCES OF BASKETBALL

Inspiring grins as infectious as their iconic theme song, "Sweet Georgia Brown," the Harlem Globetrotters play competitive basketball games filled with delightful displays of ball handling wizardry and amazing trick shots interrupted by beloved comedy routines. A reminder of American entertainment's barnstorming heritage, the "Clown Princes of Basketball" continue to break barriers and spread laughter across the world.

Composed of players estranged from the "Savoy Five," whose basketball games served as warm-up acts for dances held at Chicago's Savoy Theater, the first "Globetrotters" team, five African American players and their manager, Jewish American Abe Saperstein, hit the road in a ramshackle Model T on a tour of Illinois corn country in 1928.

Despite their iconic name, the Harlem Globetrotters were not from Harlem, and, at least in their early days, their "trotting" remained confined to America's midwestern states. The moniker was chosen in part to connect the team with America's most prominent African American neighborhood, where the Harlem Renaissance was an epicenter of Black intellectual and cultural activity. The name also served a more practical purpose, indicating to white communities in the time of Jim Crow, some of whom may had never seen a person of color before, that the visiting team featured Black athletes.

The team continually expanded its boundaries, taking on local high school and collegiate teams, as well as other barnstorming organizations. At first the Globetrotters played an exceptional, yet traditional, brand of basketball. However, over the years, they added an increasing amount of

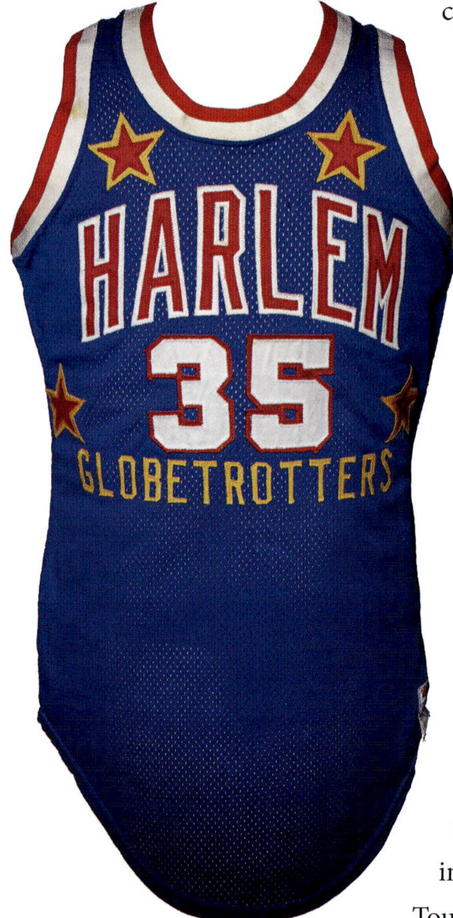

Herbert "Geese" Ausbie (b. 1938) played for the Harlem Globetrotters from 1961 to 1985. One of the team's most popular players, Ausbie was one of the few Globetrotters to assume the prestigious role of the team's "Clown Prince of Basketball." In recognition of his accomplishments, the Globetrotters retired Ausbie's number 35 in 2017.

comedy into their games. Wanting to rest tired legs, make blowout victories more entertaining, and help defuse racial tensions, the team developed an entertaining style of play that emphasized trick maneuvers and humorous skits, an addition they called "the Show."

The Show emphasized the player's skills, showcasing fancy ball control, surprising passes, and mischievous yet difficult shots that left opponents demoralized. Both zany and impressive, the Show was a unique touch that separated the team from their barnstorming peers. As the Show developed, Saperstein inserted routines that were, as was common at the time, dependent on America's racist minstrel tradition. Even as the Globetrotters humiliated their (often) white competition, they were also put into the unfortunate position of affirming negative stereotypes that presented Blacks as immature and lazy.

However, with winning streaks over one hundred games, the Globetrotters were anything but. In 1940, the Globetrotters proved themselves as one of the strongest basketball clubs in the nation, winning that year's World Professional Basketball Tournament, an invitational tournament featuring the nation's most prominent hoopsters, including teams from the all-white professional leagues. The continued success of Black teams such as the Globetrotters and the Harlem Rens against white opponents over the ensuing decade was one factor in the NBA's desegregation in 1950. High-profile wins against teams such as the Minneapolis Lakers made the Globetrotters more renowned than ever.

Over the ensuing decades, the Show became more developed, less dependent on racial stereotypes, and a bigger part of the Globetrotter games. Playing primarily against the Washington Generals, a team created to be their opposition, actual competitive play was reduced to about 20 to 30 percent of the contest. The rest of the time was reserved for fan-friendly antics and show-stopping skills.

In the course of its storied history the team has had tremendous cultural influence, including being recruited by the U.S. government to serve as cultural ambassadors on goodwill missions around the world. Featured in numerous movies and television programs, including their own animated children's series, the Globetrotters' reach has expanded outside the gym and into the popular imagination.

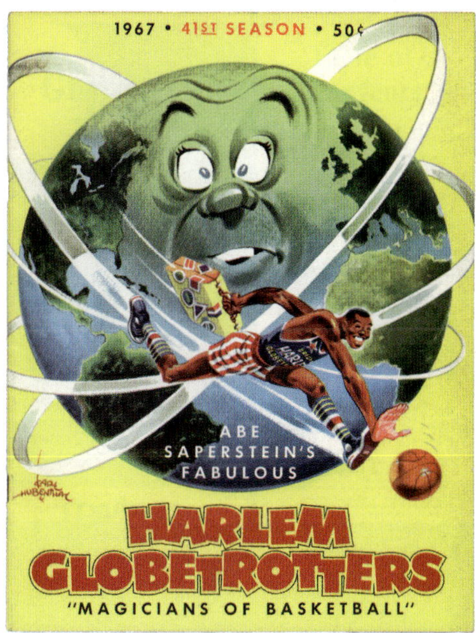

As illustrated on the cover of this program from the Globetrotters' 1967 season, the basketball team really did travel the world. They played before seventy-five thousand in Berlin's Olympic stadium on their first international tour in 1950, visited the Soviet Union at the height of the Cold War in 1959, and earned the title "Ambassadors of Goodwill" on tours supported by the U.S. State Department.

A notable example of African American entrepreneurship and innovation, the team has since fielded teams featuring diverse athletes of all backgrounds, shapes, and sizes, including some of basketball's most talented women. Playing before kings and queens, presidents and popes, the Globetrotters' unique blend of slapstick and sport has been shared in over 120 countries. Connecting generations, the team's long history and enormous reach has led some to call them the most viewed comedy troupe of all time.

Eric Jentsch

HARVEY FIERSTEIN: I AM WHO I AM

Harvey Fierstein is a playwright and actor who helped bring gay lives and stories to the Broadway stage in several groundbreaking shows, especially the semiautobiographical play *Torch Song Trilogy* and musical comedy *La Cage aux Folles*. Though both were notable and controversial for their representation of gay characters and themes, critics remarked that they were also subversively old-fashioned in their celebration of monogamous family life, running counter to dominant narratives of gay promiscuity and libertinism. As an actor, Fierstein made celebrated appearances on *Cheers* and *The Simpsons*, appeared in the films *Mrs. Doubtfire* and *Independence Day*, and returned to Broadway in *Hairspray* and the 2004 revival of *Fiddler on the Roof*; as a playwright he wrote the books for *Newsies*, *Kinky Boots*, and the 2022 revival of *Funny Girl*. Fierstein's gravelly Brooklyn voice is as unmistakable and unique as his comic voice, which has injected a flamboyant yet sincere call to self-love and empathy into American entertainment over his five-decade career.

Fierstein was born into a middle-class Jewish family in Brooklyn in 1954 and showed an artistic acuity from an early age. He moved from community theater to performing as a drag queen in his teens, and then appearing as a lesbian maid in Andy Warhol's avant-garde play *Pork* by the early

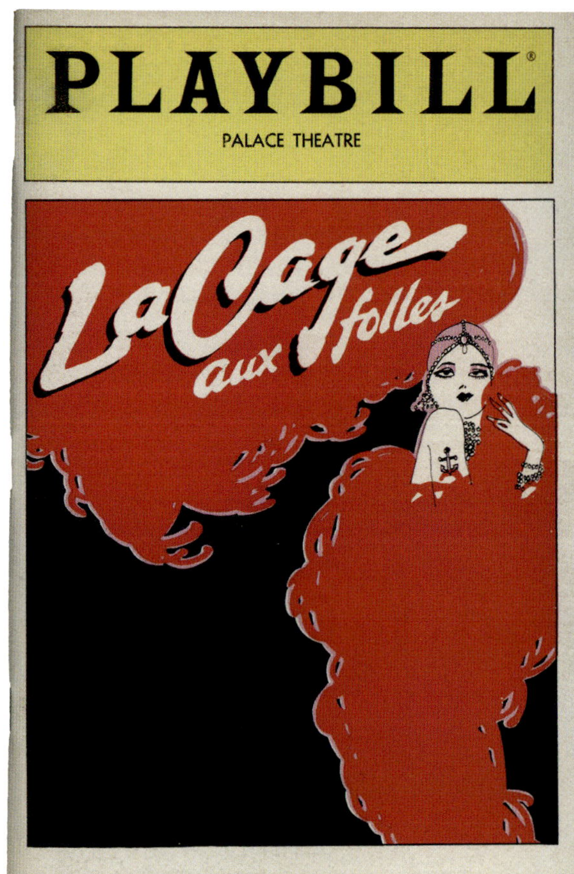

The musical *La Cage aux Folles* was groundbreaking for its representation of a loving, monogamous gay relationship, drag performance, and radical self-acceptance. The show's act 1 finale song "I Am What I Am" earned acclaim as a gay anthem.

1970s. In 1978, at the off-off-Broadway La Mama Experimental Theater Club, Fierstein wrote and starred in a play, *The International Stud*, named for a Greenwich Village gay bar with a back room for anonymous sex, but the story wasn't prurient; rather, it was a dramedy about a gay man whose heart is broken when his bisexual lover leaves him for a woman.

Fierstein wrote two follow-up plays, *Fugue in a Nursery* and *Widows and Children First!*, and combined them into a three-act play titled *Torch Song Trilogy*. In the play's three parts, Arnold Beckoff, a gay Jewish drag performer, struggles to find love, build a family, and get his mother to accept and respect him for who he is. The show opened off-Broadway in 1981 but soon moved to Broadway's Little Theatre, where it ran for 1,222 performances, earned Fierstein two Tony Awards, the first person ever to win for Best Play and Best Actor in a Play, and was heralded as the first commercially successful gay play on Broadway. It was certainly one of the first mainstream productions to feature an out gay leading character and lead, and though it garnered some homophobic reviews, it has been celebrated for its empathetic and complicated exploration of gay identity, romance, and family life in the years between the Stonewall riots and the height of the AIDS crisis.

"Arnold Beckoff, for once, wasn't a eunuch-like side-kick, but the hero of his own story," playwright Charles Busch wrote in *The Advocate*, "He was a fully realized character who had an active sex life, a tragic love, story, and a gay teenage foster son. . . . Fierstein's play gave the public a vision of gay life that was outrageous yet completely accessible."[68] Indeed, the play's intimate and heartfelt drama of underdog overcoming the odds and a son finding peace with his disappointed mother proved universal, charming even straight audiences who might not have otherwise sympathized with an effeminate, gay, drag queen protagonist.[69]

Fierstein's next major project was in a similar vein: he wrote the book for the 1983 musical adaptation of the French play *La Cage aux Folles*. The show, which opened on Broadway in 1983, directed by Arthur Laurents with a "defiantly old fashioned" score by Jerry Herman, tells the story of a gay couple, Georges and Albin, who own and perform at a

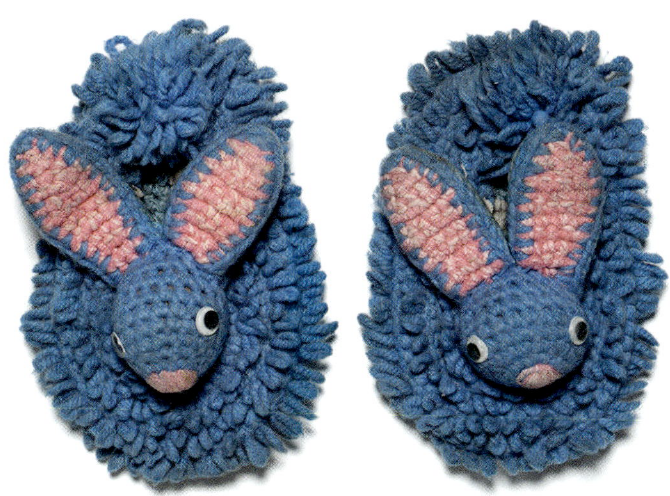

This pair of crocheted bunny slippers was worn by Harvey Fierstein in the role of Arnold Beckoff in the original Broadway production of *Torch Song Trilogy*. Arnold's fondness for rabbits was true to life for Harvey, who had long received gifts of bunny kitsch based on his name (a nod to Mary Chase's 1944 play *Harvey*), but the slippers also represented the domestic family bliss Arnold yearned for.

drag nightclub in Saint-Tropez.[70] The almost parodically butch and effeminate duo have raised an open-minded, liberal, and straight son, who nevertheless decides to marry the daughter of a homophobic and bigoted right-wing politician. When the couple brings their parents together to meet, a hilarious comedy of errors ensues.

Fierstein's sentimental script helped make the screwball farce a popular success, winning six Tony Awards from nine nominations and running for 1,761 performances in its original Broadway production, and the musical was remade again as a 1996 film, *The Birdcage*, starring Robin Williams and Nathan Lane and directed by Mike Nichols. Critics noted that Fierstein had cannily used the emotional power and sensational trappings of the old-fashioned musical to make the transgressive homosexual love at the center of the story seem somehow tame and relatable (if not trite and boring, as *New York Times* critic Frank Rich complained), leading the audience to embrace the dignity, humanity, and love expressed by the gay characters onstage.[71]

Ryan Lintelman

ALI WONG: BABY COBRA

Ali Wong's memoir, *Dear Girls: Intimate Tales, Untold Secrets, and Advice for Living Your Best Life*, is written as an extended letter to her two young daughters. More than just advice, the book is about the lessons the comedian has learned in the unforgiving world of stand-up and presents a record of how she reshaped a historically exclusionary art form.

For many, Wong's dramatic arrival came in 2016 with *Baby Cobra*. Seven months pregnant, she delivered an hour-long set that was both raunchy and razor-sharp, demolishing stereotypes of Asian American women as quiet or submissive. She vaulted into subjects often considered taboo: sexual desire, ambition, the absurdities of modern gender roles. The pregnancy was not incidental; the sight of a pregnant Asian

American woman headlining a Netflix comedy special was a cultural shift that forced audiences to confront biases about whose voices could be both authoritative and funny. She followed it with *Hard Knock Wife* (2018), again performing while visibly pregnant, examining the realities of motherhood and the myth of "having it all." In *Don Wong* (2022), she turned marriage, desire, and female rage into content worthy of serious comedic exploration. Her body of work emerged as one of the most original in modern stand-up.

The seeds of Wong's career were planted at UCLA, where she joined a group called Lapu, the Coyote that Cares (LCC), founded by David Lee, Derek Mateo, and Randall Park. "With the skills I learned from LCC, an Asian American student theater group . . . , I produced and promoted my own shows right away," she recalls. Self-produced shows like *Hustle and Pho*, *The Cameltoe Show*, and *Jungle Beaver* reflected the irreverence and ingenuity of her work early on. Hustling for herself, rather than waiting for the opportunities to find her, is a major through line in her career: "It was the only way I could headline and do an hour of material."[72]

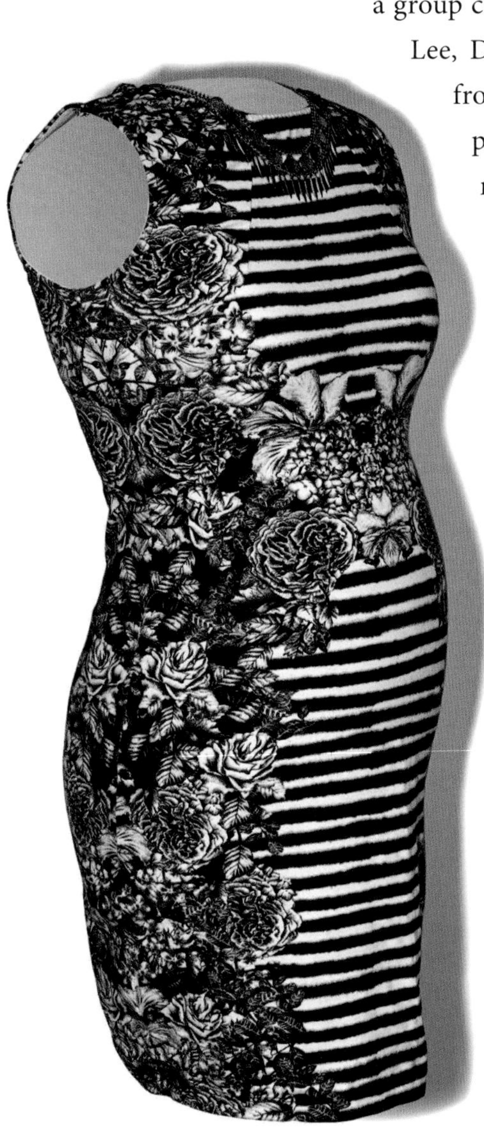

Wong wore this dress at the taping of her 2016 comedy special *Baby Cobra* when she was seven months pregnant with her first child. Fans emulated the look at Halloween and at parties.

After college, Wong returned to her hometown of San Francisco, a city she calls a "cool, progressive metropolis" where a young comic can develop their skills outside of the entertainment beacons of Los Angeles and New York City. Where to start? How about a laundromat that doubles as a comedy venue? She cut her teeth at BrainWash Café—a comedy institution where, for twenty-eight years, you could grab a beer while waiting for a load to finish. The most coveted gig was to host a show at San Francisco's Punch Line comedy club, but as much as she loved the sharp, supportive audiences of San Francisco, the city could also feel, in her words, "oppressive." She knew she needed the road to expand her craft.[73]

The road was far from glamorous. Wong recalls putting in time in the oddest of places: "Usually the back room of a Mexican restaurant in Carson. Or somebody's dog-poop-covered backyard in Silver Lake. Or an abandoned Cheesecake Factory behind an abandoned Sears."[74] The reality of stand-up, she admits, was less about applause than about endurance: "Spending hours on the Internet to book the cheapest flights possible. Eating a boatload of fried food with ranch dressing because there are no other options. Fending off creepy-ass men. Steering clear of your idols and funny colleagues who you've learned tend to sexually harass women."[75] These experiences, grueling as they were, shaped Wong into a comic unafraid of discomfort and deeply attuned to the absurdities of everyday life.

Ali Wong's place in comedy history is secure: by centering her body and her unapologetic truths, she redefined the image of the stand-up comic and used humor to transform social narratives. Her career has been both a chronicle of the perils women face in stand-up and a model of how to thrive despite them. By turning vulnerability into power and grind into brilliance, she has become one of the most popular and influential comics of her generation.

Theodore S. Gonzalves

THE BIG BANG THEORY AND *THE GUILD*

With the rapid social and technological changes of the twenty-first century leaving many feeling disconnected and isolated, fandom and fan culture has emerged as a vital way Americans can find community and identity. Having access to abundant streams of entertainments both old and new, modern audiences have an unprecedented capacity to immerse themselves in the popular culture products of their choosing, as well as the means to easily engage with others around these interests. Developing identities and seeking representation, fans use their shared passions to understand the world, challenge assumptions and share experiences.

"I'm not crazy, my mother had me tested."
—Sheldon Cooper (Jim Parsons)

Two comedies, Chuck Lorre and Bill Prady's globally popular sitcom *The Big Bang Theory* (2007–2019) and Felicia Day's groundbreaking web series *The Guild* (2007–2013), explored the "found families" that can develop, in part, around shared fandoms. A reflection of the societal mainstreaming of traditional geek culture, these programs added new wrinkles to the traditional situation comedy by exploring the dynamism and idiosyncrasies of social groups bound by their mutual interest and participation in popular culture.

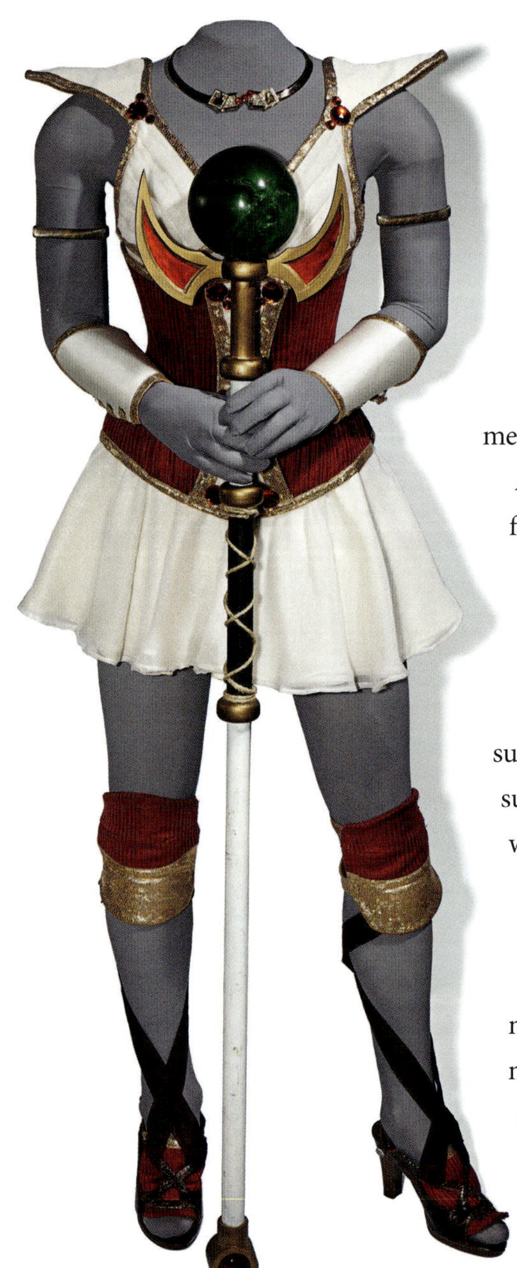

Felicia Day wore this costume in "(Do You Wanna Date My) Avatar," a music video promoting *The Guild* web series, directed by Joss Whedon. The comical song about gamer culture, written by Day and Whedon, featured the series' cast in the roles of their online alter egos. The video has reached over 27 million hits on YouTube since its 2009 release.

The Big Bang Theory centered on the nerdy adventures of two Caltech roommates, physicists Dr. Sheldon Cooper (Jim Parsons) and Dr. Leonard Hofstadter (Johnny Galecki), and their close friends, astrophysicist Dr. Raj Koothrappali (Kunal Nayyar) and engineer Howard Wolowitz (Simon Helberg). While navigating their professional and romantic lives, the four men bonded over visits to comic bookstores and conventions, playing video and board games, and immersing themselves in the worlds of science fiction and fantasy. In so doing, they found friendship and enjoyment in a world where they felt like outsiders due to their differences.

Attractive non-geek neighbor Penny (Kaley Cuoco) served as a foil for the eccentricities of the brilliant yet awkward group. With a conventional background and more common interests, Penny could be wryly judgmental of her friends' anxieties and awkwardness, as well as dismissive of their passions and convictions. As their friendship strengthened, Penny provided emotional support and street sense to her neighbors, while allowing her exposure to their intellect, curiosity, and sincerity to expand her own worldview. In so doing, Penny learned to challenge herself, and evolved from being a waitress and B-movie actress to becoming a pharmaceutical rep, eventually marrying the devoted Leonard.

Gender dynamics were further explored with the addition of neuroscientist Dr. Amy Farrah Fowler (Mayim Bialik) and Dr. Bernadette Rostenkowski (Mellissa Rauch), a microbiologist/pharmaceutical researcher. The two, who would go on to marry Sheldon and Howard, respectively, were critically lauded for their positive representation of women in STEM careers while also contributing to the show's comedy with their own complex and peculiar personalities.

In her innovative online comedy series, *The Guild,* Felica Day portrayed Cyd Sherman, a woman totally obsessed with her geeky passion: a massive multiplayer online fantasy role playing game known simply as *The Game.* Timid and isolated in real life, Sherman spent most of her free time playing online as her Avatar "Codex," a High Priestess and member of a guild of adventurers known as "The Knights of Good." Other members of the Knights included the warrior "Vork" / real name Herman Holden (Jeff Lewis), the rogue "Bladezz" / Simon Kemplar (Vincent Caso), ranger "TinkerBall" / April Lou (Amy Oduka), the Frost Mage "Clara" / Clara Beane (Robin Thornson), and "Zaboo" / Sujan Balakrishnan Goldberg

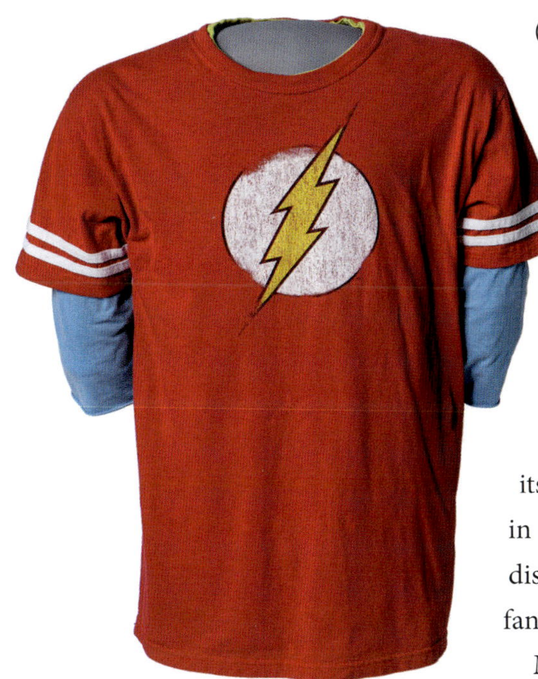

On *The Big Bang Theory*, Jim Parsons's character Dr. Sheldon Cooper wore T-shirts indicating his favorite fandoms, in this case, that of the DC Comics superhero the Flash. Cooper, a brilliant yet socially challenged (and challenging) scientist, was the series' breakout character, his popularity helping make Parsons TV's highest paid actor.

(Sandeep Parikh), a Warlock. Eccentric and often challenged by normal human interactions, the other players, like Sherman, are happier in the game than they are having normal human experiences.

The series begins with a succession of crises that force the Guild to meet in person for the first time. The show then explores the misfit groups adventures as they interject themselves increasingly in one another's lives both on and offline.

Informed by Day's own experiences, *The Guild* was venerated by members of the online gaming community, who praised its heart and authenticity. Providing a powerful voice for women in an often-misogynist community where women commonly face disparagement and abuse from men, the comedian's web series met fans where they were, on their computers.

Modern spins on the "found family" situation comedy, *The Big Bang Theory* and *The Guild* used humor and affection to celebrate diverse groups of outsiders that found meaning and friendship through their shared love of popular culture. As society seems to become more detached and divisive, they perhaps show how engagement with our own fandoms might help us find empathy and accord.

Eric Jentsch

COMEDY AT THE DAWN OF THE DIGITAL ERA

Created by reality TV pioneer Vin Di Bona, *America's Funniest Home Videos* originally aired as a one-hour TV special in the winter of 1989, hosted by comedian Bob Saget and based on a popular Japanese home movie clip show called *Fun TV with Kato-chan and Ken-chan*. The special was a surprise ratings smash, and *AFV*, as it has come to be colloquially known, has ascended to become one of the longest-running series in American television history, spanning more than six hundred episodes—and counting—with a roster of comedian hosts that includes Saget, Tom Bergeron, and Alfonso Ribeiro.

AFV's simple format involves short-form amateur home movie footage captured by everyday Americans competing to win a cash grand prize and the title of "America's Funniest Home Video" as determined by a vote of viewers. Primarily showcasing pet tricks, botched weddings, accident-prone kids, and family pranksters, the series emerged as a cultural phenomenon at the same time as affordable consumer recording technologies like the camcorder and VCR entered the marketplace on a mass scale, and while those appearing in the sort of accidental mishaps that characterize *AFV* clips aren't properly comedians themselves, the format did prove the mettle of the short-form comedy clip as a mainstay of turn-of-the-century American entertainment culture.

By the turn of the twentieth century, the internet had dramatically sped up the churn of content creation and further democratized access to media technologies, with novel formats like memes, tweets, and TikToks allowing anyone to easily manipulate and publish words, images, sounds, and videos. An explosion of shareables—from dancing hamsters to rapping bananas—heralded the arrival of a global community of comedy creators and consumers. The 2005 launch of YouTube catalyzed what may be the most significant creative renaissance in comedy history since the advent of recording technology. The low cost, wide reach, and editorial freedom afforded by the format of the viral video have challenged the authority of traditional cultural gatekeepers, equipped an entire generation of innovators with the once exceedingly rare affordances of total creative control, and prompted a global reevaluation of how—and for whom—comedy is made.

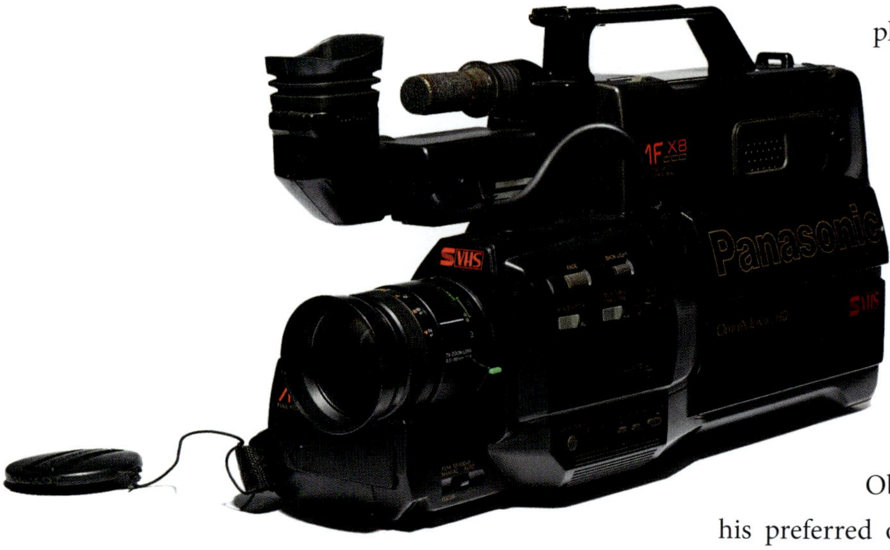

This camcorder was used to film *America's Funniest Videos'* very first winning video in November 1989.

YouTube's earliest adopters—like Andy Samberg, Bo Burnham, and Jenna Marbles—lured millions of fans to the platform and launched hugely successful comedy careers based on video plays, while amateur videos made unlikely, if fleeting, superstars of "Keyboard Cat" and "Sneezing Panda." Web series like *Bad Lip Reading* and *Between Two Ferns* emerged as cultural juggernauts (President Barack Obama deftly chose the latter as his preferred outlet for communicating with millennials about health care reform), while established TV programs, most notably the networks' late night rosters, adapted to the Internet's segmented presentation of video by uploading bite-size clips for viral viewing (see, for example, Jimmy Kimmel's viral monologue about President Trump's nonword "covfefe"). The platform has been a boon for comedians, offering a venue for trying out material and reaching new audiences, and, as with any new artistic tool, the constraints of the medium have promoted extraordinary innovation and entirely novel forms of expression and communication.

Meanwhile, having spent decades trading in user-generated comedy content long before the general public had access to webcams, smartphones, or internet connections, *AFV* has—against all odds—weathered the rise of internet culture. Even though similar content (including actual clips from *AFV*) is now freely discoverable online, millions of viewers continue to tune in faithfully, reveling in *AFV*'s unique curation of clips and the familiar rhythms that have made it a generational staple of American family viewing. The series now ties into a parallel YouTube channel of its own, as well as a portal for web submissions that funnels more than five thousand digital clip submissions per week.

Laura LaPlaca

CONCLUSION

LAURA LAPLACA

In 2018, shortly after the National Comedy Center opened its doors, I received a cold call from a neighbor of Tommy Smothers, whose voice carried the kind of urgent panicked tones that make you question whether you've stumbled into a prank. He explained that the comedian had grown weary of the dusty piles of memorabilia crowding his property and had started kidding that a phone call to 1-800-GOT-JUNK was in order. "Do you have room for this stuff?" he asked, almost breathlessly.

I hope you'll pause to contemplate the remarkable fact that there wasn't a national archive for comedy history before 2018. There was no place devoted to collecting the art form's material heritage or intervening before the proverbial junk trucks arrived. It's been my charge throughout the National Comedy Center's development and growth to champion the preservation of comedy's story and to advocate for the value of doing so. Why *do* we need to build a place for all this stuff? Because the story of comedy is inseparable from the story of freedom of expression; because comedy is a potent—perhaps the most potent—form of social commentary; because it has played a vital role in advancing progress throughout every major social movement in American history. It matters because comedy is a gateway to empathy and connection. And it matters because it helps us navigate the dislocations, injustices, and tragedies we all encounter on both global and personal scales.

It was humbling, and sort of humiliating, to articulate these points to Tommy Smothers, who, along with his brother Dick, had been martyred for his art in a quite dramatic defense of the First Amendment, as you read about earlier in this volume. He was an American hero and a comedy legend. And he agreed with me when I explained that profound experiences could unfold when groups of students on field trips or multigenerational families or aspiring creatives visited our galleries and had the opportunity to stand in the presence of these objects—comedy's DNA, our shared cultural inheritance.

A few days later we were hauling a rickety ladder to the gaping mouth of a rusted-out trailer up on blocks. Tommy, at eighty-one, climbed inside and began transferring the collection into my arms, an expression that seemed to blend pride and bemusement crossing his face. The matching red suit jackets came first, followed by a cobweb-laden box of sheet music, and piles of revisions for every episode of *The Smothers Brothers Comedy Hour*, with censors' strikethroughs faded but still glaring in red. He pried a locked briefcase open with a screwdriver to reveal the complete court filings from their landmark lawsuit against CBS. Finally, he handed over his guitar, and a quick call to Dick ensured that his bass, long in storage, would also join the collection.

One year later, four thousand people turned out to greet the Smothers Brothers with a standing ovation as we celebrated the accessioning of their remarkable collection into comedy's national archive—exactly fifty years after they'd been fired for pushing the bounds of acceptability on network television.

The National Comedy Center is a place that *you* can visit. It exists both as a monument to the great minds and unique voices that have elevated comedy to an art and as a living, ever-expanding archive of American ingenuity, courage, and excellence. The artifacts we assemble are not idle; they have hard work to do: to make you laugh, yes, but also to make you think. You will be inspired, entertained, and at times simply in awe of the enormity of our comedic heritage—its breadth, depth, and the countless innovators who have advanced its impacts across generations. Until you can visit in person, I hope you take two things from this book: an incitement to further curiosity about comedy's past, and a certainty that the art form has a rich heritage worthy of our reverence.

RYAN LINTELMAN

Tim Robinson, if you're reading this, please answer my emails.

Since we started working on this book, I've been trying to get in touch with the sketch comedian best known for his Netflix streaming series *I Think You Should Leave*, which premiered in 2019. The surreal and outrageous sketch series has captured the current zeitgeist like nothing else. It's a prime example of "cringe comedy," a successor to *Curb Your Enthusiasm*, *The Office*, *Nathan for You*, and other examples of humor based on transgression of social rules and norms that gets viewers' skin crawling with secondhand embarrassment as they watch the awkward situation play out on screen.

I Think You Should Leave is filled with short sketches in which a seemingly normal character—usually played by Robinson himself—steps over the boundary of acceptable behavior in a social situation, realizes what they've done, and then doubles down on their transgression in the most absurd way possible. These vignettes are addictively quotable, make for easy TikToks and YouTube clips, and lend themselves to memeification, making Robinson one of the most visible faces in this particular form of folk comedy on social media in recent years.

You may have seen these memes. Among the most popular are a bit from season 2, episode 3 where Robinson incredulously asks, "Are you sure about that?" and, my favorite, a bit from season 1, episode 5, where Robinson appears in a hot dog costume. In the sketch, customers at a clothing store are surprised when a car decorated like a hot dog crashes through the storefront. In the confusion, with customers struggling to make sense of the scene, Robinson, dressed in a novelty hot dog costume, attempts to blend in with the crowd, stridently arguing that "we're all trying to find the guy who did this."

I've been emailing Robinson because I think his hot dog suit belongs at the Smithsonian. Specifically, I want him to donate it to the entertainment collection at the National Museum of American History, where it would be preserved for future generations alongside George Washington's military uniform, Abraham Lincoln's stovepipe hat, and the original Star Spangled Banner, the flag that inspired the national anthem. You'd think he'd return my call.

Since he hasn't, I've been collecting memes. I use social media to keep up on the news, to learn what people are saying about current events, and to find things that make me laugh. As we've discussed throughout this book, comedy evolves to fill its cultural and sociological niche, and social media is just the latest medium in which it continues to serve its purposes. In his essay on "Traumedy," Jim Deutsch wrote about the use of folk humor like memes to help Americans cope in times of crisis. It's a version of a talk he gave as part of a Smithsonian colloquium series during the COVID-19 pandemic, and he used modern social media memes to connect to earlier moments of shared crisis and trauma. These past few years have seen plenty of both.

Robinson's hot dog costume meme has proven a remarkably robust and eminently applicable bit of folk humor these past few years. The basic joke, that an obviously guilty person resolutely proclaims their innocence despite overwhelming evidence to the contrary, comically illustrates hypocrisy, narcissism, irresponsibility, denial, cynicism, and contempt for one's fellow humans. I don't think I'm the only one who's noticed a bit more of all of these in the public sphere in recent years. In fact, I know it. I've got the receipts. I've got the memes.

In June 2020, amid national protests following the Minneapolis Police Department's killing of George Floyd, the National Football League (NFL) Twitter account posted a video featuring commissioner Roger Goodell stating that the league condemned the systemic oppression of Black people and supported Black Lives Matter. Journalist Dave Itzkoff, alluding to the NFL's mixed record on racial equality, reshared the post on Twitter and suggested that Goodell "should've just put on a hot dog costume and said, 'we're all trying to find the guy who did this.'"

By December 2020, this meme was being widely used on social media to call out corporate hypocrisy. When ExxonMobil's official Twitter account posted that the oil and gas corporation was "working collaboratively toward solutions to mitigate the risks of climate change," Minnesota Representative Ilhan Omar retweeted with an image of the meme. ExxonMobil concerned about climate change after incidents like the *Exxon Valdez* oil spill and funding of climate change denial lobbying? "We're all trying to find the guy who did this!"

The meme was perfectly suited for the political chaos following President Donald J. Trump's attempt to overturn the results of the 2020 presidential election and the resulting attack on the U.S. Capitol on January 6, 2021. Any politician who had explicitly or tacitly endorsed the effort to reject the election results and then used social media to express shock at the events of January 6 could expect at least one commentor to post the *I Think You Should Leave* meme. Journalist Timothy Burke even tweeted a photoshopped image of Missouri Senator Josh Hawley, who was photographed saluting the crowd mere hours before they overran the Capitol, wearing the hot dog suit in a congressional hearing investigating the violent attack, with closed caption reading "WE'RE ALL TRYING TO FIND THE GUY WHO DID THIS."

In February 2021, *Washington Post* politics reporter Dave Weigel suggested in a tweet that "We're All Trying to Find the Guy That Did This" might be a good title for a history of the past five years. Culture reporters for *Slate*, the *New Yorker*, and the *New York Times Magazine* have written about the hot dog guy meme and its encapsulation of our times.[1]

What better endorsements could you ask for to prove comedy's continuing relevance to our conversations about political and social change?

At the National Museum of American History, we collect comedy to document the nation's history and explore what it means to be an American. As curator of the museum's entertainment collection, I sometimes have a hard time convincing my colleagues that a comedy prop (a novelty hot dog costume, for example) holds the same weight as those other national treasures we care for. As the stories in this book prove, however, comedy in all its forms has been vitally important to the historical developments, political debates, social changes, and cultural conversations that have shaped this nation over the past two hundred fifty years. Comedy is the hammer that breaks down our biases, preconceived notions, and blind spots, opening our eyes to other perspectives, diverse experiences, and new ways of thinking. Its practitioners—the writers, actors, storytellers, artists, stand-up comics, basketball barnstormers, singers, and meme creators—have fundamentally shaped the nation's history.

So, I guess if you don't like where we are at this point in our history, take it up with them.

We're all trying to find the guy who did this.

ACKNOWLEDGMENTS

RYAN LINTELMAN

This book overcame some serious challenges on the way to publication, with the COVID-19 pandemic making the road even rockier than usual, and I'm truly grateful for the contributions, assistance, and support provided by so many friends and colleagues over the past few years. In particular, I'd like to thank Carolyn Gleason and Veronica La Du for their early support and help developing the project; Jill Corcoran, Paige Towler, and Kealy Gordon for their stewardship through the pandemic; Janet Rockenbaugh for her enthusiastic and essential assistance with collections management; Jaclyn Nash for her always-beautiful photography; Trina Brown and the NMAH library staff for their help pulling every comedy book across the institution; Kay Peterson, Franklin Robinson, and the Archives Center staff for their patience and help pulling from the incredible collections they oversee; Janice Ellis, Sunae Park Evans, Tamsin McDonagh, Meredith Sweeney, and Dawn Wallace for making sure that these objects all look their best; and each of the essay contributors from across the Smithsonian who made this such a unique and fascinating project. Finally, my deepest thanks and love to my wife Connie, who was indispensable as a brainstormer, editor, supporter, and even graphic designer throughout the process. I couldn't have done it without you.

LAURA LAPLACA

I would like to extend appreciation for the support of my colleagues, primarily including the National Comedy Center's incredibly hardworking and talented archives team helmed by collections manager Ashley Senske and archivists Olivia Ricker and Julie Livengood. Photographer Leslie Calimeri was an indispensable part of this project's success. All those at the National Comedy Center who contribute to the presentation, maintenance, and safety of our collections play a vital role in stewarding comedy history every day. I would like to especially acknowledge the constant collegiality, creative encouragement, and friendship of Malachi Livermore, Rochelle Molé, Gary Hahn, and Journey Gunderson. My greatest gratitude is reserved for the comedians, estates, collectors, and donors who have supported us in the founding of the National Comedy Center's archive—the first preservation and research center devoted solely to this great art form. Finally, to my family: Thank you for all the patient hours of comedy talk and writing time that have filled our days.

NOTES

INTRODUCTION

1. Bob Newhart, *I Shouldn't Even Be Doing This! And Other Things That Strike Me as Funny* (New York: Hyperion, 2006), 171.

CHAPTER 1. COMEDY SHAPES HOW WE SEE EACH OTHER

1. *Barney Miller*, season 3, episode 19, "Asylum," directed by Danny Arnold and Alex March, written by Roland Kibbee, Danny Arnold, Rony Sheehan, and Reinhold Weege, aired February 24, 1977, on ABC.
2. Francis Bicknell Carpenter, *Six Months at the White House* (Ann Arbor: University of Michigan Library, 2005), 48.
3. Mark Twain, *The Mark Twain Papers, Mark Twain's Letters*, vol. 3: *1869*, ed. Victor Fischer (Berkeley: University of California Press, 1992), 56.
4. John M. Harrison, *The Man Who Made Nasby: David Ross Locke* (Chapel Hill: University of North Carolina Press, 1969), 85.
5. Harrison, *Man Who Made Nasby*, 219.
6. Marcus Mills Pomeroy, *Reminiscences and Recollections of "Brick" Pomeroy* (Ann Arbor: University of Michigan Press, 1890), 60.
7. Harrison, *Man Who Made Nasby*, 77, 61.
8. David Ross Locke, *Divers Views, Opinions and Prophecies of Yoors Trooly, Petroleum V. Nasby* (Cincinnati: R. W. Carroll, 1867), 30.
9. Locke, *Divers Views*, 159.
10. Locke, *Divers Views*, 47.
11. Locke, *Divers Views*, 47.
12. David Ross Locke, *The Struggles (Social, Financial and Political) of Petroleum V Nasby* (Boston: I. N. Richardson, 1872), 117.
13. Locke, *Divers Views*, 50.
14. Locke, *Divers Views*, 32.
15. Locke, *Divers Views*, 31.
16. Locke, *Divers Views*, 336.
17. Mark Twain, *The Autobiography of Mark Twain*, vol. 1 (New York: Harper & Brothers, 1934), 147.
18. Preston Bailhache, quoted in Jeremy Prichard, "In Lincoln's Shadow: The Civil War in Springfield, Illinois" (PhD diss., University of Kansas, 2014); "Wide Awakes," *Los Angeles Daily News*, November 14, 1860.
19. Charles Godfrey Leland, *Abraham Lincoln and the Abolition of Slavery in the United States* (New York: G. P. Putnam's Sons, 1881); Elizabeth Robins Pennell, *Charles Godfrey Leland* (Boston: Houghton, Mifflin, 1906), 6.
20. Gary Scharnhorst, "'Ways That Are Dark': Appropriations of Bret Harte's 'Plain Language from Truthful James,'" *Nineteenth-Century Literature* 51, no. 3 (December 1996): 377.
21. Joy Lanzendorfer, "When Mark Twain Canceled Bret Harte," *Alta Journal*, January 4, 2022.
22. Axel Nissen, *Bret Harte: Prince and Pauper* (Jackson: University Press of Mississippi, 2000), 158.
23. S. F. Elliott, "Glimpses of Bret Harte," *Reader* 10, no. 2 (July 1907): 124, quoted in Scharnhorst, "'Ways That Are Dark,'" 377.
24. Robert W. Snyder, *The Voice of the City: Vaudeville and Popular Culture in New York*, rev. ed (Chicago: Ivan R. Dee, 2000), 99–100.
25. S. D. Trav, *No Applause—Just Throw Money; or, The Book That Made Vaudeville Famous* (New York: Faber and Faber, 2005), 112.
26. Trav, *No Applause*, 73.
27. LeRoy Ashby, *With Amusement for All: A History of American Popular Culture Since 1830* (Lexington: University Press of Kentucky, 2006), 120.
28. Trav, *No Applause*, 76.
29. Andrew L. Erdman, *Blue Vaudeville: Sex, Morals, and the Mass Marketing of Amusement, 1895–1915* (Jefferson, NC: McFarland, 2004), 2–5.
30. Trav, *No Applause*, 84.
31. Shawn Levy, *In on the Joke: The Original Queens of Stand-Up Comedy* (New York: Doubleday, 2002), 23.
32. Trav, *No Applause*, 87–88.
33. Snyder, *Voice of the City*, 43.
34. Frederick Douglass, "The Hutchinson Family—Hunkerism," *North Star* (Rochester, NY), October 27, 1848.
35. Michael Shane Breaux, "Just a Buncha Clowns: Comedic-Anarchy and Racialized Performance in Black Vaudeville, the Chop Suey Circuit, and *las Capras*" (PhD diss., City University of New York, 2019), 3.
36. W. Mosby, "Bill Dana's Senor Jiménez Plans a Season on TV," *Milwaukee Journal* 28 (April 1963).
37. Raúl Pérez, "Brownface Minstrelsy: 'José Jiménez,' the Civil Rights

Movement, and the Legacy of Racist Comedy," *Ethnicities* 16, no. 1 (2016): 41.

38. Bill Dana (comedian and writer), interview by Jenni Matz, part 1 of two-part interview for the American Comedy Archives at Emerson College, February 21, 2005, Cutler Majestic Theatre, Emerson College, Boston, video, Television Academy Foundation, The Interviews: An Oral History of Television, "Bill Dana with Emerson College," https://televisionacademy.com.
39. Bill Dana (comedian and writer), interview by Jenni Matz, part 2 of two-part interview for the American Comedy Archives at Emerson College, June 3, 2005, Los Angeles, video, Television Academy Foundation, The Interviews: An Oral History of Television, "Bill Dana with Emerson College," https://televisionacademy.com.
40. Bart Andrews and Ahrgus Julliard, *Holy Mackerel! The* Amos 'n' Andy *Story* (New York: E. P. Dutton, 1986), xvi.
41. Melvin Patrick Ely, *The Adventures of Amos 'n' Andy: A Social History of an American Phenomenon* (New York: Free Press, 1991), 5.
42. Mel Watkins, *On the Real Side: A History of African American Comedy from Slavery to Chris Rock* (Chicago: Lawrence Hill Books, 1994), 271.
43. Ely, *Adventures of Amos 'n' Andy*, 30–33.
44. Ely, *Adventures of Amos 'n' Andy*, 128.
45. Ely, *Adventures of Amos 'n' Andy*, 146.
46. William Barlow, *Voice Over: The Making of Black Radio* (Philadelphia: Temple University Press, 1999), 41–46.
47. Ely, *Adventures of Amos 'n' Andy*, 7.
48. Ely, *Adventures of Amos 'n' Andy*, 215–216.
49. Richard Severo and Peter Keepnews, "Phyllis Diller, Sassy Comedian, Dies at 95," *New York Times*, August 20, 2012.
50. Michael Kantor, interview with Phyllis Diller, *Make 'Em Laugh: The Funny Business of America*, directed by Michael Kantor, aired in 2009 on PBS.
51. Kathryn Kein, "Domestic Failure, Comic Pleasure: Phyllis Diller and the Feminist Potential of Failure, 1955–1969," *Studies in American Humor* 4, no. 1 (2018): 75–96, 79.
52. Bob Thomas, "The Story of Comedian Phyllis Diller's Life Is No Laughing Matter," Associated Press, April 10, 2005.
53. Marc Weingarten, "The Return of the Sit-Down Comedian," *New York Times*, March 30, 2003.
54. "Vaughn Meader, Satirist of Kennedy Family, Dies," Washington Post, November 1, 2004.
55. E. Alex Jung, "In Conversation: Whoopi Goldberg," *Vulture*, October 30, 2020.
56. Mel Gussow, "Whoopi Goldberg Does the Spook Show," *New York Times*, February 3, 1984.
57. Jerry Seinfeld in Marshall Fine, *Robert Klein Still Can't Stop His Leg*, directed by Marshall Fine, 2016.
58. Robert Klein, interview by Terry Gross, *Fresh Air*, National Public Radio, March 8, 1985.
59. L. H. Stallings, *Mutha' Is Half a Word: Intersections of Folklore, Vernacular, Myth, and Queerness in Black Female Culture* (Columbus: Ohio State University Press, 2007).
60. Reprinted with permission from Kenneth Cohen and John W. Troutman, *Entertainment Nation: How Music, Television, Film, Sports, and Theater Shaped the United States* (Washington, DC: Smithsonian Books, 2022).
61. Zoë Heller, "Don't Call Me Sir: Don Rickles and the Art of the Insult," *New Yorker*, August 2, 2004.
62. Raúl Pérez, "Rhetoric of Racial Ridicule in an Era of Racial Protest: Don Rickles, the 'Equal Opportunity Offender' Strategy, and the Civil Rights Movement," in *Standing Up, Speaking Out: Stand-Up Comedy and the Rhetoric of Social Change*, ed. Matthew R. Meier and Casey R. Schmitt (New York: Routledge, 2017), 71–91.
63. Peter Bradshaw, "9 to 5 Review—Dolly Parton's Quietly Radical Office Revenge Satire," *The Guardian*, November 15, 2018, https://www.theguardian.com/film/2018/nov/15/9-to-5-review-dolly-parton.
64. Deborah H. Holdstein, "*Tootsie*: Mixed Messages," *Jump Cut: A Review of Contemporary Media*, no. 28 (April 1983), https://www.ejumpcut.org/archive/onlinessays/JC28folder/Tootsie.html.
65. Richard Saul Wurman, *Hawai'i Access: A Complete Guide to the Islands* (Los Angeles: Access Press, 1982).
66. Darrell H. Y. Lum, "On Pidgin and Children in Literature," in *Infant Tongues: The Voice of the Child in Literature*, ed. Elizabeth Goodenough, Mark A. Heberle, and Naomi Sokoloff (Detroit: Wayne State University Press, 1994), 299, 301. See also Roderick N. Labrador, "'We Can Laugh at Ourselves': Hawai'i Ethnic Humor, Local Identity, and the Myth of Multiculturalism," *Pragmatics* 14, no. 2/3 (2004): 291–316.
67. Labrador, "'We Can Laugh at Ourselves,'" 299.
68. "Packed House for Bumatai," *Ke Alaka'i* [Brigham Young University, Hawai'i campus] 25, no. 12 (November 16, 1979): 2, 13.
69. Wurman, *Hawai'i Access*, 64.
70. Jerry Hopkins et al., *The Hawaiian Book of Lists; or, Fax to Da Max* (Honolulu: Bess Press, 1985), 104.
71. Frederic M. Biddle, "Ellen's Coming Out: The Inside Story," *Boston Globe*, April 23, 1997.
72. Malinda Lo, "Back in the Day: Coming Out with Ellen," *AfterEllen*, April 9, 2005, https://afterellen.com/back-in-the-day-coming-out-with-ellen/.
73. Susan J. Hubert, "What's Wrong with This Picture? The Politics of Ellen's Coming Out Party," *Journal of Popular Culture* 33, no. 2 (Fall 1999): 31.
74. Cory L. Armstrong, Jue Hou, and Kylie McLeod, "Is Ellen DeGeneres a

'DeGenerate?': How TV's First Out Lesbian Connects to Public Support for Same-Sex Marriage," *Electronic News* 14, no. 1 (2020).

75. Andrew Holleran, "The Alpha Queen," *Harvard Gay & Lesbian Review* 7, no. 3 (Summer 2000): 65.

76. Dennis Provencher, "Sealed with a Kiss: Heteronormative Strategies in NBC's *Will & Grace*," in *The Sitcom Reader, Second Edition: America Re-Viewed, Still Skewed*, ed. Mary M. Dalton and Laura R. Linder (New York: State University of New York Press, 2016), 96.

77. Howard Rosenberg, "Ready, Aim, Click!," *Los Angeles Times*, September 21, 1998.

78. Joe Reid, "The Burden of Sole Representation Led Many Viewers to Be Too Hard on *Will & Grace*," *AV Club*, November 6, 2013, https://www.avclub.com/the-burden-of-sole-representation-led-many-viewers-to-b-1798241729.

79. Edward Schiappa, Peter B. Gregg, and Dean E. Hewes, "Can One TV Show Make a Difference? *Will & Grace* and the Parasocial Contact Hypothesis," *Journal of Homosexuality* 51, no. 4 (2006): 15–37.

80. Seth Abramovitch, "Joe Biden Cites 'Will & Grace' in Endorsement of Same-Sex Marriage," *Hollywood Reporter*, May 6, 2012, https://www.hollywoodreporter.com/tv/tv-news/joe-biden-cites-will-grace-320724-0-320724/.

81. Sarah Ahern, "Ellen DeGeneres Gets Emotional Receiving Presidential Medal of Freedom," *Variety*, November 22, 2016, https://variety.com/2016/biz/awards/ellen-degeneres-presidential-medal-of-freedom-barack-obama-1201925308/.

CHAPTER 2. COMEDY CREATES AMERICAN IDENTITY

1. "To George Washington from Thomas Wignell, 22 May 1790," in *The Papers of George Washington, Presidential Series*, vol. 5: *16 January 1790–30 June 1790*, ed. Dorothy Twohig, Mark A. Mastromarino, and Jack D. Warren (Charlottesville: University of Virginia Press, 1996), 416–417.

2. Prudence Doherty, "George Washington's Bold, Clear Signature," *Silver Special Collections Blog*, University of Vermont, February 17, 2020, https://blog.uvm.edu/uvmsc-specialcollections/?p=689.

3. Judith Yaross, "Stand-Up Comedy, Social Change, and (American) Culture," in *Standing Up, Speaking Out: Stand-Up Comedy and the Rhetoric of Social Change*, ed. Matthew R. Meier and Casey R. Schmitt (New York: Routledge, 2017), xvii.

4. Will Rogers, "Our Candidate Won't Sling Mud," *Life*, October 12, 1928.

5. Cheryle Blythe and Susan Sackett, *Say Goodnight, Gracie! The Story of George Burns and Gracie Allen* (New York: Dutton, 1986), 78.

6. Ron Powers, *Mark Twain: A Life* (New York: Free Press, 2005), 6.

7. Everett Emerson, *Mark Twain: A Literary Life* (Philadelphia: University of Pennsylvania Press, 1999), 18.

8. Harry L. Katz, *Mark Twain's America: A Celebration in Words and Images* (New York: Little, Brown, 2014), 39.

9. Ernest Hemingway, *Green Hills of Africa* (New York: Charles Scribner's Sons, 1935), 22.

10. Ben Yagoda, *Will Rogers: A Biography* (New York: HarperCollins, 1994), xiii.

11. Ray Robinson, *American Original: A Life of Will Rogers* (New York: Oxford University Press, 1996), 56.

12. Yagoda, *Will Rogers*, 92–94.

13. Robinson, *American Original*, 80.

14. Yagoda, *Will Rogers*, 124.

15. Richard D. White Jr., *Will Rogers: A Political Life* (Lubbock: Texas Tech University Press, 2011), 13–15.

16. Yagoda, *Will Rogers*, 148.

17. White, *Will Rogers*, 31–32.

18. Yagoda, *Will Rogers*, 250.

19. Robinson, *American Original*, 138.

20. Amy M. Ware, *The Cherokee Kid: Will Rogers: Tribal Identity, and the Making of an American Icon* (Lawrence: University Press of Kansas, 2015), 183.

21. LeRoy Ashby, *With Amusement for All: A History of American Popular Culture Since 1830* (Lexington: University Press of Kentucky, 2006), 233.

22. White, *Will Rogers*, 79.

23. Camille F. Forbes, *Introducing Bert Williams: Burnt Cork, Broadway, and the Story of America's First Black Star* (New York: Basic Civitas, 2008), 69.

24. Forbes, *Introducing Bert Williams*, 34–35.

25. Yuval Taylor, *Darkest America: Black Minstrelsy from Slavery to Hip-Hop* (New York: Norton, 2012), 119.

26. David Hajdu and John Carey, *A Revolution in Three Acts: The Radical Vaudeville of Bert Williams, Eva Tanguay, and Julian Eltinge* (New York: Columbia University Press, 2021), 37–38.

27. Ron Magliozzi, "Bert Williams and Black Performance Culture," in *Regeneration: Black Cinema, 1898–1971*, ed. Doris Berger and Rhea L. Combs (New York: Delmonico Books, 2022), 93–95.

28. W. E. B. (William Edward Burghardt) Du Bois, "Bert Williams, ca. 1922" [draft of a eulogy], W. E. B. Du Bois Papers (MS 312), Special Collections and University Archives, University of Massachusetts Amherst Libraries.

29. Bill Keveney, "Carol Burnett Is So Glad to Have Time Together for 50th Anniversary Special," *USA Today*, November 30, 2017.

30. Linda Mizejewski, *Hysterical! Women in American Comedy* (Austin: University of Texas Press, 2017), 180.

31. Paul A. Cantor, "The Talented Mr. Dukenfield: W. C. Fields and the

American Dream," in *Pop Culture and the Dark Side of the American Dream* (Lexington: University Press of Kentucky, 2019), 33.

32. Cantor, "Talented Mr. Dukenfield," 38.

33. W. C. Fields, *Fields for President* (New York: Dodd, Mead, 1940), 8.

34. Robert Lewis Taylor, *W. C. Fields: His Follies and Fortune* (Garden City, NY: Doubleday, 1949), 275.

35. Simon Louvish, *Man on the Flying Trapeze: The Life and Times of W. C. Fields* (New York: Norton, 1997), 343–345.

36. Arthur Knight, "Introduction," in *The Films of W. C. Fields*, ed. Donald Deschner (New York: Cadillac, 1966).

37. Peter Ackroyd, *Charlie Chaplin: A Brief Life* (New York: Doubleday, 2014), 18–19.

38. Jeffrey Vance, *Chaplin: Genius of the Cinema* (London: Harry N. Abrams, 2003), 36.

39. Nicholas Sammond, *Birth of an Industry: Blackface Minstrelsy and the Rise of American Animation* (Durham, NC: Duke University Press, 2015), 70–71.

40. Peter Marks, "Television: The Brief, Brilliant Run of Nichols and May," *New York Times*, May 19, 1996.

41. *Billboard*, February 14, 1925, 52.

42. *Phonograph Monthly Review*, January 1931, 136.

43. Frank Nugent, "Laurel and Hardy and Their Twins Play Slapstick with 'Our Relations,' Now at the Rialto," *New York Times*, November 11, 1936.

44. Shawn Levy, *In on the Joke: The Original Queens of Standup Comedy* (New York: Doubleday, 2022), 99.

45. David Von Drehle, "Minnie Pearl, Opry's Jewel: The Comic Sparkle in Country Music," *Washington Post*, March 5, 1996, https://www.washingtonpost.com/archive/lifestyle/1996/03/05/minnie-pearl-oprys-jewel-the-comic-sparkle-in-country-music/19b0a225-4d10-4427-b317-184cd9c79e24/.

46. Maureen Mauk, "Politics Is Everybody's Business: Resurrecting Faye Emerson, America's Forgotten First Lady of Television," *Journal of Cinema and Media Studies* 59, no. 4 (2020): 129–152.

47. Yael Kohen, *We Killed: The Rise of Women in American Comedy* (New York: Picador, 2013), 153.

48. Richard Stengel, "Jay Leno Midnight's Mayor," *Time*, March 16, 1992.

49. Jack Gould, "Diahann Carroll Seen in N.B.C.'s Julia," *New York Times*, September 18, 1968.

50. Mary Beltran, *Latino TV: A History* (New York: New York University Press, 2021); Aniko Bodroghkozy, *Groove Tube: Sixties Television and the Youth Rebellion* (Durham, NC: Duke University Press, 2001).

51. "One Hombre's Family," *Minneapolis Tribune*, June 6–12, 1976, 5.

52. Wesley Hyatt, *Short-Lived Television Series, 1948–1978* (Jefferson, NC: McFarland, 2003), 249.

53. Yeidy M. Rivero, "Interpreting Cubanness, Americanness, and the Sitcom," in *Global Television Formats: Understanding Television Across Borders*, ed. Sharon Shahaf and Tasha Oren (New York: Routledge, 2011), 90–96.

54. "Dan Sorkin, Bob Newhart: Unbuttoned," American Masters Digital Archive (WNET), March 14, 2005, https://www.pbs.org/wnet/americanmasters/archive/interview/dan-sorkin/.

55. Bob Newhart, *I Shouldn't Even Be Doing This! And Other Things That Strike Me as Funny* (New York: Hyperion, 2006), 3.

56. Newhart, *I Shouldn't Even Be Doing This!*, 55–57.

57. Courtney J. Ruffner, "Cultural Stereotyping in *Happy Days* and *The Sopranos*," in *Teaching Italian American Literature, Film, and Popular Culture*, ed. Edvige Giunta and Kathleen Zamboni McKormick (New York: Modern Language Association of America, 2010), 233.

58. Lorne Michaels, quoted in William K. Knoedelseder Jr., "*Saturday Night Live*: From Riches to Rags?," *Los Angeles Times*, November 18, 1979.

59. Alicia Gaspar Alba, ed., *Velvet Barrios: Popular Culture and Chicana/o Sexualities*, New Directions in Latino American Cultures (New York: Palgrave Macmillan, 2003), 332.

60. Christine List, "Self-Directed Stereotyping in the Films of Cheech Marín," in *Chicanos and Film: Essays on Chicano Representation and Resistance*, ed. Chon A. Noriega (New York: Garland, 1992), 205–215.

61. Brian J. Jones, *Jim Henson: The Biography* (New York: Ballantine Books, 2013), 20–34.

62. Jones, *Jim Henson*, 41–51.

63. Michael Davis, *Street Gang: The Complete History of Sesame Street* (New York: Viking, 2008), 85.

64. Christopher Finch, *Jim Henson: The Works—The Art, the Magic, the Imagination* (New York: Random House, 1993), 22.

65. Robert W. Morrow, *Sesame Street and the Reform of Children's Television* (Baltimore: Johns Hopkins University Press, 2006), 98.

66. Christopher Finch, *Of Muppets and Men: The Making of the Muppet Show* (New York: Knopf, 1981), 27.

67. Dara Lind, "Miss Piggy Explains Why She's the Perfect Feminist Icon for 2015," *Vox*, June 4, 2015, https://www.vox.com/2015/6/4/8730099/miss-piggy-feminism.

68. Jordan Schildcrout, "The Performance of Nonconformity on the Muppet Show—Or, How Kermit Made Me Queer," *Journal of Popular Culture* 41, no. 5 (2008): 823–835, https://doi.org/10.1111/j.1540-5931.2008.00551.x.

69. Jones, *Jim Henson*, 297.

70. Michelle Ann Abate, "Taking Silliness Seriously: Jim Henson's *The Muppet Show*, the Anglo-American

Tradition of Nonsense, and Cultural Critique," *Journal of Popular Culture* 42, no. 4 (2009): 590.
71. John J. O'Connor, "Veiling Black Rage in Broad Humor on TV," *New York Times*, January 31, 1991.
72. John J. O'Connor, "Bringing a Black Sensibility to Comedy in a Series," *New York Times*, May 29, 1990.
73. *Seinfeld*, season 5, episode 2, "The Puffy Shirt," directed by Tom Cherones, written by Larry David, aired September 23, 1993, on NBC.
74. Jennifer Keishin Armstrong, *Seinfeldia: How a Show About Nothing Changed Everything* (New York: Simon & Schuster, 2016), 61.
75. Armstrong, *Seinfeldia*, 31.
76. Armstrong, *Seinfeldia*, 60.
77. *Seinfeld*, season 4, episode 11, "The Contest," directed by Tom Cherones, written by Larry David, aired November 18, 1992, on NBC.
78. *Seinfeld*, season 5, episode 10, "The Cigar Store Indian," directed by Tom Cherones, written by Tom Gammill and Max Pross, aired December 9, 1993, on NBC.
79. *Seinfeld*, season 4, episode 17, "The Outing," directed by Tom Cherones, written by Larry Charles, aired February 11, 1993, on NBC.
80. *Seinfeld*, season 9, episodes 23/24, "The Finale," directed by Andy Ackerman, written by Larry David, aired May 14, 1998, on NBC.
81. *Seinfeld*, season 6, episode 22, "The Face Painter," directed by Andy Ackerman, written by Larry David, aired May 11, 1995, on NBC.

CHAPTER 3. COMEDY PROVOKES CONVERSATIONS

1. Land, "Review: *I'm No Angel*," *Variety*, October 17, 1933.
2. Jill Watts, *Mae West: An Icon in Black and White* (New York: Oxford University Press, 2001), 52–54, 68–69, 82.
3. Mae West, *Goodness Had Nothing to Do with It* (New York: Prentice Hall, 1959), 72.
4. Simon Louvish, *Mae West: It Ain't No Sin* (New York: Thomas Dunne Books, 2005), 121–123; Watts, *Mae West*, 89.
5. Maybeth Hamilton, *"When I'm Bad, I'm Better": Mae West, Sex, and American Entertainment* (Berkeley: University of California Press, 1997), 104–120.
6. Louvish, *Mae West*, 213–214.
7. Louvish, *Mae West*, 301, 247.
8. Ramona Curry, *Too Much of a Good Thing: Mae West as Cultural Icon* (Minneapolis: University of Minnesota Press, 1996), xiii–xxii.
9. Gerald Nachman, *Seriously Funny: The Rebel Comedians of the 1950s and 1960s* (New York: Pantheon, 2003), 391.
10. Rusty Warren Collection, National Comedy Center Archives, "Press Information," Marvin Drager Inc., n.d., 3.
11. "Press Information," 3.
12. Shawn Levy, *In on the Joke* (New York: Doubleday, 2022), 147.
13. Rusty Warren Collection, National Comedy Center Archives, "Rusty Warren Earns Comedy Award" (press release), Morrey Brodsky, n.d.
14. Dick Kleiner, "Singer Rusty Warren Has No Fear About Making Big Time," *Evening News* (Beacon, NY), September 1, 1961.
15. "Rusty Warren Biography," Richard Gersh Associates Inc., November 6, 1974, 2.
16. Bambi Haggins, *Hysterical! Women in American Comedy* (Austin: University of Texas Press, 2017), 4.
17. *Whoopi Goldberg Presents Moms Mabley*, directed by Whoopi Goldberg, aired in 2013 on HBO.
18. Jess Oppenheimer, "I Love Lucy" original concept and receipt for registration of original concept for television series, 1951, Jess Oppenheimer Collection, Motion Picture, Broadcasting, and Recorded Sound Division, Library of Congress (026.01.00a) (digital ID lucy0026_01). Courtesy of Gregg Oppenheimer.
19. Jack Sher and Madeline Sher, "The Cuban and the Redhead," *American Magazine* 154 (September 1952): 100.
20. Louis A. Pérez Jr., *On Becoming Cuban: Identity, Nationality and Culture* (Chapel Hill: University of North Carolina Press, 1999).
21. Christopher Chávez, *Reinventing the Latino Television Viewer: Language, Ideology, and Practice* (Lanham: Lexington Books, 2015), 80.
22. Firmat, *Life on the Hyphen*, 43.
23. Firmat, *Life on the Hyphen*, 26.
24. David Bianculli, *Dangerously Funny: The Uncensored Story of the Smothers Brothers Comedy Hour* (New York: Touchstone, 2009), xvi.
25. Joan Barthel, "Hilarious, Brash, Flat, Peppery, Repetitious, Topical and in Borderline Taste," *New York Times Magazine*, October 1968, 33.
26. Leticia Kent, "They'll Leave You Laughing—and Thinking," *New York Times*, March 11, 1973, D17.
27. *Saturday Night Live*, season 1, episode 7, "Word Association," directed by Dave Wilson, written by Paul Mooney, featuring Richard Pryor and Chevy Chase, aired December 13, 1975, on NBC.
28. Richard Pryor and Todd Gold, *Pryor Convictions and Other Life Sentences* (New York: Pantheon Books, 1995), 94.
29. Pryor and Gold, *Pryor Convictions*, 116.
30. "Indian Museum Finds a Home on the National Mall," *Indianz.com*, September 13, 2004, https://www.indianz.com/News/2004/004185.asp.
31. Megan Minoka Hill and Norbert Hill Jr., "Norbert Seabrook Hill Sr.," in *A Nation within a Nation: Voices of the Oneidas in Wisconsin*, ed. L. Gordon McLester III and Laurence M. Hauptman (Madison: Wisconsin Historical Society Press, 2010), 224.
32. Kliph Nesteroff, *We Had a Little Real Estate Problem: The Unheralded Story of Native Americans in Comedy* (New York: Simon & Schuster, 2021), 90.

33. Nesteroff, *We Had a Little Real Estate Problem*, 142.
34. *The Richard Pryor Show*, season 1, episode 4, "Charlie Hill," directed by John Moffitt, written by David Banks, Jeffrey Barron, and Booker Bradshaw, aired October 20, 1977, on NBC.
35. Nesteroff, *We Had a Little Real Estate Problem*, 157.
36. *Goin' Native, No Reservations Needed: The American Indian Comedy Slam*, directed by Scott L. Montoya, Laugh Out Loud Comedy, 2010.
37. "Marc Maron Burns Money with Kinison," *Tiger Belly Podcast*, episode 336, YouTube, February 24, 2022, https://youtu.be/WKO-xNidWkI.
38. Tracy Greer, "Entertainment Industry Mourns Loss of Groundbreaking Native American Comedian," *KJZZ*, January 30, 2014, https://kjzz.org/content/9395/entertainment-industry-mourns-loss-groundbreaking-native-american-comedian.
39. Jim Colucci, *All in the Family: The Show That Changed Television* (New York: Universe, 2021), 22.
40. Gerard Jones, "Norman Lear Sitcoms and the 1970s," in *The Sitcom Reader, Second Edition: America Re-Viewed, Still Skewed*, ed. Mary M. Dalton and Laura R. Linder (New York: State University of New York Press, 2016), 45.
41. *All in the Family*, season 4, episode 8, "The Games Bunkers Play," directed by John Rich and Bob LaHendro, written by Susan Perkis Haven, Dan Klein, and Bernie West, featuring Carroll O'Connor, Jean Stapleton, Rob Reiner, and Sally Struthers, aired November 3, 1973, in broadcast syndication.
42. Dave Kaufman, "'All in the Family' Producer: 'Archie a Lovable Bigot,'" *Variety*, August 3, 1971.
43. Whitney M. Young Jr., "Irresponsible Television Production Aids Racism," *Los Angeles Sentinel*, February 4, 1971.
44. Jones, "Norman Lear Sitcoms," 45.
45. Lawrence E. Mintz, "Ideology in the Television Situation Comedy," in *What's So Funny? Humor in American Culture*, ed. Nancy A. Walker (Wilmington, DE: Scholarly Resources, 1998), 280.
46. Christina von Hodenberg, "Archie Bunker Actually Helped Race Relations: How 'All in the Family' Led to 'Key and Peele,'" *Salon*, September 9, 2015, https://www.salon.com/2015/09/08/archie_bunker_actually_helped_race_relations_how_all_in_the_family_led_to_key_and_peele/.
47. Dennis Tredy, "'Those Were the Days . . .': *All in the Family* and the 'Primetiming' of U.S. Diversity and Counterculture," *Revue électronique EOLLE, 2013, Expressions artistiques et politiques de la contre-culture: La contestation en images, 1955–1975* 2, no. 4 (December 2012): 84.
48. Oscar Winberg, "Archie Bunker for President: The Strange Career of a Political Icon in Moynihan's America," *PS: Political Science & Politics* 50, no. 2 (2017): 392.
49. Office of the Press Secretary, The White House, "Remarks by the President at Presentation of the National Medal of the Arts and the National Humanities Medal," September 29, 1999, https://clintonwhitehouse4.archives.gov/WH/New/html/19990929.html.
50. Mekeisha Madden Toby, "John Amos' Good Times: The Iconic Actor Reflects on His Career 45 Years After Roots Changed TV Forever," *TVLine*, February 25, 2022, https://www.yahoo.com/entertainment/john-amos-good-times-iconic-025240332.html.
51. Louie Robinson, "Bad Times on the Good Times Set," *Ebony*, September 1975, 35.
52. Norman Lear, *Even This I Get to Experience* (New York: Penguin, 2015), 276.
53. Lear, *Even This*, 277.
54. Emily Niekrasz, "*M*A*S*H*: Binding Up the Exhibit," *Smithsonian Institution Archives* blog, July 30, 2019, https://siarchives.si.edu/blog/mash-binding-exhibit.
55. Larry Gelbart, *Laughing Matters: On Writing M*A*S*H, Tootsie, Oh, God!, and a Few Other Funny Things* (New York: Random House, 1998), 27.
56. Rick Worland, "The Other Living-Room War: Prime Time Combat Series, 1962–1975," *Journal of Film and Video* 50, no. 3 (1998): 17–19.
57. Mike Budd and Clay Steinman, "*M*A*S*H* Mystified: Capitalization, Dematerialization, Idealization," *Cultural Critique* 10 (1988): 70.
58. Greg Oguss, "'Whose Barrio Is It?' Chico and the Man and the Integrated Ghetto Shows of the 1970s," *Television & New Media* 6, no. 1 (February 2005): 3–21.
59. Luis Alvarez, *Chicanx Utopias: Pop Culture and the Politics of the Possible* (Austin: University of Texas Press, 2022), 73.
60. Alvarez, *Chicanx Utopias*, 14.
61. Betty Freidan, "Television and the Feminine Mystique," *TV Guide*, February 1964, 66.
62. Marlo Thomas, quoted in Yael Kohen, *We Killed: The Rise of Women in American Comedy* (New York: Farrar, Straus and Giroux, 2012), 59.
63. Serafina Bathrick, "*The Mary Tyler Moore Show:* Women at Home and at Work," in *MTM: Quality Television*, ed. Jane Feuer, Paul Kerr, and Tise Vahimagi (London: British Film Institute, 1984), 101.
64. Bonnie Dow, *Prime-Time Feminism: Television, Media Culture, and the Women's Movement Since 1970* (Philadelphia: University of Pennsylvania Press, 1996), 24.
65. Amy Mitchell, Jeffery Gottfried, Jocelyn Kiley, and Katerina Eva Matsa, principal researchers, *Political Polarization & Media Habits* (Washington, DC: Pew Research Center, 2014).
66. James Poniewozik, "Jon Stewart, the Fake Newsman Who Made a Real Difference," *Time*, February 10, 2015,

https://time.com/3704321/jon-stewart-daily-show-fake-news/.

67. Juleanna Glover, "If Tucker Runs in 2024, Here's Who the Democrats Need," *Politico*, July 8, 2022, https://www.politico.com/news/magazine/2022/07/08/jon-stewart-2024-democrats-00044146.

68. Ken Jennings, *Planet Funny: How Comedy Ruined Everything* (New York: Scribner, 2018), 213–224.

69. S. Robert Lichter, Jody C. Baumgartner, and Jonathan S. Morris, *Politics Is a Joke! How TV Comedians Are Remaking Political Life* (Boulder, CO: Westview, 2015), 34.

70. Jody Baumgartner and Jonathan S. Morris, "The Daily Show Effect: Candidate Evaluations, Efficacy, and American Youth," *American Politics Research* 34, no. 3 (2006): 341–367.

71. Daxton Stewart, "'The Daily Show Effect' Revisited: How Satire Contributes to Political Participation and Trust in Young Audiences" (paper, Entertainment Studies Interest Group, AEJMC 2007 Annual Conference, Washington, DC, July 27, 2007), http://dx.doi.org/10.2139/ssrn.3130227.

CHAPTER 4. COMEDY BREAKS THE MOLD

1. Ryan Teague Beckwith, "Obama: The First Meme President," *San José Mercury News*, October 24, 2012.

2. John Dunning, "The Edgar Bergen/Charlie McCarthy Show," in *The Encyclopedia of Old Time Radio* (Oxford: Oxford University Press, 1998), 226–230.

3. Steve Craig, "Out of Eden: The Legion of Decency, the FCC, and Mae West's 1937 Appearance on the Chase & Sanborn Hour," *Journal of Radio Studies* 13, no. 2 (November 2006): 235.

4. Craig, "Out of Eden," 235–244.

Eric Jentsch is appreciative of the work of Kathryn H. Fuller-Seeley, whose book *Jack Benny and the Golden Age of American Radio Comedy* contributed greatly to this essay.

5. Tom Lewis, *Empire of the Air: The Men Who Made Radio* (New York: HarperCollins, 1991), 230–231.

6. Sid Caesar, with Eddy Friedfeld, *Caesar's Hours: My Life in Comedy, with Love and Laughter* (New York: PublicAffairs, 2003), 53.

7. Caesar, *Caesar's Hours*, 77.

8. David Steinberg, *Inside Comedy: The Soul, Wit, and Bite of Comedy and Comedians of the Last Five Decades* (New York: Knopf, 2021), 51.

9. David Bianculli, *The Platinum Age of Television: From* I Love Lucy *to* The Walking Dead, *How TV Became Terrific* (New York: Doubleday, 2016), 102.

10. David Margolick, "Sid Caesar's Finest Sketch," *New Yorker*, February 14, 2014.

11. Mel Tolkin, interview by Bob Claster, Archive of American Television, November 4, 1997, https://interviews.televisionacademy.com/interviews/mel-tolkin.

12. LeRoy Ashby, *With Amusement for All: A History of American Popular Culture Since 1830* (Lexington: University Press of Kentucky, 2006), 330.

13. Judith Yaross, "Stand-Up Comedy, Social Change, and (American) Culture," in *Standing Up, Speaking Out: Stand-Up Comedy and the Rhetoric of Social Change*, ed. Matthew R. Meier and Casey R. Schmitt (New York: Routledge, 2017), xvii.

14. Gerald Bordman and Thomas S. Hischak, "Adonis," in *The Oxford Companion to the American Musical* (New York: Oxford University Press, 2004), 11–12.

15. John Bush Jones, *Our Musicals, Ourselves: A Social History of the American Musical Theatre* (Lebanon, NH: University Press of New England, 2003), 52–68.

16. John Kenrick, *Musical Theatre: A History* (New York: Bloomsbury, 2008), 213.

17. Jordan Schildcrout, *In the Long Run: A Cultural History of Broadway's Hit Plays* (London: Routledge, 2020), 25.

18. Ted Merwin, "The Performance of Jewish Ethnicity in Anne Nichols' 'Abie's Irish Rose,'" *Journal of American Ethnic History* 20, no. 2 (2001): 3–37.

19. Eric Grode, "The Smart Set Sneered, but the Play Won the Day," *New York Times*, May 11, 2022, https://www.nytimes.com/2022/05/11/theater/abies-irish-rose-broadway.html.

20. Schildcrout, *In the Long Run*, 29.

21. John Lahr, "Master of Revels: Neil Simon's Comic Empire," *New Yorker*, April 26, 2010.

22. Lahr, "Master of Revels."

23. James Lipton, "Neil Simon, the Art of Theater No. 10," *Paris Review* 125 (Winter 1992).

24. Jeremy Dauber, *Jewish Comedy: A Serious History* (New York: Norton, 2017), 266.

25. Liner notes to *My Son, the Folk Singer* (Warner Bros. Records, 1962).

26. Mark Cohen, *Overweight Sensation: The Life and Comedy of Allan Sherman* (Lebanon, NH: University Press of New England, 2013), 85.

27. Dr. Demento, qtd. in Gerald Nachman, *Seriously Funny: The Rebel Comedians of the 1950s and 1960s* (New York: Pantheon, 2003), 180.

28. Tony Schwartz, "Birthplace of Comedians Has Birthday of Its Own," *New York Times*, August 19, 1982.

29. "Van Dyke's TV 'Wief' Wears the Pants," n.d., Carl Reiner Collection, National Comedy Center Archives, Jamestown, NY.

30. Frank Penn, "Goodbye to a Good Show," March 30, 1966, Carl Reiner Collection, National Comedy Center Archives, Jamestown, NY.

31. Jack Viertel, quoted in "Chicago Impromptu," *American Theater*, July 1990

32. Charna Halpern, Del Close, and Kim "Howard" Johnson, *Truth in Comedy: The Manual of Improvisation* (Denver: Meriwether, 1994), 25.

33. Halpern, Close, and Johnson, *Truth in Comedy*, 47.

34. Richard F. Shepard, "'Living Premise,' a New Revue, Tackles

Integration Problems," *New York Times*, June 14, 1963.
35. "The Living Premise," *Ebony*, November 1963, 59.
36. "The Living Premise," 59.
37. Stephen E. Kercher, *Revel with a Cause: Liberal Satire in Postwar America* (Chicago: University of Chicago Press, 2006), 176.
38. Carl Reiner, quoted in Kay Gardella, "Nobody Can See Past the Edges," *New York Daily News*, November 28, 1982, B7.
39. Chris Tuner, *Planet Simpson: How a Cartoon Masterpiece Defined a Generation* (Cambridge, MA: Da Capo, 2004), 120.
40. Tom Shales, "The Simpsons," *Washington Post*, October 11, 1990, https://www.washingtonpost.com/archive/lifestyle/1990/10/11/the-simpsons/4b6c0919-b26f-47a3-946b-1046f47fcfcf/.
41. John Ortved, *The Simpsons: An Uncensored, Unauthorized History* (New York: Faber & Faber, 2009), 82.
42. Shales, "The Simpsons."
43. Scott Williams, "Bart Simpson: Cultural Icon—Or Rebel Without a Clue?," Associated Press, May 22, 1990, https://apnews.com/article/b21a87dcb470b3d62ef4af24c35744fb.
44. Willa Paskin, "Bart Simpson Mania," *Slate Decoder Ring*, podcast audio, October 7, 2019, https://slate.com/podcasts/decoder-ring/2019/10/decoder-ring-bart-simpson-culture-wars-george-h-w-bush.
45. Ortved, *The Simpsons*, 5.
46. Isador Barmash, "The T-Shirt Industry Sweats It Out," *New York Times*, October 7, 1990, https://www.nytimes.com/1990/10/07/arts/television-overacheiver-and-learning-to-deal-with-it-man.html.
47. Jonah Goldberg, "Homer Never Nods: The Importance of The Simpsons," *National Review*, May 1, 2000.
48. "The Best of the Century," *Time*, December 31, 1999, https://content.time.com/time/subscriber/article/0,33009,993039,00.html.
49. Gene Demby, "The Fallout of a Callout," *Code Switch* podcast, National Public Radio, April 26, 2023, https://www.npr.org/sections/codeswitch/2023/04/10/1169162406/hank-azaria-and-hari-kondabolu-on-apu-and-the-fallout-of-a-callout.
50. K. Connie Kang, "*All American Girl* and Images of Asians in the Media," in *MultiAmerica: Essays on Cultural Wars and Cultural Peace*, ed. Ishmael Reed (New York: Penguin, 1997), 360.
51. Margaret Cho, *I'm the One That I Want* (New York: Ballantine Books, 2001), 106.
52. Cho, *I'm the One That I Want*, 107.
53. Cho, *I'm the One That I Want*, 140.
54. Caroline Tiger, *Margaret Cho* (New York: Chelsea House, 2007), 15.
55. Tiger, *Margaret Cho*, 89.
56. John Koegel, "Mexican Musical Theater and Movie Palaces in Downtown Los Angeles Before 1950," in *Tide Was Always High: The Music of Latin America in Los Angeles*, ed. John Koegel (Oakland: California Scholarship Online, 2018), https://doi.org/10.1525/california/9780520294394.003.0002; Nicolás Kanellos, *A History of Hispanic Theatre in the United States: Origins to 1940* (Austin: University of Texas Press, 1990); Nicolás Kanellos, ed., *Mexican American Theatre: Then and Now* (Houston: Arte Público Press, 1983).
57. Alan Dundes, "At Ease, Disease: AIDS Jokes as Sick Humor," *American Behavioral Scientist* 30, no. 1 (1987): 72.
58. Dundes, "At Ease, Disease," 80.
59. American Folklore Society, "What Is Folklore?" (n.d.), https://whatisfolklore.org.
60. Yvonne J. Milspaw, "Folklore and the Nuclear Age: 'The Harrisburg Disaster' at Three Mile Island," *International Folklore Review* 1 (1981): 61.
61. Larisa Fialkova, "Chornobyl's Folklore: Vernacular Commentary on Nuclear Disaster," *Journal of Folklore Research* 38, no. 3 (2001): 196.
62. Antonin J. Obrdlik, "'Gallows Humor': A Sociological Phenomenon," *American Journal of Sociology* 47, no. 5 (1942): 709.
63. Obrdlik, "'Gallows Humor,'" 712.
64. Dundes, "At Ease, Disease," 77–79.
65. Elliott Oring, "Jokes and the Discourse on Disaster," *Journal of American Folklore* 100, no. 297 (1987): 280.
66. Roger Simon, "The Jokes That Speak the Unspeakable," *Los Angeles Times*, February 23, 1986, K11.
67. Willie Smyth, "Challenger Jokes and the Humor of Disaster," *Western Folklore* 45, no. 4 (1986): 254.
68. Charles Busch, "Torch Song Trilogy June 1982," *The Advocate*, November 12, 2002.
69. Jordan Schildcrout, *In the Long Run: A Cultural History of Broadway's Hit Plays* (London: Routledge, 2020), 183–185.
70. John Kenrick, *Musical Theatre: A History* (New York: Bloomsbury, 2015), 349.
71. Frank Rich, "Stage: The Musical 'Cage Aux Folles,'" *New York Times*, August 22, 1983.
72. Ali Wong, *Dear Girls: Intimate Tales, Untold Secrets and Advice for Living Your Best Life* (New York: Random House, 2019), 76.
73. Wong, *Dear Girls*, 69.
74. Wong, *Dear Girls*, 65.
75. Wong, *Dear Girls*, 64.

CONCLUSION

1. Rebecca Onion, "*I Think You Should Leave*'s Hot Dog Guy Is More Than Just a Meme," *Slate*, August 18, 2020, https://slate.com/culture/2020/08/hot-dog-costume-meme-i-think-you-should-leave.html; Rachel Syme, "'I Think You Should Leave' Is a Love Language," *New Yorker*, July 26, 2021, https://newyorker.com/culture/on-television/i-think-you-should-leave-is-a-love-language; Sam Anderson, "Tim Robinson and the Golden Age of Cringe Comedy," *New York Times Magazine*, June 2, 2023, https://www.nytimes.com/2023/06/02/magazine/tim-robinson-i-think-you-should-leave.html.

CONTRIBUTORS

JAMES I. DEUTSCH is senior content coordinator for the Smithsonian Institution's *America at 250* book project, which will mark the 250th anniversary of the United States in 2026. In addition, he serves as an adjunct professor—teaching courses on American film history—in the American Studies Department at George Washington University.

THEODORE S. GONZALVES is curator at the Smithsonian's National Museum of American History. A Fulbright Scholar and past president of the Association for Asian American Studies with more than thirty years of teaching experience in the United States, Spain, and the Philippines, he has released several publications including *Smithsonian Asian Pacific American History, Art, and Culture in 101 Objects*. He has worked on Smithsonian exhibits such as *Entertainment Nation* and *Rallying Against Racism*.

JON GRINSPAN is a curator of political history at the Smithsonian's National Museum of American History. His work focuses on the deep history of American democracy during its messy, formative years in the 1800s. He is the author of the books *The Virgin Vote: How Young Americans Made Democracy Social, Politics Personal, and Voting Popular in the Nineteenth Century*, *The Age of Acrimony: How Americans Fought to Fix Their Politics, 1865–1915*, and *Wide Awake: The Forgotten Force That Elected Lincoln, Spurred Secession, and Fought the Civil War*. His scholarship on humor has appeared in the *Journal of the Civil War Era* ("Sorrowfully Amusing: The Popular Comedy of the Civil War") as well as in the *New York Times* and elsewhere.

ERIC JENTSCH serves as a curator for sports and entertainment in the Division of Culture and the Arts at the National Museum of American History. He attended Saint Louis University, where he studied American history and English literature, and received his master's in museum studies at George Washington University.

LAURA LAPLACA is the founding director of the National Comedy Center's Carl Reiner Department of Archives and Preservation in Jamestown, New York—the United States' congressionally designated home for the preservation of comedy history. An archivist, curator, and historian of popular culture, she holds a PhD in the history of film, broadcasting, and digital media from Northwestern University.

RYAN LINTELMAN is the curator of entertainment at the Smithsonian National Museum of American History, and studies the history of American film, television, and comedy, and is one of the curators of the landmark exhibition *Entertainment Nation*. He contributed essays to Smithsonian Books' *Entertainment Nation* and *Smithsonian Civil War: Inside the National Collection*.

ASHLEY OLIVA MAYOR is a public historian and curator with almost a decade of experience in the field. Currently, she works as a curatorial associate in the Division of Culture and the Arts at the Smithsonian's National Museum of American History, specializing in Latinx music and culture. She is part of the curatorial team for the landmark exhibition *Entertainment Nation / Nación del espectáculo*, which opened in December 2022. She is the codirector of the Hasta 'Bajo Project, a nonprofit and community-based organization building the first historical archive dedicated to reggaetón/urban music in Puerto Rico. She received a master's degree from George Washington University and is finishing a doctorate degree in history at Georgetown University.

ANYA MONTIEL is a curator in the history and culture department at the Smithsonian's National Museum of the American Indian. She received her doctorate and master's degrees in American studies from Yale University and a bachelor's degree in Native American studies from the University of California, Davis.

ASHLEY M. SENSKE is the collections manager at the National Comedy Center, where she oversees the preservation, digitization, and display of artifacts representing comedy's great artistic, social, and political impacts on American culture. She holds a master's degree in information and library science from the University at Buffalo and is deeply involved in local history work in Western New York.

KEVIN STRAIT is a museum curator at the Smithsonian's National Museum of African American History and Culture. Since 2010, he has worked in the museum's Office of Curatorial Affairs and was part of the core team that acquired objects and developed content for several of the museum's permanent exhibitions and interpretive spaces. He currently oversees the NMAAHC's collections related to twentieth-century political and social history and African American popular culture and is the curator of the temporary exhibition "Afrofuturism—A History of Black Futures" and the coeditor of the exhibition's companion publication. He is a graduate of Wesleyan University and received his PhD in American studies from George Washington University.

JOHN W. TROUTMAN is curator of music and musical instruments at the Smithsonian's National Museum of American History. He is the lead curator of the museum's recently opened permanent exhibition on entertainment, *Entertainment Nation*. His books include *Kīkā Kila: How the Hawaiian Steel Guitar Changed the Sound of Modern Music* and *Indian Blues: American Indians and the Politics of Music, 1879–1934*. He coedited the exhibition catalog for *Entertainment Nation* and edited Robert "Mack" McCormick's *Biography of a Phantom: A Robert Johnson Blues Odyssey*.

ILLUSTRATION CREDITS

Chapter 1, page 5
National Museum of American History, gift of Steve Landesberg and Jean Soo, catalog number 1979.1008.06.

Chapter 1, page 6
National Museum of American History, gift of Steve Landesberg and Jean Soo, catalog number 1979.1008.04.

Chapter 1, page 7
National Museum of American History, gift of Steve Landesberg and Jean Soo, catalog number 1979.1008.02.

Chapter 1, page 9
National Museum of American History, catalog number 2002.0133.39.

Chapter 1, page 12
National Museum of American History, The Ralph E Becker Collection of Political Americana, catalog number PL.227739.1860.K09.

Chapter 1, page 13
National Museum of American History, The Ralph E Becker Collection of Political Americana, catalog number PL.227739.1860.K09.

Chapter 1, page 15
National Museum of American History, gift of Jay and Emma Lewis, catalog number 1991.0735.01.

Chapter 1, page 16
National Museum of American History, gift of Nancy E. Davis, catalog number 2015.0281.07.

Chapter 1, page 18
NMAH Archives Center, George and Hart's Georgia Up To Date Minstrels Scrapbook, NMAH. AC.0576.

Chapter 1, page 19
National Museum of American History, Gift of Ellen Roney Hughes, catalog number 1977.1006.01.

Chapter 1, page 20
Photograph from the NMAH Archives Center, Jerry Maren Papers, NMAH. AC.1589.

Chapter 1, page 20
National Museum of American History, gift of Lloyd Decker, catalog number 2022.0141.01.04.

Chapter 1, page 20
National Museum of American History, gift of Lloyd Decker, catalog number 2022.0141.01.01-03.

Chapter 1, page 21
National Museum of American History, catalog number 2017.3021.031.

Chapter 1, page 22
National Museum of American History, gift of Jean P. Warner, catalog number 1998.0002.01.

Chapter 1, page 22
National Museum of American History, gift of Gloria K. Pocobello, catalog number 1990.0583.01.

Chapter 1, page 24
National Portrait Gallery, Smithsonian Institution; gift of Estrellita Karsh in memory of Yousuf Karsh © Estate of Yousuf Karsh.

Chapter 1, page 25
National Museum of American History, bequest of Julius H. Marx, catalog number 1987.0588.26 and 1987.0588.30.

Chapter 1, page 26
National Museum of American History, gift of Twentieth Century Fox, catalog number 1983.0095.009.

Chapter 1, page 28
National Comedy Center courtesy of Bob and Dolores Hope Foundation.

Chapter 1, page 30
National Museum of American History, Gift of Barry and Roberta Richter in loving memory of Mark Harris, catalog number 2020.0087.01 and 2020.0145.01.

Chapter 1, page 31
National Museum of American History, catalog number 2016.0145.01.

Chapter 1, page 32
National Museum of American History, catalog number 2017.0295.01-03.

Chapter 1, page 33
Black and Decker Collection, Archives Center, National Museum of American History, NMAH.AC.1441.

Chapter 1, page 34
National Museum of American History, gift of Dwight Blocker Bowers, catalog number 2016.3125.11.

Chapter 1, page 36
National Museum of American History, Gift of Mel J. Blanc, catalog number 1985.0247.01.

Chapter 1, page 37
National Museum of American History, Gift of Morris H. Blum, catalog number 2000.0165.0401.

Chapter 1, page 39
National Portrait Gallery, Smithsonian Institution, gift of an anonymous donor, catalog number NPG.96.205.

Chapter 1, page 40
National Museum of American History, Gift of Lucille G. and Robert G. Jensen in memory of Glenn W. Jensen, catalog number 1989.0510.01.

Chapter 1, page 44
National Museum of American History, Gift of Phyllis Diller, catalog numbers 2003.0289.05.01-04; 2003.0289.11.

Chapter 1, page 44
National Museum of American History, catalog number 2015.0280.01.

Chapter 1, page 45
National Museum of American History, Gift of Phyllis Diller, catalog numbers 2003.0289.01.01-02.

Chapter 1, page 47
National Comedy Center courtesy of Shelley and Sarah Berman.

Chapter 1, page 48
National Comedy Center courtesy of Bob Booker.

Chapter 1, page 49
National Comedy Center.

Chapter 1, page 50
National Comedy Center courtesy of Jerry Zolten.

Chapter 1, page 50
National Comedy Center courtesy of Carl Reiner.

Chapter 1, page 51
National Comedy Center courtesy of Carl Reiner.

Chapter 1, page 52
National Comedy Center.

Chapter 1, page 53
National Comedy Center courtesy of Jerry Zolten.

Chapter 1, page 55
National Museum of American History, gift of Dorothy Ebsen, catalog numbers 2019.0152.01.01-06.

Chapter 1, page 56
National Museum of American History, Gift of Joyce Darrell and Michael C. Dickerson, catalog number 2001.3099.02.

Chapter 1, page 57
National Comedy Center courtesy of The Don Rickles Estate.

Chapter 1, page 58
National Comedy Center courtesy of The Don Rickles Estate.

Chapter 1, page 60
National Museum of American History, gift of Dustin Hoffman, catalog number 1984.0549.01.

Chapter 1, page 62
National Museum of American History, gift of Theodore S. Gonzalves, catalog number 2023.0056.01.

Chapter 1, page 65
Portrait of Ellen DeGeneres, National Portrait Gallery, Smithsonian Institution, Copyright Timothy White 2023, catalog number NPG.2011.120.

Chapter 1, page 65
National Museum of American History, gift of Tammara Billik, catalog number 2019.0130.01.

Chapter 1, page 67
National Museum of American History, gift of KoMut Entertainment, catalog number 2014.0145.03.

Chapter 2, page 71
Courtesy of Silver Special Collections, University of Vermont.

Chapter 2, page 73
National Museum of American History, catalog number 2017.3021.034.

Chapter 2, page 74
Photograph by Jeremiah Gurney, ca. 1873, National Portrait Gallery, Smithsonian Institution, catalog number NPG.80.283.

Chapter 2, page 75
Photograph by Albert Bigelow Paine, 1906, National Portrait Gallery, Smithsonian Institution, catalog number NPG.79.162.

Chapter 2, page 77
National Museum of African American History and Culture, catalog number 2014.249abc.

Chapter 2, page 79
National Portrait Gallery, Smithsonian Institution, catalog number NPG.91.166.

Chapter 2, page 84
National Portrait Gallery, Smithsonian Institution, catalog number NPG.2016.118.

Chapter 2, page 86
National Museum of American History, catalog number 2015.0018.01.

Chapter 2, page 88
National Museum of American History, gift of Carol Burnett, catalog number 1984.0223.01.

Chapter 2, page 90
National Museum of American History, Gift of Bob Mackie, catalog number 2009.0078.01.

Chapter 2, page 92
National Museum of American History, gift of Will Connell, catalog number PG.8077b, copyright Will Connell.

Chapter 2, page 93
National Museum of American History, gift of Will Connell, catalog number PG.8077l, copyright Will Connell.

Chapter 2, page 95
National Portrait Gallery, Smithsonian Institution, catalog number NPG.84.114.

Chapter 2, page 98
Photograph from the Core Collection Production files of the Margaret Herrick Library, Academy of Motion Picture Arts and Sciences.

Chapter 2, page 99
National Portrait Gallery, Smithsonian Institution, catalog number NPG.86.170.

Chapter 2, page 101
National Portrait Gallery, Smithsonian Institution, catalog number NPG.2008.55.

Chapter 2, page 103
National Museum of American History, gift of Gracie and Walter Lantz, catalog number 1982.0567.18.

Chapter 2, page 103
National Museum of American History, gift of Gracie and Walter Lantz, catalog number 1982.0567.20.

Chapter 2, page 104
National Museum of American History, catalog number 2016.3009.019; 1988.0434.08.

Chapter 2, page 105
National Museum of American History, gift of Warner Brothers, catalog number 1983.0555.13.

Chapter 2, page 107
National Comedy Center courtesy of Brian and Monica Sands.

Chapter 2, page 108
National Comedy Center courtesy of Jerry Zolten.

Chapter 2, page 111
Duncan P. Schiedt Photograph Collection, Archives Center, National Museum of American History, NMAH.AC.1323.

Chapter 2, page 112
National Comedy Center courtesy of Jerry Zolten.

Chapter 2, page 113
National Comedy Center courtesy of Ben Stiller

Chapter 2, page 116
National Comedy Center courtesy of Brian and Monica Sands.

Chapter 2, page 117
National Museum of American History, gift of Chris Costello, catalog number 2005.0139.01.

Chapter 2, page 117
National Museum of American History, Gift of the Family of Jim Henson: Lisa Henson, Cheryl Henson, Brian Henson, John Henson and Heather Henson, catalog numbers 2013.0101.13-14.

Chapter 2, page 119
National Museum of American History, Gift of Minnie Pearl, catalog numbers, 1993.0457.01-02.

Chapter 2, page 120
National Museum of American History, Gift of Minnie Pearl, catalog number 1993.0457.12.

Chapter 2, page 124
National Comedy Center courtesy of Carson Entertainment Group.

Chapter 2, page 124
National Comedy Center courtesy of Carson Entertainment Group.

Chapter 2, page 125
National Comedy Center courtesy of Doc Severinsen

Chapter 2, page 126
National Museum of American History, gift of Jack Rollins, catalog number 1992.0607.01.

Chapter 2, page 129
National Museum of American History, gift of Barbara Eden, catalog number 2022.0140.01.

Chapter 2, page 130
National Comedy Center.

Chapter 2, page 131
National Comedy Center courtesy of James Comisar.

Chapter 2, page 132
National Comedy Center courtesy of The Estate of Betty White Ludden.

Chapter 2, page 133
National Museum of American History, gift of Ashley Oliva Mayor, catalog number 2023.0103.03.

Chapter 2, page 134
National Museum of American History, gift of Ashley Oliva Mayor, catalog number 2023.0103.04.

Chapter 2, page 135
National Museum of American History, gift of Ashley Oliva Mayor, catalog number 2023.0103.02.

Chapter 2, page 137
National Museum of American History, catalog number 2023.0076.01.

Chapter 2, page 138
National Museum of Natural History, gift of Bob Newhart, catalog number 2023.0059.01.

Chapter 2, page 139
National Museum of American History, catalog number 1988.3160.58.

Chapter 2, page 140
National Museum of American History, gift of Paramount Television Productions, catalog number 1980.0094.01.

Chapter 2, page 142
National Comedy Center courtesy of Alan and Robin Zweibel.

Chapter 2, page 143
National Comedy Center Courtesy of Nate Bargatze.

Chapter 2, page 146
National Museum of American History, Gift from the Family of Jim Henson, catalog number 2010.0144.02.

Chapter 2, page 147
National Museum of American History, Gift of the Family of Jim Henson: Lisa Henson, Cheryl Henson, Brian Henson, John Henson and Heather Henson, catalog number 2013.0101.04.

Chapter 2, page 148
National Museum of American History, Gift from the Family of Jim Henson, catalog numbers 2010.0144.01-10.

Chapter 2, page 148
National Museum of American History, gift of Terry Atlas, catalog number 2019.0131.01.

Chapter 2, page 149
National Museum of American History, Gift of the Family of Jim Henson: Lisa Henson, Cheryl Henson, Brian Henson, John Henson and Heather Henson, catalog number 2013.0101.12.

Chapter 2, page 150
National Museum of American History, catalog numbers 1989.0540.01 [gift of Muppets, Inc.]; 2013.0101.20, 2013.0101.13, 2013.0101.14 [gifts of the Family of Jim Henson: Lisa Henson, Cheryl Henson, Brian Henson, John Henson and Heather Henson]; 1979.0952.03, and 1979.0952.01 [Gifts of Children's Television Workshop].

Chapter 2, page 152
National Comedy Center courtesy of Tamara Rawitt.

Chapter 2, page 153
National Comedy Center courtesy of Tamara Rawitt.

Chapter 2, page 154
National Comedy Center Courtesy of Tamara Rawitt.

Chapter 2, page 155
National Museum of American History, gift of Warner Brothers Entertainment Inc., catalog number 2004.0245.01.

Chapter 3, page 164
National Museum of American History, Gift of Janet Vart, catalog number 2009.0064.14.

Chapter 3, page 164
National Portrait Gallery, Smithsonian Institution, catalog number S/NPG.95.119.

Chapter 3, page 167
National Comedy Center courtesy of Kitty Bruce.

Chapter 3, page 168
National Comedy Center courtesy of Kitty Bruce.

Chapter 3, page 169
National Comedy Center courtesy of Rusty Warren and Liz Rizzo.

Chapter 3, page 170
National Comedy Center courtesy of Rusty Warren and Liz Rizzo.

Chapter 3, page 171
National Comedy Center courtesy of Rusty Warren and Liz Rizzo.

Chapter 3, page 174
Collection of the Smithsonian National Museum of African American History and Culture, Gift of Lydia Samuel Bennett, © Universal Music Group.

Chapter 3, page 176
National Comedy Center courtesy of Desilu, too, LLC.

Chapter 3, page 177
National Comedy Center courtesy of Desilu, too, LLC.

Chapter 3, page 178
National Comedy Center courtesy of Desilu, too, LLC.

Chapter 3, page 179
National Comedy Center courtesy of Desilu, too, LLC.

Chapter 3, page 180
National Comedy Center.

Chapter 3, page 182
National Comedy Center courtesy of Desilu, too, LLC.

Chapter 3, page 183
National Comedy Center courtesy of Desilu, too, LLC.

Chapter 3, page 185
National Comedy Center courtesy of Melissa Rivers.

Chapter 3, page 186
National Comedy Center courtesy of Melissa Rivers.

Chapter 3, page 188
National Comedy Center courtesy of Melissa Rivers.

Chapter 3, page 190
National Comedy Center courtesy of Tommy and Dick Smothers.

Chapter 3, page 191
National Comedy Center courtesy of Tommy and Dick Smothers.

Chapter 3, page 192
National Comedy Center courtesy of Tommy and Dick Smothers.

Chapter 3, page 194
National Comedy Center courtesy of George Schlatter.

Chapter 3, page 195
National Comedy Center courtesy of NBCUniversal and George Schlatter.

Chapter 3, page 196
National Comedy Center courtesy of the Estate of Pat Paulsen.

Chapter 3, page 197
National Comedy Center courtesy of Lily Tomlin.

Chapter 3, page 199
[. . . *Is It Something I Said?* album] National Museum of American History. [*That N-----'s Crazy* album] National Museum of African American History and Culture, catalog number 2011.173.82abc.

Chapter 3, page 203
Photo courtesy Nasbah Hill.

Chapter 3, page 204
National Museum of the American Indian, Smithsonian Institution.

Chapter 3, page 207
National Museum of American History, gift of Pam Putch, catalog number 2017.0150.36.

Chapter 3, page 208
National Museum of American History, Gift of Tandem/TAT Productions, catalog number 1978.2146.01-06.

Chapter 3, page 212
Photograph by Bob Lucas, Johnson Publishing Company Archive. Courtesy J. Paul Getty Trust and Smithsonian National Museum of African American History and Culture.

Chapter 3, page 213
National Museum of African American History and Culture, catalog number 2014.26.1; NMAAHC 2013.145.1.

Chapter 3, page 214
National Comedy Center courtesy of Kelly Carlin.

Chapter 3, page 215
National Comedy Center courtesy of Kelly Carlin.

Chapter 3, page 216
National Comedy Center courtesy of Kelly Carlin.

Chapter 3, page 217
National Comedy Center courtesy of Kelly Carlin.

Chapter 3, page 218
National Comedy Center courtesy of Kelly Carlin.

Chapter 3, page 219
National Comedy Center courtesy of Kelly Carlin.

Chapter 3, page 220
National Museum of American History, gift of Twentieth Century Fox, catalog number 1983.0095.003.

Chapter 3, page 221
National Museum of American History, gift of Twentieth Century Fox, catalog number 1983.0095.237.

Chapter 3, page 222
National Museum of American History, gift of Evelyn and Paul A. Wurtzel, catalog number 1988.0667.03.

Chapter 3, page 223
National Museum of American History, gift of Twentieth Century Fox, catalog numbers 1983.0095.015 and 1983.0095.015.01.

Chapter 3, page 224
National Museum of American History, catalog number 2023.0083.01; 2023.0084.01.

Chapter 3, page 227
National Comedy Center.

Chapter 3, page 229
National Museum of American History, Gift of Home Box Office, Original Programming, through John Melfi, catalog number 2004.0163.01.

Chapter 3, page 231
National Museum of American History, gift of Hello Doggie Inc., catalog numbers 2016.0101.01-04.

Chapter 3, page 232
National Museum of American History, Gift of Hello Doggie Inc., catalog number 2009.3007.01.

Chapter 4, page 235
Official White House photo by Pete Souza, courtesy Barack Obama Presidential Library.

Chapter 4, page 237
National Museum of American History, gift of Bill Nye, catalog numbers 2016.0177.01 and 2016.0177.03.

Chapter 4, page 239
National Museum of American History, gift of The Bergen Foundation, catalog number 1980.0273.01.

Chapter 4, page 240
National Museum of American History, gift of Robert J. Schurk, catalog number 1980.0840.01.

Chapter 4, page 241
National Museum of American History, gift of Martin Farbenblum, catalog number 2013.0327.1467.

Chapter 4, page 246
National Comedy Center courtesy of Roland Mesa.

Chapter 4, page 247
National Museum of American History, gift of Edie Adams, catalog number 1989.0173.03.

Chapter 4, page 249
National Museum of Natural History, gift of Mark Basile and Steven Schnepp, catalog number, 2010.0137.01.

Chapter 4, page 249
National Museum of American History, catalog number 1982.0377.24.

Chapter 4, page 250
National Museum of American History, gift of Sid Caesar, catalog numbers 1989.0172.01-04 and 1989.0172.06.

Chapter 4, page 250
Photograph by Victor Keppler, National Museum of American History, catalog number 2023.0077.01, c

Chapter 4, page 252
NMAH Archives Center, Frank Schiffman Apollo Theatre Collection, NMAH.AC.0540.

Chapter 4, page 253
NMAH Archives Center, Sam DeVincent Collection of Illustrated American Sheet Music, NMAH. AC.0300.

Chapter 4, page 254
National Museum of American History, catalog number 2017.3021.014.

Chapter 4, page 255
National Museum of American History, gift of Harry Goz, catalog numbers 1983.0345.01-04.

Chapter 4, page 256
National Museum of American History, gift of Edith Lauren, catalog number 2018.3033.276.

Chapter 4, page 257
National Museum of American History, gift of Rick Lyon, catalog numbers 2019.0094.01-03.

Chapter 4, page 258
National Museum of American History, gift of Daryl Roth

Productions, catalog numbers 2019.0035.01-03.

Chapter 4, page 259
National Museum of American History, catalog number 2023.0082.01.

Chapter 4, page 260
National Museum of American History, gift of Elaine Joyce Van Simon, catalog numbers 2021.0152.01 and 2021.0152.02.

Chapter 4, page 261
National Museum of American History, catalog number 2016.0108.02.

Chapter 4, page 262
National Comedy Center courtesy of Robert Sherman.

Chapter 4, page 264
National Comedy Center courtesy of Hunter Freberg.

Chapter 4, page 265
National Comedy Center courtesy of Mark and Ali Russell.

Chapter 4, page 266
National Comedy Center courtesy of Weird Al Yankovic.

Chapter 4, page 266
National Comedy Center courtesy of Dr. Demento.

Chapter 4, page 268
National Museum of American History, catalog number 2016.3009.235.

Chapter 4, page 271
National Comedy Center courtesy of Caroline Hirsch.

Chapter 4, page 272
National Museum of American History, gift of Carl Reiner, catalog number 2017.0140.01.

Chapter 4, page 272
National Comedy Center courtesy of Carl Reiner.

Chapter 4, page 273
National Comedy Center courtesy of Carl Reiner.

Chapter 4, page 274
National Comedy Center courtesy of Jerry Kessler.

Chapter 4, page 275
National Comedy Center courtesy of Georgiana "Noopy" Guy Rodrigues.

Chapter 4, page 276
National Museum of American History, gift of Carl Reiner, catalog number 2017.0140.02.

Chapter 4, page 281
National Comedy Center courtesy of Matt Besser.

Chapter 4, page 282
National Comedy Center courtesy of the Andy Kaufman Memorial Trust.

Chapter 4, page 284
National Comedy Center courtesy of the Andy Kaufman Memorial Trust.

Chapter 4, page 285
National Museum of American History, catalog number 2023.0061.01.

Chapter 4, page 290
Photograph by Sergio Garcia.

Chapter 4, page 293
National Museum of American History, gift of Netflix, Inc. through Allie Greene, catalog numbers 2023.0017.01 and 2023.0017.03.

Chapter 4, page 296
Photo illustration by Connie Sinclair.

Chapter 4, page 298
San Francisco Examiner, October 27, 1918.

Chapter 4, page 300
National Museum of American History, gift of Hubert "Geese" Ausbie, catalog number 1985.0198.01.

Chapter 4, page 301
National Museum of American History, gift of Harlem Globetrotters Inc., catalog number 1983.0782.36.

Chapter 4, page 302
National Museum of American History, gift of Edith Lauren, catalog number 2018.3033.110.

Chapter 4, page 303
National Museum of American History, gift of Harvey Fierstein, catalog number 2018.0261.01.

Chapter 4, page 304
National Museum of American History, gift of Ali Wong, catalog number 2021.0082.01.01.

Chapter 4, page 306
National Museum of American History, gifts of Knights of Good Productions and Greg Aronowitz, catalog numbers 2017.0190.04-11 and 2017.0227.01.

Chapter 4, page 307
National Museum of American History, gift of Warner Bro. Entertainment Inc., catalog number 2019.0103.01.01.

Chapter 4, page 308
National Museum of American History, gift of Vin Di Bona, catalog number 2009.0083.01.

INDEX

Page numbers in *italics* indicate photos and illustrations.